SUPERSEDED

Cover photo provided by **Sullivan & Cromwell LLP.** Pictured (left to right) are Sullivan & Cromwell associates Perrin Clark, Soraya Tabibi, and Inosi Nyatta. The three are engaged in pro bono work for New York Presbyterian Hospital's Center for Special Studies and its related Chelsea Clinic to provide estate planning services for indigent AIDS patients, adding to the nearly 9,000 hours of free legal advice the firm has provided since 1989.

Photo credit: Dick Duane.

The Vault Guide to Law Firm Pro Bono Programs
is made possible through the generous support
of the following sponsors:

- BAKER & McKENZIE
- BINGHAM McCUTCHEN
- CADWALADER
- Cleary Gottlieb Steen & Hamilton
- CLIFFORD CHANCE
- DEBEVOISE & PLIMPTON LLP
- DEWEY BALLANTINE LLP
- FRIED FRANK HARRIS SHRIVER & JACOBSON

- GOODWIN PROCTER
- GrayCary TECHNOLOGY'S LEGAL EDGE
- HellerEhrman ATTORNEYS
- HOGAN & HARTSON LLP
- JENNER & BLOCK
- JONES DAY
- KILPATRICK STOCKTON LLP — Attorneys at Law
- KRAMER LEVIN — Kramer Levin Naftalis & Frankel LLP

LATHAM & WATKINS

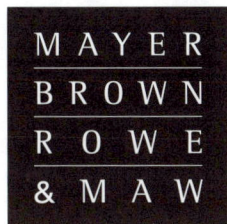

PaulHastings
ATTORNEYS

Paul | Weiss

SHEARMAN & STERLING LLP

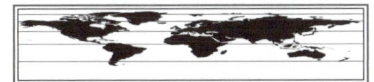

Skadden, Arps, Slate, Meagher & Flom LLP
& Affiliates

STROOCK

STROOCK & STROOCK & LAVAN LLP

SULLIVAN & CROMWELL LLP

Thelen Reid & Priest LLP
Attorneys At Law

 WEIL, GOTSHAL & MANGES LLP

WILLKIE FARR & GALLAGHER LLP

WINSTON & STRAWN LLP

The media's watching Vault!
Here's a sampling of our coverage.

"With reviews and profiles of firms that one associate calls 'spot on', [Vault's] guide has become a key reference for those who want to know what it takes to get hired by a law firm and what to expect once they get there."
- ***New York Law Journal***

"The best place on the web to prepare for a job search."
- ***Fortune***

"Vault is indispensable for locating insider information."
- ***Metropolitan Corporate Counsel***

"[Vault's guide] is an INVALUABLE Cliff's Notes to prepare for interviews."
- ***Women's Lawyer's Journal***

"For those hoping to climb the ladder of success, [Vault's] insights are priceless."
- ***Money Magazine***

"[Vault guides] make for excellent starting points for job hunters and should be purchased by academic libraries for their career sections [and] university career centers."
- ***Library Journal***

Wondering what it's like to work at a specific employer?

Read what EMPLOYEES have to say about:

- Workplace culture
- Compensation
- Hours
- Diversity
- Hiring process

Read employer surveys on THOUSANDS of top employers.

> the most trusted name in career information™

Go to www.vault.com

VAULT GUIDE TO
LAW FIRM PRO BONO PROGRAMS

© 2004 Vault Inc.

VAULT LAW CAREER LIBRARY

You are reading just one title from Vault's Law Career Library - the complete resource for legal careers. To see a full list of legal career titles, go to law.vault.com.

"With reviews and profiles of firms that one associate calls 'spot on,' [Vault's] guide has become a key reference for those who want to know what it takes to get hired by a law firm and what to expect once they get there."
– New York Law Journal

"To get the unvarnished scoop, check out Vault."
– SmartMoney magazine

> the most trusted name in career information™

"Vault is indispensable for locating insider information."
- Metropolitan Corporate Counsel

VAULT GUIDE TO LAW FIRM PRO BONO PROGRAMS

THE STAFF OF VAULT
WITH AN INTRODUCTION BY IRENE DORZBACK, ASSISTANT DEAN OF NYU SCHOOL OF LAW, OFFICE OF CAREER SERVICES
RESEARCH UNDERWRITTEN BY 29 LAW FIRMS
WITH A FOREWORD BY PENNY SHANE, CHAIR OF THE SULLIVAN & CROMWELL PRO BONO FELLOWSHIP

© 2004 Vault Inc.

ACKNOWLEDGEMENTS

Vault could not have put this guide together without the generous help of the following people: Irene Dorzback, Carrie Grimm, Mark Goldberg, Gregory A. McConnell, Teresa Schiller, and Penny Shane. A special thanks to writer extraordinaire Vera Djordjevich and the Vault sales, graphics, editorial, and IT staffs for selling, designing, editing, and programming the guide. Lastly, and especially for making the guide financially possible, a very special thanks to all of the pro bono chairs, managers, and coordinators; recruiting staff; and marketing people at the 29 sponsoring law firms.

TABLE OF CONTENTS

Introduction 1

Foreword 2

How to Use This Guide 3

PRO BONO PROFILES   7

Allen & Overy	.8
Alston & Bird LLP	.14
Arnold & Porter	.20
Baker & Hostetler LLP	.28
Baker & McKenzie	.32
Bingham McCutchen LLP	.38
Bryan Cave LLP	.44
Cadwalader Wickersham & Taft LLP	.50
Cahill Gordon & Reindel LLP	.56
Carlton Fields, P.A.	.62
Chadbourne & Parke, LLP	.68
Choate Hall & Stewart	.74
Cleary, Gottlieb, Steen & Hamilton	.80
Clifford Chance US LLP	.88
Cooley Godward LLP	.94
Covington & Burling	.100
Cravath, Swaine & Moore LLP	.106
Crowell & Moring LLP	.112
Davis Polk & Wardwell	.118
Davis Wright Tremaine LLP	.124
Debevoise & Plimpton	.128
Dechert LLP	.134
Dewey Ballantine LLP	.140
Dorsey & Whitney LLP	.146
Faegre & Benson LLP	.152

Fenwick & West LLP	158
Fish & Neave	166
Fish & Richardson P.C.	172
Fried, Frank, Harris, Shriver & Jacobson	178
Fulbright & Jaworski L.L.P.	186
Gibson, Dunn & Crutcher LLP	192
Goodwin & Procter LLP	198
Gray, Cary, Ware & Freidenrich, LLP	204
Greenberg Traurig, LLP	210
Hale and Dorr LLP	216
Heller Ehrman White & McAuliffe LLP	222
Hogan & Hartson L.L.P.	228
Holland & Hart LLP	234
Holland & Knight LLP	238
Howrey Simon Arnold & White, LLP	244
Hughes Hubbard & Reed LLP	250
Jenner & Block LLP	256
Jones Day	262
Katten Muchin Zavis Rosenman (KMZ Rosenman)	270
Kaye Scholer LLP	276
Kelley Drye & Warren LLP	282
Kilpatrick Stockton LLP	288
King & Spalding LLP	294
Kirkland & Ellis LLP	300
Kirkpatrick & Lockhart LLP	306
Kramer Levin Naftalis & Frankel LLP	312
Latham & Watkins	318
LeBoeuf, Lamb, Greene & MacRae, L.L.P.	324
Linklaters	330
Mayer, Brown, Rowe & Maw LLP	336
McDermott Will & Emery	344
McGuireWoods LLP	350
Milbank, Tweed, Hadley & McCloy LLP	354

Firm	Page
Morgan Lewis & Bockius LLP	360
Morrison & Foerster LLP	366
Munger, Tolles & Olson LLP	374
O'Melveny & Myers LLP	380
Orrick, Herrington & Sutcliffe LLP	386
Palmer & Dodge LLP	392
Patton Boggs LLP	398
Paul, Hastings, Janofsky & Walker LLP	404
Paul, Weiss, Rifkind, Wharton & Garrison LLP	410
Perkins Coie LLP	416
Pillsbury Winthrop LLP	422
Piper Rudnick LLP	428
Preston Gates & Ellis LLP	434
Proskauer Rose LLP	440
Ropes & Gray LLP	446
Schulte Roth & Zabel LLP	452
Shaw Pittman LLP	458
Shearman & Sterling LLP	464
Simpson Thacher & Bartlett LLP	470
Skadden, Arps, Slate, Meagher & Flom LLP and Associates	476
Sonnenschein Nath & Rosenthal LLP	482
Steptoe & Johnson LLP	488
Stroock & Stroock & Lavan	494
Sullivan & Cromwell LLP	500
Swidler Berlin Shereff Friedman, LLP	506
Thelen, Reid & Priest LLP	510
Torys LLP	512
Vinson & Elkins L.L.P.	518
Wachtell, Lipton, Rosen & Katz	526
Weil, Gotshal & Manges LLP	530
White & Case LLP	536
Williams & Connolly LLP	542
Willkie Farr & Gallagher LLP	548

Wilmer Cutler Pickering LLP 554
Wilson Sonsini Goodrich & Rosati 560
Winston & Strawn LLP 566

INTRODUCTION

THE REAL SCOOP

The market has fluctuated, law firms have merged and dissolved, and practice areas have been in and out of demand in my 20 years as a career services professional at NYU School of Law. But the constant in my work with students and alumni has been their strong commitment to pro bono work and the very difficult time they have in identifying and assessing opportunities. I have watched students pore over hard-copy directories and, more recently, get bleary-eyed reading scores of web sites, trying to sort out meaningful information from marketing hype. The upshot has been students making employment decisions that were not the right personal fit and, down the line, alumni leaving the legal profession because they were unable to incorporate pro bono work with other law firm work.

When Samer Hamadeh, Vault's CEO, contacted me to pitch a project idea, I asked him to literally and figuratively stop Vault's presses and consider putting this guide to pro bono together. I knew that there were fabulous pro bono programs, projects, and committed attorneys at the firms who wanted to communicate their message to students; and I knew there were students and alumni hungry for this information. It seemed logical that a guide would address this obvious disconnect.

The guide format, which presents the same information for all firms in a user-friendly way, responds to many of the questions raised in student counseling sessions over the years, as well as highlights factors "off the record" that students may not have considered asking during the interview process. In addition, the pro bono coordinators collaborated to write a "How To" section to guide readers when evaluating the various programs. As with many things, pro bono programs in firms may not be as they appear on a directory or survey form. I encourage you to take a few minutes to familiarize yourself with the hallmarks of a receptive and productive pro bono culture: Leadership, Structure, Participation, and Evaluation.

I am proud of this project, not only because of the enthusiasm with which the firms embraced the idea, but because I believe there is finally a way to disseminate great information that will benefit the careers of law students. Through pro bono work, students acquire valuable lawyering skills often not developed through traditional law firm practice, as well as establish a network of contacts in numerous areas of the law. And while skills and networks are being developed, the needs of the underrepresented are being addressed. From where I sit, it doesn't get better than that.

Irene Dorzback
Assistant Dean
Office of Career Services
NYU School of Law

FOREWORD

In remarks at the 1991 ABA Pro Bono Awards Assembly Luncheon in Atlanta, Ga., Justice Sandra Day O'Connor delivered the following "good news and bad news":

> On the one hand, there is probably more innovative pro bono work being done right now than at any time in our history; on the other hand, there has probably never been a wider gulf between the need for legal services and the availability of legal services.

The legal community has responded to Justice O'Connor's challenge in innovative ways. The American Bar Association implemented the Pro Bono Challenge, to which large firms pledge three or five percent of their total billable hours annually or 60 or 100 hours per lawyer on pro bono matters. Law firms, individual lawyers, and legal services organizations together launched Pro Bono Net (http://www.probono.net) – an online collection of web sites dedicated to matching lawyers with pro bono matters. Several law firms have developed both full-time and summer fellowship programs to respond to the growing need to serve the public good as well as fulfill law students' interest in working on these important issues. At Sullivan & Cromwell, for instance, our annual pro bono fellowship allows a litigation associate to work full time at the firm representing indigent pro se plaintiffs with actions pending in the U.S. District Court for the Southern District of New York. Many other firms, including those in this guide, have adopted other models that work well for them and their clients.

Despite these and other innovations, the ever-growing gulf between the legal needs of indigent populations and the availability of high-quality pro bono legal services continues to demand introspection and action on the part of the legal community. Organizations that deliver pro bono legal services and other services to the poor also require assistance to incorporate their organizations as not-for-profits, to obtain tax exempt status and to handle real estate, employment and a host of other issues. Law firm pro bono work, therefore, increasingly involves corporate lawyers, tax lawyers and other non-litigators. Once the organizations are up and running, they may need volunteer help in serving clients, which in many cases involves non-litigation work as well. Additionally, attorneys at law firms throughout New York City and from every practice group have worked extensively with individuals and businesses affected by the events of September 11. Day to day, large teams of law firm litigators work regularly on such matters as capital cases, domestic violence, and constitutional impact litigations, sometimes as co-counsel with legal services providers, a model Sullivan & Cromwell has employed in challenges to conditions of confinement in New York prisons as well as challenges to systemic housing discrimination.

To respond to these challenges, law firms need the help of this guide's readers – especially those just starting their legal careers. The guide promises to provide a newly comprehensive look at the pro bono programs of leading law firms. For those readers and firms dedicated to improving available legal services, this guide and other innovations in law firm pro bono work are the "good news."

Penny Shane
Partner, Pro Bono Fellowship Coordinator, & Pro Bono Committee Member
Sullivan & Cromwell, LLC

HOW TO USE THIS GUIDE

Service to clients who cannot afford legal counsel has always been an ethical imperative of lawyers. During the last few decades, large U.S. law firms collectively have devoted increasing resources to pro bono work as well as to the management and administration of those efforts. Nearly all have developed their own unique culture of service and methods of administration. This book was developed to provide law students and lawyers with the essential objective information necessary to meaningfully evaluate these firms' pro bono cultures and activities. We hope that the information contained within this guide will enable you to match your interests with an appropriate firm.

The information presented in this guide was developed through a partnership between Vault and pro bono coordinators at firms featured in this guide. Despite the natural competition among law firms, law firm pro bono coordinators often collaborate with their colleagues at other firms. Law firms recognize that these collaborations not only promote greater pro bono work within their own firms but also foster increased service within the entire legal community. The result is that the ever-increasing legal needs of the poor and disadvantaged receive greater attention.

When examining law firm pro bono culture and comparing firms, we encourage you to look beyond raw numerical data. We encourage you to examine the hallmarks of a hospitable and productive pro bono culture: Leadership and Structure, Participation, and Evaluation.

LEADERSHIP AND STRUCTURE

Once a firm has committed to create a pro bono practice, there are various ways in which the firm can structure its practice to meet that commitment. Questions 1, 2, 3, and 4 of the enclosed Law Firm Pro Bono Profiles are meant to explore firms' pro bono leadership and structure. Many firms have a pro bono coordinator and/or a pro bono committee. In order to better understand the mandate and role of the pro bono coordinator and/or committee, take the following points into consideration : How much time does the coordinator devote to pro bono? Is it a full-time or part-time position? Keep in mind that although no pro bono practice can be successful without partner support, a coordinator need not be a partner or a lawyer to be an effective volunteer manager. At the same time, a firm may not have a coordinator if it has a strong committee culture. If a firm has a committee, consider the composition of its members. Is there partner and/or associate representation? When considering how often the committee meets, be aware that in some instances, a committee that does not meet often may still be very active, communicating regularly with the coordinator and individual attorneys on an ad hoc basis.

Question 3 asks firms if they have established written pro bono policies. Many firms do, and those policies are often incorporated into their lawyers' manual. To learn more about a firm's practice, you may consider contacting the firm to request a copy. It is likely that firms' recruiting departments are prepared to disclose this information.

The next question refers to the "Law Firm Pro Bono Challenge." The Challenge is an aspirational minimum standard of pro bono service for firms with 50 or more attorneys. Signatories to the Challenge target a pro bono commitment of either 3 or 5 percent of annual billable hours or 60 or 100 hours per attorney per year. Many firms have signed on to the Challenge, and they use it as a goal for their pro bono practice. However, this does not mean that non-signatories do not have their own internal goals, particularly where a firm's pro bono program is still maturing. Moreover, every firm that accepts the Challenge does not necessarily meet it every year. The results are self-reported, and they are not published by the ABA.

PARTICIPATION

Participation means more than merely how many hours a firm devotes to pro bono work. Access to pro bono opportunities is a key to participation. The pro bono cases that lawyers enjoy most are those that meet their interests and enhance their skills. Question 5 asks firms to mention some of the areas of law in which they offer pro bono representation. A firm's pro bono work is a function of the interests of its attorneys, which can differ from office to office and class to class. Accordingly, the areas in which a firm does not practice may be more telling than the areas in which it does, since a firm may not practice in certain areas due to unavoidable conflicts of interest or ideological decisions. On the other hand, it simply may be due to a lack of attorney interest. Many firms will work with you to find a project that appeals to you, and you should explore opportunities to pursue your areas of pro bono interest with the law firm pro bono coordinator.

Pro bono statistics should be viewed in the context not only of firm size (larger firms tend to have larger total pro bono hours due to economies of scale), but also with an understanding of the extent to which the average lawyer at the firm performs pro bono work. Responses to Questions 6, 7, 8, and 9 will help you understand this better. When following up with a firm, you may wish to consider the level of involvement among partners and senior management. You may also want to examine the participation among specific offices and departments – particularly the office or department that you are considering.

EVALUATION, COMPENSATION & ADVANCEMENT

While pro bono work is meant to serve the public good and should be engaged in for altruistic rather than self-interested reasons, many associates have legitimate concerns about whether or not time spent on pro bono matters will negatively impact their compensation and advancement within the firm. Questions 12 and 13 are meant to explore how pro bono work is evaluated and compensated as compared with work for commercial clients, and the impact of such work on an associate's professional development within the firm.

Although many firms require partner supervision of pro bono matters, the level of such partners' involvement varies from firm to firm and matter to matter. For example, some firms assign one partner to all pro bono matters while other firms encourage different partners to supervise different matters. In either instance, the partner may take an active role in the case or may be only nominally involved. In addition, some firms may encourage (or require) senior associate supervision in lieu of (or in addition to) partner supervision. Whatever the case, you may want to consider whether these supervisors provide any kind of written evaluations and, if so, the function they serve in determining compensation and advancement. For example, some firms have a formal review process for commercial client work; if so, is pro bono work evaluated under the same system? If not, how is pro bono work evaluated? Is it given the same weight as commercial work in terms of contributing to your potential advancement within the firm?

Many firms have billable hours requirements for associates or use billable hours to help determine bonus levels. You may want to consider the extent to which such firms count pro bono work as "billables" in this regard. If they do not, is there some other way in which pro bono work factors into to an associate's compensation?

OUR SURVEY SAYS

This section of the firm profiles is comprised of quotes from current associates as collected in Vault's 2003 Associate Survey. In addition to the quotes, some firms have also included short "firm responses" to correct any misrepresentations regarding an aspect of the firm's pro bono program.

In conclusion, we hope that this book assists you in finding a pro bono practice that is a good match for your interests. Remember: although you can get a quick impression by flipping through these pages and looking at pro bono hours billed, and yes/no responses, the most important factor is the commitment of the partnership to meet defined pro bono goals and to structure the program to enable volunteers to meet those goals. This guide is intended to be your first step in learning how to consider a firm's pro bono commitment within the context of the firm's unique culture.

Enjoy!

Carrie Grimm, Pro Bono Coordinator, Cleary Gottlieb Steen & Hamilton
Gregory A. McConnell, Director, Public Interest Law, Winston & Strawn LLP
Mark Goldberg, Member, Pro Bono Committee, Latham & Watkins LLP
Teresa Schiller, Manager of Pro Bono and Community Programs, Clifford Chance US LLP

VAULT LAW CAREER LIBRARY

You are reading just one title from Vault's Law Career Library - the complete resource for legal careers. To see a full list of legal career titles, go to law.vault.com.

"With reviews and profiles of firms that one associate calls 'spot on,' [Vault's] guide has become a key reference for those who want to know what it takes to get hired by a law firm and what to expect once they get there."

– *New York Law Journal*

"To get the unvarnished scoop, check out Vault."

– *SmartMoney magazine*

> the most trusted name in career information™

"Vault is indispensable for locating insider information."
- *Metropolitan Corporate Counsel*

PRO BONO PROFILES

Allen & Overy

1221 Avenue of the Americas
New York, NY 10020
Phone: (212) 610-6300

One New Change
London, UK EC4M 9QQ
Phone: +44 (0) 20-7330-3000
www.allenovery.com

LOCATIONS

London (HQ) • New York, NY • Amsterdam • Antwerp • Bangkok • Bratislava • Brussels • Beijing • Budapest • Dubai • Frankfurt • Hamburg • Hong Kong • Luxembourg • Madrid • Milan • Moscow • Paris • Prague • Rome • Shanghai • Singapore • Turin • Tokyo • Warsaw

MAJOR DEPARTMENTS & PRACTICES

Antitrust
Banking
Derivatives
Employment
Environmental
International Capital Markets
Litigation
Project Finance
Real Estate
Securities
Tax

THE STATS

No. of attorneys: 2,300 +
No. of offices: 25
Managing Partner, New York: Mark Welling

EMPLOYMENT CONTACTS

Ms. Elizabeth Papas
Legal Recruitment Manager
Phone: (646) 344-6633
E-mail: elizabeth.papas@allenovery.com

Ms. Jennifer Thornton
Legal Recruitment Coordinator
Phone: (646) 344-66373
E-mail: jennifer.thornton@allenovery.com

Ms. Nicola McNeill
U.S. Liaison Manager
Phone: +44 (0) 20-7330-2447
E-mail: nicola.mcneill@allenovery.com

WHO'S WHO

Principal pro bono contact(s) at your firm:

Sarah Fels, Esq.
Senior Counsel
Phone: (212) 610-6415
E-mail: sarah.fels@allenovery.newyork.com

Does the firm have a pro bono coordinator? Yes
Sarah Fels

If yes, what percentage of his or her time is spent on pro bono work? Approximately 10 percent

Does the firm have a pro bono committee? No

If yes, how often does the committee meet? N/A

Describe the composition of the committee: N/A

THE SCOOP

Does your firm have a written pro bono policy? No

Has the firm signed on to the Law Firm Pro Bono Challenge? No

What are some of the areas of law in which your firm has performed pro bono legal work in the last two years? Individual political asylum cases; orders of protection and domestic violence; incorporation and application for 501(c)(3) status for community development, educational and artistic organizations; advising Afghanistan and drafting new law on mining and natural resources.

What are some of the areas of law in which your firm does not perform pro bono work? Criminal law.

Organizations for which your firm has performed pro bono legal services in the last two years: Lawyers Alliance for New York, inMotion, New York Lawyers for the Public Interest, Lawyers Committee for Human Rights, International Bar Association, Legal Aid Society, New York City Bar Association 9/11 committees.

List up to three pro bono matters that are representative of the pro bono work your firm participates in.

- Obtained political asylum for a former activist from Guinea, who was detained upon his arrival in New Jersey.

- Working with a group of concerned parents to establish the Brooklyn Montessori as an independent school after the YMCA withdrew funding of the program.

- Representing the Human Rights Institute of the International Bar Association in connection with the Guantanamo Bay detainees by submitting an amicus brief on the motion for certiorari and a second brief on the merits.

BY THE NUMBERS

What is the total number of hours that lawyers at your firm spent performing pro bono legal services in 2000, 2001 and 2002?

> Total number of hours in 2000: 205 hours
> Total number of hours in 2001: 600 hours
> Total number of hours in 2002: 425 hours

Average number of pro bono hours per attorney in U.S. offices per year (including associates, partners, counsels, but not summer associates):

> Average number of hours per attorney in 2000: 5.25 hours
> Average number of hours per attorney in 2001: 11 hours
> Average number of hours per attorney in 2002: 5 hours

What percentage of attorneys in this firm's U.S. offices did pro bono work in 2002? 11 percent

What percentage of attorneys in this firm's U.S. offices did at least 20 hours of pro bono work in 2002? 6 percent

Does the firm encourage its lawyers to perform a minimum number of pro bono hours? No

SUPERVISION AND EVALUATIONS

Is there partner supervision on each pro bono matter? Yes

Do partner supervisors or, if applicable, senior associates provide written evaluations of associates' work on pro bono matters? No

If so, are those evaluations taken into account in determining salary, bonuses or advancement in the firm? No

If not, does the firm consider pro bono work generally in associate evaluations? Yes

HOURS

Does the firm give billable hour credit for pro bono work? Yes

Does the firm have a maximum number of pro bono hours that can be applied toward the billable hour target? No

If so, what is the maximum? N/A

If your firm uses hours to determine bonuses, does it consider pro bono hours when determining bonuses? Not applicable

PRO BONO POINTS

What training opportunities are open to associates working on pro bono matters? Associates are able to attend trainings given by various legal service providers around the city, such as Legal Aid, inMotion, Lawyers Alliance for New York, Lawyers Committee for Human Rights, and New York City Bar Association.

Can associates bring matters of interest to the firm? Yes

Does the firm offer the use of support staff in carrying out pro bono matters? Yes

What pro bono opportunities are available for summer associates? Summer associates participate in ongoing pro bono matters with permanent associates and also may participate in externship programs with legal service providers throughout New York.

Does the firm have established programs, such as externships, that enable its associates to work in a public interest setting? Yes

If so, where and for up to how long? Externship programs are available to summer associates through NYLPI.

Has your firm won any special recognition or awards in the last two years for its pro bono work? Yes

If so, please list. Our London office has been recognized with a number of awards in the past few years, including The Lawyer Award for Best Pro Bono Activity in 2001, second place in 2002 and the Impact Endorsement Mark (endorsed by the UK Department of Trade and Industry) in 2001, 2002 and 2003.

THE FIRM SAYS

Allen & Overy's Pro Bono and Community Affairs Program is an important part of who we are as a firm and the broad range of initiatives we support is testimony to this. Lawyers in our global offices from Brussels to Warsaw participate in local pro bono and community service activities. Our pro bono work includes activities varying from the London office's representation of prisoners on death row, to helping to set up a Corporate Social Responsibility organization in Hong Kong, to advising a Cambodian children's charity in Paris. The Brussels office is leading an important project on parental abduction for the charity Child Focus, with a team of our lawyers from 11 offices. We hope that this is the first of many joint pro bono projects throughout Allen & Overy. Our community work has included: renovating and decorating an after-school center for children in Frankfurt and organizing and taking part in an activities day at a home for the elderly in Singapore. 2002 also saw the launch of the New York office's Values into Community Action Art Project where students from 12 schools throughout the city created artwork that is displayed in the office, using materials donated by the firm. We repeated this project in 2003 and inspired both the Hong Kong and London offices to initiate their own student art projects.

There is a twelve person pro bono committee in the London office, comprised of partners, senior management staff and the global Pro Bono and Community Affairs Officer. The New York office is currently considering forming a local pro bono committee to more easily monitor the various pro bono initiatives centered in New York.

Barra Little and Joanna Norland coordinate the program for research, advocacy and community service efforts for U.S. Associates based in the London office. During 2002, 8 permanent and 13 summer associates contributed a total of 80 hours to the summer pro bono program, which included a visit to the Battersea Legal Advice Centre, capital defense work for the London-based charity, Amicus and a gardening day at the Globe Centre which provides outreach services for people living with HIV.

Lawyers in the New York office substantially increased their participation in pro bono activities in 2003, logging over 2,000 hours on matters including a successful asylum application for an activist from Guinea, amicus briefs on behalf of the Guantanamo detainees and advising several women on child custody and related family and domestic violence disputes.

OUR SURVEY SAYS

"Improving — but very associate-driven rather than firm-driven."

"A committed but nascent program."

"The firm is quite committed — there are several organized programs (both legal and non-legal), and individuals also take on their own projects. The U.S. group seems less involved, though that appears to be a function of (i) individual choice and (ii) fewer opportunities to do legal pro bono work because the community we live in does not operate under U.S. law!"

"We have a very active pro bono committee."

"There's a senior person dedicated to pro bono who brings projects to our attention and solicits help."

"The firm is very committed to, and invests large amounts of time and resources in, its pro bono program. Pro bono opportunities range from legal work to volunteer work with AIDS hospices and inner city schools. Until recently the challenge for U.S. lawyers working in London has been to find pro bono opportunities that don't require English law expertise, but there are plenty of opportunities out there, some of which require legal (though not strictly English law) knowledge, and U.S. lawyers have become very involved."

"Organized pro bono seems to be just starting to move. There isn't any sort of requirement or very strong encouragement in that direction."

"There's a lot of pro bono here if you decide to get involved with it. The firm does support it."

"Being overseas does impede the ability of the U.S. lawyers to do pro bono work, and the U.S. partners don't really push the issue much. However, the firm at large in London does a lot of pro bono work and an even greater amount of general charity work in the community, winning awards for it. You can assist in a community legal clinic, read to children at a local school or serve as a board member of a charity through firm-sponsored programs."

"Good but could be better. Should be more strongly encouraged by all partners."

"Allen & Overy's Pro Bono and Community Affairs Program is an important part of who we are as a firm, and the broad range of initiatives we support is testimony to this."

— *Allen & Overy*

Alston & Bird LLP

1201 West Peachtree Street
One Atlantic Center
Atlanta, GA 30309-3424
Phone: (404) 881-7000
www.alston.com

LOCATIONS

Atlanta, GA (HQ)
Charlotte, NC
New York, NY
Raleigh, NC
Washington, DC

MAJOR DEPARTMENTS & PRACTICES

Business Transactions
E-Business
Financial Services
Government Regulation
Health Care
Intellectual Property
International
Legislation & Public Policy
Litigation & Dispute Resolution
Products Liability
Project Consulting
Tax
Workforce Management

THE STATS

No. of attorneys worldwide: 675
No. of offices worldwide: 5
Managing Partner: Ben F. Johnson III

EMPLOYMENT CONTACT

Ms. Emily S. Leeson
Director of Attorney Hiring & Development
E-mail: eleeson@alston.com

WHO'S WHO

Principal pro bono contact(s):

Judson Graves, Esq.
Chair, Pro Bono Committee
Phone: (404) 881-7279
E-mail: jgraves@alston.com

Does the firm have a pro bono coordinator? No

Does the firm have a pro bono committee? Yes

If yes, how often does the committee meet? Monthly

Describe the composition of the committee: Reflects the firm's age, gender, racial, ethnic and practice area diversity.

THE SCOOP

Does the firm have a written pro bono policy? Yes

Has the firm signed on to the Law Firm Pro Bono Challenge? Yes

What are some of the areas of law in which the firm has performed pro bono legal work in the last two years? Rotational programs at Atlanta Legal Aid and Fulton County Public Defender's office; death penalty appeals; representation of numerous status offenders at Fulton County Juvenile Court.

What are some of the areas of law in which the firm does not perform pro bono work? None

Organizations for which the firm has performed pro bono legal services in the last two years: Atlanta Legal Aid, Southern Center for Human Rights, Fulton County Public Defender's Office, Georgia Indigent Defense Council.

List up to three pro bono matters that are representative of the pro bono work the firm participates in.

- Representation of 12-year-old habitual truant who was sexually exploited; secured regular attendance of client at school and obtained placement at appropriate housing/medical facility.

- Representation, as Legal Aid Fellow on loan to legal services provider, of family being dispossessed by Housing Authority; successfully obtained reversal of dispossess order.

BY THE NUMBERS

What is the total number of hours that lawyers in U.S. offices at the firm spent performing pro bono legal services in 2000, 2001 and 2002?

Total number of hours in 2000: Approximately 27,840 hours
Total number of hours in 2001: Approximately 29,250 hours
Total number of hours in 2002: Approximately 38,610 hours

Average number of pro bono hours per attorney in U.S. offices per year (including associates, partners, counsels, but not summer associates):

    Average number of hours per attorney in 2000: Associates: 41 hours; partners: 72 hours
    Average number of hours per attorney in 2001: Associates: 31 hours; partners: 74 hours
    Average number of hours per attorney in 2002: Associates: 44 hours; partners: 73 hours

What percentage of attorneys in this firm's U.S. offices did pro bono work in 2002? Approximately 80 percent

What percentage of attorneys in this firm's U.S. offices did at least 20 hours of pro bono work in 2002? Approximately 70 percent

Does the firm encourage its lawyers to perform a minimum number of pro bono hours? Yes

If so, how many hours per year or what percentage of lawyers' billable hours? 3 percent of billable hours/minimum 50 hours per year.

SUPERVISION AND EVALUATIONS

Is there partner supervision on each pro bono matter? No

Do partner supervisors or, if applicable, senior associates provide written evaluations of associates' work on pro bono matters? Yes

If so, are those evaluations taken into account in determining salary, bonuses or advancement in the firm? Yes

If not, does the firm consider pro bono work generally in associate evaluations? N/A

HOURS

Does the firm give billable hour credit for pro bono work? Yes

Does the firm have a maximum number of pro bono hours that can be applied toward the billable hour target? Yes

If so, what is the maximum? 50 hours

If your firm uses hours to determine bonuses, does it consider pro bono hours when determining bonuses? Yes

PRO BONO POINTS

What training opportunities are open to associates working on pro bono matters? Too numerous to list

Can associates bring matters of interest to the firm? Yes

Does the firm offer the use of support staff in carrying out pro bono matters? Yes

What pro bono opportunities are available for summer associates? Too numerous to list

Does the firm have established programs, such as externships, that enable its associates to work in a public interest setting? Yes

If so, where and for up to how long? Approximately four months at Atlanta Legal Aid and Fulton County Public Defender's Office (see above).

Has your firm won any special recognition or awards in the last two years for its pro bono work? Yes

Has your firm won any special recognition or awards in the last two years for its pro bono work? Yes

Has the firm won any special recognition or awards in the last two years for its pro bono work? Yes

If so, please list. Alston & Bird received the 2003 Atlanta Bar Association Law Firm Service Award for the fifth year in a row and tenth time in the award's 17-year history. In 2002, A&B received the IMPACT Award from the Metro Atlanta Corporate Volunteer Council. A&B was ranked number 21 by The American Lawyer among the nation's 100 leading pro bono law firms in its most recent survey.

THE FIRM SAYS

Our firm's pro bono and community service program encompasses lawyers, staff and summer associates and includes senior partners through the newest recruits. The firm does not simply permit service of this type; rather, it encourages and facilitates such participation through the effort of Alston & Bird's pro bono committee. This group of lawyers — diverse in race, gender, practice area and age — has as a mission to (1) develop, facilitate and administer the firm's pro bono policy and related procedures; and (2) encourage and support the involvement of the firm's lawyers and staff in the provision of pro bono services.

For additional information about our legal pro bono and community services participation, please see answers to other parts of this survey and/or contact Judson Graves, Chair, Pro Bono Committee, Alson & Bird LLP, jgraves@alston.com.

OUR SURVEY SAYS

"The firm gives pro bono awards, strongly encourages pro bono activities [and] allows up to 50 hours of legal service pro bono hours to be counted toward the bonus."

"The firm overall is very committed. However, on an individual associate level, there is no question about what commitments should come first."

"The Truancy Intervention Project is our firm's biggest pro bono project and I can remember hearing it publicized by the firm during interviewing — the campaign for involvement only increases when you come to work here!"

"[There are] lots of pro bono activities, and the firm now gives 50 hours of pro bono legal work as credit towards earning the 2,100 billable-hour bonus."

"They love it – so long as it is in ADDITION to your 2,100 hours."

"While the firm gives pro bono work a lot of lip service, they only count 50 hours toward the billable requirement. Still, they do allow 50 hours to count toward the bonus, which is more than many firms can say."

"They let you do anything pro bono you want, as long as you have time."

"We actually can put 50 hours of pro bono work towards billables.... You'd be a fool not to find some pro bono work that you enjoy – there's no downside to doing it."

"We have the opportunity to get billable credit for some pro bono work; the problem is trying to do that on top of all the other firm work we need to get done — not enough hours in the day to do everything."

"Atlanta office, great; Charlotte, commitment is growing."

"The firm does not simply permit service of this type; rather, it encourages and facilitates such participation through the effort of Alston & Bird's pro bono committee."

— *Alston & Bird LLP*

Arnold & Porter LLP

555 Twelfth Street, NW
Washington, DC 20004
Phone: (202) 942-5000
www.arnoldporter.com

LOCATIONS

Washington, DC (HQ)
Century City, CA
Denver, CO
Los Angeles, CA
McLean, VA
New York, NY
Brussels
London

MAJOR DEPARTMENTS & PRACTICES

Antitrust
Banking
Bankruptcy
Benefits
Corporate & Securities
Environmental
Food & Drug
Governmental Contracts
Intellectual Property
Legislation
Life Sciences
Litigation
Public Policy
Real Estate
Tax & Estates
Telecommunications
Trusts

THE STATS

No. of attorneys worldwide: 700
No. of offices worldwide: 8
Chairman: Michael N. Sohn

EMPLOYMENT CONTACT

Ms. Lisa Pavia
Manager of Attorney Recruitment
Phone: (202) 942-5059
Fax: (202) 942-5999
E-mail: Lisa_Pavia@aporter.com

WHO'S WHO

Principal pro bono contact(s) at your firm:

Philip Horton, Esq.
Co-Chair
Phone: (202) 942-5787
E-mail: Philip_Horton@aporter.com

Kathleen Behan, Esq.
Co-Chair
Phone: (202) 942-5533
E-mail: Kathleen_Behan@aporter.com

Ms. Marsha Tucker
Social Worker
Phone: (202) 942-5315
E-mail: Marsha_Tucker@aporter.com

Does the firm have a pro bono coordinator? Yes
Marsha Tucker

If yes, what percentage of his or her time is spent on pro bono work? 100 percent

Does the firm have a pro bono committee? Yes

If yes, how often does the committee meet? The committee meets on a periodic basis, as needed, and communicates regularly by e-mail.

Describe the composition of the committee: The committee is comprised of 19 members consisting of partners, associates and a full-time professional social worker.

THE SCOOP

Does your firm have a written pro bono policy? Yes

Has the firm signed on to the Law Firm Pro Bono Challenge? Yes

What are some of the areas of law in which your firm has performed pro bono legal work in the last two years? The firm provides pro bono representation in matters addressing important public policy issues, for indigent or disadvantaged individuals in need of legal representation, and for nonprofit organizations. Specific areas of law in which the firm has performed pro bono legal work include: civil rights, international human rights, political asylum, women's rights, death penalty, poverty law, environmental protection, fair housing, veterans' appeals, AIDS advocacy, intellectual property, domestic violence, prisoners' rights, community economic development and other transactional matters, First Amendment and other areas of constitutional law, criminal justice reform, disability rights, employment law, homelessness, the arts, family law, children's rights, public benefits, nonprofit corporate matters and historic preservation.

What are some of the areas of law in which your firm does not perform pro bono work? As indicated, our pro bono practice is broad-based, and there are no areas in which, as a matter of policy, we do not practice.

Organizations for which your firm has performed pro bono legal services in the last two years: American Civil Liberties Union/ACLU Reproductive Freedom Project, Habitat for Humanity, Innocence Project, Lawyers Committee for Human Rights, Legal Aid Societies of the District of Columbia and New York, NAACP Legal Defense and Educational Fund, Inc., National Women's Law Center, Natural Resources Defense Council, People for the American Way, Southern Center for Human Rights.

List up to three pro bono matters that are representative of the pro bono work your firm participates in.

- Criminal Justice Reform. Arnold & Porter attorneys are representing three rural counties in suits against the State of Mississippi for failing to provide a constitutionally adequate indigent defense system by improperly shifting the funding burden from the state to financially strapped governments. The team developed a novel legal theory to challenge ineffective representation on a system-wide basis, and we are waiting for a decision in the case.

- Women's Rights. The firm initiated a first-of-its-kind lawsuit in Baltimore federal court against an international marriage broker on behalf of a "mail order bride." The lawsuit responds to concerns that brokers turn a blind eye to the heightened risk of domestic abuse facing women recruited to become "mail order brides."

- Reproductive Rights. We have served as principal outside counsel for NARAL Pro Choice America and have been involved in litigation and counseling for the organization, both in the core areas of concern relating to reproductive freedom, federal and state campaign law fundraising, judicial nominees and disclosure questions relating to NARAL's political mission, as well as on tax issues arising from NARAL's status as a tax-exempt organization. We are also representing Planned Parenthood Federation of America in connection with providing legal advice and strategy relating to Planned Parenthood's concerns about the growing trend of mergers and consolidations in the hospital industry, which often results in religiously dictated service limitations when sectarian hospitals merge with nonsectarian hospitals.

BY THE NUMBERS

What is the total number of hours that lawyers in U.S. offices at your firm spent performing pro bono legal services in 2000, 2001 and 2002?

    Total number of hours in 2000: 45,839 hours

    Total number of hours in 2001: 63,072 hours

    Total number of hours in 2002: 77,150 hours

Average number of pro bono hours per attorney in U.S. offices per year (including associates, partners, counsels, but not summer associates):

    Average number of hours per attorney in 2000: 94.3 hours

    Average number of hours per attorney in 2001: 109.6 hours

    Average number of hours per attorney in 2002: 125.9 hours

What percentage of attorneys in this firm's U.S. offices did pro bono work in 2002? 69.85 percent

What percentage of attorneys in this firm's U.S. offices did at least 20 hours of pro bono work in 2002? 52.25 percent

Does the firm encourage its lawyers to perform a minimum number of pro bono hours? Yes

If so, how many hours per year or what percentage of lawyers' billable hours? The firm encourages attorneys to spend 15 percent of their time on pro bono matters.

SUPERVISION AND EVALUATIONS

Is there partner supervision on each pro bono matter? Yes

Do partner supervisors or, if applicable, senior associates provide written evaluations of associates' work on pro bono matters? Yes

If so, are those evaluations taken into account in determining salary, bonuses or advancement in the firm? Yes

If not, does the firm consider pro bono work generally in associate evaluations? N/A

HOURS

Does the firm give billable hour credit for pro bono work? Yes

Does the firm have a maximum number of pro bono hours that can be applied toward the billable hour target? No

If so, what is the maximum? N/A (no hour target)

If your firm uses hours to determine bonuses, does it consider pro bono hours when determining bonuses? Yes

PRO BONO POINTS

What training opportunities are open to associates working on pro bono matters? The firm offers in-house trainings and allows attorneys to participate in trainings sponsored by bar associations and other groups.

Can associates bring matters of interest to the firm? Yes

Does the firm offer the use of support staff in carrying out pro bono matters? Yes

What pro bono opportunities are available for summer associates? Summer associates are actively encouraged to work on pro bono matters, and the firm makes a concerted effort to facilitate their participation.

Does the firm have established programs, such as externships, that enable its associates to work in a public interest setting? Yes

If so, where and for up to how long? The firm has two "rotation" or "loaned associate" programs, under which associates can spend six months working full-time (at full pay) for either the Legal Aid Society or the Washington Lawyers' Committee for Civil Rights and Urban Affairs. The Legal Aid rotation involves poverty law and offers excellent opportunities to get into court, while the Lawyers' Committee involves major cases alleging unlawful discrimination.

Has your firm won any special recognition or awards in the last two years for its pro bono work? Yes

If so, please list.

- Selection by *The American Lawyer* as one of only 20 of its "A-List" law firms in the United States, based on the belief that a first-rank law firm should have, in addition to a successful law practice, **a commitment to pro bono work**, to diversity in the workplace, and to development and training of its associates.

- The Human Rights Campaign Ally of Justice award in recognition of the Firm's pro bono services to HRC and its mission.

- *National Law Journal* 2002 Pro Bono Award.

- D.C. Bar Pro Bono Law Firm of the Year Award in both 1999 and 2002.

- 2002 Pro Bono Award from the State Bar of California to the Los Angeles office.

- 2002 Legal Aid Society Award to the New York office for work in connection with the September 11th tragedy.

- 2002 Colorado Lawyers Committee Law Firm of the Year Award to the Denver office for creation of the Colorado Innocence Project.

- Citation from the Washington Lawyer's Committee for Civil Rights for preparing a study of ongoing public and private discrimination against Latinos in the D.C. metropolitan area.

- Pro Bono Award from the Department of Justice's Board of Immigration Appeals for work in developing a program to provide appellate counsel to underrepresented individuals.

- Recognition from Habitat for Humanity for the Firm's long history of performing acquisition, zoning, and financing work for the organization.

- Recognition from Ayuda and Capital Area Immigrants Rights Coalition (CAIR) for the Firm's work in political asylum cases.

- Recognition from several Native American tribes for the Firm's pro bono work before the Federal Reserve and the Comptroller of the Currency in obtaining a national charter for the Native American National Bank.

- 2002 Community Partner of the Year award from the Marshall-Brennan Fellowship Program in recognition of participation in the "We the Students" Constitutional Literacy Project.

- Recognition from Ayuda for creating a pro bono project to represent battered women and assist in legalizing their immigration status.

- Tahirih Justice Center Award for continued dedication to providing pro bono services for the nonprofit group, which advocates on behalf of women facing international human rights abuses.

- Business Leadership Award from the District of Columbia Charter School Resource Center for the Firm's assistance in handling numerous legal matters on behalf of Washington, D.C. charter schools.

- Recognition from NARAL and the ACLU for the Firm's representation in connection with various pro-choice legal work.

THE FIRM SAYS

Arnold & Porter encourages both partners and associates to devote up to 15 percent of their time to pro bono work. While participation in pro bono matters is voluntary, the firm believes that pro bono work is the professional obligation of every attorney. In particular, all attorneys are urged to work on at least one pro bono case in their first three years at the firm. The firm's commitment to pro bono work is consistent with the American Bar Association's policy which states that it is "the professional obligation of all attorneys to devote a reasonable amount of time, but in no event less than at least 50 hours per year, to pro bono and other public service activities." Arnold & Porter was among the first law firms to sign the "Law Firm Pro Bono Challenge Statement of Principles" which asks law firms to contribute at least 5 percent of the firm's total billable hours to pro bono work.

I. The Pro Bono Committee

The firm has a pro bono committee, consisting of both partners and associates, as well as a full-time professional social worker, which is responsible for implementing the firm's pro bono policies and procedures. The committee seeks important and interesting pro bono opportunities, determines the matters that the firm should undertake on a pro bono basis, advertises these matters throughout the firm, encourages attorneys to undertake pro bono work and assures proper staffing of pro bono work undertaken by the firm.

II. Staffing of Pro Bono Matters

As noted, all lawyers are encouraged to spend up to 15 percent of their total working hours on such matters. It is understood, however, that a particular matter may require, for some weeks or months, a substantially greater time commitment, and that commitment is permitted. Billable equivalent hour credit is given for all time spent on pro bono activities, and attorneys' work on pro bono matters is evaluated in the same way as work on billable matters. Once the firm undertakes a pro bono matter, that matter is treated in the same manner as the firm's commercial work: the same staffing, resources and attention are given to the matter.

III. Screening of Pro Bono Opportunities

In order to obtain interesting and important pro bono matters, the pro bono committee maintains relationships with a variety of public interest organizations which have diverse goals and interests. In addition, if an attorney has a particular area of interest, the committee is available to try to find a matter in that area. If an attorney is interested in a potential pro bono matter, it must be referred to the pro bono committee for approval before it may be taken on by the firm. Generally, pro bono matters fall into three basic categories: (1) legal assistance to indigent persons; (2) matters involving significant issues of public policy; and (3) legal work for nonprofit organizations. Among the factors considered by the pro bono committee in determining whether the firm will undertake a particular matter on a pro bono basis are the following:

- the financial means of the client;
- the public policy issues involved;
- the significance and potential impact of the matter;
- whether the matter is a court appointment;
- whether the matter is for a nonprofit organization;
- whether the matter makes special use of Arnold & Porter's resources;
- the ability of the client to obtain other counsel;
- the costs to the firm of undertaking the matter;
- the location of the matter;

- whether the matter will provide helpful training for associates;
- the strength or merits of the case;
- potential conflicts;
- the firm's ability adequately to staff the matter; and
- whether the matter would further the firm's commitment to the Law Firm Pro Bono Challenge Statement of Principles

OUR SURVEY SAYS

"Everyone I know does pro bono here."

"One of the greatest assets of this firm is its commitment to pro bono. The firm has been involved in major pro bono efforts and was founded by men who believed it was important not just to service the rich and the powerful, but to fight for the rights of the poor and the meek. From defending people from McCarthyism to defending the constitutional right to an attorney, this firm leads the way. Some firms talk a lot about their pro bono, this firm shows its commitment every day. Pro bono hours count towards the pain alleviation bonus and are considered billable. Associates are encouraged to participate in pro bono projects, but in no way are we forced to do so."

"Pro bono is part of the firm's heritage and deeply important to it. People take pro bono seriously."

"I was able to spend approximately 400 hours on pro bono matters last year."

"Pro bono hours are billable, and I started working on a pro bono case in my first month here. I have the impression that you're odd here if you don't have some pro bono work going on."

"The upper echelons of the firm are constantly encouraging people to do more pro bono work."

"This firm is interesting on this issue — on the one hand, they tout themselves as deeply committed to pro bono. On the other hand, I was told by a partner recently that I needed to bill a certain number of hours a day, and if I had an extra hour or two, it should be spent on billable work, not 'wasted' on pro bono."

"There are many opportunities for pro bono service, and the firm truly does support pro bono (it has a full-time pro bono coordinator/social worker), but only to an extent. It is noted in reviews when a person 'needs to find more billable work,' which, when a significant amount of the person's time has been spent doing pro bono work, suggests that they should have done less pro bono. The firm generally wants you to spend no more than 15 percent of your time on pro bono, which I do think is generous."

"A third of my clients since arriving have been pro bono."

"There is not a better firm in the country for a young lawyer committed to doing pro bono work."

> "While participation in pro bono matters is voluntary, the firm believes that pro bono work is the professional obligation of every attorney."
> — *Arnold & Porter LLP*

Baker & Hostetler LLP

3200 National City Center
1900 East 9th Street
Cleveland, OH 44114-3485
Phone: (216) 621-0200
www.bakerlaw.com

LOCATIONS

Cleveland, OH (HQ)
Cincinnati, OH
Columbus, OH
Costa Mesa, CA
Denver, CO
Houston, TX
Los Angeles, CA
New York, NY
Orlando, FL
Washington, DC
São Paulo, Brazil*
Juarez, Mexico*

*International Affiliates

MAJOR DEPARTMENTS & PRACTICES

Business
Employment & Labor
Energy
Health Care
Hospitality
Intellectual Property
International
Litigation
Media Law
Tax, Personal Planning & Employee Benefits
Transportation

THE STATS

No. of attorneys worldwide: 526
No. of offices worldwide: 10
Executive Partners: R. Steven Kestner and Alec Wightman

EMPLOYMENT CONTACT

Ms. Dee Driscole
Attorney Recruitment and Development Manager
Phone: (216) 861-7092
Fax: (216) 861-6618
E-mail: ddriscole@bakerlaw.com

WHO'S WHO

Principal pro bono contact(s) at your firm:

Ken Snyder, Esq.
Managing Partner, Cleveland
E-mail: ksnyder@bakerlaw.com

THE SCOOP

What are some of the areas of law in which your firm has performed pro bono legal work in the last two years? See below.

What are some of the areas of law in which your firm does not perform pro bono work? N/A

Organizations for which your firm has performed pro bono legal services in the last two years: See below.

List up to three pro bono matters that are representative of the pro bono work your firm participates in.

Recent representative examples of 2003 pro bono legal services:

- Baker & Hostetler represented former President Bill Clinton in a deal between his foundation and four generic drug companies to supply developing countries in Africa and the Caribbean with deeply discounted antiretroviral AIDS medicine. At a New York press conference, President Clinton thanked attorneys from Baker & Hostetler for crafting the complex agreements with drug manufacturers in India and South Africa. The agreements cover such issues as product quality, pricing transparency and supply commitments.

- Baker & Hostetler represented former employees of CSC Ltd., a Youngstown steel company, to help them receive distributions from their employee investment plans after the company went bankrupt.

- Baker & Hostetler provides tax advice to community and charitable organizations.

- During the summer of 2003, the Columbus office was involved in pro bono immigration project in which one of the firm's summer associates used her Spanish background to translate Honduran birth certificates.

- Baker & Hostetler represented the Cincinnati Habitat for Humanity in closing land transfers.

- The Denver office's lawyers perform pro bono work with the Metro Family Law Clinic, ACLU of Colorado and the federal Pro Bono Mentorship Program.

- Baker & Hostetler provides legal services for the finalization of adoptions of dependent children in Los Angeles.

- Baker & Hostetler provided legal services to assist in the merger of the Washington Metropolitan Police Boys and Girls Club with the Boys and Girls Club of Greater Washington.

PRO BONO POINTS

Has your firm won any special recognition or awards in the last two years for its pro bono work? Yes

If so, please list. See below.

THE FIRM SAYS

Baker & Hostetler attorneys provide legal services on a pro bono basis in Cleveland and nationwide.

Community Activities

Baker & Hostetler was founded by partners who first served in municipal government. When moving on to the legal profession, they brought with them a commitment to community support. Our attorneys in each of our 10 offices continue this dedication.

You'll find Baker & Hostetler people mentoring school children in Cleveland, Houston, Los Angeles and Orlando. B.E.S.T. (Baker's Educational Service Team) works closely with schools. You may see us collecting food and building housing for the less fortunate in Columbus. In Washington and New York we raise funds for medical research. A community activities committee in Denver drives our involvement in local legal aid organizations.

Pro Bono

We act as retained counsel to boards, county commissions and municipalities of all sizes, reflecting our tradition of government and civic service.

Baker & Hostetler was recently recognized by Congressman Tim Ryan of Youngstown, Ohio, for our pro bono work for former employees of CSC Ltd., a Youngstown steel producer. Diane Wilcox of our Cleveland office was instrumental in helping former CSC salaried and union employees receive distributions from the employee investment plans in which they had participated. CSC filed bankruptcy and shut down its facilities in early 2001. Distributions from the employee investment plans were suspended in January 2002 as part of the IRS approval process. Wilcox did the work on a pro bono basis because CSC entered final liquidation before the IRS had completed the review of the applications for approval of the termination of each employee investment plan.

For other recent representative examples of Baker & Hostetler pro bono legal services, see above.

OUR SURVEY SAYS

"Litigation appears to be more committed than business."

"The firm is committed to supporting people that take on pro bono work, but there is no organized pro bono program."

"At a New York press conference, President Clinton thanked attorneys from Baker & Hostetler for crafting the complex agreements with drug manufacturers in India and South Africa."

— *Baker & Hostetler LLP*

Baker & McKenzie

One Prudential Plaza
130 East Randolph Street, Suite 2500
Chicago, IL 60601
Phone: (312) 861-8000
www.bakernet.com

LOCATIONS

Although the firm has no "main office," its administrative hub is located in Chicago.

Chicago, IL
Dallas, TX
Houston, TX
Miami, FL
New York, NY
Palo Alto, CA
San Diego, CA
San Francisco, CA
Washington, DC
Calgary
Toronto
+ 55 other offices worldwide

MAJOR DEPARTMENTS & PRACTICES

Antitrust & Trade
Banking & Finance
Corporate
Dispute Resolution
Employment
Health Care
Information Technology/Communications
Insurance
Intellectual Property
International/Communications
Major Projects & Project Finance
Real Estate, Construction, Environment & Tourism
Tax

THE STATS

No. of attorneys worldwide: 3,273
No. of offices worldwide: 66
Executive Committee Chair: Christine Lagarde

EMPLOYMENT CONTACT

Chicago: Ms. Eleonara Nikol
Phone: (312) 861-2924
E-mail: eleonora.nikol@bakernet.com

Dallas: Ms. Terry Deleon
Phone: (214) 978-3049
E-mail: terry.a.deleon@bakernet.com

Houston: Ms. Nancy Rader
Phone: (713) 427-5009
E-mail: nancy.a.rader@bakernet.com

Miami: Mr. Clement Noble
Phone: (305) 789-8908
E-mail: clement.noble@bakernet.com

New York: Ms. Anne Zagorin
Phone: (212) 891-3573
E-mail: anne.s.zagorin@bakernet.com

San Diego: Ms. Victoria Leach
Phone: (619) 235-7733
E-mail: victoria.a.leach@bakernet.com

San Francisco/Palo Alto: Ms. Andrea Carr
Phone: (415) 984-3801
E-mail: andrea.l.carr@bakernet.com

Washington, DC: Ms Jane Lint
Phone: (202) 452-7024
E-mail: jane.e.lint@bakernet.com

WHO'S WHO

Principal pro bono contact(s) at your firm:

Angela C. Vigil, Esq.
Director of Pro Bono and Public Service — North America
Phone: (312) 861-2570
E-mail: angela.c.vigil@bakernet.com

Does the firm have a pro bono coordinator? Yes
Angela C. Vigil, Esq.

If yes, what percentage of his or her time is spent on pro bono work? 100 percent

Does the firm have a pro bono committee? Yes

If yes, how often does the committee meet? The Pro Bono and Public Service Initiative functions as a pro bono committee for Baker & McKenzie's North American region.

Describe the composition of the committee: At least one partner and one associate from each of Baker & McKenzie's 11 offices in the North American region serve on the Pro Bono and Public Service Initiative of the firm. Personnel from the firm's diversity committee, professional development staff and marketing departments are also invited as participants in these calls and discussions. The managing partners of each office in North America participate in meetings at the regional and local level. The Initiative also includes working groups of partners from several offices. These working groups direct the firm's work in pro bono legal services, client partnering projects, fellowships, employee volunteerism, charitable giving and civic presence.

THE SCOOP

Does your firm have a written pro bono policy? Yes

Has the firm signed on to the Law Firm Pro Bono Challenge? Yes. The Chicago office signed the Challenge as a charter member; all other offices have since signed on.

What are some of the areas of law in which your firm has performed pro bono legal work in the last two years? Baker & McKenzie's pro bono advocacy has spanned many areas of law including: administrative law and public benefits, children's rights, contracts and business law for non-profit organizations, criminal law and death penalty advocacy, disability and elder law, estate and probate law, family law, defense of evictions and foreclosures, immigration law including naturalization and applications for political asylum, secured transactions and special education law.

What are some of the areas of law in which your firm does not perform pro bono work? There are no designated areas of law in which Baker & McKenzie refuses pro bono work. The firm concentrates provision of pro bono service to underserved and disadvantaged clients who would not otherwise have access to the justice system or to able counsel.

Organizations for which your firm has performed pro bono legal services in the last two years: National Organizations: American Bar Association, Lawyers for Children America, Council of Parent Attorneys and Advocates, Habitat for Humanity.

Local Organizations (in jurisdictions where we have offices): Capital Area Immigrants' Rights Coalition (Washington, D.C.), Catholic Charities (Houston), Center for Disability and Elder Law (Chicago), Dream League (San Francisco), Human Rights Initiative (Dallas), Jewish Community Center of San Francisco (San Francisco), Lawyers for Children America (Miami), Lawyers Committee for Human Rights (New York), Midwest Immigrant and Human Rights Center (Chicago), Elder Law & Advocacy: Senior Citizen Legal Services (San Diego).

List up to three pro bono matters that are representative of the pro bono work your firm participates in.

Advocacy on behalf of disabled children: Attorneys in Washington, D.C., Dallas, Palo Alto, Toronto and Chicago have been advocating on behalf of disabled children in several forums. The firm has drafted appeals of amicus briefs for the Federal Circuit courts on issues related to the placement of disabled students and the access of disabled students and their families to counsel. Baker & McKenzie offices advise national public interest organizations on the policy implications of filing amicus briefs before the U.S. Supreme Court on special education issues related to the exclusion of special education children from mainstream classrooms. This work has led to the firm's development of a public interest law practice in special education law, social security benefits advocacy, delinquency and criminal court representation of disabled youth, and school discipline advocacy against zero tolerance policies in public schools.

Immigration law and political asylum: Teams of attorneys in our Dallas, San Francisco, Houston, New York and Washington, D.C., offices have represented clients in political asylum applications, including claims under the Violence Against Women Act. Each of these clients feared physical and mental persecution if they returned to their home countries, but lacked the resources to obtain paid counsel to represent them before the Immigration and Naturalization Service (INS) and the Bureau of Naturalization and Immigration Services. A significant project in our Chicago office involves the presentation of applicants seeking naturalization as United States citizens. This is a project in which the firm partners with client corporations in our pro bono advocacy.

Housing work with Habitat for Humanity International: Baker & McKenzie provides pro bono services to Habitat for Humanity International, raising millions for the development of low-income housing via the securitization of existing Habitat mortgages. The sophisticated Wall Street financing device affords decent housing to families in communities in the United States and beyond. In late 2002, for example, Habitat for Humanity International and the firm announced the closing of a $1 million, 15-year interest-free loan from the New Jersey Housing and Mortgage Finance Authority. The loan was secured by mortgages held by eight Habitat affiliates in New Jersey, and, as limited by its terms, all proceeds will be used to build affordable, owner-occupied housing for homeowners earning 80 percent or less of the area median income.

BY THE NUMBERS

What is the total number of hours that lawyers in U.S. offices at your firm spent performing pro bono legal services in 2000, 2001 and 2002?

       Total number of hours in 2000: Not available
       Total number of hours in 2001: 6,592 hours
       Total number of hours in 2002: 12,555 hours

Average number of pro bono hours per attorney in U.S. offices per year (including associates, partners, counsels, but not summer associates):

       Average number of hours per attorney in 2000: Not available.
       Average number of hours per attorney in 2001: 11 hours

Average number of hours per attorney in 2002: 22.5 hours

What percentage of attorneys in this firm's U.S. offices did pro bono work in 2002? 43 percent

What percentage of attorneys in this firm's U.S. offices did at least 20 hours of pro bono work in 2002? 19.8 percent

Does the firm encourage its lawyers to perform a minimum number of pro bono hours? Yes

If so, how many hours per year or what percentage of lawyers' billable hours? As a region, the North American offices of Baker & McKenzie ask each attorney to provide at least 60 hours of pro bono service to the underserved and disadvantaged each year. Many individual offices ask for more hours of pro bono service. Each office considers at least 60 hours of pro bono time toward promotion, salary or advancement. Many offices consider pro bono work by attorneys in excess of this minimum level in evaluating attorneys for compensation and advancement.

SUPERVISION AND EVALUATIONS

Is there partner supervision on each pro bono matter? Yes

Do partner supervisors or, if applicable, senior associates provide written evaluations of associates' work on pro bono matters? Each office conducts evaluations of attorneys in different ways. In general, the quality of all of an attorney's legal work, including lawyering in pro bono matters, is assessed to determine and evaluate an attorney's compensation and advancement.

If so, are those evaluations taken into account in determining salary, bonuses or advancement in the firm? Yes

If not, does the firm consider pro bono work generally in associate evaluations? N/A

HOURS

Does the firm give billable hour credit for pro bono work? Yes

Does the firm have a maximum number of pro bono hours that can be applied toward the billable hour target? No

If so, what is the maximum? While the worldwide firm has no policy on the maximum number of hours an attorney can complete for pro bono credit, North American offices have varying policies.

If your firm uses hours to determine bonuses, does it consider pro bono hours when determining bonuses? Yes

PRO BONO POINTS

What training opportunities are open to associates working on pro bono matters? Baker & McKenzie, directly and through agencies with which the firm partners, provides associates with many opportunities for training and mentorship in pro bono projects. Each office of the firm has partnered with a select group of public interest organizations who work with office leadership and the firm's Director of Pro Bono and Public Service to provide the highest quality training to attorneys. The firm is dedicated to providing the same high quality of representation to its pro bono clients as it provides to paying clients.

Can associates bring matters of interest to the firm? Yes

Does the firm offer the use of support staff in carrying out pro bono matters? Yes

What pro bono opportunities are available for summer associates? Summer associates are invited and encouraged to be involved in any pro bono project in which firm attorneys are involved. Baker & McKenzie sees pro bono cases as a great opportunity for summer associates to demonstrate and develop their skills and to gain training and mentorship from full-time attorneys.

Does the firm have established programs, such as externships, that enable its associates to work in a public interest setting? Yes

If so, where and for up to how long? Some offices of the firm support summer public interest law internships for first-year associates to work with public interest law organizations.

Has your firm won any special recognition or awards in the last two years for its pro bono work? Yes

If so, please list. Baker & McKenzie was awarded the first ever CorporateProBono.org award for our "Partners To Serve" program in 2003. The "Partners To Serve" program has become a national model for client partnering efforts in pro bono. The firm partners with client corporations and public interest organizations to provide free legal representation for the underserved and disadvantaged. More information on the project is available at www.bakernet.com.

The firm's pro bono efforts also gained the Baker & McKenzie the 2003 Pro Bono Initiative Award given by the Public Interest Law Initiative in Chicago. This award recognizes the firm's work in direct legal service, institutionalization of a pro bono ethic within the firm, and innovative new efforts in pro bono legal services including the firm's client partnering project.

THE FIRM SAYS

Since our inception in 1949, Baker & McKenzie has been committed to returning value to the communities in which we work and live. Baker & McKenzie's commitment to pro bono work started with Russell Baker, the firm's founder, because of his belief that lawyers have a professional duty to provide the underserved with free legal services.

Today, with offices worldwide, Baker & McKenzie continues to make a positive impact through multiple avenues of service. Supported by firm leadership, Baker & McKenzie provides financial support and annually contributes a substantial amount of time to pro bono legal service and community service. Baker & McKenzie seeks out not only the best and brightest attorneys, but also those that care very deeply about the world around them. Our pro bono and public service program helps the firm leverage our resources to make a real difference in the communities in which we live and work.

Baker & McKenzie stands behind its pro bono and public service mission:

- To deliver first class legal services to the underserved by fostering an environment which encourages and promotes public service.

- To promote and sponsor activities which provide opportunities for all firm personnel, independently, and in partnership with our clients, to contribute to the well-being of the communities in which we practice and live.

The dedication of Baker & McKenzie's worldwide leadership is evident in the words of the firm's chair, Christine Lagarde:

> For over 50 years, Baker & McKenzie members have been dedicated to giving back to their communities. We see this as our commitment to the bar, and as our responsibility as citizens of our communities. Whether it is

through legal services for the disadvantaged, public service and volunteerism, community leadership or charitable giving, Baker & McKenzie attorneys and staff have recognized and embraced our civic responsibilities and have made the fulfillment of these responsibilities an essential element of firm life. Through its Pro Bono and Public Service Initiative, the firm works not only to be an active participant in the community, but also to guide and inspire clients and fellow lawyers and staff to engage in the same worthwhile activities in service to the public. We are proud of our commitment to pro bono and public service.

Baker & McKenzie has recently hired the firm's first-ever North American Director of Pro Bono and Public Service, Angela C. Vigil. The Director coordinates and facilitates legal and community service and outreach projects across the regional Firm.

The firm is also very proud of "Partners to Serve", an award-winning client partnering program already garnering success alongside participants including McDonald's Corporation and Abbott Laboratories. The program assists and advises in the development of corporate legal departments for clients desirous to increase their pro bono services.

Baker & McKenzie is a global law firm dedicated to providing public service in all regions of the globe where we practice. The global law firm Baker & McKenzie has 66 offices in 36 jurisdictions. Pro bono service provided by our global offices include: securitization and intellectual property representation in our Asia Pacific Region; business law, human rights and criminal cases, including death penalty representation in our Europe and Middle Eastern Region; and contracts and tax work on behalf of non-profit organizations in our Latin American region.

Baker & McKenzie's pro bono and public service program is growing every day and is integral to the life of the firm. We are proud of the tradition of pro bono and community service at Baker & McKenzie as we continue to strive to deepen our public service commitment.

OUR SURVEY SAYS

"We just became the first firm to hire a national pro bono director."

"We receive 50 hours of billable credit for pro bono work, and the firm staffs a local advice and referral clinic four times per year."

"We have a growing commitment to pro bono work."

"For the most part, although there are some naysayers, pro bono is accepted and sometimes encouraged. They did just add a full-time pro bono attorney on staff, so that should bring good results."

"We get 50 hours per year pro bono applied to our billable hours."

"On the one hand, they do allow 100 hours of pro bono to count toward billable hours. On the other hand, there is very little pro bono work pursued by attorneys and procedures are barely in place, which makes it hard to pursue pro bono work. Only a handful of attorneys are committed enough to pursue it, which I think is too bad. The firm should make it more or less expected of attorneys — just part of the program of working here."

"Our firm provides a non-billable hours bonus for pro bono work."

"The firm has given me full credit on more than 400 hours of pro bono this year!"

Bingham McCutchen LLP

150 Federal Street
Boston, MA 02110
Phone: (617) 951-8000
www.bingham.com

LOCATIONS

Boston, MA
Hartford, CT
Los Angeles, CA
New York, NY
Orange County, CA
San Francisco, CA
Silicon Valley, CA
Walnut Creek, CA
Washington, DC
London
Tokyo

MAJOR DEPARTMENTS & PRACTICES

Antitrust & Trade Regulation
Broker-Dealer
Corporate
Environmental & Land Use
Finance
Financial Restructuring
International
Investment Management
Intellectual Property
Litigation
Private Equity/M&A
Project/Structured Finance
Real Estate
Tax/Estate Planning
Subsidiary Businesses
    Bingham Consulting Group
    Bingham Legg Advisers
    Bingham Strategic Advisors

THE STATS

No. of attorneys worldwide: 850 +
No. of offices worldwide: 11
Chairman: Jay S. Zimmerman

EMPLOYMENT CONTACT

Fiona S. Trevelyan, Esq.
Director of Legal Recruitment
Phone: (617) 951-8608
Fax: (617) 951-8736
E-mail: legalrecruit@bingham.com

WHO'S WHO

Does the firm have a pro bono coordinator? Yes

The firm's pro bono program is coordinated by Nora Cregan, West Coast chair, in San Francisco and Neal Rosen, East Coast chair, in Boston, with administrative assistance from Hilarie Lieber, training and pro bono manager, from the San Francisco office.

Nora Cregan, Esq.
West Coast Chair, San Francisco
Phone: (415) 393-2000
E-mail: nora.cregan@bingham.com

Neal Rosen, Esq.
East Coast Chair, Boston
Phone: (617) 951-8000
E-mail neal.rosen@bingham.com

Ms. Hilarie Lieber
Training and Pro Bono Manager, San Francisco
Phone: (415) 393-2000
E-mail: hilarie.lieber@bingham.com

If yes, what percentage of his or her time is spent on pro bono work? It varies. Hilarie Lieber spends approximately 50 percent of her time on pro bono matters. The chairs spend between 10 and 15 percent of their time on pro bono matters.

Does the firm have a pro bono committee? Yes, an informal committee.

If yes, how often does the committee meet? On an ad hoc basis.

Describe the composition of the committee: The coordinators, together with other interested partners from Bingham McCutchen's offices.

THE SCOOP

Does your firm have a written pro bono policy? Yes

Has the firm signed on to the Law Firm Pro Bono Challenge? Yes

What are some of the areas of law in which your firm has performed pro bono legal work in the last two years? Adoption, civil rights, corporate nonprofit work, debt collection, environmental, estate planning, family law, health care, housing, intellectual property, political asylum, prisoners' rights, reproductive rights, uninsured motorist, unemployment compensation.

What are some of the areas of law in which your firm does not perform pro bono work? N/A

Organizations for which your firm has performed pro bono legal services in the last two years: AIDS Legal Referral Panel, American Civil Liberties Union, Law Works for People/Connecticut Bar Association, Lawyers Alliance of New York Lawyers, Clearinghouse on Affordable Housing and Homelessness, Inc./ Boston Bar Association Business Law Pro Bono Project, Lawyers' Committee for Civil Rights Under Law (San Francisco/Boston/LA Public Counsel), Planned Parenthood

Federation, Prison Law Office, Volunteer Lawyers Project of the Boston Bar Association/Legal Services Program of the San Francisco Bar, Volunteer Lawyers for the Arts.

List up to three pro bono matters that are representative of the pro bono work your firm participates in.

- ·*Valdivia v. Davis*, U.S. District Court, Eastern District of California. Bingham McCutchen attorneys are representing a class of parolees who allege that California's parole revocation system violates their due process rights by holding parolees in custody for up to 45 days, and in many cases longer. The U.S. District Court has granted summary judgment in favor of the class of more than 75,000 parolees and directed that the state make substantial changes to its parole revocation system.

- ·*Cotter v. City of Boston*, U.S. District Court for the District of Massachusetts and U.S. Court of Appeals for the First Circuit. In Cotter, the firm, in association with the Lawyers' Committee for Civil Rights Under Law of the Boston Bar Association, represents the Massachusetts Association of Minority Law Enforcement Officers (MAMLEO), whom the firm has represented on a pro bono basis for 25 years, and two African-American police officers whose promotions were challenged by a group of Caucasian police officers on reverse discrimination grounds. After successfully intervening, MAMLEO obtained in its favor in 2002 a 77-page decision by the trial court upholding the department's use of affirmative action. The First Circuit affirmed the trial court's ruling that the affirmative action promotions were lawful.

- ·Partners In Health. Bingham McCutchen serves as general counsel to Partners In Health, a 501(c)(3) public charity (PIH) that works in locations throughout the world to treat and eradicate infectious disease and provide preferential health options to the poor. In its capacity as general counsel, Bingham regularly counsels PIH on a wide range of matters, including corporate governance, employment, intellectual property, contracts and joint ventures. Bingham worked with PIH to obtain its 501(c)(3) status in conjunction with its recent reorganization, and in addition, Bingham has qualified PIH as a public charity in numerous foreign jurisdictions, including Peru, Haiti and Russia, and has assisted PIH with the state registration requirements for fundraising in all 50 states.

BY THE NUMBERS

What is the total number of hours that lawyers in U.S. offices at your firm spent performing pro bono legal services in 2000, 2001 and 2002?

       Total number of hours in 2000: N/A (pre-merger)
       Total number of hours in 2001: N/A (pre-merger)
       Total number of hours in 2002: 38,954 hours

Average number of pro bono hours per attorney in U.S. offices per year (including associates, partners, counsels, but not summer associates):

       Average number of hours per attorney in 2000: N/A (pre-merger)
       Average number of hours per attorney in 2001: N/A (pre-merger)
       Average number of hours per attorney in 2002: 55.3 hours

What percentage of attorneys in this firm's U.S. offices did pro bono work in 2002? 73.6 percent

What percentage of attorneys in this firm's U.S. offices did at least 20 hours of pro bono work in 2002? 45.5 percent

Does the firm encourage its lawyers to perform a minimum number of pro bono hours? No. The firm does not require the performance of any specific minimum number of pro bono hours, but encourages all attorneys to do pro bono work.

If so, how many hours per year or what percentage of lawyers' billable hours? N/A

SUPERVISION AND EVALUATIONS

Is there partner supervision on each pro bono matter? Yes

Do partner supervisors or, if applicable, senior associates provide written evaluations of associates' work on pro bono matters? Yes

If so, are those evaluations taken into account in determining salary, bonuses or advancement in the firm? Yes

If not, does the firm consider pro bono work generally in associate evaluations? N/A

HOURS

Does the firm give billable hour credit for pro bono work? Yes

Does the firm have a maximum number of pro bono hours that can be applied toward the billable hour target? All East Coast and most West Coast pro bono hours are creditable without limit.

If so, what is the maximum? See above.

If your firm uses hours to determine bonuses, does it consider pro bono hours when determining bonuses? Yes

PRO BONO POINTS

What training opportunities are open to associates working on pro bono matters? Bingham McCutchen offers an extensive pro bono library, which includes various training materials. Partners also offer direct supervision, and training is provided by referral agencies. In addition, a formal firm-developed pro bono training program in nonprofit incorporation and related matters is available.

Can associates bring matters of interest to the firm? Yes

Does the firm offer the use of support staff in carrying out pro bono matters? Yes

What pro bono opportunities are available for summer associates? Opportunities vary by office, but opportunities include unemployment compensation cases, cases referred by legal aid, work with the Anti-Defamation League and work on existing pro bono matters. Other examples: Homeless Advocacy Project — summer associates participate in a special program where each is responsible for a pro bono matter, which many times culminates in a hearing; Lawyers' Committee for Civil Rights — summer associates are encouraged to attend a firm-sponsored clinic at least twice during the summer to conduct intake on potential clients and help out with the pro bono matters which the firm takes on; and various ongoing impact litigation — Bingham McCutchen is always engaged in a substantial number of ongoing impact litigation and other larger-scale matters in which summer associates may participate. Summer associates are encouraged to work on matters that interest them.

Does the firm have established programs, such as externships, that enable its associates to work in a public interest setting? Yes

If so, where and for up to how long? Attorneys at the firm can gain valuable courtroom experience by participating in externships in which they serve as prosecutors at local district attorneys offices in Boston and San Francisco areas.

Has your firm won any special recognition or awards in the last two years for its pro bono work? Yes

If so, please list. The Father Cuchulain Moriarity Award, Lawyers' Committee Asylum Project, Lawyer's Committee for Civil Rights of the San Francisco Bay Area, 2003; Keta Taylor Colby Award, Lawyer's Committee for Civil Rights of the San Francisco Bay Area, 2001; Robert G. Sproul Award, Lawyer's Committee for Civil Rights of the San Francisco Bay Area, 2000; Legal Aid Society of New York's Public Service Award, 2002.

THE FIRM SAYS

When Bingham Dana and McCutchen Doyle merged in July 2002 to form Bingham McCutchen, two firms with strong pro bono traditions united and created a robust 850-attorney committed to pro bono initiatives on both coasts. Bingham McCutchen attorneys have a long and distinguished record of serving the public interest within local communities and nationwide. The firm believes that its pro bono work exemplifies the best traditions of the legal profession, and Bingham McCutchen encourages and facilitates participation by all of its attorneys. The firm's commitment to the public interest is reflected in the strength and diversity of its pro bono program. It provides pro bono services to promote a number of important interests including ensuring access to justice for those of limited means, upholding civil rights and liberties, protecting the environment, and fostering community economic and educational development.

Bingham McCutchen's pro bono initiatives include:

- ·The first major Boston firm to agree to take pro bono referrals from an AIDS law project, with cases focusing on discrimination issues, housing and public accommodations matters.

- ·Handled major impact pro bono litigation involving civil rights, including matters involving prisoners' rights, racial discrimination, desegregation of schools, voting rights, use of excessive force by police and hate crimes.

- ·Since 1999, the Los Angeles office has participated in Public Counsel's Adoption Project, a pro bono program for parents seeking the adoption of special needs children through the Department of Child and Family Services. Nearly every associate in the Los Angeles office has participated in the Adoption Project. Bingham McCutchen attorneys have handled more than 250 adoptions, including five adoptions for a single family, making the firm one of the biggest participants in the Project. Forty-nine attorneys have handled adoptions, with help from more than 30 staff members.

- ·Selected as one of the top 20 A-List law firms in the United States by The American Lawyer, based on diversity, associate satisfaction, pro bono work and revenue (September 2003).

OUR SURVEY SAYS

"One of the best parts of working here is the commitment to community — makes you feel like law is still an honored profession!"

"There are those partners that care deeply and those that don't. Most young associates take their pro bono commitment fairly seriously and are encouraged by the pro bono forces at the firm. But usually one's commitment seems to mellow as demanding work piles up. The firm has no limit on the number of hours we can devote to pro bono, so it is institutionally encouraged."

"Bingham McCutchen has a strong pro bono commitment. The Los Angeles office participates in an adoption project to help various clients finalize adoptions. The firm also works on prisoners' rights and elder law cases."

"I have never had a request to take a pro bono case turned down."

"Committed, but the San Francisco office does more pro bono 'impact' work. Most of the pro bono work in this [Los Angeles] office is for the Public Counsel Adoption Program. There could definitely be more opportunities, especially for young associates."

"Very high per-associate pro bono hours. Almost everyone participates."

"Associates get real billable hour credit for doing approved pro bono work, and this amount is not capped (although reason would suggest that you should not have too many pro bono hours at the expense of billable hours)."

"It seems with the recent merger, commitment to pro bono has gone from very little to very strong over the past year."

Bryan Cave LLP

One Metropolitan Square, Suite 3600
St. Louis, MO 63102
Phone: (314) 259-2000
www.bryancave.com

LOCATIONS

St. Louis, MO (largest office)
Chicago, IL
Irvine, CA
Jefferson City, MO
Kansas City, MO
Leawood, KS
Los Angeles, CA
New York, NY
Phoenix, AZ
Washington, DC
Dubai
Hong Kong
Kuwait City
London
Riyadh
Shanghai

MAJOR DEPARTMENTS & PRACTICES

Antitrust/U.S. Trade
Banking & Business Finance
Bankruptcy, Restructuring & Creditors' Rights
Corporate & Securities
Employee Benefits
Entrepreneurial, Technology & Commercial Practice
Environmental
Government Contracts
Health Care
Intellectual Property
International
Labor & Employment
Litigation & Dispute Resolution
Private Client
Public Finance
Real Estate & Project Finance
Regulatory Affairs, Public Policy & Legislation
Tax
Transactions

THE STATS

No. of attorneys worldwide: 840
No. of offices worldwide: 16
Chairman: Walter L. Metcalfe Jr.

EMPLOYMENT CONTACT

See firm web site for employment contacts.

WHO'S WHO

Principal pro bono contact(s) at your firm:

Bryan Cave LLP
Attn: Pro bono Committee Chair
One Metropolitan Square, Suite 3600
St. Louis, MO 63102

Does the firm have a pro bono coordinator? None other than committee members.

Does the firm have a pro bono committee? Yes. Each Bryan Cave office has a pro bono committee.

If yes, how often does the committee meet? Meeting schedules vary by office.

Describe the composition of the committee: Each pro bono committee consists of lawyers at different practice levels and in a variety of practice groups.

THE SCOOP

Does your firm have a written pro bono policy? Yes

Has the firm signed on to the Law Firm Pro Bono Challenge? Yes

What are some of the areas of law in which your firm has performed pro bono legal work in the last two years? Bryan Cave lawyers have performed pro bono work in a broad spectrum of legal areas from individual civil rights to institutional interests; from family law matters to real estate issues; and in many other areas as well.

What are some of the areas of law in which your firm does not perform pro bono work? The firm will consider pro bono work in any area of law but will not accept pro bono matters that are in conflict with other clients or matters.

Organizations for which your firm has performed pro bono legal services in the last two years: Arizona Bar Foundation; Children's Law Center (adoptions); Florence Immigration Project (asylum cases); Habitat for Humanity (real estate); Lawyers and Accountants for the Arts; Legal Advocates for Abused Women; Legal Services of Eastern Missouri; Missouri Bar and the Kansas City and local bar committees; Public Counsel; UniReach International (surgical training for Vietnamese hospitals).

List up to three pro bono matters that are representative of the pro bono work your firm participates in.

- In response to the September 11 terrorist attacks on New York City, Bryan Cave's New York office assisted families and victims in many areas, but especially in probate, family law and general commercial areas. Realizing that many of the firm's clients in the World Trade Center towers were left without offices or with heavily damaged offices, the firm's New York location also offered the use of conference rooms and equipment.

- Bryan Cave LLP's Washington, D.C., office is handling a pro bono case that tests the balance between maintaining order and respecting constitutional rights. We are representing seven George Washington University students who were swept up in mass arrests, detained and shackled for up to 30 hours during a September 2002 anti-globalization demonstration at the time of the World Bank/International Monetary Fund meeting in Washington, D.C. Three of the plaintiffs were law students at the protests to observe and document police behavior, and four others were photographers with the university's newspaper. The federal lawsuit alleges that the police violated the students' rights under the First, Fourth and Fifth Amendments. It accuses police of "abusive confinement" and of denying the detainees' access to counsel. The suit seeks to have the police "trap-and-arrest" tactic declared unconstitutional, to clear the arrests from the students' records and other damages as are appropriate.

- The St. Louis office is advising numerous start-up charities on a pro bono basis, including a Section 501(c)(6) business league that will perform educational services for federal contractors, as well as several different Section 501(c)(3) charities engaged in such activities as providing services to persons with eating disorders, serving persons who have lost a child, promoting arts in Kirkwood, Missouri, training animals for persons with disabilities, and performing as a theatre group. Lawyers also participate as attorney supervisors for the program at Washington University that assists charities on a pro bono basis with the formation of nonprofit organizations.

BY THE NUMBERS

What is the total number of hours that lawyers in U.S. offices at your firm spent performing pro bono legal services in 2000, 2001 and 2002?

Total number of hours in 2000: Approximately 23,000 hours
Total number of hours in 2001: Approximately 23,000 hours
Total number of hours in 2002: Approximately 23,000 hours

Average number of pro bono hours per attorney in U.S. offices per year (including associates, partners, counsels, but not summer associates):

Average number of hours per attorney in 2000: Not available
Average number of hours per attorney in 2001: Not available
Average number of hours per attorney in 2002: Not available

What percentage of attorneys in this firm's U.S. offices did pro bono work in 2002? Not available

What percentage of attorneys in this firm's U.S. offices did at least 20 hours of pro bono work in 2002? Not available

Does the firm encourage its lawyers to perform a minimum number of pro bono hours? No. There is no firm-required number of hours for the appropriate level of pro bono activity for each lawyer. Firm lawyers are strongly encouraged to engage in pro bono activity because we believe this work makes us better lawyers — and makes Bryan Cave a better firm.

If so, how many hours per year or what percentage of lawyers' billable hours? N/A

SUPERVISION AND EVALUATIONS

Is there partner supervision on each pro bono matter? Each pro bono file is properly staffed and supervised by lawyers knowledgeable in the area of law involved. Lawyers performing pro bono services are encouraged to consult with other firm lawyers in various fields as needed.

Do partner supervisors or, if applicable, senior associates provide written evaluations of associates' work on pro bono matters? Pro bono work is evaluated in the same manner as all legal work.

If so, are those evaluations taken into account in determining salary, bonuses or advancement in the firm? All evaluations are considered in the same manner for those purposes.

If not, does the firm consider pro bono work generally in associate evaluations? The firm considers all submitted evaluations as part of the evaluation process.

HOURS

Does the firm give billable hour credit for pro bono work? Yes

Does the firm have a maximum number of pro bono hours that can be applied toward the billable hour target? Yes

If so, what is the maximum? 50 hours

If your firm uses hours to determine bonuses, does it consider pro bono hours when determining bonuses? Pro bono hours applied toward the billable hour target are also considered in the Performance Bonus Program.

PRO BONO POINTS

What training opportunities are open to associates working on pro bono matters? The firm has an expansive firm-wide training program that covers various substantive legal fields and practice skills. All associates are invited and encourage to participate in any of the training programs.

Can associates bring matters of interest to the firm? Yes

Does the firm offer the use of support staff in carrying out pro bono matters? Yes

What pro bono opportunities are available for summer associates? Summer interns are welcome to participate in any ongoing pro bono matters during their internship. For example, last summer a summer intern in the St. Louis office assisted with a petition for recognition of a foreign adoption filed in county family court. We assisted parents who had adopted an orphaned child from Guatemala under the laws of that country by having the State of Missouri formally recognize the adoption by the court entering an order and decree of adoption.

Does the firm have established programs, such as externships, that enable its associates to work in a public interest setting? No

If so, where and for up to how long? N/A

Has your firm won any special recognition or awards in the last two years for its pro bono work? Yes

If so, please list. Phoenix associate Milagros Cisneros was selected to receive one of the Arizona Bar Foundation's Top 50 Pro Bono Attorneys in Arizona award. The award recognizes 50 attorneys who have given tirelessly of their time and expertise to help low-income Arizonans with their legal needs through Volunteer Lawyer Programs funded by the foundation. While this award recognizes the quality legal help Cisneros has given to numerous cases, it specifically notes the work Cisneros has put in on behalf of the firm to have a teenage Nicaraguan refugee granted asylum in the United States.

The St. Louis Business Journal named Bryan Cave one of the city's "most valuable volunteers," recognizing corporations and individuals who make a positive difference through the time they give to the community. The Business Journal commended Bryan Cave's volunteer work for Habitat for Humanity, fundraising efforts for breast cancer research and participation in the United Way.

THE FIRM SAYS

Bryan Cave strongly encourages all of its lawyers to engage in pro bono work. In 2000, 44 percent of partners and 67 percent of associates participated in pro bono activities. Regardless of professional prominence or workload, pro bono work is a professional responsibility and can be one of the most rewarding experiences in the life of a lawyer.

Pro bono work is professional legal service without expectation of compensation, or at significantly reduced rates. Such work can include poverty law; civil rights and public rights law; representation of charitable organizations; and administration of justice. Referrals from local legal services agencies and work for nonprofit organizations make up much of the firm's pro bono time.

Each Bryan Cave office has written policies and pro bono committees to help lawyers identify and participate in pro bono activities, coordinate firm resources on behalf of pro bono clients and assure that pro bono services are delivered capably, efficiently and effectively. The service provided to our pro bono clients is of the same quality delivered to all clients. Lawyers treat these matters with the same care and importance as any other.

OUR SURVEY SAYS

"There is a lot of encouragement to participate in pro bono, both on a moral level and because those hours count toward yearly requirements."

"Fifty hours of firm-approved pro bono work count toward the annual billable hour minimum requirement — could be more during slow economic times such as at present."

"All first-year litigation associates are encouraged very quickly to get involved with the group's 'adopted' project. But then the firm is open to other pro bono matters that an attorney may wish to work on."

"They let me work as much pro bono as I can handle — over 70 hours last year — and they count 50 of it toward a bonus."

"We have a good working relationship with many of the pro bono organizations in Phoenix. I would like to see a greater focus on this, but 50 hours of pro bono time are included in our minimum billable requirement."

"While I believe that the attorneys at the office are personally committed, I believe that the firm's policy toward pro bono does not reflect strong commitment."

"Individual lawyers are encouraged and supported in doing pro bono legal work if they desire and strongly encouraged to support Legal Aid with contributions of time and money. In addition, the firm pays for an outside attorney who is skilled in such representation to handle pro bono assignments from the court if necessary."

"If you would like to engage in pro bono work, the firm is happy to assist, but the associate must go out and find the pro bono work on her own."

"Bryan Cave has established pro bono programs that all are encouraged to participate in. If you have ideas for new projects, the firm will entertain those possibilities as well."

"[The firm is] very committed unless it starts interfering with your billable hours."

"In response to the September 11 terrorist attacks on New York City, Bryan Cave's New York office assisted families and victims in many areas, but especially in probate, family law and general commercial areas."

— *Bryan Cave LLP*

Cadwalader, Wickersham & Taft LLP

100 Maiden Lane
New York, NY 10038
Phone: (212) 504-6000
www.cadwalader.com

LOCATIONS

New York, NY (HQ)
Charlotte, NC
Washington, DC
London

MAJOR DEPARTMENTS & PRACTICES

Banking & Finance
Capital Markets
Corporate/Mergers & Acquisitions
Financial Restructuring
Health Care/Not-for-Profit
Insurance & Reinsurance
Litigation
Private Client
Real Estate
Tax

THE STATS

No. of attorneys worldwide: 502
No. of offices worldwide: 4
Chairman: Robert O. Link Jr.

EMPLOYMENT CONTACT

Ms. Monica R. Brenner
Manager of Legal Recruitment
Phone: (212) 504-6044
E-mail: monica.brenner@cwt.com

WHO'S WHO

Principal pro bono contact(s) at your firm:

Howard R. Hawkins, Esq.
Partner/Chairman, Pro Bono Committee
Phone: (212) 504-6422
E-mail: Howard.Hawkins@cwt.com

Does the firm have a pro bono coordinator? Yes
Ms. Annie Mohan
Pro Bono Assistant

If yes, what percentage of his or her time is spent on pro bono work? 100 percent

Does the firm have a pro bono committee? Yes

If yes, how often does the committee meet? Bimonthly

Describe the composition of the committee: The firm's Pro Bono Committee is comprised of four partners and eight associates from our various departments and offices as well as four administrative staff members.

THE SCOOP

Does your firm have a written pro bono policy? Yes

Has the firm signed on to the Law Firm Pro Bono Challenge? No

What are some of the areas of law in which your firm has performed pro bono legal work in the last two years? Our pro bono activities encompass legal services for not-for-profit organizations and indigent individuals in a range of areas, including corporate, bankruptcy, employment, family law, immigration, litigation, dispute resolution, real estate, health care and tax law.

What are some of the areas of law in which your firm does not perform pro bono work? Intellectual property and patent law.

Organizations for which your firm has performed pro bono legal services in the last two years: Barrier Free Living, Food Bank for New York City, Legal Services of Southern Piedmont, New York City Chapter of the National Multiple Sclerosis Society, New York Lawyers for the Public Interest, Pace University Community Economic Development Center, Restaurant Opportunities Center, Robin Hood Foundation, The Legal Aid Society and Volunteer Lawyers for the Arts.

List up to three pro bono matters that are representative of the pro bono work your firm participates in.

- With the help of the Hotel Employees and Restaurant Employees Union, the Urban Justice Center and Lincoln Square Legal Services, Inc., 40 former workers at Windows on the World are forming the Restaurant Opportunities Center of New York (ROC) to rebuild their lives. They plan on opening a co-op restaurant in Tribeca, that will not only create a new future for themselves but will also stand as a legacy to the memory of their 73 colleagues who died on September 11. Cadwalader is helping with their incorporation, tax issues and lease negotiations.

- Our pro bono client, an art expert, was accused of entering into a conspiracy with several other art experts to defame one of the world's leading sellers of a very specialized type of high-end art, by accusing a gallery of selling fakes. A Cadwalader associate successfully argued the client's position in the Second Circuit Court of Appeals. She directly addressed the judge's pointed questions concerning a Rule 8 issue, grappling with both Supreme Court precedent and a Second Circuit decision written by the judge. In a significant victory, the Second Circuit issued its opinion, affirming the trial court's dismissal of the complaint.

- The Low Income Taxpayer Clinic was established by the Legal Services of Southern Piedmont to aid low income taxpayers in the Charlotte, N.C., community. These taxpayers require aid in handling disputes they may have with the IRS or the NC Department of Revenue. The clinic employs a full-time attorney, but relies heavily on volunteer attorneys to handle many of their cases. Cadwalader is helping with cases that come to the clinic by setting up payment plans, submitting offers in compromise for tax debt, handling innocent spouse issues, and coordinating earned income tax credit appeals for low income taxpayers.

BY THE NUMBERS

What is the total number of hours that lawyers in U.S. offices at your firm spent performing pro bono legal services in 2000, 2001 and 2002?

    Total number of hours in 2000: N/A
    Total number of hours in 2001: N/A
    Total number of hours in 2002: 15,450 hours

Average number of pro bono hours per attorney in U.S. offices per year (including associates, partners, counsels, but not summer associates):

    Average number of hours per attorney in 2000: N/A
    Average number of hours per attorney in 2001: N/A
    Average number of hours per attorney in 2002: 34.2 hours

What percentage of attorneys in this firm's U.S. offices did pro bono work in 2002? 59 percent

What percentage of attorneys in this firm's U.S. offices did at least 20 hours of pro bono work in 2002? 36 percent

Does the firm encourage its lawyers to perform a minimum number of pro bono hours? Yes

If so, how many hours per year or what percentage of lawyers' billable hours? 50 hours per year

SUPERVISION AND EVALUATIONS

Is there partner supervision on each pro bono matter? Yes

Do partner supervisors or, if applicable, senior associates provide written evaluations of associates' work on pro bono matters? Yes

If so, are those evaluations taken into account in determining salary, bonuses or advancement in the firm? Yes

If not, does the firm consider pro bono work generally in associate evaluations? N/A

HOURS

Does the firm give billable hour credit for pro bono work? Yes

Does the firm have a maximum number of pro bono hours that can be applied toward the billable hour target? Yes

If so, what is the maximum? 100 hours

If your firm uses hours to determine bonuses, does it consider pro bono hours when determining bonuses? Yes

PRO BONO POINTS

What training opportunities are open to associates working on pro bono matters? Attorneys are encouraged to attend training sessions offered by the firm and pro bono legal services providers. Each attorney working on a pro bono matter is supported by a partner and/or a more senior associate who provides training and acts as a resource for the attorney.

Can associates bring matters of interest to the firm? Yes

Does the firm offer the use of support staff in carrying out pro bono matters? Yes

What pro bono opportunities are available for summer associates? In addition to helping out with existing firm pro bono matters, summer associates are also encouraged to participate in the following turnkey projects: New York Lawyers for the Public Interest's Externship Program, Sanctuary for Families' Courtroom Advocates Project (CAP) and The Association of the Bar of the City of New York's Housing Court Summer Assistance Project.

Cadwalader is also pleased to offer the Cadwalader Public Interest Fellowship to a 2L student for the summer between his/her second and third year of law school. The Fellow works as a summer associate at Cadwalader for the first half of the summer program and spends the second half working in the legal department of a public interest organization, selected by the fellow. While working at Cadwalader, the fellow will be paid Cadwalader's standard 2L weekly summer associate salary. In addition, Cadwalader will pay the fellow a lump sum of $8,000 for the time spent working at the public interest organization. At the end of the summer, the fellow will be eligible for a first-year associate offer along with the rest of the summer class.

Has your firm won any special recognition or awards in the last two years for its pro bono work? Yes

If so, please list.

- ·The New York Legal Aid Society's award in recognition of the firm's outstanding assistance to the victims of the September 11 tragedy.
- ·The New York State Senate commended Cadwalader partner Debra Brown Steinberg for the donation of her time and expertise to the victims of the September 11 tragedy.
- ·The New York State Bar Association awarded Cadwalader partner Debra Brown Steinberg with the 2003 President's Pro Bono Service Award for the First Judicial District.
- ·Cadwalader was a recipient of a Special Award from inMotion at the 3rd Annual Commitment to Justice Awards Reception.
- ·Cadwalader partner Debra Brown Steinberg was honored by New York Lawyers for the Public Interest for her work on behalf of the victims of the September 11 tragedy.
- ·Litigation associate Elizabeth Butler was honored with the "Outstanding Volunteer Service Award" for 2002 by

Volunteer Lawyers for the Arts.

THE FIRM SAYS

Cadwalader has a longstanding tradition of providing pro bono services to those in need. This commitment serves the goal of (a) meeting our professional obligation to provide legal services to those unable to afford an attorney, and (b) providing professional development opportunities for junior associates to assume principal responsibility for important matters. Our pro bono program encompasses legal assistance to those in need or without access to the justice system, volunteer service and community projects, and financial contributions to charitable organizations. Both new and experienced attorneys have the chance to help the indigent and contribute to matters and causes of public interest as well as to gain valuable personal and professional experience.

Cadwalader's pro bono programs are managed by a pro bono committee. The committee's mission is threefold: (a) to identify and maintain relationships with select public service agencies and other organizations; (b) to oversee the procedures for the supervision, management and administration of pro bono assignments; and (c) to carry out the annual fundraising campaigns for pro bono organizations. The committee meets regularly to satisfy its mission and to discuss ways in which our pro bono work can be expanded and improved. While we encourage all personnel to bring pro bono projects in which they are interested to the committee's attention, the majority of our pro bono clients come to us from the outside referral sources and legal services agencies with which we have longstanding relationships. The firm believes that our attorneys should dedicate substantial resources to pro bono matters, with an annual goal of at least 50 hours per attorney.

OUR SURVEY SAYS

"Prior to 9/11, I don't think that pro bono was particularly stressed. Since then, I believe that a new attitude has swept across both the firm and the country for dedication to service."

"I have had some wonderful pro bono opportunities."

"I think the firm is fairly supportive of people who are themselves committed to pro bono work, but I don't get the impression that the firm itself has any such commitment."

"Senior partner Don Glascoff has helped to found a human rights program at Oxford University and is happy to involve associates in international human rights cases. Litigation first-years are given mandatory pro bono projects our first week. All attorneys receive numerous e-mails per week from the firm's pro bono committee listing pre-approved pro bono projects that we may sign up for. Most importantly, we can bill the hours — the true test of Cadwalader's commitment. We can even find our own pro bono clients and obtain Cadwalader's sponsorship."

"The firm has been tremendously dedicated to its young pro bono program after receiving a shameful score in past years. Pro bono is encouraged."

"All our pro bono hours go towards our year end total billables. There are countless opportunities to take on pro bono matters and the firm has made it mandatory for litigators to take on a pro bono assignment in their first two years."

"E-mails are sent around constantly informing attorneys of available pro bono matters and attorneys are strongly encouraged to take on pro bono matters."

"I personally do a lot of pro bono (in addition to a lot of billable work)."

"Pro bono work always takes back seat to billable work, even if it means dropping a pro bono matter altogether."

"Since September 11, we have tremendously improved our commitment to pro bono work."

Cahill Gordon & Reindel LLP

80 Pine Street
New York, NY 10005
Phone: (212) 701-3000
www.Cahill.com

LOCATIONS

New York, NY (HQ)
Washington, DC
London

MAJOR DEPARTMENTS & PRACTICES

Corporate
Litigation
Pro Bono
Real Estate
Tax
Trade Regulation & Antitrust

THE STATS

No. of attorneys worldwide: 245
No. of offices worldwide: 3
Chairman: Immanuel Kohn

EMPLOYMENT CONTACT

Ms. Joyce A. Hilly
Hiring Coordinator
E-mail: jhilly@cahill.com

WHO'S WHO

Principal pro bono contact(s) at your firm:

Gerard M. Meistrell, Esq.
E-mail: GMeistrell@Cahill.com

Howard G. (Peter) Sloane, Esq.
E-mail: PSloane@Cahill.com

Does the firm have a pro bono coordinator? Yes
Gerard Meistrell and Howard G. (Peter) Sloane

If yes, what percentage of his or her time is spent on pro bono work? 10 to 25 percent

Does the firm have a pro bono committee? No

If yes, how often does the committee meet? N/A.

Describe the composition of the committee: N/A

THE SCOOP

Does your firm have a written pro bono policy? Yes

Has the firm signed on to the Law Firm Pro Bono Challenge? The firm supports the efforts of the Association of the Bar of the City of New York through Volunteers of Legal Service to provide an average of 30 (formerly 20) hours per attorney to qualifying pro bono work annually.

What are some of the areas of law in which your firm has performed pro bono legal work in the last two years? Organizations for which we have devoted substantive legal services in the recent past, and which continue to offer pro bono opportunities, include the New York County District Attorney's office (arguing appeals); U.S. District Court for the Southern District of New York Pro Bono Panel (referrals of various pro se litigants); New York Lawyers for the Public Interest (variety of cases and issues including litigation and non-litigation); Victim Services, Inc. (services to crime victims and their families); Sanctuary for Families (battered women); National Employment Law Project, Inc. (advocacy on behalf of working poor and unemployed); The Municipal Art Society (assistance on land use, zoning and other policy initiatives); Lincoln Center (variety of projects); Volunteer Lawyers for the Arts (legal services to indigent artists and not-for-profit arts organizations); MFY Legal Services (representation of indigents in eviction and other proceedings); Libel Defense Resource (drafting of briefs); and the Legal Aid Society.

We are one of the lead counsel for plaintiffs in litigation challenging the constitutionality of the Bipartisan Campaign Reform Act ("BCRA"), the most sweeping campaign finance legislation passed by Congress in the last 25 years. Cahill partner Floyd Abrams was appointed by Chief Judge Judith S. Kaye to chair New York's Commission on Public Access to Court Records. A Cahill associate acts as counsel to the commission. The commission has been charged with examining the sometimes competing interests of privacy and open access relating to information in court case files that will be filed or maintained in electronic form by New York courts in the future. The findings and recommendations of the commission will help shape the judiciary's policies regarding the future availability of court records on the Internet. The commission is comprised of 20 stellar members representing a broad spectrum of expertise, including academia, the law and the media.

We represented plaintiffs in a major precedent-setting class action on behalf of 100,000 children in New York City filed by Children Rights Inc. and Lawyers for Children in the Southern District of New York in a challenge to major aspects of New York City's child welfare system as operated by the Administration for Children Services and monitored and supervised by the New York State Office of Children & Family Services. The complaint alleged that the City and State were responsible for an extended history of neglect in all aspects of the City's child welfare operations and sought the appointment of a receiver to operate the City's child welfare system. The case was settled with the State. The settlement contains provisions that obligate the State, for the first time in its history, dramatically to alter the way it monitors the City's child welfare performance and to keep plaintiffs timely informed of what they are doing and what its investigations are uncovering. Cahill donated its entire fee recovery of $1 million dollars to Children's Rights, Inc.

What are some of the areas of law in which your firm does not perform pro bono work? Not applicable.

Organizations for which your firm has performed pro bono legal services in the last two years: See answer above.

List up to three pro bono matters that are representative of the pro bono work your firm participates in. See answer above.

BY THE NUMBERS

What is the total number of hours that lawyers in U.S. offices at your firm spent performing pro bono legal services in 2000, 2001 and 2002?

> **Total number of hours in 2000:** 5,700 hours
> **Total number of hours in 2001:** 6,200 hours
> **Total number of hours in 2002:** 7,850 hours

Average number of pro bono hours per attorney in U.S. offices per year (including associates, partners, counsels, but not summer associates):

> **Average number of hours per attorney in 2000:** 28 hours
> **Average number of hours per attorney in 2001:** 27.5 hours
> **Average number of hours per attorney in 2002:** 33 hours

What percentage of attorneys in this firm's U.S. offices did pro bono work in 2002? See firm narrative below.

What percentage of attorneys in this firm's U.S. offices did at least 20 hours of pro bono work in 2002? See firm narrative below.

Does the firm encourage its lawyers to perform a minimum number of pro bono hours? N/A

If so, how many hours per year or what percentage of lawyers' billable hours? N/A

SUPERVISION AND EVALUATIONS

Is there partner supervision on each pro bono matter? Yes

Do partner supervisors or, if applicable, senior associates provide written evaluations of associates' work on pro bono matters? Yes

If so, are those evaluations taken into account in determining salary, bonuses or advancement in the firm? Yes

If not, does the firm consider pro bono work generally in associate evaluations? Yes

HOURS

Does the firm give billable hour credit for pro bono work? Yes

Does the firm have a maximum number of pro bono hours that can be applied toward the billable hour target? No

If so, what is the maximum? Not applicable

If your firm uses hours to determine bonuses, does it consider pro bono hours when determining bonuses? Not applicable

PRO BONO POINTS

What training opportunities are open to associates working on pro bono matters? Partners supervise associate work on pro bono matters and offer training in connection with that supervision. In addition, many of the pro bono organizations for which we perform pro bono work offer training programs.

Can associates bring matters of interest to the firm? Yes

Does the firm offer the use of support staff in carrying out pro bono matters? Yes

What pro bono opportunities are available for summer associates? In addition to working on pro bono matters in the firm, Cahill has provided one-week externships for summer associates with the following organizations: New York Lawyers for the Public Interest, Brooklyn Legal Services Corporation, Bronx Legal Services for the Elderly, The Door and City-wide Task Force on Housing Court.

Does the firm have established programs, such as externships, that enable its associates to work in a public interest setting? Yes

If so, where and for up to how long? See response regarding summer associates.

Has your firm won any special recognition or awards in the last two years for its pro bono work? Yes

If so, please list. An associate, Joel Kurtzberg, received the Sanctuary for Families Award for Excellence in Pro Bono Advocacy on Behalf of Domestic Violence Victims and Their Children in November 2003. Cahill retired partner Allen Joslyn received the Legal Aid Society's 2003 pro bono publico award for his work in the area of matrimonial law.

THE FIRM SAYS

The firm encourages pro bono work by every lawyer in the firm. The firm has undertaken to support the effort of the Association of the Bar of the City of New York through Volunteers of Legal Service to provide an average of 30 hours of pro bono service annually per lawyer. We solicit the continuing assistance of all lawyers in meeting this commitment. Partners are assigned by the firm to supervise each public interest or charitable activity of a professional nature undertaken by any lawyer in the firm. This work is under the guidance of the pro bono partners, and questions are brought to their attention. Any pro bono project, including projects involving assistance to community law offices, must be discussed with

one of the pro bono partners before it is undertaken. After a project has been approved, a pro bono partner will authorize the opening of time accounts to record time spent, authorize use of the firm's facilities, including files and services of the support staff, and make such arrangements as are appropriate with respect to the handling of disbursements. Lawyers participating in pro bono activities are asked to accurately record the time they devote to such efforts. All such time is considered "billable" time in assessing associates' performance, salary and bonus.

OUR SURVEY SAYS

"The firm strongly encourages pro bono work; however, I don't know how people have time for such projects."

"You personally will have to bring your own commitment or it is not going to happen. The firm could and should do more to share its resources and could take the lead in valuing pro bono. As it is, it's the individual who takes the lead."

"Associates are definitely committed to pro bono, but in a free-market environment where you have to look for your own work, often finding billable work takes priority to looking for pro bono work."

"In a conversation with a partner, I was told that I was the type of person the firm would like to see do pro bono work. My response was, 'Fine — should I do that between 3 and 4 a.m. each day?'"

"The firm does not have a formal pro bono program and very few associates seem to work on pro bono matters."

"Pro bono is tolerated, not encouraged. Every now and then there are big pro bono cases that receive a lot of firm resources (such as the McConnell campaign finance case, which is currently occupying many litigators' time), but individual associates are not encouraged to take on minor pro bono matters. You need to seek it out."

"Some partners are very committed and encourage associates to be as well. Others don't, and frown upon associate involvement in pro bono matters."

"A lot of the pro bono work is for high-profile First Amendment cases."

"We are not outwardly encouraged to take on significant pro bono assignments but are not discouraged either. If you are dedicated to it, you can do it here. But your other billable work cannot be put to the side."

"Self-initiative required, as with anything at Cahill."

"We represented plaintiffs in a major precedent-setting class action on behalf of 100,000 children in New York City filed by Children Rights Inc. and Lawyers for Children in the Southern District of New York in a challenge to major aspects of New York City's child welfare system."

— *Cahill Gordon & Reindel LLP*

Carlton Fields, P.A.

777 South Harbour Island Boulevard
Tampa, FL 33601
Phone: (813) 223-7000
www.carltonfields.com

LOCATIONS

Tampa, FL (HQ)
Miami, FL
Orlando, FL
St. Petersburg, FL
Tallahassee, FL
West Palm Beach, FL

MAJOR DEPARTMENTS & PRACTICES

Antitrust & Trade Regulation
Appellate Practice & Trial Support
Aviation
Bankruptcy & Creditors' Rights
Business Transactions
Class Action Litigation
Construction
Corporate, Securities, Taxation & Asset-Based Financing
Environmental
ERISA
Estate Planning
Family Law
Government Law & Consulting
Health Care
Insurance Litigation & Regulation
Intellectual Property & Technology
International Trade & Transactions
Labor & Employment
Litigation & Dispute Resolution
Medical Malpractice
Mergers & Acquisitions
Private Equity & Venture Capital
Products & Toxic Tort Liability
Real Estate
Securities
Taxation
Telecommunications Law
White Collar Crime & Government Investigations

THE STATS

No. of attorneys worldwide: 210
No. of offices worldwide: 6
President and CEO: Thomas A. Snow

EMPLOYMENT CONTACT

Ms. Elizabeth Bergen Zabak
Director of Attorney Recruitment & Training and Director of Client Services
Phone: (813) 229-4130
Fax: (813) 229-4133
E-mail: ezabak@carltonfields.com

Ms. Catherine Glenn Witherspoon
Attorney Recruiting and Training Manager
Phone: (813) 229-4172
Fax: (813) 229-4133
E-mail: cwitherspoon@carltonfields.com

WHO'S WHO

Principal pro bono contact(s) at your firm:

Kathleen S. McLeroy, Shareholder
Chair of Pro Bono Committee

Does the firm have a pro bono coordinator? No

Does the firm have a pro bono committee? Yes

If yes, how often does the committee meet? Quarterly

Describe the composition of the committee: Both shareholders (partners) and associates, with all offices represented.

THE SCOOP

Does your firm have a written pro bono policy? Yes

Has the firm signed on to the Law Firm Pro Bono Challenge? Yes

What are some of the areas of law in which your firm has performed pro bono legal work in the last two years?
Work for both individuals and nonprofits, including consumer, death penalty, transactional work and civil rights litigation.

What are some of the areas of law in which your firm does not perform pro bono work? N/A

Organizations for which your firm has performed pro bono legal services in the last two years: Bay Area Legal Services, Put Something Back (Miami), Legal Services of North Florida, Florida Justice Institute Community Law Program, Inc., The Spring of Tampa Bay, Inc., Central Florida Legal Services, Legal Aid Society of Palm Beach.

List up to three pro bono matters that are representative of the pro bono work your firm participates in.
Death penalty representation of Daniel Caldwell. Representation of The Spring of Tampa Bay, Inc. (domestic violence center) in various issues. Assisting attorneys from Florida Justice Institute in litigation to improve the conditions of prisoners in close management (severe solitary confinement).

BY THE NUMBERS

What is the total number of hours that lawyers in U.S. offices at your firm spent performing pro bono legal services in 2000, 2001 and 2002?

> **Total number of hours in 2000:** 7166.5 hours
> **Total number of hours in 2001:** 8427.3 hours
> **Total number of hours in 2002:** 9017.3 hours

Average number of pro bono hours per attorney in U.S. offices per year (including associates, partners, counsels, but not summer associates):

> **Average number of hours per attorney in 2000:** 44.12 hours
> **Average number of hours per attorney in 2001:** 46.89 hours
> **Average number of hours per attorney in 2002:** 43.60 hours

What percentage of attorneys in this firm's U.S. offices did pro bono work in 2002? 72 percent

What percentage of attorneys in this firm's U.S. offices did at least 20 hours of pro bono work in 2002? 62 percent

Does the firm encourage its lawyers to perform a minimum number of pro bono hours? Yes

If so, how many hours per year or what percentage of lawyers' billable hours? 50 hours, which is just over 3 percent of billable budget.

SUPERVISION AND EVALUATIONS

Is there partner supervision on each pro bono matter? Yes

Do partner supervisors or, if applicable, senior associates provide written evaluations of associates' work on pro bono matters? Yes

If so, are those evaluations taken into account in determining salary, bonuses or advancement in the firm? Yes

If not, does the firm consider pro bono work generally in associate evaluations? Yes

HOURS

Does the firm give billable hour credit for pro bono work? Yes

Does the firm have a maximum number of pro bono hours that can be applied toward the billable hour target? Yes

If so, what is the maximum? 100 hours

If your firm uses hours to determine bonuses, does it consider pro bono hours when determining bonuses? Yes

PRO BONO POINTS

What training opportunities are open to associates working on pro bono matters? Training specific to type of work (e.g., family law procedure and substantive training) as well as general skill training (e.g., deposition training).

Can associates bring matters of interest to the firm? Yes

Does the firm offer the use of support staff in carrying out pro bono matters? Yes

What pro bono opportunities are available for summer associates? Intake for legal services program within the firm as well as work on any active pro bono matter during their tenure with the firm.

Does the firm have established programs, such as externships, that enable its associates to work in a public interest setting? No

Has your firm won any special recognition or awards in the last two years for its pro bono work? Yes

If so, please list. 2003: The Chief Justice Law Firm Commendation from the Supreme Court of Florida, Put Something Back Pro Bono Award for Exceptional Law Firm, Volunteer of the Year Award from the Tallahassee Democrat Miami Law Project, Recognition from President Bush for work to promote Welfare to Work.

THE FIRM SAYS

Carlton Fields has a rich, long-standing tradition of support for individual participation in pro bono and public service. Attorneys are encouraged to provide legal services to individuals and groups who cannot afford legal help. Recognizing the special responsibility that attorneys bear in a democratic society, and their obligations as citizens, Carlton Fields expects and encourages its attorneys to participate actively in community service, pro bono representation, and professional organizations. Carlton Fields' attorneys annually provide almost $2 million of legal services to those less fortunate in society and to organizations that serve the disadvantaged.

Carlton Fields is a charter signatory in the American Bar Association Pro Bono Challenge (n/k/a the Law Firm Pro Bono Challenge). The firm pledged to contribute an amount of time equal to three percent (3 percent) of its total billable hours to pro bono work. The firm also co-sponsored a National Association for Public Interest Law (NAPIL) Partner Fellow. The Fellow worked with the Child Victim Rapid Response School Program, a school-based violence prevention and intervention program established in conjunction with the Florida Attorney General's Office, Bay Area Legal Services, Inc., the Florida Commission on Community Service, and the Florida Department of Education. Carlton Fields is ranked among the "honored top quarter" (top 50) in The American Lawyer's 2003 list of the top 200 firms in the nation. The rankings are based on a formula that measures economic factors, pro bono hours, associate satisfaction, and diversity. Carlton Fields is the only Florida law firm named in the top 50, and is one of the few law firms of its size on the top quarter list.

Attorneys at Carlton Fields are encouraged to donate at least 50 hours per year of legal services to individuals and groups who cannot afford to pay for such assistance. In support of this commitment, the firm provides its shareholders, associates, and paralegals with substantial "billable hour credit" for pro bono legal services. Carlton Fields has also instituted a practice of selecting recipients for a firm-sponsored award recognizing a shareholder and an associate (and on some occasions groups of attorneys) within its firm who have made the most significant contributions to pro bono efforts during each year.

To coordinate pro bono and public service from office to office, Carlton Fields attorneys serve on its longstanding Pro Bono Committee. The firm's Pro Bono Committee oversees statewide participation in large pro bono or public service projects and works with community groups in the locale of each office to optimize the services provided.

Carlton Fields' pro bono and public service work have brought it both local and national recognition. Below is a representative sampling of awards received by Carlton Fields for exemplary pro bono and community service.

- In 2003, Carlton Fields was the recipient of the Chief Justice Law Firm Commendation from the Supreme Court of Florida for outstanding efforts in support of pro bono legal services.

- On April 18, 2002, President Bush and his administration honored Carlton Fields, together with several other businesses from across the country, for its commitment to hiring former welfare recipients. Carlton Fields was specifically recognized for its participation in the Miami Law Project, the goal of which is to ensure that former welfare recipients receive the training and experience necessary to be prepared for successful entry into law firm staff positions.

- In 2001, Carlton Fields received the Put Something Back Pro Bono Award for Exceptional Law Firm for its exceptional history of pro bono and community service.

- Carlton Fields received the Tallahassee Democrat's 2001 Volunteer of the Year Award for its contributions to ECHO (Emergency Community Help Organization).

OUR SURVEY SAYS

"Commitment is across the board — I don't know of anyone who doesn't have pro bono cases."

"Carlton Fields is sincere in its commitment to pro bono — it is not a line-item in the Attorney Handbook but is actually an assumed part of the culture. This is very different from other firms I am familiar with, who espouse their commitment to pro bono yet forbid associates from taking on any pro bono work or inform them that any such work will be done only after their billable requirement is met."

"Here at Carlton Fields, there is a very positive culture for participation in pro bono matters. The firm encourages all lawyers — both shareholders and associates — to participate, and most of them do."

"Although we do have high-profile pro bono cases, usually people take on pro bono matters that are important to them personally — either to assist an organization that they care about or to help an individual who otherwise could not afford it"

"I have not been pressured to take on smaller cases or to limit the resources devoted to the project. However, we all recognize that the firm will credit a certain number of pro bono hours toward billable requirements and anything beyond that is truly PRO BONO. It does not seem to have a significant impact on attorneys' selection of pro bono projects."

"It is quite refreshing to be able to spend a week on something that is not billable, knowing that when the firm looks at performance they view my pro bono work as an asset to the firm."

"The firm's dedication to pro bono work transcends department lines. It is not uncommon for a litigator to have a pro bono case but need input from the corporate/transactional department, and vice versa. Attorneys in litigation, real estate, corporate and other departments all handle their own pro bono cases."

"We have all the same resources available to us on pro bono cases as we do on other cases (e.g., ability to consult with other attorneys, Westlaw and Lexis use, copying, mailing, filing and so on). We are dedicated advocates for our clients regardless of whether they are paying or not. We are always mindful of producing quality work while controlling costs, regardless of the client."

"One of the reasons why I like my firm is its continual dedication to pro bono. If there were no Vault publication or Bar reporting requirements, the firm would still be doing pro bono. It's a culture that emanates from the top."

> "Carlton Fields' attorneys annually provide almost $2 million of legal services to those less fortunate in society and to organizations that serve the disadvantaged."
>
> — *Carlton Fields, P.A.*

Chadbourne & Parke LLP

30 Rockefeller Plaza, 31st Floor
New York, NY 10112
Phone: (212) 408-5100
www.chadbourne.com

LOCATIONS

New York, NY (HQ)
Houston, TX
Los Angeles, CA
Washington, DC
Beijing
Kyiv, Ukraine
London
Moscow
Tashkent, Uzbekistan
Warsaw

MAJOR DEPARTMENTS & PRACTICES

Bankruptcy
Corporate
Employment
Environmental
Intellectual Property
Litigation
Products Liability
Project Finance
Real Estate
Reinsurance/Insurance
Tax
Trusts & Estates

THE STATS

No. of attorneys worldwide: 355
No. of offices worldwide: 10
Managing Partner: Charles K. O'Neill

EMPLOYMENT CONTACT

Ms. Amy M. Weinstein
Manager of Legal Recruiting
Phone: (212) 408-5338
E-mail: aweinstein@chadbourne.com

WHO'S WHO

Does the firm have a pro bono coordinator? Yes

Bernard W. McCarthy, Esq.
Pro Bono Partner
Phone: (212) 408-5397
E-mail: bmccarthy@chadbourne.com

Ms. Elly Spiegel
Pro Bono Coordinator
Phone: (212) 408-5164
E-mail: espiegel@chadbourne.com

If yes, what percentage of his or her time is spent on pro bono work? Bernard McCarthy – variable; Elly Spiegel — 100 percent.

Does the firm have a pro bono committee? Yes

If yes, how often does the committee meet? Monthly

Describe the composition of the committee: 16 members (four partners, four counsel, eight associates) from three offices (New York, D.C., Los Angeles.) and all practice areas.

THE SCOOP

Does your firm have a written pro bono policy? Yes

Has the firm signed on to the Law Firm Pro Bono Challenge? Yes (one of the original signatories)

What are some of the areas of law in which your firm has performed pro bono legal work in the last two years? Political asylum, family justice, landlord/tenant, arts, elder law, prisoners' rights, criminal appeals, death penalty, 9/11-related cases, intellectual property, community development (including incorporation of nonprofits, helping micro-entrepreneurs and a partnership with the Upper Manhattan Empowerment Zone).

What are some of the areas of law in which your firm does not perform pro bono work? Plaintiffs' employment work.

Organizations for which your firm has performed pro bono legal services in the last two years: New York Lawyers for the Public Interest, The Legal Aid Society, MFY Legal Services, Volunteer Lawyers for the Arts, Volunteers of Legal Service, Lawyers Alliance for New York, Lawyers Committee for Human Rights, Sanctuary for Families, inMotion, Asian American Legal Defense and Education Fund, DC Bar Community Economic Development Project.

List up to three pro bono matters that are representative of the pro bono work your firm participates in.

- Fonkoze. A team of corporate and tax attorneys prepared a complex private offering memorandum of interests in a domestic LLC that will invest in a Haitian micro-credit bank that will make loans to small businesses in Haiti.

- LCHR Asylum Team. The most recent political asylum applicant represented by C&P is a Chinese Christian from Indonesia fleeing religious and ethnic persecution. Although her case seemed hopeless when it came to Chadbourne, as a key filing deadline had been missed and a referral for deportation proceedings already had been made, the team was successful in obtaining asylum for her.

- **Hue-Man Bookstore Team.** Real estate, corporate, tax and IP attorneys joined forces to establish the Hue-Man Bookstore, which opened on August 1, 2002, at the Harlem USA Mall, and is now one of the largest African-American bookstores in the country. The team rendered a variety of services to the client, including setting up a corporate entity, protecting IP rights, preparing an employment contract, analyzing tax issues and negotiating the lease for space at the Harlem USA Mall.

BY THE NUMBERS

What is the total number of hours that lawyers in U.S. offices at your firm spent performing pro bono legal services in 2000, 2001 and 2002?

> **Total number of hours in 2000:** 8,548 hours
> **Total number of hours in 2001:** 9,151 hours
> **Total number of hours in 2002:** 10,646 hours

Average number of pro bono hours per attorney in U.S. offices per year (including associates, partners, counsel, but not summer associates):

> **Average number of hours per attorney in 2000:** 33.3 hours
> **Average number of hours per attorney in 2001:** 32.3 hours
> **Average number of hours per attorney in 2002:** 38.2 hours

What percentage of attorneys in this firm's U.S. offices did pro bono work in 2002? 48.5 percent

What percentage of attorneys in this firm's U.S. offices did at least 20 hours of pro bono work in 2002? 33 percent

Does the firm encourage its lawyers to perform a minimum number of pro bono hours? Yes

If so, how many hours per year or what percentage of lawyers' billable hours? C&P encourages but does not require attorneys to perform 20-50 hours of pro bono work annually.

SUPERVISION AND EVALUATIONS

Is there partner supervision on each pro bono matter? Yes

Do partner supervisors or, if applicable, senior associates provide written evaluations of associates' work on pro bono matters? Yes

If so, are those evaluations taken into account in determining salary, bonuses or advancement in the firm? Yes

If not, does the firm consider pro bono work generally in associate evaluations? N/A

HOURS

Does the firm give billable hour credit for pro bono work? Yes

Does the firm have a maximum number of pro bono hours that can be applied toward the billable hour target? Yes

If so, what is the maximum? 100 hours

If your firm uses hours to determine bonuses, does it consider pro bono hours when determining bonuses? Yes

PRO BONO POINTS

What training opportunities are open to associates working on pro bono matters? Outside training sessions conducted by legal service providers; on-the-job training by senior attorneys on ongoing matters; in-house training by Pro Bono Net and various legal service providers.

Can associates bring matters of interest to the firm? Yes

Does the firm offer the use of support staff in carrying out pro bono matters? Yes

What pro bono opportunities are available for summer associates? Most are asked to work on ongoing pro bono matters.

Does the firm have established programs, such as externships, that enable its associates to work in a public interest setting? Yes

If so, where and for up to how long? The Door Legal Services Center (part of a center for troubled adolescents that offers health, education, psychological and legal services) for up to three months.

Has your firm won any special recognition or awards in the last two years for its pro bono work? Yes

If so, please list.

- May 17, 2002 proclaimed "Chadbourne & Parke Day" by New York City Mayor Bloomberg in recognition of the volunteer efforts of legal and non-legal personnel in New York and D.C. after 9/11; the firm's donation of space and services to 100 attorneys and support staff from the Office of the Corporation Counsel after 9/11; and the firm's pledge of $500,000 to assist victims of 9/11

- 2002 Special Award from The Legal Aid Society in recognition of outstanding pro bono assistance to the victims of the World Trade Center tragedy

- 2002 MFY Special Pro Bono Achievement Award

- 2002 VLA Outstanding Volunteer Service Award

- Top firm in its category in the New York City Legal Aid Society Associates' Campaign for 1999-2002 "The firm has a very strong commitment to a wide variety of pro bono work. The firm provides many opportunities to get involved in pro bono cases and training, as well as encourages us to seek out our own pro bono work."

THE FIRM SAYS

C&P has long recognized its responsibility to the community at large and encouraged involvement in pro bono and other public service activities. Pro bono is intended in the narrow sense (providing free legal services to those who cannot pay for them) and in the broader one (mentoring high school students in moot court/mock trial competitions, serving on the boards of legal service providers). C&P partners serve as directors of The Legal Aid Society, CAMBA Legal Services, New York Lawyers for the Public Interest, Advocates for Children, MFY Legal Services and The University Settlement Society. Chadbourne is one of the rare firms to have a designated pro bono partner. Attorneys may choose from regularly circulated lists of cases and training programs proposed by many legal service providers, subject to the approval of the Pro Bono Partner. Pro bono service is considered an important factor in performance reviews and when determining associate bonus eligibility.

Attorneys at Chadbourne's overseas offices are engaged in some far-reaching pro bono projects: helping disabled children get access to the public education to which they are entitled (Moscow); assisting a private humanitarian group working on refugee protection (Moscow); establishing the first non-governmental school in Uzbekistan (Tashkent); facilitating dialogue between Israeli and Palestinian women and filming such dialogue (London).

C&P's acknowledges the highest level of attorney pro bono commitment through its Outstanding Service Awards, in the form of $1,000 contributions to the legal service providers chosen by the awardees. Six such awards were given in 2002. All attorneys who perform 50+ hours of pro bono service are named to the PB Honor Roll and receive an engraved memento at an all-attorney awards ceremony.

OUR SURVEY SAYS

"I think the firm does a lot to encourage participation in pro bono work."

"[It] also depends on the person, but there is considerable 'press' on pro bono activities. First-year associates can get very involved in pro bono work."

"We receive a mixed message on pro bono work — we have committees that try to get you involved, but 'oversight' that will try to get you 'uninvolved' if it starts to take up too much time!"

"The firm does a lot of pro bono work; however, there is a limit to the amount of pro bono work that can be credited towards your minimum billable requirement."

"Even in these tougher times, the firm is committed to encouraging associates to take on pro bono work and to participate in pro bono externships at the Door."

"The firm has a dedicated partner and associate who continually recruit associates for pro bono matters. Some partners are opposed to pro bono as are some associates who 'don't believe in it.'"

"The firm has certain people who are committed to pro bono work and are allowed to do it. Most associates, however, feel that if it takes time away from billable work, it will be held against them."

"Pro bono is openly and strongly encouraged. Indeed, a significant portion of your billable hours can include pro bono."

"[There are] lots of pretty good ventures and projects to choose from, and the firm does reward and promote pro bono work."

"The firm has a very strong commitment to a wide variety of pro bono work. The firm provides many opportunities to get involved in pro bono cases and training, as well as encourages us to seek out our own pro bono work."

> "Pro bono service is considered an important factor in performance reviews and when determining associate bonus eligibility."
>
> — *Chadbourne & Parke*

Choate, Hall & Stewart

Exchange Place
53 State Street
Boston, MA 02109
Phone: (617) 248-5000
www.choate.com

LOCATIONS

Boston, MA (HQ)

MAJOR DEPARTMENTS & PRACTICES

Corporate
Health Care
Intellectual Property
Litigation
Real Estate
Trusts & Estates

THE STATS

No. of attorneys worldwide: 190
No. of offices worldwide: 1
Managing Partners: William P. Gelnaw Jr. and John A. Nadas

EMPLOYMENT CONTACT

Ms. Robin Carbone
Director of Recruiting
Phone: (617) 248-5000
Fax: (617) 248-4000
E-mail: rcarbone@choate.com

WHO'S WHO

Principal pro bono contact(s) at your firm:

Mitch Kaplan, Esq.
Partner
Phone: (617) 248-5158
E-mail: mkaplan@choate.com

Does the firm have a pro bono coordinator? No. The pro bono program is managed by one of our partners. Other partners have assumed responsibility for some of our more popular programs — e.g., PAIR, the Pine Street Inn outreach program and the Battered Women's program (all described below).

If yes, what percentage of his or her time is spent on pro bono work? N/A

Does the firm have a pro bono committee? No

If yes, how often does the committee meet? N/A

Describe the composition of the committee: N/A

THE SCOOP

Does your firm have a written pro bono policy? Yes

Has the firm signed on to the Law Firm Pro Bono Challenge? No

What are some of the areas of law in which your firm has performed pro bono legal work in the last two years?

- Presidential clemency — We have been active in the last several years in the presidential clemency program. Our representation of Dorothy Gaines of Mobile, Ala., who was granted executive clemency by President Clinton on December 22, 2000, thereby commuting her 19-plus-year sentence to time served, received both national and regional attention from the press.

- Social services — A centerpiece of our pro bono efforts is a first-of-its-kind collaboration between Choate, Hall & Stewart and Family Services of Greater Boston (FSGB), the city's oldest social service agency. Now in its third year, the program brings together the diverse legal and administrative talents of Choate staff.

- Elder protection — Through its relationship with FSGB, Choate also participates in the Suffolk County Elder Protection Roundtable, a multidisciplinary initiative of the Suffolk County district attorney's office that addresses the complicated problems that elders face when they become victims of crime.

- Criminal law — Choate's litigation department has a long-standing relationship with the Suffolk County DA's office. Through the Volunteer Prosecutor Program, one of Choate's mid-level litigators spends six months as a full-time assistant district attorney with the DA's office.

- Poverty law — We provide legal services on behalf of indigent clients in a variety of civil and criminal matters. Choate has maintained a close relationship with the Volunteer Lawyers Project of the Boston Bar Association since its inception. It was also one of the founding firms working through the Lawyers Clearinghouse on Affordable Housing, to provide outreach services to homeless residents of the Pine Street Inn and St. Francis House shelters. Through these agencies,

Choate represents clients in matters addressing housing, statutory benefits, tax problems, criminal charges and a range of other issues.

- Political asylum — Through the Political Asylum/Immigration Representation Project (PAIR), Choate attorneys have represented a number of indigent clients seeking asylum in this country because of persecution and political danger in their countries of origin.

- Domestic violence — Through the Massachusetts Women's Bar Association's Family Law Project for Battered Women, Choate attorneys have represented victims of domestic violence. This representation has gone beyond assistance in obtaining restraining orders to long-term representation on the domestic relations, child support and child custody matters that often are associated with domestic violence.

- Civil rights — Choate has had a long-standing commitment to protecting the civil rights of individuals as well as groups. From groups including the Lawyers Committee for Civil Rights and the Civil Liberties Union of Massachusetts, Choate has accepted referrals on matters involving First Amendment rights, prisoners' rights, voting rights, discrimination and other matters.

- Charitable organizations — We provide legal services to charitable, civic, governmental and educational institutions in furtherance of their charitable purposes, where payment of legal fees would significantly deplete the organization's economic resources.

- Administration of justice — We participate in organizations whose purpose is to improve the law or the legal system, increase the availability of legal services or otherwise improve the administration of justice.

What are some of the areas of law in which your firm does not perform pro bono work? N/A

Organizations for which your firm has performed pro bono legal services in the last two years: See answer above.

List up to three pro bono matters that are representative of the pro bono work your firm participates in.

- A Choate, Hall & Stewart team recently represented a very young adolescent woman who sought asylum in this country because her father was intent on forcing her marriage to a man several decades older than her. We had to prove that the customs in her country of origin were such that she would be physically and emotionally impaired were she forced to return.

- Choate, Hall & Stewart attorneys represented a class of Spanish-speaking inmates at a maximum security prison who were not provided with interpreters at disciplinary hearings or for healthcare. A consent decree was negotiated with the Massachusetts Department of Corrections requiring adequate translators at these critical events.

- Choate, Hall & Stewart attorneys represented a conservation land trust in litigation protecting the conservation easements that attached to the land and prevented any future commercial development.

BY THE NUMBERS

What is the total number of hours that lawyers in U.S. offices at your firm spent performing pro bono legal services in 2000, 2001 and 2002?

Total number of hours in 2000: 10,163 hours
Total number of hours in 2001: 9,635 hours

Total number of hours in 2002: 10,462 hours

Average number of pro bono hours per attorney in U.S. offices per year (including associates, partners, counsels, but not summer associates):

Average number of hours per attorney in 2000: 62.5 hours
Average number of hours per attorney in 2001: 54.7 hours
Average number of hours per attorney in 2002: 62.5 hours

What percentage of attorneys in this firm's U.S. offices did pro bono work in 2002? 44 percent

What percentage of attorneys in this firm's U.S. offices did at least 20 hours of pro bono work in 2002? 44 percent

Does the firm encourage its lawyers to perform a minimum number of pro bono hours? No. While the firm encourages its attorneys to participate in pro bono work, there is no required minimum.

If so, how many hours per year or what percentage of lawyers' billable hours? N/A

SUPERVISION AND EVALUATIONS

Is there partner supervision on each pro bono matter? Yes

Do partner supervisors or, if applicable, senior associates provide written evaluations of associates' work on pro bono matters? Yes

If so, are those evaluations taken into account in determining salary, bonuses or advancement in the firm? Yes

If not, does the firm consider pro bono work generally in associate evaluations? Yes

HOURS

Does the firm give billable hour credit for pro bono work? Yes

Does the firm have a maximum number of pro bono hours that can be applied toward the billable hour target? No. The firm believes that there are many reasons why its attorneys should participate in community activities and provide pro bono legal services. One of those reasons is the value of the work to one's own professional development. Therefore, we encourage associates to participate in community initiatives and pro bono projects that provide an opportunity for professional growth. The firm supports the associate's efforts in a variety of ways, including providing credit towards hourly expectations for time devoted to approved pro bono projects.

If so, what is the maximum? N/A

If your firm uses hours to determine bonuses, does it consider pro bono hours when determining bonuses? Yes

PRO BONO POINTS

What training opportunities are open to associates working on pro bono matters? Several of the pro bono programs require some formal training — e.g., PAIR cases, the domestic violence program and certain benefits cases. Continuing

Legal Education providers also run programs throughout the year in immigration, housing and other areas that associates are always free to attend at no cost to them.

Can associates bring matters of interest to the firm? Yes

Does the firm offer the use of support staff in carrying out pro bono matters? Yes

What pro bono opportunities are available for summer associates? Summer associates are always involved in the pro bono matters underway in the firm during the summer. We do not have a specific program for them as most matters take longer than our summer program.

Does the firm have established programs, such as externships, that enable its associates to work in a public interest setting? Yes

If so, where and for up to how long? One example of an established program designed to expose associates to public interest matters is our Volunteer Prosecutor Program. Through the program, during each six-month period one of Choate's mid-level litigators serves as a full-time assistant district attorney with the Suffolk County district attorney's office. The program helps to address scarce resource constraints faced by the DA's office and also offers Choate lawyers with unique and valuable training and professional development opportunities.

Has your firm won any special recognition or awards in the last two years for its pro bono work? Yes

If so, please list. See narrative below.

THE FIRM SAYS

Choate, Hall & Stewart's pro bono services range from its first-of-its-kind collaboration with Family Services of Greater Boston, the city's oldest social service agency, to the representation of individual domestic violence victims, to class action litigation on behalf of Spanish-speaking prison inmates.

In addition to providing pro bono legal services to FSGB and its clients, which include the city's neediest families, the firm has also committed $100,000 toward agency programs and infrastructure costs. For example, Choate will again serve this year as corporate underwriter for FSGB's flagship fundraiser, "Crafts at the Castle." Through our multifaceted involvement with FSGB, Choate is not only helping to fill the gap in legal services for the poor, but also supporting the agency's ideology of "Helping Families Be Families."

In the first year of operation of the Suffolk County Elder Protection Roundtable, a multidisciplinary initiative of the Suffolk County DA's office addressing problems faced by elder victims of crime, Choate attorneys and paralegals were involved in two significant matters on behalf of FSGB clients.

The firm's participation in the Volunteer Prosecutor Program, whereby a Choate litigator spends six months as an assistant district attorney at the Suffolk County district attorney's office, helps to address resource constraints faced by the DA's office and also offers Choate lawyers valuable training and professional development opportunities.

Choate's commitment to providing legal services through many of the city's legal service providers goes back many decades. Choate attorneys have long worked both for individual clients in need of personal legal assistance as well as important civil rights litigation. Choate attorneys provide pro bono legal services in areas including poverty law, political asylum, domestic violence, and civil rights and liberties. One of our partners was a founder of the Lawyers Committee for Civil Rights and an original board member of its Massachusetts chapter; another serves on its Board of Advisors. Another partner has served as general counsel of the Civil Liberties Union of Massachusetts. Presently, we represent a class of Spanish-speaking inmates seeking adequate translation services for health and disciplinary matters.

Through the Political Asylum/Immigration Representation Project, Choate attorneys have represented a number of indigent clients seeking asylum in this country because of persecution and political danger in their countries of origin. As a result of their efforts, Choate was awarded PAIR's 2000 Law Firm Pro Bono Award; and in 2001, a Choate attorney was named PAIR Pro Bono Attorney of the Year for his efforts in obtaining refuge for an immigrant facing imminent danger if deported.

We recognize that certain of the firm's lawyers, by reason of experience, suitability and/or opportunity, will satisfy their pro bono obligation outside the parameters identified above. The firm supports those alternative pro bono activities as well.

Choate, Hall & Stewart's long tradition of public service extends beyond the provision of pro bono legal services. Our lawyers have served as presidents of the Massachusetts and Boston Bar Associations and in other leadership positions with those organizations, as well as with the Asian-American Lawyers Association of Massachusetts, the Hispanic National Bar Association and Greater Boston Legal Services. Two of our partners have been appointed to the Massachusetts Board of Bar Overseers by the Chief Justice of our State Supreme Court. Others serve on the boards of numerous charitable organizations, including hospitals, museums and colleges and universities.

Choate personnel participates in various group public service efforts. Choate teams have participated in City-Year's Serve-A-Thon, as well as Goodwill's Clothing Collaborative for Job Trainees and the Greater Boston Legal Services Associate Fund Drive, just to name a few.

OUR SURVEY SAYS

"Pro bono hours count toward your billable requirement and many young associates are involved in pro bono work."

"[The firm] needs to make a stronger commitment to pro bono hours actually counted and not just given lip service (they say it counts, but there is some question if it really matters)."

"Many associates participate in pro bono work and it is encouraged."

"Pro bono is not encouraged. We are told it counts towards billable hours, but it is broken out separately and most partners pay no attention to it."

"The firm encourages all associates (and partners) to participate in the loads of pro bono work that our relationship with a local political asylum referral service provides. The firm is also committed to its relationship with Family Services of Greater Boston, which provides associates (and partners) with opportunities to represent poor and otherwise disadvantaged clients in a variety of domestic and other disputes. All that being said, pro bono work is non-billable, and I haven't had the time or inclination to participate because I've been busy with billable matters (and I'd rather not take the hit on hours that a protracted pro bono matter might cause)."

"Does not count toward your hours, so no one supports it."

"The firm tries to hype the pro bono initiatives but at the end of the day it is not counted. The firm states that the pro bono work is counted toward billables but our time sheets indicate otherwise (as do the reviews)."

"It is great and unusual. Pretty much anything gets approved."

Cleary, Gottlieb, Steen & Hamilton

One Liberty Plaza
New York, NY 10006-1470
Phone: (212) 225-2000
www.cgsh.com

LOCATIONS

New York, NY (HQ)
Washington, DC
Brussels
Cologne
Frankfurt
Hong Kong
London
Milan
Moscow
Paris
Rome
Tokyo

MAJOR DEPARTMENTS & PRACTICES

Antitrust & Competition
Bankruptcy & Restructuring
Litigation & Arbitration
Mergers, Acquisitions & Joint Ventures
Private Clients & Charitable Organizations
Project Finance & Infrastructure
Real Estate
Securities & Capital Markets
Sovereign Governments & International Institutions
Tax

THE STATS

No. of attorneys worldwide: 853
No. of offices worldwide: 12
Managing Partner: Peter Karasz

EMPLOYMENT CONTACT

Mr. Jaime E. Martinez
Manager of Legal Recruitment
Phone: (212) 225-3163
E-mail: jmartinez@cgsh.com

WHO'S WHO

Principal pro bono contact(s) at your firm:

Steven Horowitz, Esq.
Partner, New York Office

Lindsee Granfield, Esq.
Partner, New York Office

Ms. Carrie Grimm
Pro Bono Coordinator

Mathew Slater, Esq.
Partner, D.C. Office

Andrew Curran, Esq.
Partner, London Office

Does the firm have a pro bono coordinator? Yes
Ms. Carrie Grimm
Phone: (212) 225 3136
E-mail: cgrimm@cgsh.com

If yes, what percentage of his or her time is spent on pro bono work? 100 percent

Does the firm have a pro bono committee? Yes

If yes, how often does the committee meet? Every two months

Describe the composition of the committee: The committee is comprised of 15 members. Five partners and four associates are on the committee for a three-year term. Six partners, including the managing partner, are on the committee in an ex officio capacity. Each serves on the board of a legal services organization with which Cleary Gottlieb has a close relationship.

THE SCOOP

Does your firm have a written pro bono policy? Yes

Has the firm signed on to the Law Firm Pro Bono Challenge? Yes

What are some of the areas of law in which your firm has performed pro bono legal work in the last two years? We work in almost every area of public interest law. A large portion of our work over the past two years includes immigration and asylum law, assistance to survivors of domestic violence, affordable housing development, education and children's rights, impact litigation including voters rights and disability rights, not-for-profit assistance, arts and entertainment law, housing litigation, assistance to small businesses and representation of persons affected by the events of September 11, 2001.

What are some of the areas of law in which your firm does not perform pro bono work? We do not handle religious matters or political matters. We rarely work in the areas of predatory lending or environmental law.

Organizations for which your firm has performed pro bono legal services in the last two years: Legal Aid Society; Lawyers Alliance for New York; Lawyers Committee on Civil Rights under the Law; Lawyers Committee on Human Rights; Legal Services for New York, including Brooklyn Legal Services Corporations; Mutual Housing Association of New York; New York Immigration Coalition; New York Lawyers for the Public Interest; Sanctuary for Families; Volunteer Lawyers for the Arts.

List up to three pro bono matters that are representative of the pro bono work your firm participates in.

- Accion NY Partnership. We partner with the micro-lender Accion NY to provide pro bono corporate legal services to its clients, which are micro-businesses located in disenfranchised areas of New York City that lack access to traditional forms of business credit.

- Immigration Rights. We work with several public interest law groups to further the rights of immigrants and asylum seekers. We represent individuals applying for asylum, as well as immigrant criminal cases advocating clients habeas corpus rights. We staff special registration clinics for persons who must register with the Department of Homeland Security under the U.S. PATRIOT Act. We also partnered with Migration Policy Institute to draft a white paper on the impact of the U.S. PATRIOT Act on national security and civil liberties.

- Affordable Housing. We regularly represent community organizations in the acquisition and financing of affordable housing projects, including through the use of federal low-income housing tax credits and various federal, state and municipal subsidies. We advise our clients on 501(c)(3) issues related to these projects and negotiate the terms of joint ventures with not-for-profit and private partners. As an example, we have helped Mutual Housing Association of New York, Inc. acquire and finance the rehabilitation of over 150 properties in Brooklyn, N.Y., for affordable housing.

BY THE NUMBERS

What is the total number of hours that lawyers in U.S. offices at your firm spent performing pro bono legal services in 2000, 2001 and 2002?

      Total number of hours in 2000: 20,285 hours
      Total number of hours in 2001: 25,027 hours
      Total number of hours in 2002: 34,645 hours

Average number of pro bono hours per attorney in U.S. offices per year (including associates, partners, counsels, but not summer associates):

      Average number of hours per attorney in 2000: 48 hours
      Average number of hours per attorney in 2001: 54 hours
      Average number of hours per attorney in 2002: 70 hours

What percentage of attorneys in this firm's U.S. offices did pro bono work in 2002? 79 percent

What percentage of attorneys in this firm's U.S. offices did at least 20 hours of pro bono work in 2002? 56 percent

Does the firm encourage its lawyers to perform a minimum number of pro bono hours? No. While the firm sets no target for minimum number of pro bono hours, Cleary Gottlieb strongly encourages lawyers to undertake such work.

If so, how many hours per year or what percentage of lawyers' billable hours? N/A

SUPERVISION AND EVALUATIONS

Is there partner supervision on each pro bono matter? Yes

Do partner supervisors or, if applicable, senior associates provide written evaluations of associates' work on pro bono matters? Yes

If so, are those evaluations taken into account in determining salary, bonuses or advancement in the firm? Yes. Pro bono work is evaluated with all other work performed by associates, but this does not affect salary or bonuses.

If not, does the firm consider pro bono work generally in associate evaluations? N/A

Does the firm have a maximum number of pro bono hours that can be applied toward the billable hour target? No. Cleary Gottlieb does not have a billable hour requirement. The firm does not consider hours worked, neither billable nor pro bono, in determining associate bonuses.

If so, what is the maximum? If your firm uses hours to determine bonuses, does it consider pro bono hours when determining bonuses? N/A

PRO BONO POINTS

What training opportunities are open to associates working on pro bono matters? Cleary Gottlieb lawyers can participate in many of the legal service trainings offered throughout the year to learn about areas of pro bono law that interest them. The firm expects the lawyer to take on a pro bono matter in the applicable area within six months of the training.

Can associates bring matters of interest to the firm? Yes

Does the firm offer the use of support staff in carrying out pro bono matters? Yes

What pro bono opportunities are available for summer associates? Summer associates can participate in any open pro bono matter during their summer. The pro bono matters are assigned to summer associates based upon their statement of interest. The pro bono coordinator works with the summer associates committee to ensure that a good match is made according to the interests of the summer associate. In addition, summer associates can participate in the Courtroom Advocates Program assisting domestic violence survivors in drafting and filing orders of protection. Summer associates can also participate in our Accion NY partnership assisting small businesses with corporate legal matters.

Does the firm have established programs, such as externships, that enable its associates to work in a public interest setting? Yes

If so, where and for up to how long? Cleary Gottlieb tax partner Les Samuels was the first extern in New York City in 1968. He worked at Brooklyn Legal Services Corporation for four months. In 1969, Cleary Gottlieb established its first formal externship with MFY Legal Services, Inc., a legal services office in Manhattan,. MFY devotes much of its resources to landlord-tenant matters, often in New York City Housing Court. Since 1989, the firm has also worked with the Lawyers Alliance for New York (LANY), a public interest law group that assists not-for-profit community organizations in New York City. The externship program at LANY provides associates with corporate, real estate, tax and/or other transactional or business law experience related to the not-for-profit sector.

Both externships work in the same fashion: an associate is selected to work on a full-time basis at the offices of MFY or LANY for a four-month period. Each associate participating in the program works exclusively on MFY or LANY matters during the four-month assignment, but continues to receive his or her full salary and benefits from the firm. In essence, during the course of a year, three different associates provide an additional full-time staff lawyer position for MFY and LANY. Typically, an associate will have been with the firm for at least two years before an externship assignment is made.

In 2002, Cleary Gottlieb created a third pilot externship program to meet the request of the New York City Law Department. To date we have had two associates participate in a three-month externship in the Tort Division of the Corporation Counsel's Office, which defends the city in all the negligence claims brought against it.

Has your firm won any special recognition or awards in the last two years for its pro bono work? Yes

If so, please list. 2003 American Immigration Lawyers Association Pro bono Award, 2003 Volunteer Lawyers for the Arts Pro bono Service Award, 2003 MFY Legal Services, Inc. Scales of Justice Partnership Award, 2003 Compassion in Dying Special Recognition for Pro Bono Service, 2002 Legal Aid Society Award for Outstanding Assistance to Victims of WTC Tragedy.

THE FIRM SAYS

Cleary Gottlieb has a longstanding commitment to pro bono service based upon the belief that the legal profession has a serious obligation to support the integrity of the justice system, by assisting those with limited access to legal services. The firm is a charter member of the Law Firm Pro Bono Challenge, which requires that at least 3 percent of the firm's overall practice consist of pro bono work. We meet or exceed this challenge each year by providing quality legal assistance to a diverse range of clients. We believe that pro bono work creates an opportunity for "equal justice," enabling lawyers to address the unmet legal needs of those with limited access to legal services.

Cleary Gottlieb encourages and values pro bono work, recognizing not only the needs of the indigent, but also the needs of our lawyers to add value to the legal profession. Our firm provides lawyers with opportunities for both corporate and litigation pro bono work. Our matters include representing individuals such as domestic violence survivors and political asylum seekers, advising not-for-profit organizations and affordable housing associations and litigating class action suits. We work with several legal service providers, as well as local and international not-for-profits to present our lawyers with the most diverse range of pro bono opportunities available. Any Cleary Gottlieb lawyer can bring a new matter to the firm as long as it meets eligibility requirements and passes a conflict check. In our New York office, lawyers also have the opportunity to work full-time for a four-month rotation at one of two legal services agencies through our externship programs, and to participate in public service work through our partnership program with Washington Irving High School in lower Manhattan.

Cleary Gottlieb maintains an extensive internal Intranet site dedicated to our pro bono practice, providing our lawyers with both administrative and substantive legal resources. We have developed 12 pro bono interest groups, organized around substantive areas such as international human rights and community development, in order to support and communicate with lawyers who share common pro bono interests. Each interest group is chaired by a volunteer lawyer coordinator and maintains an internal e-mail list to facilitate communication. In the New York office, we maintain a Community Legal Assistance Committee (CLAC), comprised of partners and associates who oversee all aspects of our pro bono program. The CLAC screens and approves all New York pro bono matters and meets regularly to discuss and improve the ways in which pro bono work is conducted. We also employ a full-time pro bono coordinator who handles day-to-day administrative matters, serves as the liaison between organizations seeking pro bono volunteers and Cleary Gottlieb lawyers in search of pro bono opportunities, and works with our lawyers to ensure proper staffing on each matter in addition to maintaining contact with various bar associations, pro bono staff at other law firms and law schools.

In our Washington office, Cleary Gottlieb maintains a separate pro bono committee of partners and associates that oversees the pro bono work done in that office.

Our London office is leading our international offices with its pro bono activities. The London office also maintains a pro bono committee. On August 21, 2003, Cleary Gottlieb became the second American law firm to sign the Joint Protocol for Pro Bono Legal Work, to strengthen our support for pro bono efforts in England. Due to the different legal climate in England, the pro bono work done in London is currently limited to assisting not-for-profit community groups. Our other European offices take on matters in an ad hoc manner. Some countries laws require that each lawyer represent an indigent client as part of their admission to the bar.

For more information about our pro bono practice, please visit our web site: www.cgsh.com.

OUR SURVEY SAYS

"The firm is extremely committed to pro bono. These hours are counted in work reports, so the partnership sees each lawyer's commitment. The firm is always on the cutting edge with new projects and programs and is also very supportive of lawyers who want to take on their own projects."

"[We have a] great pro bono coordinator, really receptive to new project referrals, and pro bono clients are treated as important as paying clients."

"Cleary actively encourages pro bono work. In my experience, the partners have been very generous with their time and accommodating of junior associates' pro bono matters."

"I've always been encouraged to do pro bono, it is counted as billable hours, you can expense meals or cars that you need due to late night hours to the firm."

"Pro bono hours are treated like billables in terms of adding up each associate's hours, though since no one even seems to know how many hours are the average here, billables are clearly not a priority concern. I have spent full days working on pro bono matters and no one thinks of the work any differently. There are tons of community development and immigration-related matters that come to Cleary lawyers. We're very well connected in the pro bono networks in the city."

"The firm has a pro bono committee that actively pursues ways to increase our pro bono activities. The firm has a full-time pro bono coordinator who manages a number of various pro bono 'groups,' each with its own attorney coordinator (e.g., an art/entertainment group, a civil rights group, an asylum group, and so on). The firm has a pro bono criteria for making partner, and the firm as a whole had a goal of exceeding 3 percent of billable hours devoted to pro bono. For a 700-lawyer firm billing 2,000 hours each per year, that's 42,000 hours of pro bono."

"I have been able to do lots of pro bono work, even [projects] that I have suggested as a first-year. Partners are very accessible and willing to supervise pro bono projects."

"They don't urge you to do the work but are very receptive to people initiating the work. A lot of firm programs/opportunities are also made available to attorneys, so they facilitate your finding pro bono work."

"There are some good opportunities to do internships while keeping your law firm salary."

"Cleary's pro bono policy is something I appreciate most about the firm. Pro bono hours have the same value as billable hours and no distinction is made. You can do as much pro bono work as you want as long as the other work gets done. This sometimes means that pro bono work comes second and contributes to your long hours. One big difference between pro bono work and billable work is that you get far less supervision from partners, so you have only yourself to blame for mistakes, but only yourself and your team to congratulate on a victory."

"We believe that pro bono work creates an opportunity for 'equal justice,' enabling lawyers to address the unmet legal needs of those with limited access to legal services."

— *Cleary, Gottlieb, Steen & Hamilton*

Clifford Chance US LLP

200 Park Avenue
New York, NY 10166
Phone: (212) 878-8000
www.cliffordchance.com

LOCATIONS

Los Angeles, CA • New York, NY • Palo Alto, CA • San Diego, CA • San Francisco, CA • Washington, DC • Amsterdam • Bangkok • Barcelona • Beijing • Berlin • Brussels • Budapest • Dubai • Dusseldorf • Frankfurt • Hong Kong • London • Luxembourg • Madrid • Milan • Moscow • Munich • Padua • Paris • Prague • Rome • Sao Paulo • Shanghai • Singapore • Tokyo • Warsaw

MAJOR DEPARTMENTS & PRACTICES

Antitrust
Banking & Finance
Capital Markets
Construction
Corporate
E-commerce
Insurance
Intellectual Property
International Trade
Litigation & Dispute Resolution
Maritime
Project Finance
Public Policy
Public Private Partnership
Real Estate
Tax, Pensions & Employment
Transport

THE STATS

No. of attorneys worldwide: 3,700
No. of offices worldwide: 32
Regional Managing Partner – Americas: John K. Carroll

EMPLOYMENT CONTACT

Ms. Carolyn Older Bortner
Manager of Legal Recruiting
Phone: (212) 878-8252
Fax: (212) 878-8375
E-mail: Carolyn.Bortner@cliffordchance.com

WHO'S WHO

Principal pro bono contact(s) at your firm:

Warren L. Feldman, Esq.

Does the firm have a pro bono coordinator? Yes

Teresa Schiller, Esq.

If yes, what percentage of his or her time is spent on pro bono work? 25 percent

Does the firm have a pro bono committee? Yes

If yes, how often does the committee meet? Several times a year

Describe the composition of the committee: Partners, administrative heads, associates and pro bono coordinators are on the committee.

THE SCOOP

Does your firm have a written pro bono policy? Yes

Has the firm signed on to the Law Firm Pro Bono Challenge? No

What are some of the areas of law in which your firm has performed pro bono legal work in the last two years? Arts, children's rights, civil rights/First Amendment, criminal law, domestic violence, housing, immigration, international law and not-for-profits.

What are some of the areas of law in which your firm does not perform pro bono work? Medical malpractice and matrimonial law.

Organizations for which your firm has performed pro bono legal services in the last two years: New York Lawyers for the Public Interest, Volunteer Lawyers for the Arts, My Sisters' Place, Lawyers Committee for Human Rights, Office of the Appellate Defender, Kings County DA's Office, City Bar, International Senior Lawyers Project, Washington Lawyers Committee for Civil Rights and Urban Affairs, Thurgood Marshall Foundation.

List up to three pro bono matters that are representative of the pro bono work your firm participates in.

- A firm attorney, in conjunction with the Office of the Appellate Defender, won a reversal of a criminal conviction. The appeal was based primarily on a controversial issue related to an allegedly coercive supplemental jury charge that followed the jury's second deadlock vote. In a split decision, the appellate court found the charge to be improper and ordered a new trial. The decision and Clifford Chance's involvement in the case were covered in the *New York Law Journal*.

- Clifford Chance recently launched the Housing Access Project with New York Lawyers for the Public Interest to advocate on behalf of tenants with mobility and sensorial impairments. HAP attorneys develop expertise in negotiating with landlords and litigating in administrative hearings.

- The firm has been providing ongoing tax and corporate advice to the Lung Cancer Online Foundation, an organization dedicated to funding research and fellowships to assist in the battle against lung cancer.

BY THE NUMBERS

What is the total number of hours that lawyers in U.S. offices at your firm spent performing pro bono legal services in 2000, 2001 and 2002?

> Total number of hours in 2000: 9,812.9 hours
> Total number of hours in 2001: 16,030.95 hours
> Total number of hours in 2002: 15,707.40 hours

Average number of pro bono hours per attorney in U.S. offices per year (including associates, partners, counsels, but not summer associates):

> Average number of hours per attorney in 2000: 20 hours
> Average number of hours per attorney in 2001: 31 hours
> Average number of hours per attorney in 2002: 28 hours

What percentage of attorneys in this firm's U.S. offices did pro bono work in 2002? 53 percent

What percentage of attorneys in this firm's U.S. offices did at least 20 hours of pro bono work in 2002? 29 percent

Does the firm encourage its lawyers to perform a minimum number of pro bono hours? Yes

If so, how many hours per year or what percentage of lawyers' billable hours? 30 hours

SUPERVISION AND EVALUATIONS

Is there partner supervision on each pro bono matter? Yes

Do partner supervisors or, if applicable, senior associates provide written evaluations of associates' work on pro bono matters? Yes

If so, are those evaluations taken into account in determining salary, bonuses or advancement in the firm? Yes

If not, does the firm consider pro bono work generally in associate evaluations? N/A

HOURS

Does the firm give billable hour credit for pro bono work? Yes

Does the firm have a maximum number of pro bono hours that can be applied toward the billable hour target? No

If so, what is the maximum? N/A

If your firm uses hours to determine bonuses, does it consider pro bono hours when determining bonuses? N/A

PRO BONO POINTS

What training opportunities are open to associates working on pro bono matters? Associates receive extensive skills training internally. They also receive training from legal service providers and have free access to external CLE programs.

Can associates bring matters of interest to the firm? Yes

Does the firm offer the use of support staff in carrying out pro bono matters? Yes

What pro bono opportunities are available for summer associates? Summer associates can work on the same types of pro bono matters as associates.

Does the firm have established programs, such as externships, that enable its associates to work in a public interest setting? Yes

If so, where and for up to how long? Clifford Chance has seconded associates over the last few years to the Association of the Bar of the City of New York and the Lower Manhattan Development Corporation in the aftermath of September 11.

Has your firm won any special recognition or awards in the last two years for its pro bono work? Yes

If so, please list.

Clifford Chance has been recognized for outstanding pro bono efforts by the *New York Law Journal, The American Lawyer, The Lawyer*, the Pro Bono Institute and the Association of the Bar of the City of New York. The firm has received awards, including the Washington Lawyers' Committee for Civil Rights and Urban Affairs Outstanding Achievement Award for work with the committee's Immigrant & Refugee Rights Project.

THE FIRM SAYS

Clifford Chance encourages pro bono service in its six U.S. offices and in its 26 other offices worldwide. The firm emphasizes that pro bono clients are to be treated as if they are paying clients. Every matter is staffed with a partner and at least one associate, and some matters require teams of attorneys from domestic and international offices. Guidelines for handling matters in the U.S. are available from the firm's pro bono partner, the pro bono coordinator and the firm's intranet. Pro bono contribution is an important aspect of annual evaluations. There is no maximum number of pro bono hours that can count towards that evaluation. Attorneys handle pro bono matters referred from many legal service providers, but they are free to present other matters of interest to the firm.

Four signature projects are representative of the kinds of pro bono initiatives the firm undertakes in the United States: International Senior Lawyers Project (ISLP), the William P. Rogers Pro Bono Program ("Rogers Program"), the Housing Access Project (HAP) and the Lehmann High School project. Clifford Chance contributed to and supported the formation of the ISLP, and the firm provides office space and works with the ISLP regularly. ISLP was founded to promote democracy, protect human rights, and advance economic development in emerging democracies and developing economies. Clifford Chance created the Rogers Program to coordinate various Washington, D.C., pro bono activities, including working with the Washington Lawyers' Committee for Civil Rights and Urban Affairs, Habitat for Humanity, the Street Law Project, the Thurgood Marshall Foundation and Howard University School of Law. HAP is a joint initiative by Clifford Chance and New York Lawyers for the Public Interest to assist disabled tenants with residential accessibility problems. Firm attorneys help Lehmann High School by providing weekly training to students preparing for moot court and mock trial competitions throughout the school year.

Clifford Chance supports non-legal volunteerism in addition to pro bono service. Members of the firm's pro bono and community affairs committee work together to plan and administer programs, such as Bring a Book to Work Week and a donation drive for My Sisters' Place (MSP). Bring a Book to Work Week is a global initiative to collect books for Book Aid International, which places books in African libraries, schools, legal aid clinics, hospitals and universities. The firm has also helped MSP, a domestic violence charity, by collecting, purchasing and bagging toiletries and toys for mothers and children staying at MSP shelters. This project is one in a series of initiatives that Clifford Chance has sponsored for MSP; others include hosting a charity art auction and holiday craft fair, as well as "hands-on" volunteering at its shelters. In sum, Clifford Chance stands behind pro bono and community affairs service projects, striving to provide quality assistance to those in need.

OUR SURVEY SAYS

"The firm has really reversed itself and is now showing, I believe, a strong commitment to pro bono."

"After the famous memo fiasco — in which the associates blasted the firm for its treatment of pro bono — the official policy towards billable hours changed. Now, there's no strict quota, and pro bono work — theoretically, at least — is put on equal footing with billable work. In practice, I'm not sure whether the firm truly adheres to its stated policy — I'm sure someone with 2,500 hours of billables is still going to get a higher bonus than someone with 2,000 hours of billables and 500 of pro bono — but at least they're signaling that they'll give pro bono commitments a little more respect."

"The firm has recommitted itself to pro bono work this year in doing away with our hourly billable requirement, such that we are free to devote as many hours to pro bono matters as we wish. We are sent updated lists of pro bono matters which we may take on every week."

"There are a lot of opportunities available if you take the initiative, but the firm does not make a big push to get associates involved in pro bono."

"Pro bono is basically on your own time. It cannot interfere with responsibilities to paying clients."

"I spent an unusually large number of hours on a pro bono case in 2002 and 2001 and felt that the firm was extremely supportive."

"The firm just changed the way associates are evaluated so as to include a pro bono component. In effect, this gives credit to associates who do a lot (or any) pro bono work."

"Since 9/11 they have been a lot more committed; mostly the litigation group does pro bono. We have a group of people who are in charge of it and every week they send around e-mails, so anyone who is interested can easily do it. Also, with the hour requirement gone, I think more people will take advantage of the opportunity now."

"A lot of people talk about it, but we can only do work for 'approved' organizations. We don't have a lot of choices, and the firm has a lot of unspoken rules for what an appropriate pro bono experience would be. Unless you are doing the work with an established organization, you cannot consider it pro bono. A lot of interesting work is filtered out."

"The firm strongly encourages all attorneys to engage in pro bono work (and rewards those that do). However, no one is actually required to do pro bono work and the firm expressly accepts that pro bono is not for everyone (i.e., if you don't want to, don't — no problem)."

> "The firm emphasizes that pro bono clients are to be treated as if they are paying clients."
>
> — *Clifford Chance US LLP*

Cooley Godward LLP

Five Palo Alto Square, 4th Floor
3000 El Camino Real
Palo Alto, CA 94306-2155
Phone: (650) 843-5000
www.cooley.com

LOCATIONS

Palo Alto, CA (HQ)
Broomfield, CO
Reston, VA
San Diego, CA
San Francisco, CA

MAJOR DEPARTMENTS & PRACTICES

Antitrust & Trade Regulation
Business Crimes & Regulatory Defense
Complex Commercial Litigation
Credit Finance
Creditor's Rights & Bankruptcy
Emerging Companies
Employee Compensation & Benefits
Employment & Labor
Environmental
Estate & Family Tax Planning
Immigration
Insureds' Rights
Intellectual Property
Investment Banking
Life Sciences
Mergers & Acquisitions
Patent Counseling & Prosecution
Public Offerings
Real Estate
Securities Litigation
Tax
Technology Transactions
Trademark, Copyright & Advertising
Venture Capital

THE STATS

No. of attorneys worldwide: 500
No. of offices worldwide: 5
Chairman and CEO: Stephen C. Neal

EMPLOYMENT CONTACT

Ms. Jo Anne Larson
Director of Attorney Recruiting
Phone: (650) 843-5000
Fax: (650) 857-0663
E-mail: larsonja@cooley.com

WHO'S WHO

Does the firm have a pro bono coordinator? Yes

Maureen Alger, Esq.
Pro Bono Counsel
Phone: (650) 843-5201
E-mail: malger@cooley.com

If yes, what percentage of his or her time is spent on pro bono work? 100 percent

Does the firm have a pro bono committee? Yes

If yes, how often does the committee meet? Quarterly

Describe the composition of the committee: The committee is comprised of partners from our various offices.

THE SCOOP

Does your firm have a written pro bono policy? Yes

Has the firm signed on to the Law Firm Pro Bono Challenge? Yes

What are some of the areas of law in which your firm has performed pro bono legal work in the last two years? Prisoners' rights, capital punishment, civil rights, First Amendment, landlord-tenant disputes, contract disputes, intellectual property issues, entity formation, nonprofit mergers, environmental litigation, real estate transactional work, political asylum, guardianship matters and debtors' rights.

What are some of the areas of law in which your firm does not perform pro bono work? Personal injury.

Organizations for which your firm has performed pro bono legal services in the last two years: California Appellate Death Penalty Project, Volunteer Legal Services Program of the San Francisco Bar Association, Lawyers' Committee for Civil Rights of the San Francisco Bay Area, Legal Aid Society of San Mateo County, Stanford Community Law Clinic, Community Legal Services of East Palo Alto, Law Foundation of Silicon Valley, San Diego Volunteer Lawyer Program, Center for Justice and Accountability, Asian Pacific Islander Legal Outreach, California Lawyers for the Arts.

List up to three pro bono matters that are representative of the pro bono work your firm participates in.

- *Soko Bukai v. YMCA.* Cooley successfully represented Soko Bukai, an association of Japanese American Christian churches, in a trust and real estate dispute against the San Francisco YWCA. The case settled before trial in an agreement that required that the property be sold by the SF YWCA at a greatly reduced price to a local Japanese American childcare facility, Nihonmachi Little Friends, and the property is now permanently dedicated to charitable use.

- In *HUD v. Rucker*, Cooley represented public housing tenants in a challenge to HUD's "one strike" eviction policy. Although the U.S. Supreme Court ultimately overturned a favorable Ninth Circuit decision, we were able to achieve positive results for our individual clients and also force significant policy changes within HUD that will positively affect thousands of public housing residents.

- In *MHC, Inc. v. City of San Rafael and Contempo Marin Homeowners Association*, Cooley represented Contempo Marin Homeowners Association, a residents' association for a manufactured home community in Marin County where many lower income and elderly residents reside. We worked hand in hand with the City of San Rafael, and successfully resisted a motion to compel that would have subjected all 180 homeowners to document discovery, home inspections and depositions.

BY THE NUMBERS

What is the total number of hours that lawyers in U.S. offices at your firm spent performing pro bono legal services in 2000, 2001 and 2002?

> Total number of hours in 2000: 18,109 hours
> Total number of hours in 2001: 28,483 hours
> Total number of hours in 2002: 23,011 hours

Average number of pro bono hours per attorney in U.S. offices per year (including associates, partners, counsels, but not summer associates):

> Average number of hours per attorney in 2000: 31 hours
> Average number of hours per attorney in 2001: 46 hours
> Average number of hours per attorney in 2002: 43 hours

What percentage of attorneys in this firm's U.S. offices did pro bono work in 2002? 62 percent

What percentage of attorneys in this firm's U.S. offices did at least 20 hours of pro bono work in 2002? 34 percent

Does the firm encourage its lawyers to perform a minimum number of pro bono hours? Yes

If so, how many hours per year or what percentage of lawyers' billable hours? 60 hours

SUPERVISION AND EVALUATIONS

Is there partner supervision on each pro bono matter? Yes

Do partner supervisors or, if applicable, senior associates provide written evaluations of associates' work on pro bono matters? Yes

If so, are those evaluations taken into account in determining salary, bonuses or advancement in the firm? N/A

If not, does the firm consider pro bono work generally in associate evaluations? Yes

HOURS

Does the firm give billable hour credit for pro bono work? Yes

Does the firm have a maximum number of pro bono hours that can be applied toward the billable hour target? No

If so, what is the maximum? N/A

If your firm uses hours to determine bonuses, does it consider pro bono hours when determining bonuses? Yes

PRO BONO POINTS

What training opportunities are open to associates working on pro bono matters? Cooley provides in-house training sessions on various substantive topics that relate to our pro bono involvement. The firm also encourages attorneys to participate in training programs provided by local legal service providers.

Can associates bring matters of interest to the firm? Yes

Does the firm offer the use of support staff in carrying out pro bono matters? Yes

What pro bono opportunities are available for summer associates? We encourage our summer associates to work on a variety of pro bono matters. Summer associates are also encouraged to participate in the in-house pro bono training programs regularly offered to our attorneys. We also sponsor a Pro Bono Week each summer to showcase our pro bono work for our summer associates and introduce them to the many pro bono opportunities available at Cooley.

Does the firm have established programs, such as externships, that enable its associates to work in a public interest setting? Yes

If so, where and for up to how long? It varies, depending on the program.

Has your firm won any special recognition or awards in the last two years for its pro bono work? Yes

If so, please list. Law Foundation of Silicon Valley Founders Award (2001). Asian Pacific Islander Legal Outreach "Legal Impact" Award (2003). Many of our attorneys have also been recognized for their pro bono contributions.

THE FIRM SAYS

Commitment to pro bono work is an important part of our firm culture at Cooley Godward. We strive to give generously of our time, talents and resources in each of the communities in which we practice, and pro bono representation is one of the primary ways we fulfill this goal. Our expertise and commitment enable us to handle a wide range of pro bono matters, which are handled by attorneys from all Cooley Godward's practice groups. In 2002, Cooley attorneys participated in more than 350 different pro bono matters. We are justifiably proud of the variety of pro bono projects undertaken by Cooley attorneys and the number of individuals and organizations assisted.

OUR SURVEY SAYS

"Cooley is truly committed to its pro bono obligations and treats all pro bono work as fully billable. I have done as much pro bono work since starting here as I have wished and have never felt any push back for it."

"The firm is very committed to pro bono and actively urges people to participate in pro bono projects. We staff various clinics and there are always e-mails outlining pro bono opportunities. All pro bono work is fully billable."

"Attorneys are given unlimited billable hours credit for pro bono hours."

"The firm has made a real concerted effort to promote and encourage pro bono work. It is much better than when I first started."

"Cooley has a great commitment to its pro bono clients. Pro bono hours count as billable hours."

"Pro bono is headed up by a top Cooley partner at the Hanover office and is taken very seriously."

"Cooley's pro bono program is extraordinary. Without exaggeration, about 10 percent of my work is consistently pro bono. The crappy economy has helped to justify spending time on pro bono that would have usually been spent on paying clients."

"People are doing pro bono work all the time and the firm supports that."

"I have been strongly encouraged to seek out pro bono opportunities to get experience that I have not been able to get with my billable work."

"In my first two months here, I was put on a huge pro bono merger of two nonprofits, where I was ably trained in this type of work by a partner and a senior associate, both of whom were fantastic mentors. We do a lot of very high-profile, high-quality pro bono work, which is a great aspect of working here."

"We strive to give generously of our time, talents and resources in each of the communities in which we practice, and pro bono representation is one of the primary ways we fulfill this goal."

— *Cooley Godward LLP*

Covington & Burling

1201 Pennsylvania Avenue, NW
Washington, DC 20004-2401
Phone: (202) 662-6000
www.cov.com

LOCATIONS

Washington, DC (HQ)
New York, NY
San Francisco, CA
Brussels
London

MAJOR DEPARTMENTS & PRACTICES

Antitrust
Arbitration/ADR
Communications
Corporate, Securities, Insolvency & Real Estate
Employee Benefits
Employment
Energy
Environmental
Financial Restructuring
Food & Drug
Health Care
Information Technology, Privacy & E-Commerce
Insurance
Intellectual Property
International Legislative
Litigation (Trial & Appellate)
Mergers & Acquisitions
Patent Advice & Litigation
Sports
Tax
Transportation
White Collar Defense

THE STATS

No. of attorneys worldwide: 508
No. of offices worldwide: 5
Managing Partner: Stuart C. Stock

EMPLOYMENT CONTACT

Ms. Lorraine Brown
Director, Legal Personnel Recruiting
Phone: (202) 662-6200
E-mail: legal.recruiting@cov.com

WHO'S WHO

Principal pro bono contact(s) at your firm:

Anthony Herman, Esq.
Co-Chair, Public Service Committee
Phone: (202) 662-5280
E-mail: AHerman@cov.com

David Haller, Esq.
Co-Chair, Public Service Committee
Phone: (212) 841-1057

Ms. Jan L. Flack
Co-Coordinator of Public Service Activities
Phone: (202) 662-5044
E-mail: JFlack@cov.com

Ms. Anne C. Proctor
Co-Coordinator of Public Service Activities
Phone: (202) 662-6513
E-mail: AProctor@cov.com

Does the firm have a pro bono coordinator? Yes
Jan L. Flack
Anne C. Proctor

If yes, what percentage of his or her time is spent on pro bono work? 100 percent for both

Does the firm have a pro bono committee? Yes

If yes, how often does the committee meet? Periodically, as necessary.

Describe the composition of the committee: Approximately 30 members consisting of partners, associates and staff.

THE SCOOP

Does your firm have a written pro bono policy? Yes

Has the firm signed on to the Law Firm Pro Bono Challenge? Yes

What are some of the areas of law in which your firm has performed pro bono legal work in the last two years? Death penalty, human rights, gun control, criminal and court appointed, intellectual property, gay rights, disability, family law, First Amendment.

What are some of the areas of law in which your firm does not perform pro bono work? N/A

Organizations for which your firm has performed pro bono legal services in the last two years: ACLU, Lawyers' Committee for Human Rights, Legal Aid, Neighborhood Legal Services, Bread for the City, ABA Death Penalty Project,

Washington Lawyers' Committee for Civil Rights & Urban Affairs, Legal Counsel for the Elderly, Veteran's Law Project, Washington Humane Society.

List up to three pro bono matters that are representative of the pro bono work your firm participates in. We currently represent five death row inmates, 16 families of uniformed World Trade Center victims, and 52 plaintiffs in two race discrimination lawsuits in Missippi and Arkansas against a major restaurant chain.

BY THE NUMBERS

What is the total number of hours that lawyers in U.S. offices at your firm spent performing pro bono legal services in 2000, 2001 and 2002?

> **Total number of hours in 2000:** 35,572 hours
> **Total number of hours in 2001:** 58,405 hours
> **Total number of hours in 2002:** 66,208 hours

Average number of pro bono hours per attorney in U.S. offices per year (including associates, partners, counsels, but not summer associates):

> **Average number of hours per attorney in 2000:** 97.97 hours
> **Average number of hours per attorney in 2001:** 149.2 hours
> **Average number of hours per attorney in 2002:** 147.4 hours

What percentage of attorneys in this firm's U.S. offices did pro bono work in 2002? 88 percent

What percentage of attorneys in this firm's U.S. offices did at least 20 hours of pro bono work in 2002? 52 percent

Does the firm encourage its lawyers to perform a minimum number of pro bono hours? Yes. At our annual awards ceremony, we acknowledge lawyers whose pro bono hours total 50 hours or more.

SUPERVISION AND EVALUATIONS

Is there partner supervision on each pro bono matter? Yes

Do partner supervisors or, if applicable, senior associates provide written evaluations of associates' work on pro bono matters? Yes

If so, are those evaluations taken into account in determining salary, bonuses or advancement in the firm? Yes

If not, does the firm consider pro bono work generally in associate evaluations? N/A

HOURS

Does the firm give billable hour credit for pro bono work? Pro bono work is fully taken into account in evaluating a lawyer's workload and for the purpose of determining bonuses.

Does the firm have a maximum number of pro bono hours that can be applied toward the billable hour target? No

If so, what is the maximum? N/A

If your firm uses hours to determine bonuses, does it consider pro bono hours when determining bonuses? Yes

PRO BONO POINTS

What training opportunities are open to associates working on pro bono matters? The D.C. Bar offers a variety of training sessions throughout the year.

Can associates bring matters of interest to the firm? Yes. They are encouraged to do so.

Does the firm offer the use of support staff in carrying out pro bono matters? Yes

What pro bono opportunities are available for summer associates? Summer associates are given pro bono assignments in the same manner as billable assignments.

Does the firm have established programs, such as externships, that enable its associates to work in a public interest setting? Yes

If so, where and for up to how long? Neighborhood Legal Services — six-month, full-time rotation; Children's Law Center — six-month, full-time rotation; Bread for the City — 50 percent of one's time for six months.

Has your firm won any special recognition or awards in the last two years for its pro bono work? Yes

If so, please list. D.C. Bar Pro Bono Program, Community Economic Development Pro Bono Project; Federal Bar Council; Latin American Youth Center; Maryland Free State Justice; Washington Humane Society; Washington Lawyers' Committee for Civil Rights & Urban Affairs (two awards); Columbia Law School, Wien Prize; D.C. Appleseed; ABA Commission on Lawyers' Trust Accounts.

THE FIRM SAYS

Covington & Burling has for decades been regarded as home to many of the nation's most prominent attorneys and counsel to the world's preeminent companies. Since its founding in 1919, the firm has enjoyed a broad reputation for two paramount qualities — representation of clients according to the highest professional standards and dedication to public service. Today, Covington & Burling is a leading international law firm, with over 500 lawyers practicing in Washington, New York, San Francisco, London and Brussels. In the July 2003 issue of *The American Lawyer* magazine, Covington received the highest score and top ranking in the country for pro bono work in the publication's annual law firm survey.

Cases on the firm's current public service roster include two death penalty cases in Florida and one each in Alabama, Mississippi and Louisiana. The firm is also representing plaintiffs in employment discrimination, police brutality, custody, adoption, asylum and criminal cases. Covington recently won two disability rights cases which resulted in improved access to businesses for people who use wheelchairs. The firm also filed suit to gain accommodations for deaf and hard-of-hearing

U.S. postal workers. At the request of Mayor Giuliani, Covington took the lead in providing legal services to the families of uniformed personnel who were killed at the World Trade Center on September 11, 2001. Covington is actively working to reform a state's criminal defense system, and its debt-for-nature swaps have preserved millions of acres of land in three countries.

Additionally, through its pro bono program, Covington & Burling provides advice to over 100 nonprofit organizations. For more than 30 years, Covington & Burling has committed substantial resources to a rotation program with the District of Columbia's Neighborhood Legal Services Program. Most recently, Covington has added rotation programs to the Children's Law Center and Bread for the City. In addition, the firm's ten-year partnership with a District of Columbia high school has served as a model for law firm involvement with District of Columbia public schools.

We continue to seek the most interesting and diverse matters we can offer to our lawyers and to broaden the number of lawyers involved in pro bono work. We have found that a constant variety of case offerings keeps our program vibrant and interesting. In mid-2002, we added a second full-time pro bono coordinator to our team, to enhance our ability to accomplish these goals.

OUR SURVEY SAYS

"The pro bono program is exceptional. The firm has two full-time pro bono coordinators who are very active in making sure associates have the opportunity to work on good cases."

"We are widely regarded as a very strong pro bono firm, except that you get no credit for it in terms of your bonus, hitting your billable hour requirement and partnership decisions (despite the fact that they claim you do — not true in reality)."

"The opportunities are tremendous and the firm values the work, although the hours do not count toward the billable benchmark."

"I billed over 300 pro bono hours last year and was encouraged to do even more. Pro bono is treated exactly like billable work."

"A substantial percentage of my workload is pro bono — at the moment as much as 50 percent of my time is spent on pro bono litigation."

"Everyone does pro bono of some sort or another. People here enjoy it, and all of the happiness here seems to feed off of that enjoyment."

"Nobody can top us on this. First, the firm has FOUR full-time, six-month associate rotations going at once — no other firm can match that. The firm also puts tremendous resources into its death penalty practice. The firm is essentially open to any pro bono matter that anybody might care to bring in."

"The firm is committed to pro bono work. I would guess that more than 50 percent of the associates received an award for billing more than 50 hours of pro bono work last year. However, at least in the New York office, associates may have to do some legwork to obtain interesting pro bono work."

"The firm continues to promote pro bono work, almost to the exclusion of all else for more junior litigation associates."

"C&B is one of the best (likely, the best) in terms of promoting pro bono opportunities. Weekly matters are circulated to the firm about open pro bono matters and associates are strongly encouraged to participate."

"In the July 2003 issue of The American Lawyer magazine, Covington received the highest score and top ranking in the country for pro bono work in the publication's annual law firm survey."

— *Covington & Burling*

Cravath, Swaine & Moore LLP

Worldwide Plaza
825 Eighth Avenue
New York, NY 10019-7475
Phone: (212) 474-1000
www.cravath.com

LOCATIONS

New York, NY (HQ)
London

MAJOR DEPARTMENTS & PRACTICES

Corporate
Litigation
Tax
Trusts & Estates

THE STATS

No. of attorneys worldwide: 486
No. of offices worldwide: 2
Presiding Partner: Robert D. Joffe

EMPLOYMENT CONTACT

Ms. Lisa A. Kalen
Associate Director of Legal Personnel and Recruiting
Phone: (212) 474-3215
Fax: (212) 474-3225
E-mail: lkalen@cravath.com

WHO'S WHO

Does the firm have a pro bono coordinator? Yes

Paul Saunders, Partner
E-mail: psaunder@cravath.com

Stuart Gold, Partner
E-mail: sgold@cravath.com

Will Fogg, Partner
E-mail: wfogg@cravath.com

Sarkis Jebejian, Partner
E-mail: sjebejian@cravath.com

Robert Rifkind, Senior Counsel
E-mail: rrifkind@cravath.com

Does the firm have a pro bono committee? No

If yes, how often does the committee meet? N/A

Describe the composition of the committee: N/A

THE SCOOP

Does your firm have a written pro bono policy? Yes

Has the firm signed on to the Law Firm Pro Bono Challenge? No

What are some of the areas of law in which your firm has performed pro bono legal work in the last two years? We represent indigent individuals in criminal appeals, civil litigation and asylum proceedings. We also represent a number of environmental advocacy groups and handle corporate, tax and other matters for nonprofit clients. Under our Children's Hospital program, we represent children who are patients at the hospitals and their families in accordance with a wide range of benefits, housing, immigration and related matters.

Organizations for which your firm has performed pro bono legal services in the last two years: American Civil Liberties Union, Children's Hospital at Montefiore, The Morgan Stanley Children's Hospital of New York-Presbyterian, Covenant House, Fordham Tax Clinic, inMotion, Lawyers Committee for Civil Rights Under Law, Lawyers Committee for Human Rights, Legal Aid Society, New York Lawyers for Public Interest, Office of the Appellate Defender, Phoenix House, Volunteer Lawyers for the Arts.

List up to three pro bono matters that are representative of the pro bono work your firm participates in.

- *Harris v. State.* We represent a battered woman, currently on death row in Alabama, in proceedings seeking review of her conviction for hiring someone to kill her husband.

- *Montefiore Children's Hospital.* We represent children and their families in collaboration with The Children's Hospital at Montefiore in the Bronx in which Cravath lawyers team with doctors and social workers to offer legal services and advice.
- *USA v. Jefferson.* We represent minority fire fighters and other municipal workers in Birmingham, Ala., in litigation arising out of consent decrees that provide for race-conscious relief.

BY THE NUMBERS

What is the total number of hours that lawyers in U.S. offices at your firm spent performing pro bono legal services in 2000, 2001 and 2002?

Total number of hours in 2000: 16,567 hours
Total number of hours in 2001: 19,177 hours
Total number of hours in 2002: 36,557 hours

Average number of pro bono hours per attorney in U.S. offices per year (including associates, partners, counsels, but not summer associates):

Average number of hours per attorney in 2000: 41 hours
Average number of hours per attorney in 2001: 43 hours
Average number of hours per attorney in 2002: 79 hours

What percentage of attorneys in this firm's U.S. offices did pro bono work in 2002? 44 percent

What percentage of attorneys in this firm's U.S. offices did at least 20 hours of pro bono work in 2002? 33 percent

Does the firm encourage its lawyers to perform a minimum number of pro bono hours? No. The firm encourages its lawyers to participate in pro bono projects, but we do not have a minimum requirement of hours.

If so, how many hours per year or what percentage of lawyers' billable hours? N/A

SUPERVISION AND EVALUATIONS

Is there partner supervision on each pro bono matter? Yes

Do partner supervisors or, if applicable, senior associates provide written evaluations of associates' work on pro bono matters? No, but work on pro bono matters is considered as part of the regular evaluation of the associate.

If so, are those evaluations taken into account in determining salary, bonuses or advancement in the firm? The firm takes into account pro bono matters in making such determinations.

If not, does the firm consider pro bono work generally in associate evaluations? Yes

HOURS

Does the firm give billable hour credit for pro bono work? Not applicable, because we do not have a billable hour requirement or target. Work on pro bono matters is considered as part of the regular evaluation of the associate's work.

Does the firm have a maximum number of pro bono hours that can be applied toward the billable hour target? No, we do not have a billable hour requirement or target.

If so, what is the maximum? N/A

If your firm uses hours to determine bonuses, does it consider pro bono hours when determining bonuses? N/A

PRO BONO POINTS

What training opportunities are open to associates working on pro bono matters? All pro bono matters handled by associates must be supervised by a partner, and no associate appears in any judicial or administrative proceedings without first discussing the nature of the representation and the arguments to be made with, and having briefs to be submitted reviewed by, the partner in charge. In addition, the Firm has an extensive training program on general matters. The Firm lists on its intranet site training opportunities available from various organizations in areas directly related to that organizations' pro bono work.

Can associates bring matters of interest to the firm? Yes

Does the firm offer the use of support staff in carrying out pro bono matters? Yes

What pro bono opportunities are available for summer associates? The same opportunities that are available to all lawyers at the firm.

Does the firm have established programs, such as externships, that enable its associates to work in a public interest setting? No

Has your firm won any special recognition or awards in the last two years for its pro bono work? Yes

If so, please list. One of 35 firms that exceeded the 2002 Volunteers of Legal Services (VOLS) pro bono pledge. From the Legal Aid Society for work done on behalf of victims of September 11.

THE FIRM SAYS

Lawyers are encouraged to work on pro bono matters that have been undertaken or approved by the firm. Associates are given credit for hours spent on pro bono matters (although the firm has no hour thresholds of any sort), and work on such matters is considered as part of the evaluation of the associate. Pro bono matters are considered to be firm matters in every sense, and they are handled in the same way that all other matters are handled for firm clients. For that reason, pro bono matters being handled by associates must be accepted and supervised by a partner, and no associate appears in any judicial or administrative proceeding without first discussing the nature of the representation and the arguments to be made with, and having briefs to be submitted reviewed by, the partner in charge. Similarly, no significant legal advice is given, either orally or in writing, without first obtaining the approval of the partner in charge.

Available pro bono matters are regularly posted on the firm's intranet site. Other opportunities can usually be obtained by an associate by contacting Paul Saunders, Stuart Gold, Will Fogg, Sarkis Jebejian, Robert Rifkind or the partner(s) with whom the associate regularly works. An associate who is interested in working on a pro bono matter from one of the entities listed on the firm's intranet site should contact the partner indicated on the list. Associates are free to seek out other opportunities for pro bono representation.

OUR SURVEY SAYS

"Real work takes priority, but there are a bunch of opportunities for pro bono here."

"The firm made a big push to get associates involved in pro bono post-9/11. There was never an emphasis before that I saw. I have found partners to be supportive and accommodating when I have asked to do some pro bono work."

"No pressure to take — no pressure to drop. Do what you want."

"It's there if you look for it. I spent 1,500 hours on pro bono last year, and there is no distinction for billing purposes."

"The firm says that it encourages pro bono work, but there aren't enough hours in the day to take on a pro bono case and finish the 'billable' work that we are assigned."

"I summered at two firms prior to coming here, so I can say with authority that as far as firms go, Cravath is at the top of the list in terms of pro bono."

"Everybody I know does some pro bono work. Many high-profile trials have been pro bono, and no resources are spared. The only bad thing about Cravath's attitude about pro bono is that they take it so seriously that junior associates might not get as much responsibility as they want (partners still make the court appearances and to the major depositions, and so on)."

"It's here and I'd love to, but who's got time for it?"

"I've had a lot of pro bono opportunities and I'm in the tax department, where often they are hard to come by. The firm is very committed and treats pro bono hours the same as billables. Pro bono and paying clients are supposed to receive the same level of service."

"I am doing almost exclusively pro bono work; the firm appears not to distinguish between paying and non-paying clients."

"Under our Children's Hospital program, we represent children who are patients at the hospitals and their families in accordance with a wide range of benfits, housing, immigration and related matters."

— *Cravath, Swaine & Moore*

Crowell & Moring LLP

1001 Pennsylvania Avenue, NW
Washington, DC 20004
Phone: (202) 624-2500
www.crowell.com

LOCATIONS

Washington, DC (HQ)
Irvine, CA
Brussels
London

MAJOR DEPARTMENTS & PRACTICES

Antitrust
Aviation
Construction
Corporate
Energy
Government Contracts
Healthcare
Intellectual Property
International
Labor & Employment
Life Sciences
Litigation
Natural Resources & Environment
Securities Regulation & Enforcement
Tax
Telecommunications, Media & Technology

THE STATS

No. of attorneys worldwide: 275
No. of offices worldwide: 4
Chairman: John A. Macleod

EMPLOYMENT CONTACT

Ms. Katherine A. Arnold
Assistant Director of HR for Attorney Recruiting
Phone: (202) 624-2729
Fax: (202) 628-5116
E-mail: karnold@crowell.com

WHO'S WHO

Does the firm have a pro bono coordinator? Yes

Susan M. Hoffman, Esq.
Public Service Partner
Phone: (202) 624-2591
E-mail: shoffman@crowell.com

If yes, what percentage of his or her time is spent on pro bono work? 100 percent

Does the firm have a pro bono committee? Yes

If yes, how often does the committee meet? The committee meets approximately four times a year. Subcommittees of the full committee meet about three times a year.

Describe the composition of the committee: The committee includes partners, associates and counsel representatives and is co-chaired by the public service partner and two other partners.

THE SCOOP

Does your firm have a written pro bono policy? Yes

Has the firm signed on to the Law Firm Pro Bono Challenge? Yes

What are some of the areas of law in which your firm has performed pro bono legal work in the last two years? Civil rights (racial discrimination, disability rights); child abuse and neglect; child custody; landlord/tenant; social security disability; domestic violence; criminal defense; health law; political asylum; adoption; AIDS advocacy; community economic development.

What are some of the areas of law in which your firm does not perform pro bono work? Divorce, bankruptcy.

Organizations for which your firm has performed pro bono legal services in the last two years: Washington Lawyers Committee for Civil Rights and Urban Affairs, the Washington Legal Clinic for the Homeless, the Archdiocesan Legal Network, La Clinica del Pueblo, Children's Law Center, Whitman Walker Clinic Legal Services, the Capital Area Immigrants' Rights Coalition, the Office of the Public Defender for Montgomery County, the Lawyers' Committee for Human Rights, Children's Defense Fund.

List up to three pro bono matters that are representative of the pro bono work your firm participates in.

- Crowell & Moring is co-counsel in a major civil rights action, representing the NAACP and 42 individual plaintiffs in litigation against Cracker-Barrel Old Country Stores, Inc., alleging discriminatory treatment of African-American customers by Cracker Barrel restaurants and stores.

- Crowell & Moring initiated the Criminal Defense Representation Project with the Office of the Public Defender for Montgomery County ("MPD") in late 2001. Through this project, the MPD screens criminal felony and misdemeanor cases that it anticipates will proceed to a jury trial and refers them to the firm for pro bono representation.

- Crowell & Moring represented the Washington Legal Clinic for the Homeless and other homeless advocates in preparing litigation and, with a complaint in hand, negotiating with the District of Columbia for it to provide appropriate and adequate emergency shelter during the winter months. Through a series of negotiations and ongoing monitoring over the winter months, the firm and homeless advocates were successful in having the District open up space at three different public buildings and provide more than 250 additional beds for individuals and room for 40 additional families.

BY THE NUMBERS

What is the total number of hours that lawyers in U.S. offices at your firm spent performing pro bono legal services in 2000, 2001 and 2002?

>**Total number of hours in 2000:** 11,458 hours
>**Total number of hours in 2001:** 11,288 hours
>**Total number of hours in 2002:** 13,920 hours

Average number of pro bono hours per attorney in U.S. offices per year (including associates, partners, counsels, but not summer associates):

>**Average number of hours per attorney in 2000:** 51 hours
>**Average number of hours per attorney in 2001:** 50 hours
>**Average number of hours per attorney in 2002:** 56.8 hours

What percentage of attorneys in this firm's U.S. offices did pro bono work in 2002? 81 percent

What percentage of attorneys in this firm's U.S. offices did at least 20 hours of pro bono work in 2002? 49.7 percent

Does the firm encourage its lawyers to perform a minimum number of pro bono hours? Yes

If so, how many hours per year or what percentage of lawyers' billable hours? Associates may count up to 50 hours of pro bono time as billable regardless of their client billable hours. In addition, for associates who otherwise meet our minimum billable hours requirement, up to 200 hours of pro bono work will count as fully billable for purposes of evaluation and bonuses.

SUPERVISION AND EVALUATIONS

Is there partner supervision on each pro bono matter? Yes

Do partner supervisors or, if applicable, senior associates provide written evaluations of associates' work on pro bono matters? Yes

If so, are those evaluations taken into account in determining salary, bonuses or advancement in the firm? Yes

If not, does the firm consider pro bono work generally in associate evaluations? N/A

HOURS

Does the firm give billable hour credit for pro bono work? Yes

If so, what is the maximum? 200 hours

If your firm uses hours to determine bonuses, does it consider pro bono hours when determining bonuses? Yes. For associates who otherwise meet our minimum billable hours requirement, up to 200 hours of pro bono work will count as fully billable for purposes of evaluation and bonuses.

PRO BONO POINTS

What training opportunities are open to associates working on pro bono matters? The firm participates and offers to associates a broad array of training programs offered by the D.C. Bar Pro Bono Program in sponsorship with other legal services providers. In addition, the firm sponsors a number of specific training programs at the firm in which outside organizations, such as the Capital Area Immigrants' Rights Coalition and the Montgomery County Office of Public Defender, come in to present the training sessions, making training even more accessible for our attorneys.

Can associates bring matters of interest to the firm? Yes

Does the firm offer the use of support staff in carrying out pro bono matters? Yes

What pro bono opportunities are available for summer associates? In addition to integrating summer associates on existing pro bono matters through assignments, the firm makes available pro bono opportunities designed specifically for summer associate participation. For example, summer associates are able to perform intake and screening of low income clients at a nearby office of Law Students in Court, conduct intake interviews and complete follow-up for homeless clients at various local shelters, and participate in training and work on political asylum cases. Finally, each summer the firm conducts the "Took Tour" in which name partner Took Crowell conducts a tour of various local nonprofit organizations, such as the Mazique Parent Child Development Center, to which the firm has contributed services.

Does the firm have established programs, such as externships, that enable its associates to work in a public interest setting? Yes

If so, where and for up to how long? In 2003, the firm marked the 15th anniversary of its Summer Associate Public Interest Program in which up to 11 Crowell & Moring summer associates are able to spend five weeks of their summer working at a local public interest organization or legal service provider and the remainder of their summer at the firm. The participating groups have included the Public Defender Service of the District of Columbia, the Washington Lawyers' Committee for Civil Rights and Urban Affairs, the Children's Defense Fund, the Legal Aid Society, Legal Counsel for the Elderly, the State and Local Legal Center, the American Civil Liberties Union-Washington Office, NAACP Legal Defense and Educational Fund, Inc., the Whitman Walker Clinic, Lawyers for Children America and the National Women's Law Center. The firm pays the salary of the summer associate through grants to the participating groups.

Has your firm won any special recognition or awards in the last two years for its pro bono work? Yes

If so, please list. In 2002, the Washington Lawyers' Committee for Civil Rights and Urban Affairs honored Crowell & Moring with two Outstanding Achievement Awards — one in the field of disability rights for its work on a precedent-setting settlement against a restaurant chain for nationwide application and one in the field of immigrant & refugee rights for its work on an update report on civil rights issues affecting the city's Latino community. In 2001, Families Against Mandatory Minimums ("FAMM") awarded Crowell & Moring the first Advocates for Justice Award for its pro bono commitment and advocacy for just sentences. The Public Law Center of Orange County honored Crowell & Moring attorney Steve Rice with its Pro Bono Attorney of the Year Award in 2001-02 "for excellence and dedication in pro bono work."

THE FIRM SAYS

Crowell & Moring LLP has committed itself to assuring that citizens in our community have access to the legal system and to promoting the overall welfare of the community in which we work. This commitment is reflected in the innovative structure of the firm's proactive pro bono program, spearheaded by a full-time public service partner; the firm's leadership in sponsoring public interest fellowships for summer associates and recent law school graduates; and the partnership between Crowell & Moring and the Edward Mazique Parent-Child Development Center which has extended the firm's public service culture to include lawyers and non-lawyers. Through these and other initiatives, Crowell & Moring has promoted broad participation by the firm's attorneys and staff and has been able to serve a range of urgent community needs.

Crowell & Moring's Pro Bono Program
The firm has undertaken a wide variety of pro bono work ranging from individual landlord/tenant cases to a class action on behalf of victims of racial discrimination in taxi service to litigation on behalf of disabled individuals against a nationwide fast food chain. The bulk of the firm's pro bono work is for individual clients in traditional poverty law areas, such as child custody, public benefits, landlord/tenant, criminal defense, domestic violence and child abuse and neglect. During 2002, the firm's attorneys and legal assistants contributed more than 15,000 hours to pro bono matters, representing a value of over $4 million in donated services. The firm prides itself on having a broad-based and diverse pro bono program, having opened nearly 100 new pro bono matters during 2002 referred by more than thirty different organizations.

Structure of Pro Bono Program
In 1988, on the eve of its 10th Anniversary, Crowell & Moring adopted a series of initiatives in an effort to develop a more effective approach to delivery of volunteer legal services. Most significantly, the firm created the full-time position of public service counsel, a position that was unprecedented at the time but has since been emulated. The public service counsel has responsibility for encouraging the firm's attorneys to perform pro bono work by developing pro bono opportunities through her contacts with legal service organizations, providing the firm's attorneys with access to training in poverty law, civil rights and family law issues, providing guidance and support to attorneys who undertake pro bono representations, and developing innovative programs designed to mobilize resources inside (and outside) the firm to help meet unmet community needs. The firm further encourages pro bono work by giving associates billable hour credit for pro bono hours for purposes of annual associate evaluations.

Goals and Incentives
Crowell & Moring has undertaken to set goals for itself in the pro bono area and to meet aspirational targets set by local and national bar associations. For example, Crowell & Moring is a signatory to the Law Firm Pro Bono Challenge and has been an active member of the LAPP Project of the Litigation Section of the ABA. In 1988, Crowell & Moring joined the D.C. Bar PART ("Pro Bono Partnership") Program, committing to devote an average of 50 hours of pro bono work per attorney each year. The Public Service Committee has emphasized the goal of broadening the participation of its attorneys in pro bono work. Thus, the firm strives to encourage each attorney to undertake a pro bono representation in an area that interests him/her and that makes a valuable contribution to the community. During 2002, more than 50 percent of the firm's attorneys participated in pro bono work during the calendar year. The level of participation in 2002 is consistent with that of prior years in which Crowell & Moring attorneys have consistently worked in excess of 10,000 hours on pro bono matters, or an annual average of more than 50 hours per attorney.

OUR SURVEY SAYS

"Our firm very strongly embraces pro bono work."

"[The firm is] very committed — but the firm needs to be careful not to take bigger cases than it's able to handle. There are partners who seek the 'headliner' pro bono cases, but they then have trouble finding associates to do all the legwork due to billable-hour pressures."

"We do A LOT of pro bono here."

"It's a de facto requirement that every associate do pro bono work."

"Excellent pro bono program, but it is not equally respected when it comes time for evaluations."

"Our firm is very committed to pro bono and provides up to 200 hours of billable credit, but it doesn't seem to count as much at review time."

"Pro bono is a part of daily firm life."

Davis Polk & Wardwell

450 Lexington Avenue
New York, NY 10017
Phone: (212) 450-4000
www.dpw.com

LOCATIONS

New York, NY (HQ)
Menlo Park, CA
Washington, DC
Frankfurt
Hong Kong
London
Madrid
Paris
Tokyo

MAJOR DEPARTMENTS & PRACTICES

Corporate
Litigation
Tax
Trusts & Estates

THE STATS

No. of attorneys worldwide: 656
No. of offices worldwide: 9
Managing Partner: John R. Ettinger

EMPLOYMENT CONTACT

Ms. Bonnie Hurry
Director of Recruiting & Legal Staff Services
Phone: (212) 450-4144
Fax: (212) 450-5548
E-mail: bhurry@dpw.com

WHO'S WHO

Does the firm have a pro bono coordinator? Yes

Amy Rossabi, Esq.
Pro Bono Coordinator
Phone: (212) 450-4435
E-mail: amy.rossabi@dpw.com

If yes, what percentage of his or her time is spent on pro bono work? 100 percent

Does the firm have a pro bono committee? Yes

If yes, how often does the committee meet? We meet regularly, but have no set schedule.

Describe the composition of the committee: Litigation partners James Benkard, Sharon Katz and James Windels co-chair the pro bono committee, which includes litigation senior counsel Ogden Lewis, corporate partner John Fouhey, tax partner Michael Mollerus, pro bono coordinator Amy Rossabi and pro bono consultant Mark O'Brien.

THE SCOOP

Does your firm have a written pro bono policy? No

Has the firm signed on to the Law Firm Pro Bono Challenge? No

What are some of the areas of law in which your firm has performed pro bono legal work in the last two years?

- **Administrative appeals** — These include denials of Social Security disability benefits and those before the Board of Education to assist students with special needs attain special education placement.

- **Arts matters** — We provide advice to individual artists and arts organizations on contracts, litigation, real estate, tax and general corporate matters.

- **Capital defense** — Davis Polk currently represents an inmate on death row in Georgia in his post-conviction proceedings. The client, who is mentally retarded and was 17 at the time the crime was committed, was convicted of murder, armed robbery and kidnapping and sentenced to death. We are awaiting a decision in this matter. In addition, we successfully appealed the death sentences of inmates from Alabama and Georgia.

- **Civil rights** — In addition to our work in the area of prisoners' rights, we handle civil rights matters involving voting rights and racial discrimination.

- **Corporate, real estate and tax advice** — We provide counsel to not-for-profit community groups and organizations in the process of incorporating, obtaining tax exempt recognition, and with regard to mergers, by-laws, leases, contracts, tax and other matters.

- **Criminal appeals' prosccution and defense** — We accept the majority of our criminal appeals from The Legal Aid Society, but also take matters from the Office of the Appellate Defender and the Brooklyn and Queens district attorneys' offices.

- **General litigation** — Two examples of our recent large litigation matters are our successful representation of the New York County Lawyers' Association in an action against New York State and New York City seeking injunctive relief to raise the rates of compensation paid to assigned counsel who represent indigent litigants in family and criminal court proceedings (the rates were $25 and $40 per hour for out-of-court work and in-court work, respectively) and the unprecedented lawsuit we initiated on behalf of individuals with mental illness detained within the New York State prison system. The suit alleges a statewide failure on the part of the prison system to provide necessary mental health services to prisoners with mental illness, in violation of the Constitution and governing federal statutes.

- **Housing** — In addition to working on housing matters for Washington Heights Day Care Center and ACORN, on behalf of MFY Legal Services and The Legal Aid Society, we have represented several groups of rent-controlled tenants that sought to prevent their landlords from using a fire that partially destroyed their apartments as a pretext to convert the building into luxury apartments.

- **Matrimonial/family law** — We maintain an ongoing docket of contested and uncontested divorce cases on behalf of battered women. We also handle family law matters (custody, orders of protection, visitation, abuse/neglect) on behalf of victims of domestic violence and their children.

- **Political asylum/immigration** — We represent indigent refugees seeking political asylum in the United States. Lawyers handling these cases prepare asylum applications, provide representation in hearings before an immigration judge and pursue appeals before the Board of Immigration Appeals and federal courts when necessary. As part of our asylum program, Davis Polk, in conjunction with Columbia Law School's Center for Public Law, conducts a Political Asylum Workshop at Columbia Law School. In the workshop, Columbia law students learn about U.S. immigration law and, under the supervision of Davis Polk lawyers, represent refugees seeking asylum.

- **Trusts and estates** — Through the Volunteers of Legal Service Elder Law Program, we help indigent individuals with their life planning needs, including preparing wills, living wills, health care proxies, powers of attorney and directions for cremation. Because many of our clients are homebound, our associates travel to their homes to assist them.

What are some of the areas of law in which your firm does not perform pro bono work? We are open to all different types of pro bono.

Organizations for which your firm has performed pro bono legal services in the last two years: Asian American Legal Defense and Education Fund, Lawyers Alliance for New York, Lawyers Committee for Human Rights, The Legal Aid Society, MFY Legal Services, inMotion, Inc., New York Lawyers for the Public Interest, Sanctuary for Families, Volunteer Lawyers for the Arts, Volunteers of Legal Service.

List up to three pro bono matters that are representative of the pro bono work your firm participates in.
- We represent Larry Jenkins, a young, mentally retarded inmate on death row in Georgia, in connection with his post-conviction habeas proceedings. We have filed our post-petition brief and are awaiting a decision.
- In a statewide action, we represent individuals with mental illness detained in the New York State prison system. The suit alleges a statewide failure on the part of the prison system to provide necessary mental health services to prisoners with mental illness, in violation of the Constitution and governing federal statutes.
- Between 1999 and 2003, we represented the New York County Lawyers' Association (NYCLA) in its efforts to secure permanent injunctive relief to raise the rates of compensation paid to assigned counsel who represent children and indigent litigants in family and criminal court proceedings in New York City. Those rates were $25 and $40 hours per hour for out-of-court and in-court work, respectively. Davis Polk and NYCLA obtained a declaratory judgment and permanent injunction increasing the rates on February 3, 2003, following a bench trial in 2002. After the New York State

Legislature subsequently increased the rates to $75 and $60 per hour, effective January 1, 2004, the parties agreed to settle the litigation in November 2003.

BY THE NUMBERS

What is the total number of hours that lawyers in U.S. offices at your firm spent performing pro bono legal services in 2000, 2001 and 2002?

>**Total number of hours in 2000:** 37,868 hours
>**Total number of hours in 2001:** 39,491 hours
>**Total number of hours in 2002**: 39,379 hours

Average number of pro bono hours per attorney in U.S. offices per year (including associates, partners, counsels, but not summer associates):

>**Average number of hours per attorney in 2000:** 67 hours
>**Average number of hours per attorney in 2001:** 63 hours
>**Average number of hours per attorney in 2002:** 63 hours

What percentage of attorneys in this firm's U.S. offices did pro bono work in 2002? Nearly 40 percent

What percentage of attorneys in this firm's U.S. offices did at least 20 hours of pro bono work in 2002? 38 percent

Does the firm encourage its lawyers to perform a minimum number of pro bono hours? No

SUPERVISION AND EVALUATIONS

Is there partner supervision on each pro bono matter? Yes

Do partner supervisors or, if applicable, senior associates provide written evaluations of associates' work on pro bono matters? No

If so, are those evaluations taken into account in determining salary, bonuses or advancement in the firm? N/A

If not, does the firm consider pro bono work generally in associate evaluations? Yes

HOURS

Does the firm give billable hour credit for pro bono work? Yes

Does the firm have a maximum number of pro bono hours that can be applied toward the billable hour target? No

If so, what is the maximum? N/A

If your firm uses hours to determine bonuses, does it consider pro bono hours when determining bonuses? Not applicable

PRO BONO POINTS

What training opportunities are open to associates working on pro bono matters? We conduct pro bono training sessions throughout the year with the majority of the sessions in the fall. This fall we have trainings in handling the following types of pro bono matters: political asylum, orders of protection, uncontested divorces, contested divorces, special education, federal benefits and life planning.

Can associates bring matters of interest to the firm? Yes

Does the firm offer the use of support staff in carrying out pro bono matters? Yes

What pro bono opportunities are available for summer associates? We partner summer associates with full-time associates and after attending training sessions directed at summer associates, together they work on appeals of denial of benefits, domestic violence matters (divorces, orders of protection and custody matters), political asylum cases and a variety of elder law and corporate matters. In addition, summer associates have the opportunity to be involved in all the firm's existing pro bono matters.

Does the firm have established programs, such as externships, that enable its associates to work in a public interest setting? No

Has your firm won any special recognition or awards in the last two years for its pro bono work? Yes

If so, please list. Our firm or attorneys at our firm have received awards from the following organizations: Advocates for Children, Association of Community Organizations for Reform Now (ACORN), inMotion, Inc., Lawyers Alliance for New York, The Legal Aid Society, National Legal Aid & Defender Association, New York Legal Assistance Group, Sanctuary for Families, Volunteer Lawyers for the Arts.

THE FIRM SAYS

We provide pro bono legal services to those who cannot otherwise obtain legal representation and we do so with the same dedication and commitment to excellence with which we represent our paying clients. The goals of the firm's pro bono program are to encourage all lawyers to pursue the kind of voluntary pro bono commitment they find rewarding; to cooperate with established pro bono service providers and clearinghouses (including local courts) so that our efforts are broadly channeled and likely to benefit either deserving individuals or recognized groups; and to use pro bono as a vehicle for early client responsibility and training. With the advice and supervision of the pro bono committee, our full-time pro bono coordinator, a former litigation associate, disseminates information on current pro bono opportunities offered by courts and public interest organizations and provides in-house support and training for lawyers handling individual representation matters. In addition, lawyers interested in areas in which the firm is not involved are encouraged to present matters to the pro bono committee for consideration.

OUR SURVEY SAYS

"The firm does not get enough credit for [its] huge pro bono investment."

"The firm is genuinely proud of its pro bono projects and devotes a tremendous amount of resources to pro bono projects."

"Pro bono work, both corporate and litigation, is strongly encouraged at all levels and the firm brags about its major pro bono victories. The firm also lends its space for pro bono training to outside lawyers."

"The firm does a lot of pro bono work and a lot of that work helps the types of people that pro bono work is meant to help. However, the firm also does a lot of work (e.g., for struggling artists) that I don't think is in the true spirit of pro bono. Pro bono is meant to benefit poor persons in dire need of quality legal representation, such as many of the asylum clients that the firm represents. I don't think that helping a struggling playwright negotiate his contracts fits into the conventional definition of pro bono work."

"I spent over 650 hours on pro bono work last year, with nothing but great support."

"[The firm] will allow associates to take on pro bono projects that others might not touch with a 10-foot pole (e.g., post-9/11 detention of Arabs and Muslims)."

"Associates at the firm perform a great amount of pro bono work. It is evident that the firm is supportive of this in that, although the firm does not require a certain amount of billable hours per year, pro bono work is counted towards billable hours."

"The firm as a whole is very committed to pro bono; however, the corporate department is less so. I would estimate that 90 percent of the pro bono work here is done by the litigators."

"The pro bono commitment is ever-present and pro bono work is celebrated."

Davis Wright Tremaine LLP

1501 Fourth Avenue, Suite 2600
Seattle, WA 98101-1688
Phone: (206) 622-3150
www.dwt.com

LOCATIONS

Seattle, WA (HQ)
Anchorage, AK
Bellevue, WA
Los Angeles, CA
New York, NY
Portland, OR
San Francisco, CA
Washington, DC
Shanghai

MAJOR DEPARTMENTS & PRACTICES

Admiralty & Maritime • Aircraft Industry • Antitrust • Business & Corporate • China Practice • Communications, Media & Information Technologies • Construction & Government Contracts • Corporate Finance & Securities • Credit Recovery & Bankruptcy • Education • Emerging Business & Technology • Employment/Employee Benefits • Energy • Environmental & Natural Resources • Financial Institutions • Food & Agriculture • Health Care • Hospitality • Immigration • Intellectual Property • International Law • Internet, E-Commerce & Telecommunications • Legislation • Litigation • Municipal Finance • Real Estate & Land Use • Sports • Tax & Tax Exempt Organizations • Trusts & Estates

THE STATS

No. of attorneys worldwide: 408
No. of offices worldwide: 9
Managing Partner: Richard D. Ellingsen

EMPLOYMENT CONTACT

Ms. Carol Yuly
Recruiting Administrator, Seattle
Phone: (206) 628-3529
E-mail: carolyuly@dwt.com

Ms. Leslie Dustin
Recruiting Administrator, Portland
Phone: (503) 778-5243

WHO'S WHO

Does the firm have a pro bono coordinator? Yes

Ms. Julie Orr
Pro Bono Coordinator
Phone: (206) 628-7157
E-mail: julieorr@dwt.com

If yes, what percentage of his or her time is spent on pro bono work? 100 percent

Does the firm have a pro bono committee? Yes

If yes, how often does the committee meet? Quarterly

Describe the composition of the committee: Partner and associate representative from each U.S. office.

THE SCOOP

Does your firm have a written pro bono policy? Yes

Has the firm signed on to the Law Firm Pro Bono Challenge? Yes

What are some of the areas of law in which your firm has performed pro bono legal work in the last two years? Asylum, homelessness, nonprofit incorporation, class action, education, First Amendment rights, child welfare, domestic violence.

What are some of the areas of law in which your firm does not perform pro bono work? Employee-side employment law.

Organizations for which your firm has performed pro bono legal services in the last two years: King County Bar Association, Legal Services for Children, Public Counsel, Northwest Immigrant Rights Project, Seattle University Community Justice Centers, CASA Eastside Legal Assistance, Washington Legal Clinic for the Homeless, Legal Aid Society, American Civil Liberties Union.

List up to three pro bono matters that are representative of the pro bono work your firm participates in. Affirmative asylum, asylum appeals; free speech rights; public records access.

BY THE NUMBERS

What is the total number of hours that lawyers in U.S. offices at your firm spent performing pro bono legal services in 2000, 2001 and 2002?

    Total number of hours in 2000: 19,191 hours
    Total number of hours in 2001: 26,013 hours
    Total number of hours in 2002: 21,391 hours

Average number of pro bono hours per attorney in U.S. offices per year (including associates, partners, counsels, but not summer associates):

    Average number of hours per attorney in 2000: 53 hours
    Average number of hours per attorney in 2001: 71 hours
    Average number of hours per attorney in 2002: 55 hours

What percentage of attorneys in this firm's U.S. offices did pro bono work in 2002? 72 percent

What percentage of attorneys in this firm's U.S. offices did at least 20 hours of pro bono work in 2002? 41 percent

Does the firm encourage its lawyers to perform a minimum number of pro bono hours? Yes

SUPERVISION AND EVALUATIONS

Is there partner supervision on each pro bono matter? Yes

Do partner supervisors or, if applicable, senior associates provide written evaluations of associates' work on pro bono matters? Yes, as part of the associate evaluation process

If so, are those evaluations taken into account in determining salary, bonuses or advancement in the firm? Yes

If not, does the firm consider pro bono work generally in associate evaluations? N/A

HOURS

Does the firm give billable hour credit for pro bono work? Yes

Does the firm have a maximum number of pro bono hours that can be applied toward the billable hour target? Yes

If so, what is the maximum? 8 percent of annual budget

If your firm uses hours to determine bonuses, does it consider pro bono hours when determining bonuses? Yes

PRO BONO POINTS

What training opportunities are open to associates working on pro bono matters? All local bar trainings and other programs offering training. Resource material is available in-house.

Can associates bring matters of interest to the firm? Yes

Does the firm offer the use of support staff in carrying out pro bono matters? Yes

What pro bono opportunities are available for summer associates? CASA cases, research for pro bono projects, homeless legal intake, clinics.

Does the firm have established programs, such as externships, that enable its associates to work in a public interest setting? No

Has your firm won any special recognition or awards in the last two years for its pro bono work? Yes

If so, please list. 2002 James Madison Freedom of Information Award for Legal Counsel from the Northern California Chapter of the Society of Professional Journalists; 2002 Doris Pealy Award for Outstanding Community Support from the Center for Human Services; 2002 George A. Russill Community Service Award by Mt. Hood Habitat for Humanity; 2000 King County Bar Association Individual Award for pro bono representation; 2000 Outstanding Volunteer of the Year by Habitat for Humanity for ongoing pro bono work; 2000 David W. Soukup Award for Outstanding Legal Advocacy for Children, King County Guardian Ad Litem/CASA Program.

THE FIRM SAYS

DWT encourages its attorneys to engage in pro bono legal work. Our attorneys have the freedom to take on matters that interest them personally. As a result, DWT represents pro bono clients from a broad spectrum of socio-economic, racial and ethnic backgrounds and political persuasions. Many years ago we created a pro bono bank that represents DWT's goal of committing 3 percent of total firm-wide billable hours to pro bono work. Attorneys who perform pro bono work on behalf of people of limited means or organizations that serve the needs of people of limited means are eligible for billable hour credit from the firm's pro bono bank. Attorneys are also eligible for billable hour credit from the pro bono bank for pro bono work on behalf of nonprofit organizations whose resources are deemed insufficient to pay legal fees by the DWT pro bono and public service committee. The firm encourages all attorneys to find a way to participate in pro bono projects and to continue DWT's tradition as a leader in the community.

OUR SURVEY SAYS

"They are very committed, allowing pro bono to be billed as regular billable hours (to a grand limit)."

"We get a lot of pressure to do pro bono. A few pro bono opportunities count towards billable time. But it is a pretty personal sacrifice to add pro bono on top of all the other demands. Junior-level associates who do not have to be profitable can afford to do pro bono. More senior-level associates will not have the numbers to make partner if they actually do the pro bono that is requested."

"Associates receive can bill up to 8 percent of their billable hours requirement and receive billable credit."

"I've already done a lot and have been encouraged to continue."

"The firm has a strong commitment to pro bono, but that commitment has been weakened slightly by economic realities."

"The firm took a step backward last year by requiring 1,800 billable hours in excess of pro bono for bonus consideration. That said, the firm supports pro bono and makes it very visible."

"Overall, the firm is very active in pro bono matters. The New York office is not quite so active, in part due to the fact that it is a small office. The firm does encourage and does take on pro bono engagements, though the New York office's participation in such matters has been somewhat inconsistent."

"Too much pro bono work cuts an associate out of the running for a bonus."

"I am disappointed in the recent scaling back of pro bono hours we can bill. The firm may still have a better policy relative to other firms."

"Best pro bono program in town: billable hours credit, choose your own clients, availability of substantial work. I worked on two U.S. Supreme Court briefs in my first year."

Debevoise & Plimpton LLP

919 Third Avenue
New York, NY 10022
Phone: (212) 909-6000
www.debevoise.com

LOCATIONS

New York, NY (HQ)
Washington, DC
Frankfurt
Hong Kong
London
Moscow
Paris
Shanghai

MAJOR DEPARTMENTS & PRACTICES

Corporate
Litigation
Tax
Trusts & Estates

THE STATS

No. of attorneys worldwide: 587
No. of offices worldwide: 8
Presiding Partner: Martin Frederic Evans

EMPLOYMENT CONTACT

Ms. Ethel F. Leichti
Manager of Associate Recruitment
Phone: (212) 909-6657
E-mail: recruit@debevoise.com

WHO'S WHO

Principal pro bono contact(s) at your firm:

Christopher K. Tahbaz, Partner
Pro Bono Committee Co-Chair, Litigation Projects
Phone: (212) 909-6543
E-mail: cktahbaz@debevoise.com

Nicholas F. Potter, Partner
Pro Bono Committee Co-Chair, Corporate Projects
Phone: (212) 909-6459
E-mail: nfpotter@debevoise.com

Does the firm have a pro bono coordinator? No. Our pro bono committee, headed by partners Chris Tahbaz and Nick Potter, coordinates pro bono work at the firm.

Does the firm have a pro bono committee? Yes

If yes, how often does the committee meet? As needed.

Describe the composition of the committee: The committee consists of partners, counsel and associates representing different departments in the firm.

THE SCOOP

Does your firm have a written pro bono policy? Yes

Has the firm signed on to the Law Firm Pro Bono Challenge? Yes

What are some of the areas of law in which your firm has performed pro bono legal work in the last two years? Asylum and refugees law; reproductive rights; international human rights; prisoners' rights; indigent criminal defense; gay rights; constitutional civil rights; rights of individuals with mental disabilities; harm reduction; housing rights; labor/employment rights; corporate, tax and intellectual property advice to micro-entrepreneurs and not-for-profit organizations.

What are some of the areas of law in which your firm does not perform pro bono work? There are no areas in which we presumptively do not perform pro bono work. Rather, each individual project proposal is evaluated on its merits.

Organizations for which your firm has performed pro bono legal services in the last two years: Center for Constitutional Rights, Center for Reproductive Rights, Committee to Protect Journalists, Lawyers Committee for Human Rights, Lawyers' Committee for Civil Rights Under Law, The Legal Aid Society, New York Alliance for New Americans, New York Lawyers for the Public Interest, Inc., Robin Hood Foundation, Urban Justice Center.

List up to three pro bono matters that are representative of the pro bono work your firm participates in.

- Debevoise currently represents the Government of Mexico in its case against the United States before the International Court of Justice, in which Mexico alleges that 51 Mexican nationals now on death row in the United States were convicted and sentenced in proceedings that violated the consular notification and assistance provisions of the Vienna

Convention on Consular Relations. After a hearing in early 2003, the ICJ ordered, as provisional relief, that the United States take all steps necessary to ensure that the nationals not be executed until the Court decides the merits of the case. The case is currently pending.

- In the first half of 2003, Debevoise reached a landmark settlement in Brad H. v. City of New York, a case challenging New York City's practice of discharging city jail inmates who had been treated for mental illness while incarcerated without planning for their continued mental health care in the community. The settlement in Brad H. came after several years of litigation in which Debevoise lawyers, among other things, secured and defended on appeal a sweeping preliminary injunction against the city.

- Corporate pro bono work has included entering into partnerships with the Renaissance Business Development Center and the New York Alliance for New Americans to provide legal advice to inner-city micro-enterprises; assisting Project Reach Youth in forming a group of affiliated organizations to provide social services for teenagers; advising a Brooklyn-based organization providing seed capital to start-up companies in the health care and food industries; and providing organizational and problem-solving assistance to a New York City group devoted to providing housing, job training and day care services to homeless families.

BY THE NUMBERS

What is the total number of hours that lawyers in U.S. offices at your firm spent performing pro bono legal services in 2000, 2001 and 2002?

    Total number of hours in 2000: 33,710 hours
    Total number of hours in 2001: 35,571 hours
    Total number of hours in 2002: 37,888 hours

Average number of pro bono hours per attorney in U.S. offices per year (including associates, partners, counsels, but not summer associates):

    Average number of hours per attorney in 2000: 93.8 hours
    Average number of hours per attorney in 2001: 95.2 hours
    Average number of hours per attorney in 2002: 93.4 hours

What percentage of attorneys in this firm's U.S. offices did pro bono work in 2002? 82.3 percent

What percentage of attorneys in this firm's U.S. offices did at least 20 hours of pro bono work in 2002? 58.4 percent

Does the firm encourage its lawyers to perform a minimum number of pro bono hours? No. We strongly encourage all of our lawyers to become involved in pro bono work, but we do not specify a minimum number of hours.

If so, how many hours per year or what percentage of lawyers' billable hours? N/A

SUPERVISION AND EVALUATIONS

Is there partner supervision on each pro bono matter? Yes, partner or counsel supervision

Do partner supervisors or, if applicable, senior associates provide written evaluations of associates' work on pro bono matters? Yes

If so, are those evaluations taken into account in determining salary, bonuses or advancement in the firm? Yes

If not, does the firm consider pro bono work generally in associate evaluations? N/A

HOURS

Does the firm give billable hour credit for pro bono work? We strongly encourage pro bono work, but we do not have billable hour requirements for any associate work, so there is no "billable hour credit" to be given.

Does the firm have a maximum number of pro bono hours that can be applied toward the billable hour target? N/A

If so, what is the maximum? N/A

If your firm uses hours to determine bonuses, does it consider pro bono hours when determining bonuses? We do not determine bonuses based on lawyer hours.

PRO BONO POINTS

What training opportunities are open to associates working on pro bono matters? In addition to being able to take advantage of the full range of training provided to lawyers at the firm generally, lawyers who work on pro bono matters have opportunities to participate in training programs sponsored by legal service organizations with which we work on a regular basis. In recent years, these programs have been hosted by, among other organizations, Lawyers Committee for Human Rights, InMotion (formerly the Network for Women's Services) and The Legal Aid Society.

Can associates bring matters of interest to the firm? Yes, subject to pro bono committee approval

Does the firm offer the use of support staff in carrying out pro bono matters? Yes

What pro bono opportunities are available for summer associates? Summer associates routinely have opportunities to work on ongoing pro bono matters being handled by the firm. In addition, each year Debevoise sponsors and subsidizes one- and two-week externships for summer associates at a number of legal services organizations. In the Summer of 2003, our summer associates performed externships at Brooklyn Legal Services, Corporation A; the Legal Action Center; Mental Hygiene Legal Services; MFY Legal Services, Inc.; New York Lawyers for the Public Interest, Inc.; the Vera Institute of Justice; Legal Services for New York City; Northern Manhattan Improvement Corporation; The Legal Aid Society; and the Housing Court Summer Assistance Project of the Association of the Bar of the City of New York.

Does the firm have established programs, such as externships, that enable its associates to work in a public interest setting? No

Has your firm won any special recognition or awards in the last two years for its pro bono work? Yes

If so, please list. Within the past two years, Debevoise has been recognized for its pro bono work by a variety of organizations. In 2003, The Legal Aid Society honored Debevoise with its Outstanding Pro Bono Publico and Public Service Law Firm Award. Also in 2003, Debevoise was recognized for its pro bono efforts by the Urban Justice Center and Lawyers Committee for Human Rights. Among recognition received by the firm in 2002, the New York City Council honored Debevoise in a proclamation issued in November 2002, recognizing the firm's work on behalf of the John A. Reisenbach Charter School, a nonprofit New York City charter school that serves approximately 300 primary and secondary schoolchildren in Harlem.

THE FIRM SAYS

Debevoise has a deep and long-standing commitment to pro bono legal service. This commitment is evidenced by the large number and extensive range of pro bono matters we handle each year. It is also evidenced by our consistent ranking among the nation's top law firms for pro bono work. In 2003, we were ranked first among New York City law firms and seventh nationally in The American Lawyer's AmLaw 100 pro bono rankings. According to the AmLaw 100, we have been the number one firm in New York City for pro bono work in six of the past seven years. Debevoise is a charter signatory to the Law Firm Pro Bono Challenge. As a result, we have agreed to commit time to pro bono matters (as defined by the Challenge) equal to at least 5 percent of our billed time each year.

Our work on behalf of pro bono clients involves all areas of our practice, and our pro bono engagements range from major impact litigations of national and international import to representations of individuals in the communities in which our offices are located. We encourage our lawyers to participate in pro bono activities from the first days of their careers with the firm. We also encourage our lawyers to become involved in pro bono work even if that work falls outside their particular practice areas. Debevoise lawyers obtain pro bono work from a variety of sources. In many cases, pro bono assignments are referred to Debevoise by some of the many legal service organizations with which the firm has long-standing relationships, such as The Legal Aid Society, Lawyers Committee for Human Rights and New York Lawyers for the Public Interest, Inc. Other pro bono projects grow out of interests that our lawyers pursue outside of the firm. In all instances, lawyers are encouraged to present proposals for pro bono engagements to the firm's pro bono committee, which approves all such engagements before they are undertaken by the firm.

In addition to its long-standing commitment to pro bono legal service, Debevoise has a deep and lasting commitment to public service. One of the many ways in which this commitment manifests itself is through the number of Debevoise lawyers who serve on the boards of directors of legal service organizations, arts organizations and other charitable institutions. Among other organizations, Debevoise lawyers serve on the boards of directors of Lawyers Alliance for New York, Lawyers' Committee for Civil Rights Under Law, Lawyers Committee for Human Rights, The Legal Aid Society, Legal Services for New York, MFY Legal Services, Inc., New York Lawyers for the Public Interest, Inc., Urban Justice Center, Volunteers of Legal Service, Welfare Law Center, American Ballet Theatre, Catalyst, Inc., Citymeals on Wheels, Classic Stage Company, Freer Gallery of Art/Arthur M. Sackler Gallery, The Metropolitan Opera, Neighborhood Coalition for Shelter, The New York Historical Society, Prep for Prep and The Symphony Space Inc.

OUR SURVEY SAYS

"Unparalleled commitment to pro bono. I can bill a couple of hundred pro bono hours a year and they are always counted as billable hours. I am always encouraged to do more."

"Approaching perfection."

"Debevoise has the best pro bono program in New York, hands down. This has become a self-perpetuating tradition, because for years the firm has been attracting lawyers with a strong interest in pro bono work. The firm has billed the highest number of pro bono hours per attorney in New York for at least the last few years."

"I have done all the pro bono I could want and more — including bringing in my own projects. They take it very seriously."

"Every first-year was given a pro bono assignment and strong encouragement to take on more. This is truly impressive."

"I can't say enough about this firm's attitude towards pro bono. I have devoted a great amount of time to a variety of pro bono projects and the firm has never treated those hours any differently and it has never been stingy about resources spent on such projects. In addition, because of its reputation as a great place for pro bono, it seems to attract lots of people with progressive ideas, connections and willingness to do pro bono projects despite their heavy billable workload."

"This is hands-down the best New York corporate firm for its commitment to pro bono. Once a pro bono case is accepted, the firm's policy is that it will be worked on with as much vigor as any other case (if not more!). I have received full support for several pro bono matters and have been encouraged to take on more."

"No New York firm beats Debevoise in this department. Debevoise's commitment to pro bono work has been genuine, substantial and consistent for years. The firm is extremely encouraging of pro bono work. Pro bono work counts towards billable hours. The firm does not discourage people from working on large pro bono projects and has been engaged in several such projects. The firm takes pro bono cases of all types and is encouraging of associates who propose their own projects. During the last two years, I have worked on two amicus briefs filed before the U.S. Supreme Court."

"For my first three months here, the only work I did was pro bono, and it wasn't because there was a lack of billable work. The firm takes pro bono very, very seriously."

Dechert LLP

4000 Bell Atlantic Tower
1717 Arch Street
Philadelphia, PA 19103-2793
Phone: (215) 994-4000
www.dechert.com

LOCATIONS

Boston, MA
Charlotte, NC
Harrisburg , PA
Hartford, CT
New York, NY
Newport Beach, CA
Palo Alto, CA
Philadelphia, PA
Princeton, NJ
San Francisco, CA
Washington, DC
Brussels
Frankfurt
London
Luxembourg
Munich
Paris

MAJOR DEPARTMENTS & PRACTICES

Antitrust
Commercial Litigation
Corporate & Securities
Federal Tax
Financial Services
Intellectual Property
Labor & Employment
Mass Torts & Product Liability
Mergers & Acquisitions
Private Equity
Real Estate Finance
Securities Litigation
Securitization
State Tax
Technology

THE STATS

No. of attorneys worldwide: 730
No. of offices worldwide: 17
Chairman and CEO: Barton J. Winokur

EMPLOYMENT CONTACT

Ms. Carol S. Miller
Director of Associate Administration
Phone: (215) 994-2147
E-mail: carol.miller@dechert.com

WHO'S WHO

Does the firm have a pro bono coordinator? Yes

Suzanne Turner, Esq.
Partner
Phone: 011-44-207-775-7504
E-mail: Suzanne.Turner@dechert.com

If yes, what percentage of his or her time is spent on pro bono work? 100 percent

Does the firm have a pro bono committee? Yes

If yes, how often does the committee meet? Every six weeks.

Describe the composition of the committee: The firm-wide pro bono committee consists of a representative from every office, both in Europe and the United States. Several offices also have local pro bono committees.

THE SCOOP

Does your firm have a written pro bono policy? Yes

Has the firm signed on to the Law Firm Pro Bono Challenge? Yes

What are some of the areas of law in which your firm has performed pro bono legal work in the last two years? Prisoner civil rights litigation; asylum/immigration; capital defense; family law; international human rights; public benefits; representation of artists; civil rights; child advocacy; and corporate, real estate and tax advice for nonprofit organizations.

What are some of the areas of law in which your firm does not perform pro bono work? None.

Organizations for which your firm has performed pro bono legal services in the last two years: Dechert routinely takes referrals from legal service providers/clearinghouses in each of the cities in which we have offices. Representative examples include: Philadelphia Volunteers for the Indigent Program (Philadelphia), Homeless Advocacy Project (Philadelphia), Lawyers Alliance for New York (New York), New York Lawyers for the Public Interest (New York), Pro Bono Partnership (New York, New Jersey, Connecticut), Lawyers' Committee for Civil Rights Under Law (National), Washington Lawyers Committee for the Homeless (Washington), Volunteer Lawyers Project of the Boston Bar Association (Boston), Public Law Center (Newport Beach), LawWorks for Community Groups (London).

List up to three pro bono matters that are representative of the pro bono work your firm participates in.

- In the New York office, an associate successfully represented an Ecuadorian woman who had been a victim of human trafficking in her efforts to obtain a T-Visa (a non-immigrant visa introduced by the Victims of Trafficking and Violence Protection Act of 2000). The woman had been brought to the United States to be a nanny for a diplomat's family and was kept a virtual slave and prisoner in their home.
- A team in the Philadelphia office represents an individual on death row in Pennsylvania. The client is illiterate, mentally retarded and severely brain damaged, and his conviction and sentencing raise several constitutional questions, including claims based on invalid jury waivers and ineffective assistance of counsel.

- The firm has an ongoing project to handle prisoner civil rights appointments from the U.S. District Court for the Eastern District of Pennsylvania. During 2002, the firm worked on 12 prisoner civil rights cases, of which five resulted in jury trials, one in a non-jury trial and two were argued in the Third Circuit Court of Appeals.

BY THE NUMBERS

What is the total number of hours that lawyers in U.S. offices at your firm spent performing pro bono legal services in 2000, 2001 and 2002?

Total number of hours in 2000: 13,861 hours
Total number of hours in 2001: 17,660 hours
Total number of hours in 2002: 24,313 hours

Average number of pro bono hours per attorney in U.S. offices per year (including associates, partners, counsels, but not summer associates):

Average number of hours per attorney in 2000: 28.12 hours
Average number of hours per attorney in 2001: 31.31 hours
Average number of hours per attorney in 2002: 43.42 hours

What percentage of attorneys in this firm's U.S. offices did pro bono work in 2002? 58 percent

What percentage of attorneys in this firm's U.S. offices did at least 20 hours of pro bono work in 2002? 31 percent

Does the firm encourage its lawyers to perform a minimum number of pro bono hours? Yes

If so, how many hours per year or what percentage of lawyers' billable hours? For purposes of meeting the 1,950 billable hours expectation, interested associates are encouraged to devote up to 200 hours of their time to pro bono legal work. It is understood that a particular matter or matters may require a commitment in excess of 200 hours, and that commitment is permitted and will be credited to meeting the 1,950 hours expectation, with prior approval.

SUPERVISION AND EVALUATIONS

Is there partner supervision on each pro bono matter? Yes

Do partner supervisors or, if applicable, senior associates provide written evaluations of associates' work on pro bono matters? Yes

If so, are those evaluations taken into account in determining salary, bonuses or advancement in the firm? Yes

If not, does the firm consider pro bono work generally in associate evaluations? N/A

HOURS

Does the firm give billable hour credit for pro bono work? Yes

Does the firm have a maximum number of pro bono hours that can be applied toward the billable hour target? No

If so, what is the maximum? N/A

If your firm uses hours to determine bonuses, does it consider pro bono hours when determining bonuses? Yes

PRO BONO POINTS

What training opportunities are open to associates working on pro bono matters? The firm regularly publishes lists of external training programs offered on topics that could be useful in handling pro bono matters and encourages attorneys to attend. The firm has also conducted internal training sessions for the purposes of encouraging pro bono participation, the most recent one being on incorporating a nonprofit organization and obtaining tax exempt status.

Can associates bring matters of interest to the firm? Yes

Does the firm offer the use of support staff in carrying out pro bono matters? Yes

What pro bono opportunities are available for summer associates? Summer associates are very much encouraged to participate in pro bono matters either by working on matters already being handled by the firm or handling their own matters under the supervision of a partner. For example, associates in the Philadelphia office are encouraged to participate in Philadelphia Volunteers for the Indigent Program's Summer Associates' Day, where they are trained in a substantive area of law and often given cases. Similarly, summer associates in the firm's New York office are encouraged to participate in Sanctuary for Families Courtroom Advocates Project, where they assist victims of domestic violence obtain temporary restraining orders.

Does the firm have established programs, such as externships, that enable its associates to work in a public interest setting? Yes

If so, where and for up to how long? In July 2002, Dechert established two pro bono externships in its Washington office with the Legal Aid Society of the District of Columbia and the Washington Lawyers' Committee for Civil Rights and Urban Affairs. Under the program, one associate works in each organization for six months. At the end of each six-month period other associates rotate into the positions to make the program continuous.

Has your firm won any special recognition or awards in the last two years for its pro bono work? Yes

If so, please list. During the last two years, the firm and its lawyers have received numerous pro bono awards including the following: Geanne Zelkowitz received the inaugural Philadelphia Bar Association's Citizens Pro Bono Award; Kristin Hynd received an "outstanding volunteer service" award from the Legal Clinic for the Disabled; Suzanne Seltzer received a Cornerstone Award from the Lawyers Alliance of New York; Richard Symonds received the "Wig and Pen" award from the Young Solicitors Group; the firm received the inaugural award for "Best Contribution by a Firm" from the Solicitors Pro Bono Group (London).

THE FIRM SAYS

Dechert has a long-standing tradition of providing pro bono legal services to individuals and organizations who cannot otherwise obtain legal representation. The commitment exists throughout all of our offices — in both the United States and Europe, and opportunities exist in every area. While participation in pro bono work is voluntary, the firm encourages all attorneys and paralegals to participate. Dechert is a signatory to the Law Firm Pro Bono Challenge and has committed to contribute annually 3 percent of the firm's total billable hours to pro bono work. Additionally, the firm fully endorses the American Bar Association's House of Delegates's 1993 resolution stating that "[a} lawyer should aspire to render at least 50 hours of pro bono publico service per year."

Dechert's pro bono program is run by a firm-wide pro bono committee that includes a representative from every office. The committee promotes the firm's pro bono efforts and is responsible for, developing policies and procedures on pro bono work, cultivating a broad array of pro bono opportunities and screening potential pro bono matters, among other things. A full time pro bono partner manages the pro bono practice at the firm and chairs the firm-wide pro bono committee. Many offices also have local pro bono committees to assist in encouraging widespread participation. Pro bono matters come to the firm from many sources, including local, national and international legal services organizations and clearinghouses. Information on available pro bono opportunities is widely disseminated, and substantial support and training is given to lawyers handling pro bono matters.

Dechert has a very active pro bono practice in its European offices. In London, the firm takes a wide variety of referrals from legal service or charitable organizations, including LawWorks for Community Groups, the Free Representation Unit, the Royal Courts of Justice and the Prince's Trust. The firm also has an on-going project with the North Kensington Law Centre in which we staff evening advice sessions and provide legal services to the Law Centre itself and to local community groups that the Law Centre does not have the capacity to serve itself. Earlier this year, Dechert received the Solicitors Pro Bono Group's inaugural award for Best Contribution by a Firm for its work in London. One of our London lawyers also received the "Wig and Pen" award from the Young Solicitors Group.

OUR SURVEY SAYS

"Associates are encouraged to take pro bono cases, and the time spent on these matters is credited to your total billable hours. My complaint with respect to these cases is there is not a lot of diversity in the types of pro bono matters regularly offered."

"Pro bono has improved immensely in the Washington office. There is a partner committed to supporting the associates and circulating opportunities. I feel it has gone from nonexistent in D.C. to encouraged."

"The firm encourages pro bono work so long as it is on top of anticipated work (which is fine)."

"The firm is completely committed to pro bono and provides multiple opportunities."

"The reality is that you can do a decent amount of pro bono – about 200 hours per year, as long as you keep your total of billables and pro bono around 1,950 – but if you do anything more than that, you will be told to increase your billables and you will not get a bonus." [The firm disputes this claim.]

"There are a few attorneys very committed to pro bono, and it is generally encouraged, but more can be done."

"The D.C. office has started a pro bono externship program in addition to generally encouraging attorneys to devote time to pro bone matters on an on-going basis. They often advertise opportunities in conjunction with the D.C. bar."

"I work on a lot of pro bono matters and get full credit."

"Dechert is very committed to pro bono work. Hours spent on pro bono cases are given equal weight as billable hours. I have found the pro bono at Dechert to be extremely rewarding. The pro bono work is also a great way for junior associates to get experience with depositions, courtroom experience, drafting wills and other tasks that the associate might otherwise not see for several years."

"A team in the Philadelphia office represents an individual on death row in Pennsylvania. The client is illiterate, mentally retarded and severely brain damaged, and his conviction and sentencing raise several constitutional questions, including claims based on invalid jury waivers and ineffective assistance of counsel."

— *Dechert LLP*

Dewey Ballantine LLP

1301 Avenue of the Americas
New York, NY 10019
Phone: (212) 259-8000
www.deweyballantine.com

LOCATIONS

New York, NY (HQ)
Austin, TX
Houston, TX
Los Angeles, CA
Palo Alto, CA
Washington, DC
Budapest
Frankfurt
London
Prague
Warsaw

MAJOR DEPARTMENTS & PRACTICES

Bankruptcy
Capital Markets
Corporate
Energy & Utility
Environmental
ERISA
Insurance
Intellectual Property
International Trade
Investment Management
Litigation
Mergers & Acquisitions
Project Finance
Real Estate
Structured Finance
Tax & Private Clients

THE STATS

No. of attorneys worldwide: 550
No. of offices worldwide: 11
Co-Chairs: Morton A. Pierce, Sanford W. Morhouse

EMPLOYMENT CONTACT

Ms. Nicole Gunn
Manager of Legal Recruitment
Phone: (212) 259-7050
Fax: (212) 259-6333
E-mail: db.recruitment@deweyballantine.com

WHO'S WHO

Does the firm have a pro bono coordinator? Yes

Fiona A. Brett, Esq.
Pro Bono Coordinator
Phone: (212) 259-7481
E-mail: fbrett@dbllp.com

If yes, what percentage of his or her time is spent on pro bono work? 10 percent

Does the firm have a pro bono committee? Yes

If yes, how often does the committee meet? As needed.

Describe the composition of the committee: The committee is composed of partners from different departments and offices with the firm.

THE SCOOP

Does your firm have a written pro bono policy? Yes

Has the firm signed on to the Law Firm Pro Bono Challenge? Yes

What are some of the areas of law in which your firm has performed pro bono legal work in the last two years? Criminal defense (trial and appellate, state and federal); Hague Convention (return of abducted children); welfare law; compensation for September 11 victims; immigration and asylum law; corporate governance; tax; landlord-tenant disputes.

Organizations for which your firm has performed pro bono legal services in the last two years: Office of the Appellate Defender, Welfare Law Center, Legal Aid Society, September's Mission, Archdiocesan Legal Network of Catholic Charities, National Center for Missing and Exploited Children, National Center on Addiction and Substance Abuse at Columbia University, New York State Defenders Association's Immigration Defense Project, Abounding Grace Ministries, Alliance to Save Energy.

List up to three pro bono matters that are representative of the pro bono work your firm participates in.

- *United States v. Calero.* The firm provided pro bono representation to the defendant in a federal criminal case, culminating in a jury trial in the Southern District of New York in September 2003.

- *British Memorial Garden.* We are providing pro bono legal advice to the St. George's Society of New York on the formation of a not-for-profit trust, the British Memorial Garden Trust, and on obtaining for it tax-exempt and charitable status.

- *Gitter v. Gitter.* Dewey Ballantine has represented a custodial father petitioning for the return of his son to Israel pursuant to the Hague Convention on the Civil Aspects of International Child Abduction at trial in the U.S. District Court for the Eastern District of New York.

BY THE NUMBERS

What is the total number of hours that lawyers in U.S. offices at your firm spent performing pro bono legal services in 2000, 2001 and 2002?

    Total number of hours in 2000: 10,829 hours
    Total number of hours in 2001: 12,455 hours
    Total number of hours in 2002: 18,000 hours

Average number of pro bono hours per attorney in U.S. offices per year (including associates, partners, counsels, but not summer associates):

    Average number of hours per attorney in 2000: 25.6 hours
    Average number of hours per attorney in 2001: 28.6 hours
    Average number of hours per attorney in 2002: 42.2 hours

What percentage of attorneys in this firm's U.S. offices did pro bono work in 2002? Approximately 40 percent

What percentage of attorneys in this firm's U.S. offices did at least 20 hours of pro bono work in 2002? 36.8 percent

Does the firm encourage its lawyers to perform a minimum number of pro bono hours? No

SUPERVISION AND EVALUATIONS

Is there partner supervision on each pro bono matter? Yes

Do partner supervisors or, if applicable, senior associates provide written evaluations of associates' work on pro bono matters? No

If so, are those evaluations taken into account in determining salary, bonuses or advancement in the firm? N/A

If not, does the firm consider pro bono work generally in associate evaluations? Yes

HOURS

Does the firm give billable hour credit for pro bono work? Yes

Does the firm have a maximum number of pro bono hours that can be applied toward the billable hour target? No

If so, what is the maximum? N/A

If your firm uses hours to determine bonuses, does it consider pro bono hours when determining bonuses? Not applicable

PRO BONO POINTS

What training opportunities are open to associates working on pro bono matters? Many of the legal services organizations with which we work provide training programs which our associates attend. In addition, partners and more senior associates provide individual training in specific practice areas.

Can associates bring matters of interest to the firm? Yes

Does the firm offer the use of support staff in carrying out pro bono matters? Yes

What pro bono opportunities are available for summer associates? Summer associates are given the opportunity to work on pro bono matters to the same extent as billable matters. In addition, we place a number of our summer associates in externships with pro bono clients.

Does the firm have established programs, such as externships, that enable its associates to work in a public interest setting? Yes

If so, where and for up to how long? King's County (Brooklyn) District Attorney's Office Partners in Prosecution — an associate works full time for four-to-six months as an assistant district attorney in a trial bureau of the district attorney's office in Brooklyn. Summer associates participate in two-week externships at organizations such as the Legal Aid Society, Asian American Legal Defense and Education Fund, Hebrew Immigrant Aid Society and WNYC public radio.

Has your firm won any special recognition or awards in the last two years for its pro bono work? Yes

If so, please list. In 2003, Dewey Ballantine was honored for its legal work on behalf September's Mission. In 2003, the Alzheimer's Association presented Dewey Ballantine with an award for its representation of the organization over the past decade. In 2002 and 2003, Dewey Ballantine received the John Carroll Society Pro Bono Legal Service Award for outstanding contributions to the Archdiocesan League of Catholic Charities. In 2002, one of our associates received an award from the Legal Aid Society for pro bono excellence and others were recognized for work for September 11 victims. In 2002, one of our associates received the Hudson Guild Outstanding Volunteer Award for exceptional pro bono legal services on behalf of the organization.

THE FIRM SAYS

Dewey Ballantine is proud of its long history of pro bono service. Attorneys in all our offices, both partners and associates, participate in pro bono projects. Whether it's representing an indigent defendant facing criminal prosecution, helping an immigrant gain asylum status, incorporating a not-for-profit organization or securing benefits for the elderly or disadvantaged, the firm encourages its attorneys to donate their time to a variety of pro bono projects to assist those in need or to benefit society as a whole.

OUR SURVEY SAYS

"Pro bono work is encouraged."

"The firm does some, people mean well, but there certainly could be a lot more."

"E-mails go around almost weekly from partners who have information about potential pro bono work. Associates can go outside this route and volunteer for pro bono work through organizations they are familiar with and apply for that work to become firm pro bono work, meaning the hours spent on it count towards the associate's total hours."

"Pro bono is available but not encouraged."

"Everyone knows that once you start working on pro bono cases, you are on your way out the door."

"They are pretty good on this, particularly as work has otherwise been slow. Great chance to go to court."

"Everyone in the firm goes to great lengths to do pro bono, and as young associates we are given many opportunities to take on our own pro bono responsibilities."

"Whether it's representing an indigent defendant facing criminal prosecution, helping an immigrant gain asylum status, incorporating a not-for-profit organization or securing benefits for the elderly or disadvantaged, the firm encourages its attorneys to donate their time to a variety of pro bono projects to assist those in need or to benefit society as a whole."

— *Dewey Ballantine LLP*

Dorsey & Whitney LLP

50 South Sixth Street, Suite 1500
Minneapolis, MN 55402-1498
Phone: (612) 340-2600
www.dorsey.com

LOCATIONS

Anchorage, AK • Denver, CO • Des Moines, IA • Fargo, ND • Great Falls, MT • Irvine, CA • Minneapolis, MN • Missoula, MT • New York, NY • Palo Alto, CA • Salt Lake City, UT • San Francisco, CA • Seattle, WA • Washington, DC • Hong Kong • London • Shanghai • Tokyo • Toronto • Vancouver

MAJOR DEPARTMENTS & PRACTICES

Business Groups
Banking & Commercial • Broker-Dealer • Business Restructuring & Bankruptcy • Corporate & Securities • Emerging Companies • Employee Benefits • Funds • Health • M&A • Nonprofit & Tax-Exempt Organizations • Project Development & Finance • Public Finance • Real Estate & Land Use • Securitization • Tax & Estate Planning • Technology Commerce • Trademark, Copyright & Brand Management

Trial & Regulatory Groups
Antitrust • Appellate • Commercial/Contract • Construction/Real Estate • Environmental, Natural Resources & Energy • ERISA • Government Contracts/Procurement • Insurance • Intellectual Property • International Arbitration & Litigation • Iraq Practice • Labor & Employment • Products & Technology Liability • Professional Malpractice • Securities & Financial Institutions • Tax, Trust & Estate • Telecommunications • White Collar Crime & Civil Fraud

THE STATS

No. of attorneys worldwide: 705
No. of offices worldwide: 20
Managing Partner: Peter S. Hendrixson

EMPLOYMENT CONTACT

Ms. Kelsey Shuff
Manager of Lawyer Recruiting
Phone: (612) 340-2868
E-mail: shuff.kelsey@dorsey.com

WHO'S WHO

Principal pro bono contact(s) at your firm:

Steve Carlson, Esq. and Lyn Dee Wells, Esq.
Pro Bono Partners
E-mail: carlson.steve@dorsey.com; wells.lyndee@dorsey.com

Bricker Lavik, Esq.
Pro Bono Director
E-mail: lavik.bricker@dorsey.com

Does the firm have a pro bono coordinator? Yes
In Minneapolis, Pam Wiehoff-Kaufman. Each regional office has its own coordinator.

If yes, what percentage of his or her time is spent on pro bono work? In Minneapolis, 100 percent.

Does the firm have a pro bono committee? No

THE SCOOP

Does your firm have a written pro bono policy? Yes

Has the firm signed on to the Law Firm Pro Bono Challenge? Yes

What are some of the areas of law in which your firm has performed pro bono legal work in the last two years? Dorsey provides pro bono representation in virtually all areas of civil law. Our attorneys work on projects they are interested in and passionate about.

What are some of the areas of law in which your firm does not perform pro bono work? We have not excluded any area of civil law and review each request for service.

Organizations for which your firm has performed pro bono legal services in the last two years: The firm has provided pro bono legal services for scores of organizations throughout the country. Examples include the Volunteer Lawyers' Network in Minneapolis, The Lawyers' Committee for Civil Rights Under Law, Project Enterprise, Minnesota Justice Foundation, Minnesota Advocates for Human Rights, Children's Law Center, and Metropolitan Economic Development Association, to name a few.

List up to three pro bono matters that are representative of the pro bono work your firm participates in.
Dorsey currently represents, along with the Lawyers' Committee for Civil Rights Under Law, a group of African American parents in their efforts to desegregate the Thomasville, Georgia, School District. Dorsey attorneys also work on the case of Joe Lee Guy, who is on death row in Texas. The firm was asked by the ABA Commission on Immigration to research and draft a study on immigration appeals policies and procedures. For details, check our web site for pro bono publications including the monthly newsletter and the pro bono annual report.

BY THE NUMBERS

What is the total number of hours that lawyers in U.S. offices at your firm spent performing pro bono legal services in 2000, 2001 and 2002?

Total number of hours in 2000: 40,493 hours
Total number of hours in 2001: 43,283 hours
Total number of hours in 2002: 43,106 hours
Total number of hours in 2003: 37,979 hours

Average number of pro bono hours per attorney in U.S. offices per year (including associates, partners, counsels, but not summer associates):

Average number of hours per attorney in 2000: 51 hours
Average number of hours per attorney in 2001: 44 hours
Average number of hours per attorney in 2002: 49 hours
Average number of hours per attorney in 2003: 58 hours

What percentage of attorneys in this firm's U.S. offices did pro bono work in 2003? 78 percent

What percentage of attorneys in this firm's U.S. offices did at least 20 hours of pro bono work in 2003? 48 percent

Does the firm encourage its lawyers to perform a minimum number of pro bono hours? Yes

If so, how many hours per year or what percentage of lawyers' billable hours? Approximately 50 hours per lawyer

SUPERVISION AND EVALUATIONS

Is there partner supervision on each pro bono matter? Yes

Do partner supervisors or, if applicable, senior associates provide written evaluations of associates' work on pro bono matters? Yes

If so, are those evaluations taken into account in determining salary, bonuses or advancement in the firm? Yes

If not, does the firm consider pro bono work generally in associate evaluations? N/A

HOURS

Does the firm give billable hour credit for pro bono work? Yes on some matters and for bonus purposes on all matters

Does the firm have a maximum number of pro bono hours that can be applied toward the billable hour target? Yes

If so, what is the maximum? 50 hours

If your firm uses hours to determine bonuses, does it consider pro bono hours when determining bonuses? Yes

PRO BONO POINTS

What training opportunities are open to associates working on pro bono matters? Dorsey has several legal clinics that we train associates for. We also have in-house training on issues such as housing law, nonprofits and business pro bono projects.

Can associates bring matters of interest to the firm? Yes

Does the firm offer the use of support staff in carrying out pro bono matters? Yes

What pro bono opportunities are available for summer associates? Summer associates are encouraged to participate in a variety of projects, including housing court, asylum appeals and clinics.

Does the firm have established programs, such as externships, that enable its associates to work in a public interest setting? Yes

If so, where and for up to how long? Dorsey associates in the trial department work in the Minneapolis City Attorney's Office for three-month stints where prosecuting misdemeanors.

Has your firm won any special recognition or awards in the last two years for its pro bono work? Yes

If so, please list. Steve Carlson will receive the Hennepin County Bar Association's Distinguished Service Award in March, 2004, for his tremendous work with Minnesota Advocates for Human Rights for the past 14 years spearheading a committee for a Phillipine refugee to receive humanitarian parole the Bosnian War Crimes Project, the Child Mortality Project, the Saudi Arabia Project and his leadership as the chair of MAHR's board.

The firm also has its own pro bono awards; the Scales of Justice are given to those who have made a difference to the disadvantaged in our communities. You can see more on this in the 2002 Pro Bono Annual report online at www.dorsey.com.

THE FIRM SAYS

This last question is best summed up by our managing partner, Peter Hendrixson:

Community service has always been a hallmark of Dorsey & Whitney, and 2002 was our strongest year yet for pro bono work and volunteer service. All across the firm our lawyers and staff devoted themselves in myriad creative ways to serving disadvantaged individuals, and to improving the communities in which we work.

I'm very proud that Dorsey once again has met the Law Firm Pro Bono Challenge, contributing more than 3 percent of our hours to serving people who need legal advice but are unable to afford it. We've met the challenge each year since it was launched in 1993.

It's an impressive accomplishment, not only for our lawyers, but for the many paralegals, legal secretaries and other support staff who contribute their time to support the lawyers' efforts.

I often tell other law firms who are contemplating pro bono work that they don't have to worry about pro bono efforts taking away from a firm's billable hours. To the contrary: There are only positive returns — more energized lawyers and staff, closer ties with the community, terrific skill development and real pride.

When we get focused and passionate about an important issue, we can move mountains.

OUR SURVEY SAYS

"The firm excels in this area. It has met the Law Firm Pro Bono Challenge every year since its inception. The firm's pro bono work covers the gamut of social issues and if someone wants to work on some new issue, that's fine too."

"The firm's commitment is strong and the opportunities are plentiful, with strong involvement and guidance from partners and senior attorneys."

"They publish a monthly pro bono newsletter highlighting the projects around the firm."

"It's easy to be committed to pro bono when you don't have billable work."

"The firm gives 'good time' to at least 50 hours of pro bono time each year. The firm is highly committed to pro bono issues, and many of our partners are involved in various nonprofit agencies and organizations around the area."

"The firm is committed and wants associates to do pro bono, but they don't compensate you for the hours."*

"Lots of it floating around, and they'll let you bring in your own pet causes."

"They have a pro bono program and permit associates to bill (in lieu of the required billables) 50 hours a year to pro bono projects – it's unclear whether associates who use 50 pro bono hours are viewed negatively."

"The firm is strongly committed to doing pro bono projects. I personally do pro bono through a criminal program and for the firm's staff who need legal advice."

* The firm notes that it does compensate for pro bono hours; if the associate has met the billable floor first, then pro bono hours are considered as a bonus compensation at the end of the year.

"Dorsey provides pro bono representation in virtually all areas of civil law. Our attorneys work on projects they are interested in and passionate about."

— *Dorsey & Whitney LLP*

Faegre & Benson LLP

2200 Wells Fargo Center
90 South 7th Street
Minneapolis, MN 55402
Phone: (612) 766-7000
www.faegre.com

LOCATIONS

Minneapolis, MN (HQ)
Boulder, CO
Denver, CO
Des Moines, IA
Frankfurt
London
Shanghai

MAJOR DEPARTMENTS & PRACTICES

Advertising • Antitrust & Trade Regulation • Banking & Financial Institutions • Bankruptcy/Insolvency • Construction • Corporate Finance & Securities • Data Privacy • Distribution & Franchise Litigation • E-Commerce • Emerging Companies • Employee Benefits & Executive Compensation • ERISA Litigation • Export Controls & Compliance • Family & Closely-Held Businesses • Government Contracts • Government Relations • HIPAA Privacy Compliance • Housing Development • Immigration • Insurance • Intellectual Property • International Business • Labor & Employment • Land Use/Zoning/Environmental Review • Litigation, Appellate & Alternative Dispute Resolution • Mergers & Acquisitions • Natural Resources & Water Quality • Pro Bono & Community Service • Product Liability • Public Finance • Real Estate • Records Management & Electronic Discovery • Securities Litigation • Structured Finance • Tax • Technology & Licensing Transactions • Trusts & Estates • White Collar Criminal Defense

THE STATS

No. of attorneys worldwide: 475
No. of offices worldwide: 7
Chairman: Phil Garon

EMPLOYMENT CONTACT

Ms. Joanne Jaensch
Director of Legal Personnel Services
Phone: (612) 766-7000
E-mail: jjaensch@faegre.com

WHO'S WHO

Principal pro bono contact(s) at your firm:

Ms. Jodie M. Boderman
Pro Bono Coordinator
Phone: (612) 766-8601
E-mail: jboderman@faegre.com

Does the firm have a pro bono coordinator? Yes
Ms. Jodie M. Boderman, Pro Bono Coordinator and
Dianne C. Heins, Esq., Pro Bono Counsel

If yes, what percentage of his or her time is spent on pro bono work? 100 percent

Does the firm have a pro bono committee? Yes

If yes, how often does the committee meet? The Community Service Committee meets monthly.

Describe the composition of the committee: The Community Service Committee consists of partners and associates representing the firm's various offices and the range of practice groups.

THE SCOOP

Does your firm have a written pro bono policy? Yes

Has the firm signed on to the Law Firm Pro Bono Challenge? Yes

What are some of the areas of law in which your firm has performed pro bono legal work in the last two years? Business/transactional — a wide range of services are offered to micro-entrepreneurs and nonprofit organizations, including entity formation, counseling, contracts, employment & benefits, real estate and intellectual property. Human rights — asylum, immigration, refugees, death penalty & Innocence Project appeals. Public interest advocacy for wilderness conservation and wildlife protection. Multiple community-based clinics to benefit the disadvantaged in basic legal needs (i.e., housing, family, consumer law). Housing advocacy — development and preservation of low-income housing; litigation of behalf of victims of fraudulent real estate practices (flipping/equity stripping). Media law and protection of free speech. Juvenile court matters relating to abused and neglected children.

What are some of the areas of law in which your firm does not perform pro bono work? Plaintiff-side employment law. With a few exceptions, we generally do not provide services in the areas of family law and criminal defense.

Organizations for which your firm has performed pro bono legal services in the last two years: Minneapolis — Minnesota Advocates for Human Rights, Minnesota Indian Women's Resource Center Legal Clinic, Metropolitan Economic Development Association, The Wilderness Society, American Refugee Committee. Colorado — Colorado Lawyer's Committee, Boulder Shelter for the Homeless, The Reporter's Committee for Freedom of the Press. Des Moines — The Homestead – Des Moines Public Library Foundation..

List up to three pro bono matters that are representative of the pro bono work your firm participates in.

- ·Representation of an East African immigrant entrepreneur in Minneapolis to establish a small, ethnic food manufacturing company. Provided client with advice and representation on entity formation, contracts, patent and real estate matters.

- ·Representation by a small team of lawyers of a neighborhood tenant organization to bring an action against an owner of an apartment building, mostly inhabited by Somali immigrant families. The building had a multitude of housing code violations and the building was about to be condemned. The lawyers secured a court-appointed administrator to collect the rent and make the repairs to the building to ensure the families could remain in their housing in a tight market.

- ·Representation of a guardian ad litem in a juvenile court state ward matter to ensure that a three-year-old girl with special medical needs was adopted by loving relatives in another state rather than being placed in a non-relative home.

BY THE NUMBERS

What is the total number of hours that lawyers in U.S. offices at your firm spent performing pro bono legal services in 2000, 2001 and 2002?

  Total number of hours in 2000: 18,700
  Total number of hours in 2001: 20,200
  Total number of hours in 2002: 22,000

Average number of pro bono hours per attorney in U.S. offices per year (including associates, partners, counsels, but not summer associates):

  Average number of hours per attorney in 2000: 43 hours
  Average number of hours per attorney in 2001: 48 hours
  Average number of hours per attorney in 2002: 51 hours

What percentage of attorneys in this firm's U.S. offices did pro bono work in 2002? 904 percent

What percentage of attorneys in this firm's U.S. offices did at least 20 hours of pro bono work in 2002? 20 percent

Does the firm encourage its lawyers to perform a minimum number of pro bono hours? Yes

If so, how many hours per year or what percentage of lawyers' billable hours? The firm is a signatory to the Pro Bono Challenge and delivers pro bono legal services that annually exceed 3 percent of the firm's total billable hours. The firm encourages lawyers to met the 50 hours per year goal, consistent with the aspirational goal set forth in the Minnesota Rules of Professional Responsibility 6.1.

SUPERVISION AND EVALUATIONS

Is there partner supervision on each pro bono matter? Yes

Do partner supervisors or, if applicable, senior associates provide written evaluations of associates' work on pro bono matters? Yes

If so, are those evaluations taken into account in determining salary, bonuses or advancement in the firm? Yes

If not, does the firm consider pro bono work generally in associate evaluations? Yes

HOURS

Does the firm give billable hour credit for pro bono work? Yes

Does the firm have a maximum number of pro bono hours that can be applied toward the billable hour target? No

If so, what is the maximum? N/A

If your firm uses hours to determine bonuses, does it consider pro bono hours when determining bonuses? Yes

PRO BONO POINTS

What training opportunities are open to associates working on pro bono matters? In addition to seminars offered by legal services providers and volunteer attorney programs, the firm develops internal seminars to support the projects and clinics in which our lawyers participate.

Can associates bring matters of interest to the firm? Yes

Does the firm offer the use of support staff in carrying out pro bono matters? Yes

What pro bono opportunities are available for summer associates? All pro bono matters are open for summer associate participation. In addition, we offer structured pro bono opportunities through clinics operated by legal services providers in our communities.

Does the firm have established programs, such as externships, that enable its associates to work in a public interest setting? No

Has your firm won any special recognition or awards in the last two years for its pro bono work? Yes

If so, please list.

- ·To Nancy Sagstetter (Minneapolis): Minnesota Justice Foundation's 2003 Outstanding Advocate/Support Staff Award recognizing pro bono efforts to preserve affordable housing in the Twin Cities through addressing fraudulent and predatory home sales and financing.

- ·To Jennifer Sullivan (Boulder): Boulder County Bar Association's "Young Lawyer of the Year" award recognizing pro bono involvement with the Boulder Shelter for the Homeless and the Colorado Innocence Project.

- ·To Michael Giudicessi (Des Moines): Iowa Freedom of Information Council 2002 Skip Weber Friend of the First Amendment Award recognizing service "above and beyond the call of duty" to the First Amendment and open access to government in Iowa.

- ·To Faegre & Benson Minneapolis Office: Twin Cities Rise! 2002 "Pillar Award" recognizing longtime contribution of pro bono counsel and service.

- ·To Nancy Sagstetter: 2001 Volunteer Lawyers Network "Volunteer of the Year" for pro bono service with VLN's Real Estate Flipping Project.

THE FIRM SAYS

Faegre & Benson has 475 lawyers in a full range of practice groups, with experience handling legal matters throughout the United States, as well as Europe and Asia. Established in Minneapolis in 1886, the firm has evolved into one of the 100 largest law firms in the United States, with offices in Minnesota, Colorado, Iowa, London, Frankfurt and Shanghai. The firm is the second-largest law firm in Minnesota and one of the largest firms in the Rocky Mountain region. Faegre & Benson has a long and rich tradition of providing both pro bono legal services and generous financial support to charitable institutions. The firm strongly encourages its lawyers and staff to volunteer in community activities, including social service, environmental, educational, civic and religious organizations.

Faegre & Benson is a signatory to the Pro Bono Challenge and a founding member of the Pro Bono Institute. The firm has codified its history and culture in a formal Pro Bono Policy & Procedures manual. Faegre & Benson's Policy Statement emphasizes that the firm regards pro bono legal service to be "as important as other services that the firm renders," and that the firm expects pro bono service to be "completed with the same commitment and use of the firm's resources that the firm expects with respect to its services generally." This commitment is supported by a leadership structure has matured and expanded over the past decade and is now supported by a unique staffing model for the pro bono practice. The day-to-day activities of the public service practice is administered by a team, consisting of a pro bono counsel, a non-lawyer pro bono coordinator, a community service coordinator and an administrative assistant, with each contributing specialized qualifications and roles. Leadership is provided by a nine-member community service committee, consisting of highly respected lawyers from the firm's various offices and practice groups. These innovations in infrastructure serve to highlight the commitment of the firm's top leaders and underscore the firm's policy that the public service practice be provided a level of tangible support equivalent to the firm's other practice groups. This investment also allows the firm to effectively harness, direct and sustain the efforts in a manner that deliberately integrates its pro bono legal services, community service projects and charitable giving. An equally strong commitment to public service by individual lawyers is reflected in the continued growth of the participation rates, from a respectable 65 percent in 1995 to a record 90 percent in 2002.

In many of its pro bono projects, Faegre & Benson utilizes a team model, which encourages lawyers to cut across practice groups, expand the scope of their practice beyond their individual specialization, and work creatively and collaboratively with colleagues from throughout the firm. The frequent use of team models increases the speed, efficiency and capacity of the firm to provide an effective response to pro bono requests and proactively develop projects. As a result, Faegre & Benson has developed a pro bono practice of extraordinary depth and breadth. The firm has developed an outstanding, nationally-recognized environmental law practice focusing on protection of the wilderness and endangered species. The firm also routinely handles representation of clients in cases involving human and civil rights, protection of First Amendment and free speech rights, death penalty appeals, refugee and asylum matters. On the transactional side, the firm's extensive practice includes representation and counseling of nonprofit organizations, consumer law matters, as well as business transactional, real estate and intellectual property matters. In addition, the firm operates community-based clinics in Minneapolis and Denver, which respond to the needs of low income persons for assistance in a wide variety matters.

OUR SURVEY SAYS

"The firm's commitment to pro bono work is very strong. Partners and associates at all levels actively participate in pro bono work in a variety of areas. Not only is pro bono work done by almost every lawyer in the firm, it is also encouraged by the firm's management and is a factor that is considered in annual evaluation and compensation decisions."

"I'm astounded by the level of commitment. Within the domestic offices, I'd guess that the percentage of participants is somewhere in the 80-to-90 percent range across the firm, including partners and associates."

"The attorneys at Faegre & Benson treat a pro bono case as if it's any other case. I was told by one of the most respected business attorneys in our firm that the case shouldn't be referred to as a 'pro bono' case because Faegre attorneys give their best efforts to all clients whether or not the client is pro bono."

"Pro bono opportunities are readily available in areas outside a lawyer's typical practice areas, and they offer a good opportunity for the lawyer to gain experience in other areas of the law. The firm has some relatively high-profile pro bono clients, but most of the firm's pro bono efforts are aimed directly at local individuals with important needs who lack the financial means necessary to pursue their causes."

"Pro bono efforts are taken into consideration during the annual evaluation and compensation process. Senior partners in the firm, including members of the firm's management committee, are the source of much of my pro bono opportunities, and those partners remain engaged and active throughout our representation of pro bono clients."

"Associates have a lot of autonomy and input, and I've found that is not typically true. Often, committees are staffed by managing partner-type people. But here, we get to bring in our own projects and direct our own projects. People have the ability to run cases (although they're certainly supervised)."

"Most of the attorneys in my office participate at some level in pro bono representation. I've been with the firm for a little over one year and have been involved in two pro bono projects."

Fenwick & West LLP

Silicon Valley Center
801 California Street
Mountain View, CA 94041
Phone: (650) 988-8500
www.fenwick.com

LOCATIONS

Mountain View, CA (HQ)
Boise, ID
San Francisco, CA

MAJOR DEPARTMENTS & PRACTICES

Corporate
Employment & Labor Law
Intellectual Property
Litigation
Privacy & Information Security
Tax

THE STATS

No. of attorneys: 250 +
No. of offices: 3
Chairman: Gordon K. Davidson

EMPLOYMENT CONTACT

Ms. Karen Amatangelo-Block
Attorney Recruitment Manager
Phone: (650) 335-4949
Fax: (650) 938-5200
E-mail: recruit@fenwick.com

WHO'S WHO

Principal pro bono contact(s) at your firm:

Kathryn J. Fritz, Esq.
Phone: (415) 875-2328
E-mail: kfritz@fenwick.com

Patrick E. Premo, Esq.
Phone: (650) 335-7963
E-mail: ppremo@fenwick.com

Does the firm have a pro bono coordinator? Yes
Kathryn J. Fritz and Patrick E. Premo

If yes, what percentage of his or her time is spent on pro bono work? 10 percent

Does the firm have a pro bono committee? Yes

If yes, how often does the committee meet? The pro bono committee meets on an as-needed basis.

Describe the composition of the committee: The committee consists of partners and associates from corporate, intellectual property, litigation and tax practice groups.

THE SCOOP

Does your firm have a written pro bono policy? Yes

Has the firm signed on to the Law Firm Pro Bono Challenge? No

What are some of the areas of law in which your firm has performed pro bono legal work in the last two years? Child advocacy, consumer rights, landlord/tenant disputes, advising start-up companies and entrepreneurs, Ninth Circuit pro bono appeals, AIDS project, death penalty, intellectual property/arts, tax, political asylum/immigration.

What are some of the areas of law in which your firm does not perform pro bono work? It's a case-by-case determination.

Organizations for which your firm has performed pro bono legal services in the last two years: The firm works with a wide variety of legal and not-for-profit organizations to perform pro bono legal services. Below is a partial list:

- LACY Guardianship Panel. Legal Advocates for Children & Youth, a project of the Law Foundation of Silicon Valley, provides legal assistance to minors seeking legal guardianship in part by matching them with pro bono attorneys from area firms. Fenwick attorneys have represented a number of "at risk" minors in a variety of challenging circumstances.

- Lawyers in the Library. This program, coordinated and sponsored by the Pro Bono Project Silicon Valley, helps low-income members of Santa Clara County by connecting with private attorneys willing to help with their cases on a pro bono basis. Fenwick is the only law firm in the San Francisco Bay Area that hosts the site for the drop-in clinic.

- AIDS Legal Referral Panel. ALRP serves persons living with HIV disease or AIDS in seven Bay Area counties. ALRP handles insurance disputes, guardianship and employment discrimination cases, advocates on behalf of people whose Social Security applications have been denied, fights unfair evictions, and provides wills and durable powers of attorney.

- Equal Justice Works Fellowships. Fenwick & West sponsors a fellow to work for two years on social issues such as homelessness, access to healthcare, consumer rights, domestic violence, community development, civil rights, discrimination in housing and employment, worker's rights, and children's health and welfare issues.

- Women's Technology Cluster. The WTC is an incubator for information technology businesses run by women entrepreneurs and provides office space, shared facilities, and management assistance and mentoring. In exchange for this support, WTC asks its portfolio companies to commit a percentage of their equity to a charitable Venture Philanthropy Fund. Fenwick attorneys advise the WTC and counsel WTC members in starting up their own businesses.

- VLSP's Low Income Tax Clinic and Landlord Tenant Clinic. The Volunteer Legal Services Program was established by the San Francisco Bar Association to provide free legal aid to low-income and disadvantaged people. Fenwick tax attorneys are a major source of volunteer hours for VLSP's Low-Income Taxpayer Clinic. The firm also assists with cases referred from the Landlord Tenant Clinic.

- Samuelson Law, Technology & Public Policy Clinic. Fenwick & West works closely with the Samuelson Clinic at UC Berkeley School of Law, through which students work with nonprofit organizations, the government and individuals to give a voice to the public interest on cutting-edge technology issues.

- API Legal Outreach. API Legal Outreach combines the commitment of a nonprofit, community-based organization with the professional services of a law office to work against the long-standing barriers which have denied Asian and Pacific Islander people equal justice and equal access to the legal system.

- Ninth Circuit Pro Bono Program. In 2001, Fenwick & West joined the Ninth Circuit's Pro Bono Program, formed to assist the Court in processing pro se civil appeals more equitably and efficiently. Fenwick attorneys have briefed and argued a number of cases, including appeals on behalf of a Romanian woman seeking asylum to escape political prosecution, prisoners seeking habeas corpus relief and a destitute small-businessperson seeking patent royalties.

- Volunteer Attorney Program, East Palo Alto Community Legal Services. The Volunteer Attorney Program, started in 1985 by attorneys from several Silicon Valley law firms, refers cases to attorneys in areas not handled by staff attorneys for Community Legal Services. Fenwick & West was one of VAP's earliest members and staffs VAP every six weeks on a rotating basis.

List up to three pro bono matters that are representative of the pro bono work your firm participates in.

- Pallotta TeamWorks. In April 2002, Fenwick & West filed a class action lawsuit in San Francisco Superior Court against Pallotta TeamWorks (PTW), the for-profit company that organizes "HIV/AIDS Vaccine Rides." Fenwick's class action was brought to ensure that proceeds of these rides go to organizations that conduct vaccine research.

- Patient Doe v. City and County of San Francisco, et. al. In the course of Patient Doe's treatment for AIDS and related illnesses, a billing dispute arose and the hospital disclosed Patient Doe's intimate medical details to a collection agency it had engaged. This case not only succeeded in securing a monetary award for Patient Doe; it has resulted in the issuance of a written directive to all Bureau of Delinquent Revenue ("BDR") employees that all medical records regarding a patient's diagnosis or treatment or billing may only be released to that patient.

- GranDelusion LLC. The firm worked with filmmakers on production of the full-length documentary film The Cockettes about the 1970's San Francisco performance art group.

BY THE NUMBERS

What is the total number of hours that lawyers at your firm spent performing pro bono legal services in 2000, 2001 and 2002?

    Total number of hours in 2000: 2,053 hours
    Total number of hours in 2001: 7,206 hours
    Total number of hours in 2002: 5,675 hours

Average number of pro bono hours per attorney in U.S. offices per year (including associates, partners, counsels, but not summer associates):

    Average number of hours per attorney in 2000: 7 hours/attorney
    Average number of hours per attorney in 2001: 25 hours/attorney
    Average number of hours per attorney in 2002: 22 hours/attorney

What percentage of attorneys in this firm's U.S. offices did pro bono work in 2002? 54 percent

What percentage of attorneys in this firm's U.S. offices did at least 20 hours of pro bono work in 2002? 26 percent

Does the firm encourage its lawyers to perform a minimum number of pro bono hours? Yes

If so, how many hours per year or what percentage of lawyers' billable hours? 50 hours per year

SUPERVISION AND EVALUATIONS

Is there partner supervision on each pro bono matter? Yes

Do partner supervisors or, if applicable, senior associates provide written evaluations of associates' work on pro bono matters? Yes

If so, are those evaluations taken into account in determining salary, bonuses or advancement in the firm? Yes

If not, does the firm consider pro bono work generally in associate evaluations? N/A

HOURS

Does the firm give billable hour credit for pro bono work? Yes

Does the firm have a maximum number of pro bono hours that can be applied toward the billable hour target? No

If so, what is the maximum? N/A

If your firm uses hours to determine bonuses, does it consider pro bono hours when determining bonuses? Yes

PRO BONO POINTS

What training opportunities are open to associates working on pro bono matters? Attorneys are encouraged to attend and receive pro bono credit for participation in any training seminars offered by nonprofit legal organizations in the San Francisco Bay Area.

Can associates bring matters of interest to the firm? Yes

Does the firm offer the use of support staff in carrying out pro bono matters? Yes

What pro bono opportunities are available for summer associates? Summer associates are encouraged to participate in any existing pro bono matters being handled by attorneys in the office, including any impact litigations or appeals currently pending. They may also participate in the Lawyers in the Library program, which is the drop-in advice clinic that the firm sponsors once a week, or in addition, the Volunteer Attorney Program at the East Palo Community Legal Service, which the firm staffs every six weeks.

Does the firm have established programs, such as externships, that enable its associates to work in a public interest setting? No

If so, where and for up to how long? N/A

Has your firm won any special recognition or awards in the last two years for its pro bono work? Yes

If so, please list. William Colgin, partner in the tax group, was awarded Outstanding Volunteer in Public Service for 2002 and 2003 from the Volunteer Legal Services Program sponsored by the San Francisco County Bar Association for his work on the VLSP's Low Income Tax Clinic.

THE FIRM SAYS

Fenwick's Pro Bono Policy

The firm will recognize all approved pro bono work as "billable" hours for all purposes. The firm strongly supports pro bono work and encourages attorneys to take advantage of opportunities such as these to earn billable hours while performing a worthwhile community service.

Preliminary Statement

Fenwick & West recognizes that providing pro bono legal services is an important part of our professional responsibility as individuals and as a firm. Pro bono work also benefits those who participate. Individuals can gain valuable practical experience, learn new areas of the law and contribute to their community.

Fenwick & West encourages and supports the work performed by its legal staff on pro bono matters.

Fenwick & West suggests that each individual attorney set aside time each year to devote to pro bono work, recognizing that the number of hours devoted to pro bono work will vary depending on the type of matter(s) undertaken. The California State Bar has suggested a guideline of 50 hours per year. The maximum amount of time an individual may devote to pro bono matters has not been predetermined, although each attorney must be mindful of his/her responsibilities to our clients, to the firm and to his or her own professional development in his or her own substantive areas.

Fenwick & West also recognizes that each individual has particular interests and commitments, and will choose to devote his or her time differently. Although the firm encourages all of its legal staff, partners as well as associates, to participate, the firm's pro bono program is voluntary.

Definition of Pro Bono Legal Services

A. Pro bono legal services are defined as the provision of legal services to individuals, charitable organizations or a community that cannot afford to hire legal counsel and otherwise might go unrepresented, or to charitable organizations serving the public interest.

Although not an exhaustive list, pro bono activities can include representing or advising indigent individuals, providing advice or assistance to a community that cannot afford counsel or to charitable organizations serving the public interest, or engaging in community education efforts on issues of importance to those who cannot afford legal counsel. (Other noteworthy and uncompensated activities such as participation in civic and professional activities do not fall within the firm's definition of pro bono legal services.)

B. Because it is difficult to define pro bono legal services precisely, the firm's pro bono review committee will determine in its discretion whether and on what terms the firm will accept a particular matter as pro bono.

Pro Bono Committee

A. Objective: The objective of the pro bono committee is to develop an effective pro bono program and integrate that program into the practice and culture of the firm. The pro bono committee will provide information, coordination, supervision and direction to individuals who want to undertake pro bono work. The managing partners will oversee the work of the pro bono committee.

B. Proposals: Individuals interested in undertaking a pro bono matter on behalf of the firm must submit a proposal to the pro bono review committee. The proposal should include a description of the matter, the contribution such work will make to the community, an estimate of the time and expense commitment that such matter will require, and a description of how the matter will contribute to the individual's development. Individuals may also express an interest in a particular subject area and request that the committee assist them in developing pro bono work in that area.

OUR SURVEY SAYS

"The firm is committed to pro bono, allowing up to 100 hours of pro bono work to count toward total billables. But when it is busy in litigation, pro bono work takes second billing."

"The firm leaves it up to the individual as to whether to do pro bono work (giving up to 100 billable hours of credit). Some people do a lot; some do none."

"It's a joke to some, but some people really take it seriously. We're doing a death penalty case now, and it's a big deal here."

"[The firm is] committed but [has] trouble getting associates motivated for some reason. More partners should take it seriously."

"There is pro bono work for those who want it, and we get credit for up to 100 hours."

* The firm notes that these associate quotes were made under the firm's former policy of capping pro bono credit at 100 hours. The firm points out that it has since removed that cap.

> "Fenwick & West recognizes that providing pro bono legal services is an important part of our professional responsibility as individuals and as a firm."
>
> — *Fenwick & West LLP*

Fish & Neave

1251 Avenue of the Americas
New York, NY 10020
Phone: (212) 596-9000
www.fishneave.com

LOCATIONS

New York, NY (HQ)
Palo Alto, CA
Washington, DC

MAJOR DEPARTMENTS & PRACTICES

Intellectual PropertyLitigation (Patents, Trademarks, Copyrights, Trade Secrets, Licensing Disputes, Patent Misuse, Antitrust Issues, Unfair Competition)
Patent Prosecution & Interference Work
Trademark Prosecution

THE STATS

No. of attorneys worldwide: 185
No. of offices worldwide: 3
Managing Partner: Jesse J. Jenner

EMPLOYMENT CONTACT

Ms. Heather C. Fennell
Legal Recruitment Manager
Phone: (212) 596-9121
E-mail: hfennell@fishneave.com

WHO'S WHO

Principal pro bono contact(s) at your firm:

Richard A. Inz, Esq.
Partner
Phone: (212) 596-9130
E-mail: rinz@fishneave.com

A. Joy Arnold, Esq.
Partner
Phone: (212) 596-9140
E-mail: jarnold@fishneave.com

Does the firm have a pro bono coordinator? No

Does the firm have a pro bono committee? Yes

If yes, how often does the committee meet? As needed.

Describe the composition of the committee: Partners and associates.

THE SCOOP

Does your firm have a written pro bono policy? Yes

Has the firm signed on to the Law Firm Pro Bono Challenge? No

What are some of the areas of law in which your firm has performed pro bono legal work in the last two years? Litigations involving discrimination against persons with disabilities (against Duane Reade Inc.) and against Latinos (discriminatory housing code violation enforcement); nonprofit incorporations and tax exempt status; trademark registration applications; patent applications.

What are some of the areas of law in which your firm does not perform pro bono work? Criminal law; contested marital and child custody matters.

Organizations for which your firm has performed pro bono legal services in the last two years: Disabled in Action of Metropolitan New York, Inc.; People's Baptist Church; Public Education Network; New York Lawyers for the Public Interest (as client and clearinghouse); The Bay Cup; Advocates For Children of New York, Inc. (co-counsel); The Ogichidaa Scholarship Fund, Inc.; Civil Rights Bureau of the Attorney General of New York State (associated counsel); The Legal Aid Society (clearinghouse), including the Immigrant Youth Representation Project; Johns Hopkins University; The Rocky Mountain Cherokee Indian Association; Fragile X Association of New York, Inc.; The National Neurofibromatosis Foundation, Inc.

List up to three pro bono matters that are representative of the pro bono work your firm participates in.

- ·Fish & Neave (with co-counsel NYLPI) represents plaintiff Disabled in Action of Metropolitan New York, Inc. and individual plaintiffs against Duane Reade Inc., a major drugstore chain in New York City. The plaintiffs charge Duane Reade with violating their civil rights under the Americans with Disabilities Act, the Rehabilitation Act of 1973 and the

New York City Human Rights Law. They seek an injunction that would require Duane Reade to make all necessary changes to the layouts of their stores, guaranteeing access to all services, especially the pharmacy, to disabled persons, specifically those with mobility challenges. Fish & Neave attorneys have been involved in all aspects of the litigation, drafting the complaint, appearing in federal court and participating in settlement discussions.

- ·At the request of NYLPI, Fish & Neave associates are representing witnesses at depositions who were subjected to discriminatory housing code enforcement in an action brought by the Office of the Attorney General of the State of New York against The Village of Freeport, Long Island.

- ·Fish & Neave successfully defended the People's Baptist Church in a breach-of-contract action involving a construction project at the church. After a one-day trial, first-chaired by a Fish & Neave associate, the court dismissed the plaintiff's complaint.

BY THE NUMBERS

What is the total number of hours that lawyers in U.S. offices at your firm spent performing pro bono legal services in 2000, 2001 and 2002?

    Total number of hours in 2000: 2,365 hours
    Total number of hours in 2001: 4,520 hours
    Total number of hours in 2002: 2,475 hours

Average number of pro bono hours per attorney in U.S. offices per year (including associates, partners, counsels, but not summer associates):

    Average number of hours per attorney in 2000: N/A
    Average number of hours per attorney in 2001: N/A
    Average number of hours per attorney in 2002: N/A

What percentage of attorneys in this firm's U.S. offices did pro bono work in 2002? About 21 percent.

What percentage of attorneys in this firm's U.S. offices did at least 20 hours of pro bono work in 2002? N/A

Does the firm encourage its lawyers to perform a minimum number of pro bono hours? N/A

If so, how many hours per year or what percentage of lawyers' billable hours? N/A

SUPERVISION AND EVALUATIONS

Is there partner supervision on each pro bono matter? Yes

Do partner supervisors or, if applicable, senior associates provide written evaluations of associates' work on pro bono matters? Yes

If so, are those evaluations taken into account in determining salary, bonuses or advancement in the firm? Yes

If not, does the firm consider pro bono work generally in associate evaluations? N/A

HOURS

Does the firm give billable hour credit for pro bono work? Yes

Does the firm have a maximum number of pro bono hours that can be applied toward the billable hour target? No

If so, what is the maximum? N/A

If your firm uses hours to determine bonuses, does it consider pro bono hours when determining bonuses? Not applicable

PRO BONO POINTS

What training opportunities are open to associates working on pro bono matters? Training often is available from the clearinghouse; CLE seminars are available for pro bono subjects.

Can associates bring matters of interest to the firm? Yes

Does the firm offer the use of support staff in carrying out pro bono matters? Yes

What pro bono opportunities are available for summer associates? NYLPI. In the summer of 2003, summer associates participated in NYLPI's summer internship program. Three associates spent a week under the supervision of the City-Wide Task Force on Housing Court, two spent a week under the supervision of the Mental Hygiene Legal Service and two spent a week under the supervision of cases.org. During the internships, the summer associates assisted attorneys in providing services including clarification of legal documents, education about tenant rights and proper court procedure, advocacy of individual cases, referral to community-based housing organizations and various other services.

Does the firm have established programs, such as externships, that enable its associates to work in a public interest setting? No

Has your firm won any special recognition or awards in the last two years for its pro bono work? No

THE FIRM SAYS

Based on each individual's interests, partners, associates and summer associates alike are given the freedom to choose which pro bono matters they wish to be involved in. Many of our attorneys have availed themselves of this opportunity and are currently involved in a number of diverse and rewarding projects, some being intimately related to our general practice area and some far afield.

In line with our efforts of supporting our community through charitable work, Fish & Neave has partnered with various organizations such as New York Lawyers for the Public Interest (NYLPI), Sanctuary for Families, the Federal Pro Bono Project of the U.S. District Court for the Northern District of California and the Santa Clara County Bar Association. In the past, several attorneys in our Palo Alto office have received certificates "in recognition of outstanding contributions to the delivery of pro bono legal services in Santa Clara County." Also, the firm brought in Federal District Judge James J. Ware to moderate a training session at our Palo Alto office, designed to help provide information to our attorneys about the Pro Bono Project and its policies.

In addition to working with the organizations listed above, many of our attorneys are also associated as members and officers, with several having served on the board of directors and other committees. Examples of such relations include the NYLPI, where one of our partners recently served as Chair of the Board; The Legal Aid Society and Legal Services for the City of New York, where several Fish & Neave attorneys served on the boards of each organization; the Hudson Highlands Land Trust; and numerous other bar associations and civic groups.

As mentioned above, in a highly publicized suit, Fish & Neave attorneys are representing Disabled in Action of Metropolitan New York, Inc. against the Duane Reade drug store chain, charging Duane Reade with civil rights violations. And in a recently completed litigation, Fish & Neave successfully defended the People's Baptist Church in a breach-of-contract action involving a construction project at the church. This action, in New York State Civil Court, involved a one-day trial first-chaired by a Fish & Neave associate.

Fish & Neave attorneys also successfully took on the New York State Education Department, compelling the Department to comply with its regulations governing responding to requests for accommodations for high-school-equivalency-diploma testing.

Fish & Neave attorneys have tried a prisoner's rights case, prepared a habeas corpus petition seeking a stay of execution in capital punishment matters, represented handicapped students in an access to education case and counseled environmental groups. They have also represented a former prisoner in an access to medical treatment case and a former prison guard in a harassment and discrimination case. Recently, some of our attorneys took on a New York City Department of Education special education matter, acquired through our affiliation with NYLPI.

Fish & Neave attorneys were co-counsel with the Public Interest Law Firm (a project of the Santa Clara County Bar Association Law Foundation) and obtained a settlement halting a new policy that would have permitted jail officials to monitor without permission telephone calls between inmates and their attorneys, physicians and clergy.

Pro bono matters are staffed as would any matter at the firm. Small matters would have one, or maybe two, associates, with a supervising partner. More involved matters, such as the litigation involving Duane Reade, involve more attorneys. Pro bono matters are done on a voluntary basis; no one is assigned to a pro bono matter.

OUR SURVEY SAYS

"Let's see: I can volunteer to draft and prosecute biotech patent applications for the homeless? Not likely. And I think that explains the absence of pro bono work."

"Very few opportunities."

"Some attempt to get pro bono matters, but not much real commitment to pursue them."

"The firm is not very involved with pro bono activities, but I do not perceive this as a negative trait."

"Fish has a limited pro bono program. Because of insurance reasons we are not allowed to pursue pro bono opportunities in any area of criminal law."

"I don't know of any pro bono cases worked on right now."

The firm responds that, while it may not "prosecuted a biotech patent application for the homeless," an associate and a apartner recently obtained a patent on behalf of The National Neurofibromatosis Foundation, Inc., a non-profit organization devoted to education and research conerning this disease. And the firm provided incorporation, tax-exempt status and ongoing advice for this and many other non-profit organizations, as wellas undertaking substantial pro bono litigation projects. The firm regrets that it apparently has not suggiciently publicized these activities within the firm.

Fish & Richardson P.C.

225 Franklin Street
Boston, MA 02110-2804
Phone: 617-542-5070
www.fr.com

LOCATIONS

We have no main office; we have full service offices in eight cities. The pro bono chair is resident in Boston.

Boston, MA
Dallas, TX
Minneapolis, MN
New York, NY
Redwood City, CA
San Diego, CA
Washington, DC
Wilmington, DE

MAJOR DEPARTMENTS & PRACTICES

Appellate
Corporate & Securities
Entertainment & Media
International Regulatory Group
Litigation & Dispute Resolution
Patent Prosecution & Strategic Counseling
Trademarks & Copyrights
U.S. International Trade Commission
Proceedings

THE STATS

No. of attorneys worldwide: 300 +
No. of offices worldwide: 8
President: Peter J. Devlin

EMPLOYMENT CONTACT

Ms. Jill E. McDonald
Firm-wide Director of Attorney Hiring
Phone: (858) 678-5070
Fax: (858) 678-5099
E-mail: work@fr.com

WHO'S WHO

Does the firm have a pro bono coordinator? Yes

Heidi E. Harvey, Esq.
Principal
Phone: (617) 521-7815
E-mail: harvey@fr.com

If yes, what percentage of his or her time is spent on pro bono work? 10 percent

Does the firm have a pro bono committee? Yes

If yes, how often does the committee meet? Four times a year.

Describe the composition of the committee: The pro bono committee is made up of principals and associates representing each office of the firm as well as ex officio membership by the firm's practice group leaders.

THE SCOOP

Does your firm have a written pro bono policy? Yes

Has the firm signed on to the Law Firm Pro Bono Challenge? No

What are some of the areas of law in which your firm has performed pro bono legal work in the last two years? Veterans' rights; asylum and immigration; federal criminal defense; environmental law; First Amendment; artists' rights; family law; special prosecutor appointment; patent, copyright and trademark counseling and litigation; corporate counseling; death penalty representation.

What are some of the areas of law in which your firm does not perform pro bono work? ERISA, tax.

Organizations for which your firm has performed pro bono legal services in the last two years: Volunteer Lawyers for the Arts, Disabled American Veterans, Political Asylum and Immigration Representation Project, ACLU.

List up to three pro bono matters that are representative of the pro bono work your firm participates in.

- ·Immigration — The firm represents individuals in asylum matters before the BCIS and the United States District Courts, including appeals to the BIA and the Courts of Appeal.

- ·Federal Criminal Defense — The firm represents, by appointment from the U.S. District Court, criminal defendants in federal matters.

- ·Artists' Rights — The firm advises artists, authors and other individuals regarding intellectual property, corporate and contract matters through artists legal services organizations, including in litigation in selected cases.

BY THE NUMBERS

What is the total number of hours that lawyers in U.S. offices at your firm spent performing pro bono legal services in 2000, 2001 and 2002?

> Total number of hours in 2000: not tracked
> Total number of hours in 2001: 1,000 hours
> Total number of hours in 2002: 1,700 hours

Average number of pro bono hours per attorney in U.S. offices per year (including associates, partners, counsels, but not summer associates):

> Average number of hours per attorney in 2000: not tracked
> Average number of hours per attorney in 2001: 4 hours
> Average number of hours per attorney in 2002: 5 hours

What percentage of attorneys in this firm's U.S. offices did pro bono work in 2002? 25 percent

What percentage of attorneys in this firm's U.S. offices did at least 20 hours of pro bono work in 2002? 8 percent

Does the firm encourage its lawyers to perform a minimum number of pro bono hours? Yes

If so, how many hours per year or what percentage of lawyers' billable hours? The firm gives up to 50 hours billable credit to associates toward bonus goal levels.

SUPERVISION AND EVALUATIONS

Is there partner supervision on each pro bono matter? Yes

Do partner supervisors or, if applicable, senior associates provide written evaluations of associates' work on pro bono matters? Yes

If so, are those evaluations taken into account in determining salary, bonuses or advancement in the firm? Yes

If not, does the firm consider pro bono work generally in associate evaluations? N/A

HOURS

Does the firm give billable hour credit for pro bono work? Yes

Does the firm have a maximum number of pro bono hours that can be applied toward the billable hour target? Yes

If so, what is the maximum? 50 hours

If your firm uses hours to determine bonuses, does it consider pro bono hours when determining bonuses? Yes

PRO BONO POINTS

What training opportunities are open to associates working on pro bono matters? The firm encourages and pays for training offered by legal services organizations and continuing legal education in areas of pro bono representation; the firm will also pay for "of counsel" services of experts in complex matters to support pro bono cases.

Can associates bring matters of interest to the firm? Yes

Does the firm offer the use of support staff in carrying out pro bono matters? Yes

What pro bono opportunities are available for summer associates? All of the same opportunities available to counsel; appearance in court contingent upon the local rules regarding appearances of non-attorneys.

Does the firm have established programs, such as externships, that enable its associates to work in a public interest setting? Yes

If so, where and for up to how long? The firm has funded an externship for incoming associates to work in legal services in South Africa; this is the first year of the program and the firm hopes to expand its support for this and other externship programs.

Has your firm won any special recognition or awards in the last two years for its pro bono work? No

THE FIRM SAYS

Fish & Richardson is committed to dispelling the myth that firms with significant IP practices don't do pro bono. Through a grassroots effort formally organized in 2001, the firm's associates are the principal movers behind a firm-wide expansion of pro bono representation and increase in the firm's overall pro bono representation. The matters the firm handles in pro bono today reflect the diversity of the firm's attorneys and experience, and the firm handles matters in any area where the firm is able to provide training and supervision with the same level of competence as its core practices of intellectual property, litigation and corporate law. Some of these areas include criminal defense, environmental law, immigration, artist's rights, veteran's rights, and labor and employment law.

In the past two years of formal oversight and tracking, the number of firm attorneys who actively represent pro bono matters has increased from a handful to 33 percent of the firm's attorneys, and the total number of new pro bono matters and hours has doubled. In the coming year, the firm's goal is to achieve an average of 20 pro bono hours per attorney and to increase participation of the firm's attorneys in pro bono representation to 60 percent, as well as to increase the billable hour credit for pro bono work and the budget to support pro bono.

The firm will consider any pro bono matter that can be competently supervised, and associates are encouraged to bring pro bono matters to the firm as well as to establish ongoing liaison relationships with legal services organizations in each community where the firm has offices. Associates serve on the pro bono committee and coordinate local matters, and the associates of the firm and the young attorneys entering the firm will be a driving force in setting the firm's pro bono policies and direction in the future.

OUR SURVEY SAYS

"As an IP boutique, we do not regularly practice in an area that has opportunities for pro bono."

"The commitment from the firm to pro bono support is growing significantly. The firm now provides a limited credit for approved pro bono toward hours-based bonuses."

"The firm encourages pro bono participation and last year instituted a policy that 50 percent of pro bono hours could count towards the hours-based bonus. However, everyone seems so busy with billable work that pro bono seems to have been forgotten."

"The firm is very committed to 'allowing' its associates to do pro bono work, but there is no formal program and so the opportunities are not presented unless you go out and find [them] yourself."

"Fifty-percent credit for hours worked on pro bono cases, as long as you've first met your billable goal. I'm not sure how this compares to other firms. Basically, the feeling is that you can take on a pro bono project, but you'll probably be doing it on your own time."

"If only I could pry myself from all this work...."

"A small group of people are very committed to pro bono and are working to make the firm culture more accepting."

"It varies from person to person, but overall does not appear to be a high priority."

"The firm only gives 'credit' for pro bono work AFTER you have met your annual billable goal (and then only at a rate of 50 percent of actual time billed). Time billed in excess of the annual goal goes toward meeting various bonus levels."

"This is probably the area that could use the most improvement at a firm-wide level. There are individuals here [who are] very committed to pro bono."

"Fish & Richardson is committed to dispelling the myth that firms with significant IP practices don't do pro bono."

— *Fish & Richardson P.C.*

Fried, Frank, Harris, Shriver & Jacobson LLP

One New York Plaza
New York, NY 10004
Phone: (212) 859-8000
www.friedfrank.com

LOCATIONS

New York, NY (HQ)
Los Angeles, CA
Washington, DC
London
Paris

MAJOR DEPARTMENTS & PRACTICES

Antitrust
Arbitration & Alternative Dispute Resolution
Asset Management
Bankruptcy & Restructuring
Benefits & Compensation
Capital Markets
Corporate
Electronic Commerce
Environmental
Finance
Insurance
Intellectual Property & Technology
International Trade
Litigation
Mergers & Acquisitions
Private Equity
Real Estate
Securities Regulation, Compliance & Enforcement
Tax
Trusts & Estates
White Collar Crime

THE STATS

No. of attorneys worldwide: 550
No. of offices worldwide: 5
Co-Managing Partners: Valerie Ford Jacob and Paul M. Reinstein

EMPLOYMENT CONTACT

New York
Elizabeth M. McDonald, Esq.
Director of Legal Recruitment
Phone: (212) 859-8621
E-mail: elizabeth.mcdonald@friedfrank.com

Los Angeles
Ms. Marian Wilk Gibbs
Recruiting Administrator
Phone: (213) 473-2049
E-mail: marian.wilk.@friedfrank.com

Washington
Ms. Niki Kopsidas
Recruitment Manager
Phone: (202) 639-7286
E-mail: niki.kopsidas@friedfrank.com

WHO'S WHO

Principal pro bono contact(s) at your firm:

New York Office:
Jennifer L. Colyer, Special Counsel
Phone: (212) 859-8285
E-mail: jennifer.colyer@friedfrank.com

Lois F. Herzeca, Partner
Phone: (212) 859-8076
E-mail: lois.herzeca@friedfrank.com

Lee Parks, Partner
Phone: (212) 859-8142
E-mail: lee.parks@friedfrank.com

Mark J. Stein, Partner
Phone: (212) 859-8552
E-mail: mark.stein@friedfrank.com

Washington Office:
Karen T. Grisez, Special Counsel for Public Service
Phone: (202) 639-7043
E-mail: karen.grisez@friedfrank.com

David L. Ansell, Partner
Phone: (202) 639-7011
E-mail: david.ansell@friedfrank.com

Douglas W. Baruch, Partner
Phone: (202) 639-7052
E-mail: douglas.baruch@friedfrank.com

Does the firm have a pro bono coordinator? Yes
New York Office: Jennifer L. Colyer, Esq.
Washington Office: Karen T. Grisez, Esq.

If yes, what percentage of his or her time is spent on pro bono work? Ms. Colyer: 50 percent; Ms. Grisez: 100 percent.

Does the firm have a pro bono committee? Yes

If yes, how often does the committee meet? Three to six times per year.

Describe the composition of the committee: New York office: The committee is comprised of 19 partners, counsel and associates drawn from various departments and practices within the firm. The director of marketing and the executive director of associate affairs also sit on the committee.

Washington office: The committee consists of three partners from the litigation and corporate departments, the special counsel for public Service, the director of associate development and five associates, drawn from all practice groups and seniority levels.

THE SCOOP

Does your firm have a written pro bono policy? Yes

Has the firm signed on to the Law Firm Pro Bono Challenge? New York office: No. Washington office: Yes.

What are some of the areas of law in which your firm has performed pro bono legal work in the last two years? Immigration (focusing on asylum); family/domestic violence/children's law; micro-entrepreneurs and not-for-profit; entertainment and the arts; predatory lending litigation; insurance litigation; criminal law; community economic development; September 11, 2001 Victim's Compensation Fund; trusts/estates.

What are some of the areas of law in which your firm does not perform pro bono work? Subject to conflict issues, the firm takes on pro bono projects where it feels it can provide effective assistance in areas of need. There is no specific prohibition on any type of pro bono activity.

Organizations for which your firm has performed pro bono legal services in the last two years: New York Office: Lawyers Committee for Human Rights, National Foundation for Teaching Entrepreneurship, NAACP Legal Defense and Education Fund, Mexican American Legal Defense and Education Fund, Office of the Appellate Defender, Volunteer Lawyers for the Arts, Legal Aid Society of New York, inMotion, New York Lawyers for the Public Interest, Gay Men's Health Crisis.

Washington Office: Lawyers Committee for Human Rights, Families Against Mandatory Minimums, D.C. Bar Pro Bono Program, U.S. District Court Civil Pro Bono Panel, Whitman Walker Clinic, Children's Law Center, Legal Aid Society of D.C., Legal Counsel for the Elderly, National Veterans Legal Services Program, Washington Area Lawyers for the Arts.

List up to three pro bono matters that are representative of the pro bono work your firm participates in.

New York office: Representation of asylum seekers from various nations to obtain asylum protection from persecution based primarily on political opinion and sexual orientation. Representation of Ms. L., an elderly woman who was a victim of a predatory lending scheme, in a civil lawsuit. Transactional legal assistance to Harlem RBI, an organization dedicated to preserving and promoting baseball for inner city children.

Washington office: We have been involved since the mid-1980's in the post conviction appeals of a Texas death row inmate. A Fifth Circuit panel reversed the conviction and sentence, but the en banc court reversed the panel decision. We await the panel's decision after reargument on remand. We recently successfully represented D.C. prison inmates in having the existing system for scheduling parole revocation hearing ruled unconstitutional and in obtaining a consent decree that redesigned the entire system. Finally, we represented several asylum seekers in obtaining protection from the risk of persecution in their home countries, with a particular emphasis on representing women facing gender-based persecution.

BY THE NUMBERS

What is the total number of hours that lawyers in U.S. offices at your firm spent performing pro bono legal services in 2000, 2001 and 2002?

    Total number of hours in 2000: 37,478 hours
    Total number of hours in 2001: 40,958 hours
    Total number of hours in 2002: 38,723 hours

Average number of pro bono hours per attorney in U.S. offices per year (including associates, partners, counsels, but not summer associates):

    Average number of hours per attorney in 2000: 81 hours
    Average number of hours per attorney in 2001: 80 hours
    Average number of hours per attorney in 2002: 74 hours

What percentage of attorneys in this firm's U.S. offices did pro bono work in 2002? 65 percent

What percentage of attorneys in this firm's U.S. offices did at least 20 hours of pro bono work in 2002? 50 percent

Does the firm encourage its lawyers to perform a minimum number of pro bono hours? No, but we encourage all those who are interested to participate in the pro bono program. The Washington office does have an hours expectation, as described in the firm narrative below.

If so, how many hours per year or what percentage of lawyers' billable hours? N/A

SUPERVISION AND EVALUATIONS

Is there partner supervision on each pro bono matter? Yes

Do partner supervisors or, if applicable, senior associates provide written evaluations of associates' work on pro bono matters? Yes

If so, are those evaluations taken into account in determining salary, bonuses or advancement in the firm? Pro bono matter evaluations do not affect salary and do not directly affect bonuses. They play a role in decisions about advancement, just as evaluation of work on billable matters does.

If not, does the firm consider pro bono work generally in associate evaluations? Yes, as noted above

HOURS

Does the firm give billable hour credit for pro bono work? Yes

Does the firm have a maximum number of pro bono hours that can be applied toward the billable hour target? New York office: No. Washington office: Up to 150 hours can count toward bonuses, with permission given in appropriate circumstances for a higher number of hours to be credited.

If so, what is the maximum? See above

PRO BONO POINTS

What training opportunities are open to associates working on pro bono matters? Virtually all of our partner organizations offer training for their matters and ongoing support for associates, notably InMotion, Lawyers Committee for Human Rights, The Legal Aid Society, the D.C. Bar Pro Bono Program and the Office of the Appellate Defender. Information about appropriate training opportunities is regularly circulated to attorneys via e-mail, in memos and in the Pro Bono newsletter.

Can associates bring matters of interest to the firm? Yes

Does the firm offer the use of support staff in carrying out pro bono matters? Yes

What pro bono opportunities are available for summer associates? New York office: Summer associates are staffed on a variety of pro bono matters depending on need and on the summer associates' interests. In addition to integrating summer associates into existing projects, there are several programs tailored specifically for summer associates, including the Courtroom Advocates Project of Sanctuary for Families, which allows summer associates to appear in Family Court on behalf of indigent women seeking orders of protection. We also work with InMotion, which assists indigent and abused women in obtaining uncontested divorces. Summer associates also may participate in a number of externships with different organizations, which have in the past included the Legal Aid Society and the Pro Bono Asylum Representation Project ("ProBAR"). Last summer the ProBAR project involved two summer associates from each of our New York and Washington offices, who spent two weeks at ProBAR in Texas, successfully representing two detained clients in their Immigration Court hearings.

Washington office: Summer associates are each expected to work on at least one pro bono matter of their choosing during the summer. This can involve integration to an existing pro bono project team, bringing in new matters to accommodate summer associate preferences, or taking on special projects designed specifically for summer associate participation, such as the ProBAR project, described above.

Does the firm have established programs, such as externships, that enable its associates to work in a public interest setting? Yes

If so, where and for up to how long? We have several externships and fellowships. The Legal Aid Society Externship is a four-month rotating externship that is open to mid-level associates. The associates work in the offices of the Legal Aid Society's Community Development Office assisting small business owners with a variety of transactional issues, including incorporation, financing and lease negotiation.

The NAACP Legal Defense and Education Fund (LDF) and The Mexican American Legal Defense and Education Fund (MALDEF) Fellowships are each awarded to one applicant per year. Fellows spend two years as associates in the firm's litigation department. They then spend a subsequent term of two years in one of MALDEF's or LDF's offices. After a fellow successfully completes the four-year program, he or she may opt to return to Fried Frank as a fifth-year litigation associate.

Has your firm won any special recognition or awards in the last two years for its pro bono work? Yes

If so, please list.

New York office: In November 2003, the firm was honored when the National Center on Poverty Law renamed itself the Sargent Shriver National Center on Poverty Law in honor of firm partner Sargent Shriver. An award in Recognition of Outstanding Service was presented to partners Lois Herzeca and Sanford Krieger from the National Foundation for

Teaching Entrepreneurship in 2002. Litigation partner Janice MacAvoy was presented with the 2002 Commitment to Justice Award from InMotion. In 2002 and 2003, associates and partners have been presented with Pro Bono Publico awards from the Legal Aid Society in recognition for service. In 2002 Fried Frank was also presented with the Law Firm Access to Justice Award.

Washington office: In fall 2002, we won a Law Firm Award from the Washington Council of Lawyers. In April 2003, we were one of seven firms honored by the Judicial Conference of the D.C. Circuit with its "40 at 50" award, for having more than 40 percent of our individual lawyers meeting the Circuit's 50-hour requirement for pro bono service. In January 2004, the Washington office received the inaugural Marvin Frankel Award for its outstanding contribution to the Lawyers Committee for Human Rights' asylum program.

THE FIRM SAYS

New York Office

Fried Frank's pro bono program continues the firm's long-standing tradition of public service. This commitment is reflected in the wide-ranging pro bono work performed over the years by attorneys, summer associates and legal assistants in such areas as representing indigent individuals accused of crimes, assisting micro-entrepreneurs and non-profits with corporate, intellectual property, tax and real estate issues, representing non-citizens who seek to enter or remain in this country or are threatened with denial of basic civil liberties, working on behalf of victims of predatory lending practices and representing other persons in desperate need of legal assistance.

The firm believes that pro bono and public service work is the professional obligation of the firm and each of our individual lawyers. While pro bono work is not required by the New York State Bar Association, the firm encourages each attorney in the New York office to devote substantial attention each year to one or more pro bono or public service matters. To that end, our pro bono committee is available to assist every attorney in finding pro bono projects consistent with their areas of substantive interest, level of experience and public policy preferences. In addition to those programs and organizations with which the firm has established partnerships, the firm also circulates pro bono matters which have been referred to the firm for possible representation. Various organizations routinely sponsor seminars on substantive areas of the law such as asylum, landlord/tenant, immigration, family law, AIDS advocacy, prisoners' rights, and many others, which may also result in referrals.

Moreover, many of the lawyers at the firm have commitments to organizations or issues which generate pro bono opportunities. The firm recognizes that pro bono activities and public service to a large extent are a matter of individual choice and strives to allow attorneys to select the matters to which they devote their energies. Attorneys are therefore encouraged to bring these opportunities to the pro bono committee for consideration and approval. The firm uses the ABA guidelines to determine which matters qualify for approval.

At Fried Frank, pro bono clients are firm clients and, as a matter of policy, the firm provides the same level of professional commitment and zealous representation to pro bono clients as are devoted to billable matters. The firm's resources are available on an equal basis to attorneys working on pro bono matters.

Washington Office

The Washington office has an expectation, drawn from Rule 6.1 of the D.C. Rules of Professional Conduct, that each attorney will devote a minimum of 50 hours per year to pro bono service. It has also signed on to the Law Firm Pro Bono Challenge.

The Special Counsel for Public Service keeps attorneys informed about pro bono opportunities available in Washington, matches attorneys with appropriate projects based on individual interests and skill levels, and publicizes relevant training programs. Attorneys may propose particular matters to the pro bono committee. Up to 150 pro bono hours can count toward bonuses, with permission given in appropriate circumstances for higher number of hours to be credited.

Representative matters include landlord/tenant cases; family law matters, including adoptions, guardianship and GAL matters; Social Security disability; veterans' benefits cases; political asylum and other immigration matters; death penalty and other prisoners litigation; general corporate counseling of nonprofits; community economic development work; transactional work, including financing for purchase and renovation of a building by a tenant cooperative; debt counseling; and government contracts work for low-income housing providers.

OUR SURVEY SAYS

"The firm is very strongly committed to pro bono and you can easily get pro bono work if you want it. The firm has received awards for its pro bono work and is generally very good about attending events promoting or recognizing worthy causes."

"This is the best firm for pro bono I've ever run across! There is a dedicated counsel who does pro bono and helps associates do it. This isn't just a lip service situation. There is a [D.C. jurisdictional] requirement to do 50 hours a year and the ability to do much, much more. Fried Frank should be applauded for their very real commitment to 'give back' to the community through their pro bono service!"

"I have already completed two pro bono assignments in six months."

"I have had amazing opportunities in pro bono work including WTC relief efforts and federal criminal cases. We don't just talk, we do, and hours are hours whether pro bono or billable."

"Pro bono work is strongly encouraged. Excellent, excellent externship opportunities are available as well in all areas of practice. There are many partners who put in significant time. I do believe that Fried Frank's commitment is genuine and goes beyond the mercenary pursuit of good PR."

"Many attorneys do pro bono work here — and it is certainly supported. We have a full-time pro bono coordinator who is great. However, despite what is on the recruiting brochures, not all partners believe that pro bono hours should be treated as or viewed as carrying the same weight as billables."

"I can take on all the pro bono I want (workload allowing), [and] the hours count towards my billables. Several partners set a fantastic example of being dedicated to pro bono matters."

"The firm is very committed to pro bono work, not only of the litigation variety, but also for corporate associates to help with as well."

"I have been able to take on pro bono work as often as I would like."

"Fried Frank has just begun a four-month externship for junior associates at The Legal Aid Society. Fried Frank sends a second-, third- or fourth-year associate (usually from the corporate department) to work exclusively at The Legal Aid Society for four months. It's pretty amazing."

"At Fried Frank, pro bono clients are firm clients and, as a matter of policy, the firm provides the same level of professional commitment and zealous representation to pro bono clients as are devoted to billable matters."

— *Fried, Frank, Harris, Shriver & Jacobson*

Fulbright & Jaworski L.L.P.

1301 McKinney Street, Suite 5100
Houston, TX 77010-3095
Phone: (713) 651-5151
www.fulbright.com

LOCATIONS

Houston, TX (HQ)
Austin, TX
Dallas, TX
Los Angeles, CA
Minneapolis, MN
New York, NY
San Antonio, TX
Washington, DC
Hong Kong
London
Munich

MAJOR DEPARTMENTS & PRACTICES

Admiralty • Antitrust, Marketing & Trade Regulation • Appellate • Arbitration & ADR • Aviation • Bankruptcy, Reorganization & Creditors' Rights • Construction • Corporate, Securities & Transactions • Employee Benefits • Energy • Entertainment & Sports • Environmental • Family Law • Franchise • Government Investigations & Enforcement • Health Care • Information Technology • Insurance • Intellectual Property & Technology • International • Labor & Employment Law • Legislative & Public Policy • Litigation • Product Liability • Professional Services Liability • Public Finance • Real Estate • Securities Litigation & Enforcement • Structured & Project Finance • Tax • Trusts & Estates • Technology & Emerging Companies • Toxic, Mass Tort & Environmental Litigation • Transportation

THE STATS

No. of attorneys worldwide: 800+
No. of offices worldwide: 11
Executive Committee Chairman: Steven B. Pfeiffer

EMPLOYMENT CONTACT

Ms. Katie Eleazer
Recruiting Coordinator
Phone: (713) 651-3715
Fax: (713) 651-5246
E-mail: keleazer@fulbright.com

WHO'S WHO

Does the firm have a pro bono coordinator? Yes

Stewart W. Gagnon, Esq.
Partner
Phone: (713) 651-5603
E-mail: sgagnon@fulbright.com

If yes, what percentage of his or her time is spent on pro bono work? 25 percent

Does the firm have a pro bono committee? Yes

If yes, how often does the committee meet? Each office has its own subcommittee that meets frequently. The firm-wide committee meets twice a year.

Describe the composition of the committee: It is made up of representatives of all of the firm's offices and representatives of all of the firm's practice groups.

THE SCOOP

Does your firm have a written pro bono policy? Yes

Has the firm signed on to the Law Firm Pro Bono Challenge? No

What are some of the areas of law in which your firm has performed pro bono legal work in the last two years? Family law, community development organizations, victims' rights, assistance of military personnel, death penalty appeals, civil rights, consent to abortion, estate planning for the elderly, assistance regarding 9/11 claims, child custody.

What are some of the areas of law in which your firm does not perform pro bono work? We normally do not represent parties in criminal matters unless appointed by a court, and do not represent clients when the matter could generate a fee.

Organizations for which your firm has performed pro bono legal services in the last two years: Texas Special Olympics, Gospel Rescue Mission, Roman Catholic Diocese, Public Education Legal Services, Boy Scouts of America, District of Columbia Social Services Commission, YMCA, Junior Achievement, People's Health Clinic, Houston Area Women's Center, Reading to Learn, Brian Kelly Foundation, Community Justice Foundation, Dallas Volunteer Attorneys Program, Houston Volunteer Lawyers Program, Volunteer Legal Services of Central Texas, Inner City Law Center, Southern Minnesota Legal Regional Services, Lawyer's Committee on Human Rights, Bexar County Legal Aid, Lawyers for Children America, Lawyers for the Arts.

List up to three pro bono matters that are representative of the pro bono work your firm participates in.

Provided legal services in setting up the Brian Kelly Foundation, assisting 9/11 victims; represented a Pakistani national after her husband sued for divorce and received a $1.6 million award of damages; established a homeless shelter and acquired a "crack hotel" for its use.

BY THE NUMBERS

What is the total number of hours that lawyers in U.S. offices at your firm spent performing pro bono legal services in 2000, 2001 and 2002?

> Total number of hours in 2000: 24,873 hours
> Total number of hours in 2001: 29,912 hours
> Total number of hours in 2002: 38,845 hours

Average number of pro bono hours per attorney in U.S. offices per year (including associates, partners, counsels, but not summer associates):

> Average number of hours per attorney in 2000: 30 hours
> Average number of hours per attorney in 2001: 37 hours
> Average number of hours per attorney in 2002: 47 hours

What percentage of attorneys in this firm's U.S. offices did pro bono work in 2002? 58 percent

What percentage of attorneys in this firm's U.S. offices did at least 20 hours of pro bono work in 2002? 39 percent

Does the firm encourage its lawyers to perform a minimum number of pro bono hours? No

SUPERVISION AND EVALUATIONS

Is there partner supervision on each pro bono matter? Yes

Do partner supervisors or, if applicable, senior associates provide written evaluations of associates' work on pro bono matters? No

If so, are those evaluations taken into account in determining salary, bonuses or advancement in the firm? N/A

If not, does the firm consider pro bono work generally in associate evaluations? Yes

HOURS

Does the firm give billable hour credit for pro bono work? No

Does the firm have a maximum number of pro bono hours that can be applied toward the billable hour target? No

If so, what is the maximum? N/A

If so, what is the maximum? Yes

PRO BONO POINTS

What training opportunities are open to associates working on pro bono matters? Regular evening clinics are held where opportunities are made available. Partner and experienced attorney assistance is available at any time.

Can associates bring matters of interest to the firm? Yes

Does the firm offer the use of support staff in carrying out pro bono matters? Yes

What pro bono opportunities are available for summer associates? In the past summer associates in several offices have had the opportunity to work on pro bono cases and, in the case of Houston, were able to accept a pro bono divorce case and work with the assistance of an attorney in concluding the case.

Does the firm have established programs, such as externships, that enable its associates to work in a public interest setting? No

Has your firm won any special recognition or awards in the last two years for its pro bono work? Yes

If so, please list.

W. Frank Newton Award of State Bar of Texas, Washington Lawyers Committee for Civil Rights under Law Outstanding Achievement Award, Volunteer Legal Services of Central Texas award, Scurlock Award of State Bar of Texas, Foot Soldiers in the Sands award of the NAACP.

THE FIRM SAYS

Pro bono is a legacy at Fulbright & Jaworski propelled by its leaders, including the late Leon Jaworski who gave countless hours to serving the needs of the nation in critical times of crisis. Fulbright lawyers began the Texas Medical Center and have continued making its communities better through today. At Fulbright each attorney is encouraged to contribute time and talents to providing legal services to the poor and are recognized annually for their contributions.

OUR SURVEY SAYS

"The firm has always had a strong commitment to community involvement and participation in pro bono or board activities is highly encouraged."

"It would be more encouraging if the firm offered billable hours for it, like some firms. Otherwise, it seems to just get in the way."

"The firm expects its attorneys to perform pro bono work. The firm takes on more cases from the Houston Volunteer Lawyers Program than any other firm in Houston. Additionally, the firm actively volunteers to take cases pro bono when assigned by the local federal judiciary."

"The firm strongly encourages us to do pro bono work, and our pro bono time, to a certain number of hours, are considered in merit bonuses based on hours. However, we have so much paying work that pro bono work is hard to fit in."

"Pro bono opportunities are available, but not strongly encouraged. It really comes down to a matter of personal choice. We are doing better, I think, with some community involvement efforts."

"The amount of pro bono work totally depends on whether you want to become proactive. The firm does not require any pro bono time at all. People generally are supportive of pro bono projects, but it does not appear to be a high priority."

"Pro bono work is not counted toward billable hours. As a result, participation in pro bono projects is extremely limited. Each year, the same small handful of attorneys agree to take on new pro bono cases."

"Pro bono is encouraged, but you essentially do it on your own time. Recognition is nearly nonexistent."

"I am constantly being urged to take more pro bono work."

"I haven't heard a thing about pro bono since starting here."

"Pro bono is a legacy at Fulbright & Jaworski propelled by its leaders, including the late Leon Jaworski who gave countless hours to serving the needs of the nation in critical times of crisis."

— *Fulbright & Jaworski L.L.P.*

Gibson, Dunn & Crutcher LLP

333 South Grand Avenue
Los Angeles, CA 90071-3197
Phone: (213) 229-7000
www.gibsondunn.com

LOCATIONS

Los Angeles, CA (HQ)
Century City, CA
Dallas, TX
Denver, CO
Irvine, CA
New York, NY
Palo Alto, CA
San Francisco, CA
Washington, DC
Brussels
London
Munich
Paris

MAJOR DEPARTMENTS & PRACTICES

Antitrust
Corporate
Environmental
Financial Restructuring
International
Labor & Employment
Litigation
Public Law & Policy

THE STATS

No. of attorneys worldwide: 830
No. of offices worldwide: 13
Chairman and Managing Partner: Kenneth M. Doran

EMPLOYMENT CONTACT

Ms. Leslie E. Ripley
Director, Professional Development & Recruiting
Phone: (213) 229-7273
Email: lripley@gibsondunn.com

WHO'S WHO

Principal pro bono contact(s) at your firm:

James P. Clark, Esq.
Partner
Phone: (213) 229-7941
E-mail: jclark@gibsondunn.com

Ms. Leslie E. Ripley
Director, National Recruiting and Professional Development
Phone: (213) 229-7273
E-mail: lripley@gibsondunn.com

Ms. Aleisha C. Gravit
Director of Marketing
Phone: (303) 298-5754
E-mail: agravit@gibsondunn.com

Does the firm have a pro bono coordinator? No

If yes, what percentage of his or her time is spent on pro bono work? N/A

Does the firm have a pro bono committee? No

If yes, how often does the committee meet? N/A

Describe the composition of the committee: N/A

THE SCOOP

Does your firm have a written pro bono policy? Yes

Has the firm signed on to the Law Firm Pro Bono Challenge? No

What are some of the areas of law in which your firm has performed pro bono legal work in the last two years? Gibson Dunn's pro bono legal representations have included a wide variety of cases involving issues of child custody and adoption, landlord-tenant disputes, conservatorships and guardianships, wage claims, voter redistricting, public school system reform plans, political asylum, human rights, First Amendment rights, civil rights, endangered species and hate crimes. We have filed numerous amicus briefs on a pro bono basis in cases before the U.S. Supreme Court. In addition, our attorneys provide pro bono counsel to organizations which assist low-income and indigent individuals with a wide range of legal needs. We support groups such as Bet Tzedek and the Western Center on Law and Poverty, Public Counsel, Adoption Saturday and The Alliance for Children's Rights, The Lawyers' Committee for Civil Rights Under Law, The Legal Aid Society, Habitat for Humanity, the Sanctuary for Families' Center for Battered Women's Legal Services and many others, assuming leadership roles in addition to providing pro bono legal assistance.

Organizations for which your firm has performed pro bono legal services in the last two years: Organizations include Public Counsel Law Center, Western Center on Law and Poverty, Bet Tzedek, Rachael's Women's Center, American Civil Liberties Union, A.R.T./NY, San Francisco Volunteer Legal Services Program, Denver Metro Volunteer Lawyers, Daniel

Pearl Foundation, Los Angeles Jewish Community Center, Planned Parenthood, Lawyers Committees for Civil Rights, Atlantic Salmon Federation, Sanctuary for Families, America's Promise, The Alliance for Children's Rights, The Legal Aid Society, Habitat for Humanity and many others.

List up to three pro bono matters that are representative of the pro bono work your firm participates in.

- The Adoption Saturday Project helps to expedite the adoption from foster care in Los Angeles County of abused and severely neglected children. More than 400 Gibson Dunn lawyers, paralegals and staff have volunteered more than 10,000 hours and placed more than 3,800 foster children with adoptive parents in Los Angeles County alone. The program has expanded to the firm's Dallas office.

- A team of Gibson, Dunn & Crutcher lawyers were successful in obtaining a preliminary injunction in federal court in Albany, N.Y., on behalf of the Albany County NAACP, the Arbor Hill Concerned Citizens Neighborhood Association and several minority voters. The injunction prevents the Albany County Legislature's 2003 election from going forward because it is likely the current districting plan illegally dilutes minority voting strength in violation of the Voting Rights Act of 1965.

- Gibson Dunn was honored to have been part of the creation of the Daniel Pearl Foundation, which was formed in memory of journalist Daniel Pearl, the Wall Street Journal reporter slain by militants in Pakistan in 2002, to further the ideals that inspired Daniel's life and work.

BY THE NUMBERS

What is the total number of hours that lawyers in U.S. offices at your firm spent performing pro bono legal services in 2000, 2001 and 2002?

      Total number of hours in 2000: Over 21,000 hours
      Total number of hours in 2001: Over 21,000 hours
      Total number of hours in 2002: Over 21,000 hours

Average number of pro bono hours per attorney in U.S. offices per year (including associates, partners, counsels, but not summer associates):

      Average number of hours per attorney in 2000: Approximately 30 hours
      Average number of hours per attorney in 2001: Approximately 30 hours
      Average number of hours per attorney in 2002: Approximately 30 hours

What percentage of attorneys in this firm's U.S. offices did pro bono work in 2002? Approximately two-thirds

What percentage of attorneys in this firm's U.S. offices did at least 20 hours of pro bono work in 2002? Approximately one-third

Does the firm encourage its lawyers to perform a minimum number of pro bono hours? No. The firm encourages each of its lawyers to do pro bono work, but there is not a specified number of hours.

If so, how many hours per year or what percentage of lawyers' billable hours? N/A

SUPERVISION AND EVALUATIONS

Is there partner supervision on each pro bono matter? Yes

Do partner supervisors or, if applicable, senior associates provide written evaluations of associates' work on pro bono matters? Yes

If so, are those evaluations taken into account in determining salary, bonuses or advancement in the firm? Yes

If not, does the firm consider pro bono work generally in associate evaluations? N/A

HOURS

Does the firm give billable hour credit for pro bono work? Yes

Does the firm have a maximum number of pro bono hours that can be applied toward the billable hour target? No

If so, what is the maximum? N/A

If so, what is the maximum? Yes

PRO BONO POINTS

What training opportunities are open to associates working on pro bono matters? The firm offers myriad opportunities for associates to participate in legal representations involving issues such as child custody and adoption, landlord-tenant disputes, conservatorships and guardianships, wage claims, voter redistricting, public school system reform plans, political asylum, human rights, First Amendment rights, civil rights, endangered species and hate crimes. Opportunities also are available to develop and maintain leadership roles in community-based organizations such as Public Counsel, Bet Tzedek, the Western Center on Law and Poverty, Adoption Saturday and The Alliance for Children's Rights, The Lawyers' Committee for Civil Rights Under Law, The Legal Aid Society, Habitat for Humanity, the Sanctuary for Families' Center for Battered Women's Legal Services and many others.

Can associates bring matters of interest to the firm? Yes

Does the firm offer the use of support staff in carrying out pro bono matters? Yes

What pro bono opportunities are available for summer associates? Examples of pro bono opportunities include Public Counsel, Bet Tzedek, Adoption Saturday and Habitat for Humanity. However, numerous other pro bono opportunities are available throughout the summer.

Does the firm have established programs, such as externships, that enable its associates to work in a public interest setting? No

Has your firm won any special recognition or awards in the last two years for its pro bono work? Yes

If so, please list.

- Gibson Dunn was awarded the 2003 Commitment to Justice Award by Bet Tzedek.

- Gibson Dunn was chosen as the 2002 Pro Bono Law Firm of the Year by the Public Counsel Law Center, the country's largest public interest law firm.

- Olga Fuentes in New York received the first annual Award for Excellence in Pro Bono Advocacy from the Sanctuary for Families' Center for Battered Women's Legal Services' Associates Committee, in honor of her extraordinary pro bono work.

- Gibson Dunn was selected as the Pro Bono Law Firm of the Year in 2001 by Bet Tzedek Legal Services.

- Jim Clark and Seth Miller were honored with the 2001 Attorney Volunteer of the Year Award by Bet Tzedek Legal Services.

- The Rachael's Women's Center honored Gibson Dunn's Washington, D.C., office with its 2002 Corporate Supporter of the Year Award.

- Ted Boutrous and Tanya Acker received the ACLU of Southern California's 2002 First Amendment Award for a case they handled for the ACLU in 2001. The team filed an amicus brief and presented oral argument in support of a homeless Santa Barbara man who, unable to find a space at a non-religious shelter, was sleeping on the streets and ultimately arrested for vagrancy.

- Andy Lance received the Alliance of Resident Theatres/New York (A.R.T./NY) Local Hero Award for the pro bono work he and other Gibson Dunn lawyers have performed for A.R.T./NY. The project was groundbreaking in terms of New York City support for arts organizations in difficult economic times.

- Jennifer Chaloemtiarana received the Award of Merit from the Bar Association of San Francisco and the Wiley W. Manuel Award for Pro Bono Legal Services from the State Bar of California for her service to the legal community and her significant pro bono work with the S.F. Bar's Volunteer Legal Services Program, as part of VLSP's Community Organization Representation Project.

- Stephen McKenna was honored by the Denver Bar Association for his extraordinary efforts and dedication to Metro Volunteer Lawyers (MLV). MLV provides free legal services to the poor.

- The Bar Association of San Francisco's Volunteer Legal Services Program named Ethan Dettmer an "outstanding volunteer in public service" in recognition of his successful pro bono representation of a local nonprofit corporation in a contract dispute.

THE FIRM SAYS

At Gibson, Dunn & Crutcher, we recognize that our obligations extend not only to our clients but to our communities as well. We believe that pro bono work is not just a good idea in theory, we make it our practice. In fact, we recently were chosen as the Pro Bono Law Firm of the Year by the Public Counsel Law Center, the country's largest public interest law firm, and we have been honored by Bet Tzedek with their 2003 Commitment to Justice Award. Among the areas cited was our nationally recognized, groundbreaking "Adoption Saturday" program, which thus far has placed more than 3,800 foster children with adoptive parents.

Gibson Dunn's pro bono legal representations have included a wide variety of cases involving issues of child custody and adoption, landlord-tenant disputes, conservatorships and guardianships, wage claims, voter redistricting, public school system reform plans, political asylum, human rights, First Amendment rights, civil rights, endangered species and hate crimes. We have filed numerous amicus briefs on a pro bono basis in cases before the U.S. Supreme Court.

In addition, our attorneys provide pro bono counsel to organizations which assist low-income and indigent individuals with a wide range of legal needs. We support groups such as Bet Tzedek and the Western Center on Law and Poverty, Public Counsel, Adoption Saturday and The Alliance for Children's Rights, The Lawyers' Committee for Civil Rights Under Law, The Legal Aid Society, Habitat for Humanity, the Sanctuary for Families' Center for Battered Women's Legal Services, and many others, assuming leadership roles in addition to providing pro bono legal assistance. In connection with the events of September 11, Gibson Dunn firm personnel raised more than $160,000 for the Twin Towers Fund established by New York City Mayor Giuliani, and the firm then matched those contributions.

The firm and its lawyers and staff give generously of their time, financial support, expertise and leadership skills in order to give back to the communities in which we live and work.

OUR SURVEY SAYS

"For a conservative law firm, Gibson Dunn really works hard at fostering pro bono commitments."

"This is the source of some discontent. Previously, pro bono hours were one-for-one billable only after you met the billable requirement of 1,950. Now there is no formal billable requirement, and nobody knows how much credit will be awarded for pro bono work."

"The firm allows lawyers to do pro bono work, but it is not especially encouraged at an institutional level. If people want to do it, fine; if not, then that's fine too."

"I have put in hundreds of pro bono hours per year and continue to be encouraged to do so by the partnership."

"The firm supports pro bono work but the level of commitment is minimal. The New York office has started an ad hoc community affairs committee to help associates pick up pro bono projects."

"Pro bono work is encouraged in all areas of practice."

"Pro bono is available, but the hours requirement makes it difficult to do pro bono and to bill enough hours (pro bono does not count toward the billable requirements)."

"The firm fully supports all of my pro bono work (which is extensive) and always thanks me for my efforts in my year-end reviews. I am not sure how much my pro bono efforts 'count' in terms of evaluation of me as a potential candidate for partner, bonuses and so on, and suspect they do not."

"So long as you work 2,000 hours, the firm likes pro bono work."

"While there is widespread participation in the firm's national adoption day program, there is a lot of paperwork to get through before other pro bono projects may be worked on."

Goodwin Procter LLP

Exchange Place
53 State Street
Boston, MA 02109
Phone: (617) 570-1000
www.goodwinprocter.com

LOCATIONS

Boston, MA (HQ)
New York, NY
Roseland, NJ
Washington, DC

MAJOR DEPARTMENTS & PRACTICES

Corporate
Environmental
ERISA & Employee Benefits
Estate Planning & Administration
Financial Services
Intellectual Property
Labor & Employment
Litigation
Real Estate
Tax

THE STATS

No. of attorneys worldwide: 500
No. of offices worldwide: 4
Chairman and Managing Partner: Regina M. Pisa

EMPLOYMENT CONTACT

Ms. Maureen A. Shea
Director of Legal Recruitment
Phone: (617) 570-1288
Fax: (617) 523-1231
E-mail: mshea@goodwinprocter.com

WHO'S WHO

Principal pro bono contact(s) at your firm:

Carolyn Rosenthal, Esq.
Pro Bono Manager
Phone: (617) 570-1481
E-mail: crosenthal@goodwinprocter.com

William P. Mayer, Esq.
Chair, Pro Bono Committee
Phone: (617) 570-1534
E-mail: wmayer@goodwinprocter.com

Does the firm have a pro bono coordinator? Yes
Carolyn Rosenthal

If yes, what percentage of his or her time is spent on pro bono work? 50 percent

Does the firm have a pro bono committee? Yes

If yes, how often does the committee meet? Monthly

Describe the composition of the committee: It is composed of partners from each of our offices and from many of the departments throughout the firm.

THE SCOOP

Does your firm have a written pro bono policy? Yes

Has the firm signed on to the Law Firm Pro Bono Challenge? Yes

What are some of the areas of law in which your firm has performed pro bono legal work in the last two years? Assistance to inner city entrepreneurs, asylum law, criminal law, civil rights law, real estate law, elder law, employment law, intellectual property law, family law and corporate/nonprofit law.

What are some of the areas of law in which your firm does not perform pro bono work? We do not take on plaintiff's cases against employers.

Organizations for which your firm has performed pro bono legal services in the last two years: Legal services organizations for which we have performed pro bono work include Economic Justice Project, Elder Law Project, Lawyers Alliance for New York, Lawyers Clearinghouse on Affordable Housing and Homelessness, Political Asylum/Immigration Representation Project (PAIR), Pro Bono Partnership, Trust for Public Land, Lawyers Committee for Civil Rights Under the Law, Volunteer Lawyers for the Arts (VLA), Volunteer Lawyers Project (VLP) and the Rape Survivors' Law Project.

List up to three pro bono matters that are representative of the pro bono work your firm participates in.

We provide corporate and intellectual property assistance to a nonprofit that promotes economic growth in Africa through the creation of new businesses and jobs; we work with Habitat for Humanity to provide representation to individuals in connection with the purchase of homes and in the acquisition of property for future use; and in the firm's last fiscal year, we provided assistance to more than 50 individuals in criminal defense matters, including a number of appeals.

BY THE NUMBERS

What is the total number of hours that lawyers in U.S. offices at your firm spent performing pro bono legal services in 2000, 2001 and 2002?

>   **Total number of hours in 2000:** 14,000 hours
>   **Total number of hours in 2001:** 16,000 hours
>   **Total number of hours in 2002:** 21,800 hours

Average number of pro bono hours per attorney in U.S. offices per year (including associates, partners, counsels, but not summer associates):

>   **Average number of hours per attorney in 2000:** 34.3 hours
>   **Average number of hours per attorney in 2001:** 35.0 hours
>   **Average number of hours per attorney in 2002:** 42.5 hours

What percentage of attorneys in this firm's U.S. offices did pro bono work in 2002? 67 percent

What percentage of attorneys in this firm's U.S. offices did at least 20 hours of pro bono work in 2002? 36.6 percent

Does the firm encourage its lawyers to perform a minimum number of pro bono hours? Yes

If so, how many hours per year or what percentage of lawyers' billable hours? As a firm, we try to dedicate at least 3 percent of our billable hours to pro bono matters.

SUPERVISION AND EVALUATIONS

Is there partner supervision on each pro bono matter? Yes

Do partner supervisors or, if applicable, senior associates provide written evaluations of associates' work on pro bono matters? Yes, we follow the same policy for pro bono and for billable matters.

If so, are those evaluations taken into account in determining salary, bonuses or advancement in the firm? Yes

If not, does the firm consider pro bono work generally in associate evaluations? N/A

HOURS

Does the firm give billable hour credit for pro bono work? Yes

Does the firm have a maximum number of pro bono hours that can be applied toward the billable hour target? No

If so, what is the maximum? N/A

If so, what is the maximum? Yes

PRO BONO POINTS

What training opportunities are open to associates working on pro bono matters? Each year we hold several relevant training programs at the firm. These include eviction training, nonprofit training, asylum law training, children's law training, elder law training and a program on advising inner-city entrepreneurs. We also publicize outside training programs to our attorneys.

Can associates bring matters of interest to the firm? Yes

Does the firm offer the use of support staff in carrying out pro bono matters? Yes

What pro bono opportunities are available for summer associates? All of the above pro bono opportunities. In the summer of 2002, 73 percent of the summer associate class worked on at least one pro bono matter and collectively dedicated over 500 hours to pro bono cases. In the summer of 2003, 74 percent of the summer associate class worked on at least one pro bono matter and collectively dedicated over 1,100 hours to pro bono cases.

Does the firm have established programs, such as externships, that enable its associates to work in a public interest setting? Yes

If so, where and for up to how long? We provide an extern to the Trust for Public Land for three to four months at a time; we provide three associates to the Bar Advocate Program each year; and we provide two attorneys for six-month rotations each to the Middlesex County District Attorney's Office.

Has your firm won any special recognition or awards in the last two years for its pro bono work? Yes

If so, please list.

Selection of Litigation Partner Christopher Moore to the Boston Bar Association's Public Interest Leadership Program, September 2003. The Robert B. Fraser Award for Pro Bono Excellence from the Volunteer Lawyers for the Arts of Massachusetts, Inc., June 2003. Shining Star Award from the Victim Rights Law Center on behalf of the Rape Survivors' Law Project, April 2003. Pro Bono Award for Law Firm from the Massachusetts Bar Association and Massachusetts Bar Foundation, January 2003. Attorney Special Recognition Award to John Mercer from the Massachusetts Housing Partnership for the Soft Second Legal Services Program, January 2003. Goodwin Procter's Pro Bono Annual Report 2001 received the Award for Excellence from the International Association of Business Communicators (IABC), October 2002. Lawyers Alliance for New York Cornerstone Awards to Gregory Patchen, Sharon Mousserie and Lonnie Halpern, September 2002. National Public Service Award from the American Bar Association, April 2002. Friends of Boston's Homeless Award, April 2002. Habitat for Humanity's Golden Hammer Award to MaryAnn Peterson Kanary, January 2002.

THE FIRM SAYS

The prevailing philosophy of Goodwin Procter is that the provision of legal services for the benefit of those in need is the responsibility of every lawyer and at the same time provides compelling opportunities for professional and personal growth for those who do it. In short, Goodwin Procter expects its attorneys to do pro bono work. Our pro bono work is facilitated by a pro bono committee and a program manager. We consistently take initiatives to make pro bono opportunities and activities accessible to our lawyers. By identifying the interests of individual lawyers and publicizing opportunities, we are able to match individuals with opportunities that interest them and provide training and supervision. In addition to working with legal services groups, many of the matters for nonprofit organizations we take on a pro bono basis come into the firm through connections with our attorneys, support staff and clients. In fiscal year 2002 (ends September 30), our attorneys dedicated over 21,800 pro bono hours with a docket of 260 matters. In this year alone, the firm initiated over 140 matters, ranging from transactional work for nonprofit organizations to cases for individuals referred by bar association programs and the court system.

Goodwin Procter's pro bono activities address many community needs. We have assisted indigent individuals on issues involving housing, elder law, immigration and criminal defense, as well as nonprofit organizations on real estate, tax, environmental, intellectual property, corporate and commercial law matters. In addition, we serve the local communities in which we practice and have provided assistance to a number of nonprofit organizations in other countries, including Kenya, Poland, Mongolia, Tanzania and Chile. Attorneys working on approved pro bono matters receive billable credit for this work. And through awards and individual performance reviews, we recognize those individuals at Goodwin Procter who do pro bono work. For the more senior attorneys at the firm, direct involvement in these matters, or involvement at a supervisory level, provides them a chance to use their special skills to help people in need. For newer attorneys, this work allows substantial hands-on experience and training and a chance to manage a case or matter at an early stage in their careers. We believe that our pro bono efforts have made a difference, and we look forward to expanding our commitment to those in need.

OUR SURVEY SAYS

"Pro bono hours count as billables, a full-time pro bono coordinator constantly bombards associates with opportunities and even the management has aggressively pushed pro bono work."

"The firm is definitely VERY supportive of pro bono, both in allowing associates to spend time (hours count 100 percent toward minimum billables) and in spending money on experts, and so on, to litigate cases effectively."

"I've billed hundreds of hours per year on pro bono litigation and been uniformly praised for it. And it counts towards billables."

"The firm as a whole is very strongly committed to pro bono, but the commitment of specific attorneys and departments vary. Whether an associate can comfortably spend significant time on pro bono will depend on which department the associate works in and which attorneys the associate works with most frequently."

"I do hundreds of hours of pro bono work that is encouraged by almost all the partners and is counted towards my bonus in terms of hours."

"Full credit for all pro bono work. This sets Goodwin apart from a lot of other firms that talk a big game but never put their money where their mouth is. I have billed almost one-fourth of my 'billable hours' to pro bono work for each of the past three years and I have always received one of the top bonuses. Goodwin has made a commitment to pro bono work and they mean it. It is what has kept me here."

"With the firm's strong encouragement, I have regularly participated in a pro bono project relating to housing court and have worked on a number of pro bono matters. Within the last few years, the firm hired a full-time pro bono coordinator, so there is a pretty steady flow of pro bono opportunities."

"The firm is undoubtedly the most dedicated large firm in Boston and has won several pro bono awards over the past year."

"The firm is extremely committed to pro bono work. Associates are allowed to bill pro bono time in the same manner as billable time, and there are a wide variety of projects to choose from."

"The firm has a strong commitment to pro bono. However, being a first-year, it is often difficult to become involved in projects because you need to have a partner and/or senior associate advisor. There have been a number of instances where I was unable to take on a matter given the lack of partners willing to supervise."

Gray Cary Ware & Freidenrich LLP

2000 University Circle
East Palo Alto, CA 94303-2248
Phone: (650) 833-2000
www.graycary.com

LOCATIONS

East Palo Alto, CA (HQ)
Austin, TX
La Jolla, CA
Sacramento, CA
San Diego, CA
San Francisco, CA
Seattle, WA
Washington, DC

MAJOR DEPARTMENTS & PRACTICES

Antitrust • Appellate • Aviation • Bankruptcy & Insolvency • Capital Markets • Consumer Class Actions • Corporate & Securities • Debt Finance • Employee Benefits & Compensation • Employment • Environmental • Estate Planning • First Amendment & Media • Government Contracts • Insurance Coverage • Intellectual Property • International Trade • Licensing • Litigation • Mergers & Acquisitions • Patent • Privacy • Product Liability • Real Estate • Securities Litigation • Tax • Trademark • White Collar Criminal Defense

THE STATS

No. of attorneys worldwide: 405
No. of offices worldwide: 8
Chairman and CEO: J. Terence O'Malley

EMPLOYMENT CONTACT

Ms. Leslie Colvin
Professional Recruiting Director
Phone: (650) 833-2000
Fax: (650) 833-2001
E-mail: lcolvin@graycary.com

WHO'S WHO

Principal pro bono contact(s) at your firm:

Andrew Valentine, Esq.
Pro Bono Partner
E-mail: avalentine@graycary.com

Does the firm have a pro bono coordinator? Yes
Andrew Valentine, Esq.
Amanda Groves, Esq.
Mike Tracy, Esq.
Nancy Dix, Esq.

If yes, what percentage of his or her time is spent on pro bono work? 5 to 10 percent.

Does the firm have a pro bono committee? Yes

If yes, how often does the committee meet? Quarterly

Describe the composition of the committee: Includes representatives from all major practice groups.

THE SCOOP

Does your firm have a written pro bono policy? Yes

Has the firm signed on to the Law Firm Pro Bono Challenge? No

What are some of the areas of law in which your firm has performed pro bono legal work in the last two years? Representation of the poor; guardianships; legal services to civic, educational, charitable and business organizations; loan and real estate fraud; legal services to municipalities battling drug and nuisance houses; First Amendment cases.

What are some of the areas of law in which your firm does not perform pro bono work? Criminal.

Organizations for which your firm has performed pro bono legal services in the last two years: East Palo Alto Volunteer Attorney Program, Stanford Community Law Clinic, San Diego Volunteer Lawyer Program, Silicon Valley Campaign for Legal Services, Legal Aid Society of San Mateo County, Santa Clara University Community Law Center, Planned Parenthood, Global Fund for Women, Family and Childrens' Counseling Service, The Nature Conservancy.

List up to three pro bono matters that are representative of the pro bono work your firm participates in.

- Gray Cary successfully represented the general public (consisting primarily of the elderly and the poor) in an unfair competition case relating to a large scale fraudulent loan scheme. Gray Cary followed up by representing dozens of the victims in restitution proceedings. The defendant currently is in jail for being in contempt of court.

- Gray Cary works closely with Legal Aid and local pro bono organizations on dozens of guardianship cases.

- Gray Cary currently is working with the city of East Palo Alto battling and closing nuisance/drug houses.

BY THE NUMBERS

What is the total number of hours that lawyers in U.S. offices at your firm spent performing pro bono legal services in 2000, 2001 and 2002?

> Total number of hours in 2000: 5,134 hours
> Total number of hours in 2001: 4,468 hours
> Total number of hours in 2002: 6,176 hours

Average number of pro bono hours per attorney in U.S. offices per year (including associates, partners, counsels, but not summer associates):

> Average number of hours per attorney in 2000: N/A
> Average number of hours per attorney in 2001: N/A
> Average number of hours per attorney in 2002: N/A

What percentage of attorneys in this firm's U.S. offices did pro bono work in 2002? Approximately 30 percent

What percentage of attorneys in this firm's U.S. offices did at least 20 hours of pro bono work in 2002? Approximately 20 percent

Does the firm encourage its lawyers to perform a minimum number of pro bono hours? Yes

If so, how many hours per year or what percentage of lawyers' billable hours? 60 hours

SUPERVISION AND EVALUATIONS

Is there partner supervision on each pro bono matter? Yes

Do partner supervisors or, if applicable, senior associates provide written evaluations of associates' work on pro bono matters? Yes

If so, are those evaluations taken into account in determining salary, bonuses or advancement in the firm? Yes

If not, does the firm consider pro bono work generally in associate evaluations? N/A

HOURS

Does the firm give billable hour credit for pro bono work? Yes

Does the firm have a maximum number of pro bono hours that can be applied toward the billable hour target? Yes

If so, what is the maximum? 100 hours

If so, what is the maximum? Yes

PRO BONO POINTS

What training opportunities are open to associates working on pro bono matters? Training with the pro bono and public interest organizations we work with. Real life training while performing pro bono services.

Can associates bring matters of interest to the firm? Yes

Does the firm offer the use of support staff in carrying out pro bono matters? Yes

What pro bono opportunities are available for summer associates? Summer associates are exposed to and encouraged to participate in pro bono projects and to attend pro bono workshops and matter intake sessions. Last summer, most of our summer associates worked on pro bono projects, including guardianship cases and loan fraud cases.

Does the firm have established programs, such as externships, that enable its associates to work in a public interest setting? No

Has your firm won any special recognition or awards in the last two years for its pro bono work? Yes

If so, please list.

Legal Aid Society of San Mateo County Pro Bono Honoree (September/October 2003).

THE FIRM SAYS

Gray Cary strongly believes that a lawyer's professional responsibilities include public service and the provision of legal services to those unable to afford representation. Gray Cary also believes that the experience of providing pro bono legal services is important in the development and growth of mature, well-rounded legal professionals. Gray Cary strongly encourages its attorneys and paralegals to provide pro bono legal services and seeks to recognize and reward lawyers for providing pro bono services. For these reasons, Gray Cary aspires to have each lawyer within the firm contribute time each year to pro bono matters. Commitment to pro bono activities is an important consideration in the firm's decisions relating to compensation and advancement.

OUR SURVEY SAYS

"Our firm encourages pro bono work and gives a certain number of hours of pro bono work billable hours credit."

"I am currently involved in a pro bono project, as are many of my fellow associates (of all levels). The firm strongly supports and encourages pro bono work."

"It depends on the practice group. I don't think the corporate group is very committed to pro bono work, but other groups are very committed and devote a lot of time and effort to pro bono projects."

"The firm regularly receives awards for quality and quantity of pro bono work."

"Fifty hours/year billable equivalent; additional hours subject to approval."

"This varies from office to office and practice group to practice group. I think that certain offices and groups really emphasize pro bono work, others less so."

"The firm does promote pro bono work. However, pro bono work is sometimes forced upon associates."

"They seem to say they are committed and have a program, but when it comes down to it, it's not well regarded and is treated as something you must have done because you had no billable work."

"Full credit is given for pro bono towards billable hours. The firm was too committed to pro bono last year in my opinion, but the partners push it even when it eats up valuable litigator time!"

"While we are active in the community, we need more large-scale and relevant pro bono work."

"Commitment to pro bono activities is an important consideration in the firm's decisions relating to compensation and advancement."

— *Gray, Cary, Ware & Freidenrich LLP*

Greenberg Traurig, LLP

1221 Brickell Avenue
Miami, FL 33131
Phone: (305) 579-0500

200 Park Avenue
New York, NY 10166
Phone: (212) 801-9200
www.gtlaw.com

LOCATIONS

Atlanta, GA • Boca Raton, FL • Boston, MA • Chicago, IL • Dallas, TX • Denver, CO • Florham Park, NJ • Fort Lauderdale, FL • Los Angeles, CA • Miami, FL • New York, NY • Orlando, FL • Philadelphia, PA • Phoenix, AZ • Tallahassee, FL • Tysons Corner, VA • Washington, DC • West Palm Beach, FL • Wilmington, DE • Amsterdam • Zurich

MAJOR DEPARTMENTS & PRACTICES

Antitrust • Appellate • Biotechnology • Business Immigration • Corporate & Securities • Education • Employee Benefits & Executive Compensation • Energy & Natural Resources • Entertainment & Sports • Environmental • ERISA • Financial Institutions • Franchise & Distribution • Gaming • Golf & Resorts • Governmental Affairs • Government Contracts • Health Care • Insurance Coverage • Intellectual Property • International • Labor & Employment • Land Use • Litigation • Public Finance • Public Utilities • Real Estate Reorganization, Bankruptcy & Restructuring • Tax, Trusts & Estates • Technology, Media & Telecommunications • Transportation • Wealth Preservation

THE STATS

No. of attorneys worldwide: 1,100+
No. of offices worldwide: 21
President and CEO: Cesar L. Alvarez

EMPLOYMENT CONTACT

Atlanta, Boca Raton, Boston, Denver, Ft. Lauderdale, Miami, Orlando, Tallahassee, West Palm Beach, Wilmington

Ms. Janet McKeegan
Director of Recruitment
Phone: (305) 579-0855
E-mail: mckeeganj@gtlaw.com

Elizabeth A. Lee
Recruiting Manager
Phone: (212) 801-6551
E-mail: leeel@gtlaw.com

See firm web site for employment contacts for other offices.

WHO'S WHO

Does the firm have a pro bono coordinator? Yes

Holly R. Skolnick, Esq.
Litigation Shareholder/ Pro Bono Coordinator
1221 Brickell Avenue
Miami, FL 33131
Phone: (305) 579-0860
Fax: (305) 579-0717
E-mail: skolnickh@gtlaw.com

Stephen L. Saxl, Esq.
Litigation Shareholder/ Pro Bono Coordinator
885 Third Avenue, 21st Floor
New York, NY 10022
Phone: (212) 801-2184
Fax: (212) 688-2449
E-mail: saxls@gtlaw.com

Does the firm have a pro bono committee? No. The firm does not operate with committees. The firm places key shareholders in decision making positions. Our two shareholders in this area are Holly R. Skolnick and Stephen L. Saxl.

If yes, how often does the committee meet? N/A

Describe the composition of the committee: N/A

THE SCOOP

Does your firm have a written pro bono policy? Yes

Has the firm signed on to the Law Firm Pro Bono Challenge? No

What are some of the areas of law in which your firm has performed pro bono legal work in the last two years? Civil rights and affirmative action, custody and visitation, guardianship, criminal appeals, children's issues, immigration/political asylum, community economic development, domestic violence.

What are some of the areas of law in which your firm does not perform pro bono work? No policy precluding any areas of law.

Organizations for which your firm has performed pro bono legal services in the last two years: InMotion (formerly Network for Women's Services), Office of the Appellate Defender, Tannenbaum Center for Interreligious Understanding, Jewish National Fund, The Legal Aid Society, Florida Immigration Advocacy Center, Legal Service Corporation, Lawyers For Children, Cuban/American Bar Association, Center for Ethics and Public Service.

List up to three pro bono matters that are representative of the pro bono work your firm participates in.

- Representation of indigent women who were victims of domestic violence in obtaining orders of protection and resolving custody and visitation issues.

- Acted as co-counsel in the military amicus brief filed on behalf of 21 former generals and admirals, two former secretaries of defense, one former national security advisor to the president, four senators and others in support of affirmative action in the University of Michigan affirmative action cases (Grutter v. Bollinger and Gratz v. Bollinger). The Legal Times called the brief "one of the most important amicus curiae briefs ever submitted to the Supreme Court."

BY THE NUMBERS

What is the total number of hours that lawyers in U.S. offices at your firm spent performing pro bono legal services in 2000, 2001 and 2002?

>Total number of hours in 2000: 16,300 hours
>Total number of hours in 2001: 20,500 hours
>Total number of hours in 2002: 28,200 hours

Average number of pro bono hours per attorney in U.S. offices per year (including associates, partners, counsels, but not summer associates):

>Average number of hours per attorney in 2000: 25 hours
>Average number of hours per attorney in 2001: 27 hours
>Average number of hours per attorney in 2002: 35 hours

What percentage of attorneys in this firm's U.S. offices did pro bono work in 2002? 46 percent

What percentage of attorneys in this firm's U.S. offices did at least 20 hours of pro bono work in 2002? 35 percent

Does the firm encourage its lawyers to perform a minimum number of pro bono hours? Yes

SUPERVISION AND EVALUATIONS

Is there partner supervision on each pro bono matter? Yes

Do partner supervisors or, if applicable, senior associates provide written evaluations of associates' work on pro bono matters? Yes

If so, are those evaluations taken into account in determining salary, bonuses or advancement in the firm? Yes

If not, does the firm consider pro bono work generally in associate evaluations? N/A

HOURS

Does the firm give billable hour credit for pro bono work? No

Does the firm have a maximum number of pro bono hours that can be applied toward the billable hour target? No

If so, what is the maximum? N/A

If so, what is the maximum? Yes

PRO BONO POINTS

What training opportunities are open to associates working on pro bono matters? Greenberg Traurig participates in outside training by legal service providers and bar associations. Associates are encouraged to take on pro bono matters that will give them first-hand experience.

Can associates bring matters of interest to the firm? Yes

Does the firm offer the use of support staff in carrying out pro bono matters? Yes

What pro bono opportunities are available for summer associates? Summer associates are encouraged to participate in pro bono matters in all of our offices. In addition, New York summer associates are given the opportunity to take on a pro bono matter of their own in conjunction with inMotion (formerly Network for Women's Services). These matters include orders of protection and custody and visitation matters (which require a court appearance) and uncontested divorces.

Does the firm have established programs, such as externships, that enable its associates to work in a public interest setting? Yes

If so, where and for up to how long? Two years throughout the firm's national locations, including Miami, New York, Chicago and Los Angeles, among others.

Has your firm won any special recognition or awards in the last two years for its pro bono work? Yes

If so, please list.

- Florida's Children's First Award to Greenberg Traurig for its generosity in funding public interest fellowships enabling young attorneys to establish innovative child advocacy projects.

- Howard Jeruchimowitz, a litigation associate in our Chicago office, received the Chicago Lawyers' Committee for Civil Rights Under Law's 2003 Young Lawyer Award. He received the award in recognition of his unique contribution to the CLC's employment discrimination mediation program. When the U.S. Equal Employment Opportunity Commission began to mediate employment disputes, many employees, unlike employers, could not afford legal counsel. Consequently, in 1999, the EEOC asked the CLC to develop an employment mediation program for employees filing charges with the EEOC. Jeruchimowitz has handled more cases than any other CLC volunteer, obtaining reinstatement for wrongly discharged employees, sizeable monetary damages and favorable references.

- Cesar Alvarez, CEO and president, was honored by the Cuban American Bar Association for his pro bono work.

- Robert L. Grossman, a corporate and securities shareholder in our Miami office, was selected as one of the recipients of the 11th Judicial Circuit and Dade County Bar Association's 2003 Put Something Back award. The award recognizes individuals for contributions to the community through Put Something Back, a pro bono project of the 11th Judicial Circuit and the Dade County Bar Association.

- Holly R. Skolnick, a litigation shareholder in our Miami office, received "The Friend of the Center" award from the Center for Ethics and Public Service at the University of Miami School of Law. The award was presented to Skolnick in recognition of her contributions as a member of the center's advisory board and for her participation in developing two new projects: Community Economic Development and Design Project (CEDAD), a public-service project in Coconut Grove; and the Center's ethics training program for law firms, which is being piloted at Greenberg Traurig.

- Greenberg Traurig LLP was nominated as the National Philanthropy Day Outstanding Corporation for the firm's commitment to Equal Access to Justice by Legal Aid Service of Broward County.

- Adrienne Freisner Pardo, an environmental and land use shareholder in our Miami office, has received the Greater Miami Jewish Federation's 2002 Stanley C. Myers Presidents' Leadership Award. The award is presented annually to a Federation leader who demonstrates extraordinary commitment and dedication to the needs of the Greater Miami Jewish Federation and the Miami Jewish community.

THE FIRM SAYS

Greenberg Traurig is committed to supporting communities around the country by providing volunteer talent and financial contributions to numerous civic and charitable organizations in addition to the ongoing and significant pro bono work conducted by attorneys. Each of the firm's more than 1000 attorneys are supporting pro bono work either through devoting hours of legal services through an organized legal aid program, on their own to a variety of clients and/or by making a financial contribution to the Greenberg Traurig Fellowship Foundation and other legal aid organizations. One of the pro bono cases involving a domestic violence matter resulted not only in a positive outcome for the client, but also an entire domestic violence project. As a result of all that was learned through the pro bono case, Greenberg Traurig adopted a comprehensive firm policy to heighten awareness of domestic violence and its effects on the workplace. This policy has already served as a model for numerous other corporations around the country seeking to adopt domestic violence programs in the workplace. The firm's goal is to raise awareness and lead other companies to promote the health and safety of their employees by adopting similar programs.

Established in 1996, the Greenberg Traurig Fellowship Foundation is a private organization established by the law firm to provide public interest organizations with the services of an attorney through a fellowship program. Originally, the foundation selected one fellowship recipient for a period of two years. Due to an immensely successful run since its inception, the foundation has expanded its reach and we now have more than 10 Fellows working throughout our various national locations. The foundation has been able to expand its reach through partners with Equal Justice Works (formerly the National Association of Public Interest Lawyers). In addition, the firm formed the Greenberg Traurig Fellowship at the Center for Ethics and Public Service at the University of Miami School of Law and has awarded undergraduate fellowships to students involved in community economic development in distressed communities. Through these partnerships with Equal Justice Works, the Florida Bar Association and the University of Miami, Greenberg Traurig hopes to expand the opportunities available to lawyers seeking to commit their legal services to the public interest.

OUR SURVEY SAYS

"All associates are required to pay into a pro bono fund."

"The firm's attitude seems to be they would rather pay for someone else to do pro bono (i.e., a fellow) than utilize firm resources/attorneys for such work."

"All associates have plenty of pro bono opportunities available and everyone contributes to full-time fellowships."

"Associates are required either to contribute significant work towards a pro bono matter or to pay into a pro bono fund."

"The firm is very committed to doing pro bono work but does not recognize the hours spent on pro bono in the compensation structure"

"The firm encourages pro bono work, but recently took away billable hours equivalent credit for doing pro bono work."

"The firm does not give credit for pro bono work."

"Most attorneys pay the $350 instead of doing pro bono work.... There are a few attorneys who do significant pro bono work. However, by and large, most attorneys don't have time."

"The firm, like most, is billables-driven. People feel encouraged but also feel pressure to bill."

"Either do pro bono, or have $300 deducted from [your] paycheck each year."

Hale and Dorr LLP

60 State Street
Boston, MA 02109-1803
Phone: (617) 526-6000
www.haledorr.com

LOCATIONS

Boston, MA (HQ)
New York, NY
Princeton, NJ
Reston, VA
Waltham, MA
Washington, DC
London
Munich
Oxford

MAJOR DEPARTMENTS & PRACTICES

Antitrust & Trade Regulation
Commercial
Corporate
Employee Benefits
Employment Litigation
Environmental
Government & Regulatory Affairs
Immigration
Intellectual Property
International
Investment Management
Labor & Employment
Litigation
Mergers & Acquisitions
Private Client
Pro Bono
Public Offerings
Real Estate
Tax
Technology Transactions and Licensing
Venture Capital

THE STATS

No. of attorneys worldwide: 509
No. of offices worldwide: 9
Managing Partner: William F. Lee

EMPLOYMENT CONTACT

Ms. Evelyn M. Scoville
Director of Legal Personnel
Phone: (617) 526-6590
Fax: (617) 526-5000
E-mail: evelyn.scoville@haledorr.com

WHO'S WHO

Does the firm have a pro bono coordinator? Yes. John Sigel, Jack Regan and Cathleen Tottey coordinate pro bono work at the firm.

John Sigel, Senior Partner
Vice Chair, Commercial Department
Co-Chair, Public Service Committee
Phone: (617) 526-6728
E-mail: john.sigel@haledorr.com

John (Jack) Regan, Senior Partner
Co-Chair, Litigation/Intellectual Property Litigation Group
Co-Chair, Public Service Committee
Phone: (617) 526-6120

Ms. Cathleen Tottey
Public Service Manager
Phone: (617) 526-5526
E-mail: cathleen.tottey@haledorr.com

If yes, what percentage of his or her time is spent on pro bono work? John Sigel spends 5 to 7 percent of his time administering the program, particularly reviewing cases that are approved for intake. Jack Regan spends 5 percent of his time working with John Sigel in defining pro bono policies and dealing with third-party providers. Cathleen Tottey spends 100 percent of her time on pro bono and public service initiatives.

Does the firm have a pro bono committee? Yes

If yes, how often does the committee meet? The public service committee, which oversees pro bono work at the firm, meets quarterly. A subcommittee of the committee also considers each request for pro bono work.

Describe the composition of the committee: The committee is co-chaired by two senior partners and is composed of senior partners, junior partners and associates who represent all firm offices and a cross-section of firm departments. Administrative support for the committee is provided by the public service manager and public service assistant.

THE SCOOP

Does your firm have a written pro bono policy? Yes

Has the firm signed on to the Law Firm Pro Bono Challenge? Yes

What are some of the areas of law in which your firm has performed pro bono legal work in the last two years? The firm performs pro bono legal work in a number of areas including children's rights, civil rights, death penalty defense, environmental law, estate planning, IOLTA litigation, immigration and inner-city micro-enterprise development.

What are some of the areas of law in which your firm does not perform pro bono work? The firm does very limited work in the areas of domestic relations and landlord-tenant disputes.

Organizations for which your firm has performed pro bono legal services in the last two years: American Bar Association Subcommittee on International Children's Rights, The Center for Public Representation, Greater Boston Legal Services, The Hale and Dorr Legal Services Center at Harvard Law School, International AIDS Vaccine Initiative, National Lawyers Committee for Civil Rights, National Voting Rights Institute, Quincy Bar Advocates, Village Charter School, Volunteer Lawyers for the Arts.

List up to three pro bono matters that are representative of the pro bono work your firm participates in. We filed a class action lawsuit, with the Center for Public Representation and the Mental Health Legal Advisors Committee, alleging that Massachusetts has violated Medicaid law by failing to provide medically necessary home-based care to children with mental illnesses. The nine plaintiffs in the suit represent thousands of children throughout the state who have been unnecessarily institutionalized due to the Commonwealth's failure to provide federally mandated home-based services. Since 1999, the firm has been working on a post-conviction proceeding on behalf of John Lionel Neal Jr., a mentally impaired man incarcerated on death row in Alabama. Members of our Washington and Boston offices have obtained asylum for clients who feared likely persecution by the government in their home countries of Liberia and Nigeria.

BY THE NUMBERS

What is the total number of hours that lawyers at your firm spent performing pro bono legal services in 2000, 2001 and 2002?

    Total number of hours in 2000: 20,916 hours

    Total number of hours in 2001: 23,403 hours

    Total number of hours in 2002: 25,715 hours

Average number of pro bono hours per attorney in U.S. offices per year (including associates, partners, counsels, but not summer associates):

    Average number of hours per attorney in 2000: 50 hours

    Average number of hours per attorney in 2001: 53 hours

    Average number of hours per attorney in 2002: 52 hours

What percentage of attorneys in this firm's U.S. offices did pro bono work in 2002? 58 percent

What percentage of attorneys in this firm's U.S. offices did at least 20 hours of pro bono work in 2002? 32 percent

Does the firm encourage its lawyers to perform a minimum number of pro bono hours? Yes

If so, how many hours per year or what percentage of lawyers' billable hours? 60 hours or 3 percent of billable hours.

SUPERVISION AND EVALUATIONS

Is there partner supervision on each pro bono matter? Yes

Do partner supervisors or, if applicable, senior associates provide written evaluations of associates' work on pro bono matters? Partners evaluate associates who work for them, whether the work is pro bono or not.

If so, are those evaluations taken into account in determining salary, bonuses or advancement in the firm? Yes

If not, does the firm consider pro bono work generally in associate evaluations? N/A

HOURS

Does the firm give billable hour credit for pro bono work? For all attorneys, billable client hours and pro bono client hours count toward total hours.

Does the firm have a maximum number of pro bono hours that can be applied toward the billable hour target? No

If so, what is the maximum? N/A

If your firm uses hours to determine bonuses, does it consider pro bono hours when determining bonuses? Yes

PRO BONO POINTS

What training opportunities are open to associates working on pro bono matters? Associates may attend trainings offered by legal services providers, and Hale and Dorr has an extensive training program that can often aid associates in their pro bono practice.

Can associates bring matters of interest to the firm? Yes

Does the firm offer the use of support staff in carrying out pro bono matters? Yes

What pro bono opportunities are available for summer associates? Summer associates are typically staffed on pro bono matters as a matter of course when there is appropriate work to be done during their time at the firm. All summer associates have the opportunity to represent individuals in unemployment benefits hearings at the Massachusetts Department of Employment and Training, in cases referred to the firm by Greater Boston Legal Services. In addition, one to two summer associates research and write a legal memo for the Anti-Defamation League each summer. An example of a recent issue is the rights of public agencies to prevent hate groups from demonstrating or holding events in their facilities.

Does the firm have established programs, such as externships, that enable its associates to work in a public interest setting? Yes

If so, where and for up to how long? We send associates on six-month rotations to local district attorney's offices in the Boston area. There is also a part-time mentoring program for corporate associates at the Hale and Dorr Legal Services Center at Harvard Law School.

Has your firm won any special recognition or awards in the last two years for its pro bono work? Yes

If so, please list. The Massachusetts Chapter of The Association of Fundraising Professionals recognized Hale and Dorr with its Leaders in Philanthropy Award in 2002 for the firm's pro bono legal work, philanthropy and community service. In August 2003, the firm received a special pro bono award from the American Bar Association as part of the national team which successfully defended the country's IOLTA programs against Fifth Amendment constitutional challenges.* For his work as chair of the ABA's Subcommittee on the Rights of the Child, which is part of the ABA's International Human Rights Committee, counsel Cris Revaz of our Washington office received the Human Rights Award of the United Nations Association of the National Capital Area in 2002. The ABA Subcommittee advances U.S. laws and policies by promoting the rights, protection and well-being of children in the United States and abroad.

* In 2004, senior partner Richard Johnston received the Massachusetts Bar Foundation's Great Friends of Justice Award for his part in the IOLTA defense.

THE FIRM SAYS

Firm's Philosophy Regarding Pro Bono Work (excerpted from firm's pro bono policy)

Hale and Dorr has had a long and distinguished tradition of encouraging pro bono publico ("pro bono") work by its attorneys, dating back to the firm's original managing partner, Reginald Heber Smith, author of Justice and the Poor (1919) and one of the founders of the Boston Legal Aid Society. The firm has had a formal pro bono policy and a public service committee to administer and supervise pro bono work since 1970. The partners adopted a formal pro bono policy in 1993 to clarify informal guidelines which had been developed by the public service committee in 1970 and to conform the firm's pro bono practices with the principles recognized by the Pro Bono Institute in the Law Firm Pro Bono Challenge. Hale and Dorr reaffirms its institutional obligation to encourage and support the participation by its attorneys in pro bono activities. The firm expects to contribute annually an amount of time equal to at least 3 percent of the firm's billable hours to pro bono work. This expectation translates into an average of approximately 60 hours per attorney per year. While it is believed that participation in pro bono cases should remain a matter of individual choice, the firm expects that a majority of both partners and associates will participate annually in pro bono activities. The Public Service Committee will endeavor to provide pro bono opportunities for members of all departments.

Procedures for Undertaking Pro Bono Assignments

- The public service committee shall be responsible for approving, coordinating, and monitoring pro bono cases. The public service committee shall administer the firm's pro bono program in accordance with this policy and shall make periodic reports to the executive committee about the firm's pro bono activities.

- Requests by partners or associates for approval of pro bono cases shall be made utilizing the online case request form, which will be submitted to the co-chair of the public service committee with a copy to the chair of the new business committee. The public service committee will act upon the request in a timely fashion.

- Upon approval of an lawyer's request by the public service committee (and upon review by the new business committee, including for conflicts) a pro bono case shall be opened to the credit of the firm.

General Volunteering Opportunities

In 1997, Hale and Dorr expanded its philanthropic reach. To make a decisive impact on the educational opportunities available to children and teens, the firm applied the principles of venture philanthropy to create innovative partnerships with a select group of nonprofit organizations dedicated to serving inner-city youth in Boston and Washington, D.C. Through its Youth and Education Initiative, the firm contributes more than $1,100,000 over three years to these organizations, along with a broad range of administrative and in-kind assistance, pro bono legal services and active volunteer service. The firm's Youth and Education Initiative includes volunteer opportunities such as working with inner city high school students to prepare college applications, write research papers and learn negotiations skills, as well as teaching elementary school children to litigate a mock trial. In addition, the firm conducts supply and book drives, Career Days and high school summer internships. Volunteer opportunities outside the Youth and Education Initiative are posted internally for all firm members.

OUR SURVEY SAYS

"Hale and Dorr is committed to pro bono work, most clearly through the inclusion of pro bono hours in the target billable hour number for the year. There are a number of opportunities available for pro bono work and the firm is receptive to associates bringing in pro bono work."

"No doubt in my mind that the firm is highly committed — I have had numerous opportunities to work on cases of my choosing — and the hours all count towards billables."

"The firm is definitely committed to pro bono, but there seems to be confusion over whether it really counts as billable hours. Technically it does count at the end of the year, but throughout the year, it does not count as to whether or not an associate is meeting their budgeted number of hours."

"The firm is pretty good at permitting pro bono activities, but whenever push comes to shove, paying clients appear to come first."

"I have worked on several pro bono cases in my six months here. Pro bono cases are given the same time and attention and treated with the same level of respect as billable cases."

"I have yet to hear someone interested in a pro bono project being turned down. The firm encourages pro bono, especially for younger attorneys."

"Hale and Dorr meets its pro bono requirement primarily by sending four associates/junior partners per year to work for six months in the district attorney's office."

"Pro bono hours are not treated as billable hours, which is very unfortunate."

"Hale and Dorr is absolutely and firmly committed to its pro bono and community initiatives. These initiatives are well organized, with full-time professionals overseeing them, and the opportunities to participate are numerous and varied. They range from traditional pro bono legal practice to the Discovering Justice/St. Clair Project mock trials for elementary school children to partnerships with Teen Empowerment and City Year. All attorneys are actively encouraged to devote their work time to giving back to the legal community, and I'm proud to work at an institution so committed."

"Lots of opportunities for working on public service projects, but not as many for pro bono legal work."

Heller Ehrman White & McAuliffe LLP

333 Bush Street
San Francisco, CA 94104-2878
Phone: (415) 772-6000
www.hewm.com

LOCATIONS

San Francisco, CA (HQ) • Anchorage, AK • Los Angeles, CA • Madison, WI • Menlo Park, CA • New York, NY • Portland, OR • San Diego, CA • Seattle, WA • Washington, DC • Beijing (March 2004) • Hong Kong • Singapore

MAJOR DEPARTMENTS & PRACTICES

Antitrust & Trade Regulation
Appeals & Strategy
Bankruptcy
Consumer Litigation
Corporate Finance
Corporate Securities/M&A
Energy
Environmental Regulation & Litigation
Executive Compensation
FDA
Insurance Coverage
Intellectual Property Litigation
International
Labor & Employment
Life Sciences
Patents & Trademarks
Private Equity
Product Liability
Real Estate
Securities Litigation
Tax
Technology
Venture Law Group
Wealth Management
White Collar Criminal Defense

THE STATS

No. of attorneys worldwide: 720
No. of offices worldwide: 12
Chairman: Barry S. Levin
Firm-wide Managing Shareholder: Robert B. Hubbell

EMPLOYMENT CONTACT

San Francisco
Ms. Stephanie Shambroom
Professional Recruitment Manager
Phone: (415) 772-6591
Fax: (415) 772-6268
E-mail: sshambroom@hewm.com

See firm web site for contacts in other offices.

WHO'S WHO

Does the firm have a pro bono coordinator? Yes. The firm-wide coordinator is Robert Borton. Each office has a committee and committee chair responsible for overseeing the work in that office.

Robert Borton, Esq.
Firm-wide & San Francisco Committee Chair
Phone: (415) 772-6498
E-mail: rborton@hewm.com

Ronald Peterson, Esq.
Los Angeles Committee Chair
Phone: (213) 689-7605
E-mail: rpeterson@hewm.com

Lawrence Zweifach, Esq.
New York Committee Co-Chair
Phone: (212) 847-8762
E-mail: lzweifach@hewm.com

Bruce Saber, Esq.
New York Committee Co-Chair
Phone: (212) 847-8713
E-mail: bsaber@hewm.com

Matthew Geyman, Esq.
Seattle Committee Co-Chair
Phone: (206) 389-6020
E-mail: mgeyman@hewm.com

James Donohue, Esq.
Seattle Committee Co-Chair
Phone: (206) 389-6111
E-mail: jdonohue@hewm.com

Daniel Silverman, Esq.
San Diego Committee Chair
Phone: (858) 450-8466
E-mail: dsilverman@hewm.com

Robert Hawk, Silicon Valley Committee Chair
Phone: (650) 324-7165
E-mail: rhawk@hewm.com

Kenneth Chernof, Esq.
Washington, D.C. Committee Chair
Phone: (202) 912-2199
E-mail: kchernof@hewm.com

Does the firm have a pro bono committee? Yes

If yes, how often does the committee meet? Quarterly, or as needed.

Describe the composition of the committee: Partners and associates from each office make up the individual office committees. The firm-wide committee consists of all office committee members.

THE SCOOP

Does your firm have a written pro bono policy? No

Has the firm signed on to the Law Firm Pro Bono Challenge? Yes

What are some of the areas of law in which your firm has performed pro bono legal work in the last two years? Civil rights; poverty law; political asylum and immigrant rights; environmental law; prisoners rights; gay/lesbian/transgender rights; death penalty cases; First Amendment; youth and children's rights; human rights and international human rights; transactional, tax and nonprofit organization pro bono issues; among others. Our goal is to respond to the interests of each lawyer in the firm and to the needs of our clients and of the civil rights and legal services agencies with whom we work closely.

What are some of the areas of law in which your firm does not perform pro bono work? We do work in essentially all areas of pro bono practice, though more in some than in others.

Organizations for which your firm has performed pro bono legal services in the last two years: A sampling includes: Alliance for Children's Rights; American Civil Liberties Union; Asian Law Caucus; Bet Tzedek (The House of Justice); Center for Law in the Public Interest; Columbia Legal Services, San Diego Volunteer Lawyer Program, and other local legal aid offices in each of our home cities; Compassion in Dying Federation; Earthjustice Legal Defense Fund; Lambda Legal Defense and Education Fund, Inc.; Lawyers Committee for Civil Rights; and many others.

List up to three pro bono matters that are representative of the pro bono work your firm participates in. Three representative cases (among many transactional and litigation matters):

- McConnell v. Federal Election Commission. Heller Ehrman lawyers from our Madison and D.C. offices (along with a coalition of other public interest firms and organizations) represented Senators McCain and Feingold, among others, in defending the constitutionality of the historic "Bipartisan Campaign Finance Reform Act of 2002" before the United States Supreme Court. We are also counsel to the congressional sponsors in challenging the legality of the Federal Election Commission's rulemaking in connection with the Act.

- Through its New York office, Heller Ehrman represents a coalition of law schools and law professors in litigation against the Department of Defense challenging the constitutionality of the Solomon Amendment (a federal statute that threatens universities and colleges with loss of all federal funding if they — or their law and other professional schools — exclude military recruiters from campus). The law schools contend that assisting the military in its recruitment efforts would violate their non-discrimination policies because the military discriminates on the basis of sexual orientation.

- Lawyers from Heller Ehrman's Seattle office represented Laura Hernandez in a major Ninth Circuit victory for the rights of battered immigrant women. The Court of Appeals held that Hernandez' proof of emotional and psychological abuse established her right to seek political asylum and permanent resident status under the 1994 Violence Against Women Act.

BY THE NUMBERS

What is the total number of hours that lawyers in U.S. offices at your firm spent performing pro bono legal services in 2000, 2001 and 2002?

      Total number of hours in 2000: 30,097 hours
      Total number of hours in 2001: 29,696 hours
      Total number of hours in 2002: 45,169 hours

Average number of pro bono hours per attorney in U.S. offices per year (including associates, partners, counsels, but not summer associates):

      Average number of hours per attorney in 2000: 68 hours
      Average number of hours per attorney in 2001: 60 hours
      Average number of hours per attorney in 2002: 84 hours

What percentage of attorneys in this firm's U.S. offices did pro bono work in 2002? N/A

What percentage of attorneys in this firm's U.S. offices did at least 20 hours of pro bono work in 2002? 56 percent

Does the firm encourage its lawyers to perform a minimum number of pro bono hours? Not as such. There is no specific minimum; all attorneys are encouraged to do pro bono work of their choosing.

If so, how many hours per year or what percentage of lawyers' billable hours? N/A

SUPERVISION AND EVALUATIONS

Is there partner supervision on each pro bono matter? Yes

Do partner supervisors or, if applicable, senior associates provide written evaluations of associates' work on pro bono matters? Yes

If so, are those evaluations taken into account in determining salary, bonuses or advancement in the firm? Yes

If not, does the firm consider pro bono work generally in associate evaluations? N/A

HOURS

Does the firm give billable hour credit for pro bono work? The firm gives equal credit for billable and pro bono hours at all compensation levels.

Does the firm have a maximum number of pro bono hours that can be applied toward the billable hour target? No

If so, what is the maximum? N/A

If your firm uses hours to determine bonuses, does it consider pro bono hours when determining bonuses? Yes, fully at all levels.

PRO BONO POINTS

What training opportunities are open to associates working on pro bono matters? Training is done as needed for any area of specialization. Heller Ehrman sponsors trainings with legal services providers in many areas and on many issues; the firm trains legal services lawyers in its in-house associate and general attorney training programs. Pro bono cases afford even the most junior attorneys an opportunity directly to represent individual clients, to negotiate and manage transactions on their behalf, to take discovery, and to appear in court and at trial. All of this work is done under the mentoring supervision of experienced lawyers.

Can associates bring matters of interest to the firm? Yes

Does the firm offer the use of support staff in carrying out pro bono matters? Yes

What pro bono opportunities are available for summer associates? Summer associates are fully integrated into existing pro bono matters and into various low-income clinics and other service work. In several cities, the firm sponsors summer service programs, such as the staffing of The Homeless Advocacy Project Client Representation Clinic in San Francisco.

Does the firm have established programs, such as externships, that enable its associates to work in a public interest setting? Yes

If so, where and for up to how long? In San Francisco and certain other cities, Heller Ehrman participates in trial rotation programs for up to three months on an occasional basis (for example, San Francisco and San Mateo County district attorney offices).

Has your firm won any special recognition or awards in the last two years for its pro bono work? Yes

If so, please list. In 2003, Heller Ehrman received the Outstanding Law Firm Award from the San Diego Legal Aid Society; the firm was honored as the Outstanding Law Firm in Public Service by the San Francisco Bar Association; Heller Ehrman's Portland office was recognized by the Oregon State Bar with its award for the Highest Level of Pro Bono Service; the firm's San Diego office received the California State Bar President's 2003 Pro Bono Service Award for its outstanding pro bono work; Heller Ehrman is one of 20 law firms in the United States named to the American Lawyers "A-List" based upon its pro bono work, along with three other important characteristics (associate satisfaction, diversity and profitability) that are the defining characteristics of the nation's top law firms.

In 2002, Volunteers in Legal Services honored Heller Ehrman's New York office as one of the top law firms in New York City for its pro bono activity; the Seattle office received the 2002 John Miner Wisdom Public Interest and Professionalism Award from the ABA Litigation Section; individual lawyers were recognized for their pro bono contributions in Seattle (Judy Ramseyer received the 2002 President's Award from Washington Women Lawyers, and Matthew Geyman received the Washington State Bar Association Pro Bono Attorney of the Year Award), in Los Angeles (John Ulin received the ACLU of Southern California Voting Rights Award), in San Diego (Dan Silverman received Pro Bono Attorney of the Year Award from the Volunteer Lawyer Program), and in San Francisco (Robert Borton was honored with the Legal Aid Society Roll Call For Social Justice Award).

THE FIRM SAYS

Heller Ehrman traces its tradition of public service to founding members of the firm who believed that every lawyer has an obligation to give back to the community. The firm does not require pro bono work, but we encourage every lawyer, with the support of our legal assistants and staff, to do such legal work. All lawyers, including our youngest associates, are encouraged to bring to the firm their pro bono interests, issues, organizations and clients. Our lawyers also have access to a wide range of pubic interest opportunities through relationships with legal services providers in our home cities and through representation on the boards of many of the organizations with which we work.

We broadcast information about new pro bono opportunities throughout our offices. We do not limit the kinds of cases or issues that lawyers might wish to take on, other than through required limits imposed by conflicts rules and our ability effectively to staff an engagement. The full range of firm resources is devoted to our pro bono cases, exactly as it is to commercial cases, and every lawyer recognizes the same duty and obligation to the individual pro bono client as to the largest of our corporate clients. Pro bono engagements give lawyers the opportunity to learn the basic skills of working with clients, negotiating with adversaries and exercising the judgments that can only be practiced in an active case (many lawyers begin working with clients even before they receive their bar results, under the supervision of a firm partner or associate). Pro bono work represents one of Heller Ehrman's core values and is reflected in every one of our offices. The work we do runs from the largest impact case (such as those noted above) to the hundreds of small client cases and transactional matters that we handle ever year.

Heller Ehrman's tradition of public service, extending to lawyers at every level and in every office, is well reflected in the annual award given to a lawyer or lawyers at the firm in honor of their pro bono contributions. Named for the firm's long-time managing partner, Richard Guggenhime, the 2003 Guggenhime Award honored three associate attorneys. Rima Alaily and David Ward, both associates in the firm's Seattle office, work with that office's "Domestic Violence Revision Team." Rima recently achieved a significant victory for a victim of domestic violence after pursuing her case and her abuser, over the course of several years and through every level of the state court system, including the Washington State Supreme Court. David Ward co-counseled with Rima and is also the deputy director of the domestic violence team. He was particularly recognized for his work with many abused and traumatized clients who struggle with limited English skills and must often overcome cultural barriers to seek help from a lawyer. These clients could not possibly navigate the complex court system without the assistance of a dedicated advocate. Mike Markman, an associate in Heller Ehrman's Silicon Valley office, has done a wide array of pro bono work, including prisoners' rights litigation and various poverty law cases. Most recently Mike led a team of Heller Ehrman lawyers and legal assistants in a lengthy and successful battle against predatory lending practices. Over the course of three years Mike and his team investigated and litigated claims against a mortgage broker and "foreclosure specialist" who had defrauded hundreds of low-income elderly, disabled and mostly minority homeowners out of millions of dollars in home equity.

In recognition of their pro bono work, the firm each year donates $5,000 to an organization of each award recipient's choice.

OUR SURVEY SAYS

"The firm strongly encourages pro bono work. Pro bono time counts towards all bonuses, even if an associate does not meet the minimum billable goal. Moreover, although the official line is that the firm wants associates to hit the minimum billable goal (1,900 hours), there is very little concern if someone does not, so long as the time is made up by pro bono hours."

"The firm counts pro bono hours exactly like billable hours."

"I don't know of any firms that do a better job. That said, there are fewer partners making a major commitment to pro bono in recent years, and that hurts the perception of support among junior associates."

"As the pressure for billables increases, the encouragement to do pro bono has dropped noticeably."

"I still think Heller Ehrman is more committed than most firms to pro bono, but much of that commitment lies in the strong commitments of individual attorneys. Systemic incentives for associates to do pro bono work are increasingly eaten away by incentives to produce billable hours."

"Lots of opportunities, some incentive, not enough time."

"I billed over 200 hours to pro bono last year and have billed over 200 already this year (and it's only March)."

"The firm, like most of its kind, takes a lot of pride in its pro bono work and backs it up by making pro bono hours count toward billable and bonus requirements. We've invested some serious time in both high-profile (McCain Feingold litigation) and high-value (death penalty representation) pro bono work."

"Many associates bill large amounts of pro bono time, although there is no pressure to do so if you don't want to."

"Pro bono is a top priority for Heller, and Heller shareholders and associates commit inordinate time and effort to pro bono projects."

Hogan & Hartson L.L.P.

555 Thirteenth Street, NW
Washington, DC 20004
Phone: (202) 637-5600
www.hhlaw.com

LOCATIONS

Washington, DC (HQ)
Baltimore, MD • Boulder, CO • Colorado Springs, CO • Denver, CO • Los Angeles, CA • McLean, VA • Miami, FL • New York, NY • Beijing • Berlin • Brussels • Budapest • London • Moscow • Paris • Prague • Tokyo • Warsaw

MAJOR DEPARTMENTS & PRACTICES

Antitrust
Business & Finance
Communications
Education
Emerging Businesses
Employee Benefits
Entertainment
Energy
Environmental
Estate Planning & Administration
Food, Drug, Medical Device & Agriculture
Government Contracts
Health
Intellectual Property
International Trade
Labor & Employment
Legislative
Life Sciences
Litigation (Trial & Appellate)
Privacy

THE STATS

No. of attorneys worldwide: 1,000
No. of offices worldwide: 19
Chairman: J. Warren Gorrell Jr.

EMPLOYMENT CONTACT

Ms. Ellen M. Purvance
Associate Recruitment & Professional Development Director
Phone: (202) 637-8601
Fax: (202) 637-5910
E-mail: empurvance@hhlaw.com

WHO'S WHO

Does the firm have a pro bono coordinator? Yes

Bob Duncan, Esq.
Community Services Department Partner
Phone: (202) 637-5758
E-mail: rbduncan@hhlaw.com

If yes, what percentage of his or her time is spent on pro bono work? 100 percent

Does the firm have a pro bono committee? No

THE SCOOP

Does your firm have a written pro bono policy? Yes

Has the firm signed on to the Law Firm Pro Bono Challenge? Yes

What are some of the areas of law in which your firm has performed pro bono legal work in the last two years? Firm lawyers have handled an extraordinary array of pro bono projects encompassing virtually every substantive area in which firm lawyers practice. Some recent pro bono projects have involved international human rights and immigration, civil rights and civil liberties, public benefits and poverty law issues, incorporation and transactional work, legislative drafting and lobbying, administrative law, environmental and community preservation, criminal law and the death penalty, health care and mental health law, child and family advocacy, advising nonprofits, homelessness and housing, Supreme Court and appellate advocacy, 9/11 and other disaster response, domestic violence, AIDs and gay rights, religious rights, landlord & tenant, consumers' rights, the elderly, the arts, disability law, education, free speech, good government, native Americans, non-violence, voting rights, women's rights, estate planning and others.

What are some of the areas of law in which your firm does not perform pro bono work? The firm considers pro bono matters on a case-by-case basis. There is no area of law in which we will not consider taking on a pro bono matter.

Organizations for which your firm has performed pro bono legal services in the last two years: NAACP Legal Defense and Education Fund, Washington Lawyers' Committee for Civil Rights and Urban Affairs, Lawyers' Committee for Human Rights, Washington Legal Clinic for the Homeless, ACLU, Whitman Walker Clinic, News York Lawyers for the Public Interest, Public Counsel, National Parks Conservation Association, MALDEF, Bazelon Center for Mental Health Law, Coalition Against Domestic Violence, Lawyers' Committee for Civil Rights Under Law, Maryland Volunteer Lawyers Society, ABA Death Penalty Representation Project, Downtown Cluster of Congregations, Appleseed, DC Employment Justice Center, Servicemembers Legal Defense Network, Tahirih Justice Center, Hoop Dreams Scholarship Fund, and so on.

List up to three pro bono matters that are representative of the pro bono work your firm participates in.

- Firm lawyers successfully handled the infamous Tulia, Texas, drug sting case in which the word of a single racist undercover agent with a checkered law enforcement past resulted in the arrest of a significant portion of the African-American population of the town, and the jailing of some. As a result of the efforts of Hogan attorneys working with the NAACP Legal Defense and Education Fund, those incarcerated have been released, those convicted have been pardoned and those charged have received monetary compensation. The case received widespread media coverage around the country.

- As the main law firm involved in the ABA Asia Division's Afghanistan Transitional Code of Commerce project, Hogan lawyers have met with Afghan President Hamid Karzai and numerous other Afghan officials and have been working to help bring Afghan law relating to commerce up to international standards in order to encourage sorely needed foreign investment in the country. Firm lawyers have provided legislative drafting advice to the fledgling government on such wide-ranging matters as trade and commerce, antitrust, bankruptcy, banking and commercial law and contracts.

- On the heels of the firm's widely applauded U.S. District Court victory on behalf of an indefinitely detained Liberian national in the first case to interpret the Supreme Court's Zadvydas decision finding detentions of more than six months presumptively unlawful, the ABA Commission on Immigration Policy, Practice and Pro Bono asked firm lawyers to prepare two extensive legal handbooks for INS detainees and to speak at the 2002 Detention Watch Network Conference.

BY THE NUMBERS

What is the total number of hours that lawyers in U.S. offices at your firm spent performing pro bono legal services in 2000, 2001 and 2002?

    Total number of hours in 2000: about 37,000 hours
    Total number of hours in 2001: about 41,000 hours
    Total number of hours in 2002: about 45,000 hours

Average number of pro bono hours per attorney in U.S. offices per year (including associates, partners, counsels, but not summer associates):

    Average number of hours per attorney in 2000: about 64 hours
    Average number of hours per attorney in 2001: about 68 hours
    Average number of hours per attorney in 2002: about 72 hours

What percentage of attorneys in this firm's U.S. offices did pro bono work in 2002? about 70 percent

What percentage of attorneys in this firm's U.S. offices did at least 20 hours of pro bono work in 2002? about 35 percent

Does the firm encourage its lawyers to perform a minimum number of pro bono hours? Yes

If so, how many hours per year or what percentage of lawyers' billable hours? The firm encourages all lawyers to seek to meet the goals and aspirations set forth by their applicable bar authority(ies).

SUPERVISION AND EVALUATIONS

Is there partner supervision on each pro bono matter? Yes

Do partner supervisors or, if applicable, senior associates provide written evaluations of associates' work on pro bono matters? Yes

If so, are those evaluations taken into account in determining salary, bonuses or advancement in the firm? Yes

If not, does the firm consider pro bono work generally in associate evaluations? N/A

HOURS

Does the firm give billable hour credit for pro bono work? Yes

Does the firm have a maximum number of pro bono hours that can be applied toward the billable hour target? Yes

If so, what is the maximum? 100 hours

If your firm uses hours to determine bonuses, does it consider pro bono hours when determining bonuses? Yes

PRO BONO POINTS

What training opportunities are open to associates working on pro bono matters? The firm offers in-house training through its H&H Academy program which is often generally applicable to pro bono work. The firm also sponsors and encourages attendance by lawyers at training presentations by various legal services organizations at the firm and outside of it.

Can associates bring matters of interest to the firm? Yes

Does the firm offer the use of support staff in carrying out pro bono matters? Yes

What pro bono opportunities are available for summer associates? Summer associates have the opportunity to work on all manner of pro bono projects in the firm at the time, from smaller "one-on-one" type cases to some of our larger impact cases. Recent opportunities have included traveling to Mississippi to interview African-American farmers about their discrimination claims against the federal government; working with Women Empowered Against Violence, Inc. to provide a broad range of services to domestic violence victims in the District of Columbia; teaching Introduction to Legal Reasoning to minority and disadvantaged students who will be entering law school in the fall; providing benefits assistance to persons living with AIDS and HIV+; conducting research and analysis concerning our effort to assist on an ABA-sponsored project to develop a transitional commercial code for Afghanistan; helping the Emmaus Service program obtain financing to support the rehabilitation of housing for the elderly; working with the National Parks and Conservation Association to assess the viability of federal legislation to expand the boundary of the Petrified Forest National Park in Arizona; helping to develop two important immigration pro se handbooks for INS detainees suffering indefinite detainment or abuse; providing research and drafting assistance, as well as attending and helping to prepare for hearings and client meetings, in connection with a number of CSD cases involving issues ranging from civil rights and disability discrimination to immigration and the death penalty.

Does the firm have established programs, such as externships, that enable its associates to work in a public interest setting? Yes

If so, where and for up to how long? We do not have externships, preferring instead to allow several D.C. office associates at any given time to spend "rotation" periods doing pro bono work full time. In doing so, they not only serve the public interest and become acquainted with a number of public interest and legal services organizations in the community, but they also obtain valuable training, experience and a sense of shared responsibility to discharge our professional obligation to help those in need of legal services.

Has your firm won any special recognition or awards in the last two years for its pro bono work? Yes

If so, please list. Hogan's CSD has received much national and local acclaim and many awards over the years, including the ABA's and D.C. Bar's pro bono firm of the year awards. Recent honors include Outstanding Achievement Awards from the Washington Lawyers' Committee; the Glinda Award from the Servicemembers Legal Defense Fund; a Certificate of Appreciation from the DC Employment Justice Center; recognition from the District of Columbia Bar for our work on a pro bono website; the National Pro Bono Paralegal Award from the National Federation of Paralegal Associations was presented to a Hogan legal assistant; Parents, Families, and Friends of Lesbians and Gays awarded the firm its Outstanding Community Service Award; recognition from Emmaus Services for the Aging for the firm's corporate, tax, real estate, nonprofit and environmental help; the Lawyers Alliance for New York honored a firm partner with its 2002 Cornerstone Award; and the Maryland Bar Association and the National Asian Pacific American Legal Consortium also recently bestowed awards on the firm.

THE FIRM SAYS

Thirty years ago, Hogan became the first major law firm to establish a separate practice group devoted to pro bono legal services. Since its inception, the Community Services Department, now widely known as Hogan's "CSD," has been charged with developing and staffing both high-profile matters involving issues of public importance and smaller projects addressing individual problems, needs and rights of the disadvantaged and mistreated. The firm has been a leader in the provision of legal services in the public interest since the CSD was founded, and it has been the recipient of the ABA Pro Bono Publico Award and widespread recognition from bar associations and community and legal services organizations. Today, the CSD combines the full-time commitment of a partner and several associates with the part-time contributions of hundreds of lawyers working out of the firm's offices around the world, to provide legal services of virtually every kind to a diverse array of pro bono clients.

CSD lawyers have forced the dismantling of an "urban renewal" program that displaced minority communities, fought to include Mexican Americans under the Voting Rights Act, and challenged the constitutionality of limiting jury service to men before the Supreme Court. The CSD favorably settled two of the largest public accommodation race discrimination class action cases in history, handled landmark school desegregation litigation and argued a milestone Supreme Court case prohibiting discrimination against gays. In just the last couple of years, the CSD prosecuted the claims of numerous individual farmers in the largest discrimination case in history, and achieved a historic victory in the now infamous Tulia, Texas, drug sting case. Firm lawyers recently established a children's hospital in Warsaw, preserved natural resources in Colorado, developed a guardian ad litem program for Florida, litigated a forced labor case in Virginia and obtained sweeping injunctive relief for female detainees enduring intolerable heat and inadequate ventilation at a Baltimore detention center. Following the extraordinary human tragedies of September 11, 2001, lawyers from many of the firm's offices joined with those in New York and D.C. to assist families of victims and establish funds and programs to the families and rescue workers.

The CSD has litigated high-profile Grand Canyon and Glacier Bay environmental cases, obtained a Supreme Court decision striking down a Missouri ballot labeling law and prepared amicus briefs in various first amendment and other important cases. CSD lawyers handled civil liberties cases limiting censorship on the internet, protecting the one person/one vote guarantee, pressing for full voting rights for the District of Columbia and ensuring accessible voting machines for those with visual and manual impairments. The CSD defended the right of the mentally ill to appropriate treatment and is helping salvage D.C.'s mental health program. CSD lawyers are working on legislation to ensure adequate protection and services for homeless men and women and have represented numerous men facing execution on federal and state death rows.

CSD lawyers around the world are working with the ABA and the Afghani government to develop a new code of commerce for that desperate country. The CSD conducted successful international human rights litigation to force Guatemala to prosecute military officers who ordered the death of a "troublesome" anthropologist and secured a $71 million federal court judgment against the president of Zimbabwe for campaigns of violence designed to influence election outcomes. And the CSD obtained a class action victory in the Ninth Circuit forbidding the INS from stripping naturalized citizens of their citizenship without due process, earned a key victory in a case testing the Supreme Court's Zavydas decision limiting INS authority to hold aliens indefinitely and has represented dozens of applicants seeking asylum in the United States.

OUR SURVEY SAYS

"Hogan & Hartson excels at community service. Our community service department is outstanding and brings a lot of unique cases in for attorneys to work on. Pro bono is encouraged and supported by the firm. Hogan should be commended for this."

"You HAVE to do pro bono! Plus, you can count it towards your bonus."

"The firm's community services department is quite unique and provides each of us the opportunity to take on pro bono matters. It is hard to avoid pro bono work at the firm."

"Lots of opportunities, and lots of help from partners, associates and paralegals. Too bad our practice group is not as responsive."

"The firm has an entire practice area devoted to pro bono work, and most of the firm's attorneys engage in pro bono work at some point."

"The firm is strongly committed to having its separate pro bono department handle pro bono work, but does not appear to be very committed nowadays to having attorneys outside the department handle pro bono work."

"I've billed over 500 hours this year and it all will count toward my billable requirement."

"The firm looks committed on the surface, but it often lets the smallest and strangest conflicts (e.g., my client might not like that) prevent associates from doing important pro bono work."

"The firm has an entire department committed to pro bono work, with full-time associates and a full-time partner staffing. Attorneys are frequently encouraged to participate in pro bono work and many do. Up to 100 hours of pro bono work will count toward the 1,950 billable hour requirement once you reach 1,800 [hours]."

"The best pro bono department anywhere, bar none."

Holland & Hart LLP

555 Seventeenth Street, Suite 3200
Denver, CO 80202
Phone: (303) 295-8000
www.hollandhart.com

LOCATIONS

Denver, CO (2 offices) (HQ)
Aspen, CO
Billings, MT
Boise, ID
Boulder, CO
Cheyenne, WY
Colorado Springs, CO
Jackson, WY
Salt Lake City, UT
Santa Fe, NM
Washington, DC

MAJOR DEPARTMENTS & PRACTICES

Business
Litigation
Industry Groups (including Communications & Technology, Construction, Emerging Growth, Energy & Electricity, Health Care, Life Sciences, Mining, Oil & Gas, Native American Law, Real Estate, Telecommunications)
Natural Resources

THE STATS

No. of attorneys: 280 +
No. of offices: 12
Managing Partner: Edward H. Flitton

EMPLOYMENT CONTACT

Ms. Julie Carroll
Holland & Hart LLP
P. O. Box 8749
Denver, CO 80201-8749
Fax: (303) 295-8261

WHO'S WHO

Principal pro bono contact(s) at your firm:

David K. Broadbent, Esq.
Partner and Pro Bono Coordinator
60 East South Temple, Suite 2000
Salt Lake City, UT 84111
Phone: (801) 595-7806
E-mail: dbroadbent@hollandhart.com

Does the firm have a pro bono coordinator? Yes
David K. Broadbent

If yes, what percentage of his or her time is spent on pro bono work? 5 to 7 percent

Does the firm have a pro bono committee? No

If yes, how often does the committee meet? N/A

Describe the composition of the committee: N/A

THE SCOOP

Does your firm have a written pro bono policy? Yes

Has the firm signed on to the Law Firm Pro Bono Challenge? Yes

What are some of the areas of law in which your firm has performed pro bono legal work in the last two years? Civil rights, representation of 9/11 victims, environmental, special education, forming and assisting tax-exempt entities, post-decree death sentence appeals, rights of the mentally ill, estate planning, trust land preservation, representation of Indian tribe in drafting its probate code, assisting group for disabled acquire real estate for children's facility, guardianships and conservatorships.

What are some of the areas of law in which your firm does not perform pro bono work? N/A

Organizations for which your firm has performed pro bono legal services in the last two years: Trial Lawyers Care, Inc. (for 9/11 victims), ATLA, Metro Volunteer Lawyers, Colorado Legal Services, Utah State Bar Pro Bono Project, Idaho Volunteer Lawyers Program.

List up to three pro bono matters that are representative of the pro bono work your firm participates in.

- After the 9/11 terrorist attacks, the American Trial Lawyers Association (ATLA) set up the largest pro bono effort ever organized by attorneys across the country to provide legal assistance to the families of victims of the terrorist attacks -- Trial Lawyers Care. A number of attorneys in H&H volunteered to work on such cases. One case we took was for a man whose wife was killed in the World Trade Center on 9/11. The award eventually made by the Special Master was one of the largest awards made to date.

- We represented Trout Unlimited in the Western Water Project to conserve and restore North America's trout and salmon fisheries.

- We represented residents of the Colorado State Mental Institute in a class action to correct unsafe and inadequate conditions provided to residents. The resulting settlement requires the state to make permanent improvements in care that had, for a long time, violated constitutional and statutory standards.

BY THE NUMBERS

What is the total number of hours that lawyers at your firm spent performing pro bono legal services in 2000, 2001 and 2002?

    Total number of hours in 2000: 23,777 hours
    Total number of hours in 2001: 27,267 hours
    Total number of hours in 2002: 28,990 hours

Average number of pro bono hours per attorney in U.S. offices per year (including associates, partners, counsels, but not summer associates):

    Average number of hours per attorney in 2000: 104 hours
    Average number of hours per attorney in 2001: 106 hours
    Average number of hours per attorney in 2002: 105 hours

What percentage of attorneys in this firm's U.S. offices did pro bono work in 2002? 85 percent

What percentage of attorneys in this firm's U.S. offices did at least 20 hours of pro bono work in 2002? 78 percent

Does the firm encourage its lawyers to perform a minimum number of pro bono hours? Yes

If so, how many hours per year or what percentage of lawyers' billable hours? 3 to 5 percent of total

SUPERVISION AND EVALUATIONS

Is there partner supervision on each pro bono matter? Yes

Do partner supervisors or, if applicable, senior associates provide written evaluations of associates' work on pro bono matters? No

If so, are those evaluations taken into account in determining salary, bonuses or advancement in the firm? N/A

If not, does the firm consider pro bono work generally in associate evaluations? Yes

HOURS

Does the firm give billable hour credit for pro bono work? No

Does the firm have a maximum number of pro bono hours that can be applied toward the billable hour target? No

If so, what is the maximum? N/A

If your firm uses hours to determine bonuses, does it consider pro bono hours when determining bonuses? Not applicable

PRO BONO POINTS

What training opportunities are open to associates working on pro bono matters? All matters are supervised by partners, and regular feedback and participation are provided.

Can associates bring matters of interest to the firm? Yes

Does the firm offer the use of support staff in carrying out pro bono matters? Yes

What pro bono opportunities are available for summer associates? We actively encourage our summer associates to work on at least one pro bono matter during their term with us.

Does the firm have established programs, such as externships, that enable its associates to work in a public interest setting? No

If so, where and for up to how long? N/A

Has your firm won any special recognition or awards in the last two years for its pro bono work? N/A

If so, please list. N/A

THE FIRM SAYS

We accept as a guiding principle that this firm has a special obligation to participate in pro bono and public service activities and we expect each lawyer to accept and act upon that principle. We believe that each individual must remain free to select pro bono and public service activities of his or her own choosing. In determining whether work will be undertaken, we consider the following factors: Is the client indigent? Is the client a civic, professional, political, charitable or educational organization? Does the work contribute to the general welfare? What is the degree of professional and personal responsibility required to do the work? Attorneys' efforts in furtherance of pro bono work are evaluated and considered in the compensation process.

Holland & Knight LLP

2099 Pennsylvania Avenue, Suite 100
Washington, DC 20006-6801
Phone: (202) 955-3000
www.hklaw.com

LOCATIONS

Annapolis, MD • Atlanta, GA • Bethesda, MD • Boston, MA • Bradenton, FL • Chicago, IL • Fort Lauderdale, FL • Jacksonville, FL • Lakeland, FL • Los Angeles, CA • Miami, FL • New York, NY • McLean, VA • Orlando, FL • Portland, OR • Providence, RI • San Antonio, TX • San Francisco, CA • Seattle, WA • St. Petersburg, FL • Tallahassee, FL • Tampa, FL • Washington, DC • West Palm Beach, FL • Caracas* • Helsinki • Mexico City • Rio de Janeiro • São Paulo • Tel Aviv* • Tokyo

* Representative offices

MAJOR DEPARTMENTS & PRACTICES

Antitrust
Bankruptcy, Financial Services & Restructuring
Business Law
Energy & Environmental
Government Contracts
Health Care
Intellectual Property
International
Labor & Employment
Litigation & Alternative Dispute Resolution
Maritime, Shipping & Admiralty
Media & Communications
Private Wealth Services
Product Liability
Public Law
Real Estate
Taxation
Technology & Emerging Companies
Telecommunications
White Collar Crime & Corporate Compliance

THE STATS

No. of attorneys worldwide: 1,250 +
No. of offices worldwide: 31
Managing Partner: Howell W. Melton Jr.

EMPLOYMENT CONTACT

Ms. Alida Coo-Kendall
National Recruitment Coordinator
10 St. James Avenue
E-mail: alida.cookendall@hklaw.com

WHO'S WHO

Does the firm have a pro bono coordinator? Yes. The Community Services Team has 10 full-time attorneys dedicated to pro bono legal services for poor people or organizations that substantially benefit the poor:

Stephen F. Hanlon, Esq.
Community Services Team Partner, Washington, DC
Phone: (202) 828-1871
E-mail: Shanlon@hklaw.com

Christopher Nugent, Esq.
Community Services Team Administrator, Washington DC
Phone: (202) 419-2428
E-mail: christopher.nugent@hklaw.com

Robin Rosenberg, Esq.
Community Services Team Pro Bono Counsel, St. Petersberg
Phone: (727) 824-6199
E-mail: robin.rosenberg@hklaw.com

George Kendall, Esq.
Community Services Team Pro Bono Counsel, New York
Phone: (212) 513-3358
E-mail: george.kendall@hklaw.com

Zachary Potter, Esq.
Chesterfield Smith Fellow, Washington, DC

Chestefield Smith Fellows:
Jennifer Mason, Esq., Washington, DC (outgoing)
Cecily Baskir, Esq., Washington, DC (incoming)
Esme Caramello, Esq., Boston (outgoing)
Laura Fernandez, Esq., New York
David Shahoulian, Esq., Miami
Leon Fresco, Esq., Miami (incoming)
Gretchen Rohr, Esq., Atlanta

Additionally, each of our 23 offices has a pro bono partner whose responsibilities include coordinating pro bono legal services.

If yes, what percentage of his or her time is spent on pro bono work? 100 percent

Does the firm have a pro bono committee? No

If yes, how often does the committee meet? N/A

Describe the composition of the committee: N/A

THE SCOOP

Does your firm have a written pro bono policy? Yes

Has the firm signed on to the Law Firm Pro Bono Challenge? Yes

What are some of the areas of law in which your firm has performed pro bono legal work in the last two years? We provide pro bono representation to poor people and organizations that primarily serve poor people in virtually all areas of civil and criminal law. Over the last two years, the areas have included civil rights, asylum/immigration, legislative advocacy, children's rights, international law, health care, public benefits, indigent defense, death penalty, community economic development, domestic violence and domestic relations.

What are some of the areas of law in which your firm does not perform pro bono work? We do not restrict our pro bono representation by areas of law but require that the legal services are for poor people or organizations that primarily serve poor people.

Organizations for which your firm has performed pro bono legal services in the last two years: Washington Lawyers Committee for Civil Rights and Urban Affairs, Women's Commission for Refugee Women and Children, NAACP Legal Defense Fund, ACLU National Prison Project, The Constitution Project, Southern Human Rights Center, Florida Immigrant Advocacy Center, Lawyers for Children America, National Center for Missing and Exploited Children, Catholic Legal Immigration Network, Inc.

List up to three pro bono matters that are representative of the pro bono work your firm participates in.

- Holland & Knight LLP currently represents death row inmate Mr. Delma Banks pro bono in his petition before the Supreme Court based on prosecutorial misconduct and ineffective assistance of counsel. Oral argument was held in December, 2003.

- In *Henderson v. Moore*, Holland & Knightis representing the class of all Florida prisoners challenging Department of Corrections practices that deny inmates access to legal materials and law related supplies and services, which impair their abilities to access the courts as guaranteed by the Florida Constitution.

- Holland & Knight is currently representing Malik Jarno, a mentally retarded Guinean refugee orphan who has languished in immigration custody for more than three years, in his highly-publicized quest for freedom and safety in the United States.

BY THE NUMBERS

What is the total number of hours that lawyers in U.S. offices at your firm spent performing pro bono legal services in 2000, 2001 and 2002?

Total number of hours in 2000: 30,124 hours
Total number of hours in 2001: 40,800 hours
Total number of hours in 2002: 41,577 hours

Average number of pro bono hours per attorney in U.S. offices per year (including associates, partners, counsels, but not summer associates):

    Average number of hours per attorney in 2000: 32.5 hours
    Average number of hours per attorney in 2001: 37.3 hours
    Average number of hours per attorney in 2002: 35.8 hours

What percentage of attorneys in this firm's U.S. offices did pro bono work in 2002? 45 percent

What percentage of attorneys in this firm's U.S. offices did at least 20 hours of pro bono work in 2002? 39 percent

Does the firm encourage its lawyers to perform a minimum number of pro bono hours? Yes

If so, how many hours per year or what percentage of lawyers' billable hours? We encourage all lawyers to perform at least 50 hours in pro bono legal services per year consistent with the ABA Model Rule of Professional Conduct 6.1.

SUPERVISION AND EVALUATIONS

Is there partner supervision on each pro bono matter? Yes

Do partner supervisors or, if applicable, senior associates provide written evaluations of associates' work on pro bono matters? Yes

If so, are those evaluations taken into account in determining salary, bonuses or advancement in the firm? Yes

If not, does the firm consider pro bono work generally in associate evaluations? N/A

HOURS

Does the firm give billable hour credit for pro bono work? Yes

Does the firm have a maximum number of pro bono hours that can be applied toward the billable hour target? No

If so, what is the maximum? N/A

If your firm uses hours to determine bonuses, does it consider pro bono hours when determining bonuses? Yes

PRO BONO POINTS

What training opportunities are open to associates working on pro bono matters? We organize and host on-site and firm-wide trainings by partnering public interest organizations for CLE and billable hour credit. We also encourage attorneys to attend relevant off-site pro bono trainings for CLE and billable hour credit.

Can associates bring matters of interest to the firm? Yes

Does the firm offer the use of support staff in carrying out pro bono matters? Yes

What pro bono opportunities are available for summer associates? We involve summer associates in a firm-wide pro bono project and encourage them to support individual pro bono work at their respective offices.

Does the firm have established programs, such as externships, that enable its associates to work in a public interest setting? No

Has your firm won any special recognition or awards in the last two years for its pro bono work? Yes

If so, please list.

- Pro Bono Institute 2002 Laurie D. Zeldon Pro Bono Award presented by Supreme Court Justice Ruth Bader Ginsburg to firm founder, Chesterfield Smith

- Southern Center for Human Rights 2002 Frederick Douglass Award to Community Services Team George Kendall

- 2002 Department of Justice Executive Office for Immigration Review Pro Bono Award to Holland & Knight for Participation in Board of Immigration Appeals Pro Bono Project

- Florida Immigrant Advocacy Center 2003 Award to Holland & Knight for Pro Bono Work for Detained Immigrants and Asylum Seekers

- Florida Bar President 2002 Pro Bono Service Award to Leo Rydzewski

- Lawyers Alliance for New York 2003 Cornerstone Award to Andrea Marshall

- InMotion (New York) 2003 John. K. Geiger Award to Francesca Morris

- Fresh Ministries 2002 Award to Jacksonville Office

- National Center for Family Homelessness (Boston) 2003 Award to Veronica Greenbaum

- Boston Women's Bar Association/Women's Bar Foundation 2002 Pro Bono Award to Boston office

THE FIRM SAYS

Our Pro Bono Tradition
Holland & Knight encourages lawyers in all of its offices to provide legal services to poor people pro bono, that is, without charging legal fees. For almost 40 years, Chesterfield Smith, the firm's chairman emeritus, has imbued Holland & Knight lawyers with a sense of community purpose and the recognition that we have a professional duty to provide needy people and groups with free legal services.

The Community Services Team
In 1990, Holland & Knight established its Community Services Team (CST) to more effectively marshal its resources to provide legal representation to those who cannot afford it. The CST is a structured, institutionalized department within the firm, drawing on all of the firm's resources. The CST is headed by partner Stephen F. Hanlon, who joined the firm in 1990 to devote his entire efforts to pro bono work. Steve has a long history of successful civil rights litigation and advocacy for the poor. He manages the CST along with two pro bono senior counsel, George H. Kendall in New York and Robin L. Rosenberg in St. Petersburg, Florida. CST Administrator Chris Nugent is in our Washington, D.C., office. Beginning in 2001, the firm added five Chesterfield Smith Fellows to the team of attorneys working full-time on pro bono legal matters. In addition to this dedicated pro bono staff, hundreds of lawyers throughout the firm provide pro bono legal services.

Achieving System-wide Relief for Thousands

The CST lawyers and Smith Fellows concentrate their efforts on cases with significant issues affecting large numbers of people. They are frequently assisted by other lawyers throughout the firm. This institutionalized commitment to pro bono work has produced significant results. Holland & Knight has represented thousands of people with legal problems who otherwise would have been denied access to the legal system. Some of the clients in our major cases include dependent and delinquent children in Florida who need but are not receiving mental health services; African-American survivors of Rosewood, a town destroyed in 1923 by white neighbors; thousands of African-American would-be renters denied housing in a decade-long scheme; low-income pregnant women who were unwitting subjects of medical experimentation.

Making a Difference One Person at a Time
Lawyers in every Holland & Knight office provide free legal services to poor people and organizations that primarily serve poor people. The variety of cases is as broad as the needs of the communities in which we practice. Individual cases are accepted and managed by the pro bono partner in each of the firm's offices.

The Firm's Pro Bono Policy
The firm's written pro bono policy available at www.hklaw.com/cst provides that all approved pro bono work consisting of legal services for poor people or organizations that primarily serve poor people will be considered the same as any paying client work in evaluation, advancement and compensation decisions within the firm. Pro bono legal work accrues creditable hours eligible for collection credit.

OUR SURVEY SAYS

"I think there's a concerted effort to encourage all attorneys to contribute to pro bono work."

"Everyone gets 100 hours billable credit each year and the firm strongly encourages each and every person do use it. The 100 hours can be extended to 200 billable hours credit with permission."

"I have billed, and received credit for, over 100 hours of pro bono work each year I've been here. The firm is very encouraging of these efforts, and the large-scale projects taken on by the Community Services Team make it really easy to get involved."

"Fluctuates year by year. There was a big commitment, then it got scaled back, now it may be on the comeback trail. We'll see."

"The firm is strongly committed to pro bono as a whole, but does not encourage pro bono work by individual lawyers. The bonus structure discourages pro bono work because the bonus is based solely on 'collected' hours, and we never collect on pro bono work."

"In the past, this firm had an admirable commitment to pro bono work. However, with the increased focus on productivity and profits, there has been a noticeable de-emphasis on pro bono work."

"As a person who does a fair amount of pro bono work, Holland & Knight definitely lives up to its reputation. Not only is pro bono encouraged, but associates are given billable hour credit and, in some cases, the work undertaken is considered paid for profitability purposes."

"The pro bono commitment is substantial. The work gives me the opportunity to handle a matter from beginning to end, trial experience and a good feeling. I am extremely pleased that the firm supports it."

"Still good, but used to be better."

"The greatest aspect of the firm is the commitment to pro bono work. That is what makes this a great law firm."

Howrey Simon Arnold & White, LLP

1299 Pennsylvania Avenue, NW
Washington, DC 20004
Phone: (202) 783-0800
www.howrey.com

LOCATIONS

Chicago, IL
Houston, TX
Irvine, CA
Los Angeles, CA
Menlo Park, CA
San Francisco, CA
Washington, DC
Amsterdam
Brussels
London

MAJOR DEPARTMENTS & PRACTICES

Antitrust
Global Litigation
Intellectual Property

THE STATS

No. of attorneys worldwide: 570
No. of offices worldwide: 10
Managing Partner and CEO: Robert F. Ruyak

EMPLOYMENT CONTACT

Ms. Janet Brown
Manager, Attorney Recruitment
Phone: (202) 783-0800
E-mail: brownjanet@howrey.com

WHO'S WHO

Does the firm have a pro bono coordinator? Yes

Rachel Strong, Esq.
Pro Bono Counsel
Phone: (202) 383-7083
E-mail: strongr@howrey.com

If yes, what percentage of his or her time is spent on pro bono work? 100 percent

Does the firm have a pro bono committee? Yes

If yes, how often does the committee meet? We have a national pro bono committee that meets six to eight times a year.

Describe the composition of the committee: The committee is comprised of partners from each office as well as associates from different offices.

THE SCOOP

Does your firm have a written pro bono policy? Yes

Has the firm signed on to the Law Firm Pro Bono Challenge? Yes

What are some of the areas of law in which your firm has performed pro bono legal work in the last two years? We mostly take litigation cases. In the past two years, we have handled cases involving adoption, custody, domestic violence, landlord-tenant, disability discrimination, housing discrimination, voting rights, political asylum, and consumer debt, among others. We also have worked on pro bono trademark, copyright and patent cases.

What are some of the areas of law in which your firm does not perform pro bono work? We do very limited work in areas that do not involve litigation, such as community economic development.

Organizations for which your firm has performed pro bono legal services in the last two years: We have taken cases from more than 50 different organizations in the past two years, including The Children's Law Center, Legal Aid Society, Women Empowered Against Violence, Public Law Center, Houston Volunteer Lawyers Program, Chicago Volunteer Legal Services, Lawyers Committee for Civil Rights, Bazelon Center for Mental Health, Legal Counsel for the Elderly Public Counsel.

List up to three pro bono matters that are representative of the pro bono work your firm participates in.

- We successfully represented the plaintiffs in American Association of People With Disabilities v. Hood, et al., a class action on behalf of visually and manually impaired voters that went to trial on September 23 in Jacksonville, Fla. Howrey filed suit against the city of Jacksonville and the State of Florida for failing to provide accessible voting technology for the class members. The court ruled that Jacksonville and the State of Florida violated the ADA and Rehabilitation Act.

- We are representing all citizens who file complaints against police officers with the D.C. Office of Complaint and Review in administrative hearings. These can include complaints of harassment, excessive force, and so on.

- Howrey represented 59 families who sued their landlord because of the deplorable slum conditions in which they lived. Children were forced to fight off rats, and several had gotten ill from the vermin infested conditions. We negotiated one of the largest settlements in California history in a slum housing case.

BY THE NUMBERS

What is the total number of hours that lawyers in U.S. offices at your firm spent performing pro bono legal services in 2000, 2001 and 2002?

    Total number of hours in 2000: 25,000 hours
    Total number of hours in 2001: 23,000 hours
    Total number of hours in 2002: 41,000 hours

Average number of pro bono hours per attorney in U.S. offices per year (including associates, partners, counsels, but not summer associates):

    Average number of hours per attorney in 2000: N/A
    Average number of hours per attorney in 2001: N/A
    Average number of hours per attorney in 2002: N/A

What percentage of attorneys in this firm's U.S. offices did pro bono work in 2002? more than 50 percent

What percentage of attorneys in this firm's U.S. offices did at least 20 hours of pro bono work in 2002? more than 50 percent

Does the firm encourage its lawyers to perform a minimum number of pro bono hours? Yes

If so, how many hours per year or what percentage of lawyers' billable hours? We encourage each attorney to bill 5 percent of their billable hours to pro bono cases.

SUPERVISION AND EVALUATIONS

Is there partner supervision on each pro bono matter? Yes

Do partner supervisors or, if applicable, senior associates provide written evaluations of associates' work on pro bono matters? Yes

If so, are those evaluations taken into account in determining salary, bonuses or advancement in the firm? Yes

If not, does the firm consider pro bono work generally in associate evaluations? N/A

HOURS

Does the firm give billable hour credit for pro bono work? Yes

Does the firm have a maximum number of pro bono hours that can be applied toward the billable hour target? No

If so, what is the maximum? N/A

If your firm uses hours to determine bonuses, does it consider pro bono hours when determining bonuses? Yes

PRO BONO POINTS

What training opportunities are open to associates working on pro bono matters? We provide some training in house if there are enough volunteers. If not, we encourage lawyers to attend trainings put on by the local service providers and local bars.

Can associates bring matters of interest to the firm? Yes

Does the firm offer the use of support staff in carrying out pro bono matters? Yes

What pro bono opportunities are available for summer associates? We have a shortened summer session (three weeks in the office and two weeks at a Bootcamp off-site training facility). While the summer associates are in the firm, they are encouraged to work on existing pro bono cases.

Does the firm have established programs, such as externships, that enable its associates to work in a public interest setting? Yes

If so, where and for up to how long? We do not have an externship program for associates, but we do offer one for first-year law students. This past summer, Howrey introduced an innovative program that couples first-year law students with public interest organizations that need additional staffing during the summer. The program, known as "Howrey Externs for Legal Pro bono Service" (HELPS), awarded six externships to students who are drawn to pro bono and public interest work. The students are eligible for the program after completing one year in law school. They must demonstrate their commitment to pursuing a career in public interest law to be awarded an externship.

Has your firm won any special recognition or awards in the last two years for its pro bono work? Yes

If so, please list. In 2003, Howrey received the following awards: Robert F. Ruyak, the managing partner and CEO of Howrey Simon Arnold & White, received the first Cardinal James Hickey Award from the Archdiocese Legal Network. Protection & Advocacy, Inc. selected Howrey as a recipient of one of its 2003 Advocacy Achievement Awards because of all that Howrey did in 2003 to advance their mission of achieving an inclusive and barrier free world for Californians with disabilities. Public Counsel recognized Ben Davidson as "Advocate of the Year" for its Immigrants' Rights Project. The Public Law Center, one of the oldest and largest public interest law firms in Orange County, selected Howrey's Irvine office as the Law Firm of the Year.

In 2002, Howrey received the following awards: The Houston Bar Foundation presented its Mid Size Pro Bono Firm of the Year awarded to Howrey's Houston office. Howrey's D.C. office was honored by the Judge David L. Bazelon Center for Mental Health Law for its ongoing work on behalf of persons with disabilities. Howrey was selected as one of the recipients of the Washington Lawyers' Committee for Civil Rights and Urban Affairs Outstanding Achievement Award in recognition for the firm's pro bono efforts on behalf of the Committee's Immigrant and Refugee Rights Project.

In 2001, Howrey received the following awards: Howrey received the prestigious Katharine Krause Award from The Inner City Law Center for work in a slum housing case involving multiple plaintiff/tenants and the death of a child due to slum condition. The Maryland State Bar Association honored Howrey as a recipient of the 2001 Maryland Pro Bono Service Award for law firms for the firm's work benefiting the Baltimore City Public Schools. Howrey was honored by the Washington Lawyers' Committee for Civil Rights and Urban Affairs for its outstanding work on behalf of the Committee's Equal Employment Opportunity Project. Women Empowered Against Violence presented Rachel Strong with its first annual pro bono award in recognition of the outstanding pro bono work done with domestic vioence survivors.

THE FIRM SAYS

The lawyers of Howrey Simon Arnold & White, LLP ("Howrey") have a long-standing tradition of excellence in legal work and pride in being part of the legal profession. We believe that all lawyers have a professional obligation to help make the legal system accessible to all regardless of economic means. To implement this philosophy, Howrey fosters and supports pro bono activities by its lawyers and is one of the original signers of the Law Firm Pro Bono Challenge. We expressly encourage associates to take on pro bono assignments to help fill the great need for legal services to the poor and to develop professionally as lawyers. Consistent with ABA Model Rule 6.1 and the Pro Bono Challenge Statement of Principles, Howrey defines pro bono representation as activities of the firm undertaken normally without expectation of fee and not in the course of ordinary commercial practice and consisting of: delivery of legal services to persons of limited means or to charitable, religious, civic, community, governmental and educational organizations in matters which are designed primarily to address the needs of persons of limited means; the provision of legal assistance to individuals, groups or organizations seeking to secure or protect civil rights, civil liberties or public rights; and the provision of legal assistance to charitable, religious, civic, community, governmental or educational organizations in matters in furtherance of their organizational purposes, where the payment of standard legal fees would significantly deplete the organization's economic resources or would be otherwise inappropriate.

Because pro bono work can help associates acquire skills in case management, interviewing, negotiation and trial practice, we have established a pro bono program that integrates our service obligations with our attorney development efforts. The three-fold objective of the Howrey pro bono program is: (1) to provide pro bono legal assistance where Howrey can make a difference either on an individual basis or by having a broad impact; (2) to integrate the pro bono representation of the firm with the professional development of the associates; and (3) to represent pro bono clients in the same manner as if they were billable clients. To implement the objectives of the program, we have formed a pro bono committee. Among other responsibilities, the pro bono committee fosters relationships between Howrey and public interest and community organizations, and through these relationships identifies appropriate pro bono cases for the firm; screens for approval pro bono cases referred by public interest and community organizations or proposed by the firm's lawyers; obtains appropriate staffing for pro bono cases, considering attorney workload and expertise; monitors the status of pro bono cases; monitors and selects public interest and community events in which the firm may advance its pro bono policy by participating; monitors the firm's overall pro bono efforts and reports the results to the Law Firm Pro Bono Project; reports on the firm's pro bono activities to firm management; and prepares an annual report of the firm's pro bono activities.

Hours spent on firm-approved pro bono matters are treated for all purposes like hours spent on billable matters (e.g., they are fully counted in determining associate compensation and bonuses). Pursuant to the Law Firm Pro Bono Challenge, Howrey encourages its lawyers to spend up to 5 percent of their time on pro bono matters.

OUR SURVEY SAYS

"The firm does a substantial amount of pro bono work. Lawyers at all levels, including partners, take on pro bono cases. The firm also does a significant amount of non-legal volunteer work with Habitat For Humanity and other foundations."

"The firm has always been very supportive of pro bono work. And all pre-approved pro bono work counts towards the minimum billable requirement."

"Pro bono hours count as billable with no limit. I billed almost 1,000 hours to pro bono last year and still got the exact same bonus as everyone else in my class with similar total hours. The firm also pays expenses for big cases, including expert fees and witness travel. I cannot say enough about this firm's commitment to pro bono and those who do it."

"[The firm is] committed to almost a ridiculous degree. It will give 100 percent billable hour credit for doing approved pro bono work."

"I have worked on three pro bono cases in the last six months. I feel that I am getting the opportunity to do as much pro bono as I am willing to take on. As a show of my firm's commitment to pro bono, they have made the hours that an associate spends on a pro bono case count towards that associate's billable goal. This is very encouraging for those interested in doing pro bono work."

"Almost every associate I know has at least one pro bono case."

"One respectable thing about the firm is that they are very supportive of pro bono efforts. The problem is that the vast majority of these must be in line with the politics of the D.C. partners in order to be approved for pro bono credit."

"It seems like we have partners or senior associates sending out pro bono e-mails every other day. We have a great policy which allows us to bill many of our pro bono hours. And if we run out of hours, we can request more."

"Pro bono is encouraged, and I have never been penalized for not working enough on billable matters because of pro bono commitments. (Of course, pro bono is the only courtroom experience a Howrey litigation associate will ever get, so Howrey knows it needs to be supportive.)"

"Howrey has a very strong commitment to pro bono. Associates are given full billable credit for pro bono cases. The firm seeks out this type of work to ensure its associates have the opportunity to participate in unique and fulfilling pro bono projects."

Hughes Hubbard & Reed LLP

One Battery Park Plaza
New York, NY 10004-1482
Phone: (212) 837-6000
www.hugheshubbard.com

LOCATIONS

New York, NY (HQ)
Jersey City, NJ
Los Angeles, CA
Miami, FL
Washington, DC
Paris
Tokyo

MAJOR DEPARTMENTS & PRACTICES

Antitrust
Arbitration & Alternative Dispute Resolution
Aviation
Capital Markets
Corporate
Corporate Reorganization
Employee Benefits
Entertainment & Media Law
Environmental Law
Financial Services
Insurance
Intellectual Property & Technology
Internal Investigations & Government
Investigations
International
Joint Ventures & Other Strategic Alliances
Labor & Employment Law
Litigation
Mergers & Acquisitions
Personal Affairs
Pharmaceuticals & Healthcare
Product Liability & Toxic Torts
Real Estate
Tax
White Collar Crime & Corporate Compliance

THE STATS

No. of attorneys worldwide: 300
No. of offices worldwide: 7
Chair: Candace K. Beinecke
Managing Partner: Charles H. Scherer

EMPLOYMENT CONTACTS

Lateral Hiring
Mr. Adrian Cockerill
Director of Legal Employment
Phone: (212) 837-6131
E-mail: cockerill@hugheshubbard.com

Law Student Hiring
Ms. Bianca Torres
Recruitment Coordinator
Phone: (212) 837-6131
E-mail: torres@hugheshubbard.com

WHO'S WHO

Principal pro bono contact(s) at your firm:

Vilia B. Hayes, Esq.
Pro Bono Chair
Phone: (212) 837-6839
E-mail: hayes@hugheshubbard.com

Ms. Nellie So
Pro Bono Paralegal
Phone: (212) 837-6694
E-mail: so@hugheshubbard.com

Does the firm have a pro bono coordinator? Yes

Greg Koerner, Esq.
Senior Associate, Pro Bono Coordinator
Phone: (212) 837-6296
E-mail: koerner@hugheshubbard.com

Damon Rowe, Esq.
Associate, Pro Bono Coordinator
Phone: (212) 837-6106
E-mail: rowe@hugheshubbard.com

If yes, what percentage of his or her time is spent on pro bono work? Approximately 15 percent

Does the firm have a pro bono committee? Yes

If yes, how often does the committee meet? Periodically

Describe the composition of the committee: Partners George A. Davidson, Vilia B. Hayes, Seth D. Rothman, Carla A. Kerr.

THE SCOOP

Does your firm have a written pro bono policy? Yes

Has the firm signed on to the Law Firm Pro Bono Challenge? Yes

What are some of the areas of law in which your firm has performed pro bono legal work in the last two years? Some areas of law in which Hughes Hubbard has performed pro bono legal work include family law, prisoner rights appeals, housing issues, Social Security issues, artist representation cases and immigration law.

What are some of the areas of law in which your firm does not perform pro bono work? Criminal cases.

Organizations for which your firm has performed pro bono legal services in the last two years: The Legal Aid Society, Beth Israel Hospital, Volunteer Lawyers for the Arts, New York Lawyers for the Public Interest, inMotion,

Sanctuary for Families, Victim Services, Lawyers Committee for Human Rights, Compassion In Dying, Center for Reproductive Law and Policy.

List up to three pro bono matters that are representative of the pro bono work your firm participates in.

- Representation of HIV patients with respect to various legal issues.

- Representation of (a) individuals who have been indefinitely detained pending removal to their native country and; (b) individuals seeking asylum in the United States and relief from deportation under the Convention Against Torture Act.

- Prisoner civil rights cases.

BY THE NUMBERS

What is the total number of hours that lawyers in U.S. offices at your firm spent performing pro bono legal services in 2000, 2001 and 2002?

Total number of hours in 2000: 13,402.73 hours
Total number of hours in 2001: 12,474.45 hours
Total number of hours in 2002: 13,899.65 hours

Average number of pro bono hours per attorney in U.S. offices per year (including associates, partners, counsels, but not summer associates):

Average number of hours per attorney in 2000: 56.99 hours
Average number of hours per attorney in 2001: 53.65 hours
Average number of hours per attorney in 2002: 59.10 hours

What percentage of attorneys in this firm's U.S. offices did pro bono work in 2002? 73.3 percent

What percentage of attorneys in this firm's U.S. offices did at least 20 hours of pro bono work in 2002? 57.2 percent

Does the firm encourage its lawyers to perform a minimum number of pro bono hours? Yes

If so, how many hours per year or what percentage of lawyers' billable hours? We do not set a specific number. However, we have written goals of 30 hours of pro bono work per year for lawyers in our New York office and an overall goal of 3 percent.

SUPERVISION AND EVALUATIONS

Is there partner supervision on each pro bono matter? Yes

Do partner supervisors or, if applicable, senior associates provide written evaluations of associates' work on pro bono matters? Yes

If so, are those evaluations taken into account in determining salary, bonuses or advancement in the firm? Yes

If not, does the firm consider pro bono work generally in associate evaluations? Yes

HOURS

Does the firm give billable hour credit for pro bono work? No

Does the firm have a maximum number of pro bono hours that can be applied toward the billable hour target? N/A

If so, what is the maximum? N/A

If your firm uses hours to determine bonuses, does it consider pro bono hours when determining bonuses? Yes

PRO BONO POINTS

What training opportunities are open to associates working on pro bono matters? In addition to training and guidance by partners and associates at Hughes Hubbard, training is available from public interest organizations that the firm has partnered with in its efforts to serve the community.

Can associates bring matters of interest to the firm? Yes

Does the firm offer the use of support staff in carrying out pro bono matters? Yes

What pro bono opportunities are available for summer associates? Summer associates are encouraged to take at least one pro bono matter. The areas available include family court representation, representation of persons with AIDS, administrative hearings and uncontested divorces. Summer associates also have the opportunity to assist with pending pro bono matters being handled by admitted attorneys.

Does the firm have established programs, such as externships, that enable its associates to work in a public interest setting? Yes

If so, where and for up to how long? The firm offers a split summer Schell Fellowship to a 1L or 2L student. The fellow works as a summer associate at the New York office for the first 5-6 weeks of the summer program and spends the last part of the summer with a public interest organization of the student's choice. Any other such requests by associates would be handled on a case-by-case basis.

Has your firm won any special recognition or awards in the last two years for its pro bono work? Yes

If so, please list. New York Blood Center, Silver Award 2002. The Legal Aid Society, In Recognition of Outstanding Pro Bono Assistance to the Victims of the WTC Tragedy, November 25, 2002. Federal Bar Council Public Service Committee, Award for WTC Legal Services Program, 2002. Damon Rowe, The Legal Aid Society 2002 Pro Bono Award. Hebba Hassanein, The Legal Aid Society 2002 Pro Bono Award. Shep DiCesare, The Legal Aid Society 2002 Pro Bono Award. Sarah Loomis Cave, The Legal Aid Society 2003 Pro Bono Award. Compassion In Dying, In Recognition for Legal Work, 2003.

THE FIRM SAYS

Hughes Hubbard & Reed considers pro bono cases and counseling to be an important part of the firm's ongoing work. The firm believes that it is part of a lawyer's professional responsibilities to provide free legal services for the benefit of the public. Moreover, the exposure to areas of law, procedures, clients and experiences available in pro bono work results in a lawyer of increased depth, understanding and ability. Pro bono work is firm-wide work and is carried on in the U.S.

offices as well as our international offices in Paris and Tokyo. The pro bono committee has responsibility in consultation with the executive committee for determining whether and on what terms the firm accepts a particular matter as pro bono. Once accepted, pro bono matters are given the same staffing, attention and resources as any other matter in which the firm provides representation for its clients. Pro bono matters are reviewed by the supervising partner or associate and are part of the regular annual evaluation of each attorney. While volunteering opportunities outside legal services does not qualify as pro bono work, the firm encourages attorneys to participate in such worthy activities as well. In the past, the firm and its employees have taken part in blood drives, walkathons, and made monetary contributions to public interest organizations.

OUR SURVEY SAYS

"The commitment is unquestionable."

"It seems like everyone has at least one pro bono case, and we have great relationships with many of the legal services organizations that provide many unusual pro bono opportunities."

"You are expected to do pro bono. If you want to take on more pro bono, it is encouraged."

"The firm is very involved in Legal Aid and has formal pro bono programs and clinics that all lawyers may (and are encouraged to) participate in. However, the firm only credits pro bono hours towards bonuses once all productive, non-billable hours (including pro bono, assigned article writing, and so on) exceed 200 hours per year. Many associates think this undermines the firm's commitment — they are vocal about it and willing to encourage opportunities to do pro bono work in the firm's name, but they aren't willing to put their money where their mouth is."

"The firm is proud of [its] pro bono work and it is certainly encouraged."

"The firm is strongly committed to pro bono work but does not count time spent on pro bono matters towards billable hours. Therefore, many associates who would otherwise take on pro bono opportunities are discouraged from doing so."

"Many people do a ton of pro bono here."

"Almost a little too committed. The firm forces everyone to take on cases, and often you do not have a choice as to what case you will be assigned. [You are] required to work on a pro bono case, no matter how busy you are. Saying no is not an option."

"Pro bono is very much encouraged. However if your billable workload is high you will find it difficult to fit in and you will not be given time off a billable project to work on pro bono."

"I have been encouraged on the two pro bono projects I have worked on since I started."

"The exposure to areas of law, procedures, clients and experiences available in pro bono work results in a lawyer of increased depth, understanding and ability."

— *Hughes Hubbard & Reed LLP*

Jenner & Block LLP

One IBM Plaza
Chicago, IL 60611-7603
Phone: (312) 222-9350
www.jenner.com

LOCATIONS

Chicago, IL (HQ)
Dallas, TX
Washington, DC

MAJOR DEPARTMENTS & PRACTICES

Antitrust & Trade Regulation • Appellate & Supreme Court Practice • Arbitration (Domestic & International) • Association Practice • Bankruptcy/Corporate Restructuring • Class Action Litigation • Commercial Law & Uniform Commercial Code • Construction Law • Corporate • Corporate Finance • Defense & Aerospace • Employee Benefits & Executive Compensation • Entertainment & New Media • Environmental, Energy & Natural Resources Law • ERISA Litigation • Estate Planning & Administration • Family Law • Government Contracts • Health Care Law • Insurance Litigation & Counseling • Intellectual Property & Technology Law • Labor & Employment • Litigation Practice • Media & First Amendment Practice • Mergers & Acquisitions • Products Liability & Mass Tort Defense • Professional Liability Litigation • Real Estate • Reinsurance Practice • Securities Litigation • Tax Controversy Practice • Tax Practice • Telecommunications • Trade Secrets & Unfair Competition • White Collar Criminal Defense & Counseling

THE STATS

No. of attorneys worldwide: 409
No. of offices worldwide: 3
Chairman: Jerold S. Solovy
Managing Partner: Robert L. Graham

EMPLOYMENT CONTACT

Ms. Shannon Christopher
Manager of Legal Recruiting
Phone: (312) 923-2617
Fax: (312) 840-7616
E-mail: schristopher@jenner.com

WHO'S WHO

Principal pro bono contact(s) at your firm:

Barry Levenstam, Chicago Partner
Pro Bono Committee Co-Chair
Phone: (312) 923-2735
E-mail: blevenstam@jenner.com

David DeBruin, D.C. Partner
Pro Bono Committee Co-Chair
Phone: (202) 639-6015
E-mail: ddebruin@jenner.com

Does the firm have a pro bono coordinator? Yes
Ms. Kristin Wilde

If yes, what percentage of his or her time is spent on pro bono work? 30 percent

Does the firm have a pro bono committee? Yes

If yes, how often does the committee meet? Once a month

Describe the composition of the committee: There are two co-chairs and nineteen additional attorneys serving on a regular basis.

THE SCOOP

Does your firm have a written pro bono policy? Yes

Has the firm signed on to the Law Firm Pro Bono Challenge? Yes

What are some of the areas of law in which your firm has performed pro bono legal work in the last two years? Asylum/immigration; class action; criminal trials, appeals, post-conviction petitions, habeas petitions, death penalty litigation; contract; corporate; corporate governance; civil rights; disability rights; domestic/family law; elder law; environmental; housing/real estate/landlord/tenant; tax.

What are some of the areas of law in which your firm does not perform pro bono work? N/A

Organizations for which your firm has performed pro bono legal services in the last two years: Center for Elder and Disability Law, Chicago Lawyers' Committee for Civil Rights Under Law, Chicago Volunteer Legal Services, Cabrini Green Legal Aid Clinic, Community Economic Development Law Project, First Defense Legal Aid, Lawyers' Committee for Better Housing, Legal Assistance Foundation of Chicago, Midwest Immigrant and Human Rights Center, United States Holocaust Museum.

List up to three pro bono matters that are representative of the pro bono work your firm participates in.

- Grutter v. Bollinger and Gratz v. Bollinger, in which the justices relied heavily upon a Jenner & Block amicus brief on behalf of 65 corporations and upheld the University of Michigan Law School's affirmative action admissions policy.

- Lawrence v. Texas, in which Jenner & Block partner Paul Smith was co-lead counsel with Lambda Legal Defense & Education Fund in a civil rights decision overturning a Texas anti-sodomy law, a ruling that's widely considered the most important gay rights decision in a generation.

- Wiggins v. Smith, in which Jenner & Block partners persuaded the Supreme Court to take a major step toward dealing with the pervasive and persistent problem of inadequate representation for indigent capital murder defendants.

BY THE NUMBERS

What is the total number of hours that lawyers in U.S. offices at your firm spent performing pro bono legal services in 2000, 2001 and 2002?

    Total number of hours in 2000: 38,267 hours
    Total number of hours in 2001: 33,147 hours
    Total number of hours in 2002: 33,334 hours

Average number of pro bono hours per attorney in U.S. offices per year (including associates, partners, counsels, but not summer associates):

    Average number of hours per attorney in 2000: 103.26 hours
    Average number of hours per attorney in 2001: 92.64 hours
    Average number of hours per attorney in 2002: 86.92 hours

What percentage of attorneys in this firm's U.S. offices did pro bono work in 2002? 86 percent

What percentage of attorneys in this firm's U.S. offices did at least 20 hours of pro bono work in 2002? 69 percent

Does the firm encourage its lawyers to perform a minimum number of pro bono hours? No. Pro bono work is enthusiastically encouraged and over two-thirds of our attorneys did 20 hours of pro bono work, and many did far more. Consequently, we do not subscribe to any "minimum" where pro bono work is involved.

If so, how many hours per year or what percentage of lawyers' billable hours? N/A

SUPERVISION AND EVALUATIONS

Is there partner supervision on each pro bono matter? Yes

Do partner supervisors or, if applicable, senior associates provide written evaluations of associates' work on pro bono matters? Yes

If so, are those evaluations taken into account in determining salary, bonuses or advancement in the firm? Yes

If not, does the firm consider pro bono work generally in associate evaluations? N/A

HOURS

Does the firm give billable hour credit for pro bono work? Yes

Does the firm have a maximum number of pro bono hours that can be applied toward the billable hour target? N/A

If so, what is the maximum? N/A

If your firm uses hours to determine bonuses, does it consider pro bono hours when determining bonuses? Yes

PRO BONO POINTS

What training opportunities are open to associates working on pro bono matters? Associates working on pro bono matters are required to have a supervising partner on all matters. The supervising partner provides guidance, assistance and training as needed on all pro bono assignments. In addition, we work with a variety of different pro bono agencies that provide training specific to the types of cases they make available. Jenner & Block attorneys have participated in training sessions sponsored by the Community Economic Development Law Project for CHAC (an organization providing housing for low income residents) residential real estate closings; the Midwest Immigrant and Human Rights Center for asylum and immigration work; and Lawyers' Committee for Better Housing for landlord/tenant pro bono work. From time to time, Jenner & Block sponsors training sessions for these agencies at our office. Communications from different agencies regarding their upcoming training sessions are sent to all associates via e-mail and other communication venues as appropriate. Jenner & Block also sponsors lunches for its attorneys, at least quarterly, at which representatives from one or more of their agencies make presentations about their practice areas and the opportunities for pro bono work they make available.

Can associates bring matters of interest to the firm? Yes

Does the firm offer the use of support staff in carrying out pro bono matters? Yes

What pro bono opportunities are available for summer associates? In 2003, summer associates worked on the following types of pro bono cases: criminal (trials, appeals, post-conviction petitions, habeas corpus, and so on) (72 cases); civil (three cases); corporate (three cases); estate (one case); asylum (one case); real estate (three cases); litigation work (nine cases). In addition, the summer associates participated in two pro bono panel lunches this summer, one featuring speakers from different pro bono agencies, and one featuring Jenner & Block attorneys sharing their pro bono experiences. The summer associates also conducted volunteer client intake interviews at Cabrini Green Legal Aid. Summer associates in the firm's D.C. office also were involved in a variety of pro bono cases. In addition, D.C. summer associates worked on cases from the DC Bar Pro Bono Clinic.

Does the firm have established programs, such as externships, that enable its associates to work in a public interest setting? Yes

If so, where and for up to how long? Yes, Public Interest Law Initiative fellowships are available. We had five fellows in 2002 and two in 2003 in our Chicago office. Various Chicago pro bono agencies for 10 weeks over the summer for new associates studying for the bar.

Has your firm won any special recognition or awards in the last two years for its pro bono work? Yes

If so, please list.

- Partners David DeBruin and Deanne Maynard were this year's recipients of the Minority Corporate Counsel Association's Rainbowmaker Award for having led 65 major companies in filing the above-noted influential Supreme Court brief supporting diversity at the University of Michigan.

- Partner Thomas Sullivan was this year's recipient of the American Bar Association's John Minor Wisdom Award for "Lifelong commitment to community service."

- Partner Terri L. Mascherin in 2003 received an "Outstanding Legal Service" award from the National Coalition Against the Death Penalty.

- The 12,000 associates surveyed by Vault Inc. in 2003 ranked Jenner & Block's pro bono program as No. 1 in the country.

- *The American Lawyer* magazine included Jenner & Block in its 2003 "A-List" of the 20 most "elite" law firms in the nation based on various areas including diversity and pro bono representation.

- *The National Law Journal's* coveted Pro Bono Award for 2002

- The American Bar Association Pro Bono Publico Award

- The District of Columbia Bar's Pro Bono Law Firm of the Year Award

- The Seventh Circuit Bar Association's Pro Bono Service Award

- The Illinois State Bar Association's Business-Education Partnership Award

- The Jeanne and Joseph Sullivan Human Rights Award

- The Lawyers' Committee for Better Housing Award

- The Constitutional Rights Foundation BRIA Award

- Leadership Greater Chicago's Leadership Vision Award

- The MALDEF (Mexican American Legal Defense and Educational Fund) Legal Services Award

- The District of Columbia Bar's Best Bar Project Award

THE FIRM SAYS

Providing legal services to those in critical need of help has always been a core value at Jenner & Block. In fact, so consistent and pronounced has this commitment been, that *The American Lawyer* magazine has referred to Jenner & Block's pro bono program as "legendary." Indeed, every year the firm takes — and meets — the American Bar Association's pledge to dedicate more than 5 percent of its billable hours to pro bono representation. And this has led to its attorneys spending tens of thousands of hours providing legal services to individuals and organizations who otherwise could not afford it.

Jenner & Block is also uncommon in the extent to which it encourages all of its attorneys to participate in this remarkable pro bono effort, from the most senior partner to its youngest associate. The firm does not have a pro bono manager or team of pro bono specialists to handle its volunteer work. Instead, Jenner & Block's pro bono committee, which is made up of partners and associates from a wide range of practice areas, serves as a sort of clearinghouse of pro bono opportunities that are broadcast to all offices. Partners and associates review their regular pro bono opportunity memos and select pro bono matters based on their interests and skill set. The firm funds their pro bono cases, hiring investigators, translators and other experts and paying any other necessary expenses out of pocket; the firm also respects the demands of pro bono matters when attorneys are called upon to try pro bono cases, argue pro bono appeals or close pro bono transactions. Further, the legal team's pro bono service is a consideration to be taken into account in evaluating their work for purposes of determining their individual bonus.

Nor is the firm's commitment to community service limited to providing legal work to the indigent. An extraordinarily large number of Jenner & Block's partners teach at nearby law schools and hold leadership positions in the various local, state and national bar associations. Many of the firm's attorneys serve on the boards of nonprofit organizations. And still others are elected or appointed members of government entities and volunteer in their local communities for a wide range of educational, recreational and social service organizations. Jenner & Block's passion for serving others, then, is positioned to continue unabated well into the future — and proudly so.

OUR SURVEY SAYS

"Everyone here takes pro bono very seriously, and the firm provides great resources."

"The firm is regularly at the top of pro bono recognition because it encourages pro bono work, rather than just tolerating it. Junior associates have argued cases in trial and appellate courts, including first degree murder cases and matters involving difficult constitutional issues."

"If you want to do pro bono work at a large law firm in Chicago, there is nowhere else that is better than Jenner. The firm is supportive, has a wealth of institutional knowledge on how to represent pro bono clients and has great contacts to get interesting and varied work."

"The firm does a tremendous amount of pro bono work in a variety of jurisdictions and courts, including the Supreme Court. By way of example, firm attorneys were lead counsel in two pro bono Supreme Court cases this term. The firm has long been a national leader in terms of the number of pro bono hours its attorneys work."

"It's one of our biggest, if not our biggest, selling points. I very much support our pro bono activities, not only for their community-enhancing positive aspects, but also because they provide associates valuable experience and training they might not otherwise receive at this stage of their careers."

"Jenner goes so far as forcing people to do pro bono work."

"The firm is strongly committed to pro bono and offers new associates a pro bono fellowship to work in a public interest group before joining the firm. The pro bono cases the firm takes on are top-notch. Pro bono hours do not count in the 2,000 hour billable minimum, however."

"The firm now allows 100 hours of pro bono work to go towards bonuses."

"Pro bono work is part of the firm's culture. It is expected and encouraged, not merely tolerated. The firm treats pro bono clients with the same level of professionalism and dedication as it does its paying clients."

Jones Day

North Point – 901 Lakeside Avenue
Cleveland, OH 44114-1190
Phone: (216) 586-3939
www.jonesday.com

LOCATIONS

Atlanta, GA
Chicago, IL
Cleveland, OH
Columbus, OH
Dallas, TX
Houston, TX
Irvine, CA
Los Angeles, CA
Menlo Park, CA
New York, NY
Pittsburgh, PA
San Francisco, CA
Washington, DC
Beijing
Brussels
Frankfurt
Hong Kong
London
Madrid
Milan
Munich
Paris
Shanghai
Singapore
Sydney
Taipei
Tokyo

MAJOR DEPARTMENTS & PRACTICES

Business Practice
Energy
Government Regulation
Health Care
Litigation
Tax
Technology Issues

THE STATS

No. of attorneys worldwide: 2,000 +
No. of offices worldwide: 27
Managing Partner: Stephen J. Brogan

EMPLOYMENT CONTACT

Ms. Jolie A. Blanchard
Firm Director of Recruiting
Phone: (202) 879-3788
Fax: (202) 626-1738
E-mail: jablanchard@jonesday.com

WHO'S WHO

Does the firm have a pro bono coordinator? Yes

Pro Bono Practice Chair: Robert H. Klonoff, Of Counsel
Phone: (202) 879-3939
E-mail: rhklonoff@jonesday.com

Atlanta Coordinator: Janine Cone Metcalf, Partner
Phone: (404) 521-3939
E-mail: jmetcalf@jonesday.com

Chicago Coordinator: Lee Ann Russo, Partner
Phone: (312) 782-3939
E-mail: larusso@jonesday.com

Cleveland Coordinator: James E. Young, Partner
Phone: (216) 586-3939
E-mail: jameseyoung@jonesday.com

Columbus Coordinator: Shawn J. Organ, Partner
Phone: (614) 469-3939
E-mail: sjorgan@jonesday.com

Dallas Coordinator: Sally L. Crawford, Partner
Phone: (214) 220-3939
E-mail: scrawford@jonesday.com

Houston Coordinator: Hugh R. Whiting, Partner
Phone: (832) 239-3939
E-mail: hrwhiting@jonesday.com

Irvine/Los Angeles: Philip E. Cook, Partner
Phone: (213) 489-3939
E-mail: pcook@jonesday.com

New York Coordinator: Randi L. Strudler, Partner
Phone: (212) 326-3939
E-mail: strudler@jonesday.com

Pittsburgh Coordinator: Peter D. Laun, Partner
Phone: (412) 391-3939
E-mail: pdlaun@jonesday.com

San Francisco Coordinator: Caroline N. Mitchell, Partner
Phone: (415) 626-3939
E-mail: cnmitchell@jonesday.com

Washington, D.C., Coordinator: Donald B. Ayer, Partner
Phone: (202) 879-3939
E-mail: dbayer@jonesday.com

If yes, what percentage of his or her time is spent on pro bono work? It varies.

Does the firm have a pro bono committee? Yes

If yes, how often does the committee meet? The committee consisting of the office coordinators meets once per year and as needed. Many of the offices also have committees that meet much more frequently; for example, the committee in the Washington, D.C., office meets monthly.

Describe the composition of the committee: The committee consisting of the office coordinators is made up of partners from each of the domestic offices. The committees in each office vary by office.

THE SCOOP

Does your firm have a written pro bono policy? Yes

Has the firm signed on to the Law Firm Pro Bono Challenge? No

What are some of the areas of law in which your firm has performed pro bono legal work in the last two years? Jones Day attorneys in every domestic office are involved with local bar and community services as well as representing individuals and, on occasion, nonprofit organizations in both civil and criminal litigation. We also practice before a variety of courts and in adversarial settings before administrative agencies such as the Immigration and Naturalization Service ("INS"). Additionally, firm attorneys in virtually every domestic office are involved with local bar or community pro bono legal services clinics that directly service the needs of the underprivileged members of our communities. These legal clinics, which offer free legal advice to the poor on such matters as landlord/tenant law, public benefits, immigration, probate, family law and consumer fraud, have positively impacted the lives of the clients they serve.

Jones Day's pro bono practice includes:

- Political Asylum Claims. Jones Day attorneys routinely handle asylum and immigration matters, from the filing of the initial asylum application to appearing before the immigration officer, representing the applicant in Immigration Court and, if necessary, appealing the matter to the Board of Immigration Appeals and, possibly, the federal courts of appeals. Over the years, attorneys from the firm have represented numerous individuals seeking asylum from countries around the world including Bangladesh, Burma, Cameroon, China, Columbia, Ethiopia, Gambia, Haiti, Ivory Coast, Kenya, Kosovo, Mexico, Republic of the Congo, Russia, Rwanda, Syria and Uganda.

- Litigation and Transactional Work. Jones Day lawyers are involved in a wide array of litigation-related pro bono matters throughout the country, including routinely representing individuals in landlord-tenant disputes, and participating in a variety of innovative legal aid initiatives to counsel poor tenants. Attorneys in the firm's Atlanta, Cleveland, Los Angeles, New York and Washington offices also handle the transactional and contractual needs of a variety of nonprofit institutions serving the needs of the homeless, inner-city youth and the arts.

- Appellate Pro Bono Services. Jones Day has a vital appellate pro bono practice that has resulted in a number of oral arguments and impressive victories. Attorneys in a number of Jones Day offices have appeared in pro bono matters before the U.S. Supreme Court and various U.S. Courts of Appeals for various circuits. Moreover, in addition to the firm's federal appellate practice, attorneys in the Chicago, Columbus and Washington offices are handling appeals at the state court level.

What are some of the areas of law in which your firm does not perform pro bono work? Jones Day does not undertake pro bono cases where there is a client conflict or a substantial issue conflict. The firm also does not undertake cases involving domestic relations or custody cases.

Organizations for which your firm has performed pro bono legal services in the last two years: The Space Shuttle Children's Trust Fund, American Civil Liberties Union, Lawyers' Committee for Civil Rights and Urban Affairs, Public Counsel, Habitat for Humanity, Truancy Intervention Project (Atlanta Office), Community Economic Development Law Project, Chicago Lawyers' Committee for Civil Rights Under Law, Center for Educational Achievement (Los Angeles Office), Foreign Affairs Museum Council.

List up to three pro bono matters that are representative of the pro bono work your firm participates in.

- In the Matter of A- M-. Jones Day successfully assisted a Kosovar-Albanian teacher, who had been imprisoned, tortured and raped in Kosovo, in her fight to gain political asylum in the United States. Jones Day worked diligently to find a world-class expert to establish the factual and legal bases for the client's well-founded fear of persecution in Kosovo, and the Administrative Law Judge ruled in an unusually lengthy opinion that NATO's temporary presence in Kosovo did not eliminate the client's well-founded fear.

- The Space Shuttle Children's Trust Fund. Jones Day serves as general counsel to this nonprofit, tax exempt foundation that provides for the health, education and support of the children of the astronauts who perished in the Challenger tragedy and of astronauts who might perish in the future while actively involved in space exploration and travel. Jones Day provides advice on nonprofit corporate and tax issues, government relations, legislation and media relations, and since the recent tragic accident is working actively to assist the children of the Space Shuttle Columbia astronauts.

- Eldred v. Reno, 239 F.3d 372 (D.C. Cir. 2001); Eldred v. Ashcroft, 537 U.S. 186 (2003). Along with Professor Lawrence Lessig of Stanford University Law School and others, Jones Day represented a group of sheet music publishers, movie archives, small book publishers and individuals who depend upon the availability of works in the public domain in a challenge to the constitutionality of the 1998 Copyright Term Extension Act. Arguing that Congress does not have the power to extend the term of existing copyrights, Jones Day pursued the case all the way from the D.C. District Court in 1999 to the United States Supreme Court.

BY THE NUMBERS

What is the total number of hours that lawyers in U.S. offices at your firm spent performing pro bono legal services in 2000, 2001 and 2002?

    Total number of hours in 2000: 9,717 hours
    Total number of hours in 2001: 21,472 hours
    Total number of hours in 2002: 33,078 hours

Average number of pro bono hours per attorney in U.S. offices per year (including associates, partners, counsels, but not summer associates):

    Average number of hours per attorney in 2000: Not available
    Average number of hours per attorney in 2001: Not available
    Average number of hours per attorney in 2002: Not available

What percentage of attorneys in this firm's U.S. offices did pro bono work in 2002? Not available

What percentage of attorneys in this firm's U.S. offices did at least 20 hours of pro bono work in 2002? Not available

Does the firm encourage its lawyers to perform a minimum number of pro bono hours? No, but see below.

If so, how many hours per year or what percentage of lawyers' billable hours? Lawyers are actively urged to be involved in pro bono work, and pro bono involvement is regarded as an important contribution. The firm does not prescribe a specific number of hours as a minimum but urges involvement at a level that allows one to make a significant and important, and not merely a token, contribution.

SUPERVISION AND EVALUATIONS

Is there partner supervision on each pro bono matter? Yes

Do partner supervisors or, if applicable, senior associates provide written evaluations of associates' work on pro bono matters? Yes

If so, are those evaluations taken into account in determining salary, bonuses or advancement in the firm? Yes

If not, does the firm consider pro bono work generally in associate evaluations? N/A

HOURS

Does the firm give billable hour credit for pro bono work? Yes

Does the firm have a maximum number of pro bono hours that can be applied toward the billable hour target? No

If so, what is the maximum? N/A

If your firm uses hours to determine bonuses, does it consider pro bono hours when determining bonuses? N/A

PRO BONO POINTS

What training opportunities are open to associates working on pro bono matters? Substantial training is provided jointly by the firm and by advocacy organizations with whom we work closely. In recent years, training programs, open to the entire firm, have been conducted on the areas of veterans law, asylum law, criminal defense and predatory lending counseling.

Can associates bring matters of interest to the firm? Yes

Does the firm offer the use of support staff in carrying out pro bono matters? Yes

What pro bono opportunities are available for summer associates? Summer associates are regularly involved in a broad range the firm's pro bono work.

Does the firm have established programs, such as externships, that enable its associates to work in a public interest setting? No, but see below.

If so, where and for up to how long? The firm has established relationships with organizations that offer different types of pro bono experiences. We participate actively in a Saturday morning legal clinic, which Jones Day was instrumental in founding; we accept appointments from numerous courts to represent public agencies and indigent clients (e.g., Third Circuit, Ninth Circuit, D.C. Circuit, D.C. Court of Appeals, Court of Appeals for Veterans Claims, Montgomery County (Md.) state courts); and we represent many indigent clients in a broad range of proceedings, including asylum and landlord-tenant matters.

Has your firm won any special recognition or awards in the last two years for its pro bono work? Yes

If so, please list. On June 24, 2002, Mauricio Paez received the Volunteers Lawyers for the Arts Outstanding Volunteer Service Award in connection with his representation of Providence Productions International, Inc., a nonprofit theater production company involved in the production of socially conscious theater productions. On May 17, 2001, Noreen

English received the Cornerstone Award from the Lawyers Alliance for New York for her work on behalf of the firm with Habitat for Humanity. The Cornerstone Award honors outstanding contributions in pro bono service by members of New York's legal community. On April 26, 2001, Randi Strudler was honored for her work with Project Teen Aid Family Services, Inc., an organization in Brooklyn that provides Head Start programs and special services to teenage mothers in the Bedford-Stuyvesant area of Brooklyn.

THE FIRM SAYS

Jones Day is a collegial, team-oriented work environment where lawyers work cooperatively in ad hoc groups to address complex legal problems. Our pro bono practice is an integrated part of our overall practice, and the experience of lawyers doing pro bono work reflects that fact. While the firm strongly endorses involvement in pro bono work, the decision to involve oneself in any particular pro bono project belongs to each individual attorney. Given the high volume of pro bono work under way at any time, and the firm's extensive contacts with numerous public advocacy and intermediary organizations, opportunities to volunteer for pro bono projects is essentially unlimited. Work on pro bono matters is evaluated in exactly the same way, and with the same rigor, as paying work. Involvement in pro bono work is often a strong enhancement to a lawyer's career, in view of the excellent and early experience that it may afford. Pro bono work also counts for all purposes toward an attorney's billable hours. At the same time, all attorneys are expected to exercise sound judgment and common sense, and thus to ensure their continuing viability as a participant in an economic enterprise.

OUR SURVEY SAYS

"Habitat for Humanity is one of our biggest clients, and every first-year that I know has worked on at least one pro bono project this year. I am currently working on two different pro bono matters and find that such work is very well received."

"About one-fifth of my time is spent on pro bono work. The firm is very supportive and encouraging of pro bono work. Even first-year associates are encouraged to take on their own pro bono clients."

"The firm is very committed to pro bono work, but it does not give credit for the hours. In other words, if you want to do pro bono, you still need to reach your 2,000 hour goal based on billable hours."

"There's no formal support, but you can do whatever it is you want, so long as it is approved and you meet your other obligations."

"Since The American Lawyer ran a piece that was mildly critical of Jones Day's pro bono practice, there has been a real push to get lawyers involved in pro bono projects, at least in the Washington office. The firm participates in a number of programs offered by appellate courts, which reliably generate argument opportunities for associates."

"The firm has been supportive of my involvement in both legal pro bono work and community activities. I have also found that the firm willingly offers financial support for a number of causes without the need for extensive requests or forms."

"Jones Day has a strong commitment to pro bono. We have no ceiling (other than 'reasonable,' which is generally thought to not exceed 200) on pro bono hours that will count toward the billable goal."

"Although I am a junior associate, I have already been able to bring my own pro bono work into the firm. The firm has been very supportive of this."

"As an institution the firm still sends mixed messages about pro bono work and the extent to which it counts toward billable hours. But the firm's commitment to individual pro bono matters is beyond question — I have billed hundreds of hours (and incurred similarly large expenses) on individual cases with the full and enthusiastic support of the firm."

"Jones Day encourages pro bono work, counts the hours exactly the same as client billables and puts all the firm's resources at the disposal of pro bono clients. Associates can do almost any type of pro bono work they choose. However, the firm does not do a particularly good job of offering organized pro bono opportunities and leaves it to individual lawyers to find their own."

"Involvement in pro bono work is often a strong enhancement to a lawyer's career, in view of the excellent and early experience that it may afford."

— *Jones Day*

Katten Muchin Zavis Rosenman

525 West Monroe Street, Suite 1600
Chicago, IL 60661-3693
Phone: (312) 902-5200
www.kmzr.com

LOCATIONS

Chicago, IL (HQ)
Charlotte, NC
Los Angeles, CA
New York, NY
Newark, NJ
Palo Alto, CA
Washington, DC

MAJOR DEPARTMENTS & PRACTICES

Corporate
Customs & International Trade
Entertainment
Environment
Financial Services
Health Care
Intellectual Property
Litigation
Real Estate
Sports Law & Sports Facilities
Tax
Wealth Management

THE STATS

No. of attorneys worldwide: 600 +
No. of offices worldwide: 7
National Managing Partner: Vincent A.F. Sergi

EMPLOYMENT CONTACTS

Chicago
Ms. Elizabeth Ciula
Director of Attorney Recruiting and Development
Phone: (312) 902-5547
E-mail: elizabeth.cibula@kmzr.com

Los Angeles
Ms. Annette Roe
Director of Attorney Recruiting and Development
Phone: (312) 902-5547
E-mail: annette.roe@kmzr.com

New York & Charlotte
Ms. Kim McHugh
Legal Recruiting Manager
Phone: (212) 940-9386
E-mail: kim.mchugh@kmzr.com

Washington, DC
Ms. Judy Brown
Office Manager
Phone: (202) 625-3652
E-mail: judy.brown@kmzr.com

WHO'S WHO

Does the firm have a pro bono coordinator? Yes

Jonathan K. Baum, Esq.
Director of Pro Bono Services
Phone: (312) 902-5479
E-mail: jonathan.baum@kmzr.com

If yes, what percentage of his or her time is spent on pro bono work? 100 percent

Does the firm have a pro bono committee? Yes

If yes, how often does the committee meet? Irregularly, as needed.

Describe the composition of the committee: There are pro bono committees for each of the firm's offices composed of interested attorneys from that office. The chairs of each of the local office pro bono committees in turn constitute a national pro bono committee.

THE SCOOP

Does your firm have a written pro bono policy? Yes

Has the firm signed on to the Law Firm Pro Bono Challenge? No

What are some of the areas of law in which your firm has performed pro bono legal work in the last two years? Civil rights, consumer and criminal litigation; corporate, tax, labor, employee benefits and intellectual property matters for nonprofit organizations and microbusinesses; political asylum cases; domestic violence cases; landlord-tenant cases.

What are some of the areas of law in which your firm does not perform pro bono work? Plaintiffs' employment discrimination cases; death penalty cases; banking matters.

Organizations for which your firm has performed pro bono legal services in the last two years: Lawyers' Committee for Civil Rights Under Law, Pro Bono Advocates, Midwest Immigrant & Human Rights Center, Center for Disability & Elder Law, Lawyers for the Creative Arts, Legal Assistance Foundation of Metropolitan Chicago, Lawyers Alliance, New York Lawyers for the Public Interest, Community Economic Development Law Project, Public Counsel.

List up to three pro bono matters that are representative of the pro bono work your firm participates in.

- An attorney in our Chicago office drafted incorporation documents and obtained tax-exempt status for two camps that serve physically challenged children.

- Attorneys in our Los Angeles office participate in the Adoptions Project of Public Counsel in which persons seeking to adopt children in foster care are assisted with the adoption process and in obtaining benefits and special services for the children.

- An attorney in our New York office represents a prisoner in a federal appeal presenting questions of first impression under the Prison Litigation Reform Act.

BY THE NUMBERS

What is the total number of hours that lawyers in U.S. offices at your firm spent performing pro bono legal services in 2000, 2001 and 2002?

>Total number of hours in 2000: 11,536 hours
>Total number of hours in 2001: 14,058 hours
>Total number of hours in 2002: 22,747 hours

Average number of pro bono hours per attorney in U.S. offices per year (including associates, partners, counsels, but not summer associates):

>Average number of hours per attorney in 2000: 25.9 hours
>Average number of hours per attorney in 2001: 32.5 hours
>Average number of hours per attorney in 2002: 37.4 hours

What percentage of attorneys in this firm's U.S. offices did pro bono work in 2002? Approximately 50 percent

What percentage of attorneys in this firm's U.S. offices did at least 20 hours of pro bono work in 2002? 34.6 percent

Does the firm encourage its lawyers to perform a minimum number of pro bono hours? Yes

If so, how many hours per year or what percentage of lawyers' billable hours? The firm has a goal of an average of 35 hours per attorney per year of pro bono work; the first 100 hours of pro bono work per year are automatically counted toward minimum billable hours requirements; additional billable hour credit is available upon prior approval by firm management.

SUPERVISION AND EVALUATIONS

Is there partner supervision on each pro bono matter? Yes

Do partner supervisors or, if applicable, senior associates provide written evaluations of associates' work on pro bono matters? Yes

If so, are those evaluations taken into account in determining salary, bonuses or advancement in the firm? Yes

If not, does the firm consider pro bono work generally in associate evaluations? N/A

HOURS

Does the firm give billable hour credit for pro bono work? Yes

Does the firm have a maximum number of pro bono hours that can be applied toward the billable hour target? No

If so, what is the maximum? N/A

If your firm uses hours to determine bonuses, does it consider pro bono hours when determining bonuses? Yes

PRO BONO POINTS

What training opportunities are open to associates working on pro bono matters? Training is provided both through informal mentoring by more senior attorneys with experience in the relevant area of practice and through formal training sessions by public interest practitioners where the relevant expertise is not present in the firm.

Can associates bring matters of interest to the firm? Yes

Does the firm offer the use of support staff in carrying out pro bono matters? Yes

What pro bono opportunities are available for summer associates? In addition to involving summer associates in ongoing pro bono matters, the firm offers special opportunities for summer associates to appear in court as licensed law students under the supervision of public interest agencies, principally in the areas of domestic violence and landlord-tenant work.

Does the firm have established programs, such as externships, that enable its associates to work in a public interest setting? Yes

If so, where and for up to how long? The firm has long participated in the Public Interest Law Initiative (PILI) Fellowship Program, in which the firm pays incoming first-year associates to work for public interest agencies during the summer while they are studying for the bar exam. In addition, the firm has just initiated a First Year Public Service Fellowship Program, under which new associates may spend their first year with the firm working full-time for a public interest agency.

Has your firm won any special recognition or awards in the last two years for its pro bono work? Yes

If so, please list. Mexican American Legal Defense & Educational Fund (MALDEF) Legal Service Award; Lawyers Alliance for New York Cornerstone Award; Chicago Lawyers' Committee for Civil Rights Under Law Pro Bono Award.

THE FIRM SAYS

KMZ Rosenman strongly encourages pro bono service by its attorneys in several ways. It was one of the first law firms in the nation to have a partner whose full-time responsibility is to engage in and facilitate pro bono work. Attorneys joining the firm are surveyed for their areas of pro bono interest and periodically forwarded pro bono opportunities responsive to those interests. At least the first 100 hours per year of pro bono work (and more with prior approval) are credited toward minimum billable hours requirements and firm bonuses. Pro bono work is evaluated with billable work as part of the regular review process. The firm recognizes individual attorneys' pro bono service with annual Pro Bono Service Awards. As a result of these efforts, KMZ Rosenman attorneys render pro bono service in almost every area of practice, from litigation and corporate work to employee benefits and patent work.

OUR SURVEY SAYS

"In my first year, I spent several hundred hours on various pro bono projects — both that were assigned to me and those I chose to take on myself — and every hour of that time was counted toward my minimum billing requirements. I believe this is not rare and that the firm's commitment to pro bono service is real."

"This is one of the better firms for pro bono work. Granted, to a large extent, it is up to individuals to take the initiative, but once you do, there is an incredible amount of opportunity and support."

"During the initial formal training, the firm describes how committed it is to pro bono work. Associates fill out a survey of interests so they can be matched with quality pro bono opportunities. Hours for pro bono work are counted towards the billable hour requirement. I have already worked on two pro bono cases (relating to the same issue) since I started less than a year ago."

"I have completed several pro bono projects and received full credit in terms of billable hours for doing so. It is not only possible but encouraged."

"The firm let me go to Switzerland for a year to work on a project related to Holocaust reparations. During that time the firm continued my benefits and paid the difference between the salary I was making abroad and my salary as an associate."

"Pre-merger, all pro bono hours counted as billable hours in with respect to associate compensation. However, post-merger, although the firm expresses a strong commitment to pro bono work, it has placed a cap on the number of pro bono hours which can count towards the billable hour requirement. This to me is an expression that pro bono work is not a high priority."*

"One hundred hours are credited towards billable hours and the firm will give more if you need it."

"The firm expects associates to do extensive pro bono work. They do not apply all hours spent doing pro bono work toward minimum billing requirements, which is unfortunate."

"If you want your own pro bono case or cases as a first year, come here. I am arguing my own Second Circuit appeal in a few months."

"KMZ Rosenman attorneys render pro bono service in almost every area of practice, from litigation and corporate work to employee benefits and patent work."

— *Katten Muchin Zavis Rosenman*

Kaye Scholer LLP

425 Park Avenue
New York, NY 10022
Phone: (212) 836-8000
www.kayescholer.com

LOCATIONS

New York, NY (HQ)
Chicago, IL
Los Angeles, CA
Washington, DC
West Palm Beach, FL
Frankfurt
Hong Kong
London
Shanghai

MAJOR DEPARTMENTS & PRACTICES

Antitrust
Business Reorganization
Corporate & Finance
Employment & Labor
Entertainment, Media & Communications
Intellectual Property
International
Legislative & Regulatory
Litigation
Product Liability
Real Estate
Tax
Technology & E-Commerce
Trust & Estates
White collar Crime
Wills & Estates

THE STATS

No. of attorneys worldwide: 467
No. of offices worldwide: 9
Executive Committee Chair: David Klingsberg
Managing Partner: Barry Willner

EMPLOYMENT CONTACT

Ms. Wendy Evans
Director of Legal Personnel
Phone: (212) 836-8000
Fax: (212) 836-8689
E-mail: wevans@kayescholer.com

WHO'S WHO

Principal pro bono contact(s) at your firm:

John D. Geelan, Esq.
Co-chair, Pro Bono Committee
Phone: (212) 836-8121
E-mail: jgeelan@kayescholer.com

Alison King, Esq.
Co-chair, Pro Bono Committee
Phone: (212) 836-7037
E-mail: aking@kayescholer.com

Does the firm have a pro bono coordinator? Yes

Does the firm have a pro bono committee? Yes

If yes, how often does the committee meet? As necessary.

Describe the composition of the committee: The committee is comprised of partners, counsel and associates from various practice areas within the firm who have demonstrated a strong commitment to pro bono work.

THE SCOOP

Does your firm have a written pro bono policy? Yes

Has the firm signed on to the Law Firm Pro Bono Challenge? Yes

What are some of the areas of law in which your firm has performed pro bono legal work in the last two years?

- Over the past three years, Kaye Scholer attorneys have worked successfully in conjunction with the Legal Aid Society to represent the displaced residents of the Neponsit Nursing Care Facility in Rockaway, Queens. Hundreds of elderly residents were transferred, in the middle of the night, to facilities poorly equipped to handle their long term needs. Kaye Scholer attorneys acted as co-counsel in the case (Brown v. Giuliani), which resulted in improving the quality of nursing home facilities and assuring the health and safety of hundreds of residents.

- In 2001, Kaye Scholer and co-counsel, the Brennan Center for Justice, won a landmark constitutional victory in the United States Supreme Court on behalf of their pro bono clients, Legal Services lawyers and their indigent clients. In its 5-4 decision in Legal Services Corporation v. Velazquez, the high court affirmed the Second Circuit's decision striking down a 1996 amendment to the Legal Services Corporation Act which prohibited legal services organizations that receive federal funds from providing any legal representation involving efforts to challenge the constitutionality or legality of existing welfare laws.

- The firm also has a long history of representing indigent death row inmates who have been sentenced to death under circumstances which violate their constitutional rights. In 1998, Kaye Scholer and eight of our partners and associates were honored by the Association of the Bar of the City of New York with the prestigious Thurgood Marshall Award on behalf of their work in this area, and we are currently working on active death penalty cases in Alabama.

- Kaye Scholer attorneys have also spent significant time on World Trade Center-related matters, ranging from counseling small businesses that suffered from the attack, to probating the wills of the deceased and distributing their assets to beneficiaries, to assisting the widows of firefighters as they assert claims before the Victims Compensation Fund. The firm also provided pro bono consulting to several charitable organizations, including the United Way and the New York City Patrolmen's Benevolent Association Widow's and Children's Fund.

Organizations for which your firm has performed pro bono legal services in the last two years: The Legal Aid Society, Sanctuary for Families, Volunteer Lawyers for the Arts, inMotion, New York Lawyers for the Public Interest.

BY THE NUMBERS

What is the total number of hours that lawyers in U.S. offices at your firm spent performing pro bono legal services in 2000, 2001 and 2002?

> Total number of hours in 2000: 11,141 hours
> Total number of hours in 2001: 12,826 hours
> Total number of hours in 2002: 12,252.24 hours

Average number of pro bono hours per attorney in U.S. offices per year (including associates, partners, counsels, but not summer associates):

> Average number of hours per attorney in 2000: 31.49 hours
> Average number of hours per attorney in 2001: 32.9 hours
> Average number of hours per attorney in 2002: 28.9 hours

What percentage of attorneys in this firm's U.S. offices did at least 20 hours of pro bono work in 2002? 24.8 percent

Does the firm encourage its lawyers to perform a minimum number of pro bono hours? No

SUPERVISION AND EVALUATIONS

Is there partner supervision on each pro bono matter? Yes

Do partner supervisors or, if applicable, senior associates provide written evaluations of associates' work on pro bono matters? Yes

If so, are those evaluations taken into account in determining salary, bonuses or advancement in the firm? Yes

If not, does the firm consider pro bono work generally in associate evaluations? N/A

HOURS

Does the firm give billable hour credit for pro bono work? Yes

Does the firm have a maximum number of pro bono hours that can be applied toward the billable hour target? No

If so, what is the maximum? N/A

If your firm uses hours to determine bonuses, does it consider pro bono hours when determining bonuses? Yes

PRO BONO POINTS

What training opportunities are open to associates working on pro bono matters? The firm sponsors certain Legal Aid training seminars for its associates and publicizes trainings sponsored by other organizations.

Can associates bring matters of interest to the firm? Yes

Does the firm offer the use of support staff in carrying out pro bono matters? Yes

What pro bono opportunities are available for summer associates? Our summer associates are encouraged to participate in pro bono matters; they are given the opportunity to work on uncontested divorce cases, SSI matters, to work on the incorporation of not-for-profit entities and to participate in the Courtroom Advocates Project, which is focused on assisting battered women. These matters typically commence and conclude within the course of the summer program and thus afford the participants the opportunity to get meaningful hands-on experience. Additionally, summer associates are welcome to become involved in our larger ongoing pro bono matters which vary year to year. This diversity of opportunity reflects our longstanding commitment to both pro bono and to the development of new associates.

Does the firm have established programs, such as externships, that enable its associates to work in a public interest setting? No

Has your firm won any special recognition or awards in the last two years for its pro bono work? Yes

If so, please list. On November 25, 2002, the Legal Aid Society presented Kaye Scholer with the Society's Pro Bono Publico and Public Service Law Firm Award. Chief Judge Judith S. Kaye presided over the ceremony and presented the award to the firm in recognition of the exemplary pro bono representation and assistance Kaye Scholer attorneys have provided Legal Aid. In addition, Executive Committee Chairman David Klingsberg was singled out for his leadership in establishing the Helen L. Buttenwieser Senior Lawyer Project, which provides retired attorneys opportunities to volunteer with Legal Aid. Kaye Scholer was also recognized for providing pro bono legal services to victims of the World Trade Center attacks. We have also recently won an award from the Sanctuary for Families for representing women who have been battered by their spouses, and from the Legal Aid Society Criminal Appeals Bureau for arguing criminal appeals before appellate courts.

THE FIRM SAYS

Kaye Scholer considers pro bono work as an important part of its mission as a major U.S. law firm. The firm has a long history of representing indigent clients in civil and criminal matters. The firm partners with several pro bono agencies, including Legal Aid, Sanctuary for Families and Volunteers of Legal Services to ensure that its attorneys have a variety of opportunities to undertake pro bono legal services.

OUR SURVEY SAYS

"Including pro bono hours as part of the associates' bonus calculations is a strong sign of the firm's commitment."

"The firm does lots of excellent pro bono work and fully encourages associates to do pro bono work. Pro bono hours are counted the same as billable hours for bonus purposes."

"In 2001, I billed over 700 hours to a massive pro bono matter. The firm was very encouraging although it took up approximately one-third of my time for the year. Last year, I billed over 300 hours on the same matter."

"Pro bono counts as billable hours. The firm is not only committed but encourages pro bono. It is treated as equally important as our highest paying client and everyone likes being involved."

"The firm encourages pro bono work and counts pro bono hours for year-end bonuses. However, billable work still comes first."

"The firm is strongly committed to pro bono and puts its money where its mouth is. [There's] no limit on the amount of pro bono hours that can count towards billable hours and bonus requirements."

"Pro bono hours count towards billables. Can't ask for more."

"The firm has two partners and an associate who coordinate pro bono efforts. It really is encouraged — I've worked on several pro bono matters and the firm looks very favorably upon it. Kaye Scholer has won various awards for its commitment to pro bono work."

"Pro bono hours count toward your billable hours and it is strongly encouraged, as evidenced by the monthly memo circulated listing the various opportunities to get involved."

"My firm is very committed to pro bono — which is wonderful."

"The firm also has a long history of representing indigent death row inmates who have been sentenced to death under circumstances which violate their constitutional rights."

— *Kaye Scholer LLP*

Kelley Drye & Warren LLP

101 Park Avenue
New York, NY 10178
Phone: (212) 808-7800
www.kelleydrye.com

LOCATIONS

New York, NY (HQ)
Chicago, IL
Parsippany, NJ
Stamford, CT
Tyson's Corner, VA
Washington, DC
Bangkok *
Brussels
Jakarta*
Mumbai*
Tokyo*

*Affiliate (Independent) Offices

MAJOR DEPARTMENTS & PRACTICES

Antitrust/Trade Regulation
Broker-Dealer
Commercial Litigation
Corporate
Employee Benefits & Executive Compensation
Environmental Law
Financial Institutions
Health Care
Immigration
Intellectual Property
Labor/Employment Law
Mergers & Acquisitions
Private Clients
Products Liability
Project Finance
Real Estate
Restructuring, Bankruptcy & Creditors' Rights
Tax
Telecommunications
Venture Capital, Private Equity & Emerging Companies
White Collar Crime

THE STATS

No. of attorneys worldwide: 325 +
No. of offices worldwide: 11
Chairman: John M. Callagy

EMPLOYMENT CONTACT

Mr. Randy J. Liss
Recruiting Coordinator
Phone: (212) 80-7721
Fax: (212) 808-7897
E-mail: rliss@kelleydrye.com

WHO'S WHO

Does the firm have a pro bono coordinator? Yes

Robert E. Crotty, Esq.
Phone: (212) 808-7847
E-mail: rcrotty@kelleydrye.com

Does the firm have a pro bono committee? Yes

Describe the composition of the committee: Litigation partners, including a former New York Supreme Court justice.

THE SCOOP

Does your firm have a written pro bono policy? No

Has the firm signed on to the Law Firm Pro Bono Challenge? Yes

What are some of the areas of law in which your firm has performed pro bono legal work in the last two years? Litigation, corporate, tax, ERISA, labor.

Organizations for which your firm has performed pro bono legal services in the last two years: Kelley Drye's lawyers represent impoverished or domestically abused women through referrals from inMotion (formerly Network for Women's Services), a New York City-based nonprofit organization that provides low-income, under-served or abused women with free, quality legal services. For each of the following not-for-profit organizations listed below, Kelley Drye & Warren LLP provided assistance with respect to tax matters on a pro bono basis. In each instance, Kelley Drye successfully procured an exemption from federal income tax on the basis that the organization is dedicated to serving a charitable purpose. In addition, the firm's attorneys attended to certain tax related state and local filings required by law.

- Alliance for Young Urban Design and the Arts, Inc. (AYUDA). AYUDA provides needy urban youths with scholarships to pursue studies in design and the arts at institutions for higher learning.

- Intercultural Alliance of Artists & Scholars, Inc. (IAAS). IAAS is a literary organization dedicated to raising awareness and understanding about the cultural heritage of people in the United States.

- Friends of Columbus Park. Friends of Columbus Park is devoted to the renovation of Columbus Park in lower Manhattan and to the enhancement of the park's vitality as a center for cultural activity.

- UNAHI-USA, Inc. UNAHI-USA, Inc. is dedicated to preserving the culture of the Higaonon Tribe and their home in the rainforests of the Philippines and promotes the use of agro-forestry technology to reclaim areas in need of reforestation and to sustain the existing rainforests.

List up to three pro bono matters that are representative of the pro bono work your firm participates in.

- Kelley Drye acted as pro bono counsel for New York Lawyers for the Public Interest (NYLPI) in an Article 78 proceeding against the New York Power Authority (NYPA), the Department of Environmental Conservation and the State Board on Electric Generation Siting and the Environment. NYLPI challenged the locations of six power plants in the New York area, alleging that NYPA failed to consider certain potentially adverse environmental and health ramifications of the construction and operation of the plants, therefore violating the State Environmental Quality Review Act.

- Kelley Drye successfully represented, pro bono, a national of the Republic of Eritrea, Africa in his application for asylum before the Immigration Court, which was recently transferred to the Department of Homeland Security. The client, who was subject to persecution in Eritrea due to his religious beliefs, national origin and political opposition to the practices of the Eriterean ruling party, was held in detention by the Immigration and Naturalization Service for seven months.

- Kelley Drye successfully obtained awards from the New York Workers' Compensation Board (WCB) on behalf of two Kelley Drye pro bono clients whose fiancés were killed in the 9/11 terrorist attacks on the World Trade Center.

SUPERVISION AND EVALUATIONS

Is there partner supervision on each pro bono matter? Yes

Do partner supervisors or, if applicable, senior associates provide written evaluations of associates' work on pro bono matters? Yes

If so, are those evaluations taken into account in determining salary, bonuses or advancement in the firm? Yes

If not, does the firm consider pro bono work generally in associate evaluations? N/A

HOURS

Does the firm give billable hour credit for pro bono work? Yes

Does the firm have a maximum number of pro bono hours that can be applied toward the billable hour target? No

If so, what is the maximum? N/A

If your firm uses hours to determine bonuses, does it consider pro bono hours when determining bonuses? Yes

PRO BONO POINTS

What training opportunities are open to associates working on pro bono matters? The Association of the Bar of the City of New York (ABCNY), New York Lawyers for the Public Interest (NYLPI).

Can associates bring matters of interest to the firm? Yes

Does the firm offer the use of support staff in carrying out pro bono matters? Yes

What pro bono opportunities are available for summer associates? The Kelley Drye Pro Bono Fellowship, which is offered to one summer associate each year, allows Kelley Drye summer associates to split their time at organizations such as the Legal Aid Society and Amnesty International/USA. The 2002 Kelley Drye Pro Bono Fellow volunteered her time at South Brooklyn Legal Services (SBLS) in the governmental benefits division. SBLS provides legal services, information and counseling in civil cases to low income individuals in Southern and Western Brooklyn. SBLS focuses on ways to effectively serve the community and strives to empower the financially disadvantaged so that they are able to identify and tackle the issues that can lead to poverty. During the 2003 summer program, Kelley Drye took on two cases through inMotion specifically for summer associates. While work on those cases was supervised by Kelley Drye associates, summer associates had the opportunity to attend training seminars, conduct client meetings and attend court appearances.

Does the firm have established programs, such as externships, that enable its associates to work in a public interest setting? Yes

If so, where and for up to how long? A Kelley Drye associate spent six months with the Bar Association of the City of New York's September 11 Legal Relief Initiative, coordinating the ABCNY's Individual & Family Program as one of two staff attorneys.

Has your firm won any special recognition or awards in the last two years for its pro bono work? Yes

If so, please list. One year after the 9/11 terrorist attacks, The American Lawyer's September 2002 issue reflected on the increased interest in pro bono work nationwide, citing Kelley Drye as a prime example.

THE FIRM SAYS

Kelley Drye has advised on numerous pro bono matters for a variety of charitable and nonprofit organizations dedicated to supporting health-related causes, disadvantaged individuals, education and the arts. The firm's lawyers have also provided counsel to individuals in need of assistance with legal issues related to asylum, child custody, civil rights and testamentary matters. Kelley Drye attorneys have provided litigation, corporate, tax, ERISA and labor assistance to clients that include Center for Arts Education, a nonprofit group that promotes arts education in New York City public schools; Circle of Life Children's Center, which provides physical and psychological assistance to children with life-limiting illnesses; Friends For Steven, a nonprofit, volunteer organization raising money and awareness in the battle against the pediatric cancer known as neuroblastoma; Jewish Board of Family and Children's Services, Division for the Developmentally Disabled, one of the nation's largest nonprofit mental health and social service agencies; Joy of the Game Foundation, which coordinates sports clinic camps for disadvantaged youths and provides financial sponsorship for tournaments to the underprivileged; Make a Wish Foundation, which grants the wishes of children with life-threatening medical conditions; Mount Sinai Medical Center, one of the country's oldest and largest voluntary teaching hospitals; Stamford Symphony Orchestra, a classical concert series focused on new music and education programs; and others.

In addition, the firm has worked with the families of victims and others directly affected by the events of September 11, 2001 to provide legal counsel on a variety of issues faced by these individuals. As part of the 9/11 pro bono relief effort, one associate worked full time at the Association of the Bar of the City of New York, where she coordinated the Individual & Family Program for six months as one of two staff attorneys. Numerous other attorneys at the firm continue to provide legal counsel to the victims' families; specific ongoing matters include the representation of the fiancés of those who perished on September 11 with respect to their eligibility for the Federal Compensation Fund and other assistance programs. Attorneys also provided legal assistance to family members of victims who were employees of Keefe, Bruyette & Woods, a securities firm and investment bank that was located in the World Trade Center.

OUR SURVEY SAYS

"Our pro bono coordinator, Bob Crotty, is great and very active; and people can do as much pro bono as they want (so long as they get their other work done); I even brought in a pro bono client myself and appreciated that doing so was an option."

"Very generous [program]. Lots of pro bono hours can be counted as billable."

"Those who perform pro bono work seem to be a self-selective group. There is not strong encouragement by the firm to do so, but there is not discouragement either. There is a partner who forwards messages on pro bono opportunities firm-wide."

"If the firm is not going to count pro bono work in terms of overall hours, how committed can they be?"

"Kelley Drye was one of seven firms within New York City that gave one associate to the NYC World Trade Center law project. This associate worked for one year meeting victim needs. Associate time is deemed 'accountable' and goes to meeting the 2,000 hour billing requirement (hours count toward determining your bonus)."

"There are ample opportunities for pro bono work. It is not encouraged, nor is it discouraged."

"This is an office-specific question. Our office does not do much pro bono work. Our main office is very committed."

"The firm counts an associate's pro bono hours towards the minimum billable requirement."

"Constant e-mails are going out about opportunities, but no real effort seems to be made to bring in young associates in particular. A greater effort could be made to help young associates find and take advantage of opportunities or to get involved with pre-existing pro bono cases."

"My impression is that pro bono work is not encouraged outside of the New York office."

"Kelley Drye successfully obtained awards from the New York Workers' Compensation Board (WCB) on behalf of two Kelley Drye pro bono clients whose fiancés were killed in the 9/11 terrorist attacks on the World Trade Center."

— *Kelley Drye & Warren LLP*

Kilpatrick Stockton LLP

1100 Peachtree Street, Suite 2800
Atlanta, GA 30309-4530
Phone: (404) 815 6500
www.kilpatrickstockton.com

LOCATIONS

Atlanta, GA (HQ)
Augusta, GA
Charlotte, NC
Raleigh, NC
Washington, DC
Winston-Salem, NC
London
Stockholm

MAJOR DEPARTMENTS & PRACTICES

Construction Law & Public Contracts
Corporate & Business
Employee Benefits
Environment, Energy & Land Use
Finance
Financial Restructuring
Intellectual Property
Labor & Employment
Litigation
Real Estate
Tax/Trusts & Estates
Technology

THE STATS

No. of attorneys worldwide: 441
No. of offices worldwide: 8
Managing Partner: William H. Brewster

EMPLOYMENT CONTACT

Ms. Lea W. Hughes
Recruiting Coordinator
Phone: (404) 532-6887
Fax: (404) 541-4668
E-mail: lelughes@KilpatrickStockton.com

WHO'S WHO

Does the firm have a pro bono coordinator? Yes

Debbie Segal, Esq.
Pro Bono Partner
Phone: (404) 815-6167
E-mail: dsegal@kilpatrickstockton.com

If yes, what percentage of his or her time is spent on pro bono work? 100 percent

Does the firm have a pro bono committee? Yes

If yes, how often does the committee meet? As needed to address issues which arise related to Kilpatrick Stockton's pro bono commitment.

Describe the composition of the committee: Partner and associate from each office, firm-wide representatives, with representation from most practice groups.

THE SCOOP

Does your firm have a written pro bono policy? Yes

Has the firm signed on to the Law Firm Pro Bono Challenge? Yes

What are some of the areas of law in which your firm has performed pro bono legal work in the last two years? We've handled the gamut of representation of low income clients, including landlord-tenant, consumer, insurance and car issues, victims of domestic violence, guardian ad litem, grandparent adoption, wills and advance directives for senior citizens, civil rights, habeas death penalty. We represent over 100 nonprofit organizations in all areas, including employment, employee benefits, real estate, corporate, tax, environmental and intellectual property. We represent parents in international kidnapping cases. We represent community groups in all issues facing their members.

What are some of the areas of law in which your firm does not perform pro bono work? Work adverse to banks; trial level criminal defense work; divorces.

Organizations for which your firm has performed pro bono legal services in the last two years: Legal Aid, Pro Bono and Children's Programs in each city where we maintain an office, over 100 nonprofit organizations, civil rights organizations, farmer organizations, community revitalization organizations, arts organizations, immigration support groups.

List up to three pro bono matters that are representative of the pro bono work your firm participates in. In all of our offices, we represent low-income grandparents and relative caregivers who seek to adopt the children left in their care. We provide legal representation to a community revitalization organization, most recently handling the legal work for an affordable housing deal and to develop a childcare facility. We recently represented an organization which opposed the dissolution of a public school integration order.

BY THE NUMBERS

What is the total number of hours that lawyers in U.S. offices at your firm spent performing pro bono legal services in 2000, 2001 and 2002?

> Total number of hours in 2000: 7,900 hours
> Total number of hours in 2001: 17,264 hours
> Total number of hours in 2002: 16,824 hours

Average number of pro bono hours per attorney in U.S. offices per year (including associates, partners, counsels, but not summer associates):

> Average number of hours per attorney in 2000: N/A
> Average number of hours per attorney in 2001: 36.2 hours
> Average number of hours per attorney in 2002: 38.6 hours

What percentage of attorneys in this firm's U.S. offices did pro bono work in 2002? 81 percent

What percentage of attorneys in this firm's U.S. offices did at least 20 hours of pro bono work in 2002? 41 percent

Does the firm encourage its lawyers to perform a minimum number of pro bono hours? Yes

If so, how many hours per year or what percentage of lawyers' billable hours? 50 hours

SUPERVISION AND EVALUATIONS

Is there partner supervision on each pro bono matter? Yes

Do partner supervisors or, if applicable, senior associates provide written evaluations of associates' work on pro bono matters? Yes

If so, are those evaluations taken into account in determining salary, bonuses or advancement in the firm? Yes

If not, does the firm consider pro bono work generally in associate evaluations? N/A

HOURS

Does the firm give billable hour credit for pro bono work? Yes

Does the firm have a maximum number of pro bono hours that can be applied toward the billable hour target? Yes

If so, what is the maximum? 20 hours

If your firm uses hours to determine bonuses, does it consider pro bono hours when determining bonuses? Yes

PRO BONO POINTS

What training opportunities are open to associates working on pro bono matters? We provide frequent in-house training for many substantive areas in which pro bono work is performed. We offer the opportunity to attend outside training events for pro bono work and provide supervision and mentoring on all pro bono matters.

Can associates bring matters of interest to the firm? Yes

Does the firm offer the use of support staff in carrying out pro bono matters? Yes

What pro bono opportunities are available for summer associates? Summer associates are trained to represent (under supervision) low-income clients in landlord-tenant and consumer cases, domestic violence cases, grandparent adoption cases and to draft wills and advance directives for elderly clients. They also have the opportunity to work with KS lawyers on the wide variety of pro bono matters the lawyers are handling.

Does the firm have established programs, such as externships, that enable its associates to work in a public interest setting? Yes

If so, where and for up to how long? Fellowships for associates and summer students at legal aid and pro bono programs, for up to six months for associates and 10 weeks for summer associates.

Has your firm won any special recognition or awards in the last two years for its pro bono work? Yes

If so, please list. North Carolina Bar Association Large Law Firm Award, 2003; NC Bar Association Young Lawyer Award, 2002; Mecklenburg Bar Outstanding Law Firm Award, 2002; Mecklenburg Bar Legal Services to the Elderly Award, 2002; Mecklenburg Bar Pro Bono Lawyer of the Year Award, 2002; Legal Aid of NW North Carolina Law Firm of the Year Award, 2002; Legal Aid of NW North Carolina Lawyer of the Year Award, 2002.

THE FIRM SAYS

In January 2001, Kilpatrick Stockton hired an attorney whose full-time responsibility is to bring in, allocate, approve and supervise pro bono work throughout the firm. In 2002, KS further demonstrated that pro bono was an core value of the firm by electing her to the partnership. Since early 2001, the firm has approved a new pro bono policy, which emphasized the firm's commitment to provide pro bono representation to those who cannot afford to hire an attorney, and reiterated the firm's long-held position that pro bono work clients are entitled to the same highest quality representation and resources as are paying clients. Training is regularly provided for pro bono representation, and supervision and mentoring are the norm. Partners as well as associates in all offices participate in the pro bono program.

While a significant portion of the firm's pro bono work is for low-income clients and involves litigation, a greater portion requires the skills of transactional lawyers, who often serve as general counsel to nonprofit organizations. Kilpatrick Stockton sets a minimum goal for each lawyer of 50 hours of pro bono per year and recognizes each lawyer as he or she reaches that goal. Firm-wide awards are awarded in a variety of categories. Associates who exceed the minimum goal are eligible for pro bono bonuses. In 2002, Kilpatrick Stockton signed onto the Law Firm Pro Bono Challenge, agreeing to reach its goal of committing 3 percent of total billables to pro bono work by the end of 2004. As of October 2003, the firm has performed pro bono representation equal to 2.9 percent of billables.

OUR SURVEY SAYS

"[We have a] full-time pro bono partner. Enough said."

"Training is regularly provided for pro bono representation, and supervision and mentoring are the norm."

— *Kilpatrick Stockton LLP*

King & Spalding LLP

191 Peachtree Street, Suite 4900
Atlanta, GA 30303-1763
Phone: (404) 572-4600
www.kslaw.com

LOCATIONS

Atlanta, GA (HQ)
Houston, TX
New York, NY
Washington, DC
London

MAJOR DEPARTMENTS & PRACTICES

Business Litigation
Construction & Procurement
Corporate & Finance
Employee Benefits & Executive Compensation
Energy
Environmental
Financial Restructuring
Financial Transactions
Food & Drug
Global Projects & Transactions
Government Practice
Governmental & Regulatory
Health Care
Intellectual Property
International Trade & Litigation
Labor & Employment
Litigation
Special Matters
Litigation & Trade
Mergers & Acquisitions
Private Equity
Public Finance
Real Estate
Tax
Tort Litigation
Trusts & Estates

THE STATS

No. of attorneys worldwide: 700 +
No. of offices worldwide: 5
Chairman: Walter W. Driver Jr.

EMPLOYMENT CONTACTS

Atlanta
Ms. Rebecca McClain Newton
Director of Recruiting
Phone: (404) 572-3395
Fax: (404) 572-5100
E-mail: rnewton@kslaw.com

Houston
Ms. Ann Harris
Recruiting Manager
Phone: (713) 751-3200
E-mail: aharris@kslaw.com

New York
Ms. Kristan A. Lassiter
Recruiting Manager
Phone: (212) 556-2138
E-mail: klassiter@kslaw.com

Washington, DC
Ms. Kara O'Connor
Recruiting Manager
Phone: (202) 626-2387
E-mail: koconnor@kslaw.com

WHO'S WHO

Principal pro bono contact(s) at your firm:

William E. Hoffmann, Esq.
Pro Bono Chair, Atlanta
Phone: (404) 572-3383
E-mail: BHoffmann@kslaw.com

Mark K. Glasser, Esq.
Pro Bono Chair, Houston
Phone: (713) 751-3212
E-mail: MGlasser@kslaw.com

Charles S. Detrizio, Esq.
Pro Bono Chair, New York
Phone: (212) 556-2297
E-mail: CDetrizio@kslaw.com

Jane C. Luxton, Esq.
Pro Bono Co-Chair, Washington, D.C.
Phone: (202) 626-2627
E-mail: JLuxton@kslaw.com

Andrew C. Lynch, Esq.
Pro Bono Co-Chair, Washington, D.C.
Phone: (202) 626-5614
E-mail: ALynch@kslaw.com

Ms. Linda A. Parrish
Director of Community Affairs
Phone: (404) 572-4670
E-mail: Lparrish@kslaw.com

Does the firm have a pro bono coordinator? Yes
Linda A. Parrish

If yes, what percentage of his or her time is spent on pro bono work? 33 percent

Does the firm have a pro bono committee? Yes

If yes, how often does the committee meet? Quarterly and more often as needed.

Describe the composition of the committee: Firm-wide committee with pro bono chairs from each office; each office has a pro bono committee with partners and associates.

THE SCOOP

Does your firm have a written pro bono policy? Yes

Has the firm signed on to the Law Firm Pro Bono Challenge? Yes (D.C. office)

What are some of the areas of law in which your firm has performed pro bono legal work in the last two years? Indigent defense, prisoners' rights, death penalty post-conviction remedies, domestic violence, eviction defense and other landlord/tenant, political asylum and immigration appeals, community economic development, First Amendment, truancy intervention, nonprofit formation and representation, tax assistance, wills projects, family law.

What are some of the areas of law in which your firm does not perform pro bono work? All cases evaluated on an individual basis.

Organizations for which your firm has performed pro bono legal services in the last two years: Atlanta Legal Aid Society, Atlanta Volunteer Lawyers Foundation, Board of Immigration Appeals Pro Bono Project, inMotion, Inc., Lawyers Alliance for New York, Lawyers' Committee for Civil Rights Under Law, Southern Center for Human Rights, Texas C-Bar, Washington Lawyers' Committee for Civil Rights, Women Empowered Against Violence.

List up to three pro bono matters that are representative of the pro bono work your firm participates in. Handled a wrongful death suit, in a prisoners' rights case, on behalf of the family of a prisoner who was beaten to death by other inmates due to inadequate security. Represented low-income women in seeking orders of protection, spousal support, and divorces from abusive spouses, and in child custody disputes. Represented indigent tenants in semi-weekly eviction proceedings, resulting in agreements satisfactory in about 90 percent of the cases. Negotiated a lease for a nonprofit community development corporation founded to address the unmet needs of low-income residents (such as forming community childcare centers).

BY THE NUMBERS

What is the total number of hours that lawyers in U.S. offices at your firm spent performing pro bono legal services in 2000, 2001 and 2002?

    Total number of hours in 2000: 6,700 hours
    Total number of hours in 2001: 11,000 hours
    Total number of hours in 2002: 23,400 hours

Average number of pro bono hours per attorney in U.S. offices per year (including associates, partners, counsels, but not summer associates):

    Average number of hours per attorney in 2000: 11.7 hours
    Average number of hours per attorney in 2001: 16.6 hours
    Average number of hours per attorney in 2002: 33.7 hours

What percentage of attorneys in this firm's U.S. offices did pro bono work in 2002? 58 percent

What percentage of attorneys in this firm's U.S. offices did at least 20 hours of pro bono work in 2002? 32 percent

Does the firm encourage its lawyers to perform a minimum number of pro bono hours? We encourage lawyers to meet the annual aspirational pro bono goals set by their local or state bar associations.

SUPERVISION AND EVALUATIONS

Is there partner supervision on each pro bono matter? Yes

Do partner supervisors or, if applicable, senior associates provide written evaluations of associates' work on pro bono matters? Included in general evaluation

If so, are those evaluations taken into account in determining salary, bonuses or advancement in the firm? Yes

If not, does the firm consider pro bono work generally in associate evaluations? Yes

HOURS

Does the firm give billable hour credit for pro bono work? No

Does the firm have a maximum number of pro bono hours that can be applied toward the billable hour target? No

If so, what is the maximum? N/A

If your firm uses hours to determine bonuses, does it consider pro bono hours when determining bonuses? Yes

PRO BONO POINTS

What training opportunities are open to associates working on pro bono matters? Courtroom experience, depositions (including expert witnesses), brief writing, negotiation skills and client management.

Can associates bring matters of interest to the firm? Yes

Does the firm offer the use of support staff in carrying out pro bono matters? Yes

What pro bono opportunities are available for summer associates? Assignments available to all interested summer associates. Some offices also offer a one-week pro bono rotation for summer associates at the firm for eight or more weeks. Firm-paid public interest externships in second half of summer.

Does the firm have established programs, such as externships, that enable its associates to work in a public interest setting? No

Has your firm won any special recognition or awards in the last two years for its pro bono work? Yes

If so, please list. S. Phillip Heiner Award from Atlanta Volunteer Lawyers Foundation in 2002 for the Eviction Defense and Emergency Services Personnel Wills Projects. 2003 Wiley A. Branton Outstanding Achievement Award from Washington Lawyers' Committee for Civil Rights & Urban Affairs for political asylum cases and matters affecting juvenile immigrants. State Bar of Georgia's William B. Spann Jr. Award for the Eviction Defense Project in 2003. 2003 Commitment to Justice Award from New York-based inMotion, Inc. for representing low-income, underserved women in family law cases. Associate Benjamin Newland received the 2003 Cornerstone Award from Lawyers Alliance for New York for his work with the Ethical Community Charter School Foundation. Associate Morgan Warren received a 2003 Community Builder Award from Texas C-Bar for her leadership in the formation of tax-exempt nonprofit organizations.

THE FIRM SAYS

Pro bono legal service is an important institutional commitment of King & Spalding LLP. In recognition of the special needs of the poor for legal services, we believe that the firm's pro bono activities should be particularly focused on providing access to the justice system for persons otherwise unable to afford it and that the majority of the firm's pro bono time should consist of the delivery of legal services on a pro bono basis to persons of limited means or to charitable, religious, civic, community, governmental and educational organizations in matters which are designed primarily to address the needs of persons of limited means. Our Washington, D.C., office met the Law Firm Pro Bono Challenge by contributing 3 percent or more of total billable hours to pro bono representation in 2002. The firm strongly encourages attorneys in our other domestic offices to meet or exceed the annual aspirational goals for pro bono hours set forth by the ABA and state bar associations in their states.

Although the firm has established strong relationships with many legal service providers, we have developed several signature projects such as the Eviction Defense Program and the Indigent Defense Project. Associates are encouraged to bring in pro bono matters of interest to them. Lawyers are also encouraged to serve on the boards of legal service providers and other nonprofit organizations, which strengthens these groups and provides referral opportunities. King & Spalding contributes to community leadership efforts through service on more than 150 nonprofit boards. Over 900 people in our four domestic offices volunteered their time outside pro bono legal representation, contributing an additional 20,000 hours of volunteer service to our communities. Direct service projects and activities include building Habitat for Humanity houses; renovating homes for low-income, elderly or disabled homeowners; reading programs, career days and job shadow days for inner-city students; food, clothing, book and school supply drives; meals for the homeless; participation in city-wide days of service such as New York Cares Day and Hands On Atlanta Day; coaching high school mock trial teams and providing other law-related enrichment activities; in-house blood drives; special projects for senior citizens, veterans and international aid organizations; numerous walks and races including AIDS walks and the Susan G. Komen Breast Cancer Foundation's Race for the Cure; and various holiday projects benefiting children and families in need.

King & Spalding was recognized by the Atlanta Council of Volunteer Administrators as "Business of the Year" in 2002 for demonstrated excellence in its commitment to and support of volunteerism in metro Atlanta and among its employees. The Washington, D.C., office was recognized as the leading law firm out of 65 participating firms in the Salvation Army's Angel Tree Program.

OUR SURVEY SAYS

"The firm has a strong pro bono commitment, but does not count pro bono hours as billable hours. There is a separate bonus pool that is used to reward associates who devote a significant amount of time to pro bono work, but most associates struggle with time issues. When you work as hard as full-time associates do, it takes a real commitment to take on pro bono case that will mean incremental work."

"I am actively involved in pro bono activities, and the emphasis on such work is ever increasing."

"The firm is highly committed to pro bono and has committed each attorney to fulfilling a requisite number of pro bono hours each year. Pro bono clients are treated with the same respect and care as paying clients. If billable hours are low due to work on a pro bono case, you are not penalized. On the contrary, the firm has a discretionary bonus program to reward the extraordinary pro bono efforts of attorneys."

"While I agree that it is our 'duty' to give back, I think it's a little unfair and unrealistic to expect associates aiming for 2,050 billable hours a year to also meet the pro bono recommended hours without providing more incentive. Money talks and the fact that the firm is unwilling (at this point) to help associates by giving some billable credit for their pro bono work says a lot."

"[There has been] a new emphasis on pro bono in the last year. The pro bono committee has become very active in soliciting associates to take on work, [with] weekly updates on available cases or corporate-side opportunities."

"The firm strongly encourages and supports pro bono and other civic and charitable activities. The firm pays a bonus to those who have made 'significant contributions' in these areas."

"[The firm is] committed for litigators but transactional people get a lot of flak for doing pro bono."

"The firm puts a great emphasis on pro bono work, and is involved in excellent pro bono projects. I have already had some excellent experiences through pro bono programs. However, no portion of pro bono hours counts towards the billable hours bonus. Arguably, there should be no financial incentive involved in pro bono, but this practice creates a disincentive for doing pro bono."

"The D.C. office is really making strides because they are realizing that in order to stay competitive in our market, they have to improve their pro bono record. Last year the managing partner committed to the 'D.C. Pro Bono Initiative' and achieved our goal of over 50 hours per attorney."

Kirkland & Ellis LLP

200 East Randolph Drive
Chicago, IL 60601-6636
Phone: (312) 861-2000
www.kirkland.com

LOCATIONS

Chicago, IL (largest office)
Los Angeles, CA
New York, NY
San Francisco, CA
Washington, DC
London

MAJOR DEPARTMENTS & PRACTICES

Bankruptcy
Intellectual Property
Interdisciplinary
Litigation
Tax & Planning
Transactional

THE STATS

No. of attorneys worldwide: 900 +
No. of offices worldwide: 6
Firm Administrator: Douglas O. McLemore

EMPLOYMENT CONTACT

Ms. Norah F. Scott
Attorney Recruiting Manager
Phone: (312) 861-8532
Fax: (312) 861-2200
E-mail: nscott@kirkland.com

WHO'S WHO

Does the firm have a pro bono coordinator? Yes

Barry E. Fields, Esq. (principal pro bono contact)
Chicago Office
Phone: (312) 861-2081
E-mail: bfields@kirkland.com

Marjorie P. Lindblom, Esq. (New York Office)
Matthew H. Hurlock, Esq. (London Office)
Eric R. Lamison, Esq. (San Francisco Office)
Tony L. Richardson, Esq. (Los Angeles Office)
Steven M. Wellner, Esq. (Washington, D.C. Office)

If yes, what percentage of his or her time is spent on pro bono work? 5 percent or less.

Does the firm have a pro bono committee? No

THE SCOOP

Does your firm have a written pro bono policy? Yes

Has the firm signed on to the Law Firm Pro Bono Challenge? Yes

What are some of the areas of law in which your firm has performed pro bono legal work in the last two years? The firm has performed work in a variety of areas, including civil rights litigation, criminal appellate litigation, immigration litigation, intellectual property consultation and housing.

What are some of the areas of law in which your firm does not perform pro bono work? Usually, the firm does not handle major criminal cases at the trial level.

Organizations for which your firm has performed pro bono legal services in the last two years: Cabrini Green Legal Aid Clinic, Midwest Immigration and Human Rights Center, Chicago Lawyers' Committee for Civil Rights Under Law, Children's Rights Organization, Volunteer Lawyers for the Arts, Artists For A New South Africa, Lutheran Family and Community Services, Archdiocesan Legal Network, Washington Lawyers' Committee for Civil Rights & Urban Affairs, D.C. Appleseed Center.

BY THE NUMBERS

What is the total number of hours that lawyers in U.S. offices at your firm spent performing pro bono legal services in 2000, 2001 and 2002?

Total number of hours in 2000: N/A
Total number of hours in 2001: N/A
Total number of hours in 2002: 24,690 hours

Average number of pro bono hours per attorney in U.S. offices per year (including associates, partners, counsels, but not summer associates):

Average number of hours per attorney in 2000: N/A
Average number of hours per attorney in 2001: N/A
Average number of hours per attorney in 2002: N/A

What percentage of attorneys in this firm's U.S. offices did pro bono work in 2002? 33 percent

What percentage of attorneys in this firm's U.S. offices did at least 20 hours of pro bono work in 2002? N/A

Does the firm encourage its lawyers to perform a minimum number of pro bono hours? No

If so, how many hours per year or what percentage of lawyers' billable hours? N/A

SUPERVISION AND EVALUATIONS

Is there partner supervision on each pro bono matter? Yes

Do partner supervisors or, if applicable, senior associates provide written evaluations of associates' work on pro bono matters? Yes

If so, are those evaluations taken into account in determining salary, bonuses or advancement in the firm? Yes

If not, does the firm consider pro bono work generally in associate evaluations? N/A

HOURS

Does the firm give billable hour credit for pro bono work? Yes

Does the firm have a maximum number of pro bono hours that can be applied toward the billable hour target? No

If so, what is the maximum? N/A

If your firm uses hours to determine bonuses, does it consider pro bono hours when determining bonuses? Yes

PRO BONO POINTS

What training opportunities are open to associates working on pro bono matters? Various organizations with which the firm works offer training opportunities (including at K&E's offices). These training opportunities are open and available to associates. Additionally, associates participate in the firm's formal training programs.

Can associates bring matters of interest to the firm? Yes

Does the firm offer the use of support staff in carrying out pro bono matters? Yes

What pro bono opportunities are available for summer associates? Summer associates have the same pro bono opportunities as attorneys at the firm.

Does the firm have established programs, such as externships, that enable its associates to work in a public interest setting? Yes

If so, where and for up to how long? For example, Public Interest Law Initiative Fellowships (10 weeks).

Has your firm won any special recognition or awards in the last two years for its pro bono work? Yes

If so, please list. Volunteer Attorneys of the Year (Western Law Center for Disability Rights); Volunteer Lawyer Award (John Carroll Society).

THE FIRM SAYS

Kirkland & Ellis ("K&E") historically has been engaged in providing legal assistance on a pro bono basis. Although K&E does not require lawyers to work on pro bono matters, we do encourage each lawyer at the firm to spend time working on such matters. Pro bono activities have the same priority as "billable" client work when balancing work loads within a department or firm-wide. In determining the compensation of lawyers and in evaluating associates' progress toward partnership, the quality of legal work performed on a pro bono matter is given the same consideration as comparable work for the firm's regular, paying clients. Moreover, pro bono work performed by associates is supervised by a partner, and the firm expects the level of supervision to be comparable to that received by associates working on matters for paying clients. K&E also encourages its lawyers to participate in the activities of professional associations, not-for-profit corporations, community organizations and the like.

OUR SURVEY SAYS

"The firm takes on all sorts of diverse and challenging pro bono opportunities, from immigration matters before an immigration court, to prisoner's litigation, to cases that federal courts sometimes contact us for and ask that we handle pro bono. You get one-for-one credit on the hours devoted to pro bono time, a sure sign that the firm truly believes in giving back to the community. Plus, in addition to all the other training and experience you receive via formal training programs and our 'paid' cases, the partnership quite willingly endorses pro bono activities as yet another way to get excellent experience."

"I've never had a prospective pro bono client rejected. Once the firm accepts the prospective party as a client, the same resources are available as for paying clients. It also helps that pro bono hours are billable hours."

"I've never heard back about the one pro bono effort that I expressed interest in pursuing. Projects are often turned down by the firm."

"They talk the talk and certainly permit you to do pro bono, but better that it not interfere with your billable hours too much."

"Great quality stuff, and plenty of it: death penalty appeals, political projects, think tanks, criminal work and so on. It's abundant."

"No requirements, but unlimited billable hours for approved pro bono. Great system."

"The firm supports pro bono activities in the office by allowing associates to take on pre-approved pro bono projects that are entirely financed by the firm, but that is about the extent of it. The onus is on the associate to find the project they want to work on, to get the necessary approvals and to get a partner to support it. Generally, the firm is open to all sorts of pro bono projects but the work load in the office simply does not allow associates to take on many pro bono assignments. While the firm gives associates billable credit for all pro bono matters, the reality is that few associates can push aside billable client work for a pro bono project without sacrificing lots of sleep in the process."

"My first year as an associate, I billed 800 hours to a pro bono case. The firm counts pro bono hours as billable hours and treats all pro bono matters the same as billable matters."

"The firm is very supportive of associates' pro bono work. However, the system is largely unstructured, which has the flexibility of freedom but requires more associate initiative."

"You can do it if you can find the time. One nice thing is that pro bono hours count towards billables."

"In determining the compensation of lawyers and in evaluating associates' progress toward partnership, the quality of legal work performed on a pro bono matter is given the same consideration as comparable work for the firm's regular, paying clients."

— *Kirkland & Ellis LLP*

Kirkpatrick & Lockhart LLP

Henry W. Oliver Building
535 Smithfield Street
Pittsburgh, PA 15222
Phone: (412) 355-6500
www.kl.com

LOCATIONS

Boston, MA
Dallas, TX
Harrisburg, PA
Los Angeles, CA
Miami, FL
New York, NY
Newark, NJ
Pittsburgh, PA
San Francisco, CA
Washington, DC

MAJOR DEPARTMENTS & PRACTICES

Antitrust & Trade Regulation • Appellate • Bank Regulatory & Compliance • Bankruptcy • Class Action Litigation Defense • Construction Industry • Corporate • Electronic Commerce • Employee Benefits • Employment & Labor • Energy, Environment & Natural Resources • Financing • Food Drug Medical Device & Cosmetic Practice • Government Affairs • Health Care • Homeland Security • Insurance • Intellectual Property • International • Investment Management • Land Use Planning & Zoning • Life Sciences • Litigation • M&A • Nonprofit Organizations • Product Liability • Professional Liability • Project Finance • Public Utility • Publishing Industry/Media • Real Estate • Securities • Tax • Technology & Emerging Growth Companies • Transportation • Trusts & Estates • White Collar Crime/Criminal Defense

THE STATS

No. of attorneys worldwide: 732
No. of offices worldwide: 10
Chairman: Peter J. Kalis

EMPLOYMENT CONTACT

See firm web site for contacts in each office.

WHO'S WHO

Principal pro bono contact(s) at your firm:

Carleton O. Strouss, Esq.
Partner
Phone: (717) 231-4500
E-mail: cstrouss@kl.com

Does the firm have a pro bono coordinator? Yes
Boston: Irene C. Freidel, Esq.
Dallas: Michael D. Napoli, Esq.
Harrisburg: David R. Fine, Esq.
Los Angeles: Jill L. Varon, Esq.
Miami: Daniel A. Casey, Esq.
New York: Eva M. Ciko, Esq.
Newark: Stephen A. Timoni, Esq.
Pittsburgh: Kenneth M. Argentieri, Esq.
San Francisco: Dirk Michels, Esq.
Washington: Philip H. Hecht, Esq. and A. Thomas Morris, Esq.

Does the firm have a pro bono committee? Yes

If yes, how often does the committee meet? The firm-wide committee meets quarterly or as necessary.

Describe the composition of the committee: The committee is comprised of three partners. The committee chair also sits on the firm's management committee.

THE SCOOP

Does your firm have a written pro bono policy? Yes

Has the firm signed on to the Law Firm Pro Bono Challenge? No

What are some of the areas of law in which your firm has performed pro bono legal work in the last two years? Litigation, civil rights, family law including adoption, PFA's, landlord/tenant, contracts, health and human services, criminal appeals, public benefits, general business, immigration.

What are some of the areas of law in which your firm does not perform pro bono work? There are no categorical exclusions.

Organizations for which your firm has performed pro bono legal services in the last two years: The Boston Bar Association, Lawyers Committee for Civil Rights; Dallas Bar Association and Legal Aid of North West Texas; Dauphin County Bar Association Pro Bono Program; Los Angeles County Children's Court; Miami-Dade County Bar Association; Lawyer's Committee on Human Rights; Neighborhood Legal Services Association; Women Empowered Against Violence (WEAVE).

List up to three pro bono matters that are representative of the pro bono work your firm participates in. Representing victims of domestic violence. Represent individuals and nonprofit organizations in actions to defend, protect and/or preserve civil rights. Represent applicants for asylum.

BY THE NUMBERS

What is the total number of hours that lawyers in U.S. offices at your firm spent performing pro bono legal services in 2000, 2001 and 2002?

    Total number of hours in 2000: N/A
    Total number of hours in 2001: N/A
    Total number of hours in 2002: 6,854 hours

Average number of pro bono hours per attorney in U.S. offices per year (including associates, partners, counsels, but not summer associates):

    Average number of hours per attorney in 2000: N/A
    Average number of hours per attorney in 2001: N/A
    Average number of hours per attorney in 2002: 11.2 hours

What percentage of attorneys in this firm's U.S. offices did at least 20 hours of pro bono work in 2002? 17 percent

Does the firm encourage its lawyers to perform a minimum number of pro bono hours? No

If so, how many hours per year or what percentage of lawyers' billable hours? N/A

SUPERVISION AND EVALUATIONS

Is there partner supervision on each pro bono matter? Yes

Do partner supervisors or, if applicable, senior associates provide written evaluations of associates' work on pro bono matters? N/A

If so, are those evaluations taken into account in determining salary, bonuses or advancement in the firm? N/A

If not, does the firm consider pro bono work generally in associate evaluations? Yes

HOURS

Does the firm give billable hour credit for pro bono work? Yes

Does the firm have a maximum number of pro bono hours that can be applied toward the billable hour target? Yes

If so, what is the maximum? Typically 30 hours.

If your firm uses hours to determine bonuses, does it consider pro bono hours when determining bonuses? Yes

PRO BONO POINTS

What training opportunities are open to associates working on pro bono matters? In-house training is available. In some cases, agency training programs are also available.

Can associates bring matters of interest to the firm? Yes

Does the firm offer the use of support staff in carrying out pro bono matters? Yes

What pro bono opportunities are available for summer associates? The same opportunities are available to summer associates as are available to firm lawyers generally.

Does the firm have established programs, such as externships, that enable its associates to work in a public interest setting? No

Has your firm won any special recognition or awards in the last two years for its pro bono work? Yes

If so, please list. K&L was recognized by the Neighborhood Legal Services Association of Pittsburgh for K&L's representation over the past ten years of more than 1,500 victims of domestic violence. In 2002, K&L's Pittsburgh office received the Allegheny County Bar Foundation's (ACBF) Public Service Award for pro bono work by a law firm.

THE FIRM SAYS

The firm undertakes pro bono work on the same parameters as billable work. Pro bono work is considered for bonus and compensation purposes.

OUR SURVEY SAYS

"The firm seems committed to pro bono activity and has in place a committee to introduce pro bono to all attorneys."

"I do pro bono work and the firm is supportive."

"It seems that pro bono work is basically an individual attorney's choice, and while the firm is supportive of taking on pro bono work, there is not the sense that every lawyer should participate in pro bono efforts."

"They are quite accommodating and count the hours toward bonuses."

"The firm is committed to pro bono in the sense that we have a pro bono committee, make donations to charities and have a strong contingent of attorneys who take on pro bono projects. Pro bono work is not an overwhelming presence in the firm's daily activities, nor is it high-profile, but there are always pro bono opportunities made available and pro bono work is encouraged."

"The firm encourages associates to get involved in pro bono activities, and such activities count towards the billable hour requirement."

"I have the ability to work on pro bono material and currently do; many more projects will be forthcoming."

"There are pro bono opportunities presented on a pretty regular basis, but it does not seem to be a priority for the entire firm. Rather, it seems there are a few attorneys who are committed to pro bono work, and the rest just seem to lay low when the e-mail requests come around."

"I have encountered some slight resistance in regard to my pro bono activities. Nothing that can't be managed, however."

"The firm has recently rolled out a new pro bono initiative to improve our track record in this regard."

"K&L was recognized by the Neighborhood Legal Services Association of Pittsburgh for K&L's representation over the past ten years of more than 1,500 victims of domestic violence."

— *Kirkpatrick & Lockhart LLP*

Kramer Levin Naftalis & Frankel LLP

919 Third Avenue
New York, NY 10022-3852
Phone: (212) 715-9175
www.kramerlevin.com

LOCATIONS

New York, NY (HQ)
Paris

MAJOR DEPARTMENTS & PRACTICES

Advertising
Antitrust
Appellate & Constitutional Litigation
Banking
Corporate
Creditors' Rights & Bankruptcy
Employee Benefits
Employment & Labor
Financial Services
Information Technology & E-Commerce
Insurance Litigation
Intellectual Property
International
Land Use
Litigation
Real Estate
Securities & Shareholder Litigation
Securitization
Tax
White Collar Criminal Defense

THE STATS

No. of attorneys worldwide: 280 +
No. of offices worldwide: 2
Firm Co-Chairs: Ezra G. Levin, Gary P. Naftalis, Thomas E. Constance
Managing Partner: Paul S. Pearlman

EMPLOYMENT CONTACT

Ms. Pamela H. Nelson
Associate Director of Legal Recruiting
Phone: (212) 715-9213
Fax: (212) 715-8000
E-mail: pnelson@kramerlevin.com

WHO'S WHO

Principal pro bono contact(s) at your firm:

Jeffrey S. Trachtman, Esq.
Partner & Chair of Pro Bono Committee
Phone: (212) 715-9175
E-mail: jtrachtman@kramerlevin.com

Does the firm have a pro bono coordinator? No

Does the firm have a pro bono committee? Yes

If yes, how often does the committee meet? Two to three times per year, but frequent consults by e-mail.

Describe the composition of the committee: Partners and associates from representative departments.

THE SCOOP

Does your firm have a written pro bono policy? Yes

Has the firm signed on to the Law Firm Pro Bono Challenge? Yes

What are some of the areas of law in which your firm has performed pro bono legal work in the last two years? Political asylum, landlord-tenant, civil rights, lesbian and gay rights, Social Security disability, Medicaid rights, nonprofit incorporation, aid to 9/11 victims, criminal defense.

What are some of the areas of law in which your firm does not perform pro bono work? We have no specific bar on any area of pro bono work. We have done relatively little prisoners' rights work recently, but have done some in the past; same with criminal defense trial work. We have not gotten involved yet in micro-entrepreneur counseling, but may in the future.

Organizations for (or with) which your firm has performed pro bono legal services in the last two years: Lawyers Committee for Human Rights, Lambda Legal Defense, Volunteer Lawyers for the Arts, Lawyers Alliance for New York, Center for Disability Advocacy Rights, South Brooklyn Legal Services, New York Legal Assistance Group, inMotion, Brennan Center, Volunteers of Legal Service (VOLS), New York Lawyers for the Public Interest (NYLPI).

List up to three pro bono matters that are representative of the pro bono work your firm participates in.

- Our Associate Service Program, through which associates work full time staffing a housing court position at South Brooklyn Legal Services, exemplifies our commitment to providing efficient and effective direct representation to the poor.

- Our recently completed class action on behalf of homeless children in the New York City shelter system suffering from asthma is a great example of using our resources to tackle a bigger problem — in this case, the failure of the city and state to honor their Medicaid obligations to screen and treat kids with asthma. We achieved a great settlement after three years of litigation.

- While it's hard to pick any one matter of dozens of individual cases, our representation over many years of Patrick Mkhizi, a young man seeking political asylum from Congo, exemplifies our commitment in this area. The case required

2,000 attorney hours over several years and briefing of many difficult issues before we finally won him asylum. There are many other examples in the asylum, gay rights, housing and other areas showing our commitment and expertise.

BY THE NUMBERS

What is the total number of hours that lawyers in U.S. offices at your firm spent performing pro bono legal services in 2000, 2001 and 2002?

> **Total number of hours in 2000:** 15,136 hours
> **Total number of hours in 2001:** 14,381 hours
> **Total number of hours in 2002:** 11,224 hours

Average number of pro bono hours per attorney in U.S. offices per year (including associates, partners, counsels, but not summer associates):

> **Average number of hours per attorney in 2000:** 75 hours
> **Average number of hours per attorney in 2001:** 64 hours
> **Average number of hours per attorney in 2002:** 48 hours

What percentage of attorneys in this firm's U.S. offices did pro bono work in 2002? 65 percent

What percentage of attorneys in this firm's U.S. offices did at least 20 hours of pro bono work in 2002? 33 percent

Does the firm encourage its lawyers to perform a minimum number of pro bono hours? No

If so, how many hours per year or what percentage of lawyers' billable hours? We do not encourage a specific minimum, but we fully count pro bono as billable, with no fixed maximum.

SUPERVISION AND EVALUATIONS

Is there partner supervision on each pro bono matter? Pro bono matters are supervised in the same manner as any other work, which means by a partner or senior associate depending on size and complexity.

Do partner supervisors or, if applicable, senior associates provide written evaluations of associates' work on pro bono matters? Yes

If so, are those evaluations taken into account in determining salary, bonuses or advancement in the firm? Yes

If not, does the firm consider pro bono work generally in associate evaluations? Yes

HOURS

Does the firm give billable hour credit for pro bono work? Yes

Does the firm have a maximum number of pro bono hours that can be applied toward the billable hour target? No

If so, what is the maximum? N/A

If your firm uses hours to determine bonuses, does it consider pro bono hours when determining bonuses? Yes

PRO BONO POINTS

What training opportunities are open to associates working on pro bono matters? Associates are encouraged to take advantage of any available training offered by pro bono organizations, and we do some training in house in areas where we do a lot of work (e.g., SSI, asylum).

Can associates bring matters of interest to the firm? Yes

Does the firm offer the use of support staff in carrying out pro bono matters? Yes

What pro bono opportunities are available for summer associates? We were one of the first firms to fully incorporate pro bono into our summer programs. Every summer associate is offered a choice of pro bono matters. Most choose to work on SSI hearings or asylum cases, but we have also over the years involved summers in divorce cases, drafting wills for low-income elderly persons, transactional work for nonprofits, work on amicus briefs in the gay rights and other areas, and whatever other pro bono work is in the office.

Does the firm have established programs, such as externships, that enable its associates to work in a public interest setting? Yes

If so, where and for up to how long? Full-time four-month placement at South Brooklyn Legal Services doing housing court work. Full salary, benefits, time counts towards partnership, and so forth.

Has your firm won any special recognition or awards in the last two years for its pro bono work? Yes

If so, please list. Legal Aid Society Exceptional Pro Bono Publico and Public Service Law Firm Award; Real Estate Partner Larry Loeb received Cornerstone Award from Lawyers Alliance for New York; and Lawyers Committee for Human Rights created Marvin Frankel Fellowship and the Marvin Frankel Pro Bono Awards to honor our late firm chairman and chairman of the organization, who passed away in 2002.

THE FIRM SAYS

Kramer Levin is proud to have a long tradition of treating pro bono as an important part of our practice. We have a long history of permitting attorneys to pursue pro bono matters of personal interest to them, believing that pro bono works best when it reflects the passions and commitments of individual attorneys. We therefore have always been involved in a wide range of activities, from individual poverty law cases to civil rights amicus briefs to transactional projects for nonprofits. We also have undertaken larger, more coordinated projects to leverage our resources most effectively, including our full-time externship position at South Brooklyn Legal Services and class actions on behalf of homeless children with asthma, children SSI claimants and others. We have particularly distinguished ourselves in the SSI area, where we have represented dozens of claimants and argued two important Second Circuit appeals, and gay rights, where we have participated in the landmark Dale and Lawrence cases, brought the case that established the right to second parent adoption in Delaware, and are now actively involved in work on the recognition of same sex marriages.

We support our pro bono work by counting the hours for all firm purposes, including bonuses, and insisting that pro bono work be supervised and evaluated like any other work. Attorneys are free to propose pro bono matters, which are approved by the chair of the pro bono committee and, if requiring a particularly significant devotion of resources, others in management. All firm resources are made available to support pro bono work as regular firm work. We also encourage attorneys to become involved in other community service activities that use their skills and talents as lawyers, including nonprofit board service, participation in high school mentoring and teaching programs and other nonprofit service. This time is also credited as billable time.

OUR SURVEY SAYS

"Historically, Kramer Levin has had a tremendous commitment to pro bono. This has tempered somewhat as the firm transitioned into a modern, large New York law firm, but it remains a deep and vibrant program and one of the firm's signature characteristics."

"The litigation department is the most committed to pro bono and has been involved in major projects of nationwide scope."

"All departments can participate in pro bono matters. Pro bono also provides an opportunity to explore areas other than those one practices daily. For instance, I am in litigation and have done pro bono work in estate planning, corporate structure counseling and new media issues."

"As the firm has gotten busier, it is not as encouraging of pro bono work as [it] used to be."

"I have always been satisfied with my pro bono experiences. They have allowed me to obtain practical experience (i.e., depositions, witness preparations, hearings in federal court) as well as made me feel good about being an attorney. The firm has been extremely supportive even in years when I have worked disproportionately on pro bono cases."

"While there are a handful of partners who may not be entirely supportive, I can think of several partners who not only are willing to supervise associate's pro bono efforts, but also are actively involved in litigating pro bono matters themselves."

"In my experience, once a case is taken on, that case is treated like any other case. All of the firm's resources are available (which could theoretically mean that a pro bono client gets resources that a paying client might not be able to afford). Any issues that arise are addressed by attorneys in other departments as well, so that the pro bono client's representation is full and complete, within the scope of the matter accepted."

"I have billed 100 to 200 hours to pro bono matters every year I have been here and feel that no one has had a problem with that."

"To me, one of the nicest things about the program is that while there are certain structured aspects — such as ongoing relationships with groups like the Lawyers Committee for Human Rights, which offers regular political asylum work for those who are interested — the program is also flexible enough that if an attorney has an interest in a particular area, the firm will foster that associate's interest."

"Every firm pitches itself as committed to pro bono. I think the reality here is going to match what's on paper and in the recruiting materials."

"We have a long history of permitting attorneys to pursue pro bono matters of personal interest to them, believing that pro bono works best when it reflects the passions and commitments of individual attorneys."

— *Kramer Levin Naftalis & Frankel LLP*

Latham & Watkins LLP

633 West Fifth Street, Suite 4000
Los Angeles, CA 90071-2007
Phone: (213) 485-1234
www.lw.com

LOCATIONS

Boston, MA
Chicago, IL
Costa Mesa, CA
Los Angeles, CA
Menlo Park, CA
Newark, NJ
New York, NY
Reston, VA
San Diego, CA
San Francisco, CA
Washington, DC
Brussels
Frankfurt
Hamburg
Hong Kong
London
Milan
Moscow
Paris
Singapore
Tokyo

MAJOR DEPARTMENTS & PRACTICES

Corporate (including Communications, Government Relations, Health Care and Venture & Technology)
Environment, Land & Resources
Finance & Real Estate
Litigation
Tax

THE STATS

No. of attorneys worldwide: 1,532
No. of offices worldwide: 21
Chairman and Managing Partner: Robert M. Dell

EMPLOYMENT CONTACT

Ms. Debra Clarkson
701 B Street, Suite 2100
San Diego, CA 92101
Phone: (619) 236-1234
E-mail: debra.clarkson@lw.com

WHO'S WHO

Does the firm have a pro bono coordinator? Yes

Steven Schulman, Esq.
Pro Bono Counsel
555 11th Street, NW
Washington, DC 20004
Phone: (202) 637-2184
E-mail: steve.schulman@lw.com

If yes, what percentage of his or her time is spent on pro bono work? 50 percent

Does the firm have a pro bono committee? Yes

If yes, how often does the committee meet? Every other month by phone.

Describe the composition of the committee: Typically one partner and one associate in each U.S. office and most international offices.

THE SCOOP

Does your firm have a written pro bono policy? Yes

Has the firm signed on to the Law Firm Pro Bono Challenge? Yes

What are some of the areas of law in which your firm has performed pro bono legal work in the last two years? Human rights & refugee issues; representation of victims of 9/11 before the federal Victims Compensation Fund; community economic development; nonprofit corporation counseling; mergers of legal services organizations; public benefits; landlord-tenant issues; civil rights; death penalty.

What are some of the areas of law in which your firm does not perform pro bono work? Employee-side employment discrimination.

Organizations for which your firm has performed pro bono legal services in the last two years: Public Counsel (Los Angeles); Lawyers Committee for Human Rights (D.C. & New York); Lawyers Committee for Civil Rights (Chicago & San Francisco); Public Law Center (Orange County); Washington (D.C.) Legal Clinic for the Homeless; Appleseed Foundation and DC Center; Legal Aid of San Mateo County; San Diego Volunteer Lawyer Program; International Rescue Committee; Ashoka.

List up to three pro bono matters that are representative of the pro bono work your firm participates in.

- Child Refugee Project: representation of unaccompanied refugee children in the United States, legislative counsel and systemic reform work on related issues.

- A Place Called Home: corporate counsel to youth shelter in South Central Los Angeles providing after-school programming to 5,000 children.

- Victims Compensation Fund: counsel to more than 50 families seeking compensation from the fund, in partnership with National Economic Research Associates.

BY THE NUMBERS

What is the total number of hours that lawyers in U.S. offices at your firm spent performing pro bono legal services in 2000, 2001 and 2002?

    Total number of hours in 2000: 63,239 hours
    Total number of hours in 2001: 90,706 hours
    Total number of hours in 2002: 131,048 hours

Average number of pro bono hours per attorney in U.S. offices per year (including associates, partners, counsels, but not summer associates):

    Average number of hours per attorney in 2000: 64.4 hours
    Average number of hours per attorney in 2001: 80.4 hours
    Average number of hours per attorney in 2002: 106 hours

What percentage of attorneys in this firm's U.S. offices did pro bono work in 2002? 77 percent

What percentage of attorneys in this firm's U.S. offices did at least 20 hours of pro bono work in 2002? 55 percent

Does the firm encourage its lawyers to perform a minimum number of pro bono hours? Yes

If so, how many hours per year or what percentage of lawyers' billable hours? 60 hours per attorney.

SUPERVISION AND EVALUATIONS

Is there partner supervision on each pro bono matter? Yes

Do partner supervisors or, if applicable, senior associates provide written evaluations of associates' work on pro bono matters? Yes

If so, are those evaluations taken into account in determining salary, bonuses or advancement in the firm? Yes

If not, does the firm consider pro bono work generally in associate evaluations? N/A

HOURS

Does the firm give billable hour credit for pro bono work? Yes

Does the firm have a maximum number of pro bono hours that can be applied toward the billable hour target? No

If so, what is the maximum? N/A

If your firm uses hours to determine bonuses, does it consider pro bono hours when determining bonuses? Yes

PRO BONO POINTS

What training opportunities are open to associates working on pro bono matters? Attorneys are encouraged to go to training sessions by local bar associations or legal services providers, and some in-house training on specific issues (e.g., asylum) is provided.

Can associates bring matters of interest to the firm? Yes

Does the firm offer the use of support staff in carrying out pro bono matters? Yes

What pro bono opportunities are available for summer associates? Summer associates are encouraged to work on pro bono matters that are at the firm already, just like commercial matters.

Does the firm have established programs, such as externships, that enable its associates to work in a public interest setting? No

Has your firm won any special recognition or awards in the last two years for its pro bono work? Yes

If so, please list. 2003 New York Volunteer Lawyers for the Arts Pro Bono Law Firm of the Year; 2003 California State Bar President's Pro Bono Service Award; 2003 Bet Tzedek (Los Angeles) Law Firm of the Year Award; 2003 Recipient of the American Bar Association's Pro Bono Publico Award; 2003 Voices of Courage Award from the Women's Commission for Refugee Women and Children; 2003 Honors from the Foundation for the Junior Blind (Los Angeles); 2003 Katherine Krause Award, Inner City Law Center (Los Angeles); 2003 Honors from Legal Services for Children (San Francisco); 2003 Legal Aid Society of San Mateo County, Outstanding Pro Bono Attorney for March/April (Silicon Valley associate Christopher Jaap); 2002 Honors from The Appleseed Foundation and the Washington, D.C. Appleseed Center; 2002 Legal Impact Award, Asian Pacific Islander Legal Outreach; 2002 Outstanding Volunteer in Public Service Award, San Francisco Bar Association's Volunteer Legal Services Program (San Francisco partner Peter Huston); 2002 Law Firm of the Year Award, Orange County Public Law Center; 2002 New York Legal Aid Society (for work with victims of 9/11); 2002 Spirit of Greenwich House Award (New York); 2002 Advocate of the Year Award, Public Counsel (Los Angeles associate Amos Hartston); 2002 Pro Bono Lawyer of the Year Award, District of Columbia Bar Association (associate Andrew Morton); 2002 National Coalition on Black Civic Participation (D.C. and Chicago); 2002 Honors from The Florence Immigrant & Refugee Rights Project (13 Latham lawyers from around the firm); 2001 National Law Journal Pro Bono Award; 2001 Law Firm of the Year Award, Volunteer Legal Services Program (San Francisco); 2001 Law Firm of the Year Award, District of Columbia Bar Association; 2001 Law Firm of the Year Award, Public Counsel (Los Angeles).

THE FIRM SAYS

Latham & Watkins recognizes that as lawyers we have a duty to help ensure that the doors of justice are open to all persons, regardless of income. The goal of the firm's pro bono practice is to provide free legal services to those in our communities least able to pay and most in need of those services. The common thread that ties our pro bono clients together is the need for quality legal representation to protect rights or interests that they or their constituencies would otherwise lose. Accordingly, the focus of our pro bono work is to provide needed legal services to low-income individuals and organizations that serve the community by providing services to low income individuals, by furthering economic development in low-income areas or by pursuing other charitable endeavors. Specifically, our pro bono resources are devoted to: (i) representing low-income individuals in matters of immediate concern; (ii) providing legal services to organizations that serve the interests of low-income individuals; (iii) representing organizations or individuals advocating for public, civil or human rights; (iv) assisting not-for-profit organizations that would not otherwise be able to afford legal representation, or where the payment of legal fees would significantly interfere with that organization's mission; and (v) in some circumstances, representing small for-profit businesses that cannot afford legal services and seek to fulfill a commercial need in an economically-challenged neighborhood or to serve low-income customers.

In selecting and attracting pro bono matters, the firm gives priority to complex legal matters that require the pro bono participation of a large law firm with national and international resources, and that are likely to improve the lives of the poor or that serve the cause of human rights, civil liberties or public rights. In order to attract high-quality pro bono matters, the firm creates and maintains strong relationships with local, national and international legal services providers, bar associations and human rights and civil rights organizations that can attract, screen and refer potential pro bono matters to the firm. Because we rely on these organizations to provide quality pro bono opportunities, the firm also provides financial support to these organizations, to the extent appropriate. Attorneys are encouraged to establish relationships with new legal services organizations and to bring new pro bono clients to the firm in areas of interest.

As a signatory to the Law Firm Pro Bono Challenge, the firm has committed to provide, at a minimum, the equivalent of 60 hours per U.S. attorney per year in pro bono legal services. We have met this goal every year since 2000, when we made the commitment. The firm strongly encourages all U.S. attorneys to help the firm meet this goal. Non-U.S. attorneys are also encouraged to provide pro bono legal services to the extent appropriate in their communities. A successful pro bono program requires the steady support of firm management, and internal firm policies that support and encourage attorneys, paralegals and other employees who serve pro bono clients. Attorneys, paralegals and other employees who work on pro bono matters must treat our pro bono clients as they would all other clients by providing excellent service that meets the highest ethical and professional standards, and that is performed in an efficient manner. Accordingly, time spent on pro bono client work is credited to the same extent as time spent on commercial client work, with no cap on credit for time spent on approved pro bono matters.

OUR SURVEY SAYS

"The commitment to pro bono could not be higher. I think we have the best program in the country."

"Pro bono hours are considered billable hours for all purposes. Young lawyers are especially encouraged to do pro bono work to get experience and give back to the community. All lawyers here treat pro bono clients as regular clients."

"Pro bono is strongly encouraged and we get full billing credit towards our hours. One hour of pro bono equals one hour of billable. That is amazing."

"One hundred percent is counted toward billables. It is really considered a requirement to meet the pro bono challenge by year's end."

"We get full credit for our pro bono hours (they count as billables for our minimum) — if that isn't dedicated, what is? I billed hundreds and hundreds of pro bono hours and no one has said a word to me, except to congratulate me on pro bono successes."

"The firm as a whole is very committed, the San Francisco office less so."

"As a first-year associate I'm currently staffed on one large pro bono cases and I have two others of my own."

"Latham is absolutely the best in the industry with its commitment to pro bono. Pro bono opportunities are circulated weekly; work for 'paying clients' is never prioritized over pro bono matters; and pro bono hours count 100 percent in terms of meeting associates billable hours requirements and count 100 percent in determining the component of our bonuses that is linked to billable hours."

"This firm is extremely committed to pro bono — to the point that it is seamlessly integrated into our billable day."

"There is so much pro bono it is impossible to staff all of the projects."

LeBoeuf, Lamb, Greene & MacRae, L.L.P.

125 West 55th Street
New York, NY 10019-5389
Phone: (212) 424-8000
www.llgm.com

LOCATIONS

New York, NY (HQ) • Albany, NY • Boston, MA • Denver, CO • Harrisburg, PA • Hartford, CT • Houston, TX • Jacksonville, FL • Los Angeles, CA • Newark, NJ • Pittsburgh, PA • Salt Lake City, UT • San Francisco, CA • Washington, DC • Almaty, Kazakhstan • Beijing Bishkek, Kyrgyzstan • Brussels • Johannesburg • London • Moscow • Paris • Riyadh, Saudi Arabia

MAJOR DEPARTMENTS & PRACTICES

Bankruptcy & Restructuring
Corporate
Energy
Environmental, Health & Safety
Executive Compensation, Employee Benefits & ERISA
Insurance
Intellectual Property & Technology
International
Litigation
Real Estate
Reinsurance
Tax
Telecommunications
Trusts & Estates

THE STATS

No. of attorneys worldwide: 650
No. of offices worldwide: 23
Chairmen: Steven H. Davis and Peter R. O'Flinn

EMPLOYMENT CONTACT

Ms. Jill Cameron
Legal Recruiting Coordinator
Phone: (212) 424-8266
Fax: (212) 424-8500
E-mail: jcameron@llgm.com

WHO'S WHO

Does the firm have a pro bono coordinator? Yes. The two firm co-chairs (who are partners in the corporate and litigation departments, respectively):

Rachel B. Coan, Esq.
Pro Bono Co-Chair
Phone: (212) 424-8106
Fax: (212) 424-8500
E-mail: rbcoan@llgm.com

John M. Aerni, Esq.
Pro Bono Co-Chair
Phone: (212) 424-8231
Fax: (212) 424-8500
E-mail: jaerni@llgm.com

If yes, what percentage of his or her time is spent on pro bono work? Approximately 10 to 15 percent.

Does the firm have a pro bono committee? No

If yes, how often does the committee meet? N/A

Describe the composition of the committee: N/A

THE SCOOP

Does your firm have a written pro bono policy? Yes

Has the firm signed on to the Law Firm Pro Bono Challenge? No

What are some of the areas of law in which your firm has performed pro bono legal work in the last two years? Prisoners' rights; general litigation; bankruptcy; landlord/tenant; intellectual property; real estate; corporate (transactional work, corporate governance advice and formation of not-for-profit corporations); tax (including obtaining 501(c)(3) status); employment and labor issues; environmental.

What are some of the areas of law in which your firm does not perform pro bono work? None specifically excluded.

Organizations for which your firm has performed pro bono legal services in the last two years: Lawyers Alliance for New York, Volunteers of Legal Services, Jazz at Lincoln Center, Aaron Diamond AIDS Research Center, Volunteer Lawyers for the Arts, inMotion (formerly Network for Women's Legal Services), Women's Business Center (affiliated with the Local Development Corporation of East New York), South Brooklyn Legal Services, Citizens Committee for New York, Juvenile Law Project – Hartford, CT.

List up to three pro bono matters that are representative of the pro bono work your firm participates in.

- Clearpool, Inc. We have served for approximately 40 years as pro bono general counsel to Clearpool, Inc., a New York not-for-profit corporation that operates an educational camp for underprivileged children, primarily from the New York City area. During the past year and a half, the organization faced a number of serious problems relating to a decline in contributions following the events of September 11 and the need to obtain additional financing for its activities to remain in existence. Attorneys from virtually all of the firm's practice groups, including the corporate, tax, litigation, real estate, environmental and employment matters departments, have worked with Clearpool to restructure its mortgage loans and certain other contracts; address various corporate governance issues; defend lawsuits; negotiate its office lease; finalize and close the sale of a conservation easement with the New York City Department of Environmental Protection; and provide counsel to it on employment issues.

- Jacksonville City Zoo Foundation. Our Jacksonville office serves as general pro bono counsel to the Jacksonville City Zoo Foundation, and has recently represented the foundation in the preparation and negotiation of a 30-year operating agreement with the City of Jacksonville for the zoo and a purchase of real property. The firm also regularly counsels the foundation on employment and human resources matters, as well as intellectual property issues in connection with its sales of products and maintenance of its web site. We are currently involved with assisting the foundation in its $25,000,000 capital campaign to establish an exhibit focusing on South American Rain Forest Conservation, one of the goals of which is to have the largest collection of jaguars anywhere in the world.

- Donors Choose, Inc. Based in New York City, DonorsChoose, Inc. established an internet web site to match educational projects proposed by public school teachers for which school funds are not available with donors willing to contribute to realize these projects. The proposals cover a wide range of subject matter areas, including such activities as taking a class to a baseball game to provide practical examples and exercises using mathematical concepts. We have helped form the organization, facilitated the creation of branches in other states and cities and advised it on various corporate, intellectual property, real estate and tax issues.

BY THE NUMBERS

What is the total number of hours that lawyers in U.S. offices at your firm spent performing pro bono legal services in 2000, 2001 and 2002?

      Total number of hours in 2000: 17,826 hours
      Total number of hours in 2001: 17,492 hours
      Total number of hours in 2002: 14,054 hours

Average number of pro bono hours per attorney in U.S. offices per year (including associates, partners, counsels, but not summer associates):

      Average number of hours per attorney in 2000: 30 hours
      Average number of hours per attorney in 2001: 30 hours
      Average number of hours per attorney in 2002: 29 hours

What percentage of attorneys in this firm's U.S. offices did pro bono work in 2002? 42.4 percent

What percentage of attorneys in this firm's U.S. offices did at least 20 hours of pro bono work in 2002? 25.9 percent

Does the firm encourage its lawyers to perform a minimum number of pro bono hours? No. The firm encourages all lawyers to devote some time to pro bono work but does not prescribe a specific minimum number of hours.

If so, how many hours per year or what percentage of lawyers' billable hours? N/A

SUPERVISION AND EVALUATIONS

Is there partner supervision on each pro bono matter? Yes

Do partner supervisors or, if applicable, senior associates provide written evaluations of associates' work on pro bono matters? Yes

If so, are those evaluations taken into account in determining salary, bonuses or advancement in the firm? Yes

If not, does the firm consider pro bono work generally in associate evaluations? N/A

HOURS

Does the firm give billable hour credit for pro bono work? Yes

Does the firm have a maximum number of pro bono hours that can be applied toward the billable hour target? Yes, with individual exceptions for special circumstances.

If so, what is the maximum? 200 hours per year.

If your firm uses hours to determine bonuses, does it consider pro bono hours when determining bonuses? Yes, combined with other criteria.

PRO BONO POINTS

What training opportunities are open to associates working on pro bono matters? Associates can participate in training programs sponsored by various pro bono clearinghouses. In addition, the firm has invited organizations to provide training on particular types of work at our offices.

Can associates bring matters of interest to the firm? Yes

Does the firm offer the use of support staff in carrying out pro bono matters? Yes

What pro bono opportunities are available for summer associates? Summer associates can assist with active pro bono matters the firm is handling and can also participate in specific summer programs established by organizations such as the Courtroom Advocacy Project.

Does the firm have established programs, such as externships, that enable its associates to work in a public interest setting? Yes

If so, where and for up to how long? The firm sponsors three externship programs, two in New York (one of which is a fellowship program for two summer associates) and one in our Salt Lake City office.

South Brooklyn Legal Services Housing Externship. Since 1988, LeBoeuf's New York City office has sponsored an externship program through which second- to fifth-year associates work for four months in the housing litigation unit at South Brooklyn Legal Services (SBLS), a community legal services office. LeBoeuf rotates externs through SBLS's offices one at a time, with a week of overlap to maintain continuity. The associate "on loan" assumes primary responsibility for a full docket of cases (typically 30 to 40) and deals directly with clients, witnesses and opposing counsel.

Summer Externships. The New York office sponsors fellowships for two summer associates per year. Summer associates may apply to split their summer, spending the first half with LeBoeuf and the second half with an approved public interest organization for whom the associate works pro bono. The two summer associates who are selected for the externship receive a full salary from LeBoeuf for the entire summer. They are selected based upon the same criteria as other summer associates.

Utah Legal Services Externship. In 1999, the Salt Lake City office initiated a pro bono externship through which associates in that office are seconded to the staff of Utah Legal Services for three months. As with all LeBoeuf externships, attorneys are paid full salary while participating.

Has your firm won any special recognition or awards in the last two years for its pro bono work? Yes

If so, please list. In 2002, inMotion – Justice for All Women honored Andrianne Payson, an associate in the New York City office, for her commitment to the protection of rights of women and children who are victims of domestic violence. In 2003, Lawyers Alliance for New York honored Louis Goldberg, an associate in the New York City office, for his work since 1995 with Child Care, Inc. as part of the co-general counsel arrangement established by the Firm and ITT Corporation with respect to this organization. The matters on which Louis has worked include counseling on legislative initiatives, corporate governance issues, contract negotiation and review, employment and personnel matters, intellectual property issues and real estate leases.

THE FIRM SAYS

LeBoeuf, Lamb, Greene & MacRae is strongly committed to the delivery of pro bono legal services and encourages all attorneys to participate in this fundamental aspect of the firm culture. We recognize that, because the legal profession enjoys a monopoly on the delivery of legal services, we have a professional and moral obligation to serve not only paying clients, but also those who cannot afford legal representation.

Pro bono work allows our attorneys to pursue matters of interest and to provide professional services that are most satisfying to them. This work fosters early client responsibility and provides junior attorneys with valuable training and experience.

LeBoeuf's commitment to pro bono is evidenced by the thousands of hours of pro bono service the firm's attorneys have donated (including 281 hours contributed by our foreign offices in 2002), and the standards we hold for our attorneys to do this kind of work. At LeBoeuf, pro bono matters are treated on a par with paying matters. Billable hours reflect time spent on both paying and pro bono matters without distinction. Performance evaluations take into account an attorney's pro bono work and achievements.

Pro bono matters are referred to us directly by the courts, by paying clients and by various pro bono clearinghouse organizations. Individual attorneys also bring projects to the firm through their relationships with civic, cultural, educational and religious organizations. Finally, attorneys with interests in particular types of issues can choose specific organizations or matters to work on based on the case lists distributed by probono.net and various legal services providers.

OUR SURVEY SAYS

"Lots of encouragement in both word and by example to do pro bono work. Initiating pro bono work is highly encouraged."

"Up to 200 hours of pro bono work counts toward the 2,000 billable hour requirement. I have heard firm management say that they are committed to continuing this policy."

"As a first-year I have done a great deal of pro bono work and have been to court numerous times. It is easy to get a pro bono assignment at my firm, and we get 200 hours of pro bono work that counts as billable hours."

"Some attorneys are very committed while others do not do any pro bono. The partners in charge seem truly committed."

"There is not a great deal of pro bono work done, but the firm does encourage pro bono work — e.g., through Public Counsel, and up to 200 pro bono hours are counted against the 2,000 billable bogey."

"Because we are understaffed, very few associates have time to do pro bono work. Nonetheless, at least once a year, several associates participate in pro bono clinics where they pick up cases."

"The firm allows up to 200 hours of pro bono work to be credited towards our billable requirement (and more in unusual circumstances, such as if a case goes to trial). It also has relationships with certain legal aid clinics/entities from which we often take on pro bono matters."

"The commitment to pro bono work is mixed . There are a number of partners who champion pro bono work, and an equal number who feel it is irrelevant to the firm and associate development."

"Though the firm seems to do a substantial amount of pro bono work, it is hard to get involved as an associate in a branch office."

Linklaters

One Silk Street
London, EC2Y 8HQ
Phone: 011 44 207 456 2000

1345 Avenue of the Americas
New York, NY 10105
Phone: (212) 424-9000
www.linklaters.com

LOCATIONS

London (Firm HQ)
New York, NY (U.S. HQ)
Alicante, Spain • Amsterdam • Antwerp • Bangkok • Beijing • Berlin • Bratislava • Brussels • Bucharest • Budapest • Cologne • Frankfurt • Hong Kong • Lisbon • London • Luxembourg • Madrid • Milan • Moscow • Munich • Paris • Prague • Rome • São Paulo • Shanghai • Singapore • Stockholm • Tokyo • Warsaw

MAJOR DEPARTMENTS & PRACTICES

Asset Finance
Banking
Capital Markets
Corporate/M&A
Employment, Pensions & Incentives
Environment & Planning
EU/Competition
Financial Markets
Intellectual Property
Investment Management
IT & Communications
Litigation & Arbitration
Projects
Real Estate & Construction
Restructuring & Insolvency
Sectors
Tax

THE STATS

No. of attorneys worldwide: 2,000+
No. of offices worldwide: 31
Firm-wide Managing Partner: Tony Angel
National Managing Partner, New York: Stephen Land

EMPLOYMENT CONTACT

Mr. Michael McEvoy
Recruitment Coordinator, New York
Phone: (212) 632-9859
Fax: (212) 632-9863
E-mail: uspractice.recruitment@linklaters.com

WHO'S WHO

Principal pro bono contact(s) at your firm:

Ms. Natasha Branston
Community Investment Manager
Phone: 011 44 207 456 3732
E-mail: natasha.branston@linklaters.com

Ms. Vicki Doughty
Community Investment Manager
Phone: 011 44 207 456 5106
E-mail: vicki.doughty@linklaters.com

In the U.S.:
Mary Warren, Partner
Phone: (212) 424-9031
E-mail: mary.warren@linklaters.com

Mary Schinke, Associate
Phone: (212) 424-9067
E-mail: mary.schinke@linklaters.com

Does the firm have a pro bono coordinator? Yes
Ms. Sarah Barnes
In the U.S., Mr. Matthew Chin

If yes, what percentage of his or her time is spent on pro bono work? Sarah Barnes: 100 percent; Matthew Chin: 15 percent.

Does the firm have a pro bono committee? Yes

If yes, how often does the committee meet? The global committee meets quarterly. The New York committee meets quarterly.

Describe the composition of the committee: The global committee consists of the senior partner, partnership secretary and the partners from each office that lead community service activities in their location. The New York committee consists of the community investment partner, community investment administrator, and attorney and staff volunteer committee members.

THE SCOOP

Does your firm have a written pro bono policy? Yes

Has the firm signed on to the Law Firm Pro Bono Challenge? Yes

What are some of the areas of law in which your firm has performed pro bono legal work in the last two years?
Linklaters attorneys have represented nonprofits and individuals with respect to matters involving tax, environmental,

asylum, estate planning, real estate, finance, custody/visitation, post-9/11 matters, general contract issues and the death penalty.

What are some of the areas of law in which your firm does not perform pro bono work? Linklaters does not have specific prohibitions.

Organizations for which your firm has performed pro bono legal services in the last two years: Lawyers Alliance for New York, Volunteer Lawyers for the Arts, Office of the New York Appellate Defender, New York Lawyers for the Public Interest, Lawyers Committee for Human Rights, Volunteers of Legal Service, Safe Horizon, inMotion, Women's Housing and Economic Development Corporation, Refugee and Immigrant Fund, TransFair and Harriet Tubman Charter School.

List up to three pro bono matters that are representative of the pro bono work your firm participates in. Drafting and negotiating leases for a charter school; representing immigrants applying for asylum; incorporation and tax-exemption applications for numerous not-for-profit corporations.

BY THE NUMBERS

What is the total number of hours that lawyers in U.S. offices at your firm spent performing pro bono legal services in 2000, 2001 and 2002?

> **Total number of hours in 2000:** Not calculated
> **Total number of hours in 2001:** In the U.S., 1275.47 hours
> **Total number of hours in 2002:** In the U.S., 3.1 percent of billable hours

Average number of pro bono hours per attorney in U.S. offices per year (including associates, partners, counsels, but not summer associates):

> **Average number of hours per attorney in 2000:** Not calculated
> **Average number of hours per attorney in 2001:** Not calculated
> **Average number of hours per attorney in 2002:** Not calculated

What percentage of attorneys in this firm's U.S. offices did pro bono work in 2002? In the U.S., 62.3 percent

What percentage of attorneys in this firm's U.S. offices did at least 20 hours of pro bono work in 2002? Not calculated

Does the firm encourage its lawyers to perform a minimum number of pro bono hours? No. We do not have specified minimum hours.

If so, how many hours per year or what percentage of lawyers' billable hours? N/A

SUPERVISION AND EVALUATIONS

Is there partner supervision on each pro bono matter? Yes

Do partner supervisors or, if applicable, senior associates provide written evaluations of associates' work on pro bono matters? Yes

If so, are those evaluations taken into account in determining salary, bonuses or advancement in the firm? Yes

HOURS

Does the firm give billable hour credit for pro bono work? Yes

Does the firm have a maximum number of pro bono hours that can be applied toward the billable hour target? No

If your firm uses hours to determine bonuses, does it consider pro bono hours when determining bonuses? Yes

PRO BONO POINTS

What training opportunities are open to associates working on pro bono matters? Associates participate in training programs offered by the New York state and city bar associations, the pro bono clearinghouses and the relevant legal services organizations. We do not have specific restrictions on pro bono training.

Can associates bring matters of interest to the firm? Yes

Does the firm offer the use of support staff in carrying out pro bono matters? Yes

What pro bono opportunities are available for summer associates? Summer associates assist attorneys on ongoing pro bono matters. Summer associates also participate in special summer pro bono programs offered by New York-based clearinghouses.

Does the firm have established programs, such as externships, that enable its associates to work in a public interest setting? Yes

If so, where and for up to how long? In London, Linklaters offers six-month secondments to law centers, human rights organizations and other nonprofit organizations. In the United States, Linklaters arranged an externship program with the New York City Law Department, and additional externships are under consideration.

Has your firm won any special recognition or awards in the last two years for its pro bono work? Yes

If so, please list. In London, a real estate associate won a DLA Paul Nicholls Memorial Award for her work with one of Linklaters' community partners, Toynbee Hall. In addition, the Young Solicitors Group Pro Bono Award was won by the volunteer force, supported by Linklaters lawyers, at the weekly housing advice clinic at Toynbee. The firm was named 2003 Employer of the Year by the National Mentoring Consortium for our mentoring work with students from minority ethnic communities. Linklaters is a finalist for a Law Society Gazette Centenary Award for "Best Pro Bono Endeavour." The Law Society Gazette is the official publication of the Law Society of England & Wales (the body which regulates the legal profession). The results of this award will be announced at a reception in London on November 12. In the United States, several attorneys received Cornerstone Awards from Lawyers Alliance for New York in recognition of work related to September 11. Linklaters was awarded the Corporate Leadership Award from the Federation of Protestant Welfare Agencies in recognition of non-legal volunteer work and financial support.

THE FIRM SAYS

At Linklaters, we are committed to supporting disadvantaged communities in the vicinity of our offices around the world through our community investment program. Our strategy is to create partnerships with local nonprofit organizations dedicated to the promotion of equal access to justice, education and economic and social regeneration and to work with them to find solutions to the problems faced by the people they support. There are many ways in which partners and staff can become involved, from donating money to volunteering their time. We believe that the most powerful way in which individuals can make a difference to disadvantaged communities is by contributing the skills and expertise that they have developed through their own education and professional experience. Pro bono legal work is therefore an important way in which lawyers, trainees and legal support staff can participate in our program. Participation in the firm's community investment program is voluntary but all partners and legally qualified staff are encouraged to become involved.

OUR SURVEY SAYS

"The range of pro bono work offered at Linklaters is quite extensive and appears to be available to associates in all departments; the cases range from high-profile (Texas death penalty appeals) to high-impact (September 11th Fund cases) to lower-profile cases (individual political asylum cases)."

"The New York office of the firm is extremely supportive and committed to pro bono work of all kinds. There is commitment across the board and at all levels of the firm, although by choice most of the pro bono work is done by the junior associates and partners. There is a lot of enthusiasm for pro bono work within the office, and matters are treated with great importance."

"Provided my billable work is high-quality and I continue to develop and mature in my practice area, I feel that pro bono is encouraged and looked upon favorably in the review process."

"The firm is very supportive of any pro bono work the associates are interested in and encourages people to follow their own interests."

"The firm provides associates with a menu of pro bono work. Associates can pick and choose based on their expertise (i.e., transactional vs. litigators). Associates with a pet cause stand a very good chance of obtaining management approval for the project (this recently happened in my case in the area of political asylum cases)."

"Hours spent on pro bono activities are recordable and are not capped. I have had other associates in my department volunteer to reschedule recurring meetings that they knew would conflict with my pro bono commitments. I was pleasantly surprised by this gesture as some of these colleagues do not participate in the program as avidly as I do, but clearly the work I am doing is well respected."

"Obviously, as with any firm, there are some associates and partners who do more pro bono work than others. The advantage of Linklater's program is that there is enormous flexibility within the program, as well as support at all levels."

"Linklaters has a very public-minded conception of the role of lawyers."

"We believe that the most powerful way in which individuals can make a difference to disadvantaged communities is by contributing the skills and expertise that they have developed through their own education and professional experience."

— *Linklaters*

Mayer, Brown, Rowe & Maw LLP

190 South LaSalle Street
Chicago, IL 60603-3441
Phone: (312) 782-0600
www.mayerbrownrowe.com

LOCATIONS

Chicago, IL (largest office)
Charlotte, NC
Houston, TX
Los Angeles, CA
New York, NY
Palo Alto, CA
Washington, DC
Brussels
Cologne
Frankfurt
London
Manchester
Paris

MAJOR DEPARTMENTS & PRACTICES

Antitrust & Competition • Appellate • Banking & Finance • Bankruptcy & Reorganization • Biotech, Pharma & Life Science • Corporate & Securities • Criminal Defense • Electronic Discovery • Emerging Companies • Employee Benefits • Environment • Franchise/Dealership • Government Relations & Global Trade • Health Care • Information Technology/Outsourcing • Insurance • Intellectual Property • Labor & Employment • Litigation • Pro Bono • Real Estate • Regulated Industries • Tax • Telecommunications & Media • Wealth Management

THE STATS

No. of attorneys worldwide: 1,400
No. of offices worldwide: 13
Managing Partner: Debora de Hoyos

EMPLOYMENT CONTACT

See firm web site for employment contacts in each office.

WHO'S WHO

Does the firm have a pro bono coordinator? Yes

Marc Kadish, Esq.
Director of Pro Bono Activities and Litigation Training
Phone: (312) 701-8747
E-mail: mkadish@mayerbrownrowe.com

Julie Dickins, Esq.
Pro Bono Partner/Coordinator, United Kingdom & Brussels
Phone: 011-44-207-782-8696
E-mail: jdickins@mayerbrownrowe.com

Marla K. Feinman, Esq.
Associate Development Manager, New York
Phone: (212) 506-2811
E-mail: mkfeinman@mayerbrownrowe.com

If yes, what percentage of his or her time is spent on pro bono work? Marc Kadish spends approximately two-thirds of his time on pro bono matters. Julie Dickins works part-time; of that time, approximately 85 to 90 percent is spent on pro bono and community work. Marla Feinman spends approximately 10 percent of her time on pro bono work.

Does the firm have a pro bono committee? Yes

If yes, how often does the committee meet? The committee meets formally annually. The committee meets informally by e-mail every time a lawyer in the firm seeks approval to open a pro bono project, and periodically by conference call to address policy issues.

Describe the composition of the committee: There is a firm-wide committee consisting of partners, counsel and associates from every U.S. office, plus the London office and the Frankfurt office. Each office in the U.S. is encouraged to have its own pro bono committee.

THE SCOOP

Does your firm have a written pro bono policy? Yes

Has the firm signed on to the Law Firm Pro Bono Challenge? Yes

What are some of the areas of law in which your firm has performed pro bono legal work in the last two years? The firm does pro bono work in both the litigation and transactional areas. Our most significant litigation work has been federal appellate work, federal prisoners' rights work, death penalty work on both the trial and appellate levels, and immigration work. In the transactional area, we have done international work with respect to rule of law development and human rights. We have also carried out educational programs, work on police commissions, work with the creative arts and community economic development and child adoption work.

What are some of the areas of law in which your firm does not perform pro bono work? We will do pro bono work in any area of law where an attorney in the firm wishes to volunteer and where proper supervision is available. We try to limit ourselves to work where we have some experience. We have no ideological litmus test for pro bono work. We will do work whether it is considered liberal or conservative so long as someone volunteers for the project and there are no conflicts of interest.

Organizations for which your firm has performed pro bono legal services in the last two years:

Various federal courts throughout the country, at both the District and Court of Appeals levels; Midwest Immigrant & Human Rights Center (Chicago); Central European and Eurasian Law Initiative (CEELI); Legal Aid Society (New York); Charlotte-Mecklenburg Housing Partnership; Alliance for Children's Rights (Los Angeles); Northside College Preparatory High School (Chicago); Lawyers for the Creative Arts (Chicago); New York Lawyers for the Public Interest; Neighborhood Housing Services (New York); DC Bar Pro Bono Clinic Program; Whitman-Walker Legal Clinic (D.C.); Lawyers Alliance and Human Rights First (New York).

List up to three pro bono matters that are representative of the pro bono work your firm participates in.

- In 1999, the firm initiated its Seventh Circuit Project, accepting appointments from the court on a pro bono basis. We do not accept reimbursement for fees or expenses. As of the end of September 2003, we have accepted appointments in 60 appeals. These cases are handled by associates in every office in the firm.

- We are currently involved in a number of death penalty matters. The Chicago office has two trial-level cases and one Illinois Supreme Court case pending. The Houston office is working on two federal habeas corpus death cases and is in the process of preparing to file an amicus brief in another appeal on mental health issues, which is a consolidated appeal of two other death penalty cases. The D.C. office won a case in the Georgia Supreme Court in October 2003, and will represent the client on retrial. We also wrote the amicus brief on behalf of the American Bar Association in the United States Supreme Court case that outlawed the death penalty for mentally retarded defendants.

- We are a long-time partner of the Midwest Immigrant & Human Rights Center (MIHRC). We have sponsored three Equal Justice Work Fellows with the organization. We recently resolved a year-long case involving the government's detention of a Burmese political refugee.

BY THE NUMBERS

What is the total number of hours that lawyers in U.S. offices at your firm spent performing pro bono legal services in 2000, 2001 and 2002?

> **Total number of hours in 2000:** 26,158 hours
> **Total number of hours in 2001:** 31,833 hours
> **Total number of hours in 2002:** 32,084 hours

Average number of pro bono hours per attorney in U.S. offices per year (including associates, partners, counsels, but not summer associates):

> **Average number of hours per attorney in 2000:** 31.2 hours
> **Average number of hours per attorney in 2001:** 36.9 hours
> **Average number of hours per attorney in 2002:** 35.5 hours

What percentage of attorneys in this firm's U.S. offices did pro bono work in 2002? 45 percent

What percentage of attorneys in this firm's U.S. offices did at least 20 hours of pro bono work in 2002? 24 percent

Does the firm encourage its lawyers to perform a minimum number of pro bono hours? Yes

If so, how many hours per year or what percentage of lawyers' billable hours? The firm is a signatory to the Law Firm Pro Bono Challenge administered by the Pro Bono Institute. As a signatory, we pledge to use our best efforts to collectively contribute 3 percent of the firm's total billable hours or 60 hours per attorney to pro bono work.

SUPERVISION AND EVALUATIONS

Is there partner supervision on each pro bono matter? Partner, counsel or senior associate.

Do partner supervisors or, if applicable, senior associates provide written evaluations of associates' work on pro bono matters? Pro bono cases are treated just like paying client matters. Written evaluations are provided to associates and are included in the annual evaluation of each associate. If Marc has supervised an associate's work on a case, however, he provides the associate with a case-specific evaluation for this work.

If so, are those evaluations taken into account in determining salary, bonuses or advancement in the firm? Yes

If not, does the firm consider pro bono work generally in associate evaluations? N/A

HOURS

Does the firm give billable hour credit for pro bono work? Yes. The practice varies from office to office in the firm. In some major offices, pro bono hours count toward salary goals.

Does the firm have a maximum number of pro bono hours that can be applied toward the billable hour target? No

If so, what is the maximum? N/A

If your firm uses hours to determine bonuses, does it consider pro bono hours when determining bonuses? This varies from office to office.

PRO BONO POINTS

What training opportunities are open to associates working on pro bono matters? Marc Kadish is director of pro bono activities and litigation training for the firm. His position was created to combine pro bono and training. In the Chicago office he functions as a clinical professor working with summer associates and associates on litigation matters. Associates working on pro bono matters are encouraged to participate in any training programs they believe will assist them with their pro bono cases. Associates working on pro bono matters are automatically enrolled in the firm's deposition training program. The firm does not use formal legal writing programs. We use our Seventh Circuit Project for both training and pro bono opportunities. An editor is assigned to work with an associate on every brief. Each case is mooted to a number of experienced appellate advocates prior to every oral argument.

The head of the intellectual property practice area asked Marc to find intellectual property pro bono projects so IP junior associates would learn how to be better lawyers. Marc started a program with the Community Economic Development Law Project and the Lawyers for the Creative Arts in Chicago to direct worthwhile intellectual property pro bono matters to the firm.

Can associates bring matters of interest to the firm? Yes

Does the firm offer the use of support staff in carrying out pro bono matters? Yes

What pro bono opportunities are available for summer associates? They are permitted to work on any pending pro bono project in their office. In the summer of 2003, 129 summer associates devoted a total of 3,336.25 hours to pro bono work.

Does the firm have established programs, such as externships, that enable its associates to work in a public interest setting? Yes

If so, where and for up to how long? The Chicago office of the firm participates in the PILI (Public Interest Law Initiative) Fellowship program, which was conceived by a partner of the firm. Associates who are entering in the fall are permitted to work part time at a public interest agency while they study for the bar and full time after the bar exam is over. The program normally lasts for a total of 10 weeks. The New York office, in collaboration with the Legal Aid Society, sponsors an Equal Justice Works Fellow, which enables a lawyer to work full time providing services to battered immigrant women in New York City.

Has your firm won any special recognition or awards in the last two years for its pro bono work? Yes

If so, please list.

- Andrew Worseck, the associate who worked on the Burmese political refugee immigration case with MIHRC, received the Maurice J. Weigle Award as the Outstanding Young Associate from the Chicago Bar Association at the Chicago Bar Foundation's annual luncheon in July 2003.

- The Chicago office was awarded the Walter J. Cummings Award by the Federal Bar Association at its annual luncheon in September for the Seventh Circuit Project.

- Douglas Wisner, Judy Han and Suzy Kim received the Lawyers Alliance for New York's Cornerstone Award for their work with the Neighborhood Housing Services of New York City.

- Lawyers for the Creative Arts (LCA) has honored Mayer, Brown, Rowe & Maw LLP's pro bono program and its director Marc Kadish for the firm's pro bono legal services to the arts — the first such award to a law firm by the group. "Under Marc's leadership, Mayer, Brown, Rowe & Maw lawyers have significantly contributed to providing legal expertise to artists and art organizations in Chicago who couldn't afford legal help," said LCA Executive Director William Rattner.

- We were honored at the Chicago Legal Clinic, Inc.'s Annual Awards Dinner held on May 2, 2003. The firm received an award for an "outstanding record of achievement in providing pro bono services to the indigent as well as numerous charitable organizations."

- Marc Kadish was one of only seven Illinois attorneys chosen by the Illinois Supreme Court to make up the Special Supreme Court Committee on Pro Bono Publico Legal Services, a newly formed panel devoted to finding ways to promote pro bono legal work in Illinois and to encourage attorneys across the state to volunteer their services on a daily basis.

Mayer, Brown, Rowe & Maw LLP

THE FIRM SAYS

Our managing partner, Debora de Hoyos, has said of our pro bono work: "Pro bono work at Mayer, Brown, Rowe & Maw not only helps others; it makes us better lawyers." Mayer Brown lawyers participate in a broad range of pro bono public service and community activities in the United States, the United Kingdom and throughout the world. We offer not only legal representation in trial, appellate, and transactional matters; we provide training and encouragement to junior lawyers attracted to public interest law as well as financial support to public interest organizations. "Pro bono is a critical component in the profession," according to Debora de Hoyos, "and should be a critical factor in evaluating a law firm's true breadth."

Legacy Mayer Brown & Platt created the position of a full-time director of pro bono activities in 1999, recruiting Marc Kadish for the job. Marc was a law school clinical professor for 20 years and has devoted his entire professional life to public interest activities. Marc taught evidence, criminal law and various lawyering skill courses while he was a clinical professor. He continues to teach a first-year program at Northwestern University Law School called "Lawyer as Problem Solver" and teaches annually at the clinical intensive trial advocacy program at the University of Chicago Law School. He also consults on the legal course the firm teaches at the Northside College Preparatory High School.

Marc's position was specifically created to combine pro bono and litigation training. At about the same time, Rowe & Maw appointed Julie Dickins as the partner in charge of its pro bono work. Julie had joined the firm as a trainee solicitor in 1980, and became a partner in the litigation and dispute resolution department in 1990. Following the merger, Marc and Julie have worked together in finding and coordinating worthwhile projects and cases for lawyers and nonlawyers. We do a significant amount of pro bono work in our overseas offices. The New York office has an associate development manager, Marla Feinman. She has recently expanded her activities to include coordination of pro bono efforts in that office.

Marc handles the administration of the pro bono program, but he is also actively involved in a number of pro bono litigation matters. Building on his 20-year experience as a clinical professor and his 35 years as a criminal defense attorney, Marc has worked with partners and associates on 10 murder cases since joining the firm. Eight of these started out as death penalty cases — none has yet resulted in a sentence of death. Six of these cases went to trial, resulting in two acquittals and one not guilty by reason of insanity. Marc has also consulted on the appellate death penalty cases being handled by the other offices in the firm. We are one of the few firms in the country that does death penalty work on both the trial and appellate levels. In addition to work on these cases, we also provide financial support to the ABA's National Death Penalty Project and to the Texas Defender Service.

Marc has also used his long-time interest in prisoners' issues to supervise the handling of a number of prisoners' civil rights cases. He has supervised associates who have handled two jury trials in this area. He has begun working with ProBono.Net to create a pro bono web site to assist young associates in the trial of prisoner's civil rights cases.

Working with the firm's marketing department and web site development department, Marc has created a magazine, *The Pro Bono Update*, and a pro bono web site. Nine issues of the *Update* have been published since December 1999. The *Update* not only informs lawyers in the firm and throughout the world about the activities of our program, it also serves as a forum to explore some of the political issues that are present in the pro bono world. The winter 2003 issue contained a debate on whether law firm pro bono work is inherently left-liberal and ignores conservative issues.

OUR SURVEY SAYS

"The firm does a ton of interesting pro bono work and has a full-time partner managing the pro bono cases."

"The firm does encourage associates to participate in pro bono efforts. However, the firm does not count the pro bono work towards billable hours requirements, though the firm does count the pro bono work towards creditable hours requirements." (Houston, Texas)

"We have a full-time pro bono coordinator/attorney, who actively finds transactional and litigation pro bono assignments and coordinates the work within the firm. Our daily paper lists all the new pro bono projects and the attorneys staffed thereon. Everyone from summer associates to senior partners participates (or, at least, has the opportunity to)."

"I have always gotten support for the pro bono projects I want to work on and there are many pro bono opportunities made available to us."

"All of our pro bono activities are described on the daily intranet bulletin, and there are lots of opportunities to sign up to do pro bono work. A significant amount of pro bono time is creditable."

"New efforts to make the time creditable have helped promote the pro bono projects available, but it seems that a more formal assignment system for the projects might help emphasize the commitment."

"Associates can do a great deal of pro bono work if they seek it out. However, no one is pushing people to do it."

"Pro bono is well supported and is a big deal — especially in litigation and the other litigation-like departments. A few years back the firm hired Marc Kadish, a former Chicago-Kent law professor, to be its full-time pro bono coordinator and director. The crown jewel of Mayer Brown's pro bono is its habeas project in conjunction with the Seventh Circuit: the firm gets assigned a steady stream of indigent habeas cases, and young associates prepare, brief and argue the cases under the supervision (which is actually pretty good) of the pro bono group and some of the firm's more senior appellate lawyers. It's an impressive project. There's lots of other stuff, too, which gets well publicized."

"The firm is happy to let lawyers do extensive pro bono work, but that tolerance is undercut by a focus on billable hours."

"As a transaction lawyer, I don't participate in litigation-type pro bono work; instead I've devoted pro bono time to legal assessments of proposed statutes for Central and Eastern European states: a fantastic experience."

Mayer, Brown, Rowe & Maw LLP

"We offer not only legal representation in trial, appellate, and transactional matters; we provide training and encouragement to junior lawyers attracted to public interest law as well as financial support to public interest organizations."

— *Mayer, Brown, Rowe & Maw LLP*

McDermott, Will & Emery

227 West Monroe Street
Chicago, IL 60606-5096
Phone: (312) 372-2000
www.mwe.com

LOCATIONS

Boston, MA
Chicago, IL
Irvine, CA
Los Angeles, CA
Miami, FL
New York, NY
Palo Alto, CA
San Diego
Washington, DC
Brussels
Düsseldorf
London
Milan
Munich
Rome

MAJOR DEPARTMENTS & PRACTICES

Corporate
Employee Benefits
Health Law
Intellectual Property
Private Clients
Regulation & Government Affairs
Tax
Trial

THE STATS

No. of attorneys worldwide: 1,000+
No. of offices worldwide: 15
Chairman: Harvey W. Freishtat

EMPLOYMENT CONTACT

Ms. Karen K. Mortell
Legal Recruiting Manager
Phone: (312) 984-7784
Fax: (312) 984-7700
E-mail: kmortell@mwe.com

WHO'S WHO

Principal pro bono contact(s) at your firm:

Donald B. Hilliker, P.C.
Partner & Chair of Pro Bono Committee
Phone: (312) 984-7610
E-mail: dhilliker@mwe.com

Does the firm have a pro bono coordinator? No

Does the firm have a pro bono committee? Yes

If yes, how often does the committee meet? Regularly.

Describe the composition of the committee: A chairman (must be an equity partner); at least one member from each office of MWE; and such other members as the chairman of MWE selects, subject to the approval of the management committee.

THE SCOOP

Does your firm have a written pro bono policy? Yes

Has the firm signed on to the Law Firm Pro Bono Challenge? Yes

What are some of the areas of law in which your firm has performed pro bono legal work in the last two years? Children's law, special education, disability law, elder law, health care, Social Security benefits, death penalty, prisoner civil rights, habeas corpus, representation of nonprofit organizations.

What are some of the areas of law in which your firm does not perform pro bono work? N/A

Organizations for which your firm has performed pro bono legal services in the last two years: AIDS Legal Council of Chicago, Boston Lawyers' Committee on Civil Rights, Chicago Volunteer Legal Services, Community Economic Development Law Project (Chicago), Court Appointed Special Advocates (Silicon Valley), D.C. Bar Pro Bono Clinic, New York Lawyers for the Public Interest, Public Counsel of Los Angeles, Put Something Back Program and Legal Services of Greater Miami, Washington Lawyers Committee for Civil Rights and Urban Affairs.

List up to three pro bono matters that are representative of the pro bono work your firm participates in.

- The MWE: Kids First Project involves representation of children with special education needs to assure they receive the education opportunities to which they are entitled. In one recent case, a Chicago office associate team successfully opposed the expulsion of a child with special needs and facilitated the transfer of the student to a school with outstanding special education facilities.

- In Washington, D.C., a MWE partner led an effort to successfully cause a national retail chain to take remedial steps and expend thousands of dollars to make its stores compliant with the Americans With Disabilities Act and wheelchair accessible.

- In Los Angeles, two MWE health law partners undertook a series of seminars for Los Angeles area community health clinics to explain and assist with the compliance of the privacy rights of patients under the Health Insurance Portability and Accountability Act. This effort saved thousands of dollars from being diverted from patient care and assured that the important privacy rights of low income patients were being upheld.

BY THE NUMBERS

What is the total number of hours that lawyers in U.S. offices at your firm spent performing pro bono legal services in 2000, 2001 and 2002?

    Total number of hours in 2000: 20,058 hours
    Total number of hours in 2001: 19,158 hours
    Total number of hours in 2002: 16,447 hours

Average number of pro bono hours per attorney in U.S. offices per year (including associates, partners, counsels, but not summer associates):

    Average number of hours per attorney in 2000: 23 hours
    Average number of hours per attorney in 2001: 21 hours
    Average number of hours per attorney in 2002: 17 hours

What percentage of attorneys in this firm's U.S. offices did pro bono work in 2002? 48 percent

What percentage of attorneys in this firm's U.S. offices did at least 20 hours of pro bono work in 2002? 23 percent

Does the firm encourage its lawyers to perform a minimum number of pro bono hours? Yes

If so, how many hours per year or what percentage of lawyers' billable hours? 60 hours per year

SUPERVISION AND EVALUATIONS

Is there partner supervision on each pro bono matter? Yes

Do partner supervisors or, if applicable, senior associates provide written evaluations of associates' work on pro bono matters? Yes

If so, are those evaluations taken into account in determining salary, bonuses or advancement in the firm? Yes

If not, does the firm consider pro bono work generally in associate evaluations? N/A

HOURS

Does the firm give billable hour credit for pro bono work? Yes

Does the firm have a maximum number of pro bono hours that can be applied toward the billable hour target? No

If so, what is the maximum? N/A

If your firm uses hours to determine bonuses, does it consider pro bono hours when determining bonuses? Yes

PRO BONO POINTS

What training opportunities are open to associates working on pro bono matters? Early courtroom experience and client contact are available through the pro bono program.

Can associates bring matters of interest to the firm? Yes

Does the firm offer the use of support staff in carrying out pro bono matters? Yes

What pro bono opportunities are available for summer associates? Summer associates at MWE may work on pro bono projects with associates and partners.

Does the firm have established programs, such as externships, that enable its associates to work in a public interest setting? No

Has your firm won any special recognition or awards in the last two years for its pro bono work? Yes

If so, please list.

Alternatives for Community & Environment

In 1996, and again in 1998, about 200 residents of a low-income neighborhood in Boston had their homes flooded with raw sewage. The flooding occurred during heavy rainstorms and lasted for days. Sewage overflow contaminated backyards and basements throughout the neighborhood. On behalf of the residents, MWE has pursued actions against the Massachusetts Water Resources Authority and the Boston Water and Sewer Commission. This multi-year effort is still underway. Recognizing MWE's commitment and outstanding work on this complex case, Boston's Alternatives for Community and Environmental (ACE) awarded MWE its 2003 Founder's Day Award. "McDermott, Will & Emery and Jamy Madeia [co-counsel] are performing a wonderful service for this community," said the ACE presenter of the award. "The residents endured a wretched experience and deserve compensation. Don Frederico, Brian Robinson and their colleagues are helping the Archdale Street residents to receive the justice they deserve."

Chicago Public Schools

For the past two years about 40 lawyers, paralegals and staff have traveled, often by yellow school bus, each week to William H. Brown Elementary School on Chicago's Near West Side to tutor third and fourth graders in reading. In recognition of the MWE: Partners in Reading tutoring commitment, the Chicago Public Schools and Brown School awarded MWE a Community Service Award. Brown School Principal Connie Thomas described MWE's weekly tutoring program as the most successful volunteer program at the school. She noted that reading scores were up dramatically for children in the tutoring program. In fact, the school received a $10,000 grant from Chicago Public Schools for being one of the top ten schools in Chicago for improved reading scores. The plaque presented to MWE reads: "Your diligence, patience, love and understanding of our children is part of our success story. You help give Brown students choices in life. Thank you."

Public Counsel and ABA Business Law Section

Two years ago, as the entire health care industry struggled to deal with the looming new requirements of the Health Insurance Portability and Accountability Act (HIPAA), Public Counsel, the nation's largest public interest law firm, recognized the potential impact of this legislation upon its client clinics. MWE partners Tim Blanchard and Scott Edelstein quickly agreed to address this community need by conducting a HIPAA fundamentals course for community health clinics as part of Public Counsel's Community Service Project. "It was the public service opportunity that we, as healthcare regulatory lawyers, had been looking for — a chance to use our healthcare expertise in a pro bono matter," explained Tim

Blanchard. This one-time overview soon developed into a series of seminars and workshops to help and inform the community. In honor of their efforts, Public Counsel named Tim and Scott the Outstanding Advocates of the Year in the Community Development Project for two years running (2001 and 2002). Earlier this year the Business Law Section of the American Bar Association also honored Tim and Scott for outstanding pro bono commitment at its Annual Meeting in Los Angeles.

Washington Lawyers Committee for Civil Rights and Urban Affairs
As a result of MWE working with the Disability Rights Council of Greater Washington (DRC), the DRC and Family Dollar Stores, Inc. announced an agreement which will provide greater access for customers with disabilities in over 4,700 Family Dollar stores in 42 states. The DRC and Family Dollar hailed the agreement as demonstrating the effectiveness of collaborative efforts between advocacy organizations and responsible businesses to implement the equal access promise of the ADA. Working cooperatively and in the spirit of providing improved access, representatives of Family Dollar and the DRC worked during the past two years to improve the shopping experience of customers with disabilities.

THE FIRM SAYS

Statement of MWE's Pro Bono Policy
The management committee of MWE encourages all attorneys in all offices to engage in some type of pro bono legal service. The management committee seeks to have each attorney at MWE perform pro bono legal services each year, with an objective of at least 60 hours of pro bono legal services per attorney per year.

Earlier this year, MWE issued the first annual MWE Pro Bono Report highlighting recent pro bono contributions and successes of MWE lawyers and staff. In 2003, MWE awarded the first annual "McDermott, Will & Emery Award for Outstanding Achievement and Commitment to Pro Bono Service to the Community" to partners Eugene Goldman of the Washington, D.C., office and Tim Blanchard and Scott Edelstein of the Los Angeles office.

The *MWE: Kids First Project* and other efforts during the first six months of 2003 resulted in a 41 percent increase in pro bono hours over the comparable period in 2002. In Europe, MWE's London office provides legal assistance to charities providing help to homeless people. In Dusseldorf, MWE has recently undertaken a project to assist in the formation of a kindergarten.

Pro Bono Initiatives
- MWE: Kids First Project. MWE started this pro bono initiative in all of its United States offices in 2002. The *MWE: Kids First Project*, coordinated in the firm's eight U.S. offices, focuses on representing children in need to assure they receive appropriate public education and remain in school. *MWE: Kids First*, organized in collaboration with a local referral agency in each of MWE's U.S. offices, provides legal representation for a variety of needs, including special education for eligible children, legal matters regarding children with health needs, school access and registration, school discipline, school eligibility for immigrant and undocumented children, and law reform and legislative policy.

- MWE Tutoring Program. In September 2001, MWE announced a firm-wide, volunteer tutoring program for its U.S. offices. The program focuses on developing essential reading and grammar skills of children. In June 2001, the firm received an Outstanding Achievement Award in Public Education from the Washington, D.C. Lawyers' Committee for Civil Rights, a private, nonprofit, nonpartisan organization, for its participation in an affiliated tutoring program in which 60 of the firm's Washington, D.C. employees tutored second graders at Bowen Elementary School in reading and related skills. The recognition praised MWE for its three-year partnership with the Bowen Elementary School and its involvement in its tutoring program. Earlier this year, MWE received an award for its tutoring commitment for third and fourth graders at the Brown Elementary School on Chicago's Near West Side.

OUR SURVEY SAYS

"I am staffed on a major pro bono project. I billed more hours to that project [than] many others last year and all of my hours were counted. The work is incredibly rewarding. The firm has also undertaken a major initiative on behalf of children this year. Most attorneys I know are doing some pro bono work at any given moment."

"Many opportunities are available to associates interested in pro bono work, but the firm does not actively encourage or assign pro bono assignments."

"Sixty hours of pro bono work automatically count toward billables if you meet the 2,000 mark. Additional hours will also go toward billables if your pro bono matter requires more hours and [you] let a partner know beforehand."

"Several young attorneys have briefed and argued Seventh Circuit appeals recently through pro bono representation, and the firm approved 'billable time as needed for each without a problem. Partners particularly recognize that pro bono can provide young associates with good experience and do not discourage taking advantage of pro bono opportunities."

"Our record in the past has been poor, but we are getting much better. I'm very involved in pro bono work."

"The firm gives us leeway to do pro bono work and we receive billing credit for the first 60 hours of pro bono work each year. It's not really encouraged or discouraged. It's mainly up to the individual lawyer to get involved, although the pro bono coordinator in our office has done a great job with implementing volunteer programs and ideas. We can even work on projects and get pro bono credit for projects that are not necessarily 'legal' in nature."

"I have worked on three different pro bono matters. McDermott has started an initiative across all offices to partner with agencies providing legal assistance to children. In Boston we are working with Children's Law Center to provide representation for students regarding special education and/or disciplinary matters."

"The firm counted our pro bono hours towards bonuses last year, but I wouldn't say it's a very institutionalized program. You have to go out and get it yourself."

"The firm has instituted long-standing relationships with pro bono programs. For example, MWE has a program called "Kids First" where attorneys can either volunteer to tutor elementary school children or take on cases helping children get special developmental services. I have always been able to take on any pro bono work I wanted to, including ones I sought out for myself."

"MWE is generally supportive of pro bono time. The first 60 hours will automatically count toward billable credit. Last year, every hour counted."

McGuireWoods LLP

One James Center
901 East Cary Street
Richmond, VA 23219-4030
Phone: (804) 775-1000
www.mcguirewoods.com

LOCATIONS

Richmond, VA (HQ)
Atlanta, GA
Baltimore, MD
Charlotte, NC
Charlottesville, VA
Chicago, IL
Jacksonville, FL
New York, NY
Norfolk, VA
Pittsburgh, PA
Tysons Corner, VA
Washington, DC
Almaty, Kazakhstan
Brussels

MAJOR DEPARTMENTS & PRACTICES

Commercial Litigation
Corporate Services
Financial Services
Health Care
Labor & Employment
Products Liability & Litigation Management
Real Estate & Environmental
Taxation & Employee Benefits

THE STATS

No. of attorneys worldwide: 725
No. of offices worldwide: 14
Chairman: Robert L. Burrus Jr.
Managing Partner: William J. Strickland

EMPLOYMENT CONTACTS

Ms. Ann McGhee
Attorney Recruitment Manager
Phone: (804) 775-7628
E-mail: amcghee@mcguirewoods.com

Washington, DC
Ms. Dusti L. Plunkett
Attorney Recruitment Manager
Phone: (202) 857-1739
E-mail: dplunkett@mcguirewoods.com

WHO'S WHO

Does the firm have a pro bono coordinator? Yes

Scott C. Oostdyk, Partner
Dominion Tower
625 Liberty Avenue, 23rd Floor
Pittsburgh, PA 15222-3142
Phone: (412) 667-7915
E-mail: soostdyk@mcguirewoods.com

Does the firm have a pro bono committee? Yes

If yes, what percentage of his or her time is spent on pro bono work? 5 percent

Does the firm have a pro bono committee? Yes

If yes, how often does the committee meet? Newly formed — will meet quarterly initially and transition to monthly meetings.

Describe the composition of the committee: Diverse committee balanced by region, race, gender, longevity with firm and specialty — although the majority are litigators.

THE SCOOP

Does your firm have a written pro bono policy? Yes

Has the firm signed on to the Law Firm Pro Bono Challenge? Yes

What are some of the areas of law in which your firm has performed pro bono legal work in the last two years? Litigation, real estate, criminal, debtor/creditor and numerous others.

What are some of the areas of law in which your firm does not perform pro bono work? By policy, there are no limits, but tax, corporate and environmental matters are less frequent.

Organizations for which your firm has performed pro bono legal services in the last two years: Central Virginia Legal Aid (Richmond), Charlotte-Mecklenburg Legal Aid (North Carolina), Jacksonville Legal Aid (Florida), Pro Bono Clearing House (Richmond), Christmas in April (Chicago & Richmond), Habitat for Humanity United Way, federal court-appointed counsel referrals.

List up to three pro bono matters that are representative of the pro bono work your firm participates in.

- Pro bono prosecutors – A team of eight lawyers tried child support cases against non-paying parents, assuming a portion of the Virginia Division of Child Support Enforcement caseload.

- State of Alabama v. Mr. Holly Wood – death penalty appeal.

- Wills for Heroes – Washington, D.C., and Northern Virginia bar effort to execute wills for first responders; started after 9/11 Pentagon attack.

BY THE NUMBERS

What is the total number of hours that lawyers in U.S. offices at your firm spent performing pro bono legal services in 2000, 2001 and 2002?

Total number of hours in 2000: 21,323 hours
Total number of hours in 2001: 24,183 hours
Total number of hours in 2002: 25.317 hours

Average number of pro bono hours per attorney in U.S. offices per year (including associates, partners, counsels, but not summer associates):

Average number of hours per attorney in 2000: 33 hours
Average number of hours per attorney in 2001: 37 hours
Average number of hours per attorney in 2002: 38 hours

What percentage of attorneys in this firm's U.S. offices did pro bono work in 2002? 58 percent

What percentage of attorneys in this firm's U.S. offices did at least 20 hours of pro bono work in 2002? 30 percent

Does the firm encourage its lawyers to perform a minimum number of pro bono hours? No

SUPERVISION AND EVALUATIONS

Is there partner supervision on each pro bono matter? Yes

Do partner supervisors or, if applicable, senior associates provide written evaluations of associates' work on pro bono matters? Yes

If so, are those evaluations taken into account in determining salary, bonuses or advancement in the firm? Yes

If not, does the firm consider pro bono work generally in associate evaluations? N/A

HOURS

Does the firm give billable hour credit for pro bono work? Yes

Does the firm have a maximum number of pro bono hours that can be applied toward the billable hour target? No

If so, what is the maximum? N/A

If your firm uses hours to determine bonuses, does it consider pro bono hours when determining bonuses? No

PRO BONO POINTS

What training opportunities are open to associates working on pro bono matters? Certain offices offer training in connection with local legal aid or specialty projects like landlord/tenant public benefits or protective order projects.

Can associates bring matters of interest to the firm? Yes

Does the firm offer the use of support staff in carrying out pro bono matters? Yes

What pro bono opportunities are available for summer associates? Same as for regular associates.

Does the firm have established programs, such as externships, that enable its associates to work in a public interest setting? No

Has your firm won any special recognition or awards in the last two years for its pro bono work? Yes

If so, please list. Certain individual lawyers have won recognition.

THE FIRM SAYS

McGuireWoods believes that the decision to participate in pro bono is individual with the lawyer. That being said, we encourage all lawyers to serve their communities whether by contribution of legal talent or volunteer and civic energy. We prioritize services to low-income individuals and groups that represent them and also will get involved in important public issues when they present themselves.

OUR SURVEY SAYS

"We do get billable credit for pro bono work, which is great, but that work does not count toward bonuses, which is frustrating. There could be much more emphasis on pro bono at the office and firm level."

"McGuireWoods actively encourages pro bono work but does not require it."

"The firm is more focused on revenues and billable hours — pro bono work obviously decreases those numbers."

"It's encouraged in e-mails and memos, but the way the billable hours and compensation works, it's not practical for associates to do a whole lot."

"This is the only area where I believe McGuireWoods needs to substantially improve. Pro bono hours do not count towards the billable hours required for a bonus, although they do count toward the lesser minimum billable hour requirement. In addition, there is no real promotion of or encouragement of pro bono work. Participation in pro bono activities is not part of the firm culture."

"The firm encourages it but does not reward it."

"The firm fully supports anyone who wants to do pro bono work and gives full credit to billable hours requirements. Pro bono work is a positive on associate evaluations. This being said, if you don't want to do it, no one cares."

"The firm does not provide a good understanding of how pro bono is figured into the hours requirement."

"The firm gives credit for pro bono hours as billable hours, as long as it is 'approved' pro bono. It's pretty rigorous to get some matter as an approved pro bono matter. Also, pro bono hours do not count toward your bonus. So, even if you bill 2,100 hours, and 200 of them were pro bono (putting you below the 2,000 bonus threshold), then you get no bonus."

"I have just begun doing pro bono work and the firm is incredibly helpful and supportive."

Milbank, Tweed, Hadley & McCloy LLP

One Chase Manhattan Plaza
New York, NY 10005-1413
Phone: (212) 530-5532
www.milbank.com

LOCATIONS

New York, NY (HQ)
Los Angeles, CA
Palo Alto, CA
Washington, DC
Frankfurt
Hong Kong
London
Singapore
Tokyo

MAJOR DEPARTMENTS & PRACTICES

Banking & Institutional Investment
Capital Markets
Communications & Space
Corporate Governance
Employee Benefits
Exempt Organizations
Financial Restructuring
High Yield & Acquisition Finance
Intellectual Property
Litigation & Arbitration
M&A/General Corporate
Power & Energy
Project Finance
Public Interest Law
Real Estate
Securitization
Tax
Technology
Transportation Finance
Trusts & Estates

THE STATS

No. of attorneys worldwide: 507
No. of offices worldwide: 9
Chairman: Mel M. Immergut

EMPLOYMENT CONTACT

Ms. June Chotoo
Recruiting Coordinator
Phone: (212) 530-8322
Fax: (212) 822-5064
E-mail: Jchotoo@Milbank.com

WHO'S WHO

Does the firm have a pro bono coordinator? Yes

Joseph S. Genova, Esq.
Partner, Director of Public Service
Phone: (212) 530-5532
E-mail: jgenova@milbank.com

Tony Perez Cassino, Esq.
Assistant Director of Public Service
Phone: (212) 530-5245
E-mail: acassino@milbank.com

If yes, what percentage of his or her time is spent on pro bono work? 100 percent

Does the firm have a pro bono committee? Yes

If yes, how often does the committee meet? As necessary

Describe the composition of the committee: It is a combination of partners and associates from different practice areas.

THE SCOOP

Does your firm have a written pro bono policy? Yes

Has the firm signed on to the Law Firm Pro Bono Challenge? Yes

What are some of the areas of law in which your firm has performed pro bono legal work in the last two years? Family law, asylum, housing, wills, impact litigation, employment, not-for-profit, immigration, low-income taxpayer.

What are some of the areas of law in which your firm does not perform pro bono work? Work for clients who do not meet strict eligibility criteria. For example, individuals must meet federal poverty guidelines and organizations must be truly unable (as opposed to unwilling) to pay.

Organizations for which your firm has performed pro bono legal services in the last two years: New York Lawyers for the Public Interest, inMotion, The Legal Aid Society, Sanctuary for Families, ACLU, Volunteers of Legal Service, Urban Justice Center, Public Counsel, ACLU of Southern California, Legal Services for New York.

List up to three pro bono matters that are representative of the pro bono work your firm participates in.

- Predatory Lending — we represented a low-income family that obtained a home refinance loan from a no-name mortgage lender at the incredibly high rate of 16 percent. The loan also increased their indebtedness by $70,000. The client inevitably defaulted, and the lender foreclosed. We had the foreclosure vacated and continue to litigate the matter in bankruptcy court.

- Adoption — we represented a foster mother in her efforts to adopt a four-year-old girl abandoned by her birth mother. We represented the woman at hearings dealing with the child's educational progress, mental and physical health, and visitation rights.

- Prison Abuse — we represented a woman who was raped by a corrections officer. After reporting the incident, the victim was transferred but her abuser was not disciplined. During discovery, we procured a DNA test of a piece of soiled clothing that found the officer's semen and he was eventually fired. We continue to represent the woman in her case against him and other prison officials.

BY THE NUMBERS

What is the total number of hours that lawyers in U.S. offices at your firm spent performing pro bono legal services in 2000, 2001 and 2002?

    Total number of hours in 2000: 10,554 hours
    Total number of hours in 2001: 16,630
    Total number of hours in 2002: 12,373

Average number of pro bono hours per attorney in U.S. offices per year (including associates, partners, counsels, but not summer associates):

    Average number of hours per attorney in 2000: 30 hours
    Average number of hours per attorney in 2001: 43 hours
    Average number of hours per attorney in 2002: 30 hours

What percentage of attorneys in this firm's U.S. offices did pro bono work in 2002? 40 percent

What percentage of attorneys in this firm's U.S. offices did at least 20 hours of pro bono work in 2002? 22 percent

Does the firm encourage its lawyers to perform a minimum number of pro bono hours? Yes. We encourage them to meet the Law Firm Pro Bono Challenge.

If so, how many hours per year or what percentage of lawyers' billable hours? 3 percent

SUPERVISION AND EVALUATIONS

Is there partner supervision on each pro bono matter? Yes

Do partner supervisors or, if applicable, senior associates provide written evaluations of associates' work on pro bono matters? Yes

If so, are those evaluations taken into account in determining salary, bonuses or advancement in the firm? Yes

If not, does the firm consider pro bono work generally in associate evaluations? N/A

HOURS

Does the firm give billable hour credit for pro bono work? We have no minimum, but every ABA-qualified hour is equivalent to a billable hour.

Does the firm have a maximum number of pro bono hours that can be applied toward the billable hour target? No

If so, what is the maximum? N/A

If your firm uses hours to determine bonuses, does it consider pro bono hours when determining bonuses? This is rare, but when it occurs, yes, 100 percent of ABA-qualified hours count.

PRO BONO POINTS

What training opportunities are open to associates working on pro bono matters? Many of the programs offer training, and the firm maintains a library of training materials. The regular training program for paying client matters is extensive, and it is matched, if not exceeded, for pro bono matters.

Can associates bring matters of interest to the firm? Yes

Does the firm offer the use of support staff in carrying out pro bono matters? Yes

What pro bono opportunities are available for summer associates? A number of specialized projects including uncontested divorces, wills and many of the same opportunities offered associates. We make a special effort to include and indoctrinate summer associates.

Does the firm have established programs, such as externships, that enable its associates to work in a public interest setting? Yes

If so, where and for up to how long? First-year associates can participate in a 10-week internship at a pro bono program of their choosing. In 2003, 14 associates will participate in the program. The firm also has a fourth-year internship where associates can also spend two months at a pro bono program of their choosing. Other opportunities are being devised.

Has your firm won any special recognition or awards in the last two years for its pro bono work? Yes

If so, please list. Legal Aid Society's Access to Justice Award, 2002.

THE FIRM SAYS

Milbank has a long and proud tradition of pro bono service. We have one of the oldest law firm pro bono programs in the country, and we are one of the few firms in the country to have both a full-time partner in charge of public service and an experienced attorney to coordinate pro bono. We are an early signatory to the American Bar Association's Law Firm Pro Bono Challenge, and every lawyer is encouraged to meet this standard.

Milbank's public service department works closely with individual lawyers and departments to disseminate information about pro bono opportunities and coordinates training to prepare volunteers for the challenge. Milbank lawyers can either choose a pro bono opportunity developed by the public service department or they can suggest their own. We offer an innovative first-year pro bono internship program, which enables incoming associates to spend 10 weeks working at a pro bono or legal services program of their choosing. In 2003, 14 incoming associates took advantage of this unique opportunity, and since 1990, more than one hundred associates have participated in the program. Fourth-year associates are also afforded an opportunity to participate in a similar internship.

Some of our recent public interest work includes assisting clients with adoptions; representing battered women in divorce proceedings and child custody matters; protecting animals; assisting the homeless in legal issues; assisting the elderly with wills; helping secure asylum for political refugees; and working on disability rights cases.

OUR SURVEY SAYS

"There is a pro bono department with a full-time partner and associate dedicated to just pro bono work. The work assigned through that department is varied and extremely interesting. There is also the opportunity to do a two-month pro bono rotation at a public interest organization immediately before starting the first year and after the third year. Associates are encouraged to spend 60 hours per year doing pro bono work. Overall, the firm is very committed to pro bono."

"First-year associates are allowed to spend their first nine weeks working on a pro bono internship, which means that they work for one pro bono organization full time but with full access to the firm's resources. While this is a great program, the firm is not as supportive once 'real work' starts. Pro bono is definitely supposed to be done only after your paying work is completed."

"[The firm is] very strongly committed, including having a partner in charge of the program full time and a real commitment to have everyone perform pro bono activities."

"I don't know of another large New York law firm more committed to pro bono work than Milbank. You can get involved as a summer associate and have the chance to do a pro bono rotation for the first two months of your first year (with full pay)."

"We are more committed than most of our New York peers, but come on, are any large New York firms really committed to pro bono?"

"It would help if they gave full billable credit for pro bono work, rather than keeping it in the 'chargeable equivalent' column, whatever that means."

"The firm claims one of the best pro bono practices in the city. My experience is that I know almost no one in the corporate groups who has done any pro bono work. Our partners certainly do not encourage it. Pro bono hours are not billable equivalent."

"Everyone I know at the firm does some pro bono work."

"The firm is very committed in its attempts to get associates involved in pro bono work. Many of the incoming first-year associates took advantage of a three-month pro bono rotation to kick off their careers at the firm."

"We have one of the oldest law firm pro bono programs in the country, and we are one of the few firms in the country to have both a full-time partner in charge of public service and an experienced attorney to coordinate pro bono."

— *Milbank, Tweed, Hadley & McCloy LLP*

Morgan, Lewis & Bockius LLP

1701 Market Street
Philadelphia, PA 19103-2921
Phone: (215) 963-5000
www.morganlewis.com

LOCATIONS

Boston, MA
Chicago, IL
Harrisburg, PA
Irvine, CA
Los Angeles, CA
Miami, FL
New York, NY
McLean, VA
Palo Alto, CA
Philadelphia, PA
Pittsburgh, PA
Princeton, NJ
San Francisco, CA
Washington, DC
Brussels
Frankfurt
London
Tokyo

MAJOR DEPARTMENTS & PRACTICES

Antitrust
Bankruptcy
Business & Finance
Employee Benefits & Executive Compensation
Energy
FDA/Healthcare Regulation
Intellectual Property
Investment Management
Labor & Employment Law
Life Sciences
Litigation
Media
Mergers & Acquisitions
Real Estate
Securities
Tax
Technology

THE STATS

No. of attorneys worldwide: 1,167
No. of offices worldwide: 18
Firm Chair: Francis M. Milone

EMPLOYMENT CONTACT

See careers section of firm web site for contacts at various offices.

WHO'S WHO

Does the firm have a pro bono coordinator? Yes

Kevin M. Donovan, Esq.
Chair, Public Interest Practice Committee
Phone: (215) 963-5420
E-mail: kdonovan@morganlewis.com

If yes, what percentage of his or her time is spent on pro bono work? 20 to 25 percent

Does the firm have a pro bono committee? Yes

If yes, how often does the committee meet? Periodically.

Describe the composition of the committee: Chair of firm public interest practice committee and chairs of office public interest practice committees.

THE SCOOP

Does your firm have a written pro bono policy? Yes

Has the firm signed on to the Law Firm Pro Bono Challenge? Yes

What are some of the areas of law in which your firm has performed pro bono legal work in the last two years? Capital punishment litigation; immigration litigation; corporate, real estate, finance, labor and tax counseling to nonprofits; child advocacy; advocacy on behalf of victims of domestic abuse; tax and personal law counseling to individuals of limited means; family law/custody litigation; homeless advocacy clinical work and cases; civil rights litigation; representation of the arts; landlord/tenant work on behalf of individuals of limited means; criminal defense; work for victims of September 11; education law cases.

Organizations for which your firm has performed pro bono legal services in the last two years: Philadelphia Volunteers for the Indigent, The Support Center for Child Advocates (Philadelphia), The Homeless Advocacy Project (Philadelphia), The Legal Aid Society of New York, New York Lawyers for the Public Interest, The Sanctuary for Families, Capital Area Immigration Rights Coalition (Washington, D.C.), D.C. Bar Public Service Activities Corporation, Washington Lawyers Committee for Civil Rights and Urban Affairs, San Francisco Bar Association's Volunteer Legal Services Program, Lawyers' Committee for Civil Rights of the San Francisco Bay Area, Miami/Dade County Bar Association, "Put Something Back."

List up to three pro bono matters that are representative of the pro bono work your firm participates in.

- Representation of John Thompson. This 15-year representation of a Louisiana death row inmate culminated in the acquittal of our client in May 2003 following a retrial of the murder charge against him. The trial team was lead by Morgan Lewis partners Michael Banks and J. Gordon Cooney Jr. (who had been the leaders of the Thompson representation since it was initiated in 1988). The team led by Cooney and Banks developed irrefutable evidence of our client's innocence.

- Custody case. Morgan Lewis associate Nora von Stange represented a client who was deprived of her child when the client's former spouse removed the child from the state without notice. The case involved complex legal issues (including difficult choice-of-law issues) and challenging factual issues relating to domestic violence, child sexual abuse, child abduction and parental alienation. Nora received one of only two Abely Awards presented annually by the Sanctuary for Families (the other was presented to United States Supreme Court Justice Ruth Bader Ginsberg, with whom Nora shared the podium).

- Immigration case. In a significant immigration law victory (decided in early 2003), Morgan Lewis partner Mark N. Bravin and associate Corrine A. Niosi convinced the U.S. Court of Appeals for the Ninth Circuit to take the rare step of reversing a deportation order after the deportation had already occurred. Our client was a legal resident from Mexico whose parents and siblings were United States citizens. She was deported after being convicted of criminal possession of stolen property. The government claimed that this conviction was sufficient to support deportation, but the Morgan Lewis team prevailed by convincing the Court that the government had failed to prove the requisite level of criminal intent to justify deportation.

BY THE NUMBERS

What is the total number of hours that lawyers in U.S. offices at your firm spent performing pro bono legal services in 2000, 2001 and 2002?

    Total number of hours in 2000: N/A
    Total number of hours in 2001: N/A
    Total number of hours in 2002: 31,688 hours (ABA)/38,711 hours (MLB)

Average number of pro bono hours per attorney in U.S. offices per year (including associates, partners, counsels, but not summer associates):

    Average number of hours per attorney in 2000: N/A
    Average number of hours per attorney in 2001: N/A
    Average number of hours per attorney in 2002: 31.5 hours (ABA)/38.6 hours (MLB)

What percentage of attorneys in this firm's U.S. offices did pro bono work in 2002? 58 percent

What percentage of attorneys in this firm's U.S. offices did at least 20 hours of pro bono work in 2002? 33 percent

Does the firm encourage its lawyers to perform a minimum number of pro bono hours? No

SUPERVISION AND EVALUATIONS

Is there partner supervision on each pro bono matter? Yes

Do partner supervisors or, if applicable, senior associates provide written evaluations of associates' work on pro bono matters? Yes

If so, are those evaluations taken into account in determining salary, bonuses or advancement in the firm? Yes

If not, does the firm consider pro bono work generally in associate evaluations? N/A

HOURS

Does the firm give billable hour credit for pro bono work? Yes

Does the firm have a maximum number of pro bono hours that can be applied toward the billable hour target? No

If so, what is the maximum? N/A

If your firm uses hours to determine bonuses, does it consider pro bono hours when determining bonuses? Yes

PRO BONO POINTS

What training opportunities are open to associates working on pro bono matters? The firm covers the expense of training undertaken for pro bono representations. The firm also arranges or conducts training for particular types of cases (e.g., child advocacy).

Can associates bring matters of interest to the firm? Yes

Does the firm offer the use of support staff in carrying out pro bono matters? Yes

What pro bono opportunities are available for summer associates? Summer associates are invited to participate in pending matters during their time with the firm. Numerous summer associate assignments relate to pro bono cases and these are evaluated and otherwise treated identically to assignments derived from non-pro bono relationships.

Does the firm have established programs, such as externships, that enable its associates to work in a public interest setting? Yes

If so, where and for up to how long? Through its Public Interest and Community Service ("PICS") program, summer associates are given the option of experiencing a traditional summer associate program for part of the summer and spending the remainder of the summer with a public-interest or community service organization (with Morgan Lewis paying the standard summer associate salary for the entire period). Morgan Lewis also offers a one-year fellowship opportunity through the Public Interest Fellowship program of the Philadelphia Bar Association.

Has your firm won any special recognition or awards in the last two years for its pro bono work? Yes

If so, please list. 2003 Citizens Pro Bono Award (Outstanding Large Firm Pro Bono Program in Philadelphia), awarded by Philadelphia Bar Association. Outstanding Law Firm Award, awarded to Morgan, Lewis' Miami office by Miami/Dade County Bar Association. "Put Something Back" Abely Award (presented by the Sanctuary for Families), awarded to Nora von Stange. Pennsylvania Bar Association Pro Bono Awards, awarded to Michael L. Banks, J. Gordon Cooney Jr. and Georgina O'Hara. Cornerstone Award (presented by the Lawyers Alliance for New York), awarded to Michael Armstrong. Morgan Lewis awarded "Founder Status" in recognition of its pro bono work in support of The Women in Military Service for America Memorial.

THE FIRM SAYS

Morgan Lewis has a strong commitment to the provision of pro bono legal services. The firm is a charter signatory of the Law Firm Pro Bono Challenge and endorses its goals and its definition of pro bono services. The firm allows its attorneys great flexibility in undertaking pro bono representations, but actively encourages the representation of individuals of limited means. The guiding principle of the pro bono program is that pro bono representations are treated like all other representations and that pro bono work is credited and evaluated like all other work.

OUR SURVEY SAYS

"My firm is strongly committed to pro bono work. All pro bono work, if approved by the firm, counts as billable work towards your billable hours and your annual bonus."

"All pro bono hours are billable, which is great. I billed over 100 hours of pro bono time in my first year and a little less than that in my second year. The firm encourages such activities through awards programs and by circulating frequent e-mails with pro bono opportunities."

"I've done a lot of pro bono work and have been fully supported by the firm."

"The firm takes on a number of pro bono matters and the summer program provides summer associates with the opportunity to use their time to benefit others."

"I spent substantial time last year on a pro bono assignment, and the time spent counted as billable hours. I can't think of a better way for the firm to commit itself to pro bono work."

"The firm is extremely devoted to pro bono work. It rewards partners and associates who participate in the program. All pro bono hours are billable. Most associates take on these projects during slow periods and to gain valuable trial and legal experience. I am very impressed with the program."

"The firm allows associates to do as much pro bono as they like, and several prominent partners participate as well, but overall the firm does not give pro bono top billing."

"The firm has placed a great emphasis on pro bono work for its associates, as well as summer associates."

"Pro bono is strongly encouraged. Awards are given each year for pro bono commitment. And e-mails are sent weekly regarding pro bono opportunities. In addition, all pro bono hours count towards our minimum billable hour requirement for bonuses."

"The firm has been improving in this area. A number of pro bono projects are ongoing in both the corporate and litigation departments. The New York office recently publicly acknowledged at the firm dinner certain associates who have excelled in pro bono matters."

"The guiding principle of the pro bono program is that pro bono representations are treated like all other representations and that pro bono work is credited and evaluated like all other work."

— *Morgan Lewis & Bockius LLP*

Morrison & Foerster LLP

425 Market Street
San Francisco, CA 94105-2482
Phone: (415) 268-7000
www.MoFo.com

LOCATIONS

San Francisco, CA (HQ)
Century City, CA
Denver, CO
Irvine, CA
Los Angeles, CA
McLean, VA
New York, NY
Palo Alto, CA
Sacramento, CA
San Diego, CA
Walnut Creek, CA
Washington, DC
Beijing
Brussels
Hong Kong
London
Shanghai
Singapore
Tokyo

MAJOR DEPARTMENTS & PRACTICES

Bankruptcy
Communications & Media
Corporate Finance
Financial Services
Intellectual Property & Patent
International
Labor & Employment
Land Use, Environmental & Energy
Litigation
Project Finance & Development
Real Estate
Securities
Tax
Venture Capital

THE STATS

No. of attorneys worldwide: 995
No. of offices worldwide: 19
Firm Chair: Keith C. Wetmore

EMPLOYMENT CONTACT

Ms. Jane Cooperman
Senior Recruiting Manager
Phone: (415) 268-7665
Fax: (415) 268-7522
E-mail: jcooperman@mofo.com

WHO'S WHO

Does the firm have a pro bono coordinator? Yes

Anthony Press, Esq.
Chair of the Pro Bono Committee
1880 Century Park East, Suite 1111
Los Angeles, CA, 90067-1600
Phone: (310) 203-4030
E-mail apress@mofo.com

Kathi Pugh, Esq.
Pro Bono Program Counsel
425 Market Street, 35th floor
San Francisco, CA 94105
Phone: (415) 268-6370
E-mail: kpugh@mofo.com

If yes, what percentage of his or her time is spent on pro bono work? 100 percent

Does the firm have a pro bono committee? Yes

If yes, how often does the committee meet? At least quarterly but they review pro bono approval requests and other committee business almost daily.

Describe the composition of the committee: Each of our domestic offices (except Sacramento) has at least one representative on the firm-wide pro bono committee. The committee is made up of associates, partners and of counsels. We include attorneys from the different practice groups but each department has at least one representative on the committee. Many of our offices also have their own office-wide pro bono committee which may include staff members and legal assistants from that office.

THE SCOOP

Does your firm have a written pro bono policy? Yes

Has the firm signed on to the Law Firm Pro Bono Challenge? Yes

What are some of the areas of law in which your firm has performed pro bono legal work in the last two years? Education matters, children's issues, civil rights & civil liberties, criminal justice, international human rights & political asylum, disability issues, women's rights & domestic violence, sexual orientation issues, veterans' matters, animal concerns, housing & homelessness, environmental matters, legal aid for the arts, nonprofit organizations, clinical programs.

What are some of the areas of law in which your firm does not perform pro bono work? Personal injury.

Organizations for which your firm has performed pro bono legal services in the last two years: American Civil Liberties Union, LAMBDA, Lawyers Committee for Civil Rights, Lawyers Committee for Human Rights, Legal Aid Society, NAACP Legal Defense Fund, Public Counsel, Public Law Center, San Diego Volunteer Lawyer Program, Volunteer Lawyers for the Arts

List up to three pro bono matters that are representative of the pro bono work your firm participates in.

- Williams: class-action lawsuit alleging 6.5 million California schoolchildren have been denied their fundamental right to education under the California Constitution by failing to provide them with the basic tools necessary for education.

- NRDC: obtained permanent injunction halting the U.S. Navy's use of low-frequency sonar which was causing harm and death to whales and other marine mammals.

- Romagoza: human rights claims against former military leaders of El Salvador under the federal Alien Tort Claims Act and Torture Victim Protection Act.

BY THE NUMBERS

What is the total number of hours that lawyers in U.S. offices at your firm spent performing pro bono legal services in 2000, 2001 and 2002?

    Total number of hours in 2000: 44,615 hours
    Total number of hours in 2001: 72,985 hours
    Total number of hours in 2002: 100,224 hours

Average number of pro bono hours per attorney in U.S. offices per year (including associates, partners, counsels, but not summer associates):

    Average number of hours per attorney in 2000: 56 hours
    Average number of hours per attorney in 2001: 84 hours
    Average number of hours per attorney in 2002: 119 hours

What percentage of attorneys in this firm's U.S. offices did pro bono work in 2002? 70 percent

What percentage of attorneys in this firm's U.S. offices did at least 20 hours of pro bono work in 2002? 62 percent

Does the firm encourage its lawyers to perform a minimum number of pro bono hours? Yes

If so, how many hours per year or what percentage of lawyers' billable hours? At least 50 hours.

SUPERVISION AND EVALUATIONS

Is there partner supervision on each pro bono matter? Yes

Do partner supervisors or, if applicable, senior associates provide written evaluations of associates' work on pro bono matters? Yes

If so, are those evaluations taken into account in determining salary, bonuses or advancement in the firm? Yes

If not, does the firm consider pro bono work generally in associate evaluations? N/A

HOURS

Does the firm give billable hour credit for pro bono work? Yes

Does the firm have a maximum number of pro bono hours that can be applied toward the billable hour target? No

If so, what is the maximum? N/A

If your firm uses hours to determine bonuses, does it consider pro bono hours when determining bonuses? Yes

PRO BONO POINTS

What training opportunities are open to associates working on pro bono matters? The firm actively encourages attorneys to participate in training programs sponsored by local legal service organizations. Information regarding those programs is regularly e-mailed to all attorneys. The firm covers any costs associated with the training programs. The firm also regularly sponsors in-house training programs. Some of those training programs may include local legal service providers but others may be conducted by firm attorneys. Many of these training programs are also available online and by videotape.

Can associates bring matters of interest to the firm? Yes

Does the firm offer the use of support staff in carrying out pro bono matters? Yes

What pro bono opportunities are available for summer associates? Many of our domestic offices offer some kind of pro bono clinical program especially focused on summer associates. For instance, summer associates in our Los Angeles office participate in Public Counsel's summer program assisting individuals in applying for public benefits. Summer associates in San Francisco participate in a program assisting homeless people with a wide array of problems including landlord/tenant, public benefits, arrest warrants, SSI, child support and other issues.

Does the firm have established programs, such as externships, that enable its associates to work in a public interest setting? No

If so, where and for up to how long? The firm does not have any established externships in which our associates participate on an annual basis. However, we have loaned associates to legal service organizations to work on particular projects or to serve for a particular amount of time. Most recently, two New York attorneys worked with the Brennan Center for Justice on a voting rights case. Another New York attorney worked for Volunteers Lawyers for the Arts while continuing to be employed by the firm. We also regularly lend associates to city and county attorney offices. These opportunities primarily have been offered to senior litigation associates to provide a much-needed resource to the overburdened office since many city attorney, public defender and prosecutors' offices and other governmental entities are experiencing severe budgetary constraints. Some examples of past attorney rotation programs of one to three months include the city attorney offices in Denver, Los Angeles and San Francisco; the district attorneys offices in San Francisco, Santa Clara and Palo Alto; and the public defenders office in San Francisco.

Has your firm won any special recognition or awards in the last two years for its pro bono work? Yes

If so, please list.

- San Diego Volunteer Lawyer Program Pro Bono Law Firm of the Year, October 1, 2003 — Tribute to firm's contribution to a multitude of SDVLP's pro bono programs

- Public Advocates, Inc. "Voices of Conscience," September 25, 2003 — Williams v. State of California

- American Bar Association 2003 IOLTA Litigation Team Award — Brown v. Legal Foundation of Washington

- American Bar Association Section of Individual Rights & Responsibilities Pro Bono Service Award, August 2003 — For generous, sustained support to the ABA's Section of Individual Rights & Responsibilities

- Legal Aid Society of San Diego Outstanding Service Award, June 2003 — Legal services through collaboration with the Legal Aid Pro Bono Program

- Legal Aid Society of San Diego Wiley E. Manual Award, June 2003 — For work with the Legal Aid Society's Pro Bono Program

- Anti-Defamation League 2003 Jurisprudence Award, April 2003 — For legal assistance with amicus briefs and other legal matters

- Canyon Acres Children's Services 2003 Jim Murray Service Award, April 2003 — For providing pro bono aid in financial, facility, personnel and legal issues

- Mutual of America Community Partnership Award 2002, February 2003 — HomeAid's Shelter Development Program

- Lawyers Committee for Civil Rights of the Bay Area Anthony F. Logan Award, January 2003 — Williams v. State of California

- Legal Aid Society of New York 2002 Pro Bono Award, November 2002 — For work in representing nonprofit, low-income tenant cooperatives and a new public school in Harlem

- Lawyers Club of San Francisco Legends of law (Inaugural Award), November 13, 2002 — Recognition of his career "combining superior skills — with equal devotion to his clients, professional activities and community service."

- Maternal & Child Health Access Community Room Named after Patricia Phillips, October 8 2002 — For Patricia Phillips's outstanding work on behalf of MCH Access

- Lawyers Alliance of New York Cornerstone Award, September 2002 — For work on behalf of Claremont Neighborhood Centers

- Colorado Lawyers' Committee 2003 Individual of the Year, Stephen Kaufman — For dedication to the Colorado Lawyers Committee

- American Bar Association 2002 Pro Bono Publico Award, August 2002 — Outstanding Contribution and Dedication to Providing Pro Bono Services

- Break The Cycle Pro Bono Award, July 2002 — Outstanding Contribution of Legal Services to Organization

- Legal Aid Society of San Diego Outstanding Service Award, June 2002 — Collaboration with Legal Aid Society's Pro Bono Program

- State Bar of California, Nominated by Legal Aid Society of San Diego for Wiley M. Manual Outstanding Service Award, June 2002 — For assistance with formation of new nonprofit coordinating health care to indigent residents of San Diego County

- Legal Community Against Violence Acknowledgement, June 2002 — Work to enact effective firearms policies

- HomeAid Orange County Rainbow of Hope Award, June 2002 — Efforts in Homeless Advocacy
- U.S. Northern District Court of California Public Service Award, April 2002 — For service to the court and the legal community
- Northern California Innocence Project Acknowledgement, February 2002 — For work with the Innocence Project on drafting and filing an amicus brief before the Ninth Circuit Court of Appeals

THE FIRM SAYS

Morrison & Foerster has a long history of commitment to providing free legal services to indigent persons and in matters of public interest. Our attorneys have volunteered their time and expertise in class action cases to benefit tens of thousands of people and in thousands of other cases to help individuals who otherwise would have been denied access to the justice system. Our pro bono activities cover the full range of public interest work, from staffing legal service clinics and counseling over 150 nonprofit organizations to handling high-impact litigation. Our greatest efforts have focused on assisting children in poverty, school education issues, civil rights and civil liberties cases, international human rights and political asylum matters, and issues of housing and homelessness. An essential part of what has become known as the "MoFo Difference" is our tradition that strongly encourages and values pro bono work. One of our most important policies has been to treat our pro bono work in the same manner as we treat our billable work, including applying the same quality standards and providing full credit for pro bono work towards our associates and partners' client service hours goals.

During 2001 and 2002, our domestic attorneys contributed more than 173,000 hours representing pro bono clients, which was over 6 percent of our billable time. Over the past decade, the firm's pro bono hours have averaged in excess of 5 percent of billable hours. In July 2003, The American Lawyer magazine ranked the firm No. 4 in the AmLaw 100 for its pro bono work. We were one of the charter signatory firms, and our attorneys were instrumental in the development of the Law Firm Pro Bono Challenge, which calls upon the nation's top 500 law firms to commit to specified levels of pro bono work as a percentage of billable hours. A copy of our 2003 Pro Bono Report is available upon request.

OUR SURVEY SAYS

"The firm's reputation for pro bono is real and earned. If you want to do pro bono, there is very little to hold you back."

"Most everyone does pro bono work. The hours are treated like any other billable hours."

"We have many opportunities to do pro bono work. It is strongly encouraged, but it can be hard to fit it in with your regular caseload."

"All pro bono hours count as billable hours and are applied equally towards an hours-based bonus. There is no cap whatsoever on pro bono hours. All first-year associates are even required to take on a pro bono case for an indigent client in the Bay Area. We also have a full-time coordinator organizing all of the pro bono opportunities in the Bay Area."

"Pro bono counts the same as any billable work and is very important to the partners at MoFo."

"There are many opportunities to get involved in a variety of formal programs."

"Pro bono work provides me with more satisfaction than most other clients' projects. I am happy not to be penalized for time spent on pro bono clients as opposed to the paying ones."

"[There's] plenty of opportunity for pro bono work, including a steady stream of e-mails describing projects."

"This firm encourages pro bono participation. The partners also lead by example."

"Our reputation in this respect is well deserved."

Morrison & Foerster LLP

"Our attorneys have volunteered their time and expertise in class action cases to benefit tens of thousands of people and in thousands of other cases to help individuals who otherwise would have been denied access to the justice system."

— *Morrison & Foerster LLP*

Munger, Tolles & Olson LLP

355 South Grand Avenue, 35th Floor
Los Angeles, CA 90071-1560
Phone: (213) 683-9100
www.mto.com

LOCATIONS

Los Angeles, CA (HQ)
San Francisco, CA

MAJOR DEPARTMENTS & PRACTICES

Bankruptcy
Corporate
Environmental
Labor
Litigation
Real Estate
Tax

THE STATS

No. of attorneys worldwide: 153
No. of offices worldwide: 2
Co-Managing Partners: Robert K. Johnson and R. Gregory Morgan

EMPLOYMENT CONTACT

Ms. Kevinn C. Villard
Director of Legal Recruiting
Phone: (213) 683-9242
Fax: (213) 687-3702
E-mail: villardkc@mto.com

WHO'S WHO

Principal pro bono contact(s) at your firm:

Hojoon Hwang, Esq.
Partner
Phone: (415) 512-4000
E-mail: hwanghx@mto.com

Does the firm have a pro bono coordinator? No

If yes, what percentage of his or her time is spent on pro bono work? N/A

Does the firm have a pro bono committee? Yes

If yes, how often does the committee meet? As needed.

Describe the composition of the committee: Partners and associates. The current composition of the committee includes 65 percent associate representation.

THE SCOOP

Does your firm have a written pro bono policy? Yes

Has the firm signed on to the Law Firm Pro Bono Challenge? Yes

What are some of the areas of law in which your firm has performed pro bono legal work in the last two years? Election law, constitutional law, non-profit and exempt organization advice, copyright advice, real estate leasing advice, employment law, landlord/tenant, immigration, criminal (appeal and habeas).

What are some of the areas of law in which your firm does not perform pro bono work? Contested family law proceedings.

Organizations for which your firm has performed pro bono legal services in the last two years: Bet Tzedek, ACLU, Western Law Center for Disability Rights, Public Counsel, Lawyers' Committee for Civil Rights for the Bay Area, Alliance for Children's Rights, San Francisco Homeless Ballot Initiative, Natural History Museum of Los Angeles County, Common Cause and the Bar Association of San Francisco.

List up to three pro bono matters that are representative of the pro bono work your firm participates in.

- Writing of amici briefs in two INS cases before the United States Supreme Court challenging the basis of deportation proceedings in habeas proceedings and bail hearing restrictions for detained immigrants.

- MTO represents the Senate and House sponsors of the Bipartisan Campaign Reform Act of 2002 (also known as "McCain-Feingold" or "Shays-Meehan") as intervenor-defendants in the D.C. federal court lawsuits challenging the constitutionality of that law.

- Since 2000, MTO has worked with the Alliance for Children's Rights Adoption Day program to finalize over 65 adoptions in Los Angeles County.

BY THE NUMBERS

What is the total number of hours that lawyers in U.S. offices at your firm spent performing pro bono legal services in 2000, 2001 and 2002?

> **Total number of hours in 2000:** 6,605 hours
> **Total number of hours in 2001:** 10,525 hours
> **Total number of hours in 2002:** 12,338 hours

Average number of pro bono hours per attorney in U.S. offices per year (including associates, partners, counsels, but not summer associates):

> **Average number of hours per attorney in 2000:** Approximately 50 hours
> **Average number of hours per attorney in 2001:** Approximately 70 hours
> **Average number of hours per attorney in 2002:** Approximately 80 hours

What percentage of attorneys in this firm's U.S. offices did pro bono work in 2002? 73 percent (112 out of 153)

What percentage of attorneys in this firm's U.S. offices did at least 20 hours of pro bono work in 2002? 46 percent (71 out of 153)

Does the firm encourage its lawyers to perform a minimum number of pro bono hours? No

If so, how many hours or what percentage of lawyers' billable hours? N/A

SUPERVISION AND EVALUATIONS

Is there partner supervision on each pro bono matter? Yes

Do partner supervisors or, if applicable, senior associates provide written evaluations of associates' work on pro bono matters? No. Feedback and evaluation is mostly oral.

If so, are those evaluations taken into account in determining salary, bonuses or advancement in the firm? Yes

If not, does the firm consider pro bono work generally in associate evaluations? Yes

HOURS

Does the firm give billable hour credit for pro bono work? The firm does not have a billable hour requirement.

Does the firm have a maximum number of pro bono hours that can be applied toward the billable hour target? N/A

If so, what is the maximum? N/A

If your firm uses hours to determine bonuses, does it consider pro bono hours when determining bonuses? Not applicable

PRO BONO POINTS

What training opportunities are open to associates working on pro bono matters? In addition to training by supervising attorneys, all attorneys have the opportunity to participate in training provided by the various organizations with which we partner in particular areas of law.

Can associates bring matters of interest to the firm? Yes

Does the firm offer the use of support staff in carrying out pro bono matters? Yes

What pro bono opportunities are available for summer associates? Pro bono projects are available in the same manner as projects on billable matters.

Does the firm have established programs, such as externships, that enable its associates to work in a public interest setting? Yes

If so, where and for up to how long? We have a program with local district attorneys' offices for training and outplacement. The program can be up to six months.

Has your firm won any special recognition or awards in the last two years for its pro bono work? Yes

If so, please list. 2003: Free Speech/GLBT Rights Award by the ACLU Foundation of Southern California presented to partner David Dinielli and associate Linda Burrow in recognition of their outstanding work in defending the First Amendment rights of gays and lesbians. The award also recognizes the contributions of MTO attorneys Amy Boyd, Megan La Belle, Aaron May, Michael Murphy and paralegal Raphael Sepulveda.

2003: The Margaret Sanger Leadership Award presented to Munger, Tolles & Olson LLP for pro bono service to Planned Parenthood Los Angeles.

2002: Voting Rights Award by the ACLU of Southern California.

2002: Sproul Lifetime Achievement Award, Lawyers' Committee on Civil Rights, to San Francisco partner Jeff Bleich.

THE FIRM SAYS

At Munger, Tolles & Olson LLP, we view our pro bono work as a responsibility that we have as professionals and as citizens to assure a fair and just legal system. MTO lawyers have a history of being committed to providing high quality pro bono service. The firm was one of the charter signatories to the Law Firm Pro Bono Challenge and consistently devotes more than 3 percent of all attorney time to delivering needed pro bono legal assistance. In recognition of our pro bono service, Munger Tolles received the ABA's coveted Pro Bono Publico Award. The firm has received several other honors, including the State Bar of California's law firm pro bono award, in recognition of our pro bono contributions. One of the annual awards given by the Western Law Center for Disability Rights bears the name of MTO partner Chuck Siegal, who served as president of the board of directors for several years. In 2002, individual attorneys at MTO received the 2002 Voting Rights Award of the ACLU Foundation of Southern California and the Lawyers' Committee for Civil Rights for the Bay Area's Robert Sproul Jr. Lifetime Achievement Award.

As part of our pro bono commitment, we frequently represent indigent and other under-represented individuals. We have successfully tried cases on behalf of a class of capital prisoners in Oklahoma and Texas challenging the method of execution and a class of homeless people in San Francisco who were arrested for resting or sleeping in public, and we prevailed in an appeal before the Ninth Circuit establishing that an expunged foreign criminal conviction for a minor drug possession offense cannot be the basis for deportation. We also have staffed legal clinics for Bet Tzedek, Public Counsel, the Lawyers' Committee for Civil Rights for the Bay Area and the Federal Court Referral Panel. These matters have included providing legal assistance to indigent individuals on matters involving landlord-tenant disputes, government benefits, political asylum, school expulsions, mortgage fraud and credit problems. In addition, we have successfully represented inmates in actions against the Pelican Bay State Prison, including a recent case in which an inmate sued a prison doctor for diagnosing him with Hepatitis C and then failing to tell him that he had contracted the disease or to provide him with any treatment for it, and application of the Americans with Disabilities Act and California disability rights law to the freeway callbox system.

Our commitment to pro bono also includes investing ourselves in the clients we serve. We serve as general counsel to Coro Southern California, and several attorneys serve on the boards of directors and provide direct services to organizations including the Lawyers' Committee for Civil Rights in the Bay Area, Public Counsel and the Legal Aid Society Employment Law Center. One of the annual awards given by the Western Law Center for Disability Rights bears the name of MTO partner Charles D. Siegal, who served as president of the board of directors for several years.

OUR SURVEY SAYS

"The firm is very supportive of pro bono work."

"[There is] tremendous community involvement by lawyers (for example, a Munger partner, Jeff Bleich, is currently president of the San Francisco Bar Association). People from the firm occupy leadership positions in virtually every major legal services, pro bono and bar organization in the state. The firm strongly encourages associates to become involved in pro bono and community work."

"Pro bono hours count just like billables. In excess of 20 percent of my hours last year were pro bono and I still received a nice bonus."

"This is one of the best things about the firm."

"I know some associates have spent up to hundreds of hours in the last year on such matters."

"Everyone I know does a fair amount of pro bono. The firm lets you take on what you want and treats it like any other case."

"The firm encourages attorneys to do pro bono work and counts pro bono hours toward attorneys' total billables. We have at least one attorney whose practice is almost entirely pro bono work, and his pay is commensurate with his peers."

"You can do any pro bono work you want, whenever you want, so long as there is no conflict issue."

"The firm was one of the charter signatories to the Law Firm Pro Bono Challenge and consistently devotes more than 3 percent of all attorney time to delivering needed pro bono legal assistance."

— *Munger, Tolles & Olson LLP*

O'Melveny & Myers LLP

400 South Hope Street
Los Angeles, CA 90071-2899
Phone: (213) 430-6000
www.omm.com

LOCATIONS

Los Angeles, CA (HQ)
Century City, CA
Irvine, CA
Menlo Park, CA
New York, NY
Newport Beach, CA
San Francisco, CA
Washington, DC
Beijing
Hong Kong
London
Shanghai
Tokyo

MAJOR DEPARTMENTS & PRACTICES

Antitrust & Trade Regulation
Business Counseling
Class Action Defense
Emerging Companies/Venture Capital
Employee Benefits/Executive Compensation
Entertainment, Sports & Media
Environmental Law & Natural Resources
Financing
Government Relations & Regulatory Practice
Health Care
Intellectual Property & Technology
International
Labor & Employment
Litigation
M&A
Project Finance
Real Estate
Tax & Estate Planning
Telecommunications
White Collar Criminal Defense

THE STATS

No. of attorneys worldwide: 900 +
No. of offices worldwide: 13
Chairman: Arthur B. Culvahouse Jr.

EMPLOYMENT CONTACT

Ms. Jacqueline Wilson
Recruiting Administrator
Phone: (202) 383-5300
Fax: (202) 383-5414
E-mail: jwilson@omm.com

WHO'S WHO

Does the firm have a pro bono coordinator? Yes

John Daum, Esq.
Chair, Community Legal Services Committee
Phone: (213) 430-6111
E-mail: jdaum@omm.com

David A. Lash, Esq.
Managing Counsel for Pro Bono and Public Interest Services (California)
Phone: (213) 430-8366
E-mail: dlash@omm.com

If yes, what percentage of his or her time is spent on pro bono work? 15 percent

Does the firm have a pro bono committee? Yes

If yes, how often does the committee meet? The firm's community legal services committee does not meet in person. It conducts its business through e-mail, and does so on a daily basis.

Describe the composition of the committee: Partners and associates from each of the firm's domestic offices. The committee has a total of roughly 10 members.

THE SCOOP

Does your firm have a written pro bono policy? Yes

Has the firm signed on to the Law Firm Pro Bono Challenge? Yes

What are some of the areas of law in which your firm has performed pro bono legal work in the last two years? Civil rights/discrimination, criminal defense, appellate, housing, immigration, corporate governance, nonprofit tax, consumer fraud and adoptions.

What are some of the areas of law in which your firm does not perform pro bono work? Employee rights, government benefits, most aspects of family law.

Organizations for which your firm has performed pro bono legal services in the last two years: Legal Aid Foundation of Los Angeles, Office of Public Counsel, Bet Tzedek Legal Services, Alliance for Children's Rights, Habitat for Humanity, Lawyers Committee for Civil Rights of the San Francisco Bay Area, United States Court of Appeals for the Ninth Circuit (Appellate Project), Montgomery County (Maryland) Public Defender's Office, Washington (D.C.) Area Lawyers For The Arts, Anti-Defamation League.

List up to three pro bono matters that are representative of the pro bono work your firm participates in. Wen Ho Lee: defense of accused spy. Henkle v. Gregory: representation of gay high school student being harassed because of his sexual orientation. Brown v. Legal Foundation of Washington: support of IOLTA program before U.S. Supreme Court.

BY THE NUMBERS

What is the total number of hours that lawyers in U.S. offices at your firm spent performing pro bono legal services in 2000, 2001 and 2002?

> Total number of hours in 2000: 25,031 hours
> Total number of hours in 2001: 24,223 hours
> Total number of hours in 2002: 22,455 hours

Average number of pro bono hours per attorney in U.S. offices per year (including associates, partners, counsels, but not summer associates):

> Average number of hours per attorney in 2000: 35 hours
> Average number of hours per attorney in 2001: 32 hours
> Average number of hours per attorney in 2002: 26 hours

What percentage of attorneys in this firm's U.S. offices did pro bono work in 2002? 36 percent

What percentage of attorneys in this firm's U.S. offices did at least 20 hours of pro bono work in 2002? 20 percent

Does the firm encourage its lawyers to perform a minimum number of pro bono hours? No. The minimum number of pro bono hours is left up to the discretion of the individual attorneys, the firm believing this to be a matter of personal choice. The firm's values statement, policies and pronouncements encourage all to participate and to be a part of the firm effort to achieve the standards set by the Law Firm Pro Bono Challenge. However, no stated per attorney minimum exists.

If so, how many hours per year or what percentage of lawyers' billable hours? N/A

SUPERVISION AND EVALUATIONS

Is there partner supervision on each pro bono matter? Yes

Do partner supervisors or, if applicable, senior associates provide written evaluations of associates' work on pro bono matters? Yes, to the same extent as for all other work performed by associates.

If so, are those evaluations taken into account in determining salary, bonuses or advancement in the firm? Yes

If not, does the firm consider pro bono work generally in associate evaluations? N/A

HOURS

Does the firm give billable hour credit for pro bono work? Yes

Does the firm have a maximum number of pro bono hours that can be applied toward the billable hour target? No

If so, what is the maximum? N/A

If your firm uses hours to determine bonuses, does it consider pro bono hours when determining bonuses? N/A

PRO BONO POINTS

What training opportunities are open to associates working on pro bono matters? Hands on experience — trials, depositions, oral arguments (both at trial and appellate level), brief-writing, client contact, advice and counsel.

Can associates bring matters of interest to the firm? Yes

Does the firm offer the use of support staff in carrying out pro bono matters? Yes

What pro bono opportunities are available for summer associates? Assisting with ongoing projects; special projects from local legal aid organizations.

Does the firm have established programs, such as externships, that enable its associates to work in a public interest setting? No

Has your firm won any special recognition or awards in the last two years for its pro bono work? Yes

If so, please list. The firm received a pro bono award from the American Bar Association at its 2003 annual convention for its work in support of IOLTA programs in Brown v. Legal Foundation of Washington. The firm also was honored by the Hetrick-Martin Institution at the 23rd annual Emery S. Hetrick Awards in 2002, for its work on behalf of Derek Henkle in Henkle v. Gregory.

THE FIRM SAYS

O'Melveny & Myers LLP has a long history of commitment to the community. Firm founder John O'Melveny was a co-founder of the Legal Aid Foundation of Los Angeles, the oldest and largest provider of free legal services to the poor in Southern California. Firm lawyers sit on the boards of directors of major legal services organizations in Los Angeles, New York, San Francisco and Washington, D.C. Commitment to community is a key part of the firm's articulated values.

Lawyers at O'Melveny & Myers are encouraged to participate in community activities. Primary among these activities is representing indigent clients in a pro bono capacity. All firm lawyers are given full billable credit for every hour recorded on pro bono matters, and pro bono hours may be used to fulfill all firm billing expectations, including bonus consideration. Firm lawyers are welcome to bring proposed pro bono engagements to the Community Legal Services ("CLS") Committee.

In addition, regular announcements of available pro bono opportunities come from the firm's new managing counsel of pro bono & public interest services. At the present time, these opportunities involve the firm's six California offices. All proposed pro bono engagements are forwarded to the CLS Committee for discussion and approval. Chaired by firm partner Chris Hollinger, the committee conducts its business electronically and "convenes" on an as-needed basis — generally, several days each week. Formal internal case files are opened for all approved matters, billing numbers are assigned, time is accurately recorded, full conflicts checks are done and a partner is assigned to participate in, and supervise, every such matter.

The firm encourages its litigators and non-litigators, alike, to participate in pro bono matters. As a result, the firm handles a wide variety of matters that provide diverse experiences for the lawyers and a wide impact on the under-served members of the community. New lawyers get unique hands-on experience in representing low-income clients in housing cases, adoptions, domestic violence and abuse cases, slum housing matters and much more. Others handle incorporation and tax status matters for fledgling nonprofits, or negotiate with municipal governments over child care and zoning ordinances.

Additionally, the firm is widely known for handling cases of great impact. O'Melveny attorneys represented a young man who was being brutally harassed in a public school because of his sexual orientation. Achieving an extraordinary result, the case garnered wide publicity that has affected the way schools and school districts across the country deal with gay and lesbian students. The firm also represented accused spy Wen Ho Lee, and won a great victory in this closely-watched case. Last term, the firm represented the justices of the Washington Supreme Court in one of the most important cases ever to deal with the hopes of the poor. O'Melveny lawyers succeeded in convincing the U.S. Supreme Court that Washington's IOLTA (Interest on Lawyers' Trust Account) program was a constitutionally permissible way to raise more than $150 million annually to support legal services to the poor in all 50 states.

OUR SURVEY SAYS

"The firm has a reasonably strong commitment to pro bono work. All approved pro bono work (and approval does not appear to be a problem) counts toward annual minimum billable hours. There is no limit on the number of pro bono hours that will count toward billable hours. There is pressure to take on client billable hours that can interfere with the ability to actually get involved in the pro bono program."

"There is no cap on pro bono hours and all pro bono hours go towards your minimum billables and your bonus. We have a lot of great opportunities here and the firm welcomes new pro bono clients brought in by associates."

"The firm as a whole has a huge commitment to pro bono work. This is, however, not entirely reflected in the New York office as much as in the LA office."

"O'Melveny has traditionally been very good about giving associates excellent pro bono opportunities, but there are signs that this too will give way to the increasing focus on profits. It is becoming increasingly difficult to get pro bono projects approved by the committee."

"Six or seven of us billed well over 200 hours on pro bono matters last year."

"Pro bono is a big part of the firm. The fact that all pro bono hours count towards billables is very generous."

"Pro bono work is treated as regular billable hours and pro bono projects get the same attention, quality and respect as billable projects."

"Pro bono work isn't formally encouraged, but I've never heard of anyone being encouraged against it, or feeling as though it wasn't welcome. I filled up a couple of slow months last year with pro bono work and had no difficulty with the firm as a result. And, since pro bono hours go towards our billable totals, they even helped me move to a higher bonus category."

"Our firm bills more pro bono hours than almost any of our peers — and high-impact pro bono work is celebrated and rewarded."

"Strong commitment, but with a focus on taking engagements with a very high profile and/or ones that provide great learning opportunities."

"New lawyers get unique hands-on experience in representing low-income clients in housing cases, adoptions, domestic violence and abuse cases, slum housing matters and much more."

— *O'Melveny & Myers LLP*

Orrick, Herrington & Sutcliffe LLP

Old Federal Reserve Bank Building
400 Sansome Street
San Francisco, CA 94111-3143
Phone: (415) 392-1122
www.orrick.com

LOCATIONS

San Francisco, CA (HQ)
Irvine, CA
Los Angeles, CA
Menlo Park, CA
New York, NY
Portland, OR
Sacramento, CA
Seattle, WA
Washington, DC
London
Milan
Paris
Tokyo

MAJOR DEPARTMENTS & PRACTICES

Antitrust & Competition
Bankruptcy & Debt Restructuring
Compensation & Benefits
Corporate
Employment Law
Energy & Project Finance
Institutional Finance, Banking & Private
Investment Funds
Intellectual Property
Leasing
Litigation
Mergers & Acquisitions
Public Finance
Real Estate
Structured Finance
Tax

THE STATS

No. of attorneys worldwide: 675
No. of offices worldwide: 13
Chairman and CEO: Ralph H. Baxter Jr.

EMPLOYMENT CONTACTS

San Francisco
Ms. Karen Massa
Recruiting Administrator
Phone: (415) 773-5588
Fax: (415) 773-5759
E-mail: kmassa@orrick.com

Silicon Valley
Ms. Rebecca Whittall
Recruiting Manager
Phone: (650) 614-7352
Fax: (650) 614-7401
E-mail: rwhittall@orrick.com

New York
Ms. Francesca Runge
Lateral Recruiting Manager
Phone: (212) 506-3556
Fax: (212) 506-5151
E-mail: frunge@orrick.com

Ms. Jennifer Youngquist
Recruiting Administrator
Phone: (212) 506-3553
Fax: (212) 506-5151
E-mail: jyoungquist@orrick.com

Orrick, Herrington & Sutcliffe LLP

WHO'S WHO

Principal pro bono contact(s) at your firm:

Jill Rosenberg, Esq.
Partner
Phone: (212) 506-5215
E-mail: jrose@orrick.com

Does the firm have a pro bono coordinator? Yes. The firm has one pro bono coordinator for the entire firm, and one associate and one partner-in-charge of pro bono in each of its offices in the United States.

If yes, what percentage of his or her time is spent on pro bono work? Up to 2 percent in any year (for each of the coordinators).

Does the firm have a pro bono committee? Yes

If yes, how often does the committee meet? The committee meets once every two months.

Describe the composition of the committee: The committee is composed of eight partners and nine associates. Orrick's Washington, D.C., Los Angeles, New York, Pacific Northwest, Sacramento, San Francisco and Silicon Valley offices are represented.

THE SCOOP

Does your firm have a written pro bono policy? Yes

Has the firm signed on to the Law Firm Pro Bono Challenge? Yes

What are some of the areas of law in which your firm has performed pro bono legal work in the last two years? Orrick has performed pro bono legal work in the following areas: family and matrimonial law, landlord/tenant, international human rights, employment counseling, employment litigation, general commercial litigation, criminal defense, civil rights, general corporate, including incorporation and tax exemption, real estate and intellectual property work.

What are some of the areas of law in which your firm does not perform pro bono work? None unless precluded from representing clients due to a conflict.

Organizations for which your firm has performed pro bono legal services in the last two years: Capital Appellate Project, Legal Aid Society, Lawyers Committee for Human Rights, Lawyers' Committee for Civil Rights under Law, New York City Gay and Lesbian Anti-Violence Project, The Northern California Innocence Project, inMotion, Inc., Sanctuary for Families, Lawyers Alliance for New York, Volunteer Lawyers for the Arts, New York Legal Assistance Group, Public Counsel, California Lawyers for the Arts, Bar Association of San Francisco – Volunteer Legal Services Program, New York City Bar Association, California Council for the Humanities.

List up to three pro bono matters that are representative of the pro bono work your firm participates in.

- An Orrick associate in the New York office, through his pro bono work with a tenants' group, spearheaded the drafting of a bill to preserve affordable housing in New York City.

- Orrick lawyers in the Sacramento office were victorious in reversing a death penalty sentence for an inmate, in a decision affirmed by the Supreme Court of the United States after 14 years of federal and state court litigation.
- Orrick lawyers in the New York office secured the summary dismissal of a defamation suit brought against the New York City Gay and Lesbian Anti-Violence Project.

BY THE NUMBERS

What is the total number of hours that lawyers in U.S. offices at your firm spent performing pro bono legal services in 2000, 2001 and 2002?

    Total number of hours in 2000: 12,454.98 hours
    Total number of hours in 2001: 14,437.27 hours
    Total number of hours in 2002: 15,273.01 hours

Average number of pro bono hours per attorney in U.S. offices per year (including associates, partners, counsels, but not summer associates):

    Average number of hours per attorney in 2000: 25.32 hours
    Average number of hours per attorney in 2001: 27.14 hours
    Average number of hours per attorney in 2002: 29.06 hours

What percentage of attorneys in this firm's U.S. offices did pro bono work in 2002? 43.49 percent

What percentage of attorneys in this firm's U.S. offices did at least 20 hours of pro bono work in 2002? 24.53 percent

Does the firm encourage its lawyers to perform a minimum number of pro bono hours? No

SUPERVISION AND EVALUATIONS

Is there partner supervision on each pro bono matter? Yes

Do partner supervisors or, if applicable, senior associates provide written evaluations of associates' work on pro bono matters? Yes

If so, are those evaluations taken into account in determining salary, bonuses or advancement in the firm? Yes

If not, does the firm consider pro bono work generally in associate evaluations? N/A

HOURS

Does the firm give billable hour credit for pro bono work? Yes

Does the firm have a maximum number of pro bono hours that can be applied toward the billable hour target? No

If so, what is the maximum? N/A

If your firm uses hours to determine bonuses, does it consider pro bono hours when determining bonuses? Yes

PRO BONO POINTS

What training opportunities are open to associates working on pro bono matters? New associates are encouraged to attend training sessions organized by third parties, including the Bar Association of the City of New York, Lawyers Committee for Human Rights, inMotion, Inc., Volunteer Lawyers for the Arts, Sanctuary for Families and the Legal Aid Society.

Can associates bring matters of interest to the firm? Yes

Does the firm offer the use of support staff in carrying out pro bono matters? Yes

What pro bono opportunities are available for summer associates? Summer associates in New York have the opportunity to participate in two pro bono programs in which the firm participates. First is the inMotion Family Justice Program through which teams of two associates represent indigent women who are victims of domestic violence in contested or uncontested divorce actions. Second is the Lawyers Committee for Human Rights summer associate program through which associates represent individuals seeking political asylum in the United States. Summer associates in San Francisco have the opportunity to participate in the Lawyers Committee for Civil Rights Legal Services Project for the indigent.

Does the firm have established programs, such as externships, that enable its associates to work in a public interest setting? No

Has your firm won any special recognition or awards in the last two years for its pro bono work? Yes

If so, please list. Lawyers' Committee for Human Rights of the San Francisco Bay Area's "Keta Taylor Colby Award" presented to an associate in the firm's San Francisco office, January 2003. Legal Services of Northern California's "Special Pro Bono Service Award" presented to a partner in the firm's Sacramento office, October 2002. Lawyers Alliance for New York's "Cornerstone Award" presented to an associate in the firm's New York office, May 2001. Legal Aid Society of New York's "Outstanding Contribution Award" for 2002, recognizing an associate in the firm's New York office, January 2002.

THE FIRM SAYS

Pro bono contributions are an important part of Orrick's tradition and culture. While many firms have reduced their contributions, our commitment to legal volunteerism is absolute: Orrick is one of a shrinking number of firms that counts a lawyer's pro bono hours toward their billable requirement. Including pro bono work as "billable" is intended to emphasize the firm's deep commitment to pro bono work and to encourage the pro bono efforts of our associates. We recognize that work on a pro bono matter may occupy a substantial amount of an associate's time during a particular year and we believe that it is entirely appropriate. Attorneys are given the opportunity to take on pro bono matters that they are interested in, and are never assigned to such matters. As such, attorneys, including junior-level associates, generally run their own pro bono project and thus can develop substantial professional development in the process. In addition to our pro bono work and serving on boards of various nonprofit organizations, Orrick attorneys and professional staff organize food and toy drives during the holidays, volunteer to teach in local schools and participate in a variety of fundraising and volunteer days.

OUR SURVEY SAYS

"Orrick is in the process of revamping its pro bono program in order to focus on projects and commitments where we can really make a difference. Everyone acknowledges that our pro bono efforts have not been what they should, and there is a real commitment to changing that. We are off to a great start — for example, with our commitment to pro bono partnership with the National Center for Lesbian Rights."

"Orrick is strongly committed to pro bono work, and I personally work 50 to 100 pro bono hours per year."

"It varies by individual, but the firm puts no maximum on the number of pro bono hours that count toward billables. It may be that they can afford to do this because the firm is more than half transactional and transactional lawyers do much less pro bono than litigators."

"I have never been questioned about the amount of pro bono work I do and it counts 100 percent towards my billable requirements (and bonus!)."

"There is no limit on the amount of pro bono hours that the firm will count as billable hours. We are also provided many opportunities to take on pro bono cases. However, we are very busy with our commercial work and it is sometimes hard to find time to take on pro bono cases for this reason."

"I've been very busy with pro bono work and the partners I work with have not hesitated in lending assistance and guidance."

"Our litigation department has taken on a number of time-consuming pro bono matters. As a transactional lawyer, I have never been encouraged to do pro bono work, but starting this year there's been a big push from upper management to do it."

"[The firm is] very committed in terms of giving full billable credit; very few partners participate, however, and involvement is occasionally criticized."

"Pro bono hours are counted towards the billable hours requirements needed to achieve a bonus. An unlimited amount of hours may be considered, which is great. However, there is no real pro bono program, and although pro bono work is encouraged and supported, attorneys need to be proactive if they want to take on any pro bono projects."

"Who has the time?"

"Attorneys, including junior-level associates, generally run their own pro bono project and thus can develop substantial professional development in the process."

— *Orrick, Herrington & Sutcliffe LLP*

Palmer & Dodge LLP

111 Huntington Avenue
Boston, MA 02199
Phone: (617) 239-0100
www.palmerdodge.com

LOCATIONS

Boston, MA

MAJOR DEPARTMENTS & PRACTICES

Affordable Housing Finance
Antitrust
Bankruptcy, Reorganization & Workout
Business Law
Construction
Employee Benefits & Executive Compensation
Energy
Environmental & Land Use
Finance
Information Technology
Insurance
Intellectual Property
International
Investment Management
Labor & Employment
Life Sciences
Litigation
Mergers & Acquisitions
Patent
Private Client
Probate Litigation
Product Liability & Negligence Defense
Public Law
Public Offerings & Public Companies
Real Estate
Schools & Colleges
Tax
Telecommunications
Transportation
Venture Capital & Private Equity

THE STATS

No. of attorneys worldwide: 170 +
No. of offices worldwide: 1
Managing Partner: Jeffrey F. Jones

EMPLOYMENT CONTACT

Ms. Katy von Mehren
Phone: (617) 239-0172
Fax: (617) 227-4420
E-mail: kvonmehren@palmerdodge.com

WHO'S WHO

Principal pro bono contact(s) at your firm:

Tamara Wolfson, Esq.
Pro Bono Chair
E-mail: twolfson@palmerdodge.com

Does the firm have a pro bono coordinator? No

Does the firm have a pro bono committee? Yes

If yes, how often does the committee meet? Approximately six times per year.

Describe the composition of the committee: Three partners, one counsel, two associates, one legal assistant.

THE SCOOP

Does your firm have a written pro bono policy? Yes

Has the firm signed on to the Law Firm Pro Bono Challenge? No

What are some of the areas of law in which your firm has performed pro bono legal work in the last two years? Corporate law, litigation, real estate.

What are some of the areas of law in which your firm does not perform pro bono work? Requests for pro bono representation are considered on a matter-by-matter basis, but we generally do not accept divorce and child custody matters for pro bono representation.

Organizations for which your firm has performed pro bono legal services in the last two years: Boston Bar Association Business Law Pro Bono Project, Economic Justice Project of the Lawyers Committee for Civil Rights Under Law, Greater Boston Legal Services, Habitat for Humanity, Lawyers Clearinghouse on Affordable Housing and Homelessness, Lawyers Committee for Civil Rights Under Law of the Boston Bar Association, Massachusetts Housing Partnership Fund's Soft Second Loan Program, Trust For Public Land, Volunteer Lawyers For the Arts of Massachusetts, Volunteer Lawyers Project of the Boston Bar Association.

List up to three pro bono matters that are representative of the pro bono work your firm participates in.

- Political Asylum/Immigration Representation Project (PAIR). Over the past three years, Palmer & Dodge has worked on behalf of immigrants seeking political asylum in the United States after they were forced to flee their homelands due to political persecution including torture and imprisonment. During this time, Palmer & Dodge has successfully represented individuals and families from Cameroon, Uganda and Haiti.

- Boston Community Loan Fund (BCLF). Since 1986, Palmer & Dodge has represented BCLF, a nonprofit financial intermediary that provides below-market loans to community-based organizations to create and rehabilitate affordable housing in the Boston area. Over the past 17 years, with Palmer & Dodge's assistance, BCLF has made numerous loans to nonprofit organizations, has helped to create or preserve several units of affordable housing.

- Post- Conviction Death Penalty Appeal. Since 1989, Palmer & Dodge has represented an inmate on death row in Alabama in his post-conviction challenge to his conviction and death sentence. Palmer and Dodge attorneys devoted

several thousand hours to this matter. Due to their efforts, the client was awarded an evidentiary hearing on issues raised in his petition for post-conviction relief and is awaiting a decision on that petition.

BY THE NUMBERS

What is the total number of hours that lawyers in U.S. offices at your firm spent performing pro bono legal services in 2000, 2001 and 2002?

    Total number of hours in 2000: 7,556 hours
    Total number of hours in 2001: 8,224 hours
    Total number of hours in 2002: 10,773 hours

Average number of pro bono hours per attorney in U.S. offices per year (including associates, partners, counsels, but not summer associates):

    Average number of hours per attorney in 2000: 37.4 hours
    Average number of hours per attorney in 2001: 40.5 hours
    Average number of hours per attorney in 2002: 65.3 hours

What percentage of attorneys in this firm's U.S. offices did pro bono work in 2002? 77.5 percent

What percentage of attorneys in this firm's U.S. offices did at least 20 hours of pro bono work in 2002? 46.6 percent

Does the firm encourage its lawyers to perform a minimum number of pro bono hours? Yes

If so, how many hours per year or what percentage of lawyers' billable hours? 25 hours

SUPERVISION AND EVALUATIONS

Is there partner supervision on each pro bono matter? Yes

Do partner supervisors or, if applicable, senior associates provide written evaluations of associates' work on pro bono matters? Yes

If so, are those evaluations taken into account in determining salary, bonuses or advancement in the firm? Yes

If not, does the firm consider pro bono work generally in associate evaluations? N/A

HOURS

Does the firm give billable hour credit for pro bono work? Yes

Does the firm have a maximum number of pro bono hours that can be applied toward the billable hour target? No

If so, what is the maximum? N/A

If your firm uses hours to determine bonuses, does it consider pro bono hours when determining bonuses? Yes

PRO BONO POINTS

What training opportunities are open to associates working on pro bono matters? A variety of formal and informal training opportunities are available for associates working on pro bono matters. Associates are permitted and encouraged to attend pertinent training programs put on by pro bono and continuing education organizations. Where interest in the firm warrants, Palmer & Dodge will host a training session at the firm. In addition, associates receive feedback and training from the senior associates and partners supervising the matter.

Can associates bring matters of interest to the firm? Yes

Does the firm offer the use of support staff in carrying out pro bono matters? Yes

What pro bono opportunities are available for summer associates? We offer a variety of opportunities depending on which cases are active during the summer months. Pro bono work is assigned to summer associates as part of their regular work load. In addition, all summer associates participate in the Unemployment Compensation Program, through which summer associates and first year associates, under the supervision of more senior litigation associates, represent individuals who have been denied unemployment benefits at hearings before the Massachusetts Division of Employment and Training.

Does the firm have established programs, such as externships, that enable its associates to work in a public interest setting? No

Has your firm won any special recognition or awards in the last two years for its pro bono work? Yes

If so, please list. Amy Berks received the 2003 Pro Bono Attorney Award from the Political Asylum/Immigration Representation Project for her efforts in obtaining asylum in the United States for political refugees from Uganda and Cameroon. Jen Izzo received an Attorney Special Recognition Award from the Massachusetts Housing Partnership Fund in 2003 for her representation of several first-time homebuyers through the Soft Second Legal Services Program. Christine O'Connor, Anne Robbins and Katie Davenport were the recipients of the 2003 Dennis Maguire Pro Bono Award, given annually by the Volunteer Lawyers Project of the Boston Bar Association. Chris was honored for her efforts in supervising the Unemployment Compensation Program, through which summer and first-year associates, under the supervision of more senior litigation and labor associates, represent individuals denied unemployment benefits in hearings before the Division of Employment and Training. Anne and Katie were honored for their successful representation of an elderly and disabled gentlemen in a specific performance case in which the client was at risk of losing his long-time home. Palmer & Dodge was recognized as an honoree at the June 2002 ground breaking for the Garden of Peace memorial to homicide victims. Betty Lo Cualio and Art Page assisted with the incorporation of the Garden of Peace organization and with obtaining nonprofit status for the organization.

In addition to the awards received from outside organizations, Palmer & Dodge also recognizes outstanding pro bono contributions and achievements by firm lawyers at its annual pro bono reception and award program.

THE FIRM SAYS

Palmer & Dodge has a distinguished tradition of pro bono legal services. That tradition is rooted in founding partner Moorfield Storey's dedication to anti-segretionist causes, including his nearly 20 years of service as president of the NAACP. The firm expects all of its lawyers to participate in activities that serve the pro bono obligations of the profession. The firm particularly desires to continue its strong commitment to providing legal services on behalf of indigent people who have no other effective means of obtaining counsel; unempowered groups, including children, the elderly, and persons with disabilities; and persons who have been denied their civil rights and liberties. The firm also has a long-time commitment to defense of the environment and natural resources and support of literature and the arts. The pro bono committee is responsible for encouraging lawyers in all areas of the firm to participate in pro bono activities, tracking the range and extent of pro bono activity and encouraging coordination among lawyers to assure that pro bono undertakings are carried out efficiently and effectively. Pro bono hours count in full toward the billable hours target for associates and counsel and also are considered in determining annual bonuses.

OUR SURVEY SAYS

"The firm management supports pro bono well. Some individual partners are unsupportive or against it."

"Full credit is given for pro bono work."

"Our firm strongly encourages all lawyers and paralegals to do pro bono work, and pro bono hours are billable."

"Every associate I know is deeply enmeshed in at least one pro bono case. Half of my hours last year were devoted to pro bono, and the partners were fine with that. I still got a hefty bonus. The partners are also willing to supervise associates with pro bono work. Everyone here takes it very seriously and devotes the same level of care to pro bono clients as to paying clients."

"Pro bono hours count toward the billable hour requirement and are encouraged."

"This firm is very committed to pro bono. There are lots of opportunities to do pro bono work and the firm provides awards to notable contributors. Pro bono time counts towards billable hours as well as for bonus purposes."

Palmer & Dodge LLP

"Over the past three years, Palmer & Dodge has worked on behalf of immigrants seeking political asylum in the United States after they were forced to flee their homelands due to political persecution including torture and imprisonment."

— *Palmer & Dodge LLP*

Patton Boggs LLP

2550 M Street, NW
Washington, DC 20037
Phone: (202) 457-6000
www.pattonboggs.com

LOCATIONS

Washington, DC (HQ)
Anchorage, AK
Dallas, TX
Denver, CO
McLean, VA

MAJOR DEPARTMENTS & PRACTICES

Administrative & Regulatory
Business Transactions
Communications & Technology
Litigation & Dispute Resolution
Public Policy

THE STATS

No. of attorneys worldwide: 369
No. of offices worldwide: 5
Chairman: Thomas Hale Boggs Jr.
Managing Partner: Stuart M. Pape

EMPLOYMENT CONTACT

Ms. Kara P. Reidy
Director of Professional Recruitment
Phone: (202) 457-6000
Fax: (202) 457-6315
E-mail: kreidy@pattonbogs.com

WHO'S WHO

Principal pro bono contact(s) at your firm:

Steven M. Schneebaum, Esq.
Chairman, Pro Bono Committee
Phone: (202) 457-6300
E-mail: sschneebaum@pattonboggs.com

Melanie K. Gerber, Esq.
Public Service Counsel
Phone: (202) 457-6312
E-mail: mgerber@pattonboggs.com

Does the firm have a pro bono coordinator? Yes
Melanie K. Gerber, Esq.

If yes, what percentage of his or her time is spent on pro bono work? 100 percent

Does the firm have a pro bono committee? Yes

If yes, how often does the committee meet? About once every three months.

Describe the composition of the committee: 12 partners, 11 associates and two legal assistants.

THE SCOOP

Does your firm have a written pro bono policy? Yes

Has the firm signed on to the Law Firm Pro Bono Challenge? Yes

What are some of the areas of law in which your firm has performed pro bono legal work in the last two years? Public policy, immigration, death penalty, domestic relations, international human rights, general civil litigation, landlord-tenant cases, child welfare and adoption services, civil rights.

What are some of the areas of law in which your firm does not perform pro bono work? Criminal (except death penalty).

Organizations for which your firm has performed pro bono legal services in the last two years: Archdiocesan Legal Network, Legal Counsel for the Elderly, DC Employment Justice Center, Washington Lawyers' Committee for Civil Rights & Urban Affairs, Capital Area Immigrants Rights Coalition Children's Law Center, National Center for Missing & Exploited Children, The Veterans Consortium Pro Bono Program, Washington Area Lawyers for the Arts, The Legal Aid Society for the District of Columbia.

List up to three pro bono matters that are representative of the pro bono work your firm participates in.

- Tony Barksdale death penalty case

- Consortium for Child Welfare — facilitating communication between public and private agencies that provide services & resources to children.

- NAACP Conway Branch — representing NAACP and several plaintiffs in a discrimination suit resulting from alleged discriminatory practices during Black Bike Week in Myrtle Beach, S.C.

BY THE NUMBERS

What is the total number of hours that lawyers in U.S. offices at your firm spent performing pro bono legal services in 2000, 2001 and 2002?

    Total number of hours in 2000: 18,706 hours
    Total number of hours in 2001: 20,640 hours
    Total number of hours in 2002: 23,526 hours

Average number of pro bono hours per attorney in U.S. offices per year (including associates, partners, counsels, but not summer associates):

    Average number of hours per attorney in 2000: 78.6 hours
    Average number of hours per attorney in 2001: 74.25 hours
    Average number of hours per attorney in 2002: 59.8 hours

What percentage of attorneys in this firm's U.S. offices did pro bono work in 2002? 47 percent

What percentage of attorneys in this firm's U.S. offices did at least 20 hours of pro bono work in 2002? 52 percent

Does the firm encourage its lawyers to perform a minimum number of pro bono hours? Yes

If so, how many hours per year or what percentage of lawyers' billable hours? 100 hours. Associates are each required to accumulate 100 pro bono hours per year; any hours over 100 count toward their billable hours. The firm as a whole has made a commitment to contribute per year an amount of time equal to 5 percent of the firm's total billable hours to pro bono work.

SUPERVISION AND EVALUATIONS

Is there partner supervision on each pro bono matter? Yes

Do partner supervisors or, if applicable, senior associates provide written evaluations of associates' work on pro bono matters? Yes

If so, are those evaluations taken into account in determining salary, bonuses or advancement in the firm? Yes

If not, does the firm consider pro bono work generally in associate evaluations? N/A

HOURS

Does the firm give billable hour credit for pro bono work? Yes

Does the firm have a maximum number of pro bono hours that can be applied toward the billable hour target? No

If so, what is the maximum? N/A

If your firm uses hours to determine bonuses, does it consider pro bono hours when determining bonuses? Yes

PRO BONO POINTS

What training opportunities are open to associates working on pro bono matters? Training opportunities offered by legal service providers.

Can associates bring matters of interest to the firm? Yes

Does the firm offer the use of support staff in carrying out pro bono matters? Yes

What pro bono opportunities are available for summer associates? Our full range of pro bono cases currently open.

Does the firm have established programs, such as externships, that enable its associates to work in a public interest setting? No

Has your firm won any special recognition or awards in the last two years for its pro bono work? Yes

If so, please list. Washington Lawyers' Committee for Civil Rights & Urban Affairs Outstanding Achievement Award for 2003. Dallas Bar Association — Dallas Volunteer Attorney Program Gold Award for 2003. North American Interfraternity Conference Laurel Wreath Award. Legal Assistance Distinguished Service Award — September 11 Pro Bono Legal Relief Project.

THE FIRM SAYS

Patton Boggs is in the vanguard of the legal community in terms of our commitment to pro bono work. Our program, of which we are immensely proud, has achieved a number of objectively measurable successes in recent years. For example, we have consistently met the commitment we made to the Pro Bono Institute since 1995, dedicating over 3 percent of our billable time in each year to pro bono clients and causes. Along with the other leading firms in Washington, Patton Boggs was challenged by the leadership of the D.C. Bar, and the chief judges of all of our local and federal courts, to increase the quantity and quality of our pro bono service. We accepted that challenge, and agreed to raise our commitment from 3 percent to 5 percent of our billable hours beginning in 2002.

We firmly believe that pro bono work is an important aspect of our corporate citizenship in the communities in which we live. The firm strongly urges partners and counsel also to get involved in pro bono work. They are welcome to do so in whatever hands-on capacity is consistent with their interests, their availability and their expertise, or they may participate in primarily supervisory roles. We strive to provide associates in pro bono cases with mentors and supervisors, as appropriate, but we encourage associates to take on as much responsibility in these cases as they feel they can handle. We are always looking for ways to continue to grow a pro bono program that is as diverse and varied as the firm itself. Our public service counsel and pro bono committee make special efforts to bring in interesting pro bono work in other areas than the traditional ones and, in particular, in areas other than litigation.

We believe firmly in the educational and training aspects of pro bono work. All associates, in all offices, are expected to perform 100 hours of pro bono work each year. This expectation, which is in addition to billable hour requirements, applies to every associate and to every person treated as an associate. An associate's approved pro bono hours in excess of 100 annually are treated for all purposes just as if they were billable hours. Pro bono work is important to all of us individually, and to the firm as an institution. We believe that it is in the interest of all of our lawyers, from the youngest to the most experienced, to dedicate part of our work to those who are in need.

OUR SURVEY SAYS

"The firm requires all associates to complete at least 100 pro bono hours per year. This is in addition the 1,900 billable [hours] requirement and in some respects it is even more important. There are announcements nearly every day about pro bono opportunities. The firm has regular programs that it works with and you can also choose to participate in one of your own choosing."

"Associates are required to do 100 hours of pro bono each year, and this is tied to bonus eligibility. The firm makes lots of pro bono opportunities available, small-scale and long-term, in a wide variety of legal areas."

"The firm pro bono partner and chair of the pro bono committee are great, but you wonder if they are really getting the firm's support."

"The firm is very pro bono positive, and they put their money where their mouth is about the program. There is some griping from associates that the firm's position is not sincere (whatever that means), but I can say from experience without hesitation that the firm is extremely committed to its pro bono obligations."

"I applaud the firm's strong commitment to pro bono work, but do not agree with the firm's 'requirement' that associates must bill 100 pro bono hours per year."

"We have tremendous flexibility with regard to our pro bono projects. The firm expects 100 hours of pro bono per year and claims that it counts additional hours toward our billable target."

"There are some partners who are very committed to pro bono, and others who clearly are not."

"The firm requires each associate to bill at least 100 pro bono hours. Anything above and beyond 100 hours is included with your billable hours for purposes of determining bonuses, and so on. The firm has monthly pro bono meetings and encourages everyone from attorneys to staff to get involved."

"In the six months that I have been here, I have billed at least 200 hours of pro bono service. The firm rewards its associates who do pro bono work and accords a tremendous amount of recognition to all attorneys and staff members who contribute their time and skills to such undertakings."

"We appear to be strongly committed, and I get the impression that associates here do more pro bono than at most firms, but when I look at the numbers that get published each year, they seem to be middle-of-the-pack."

"We strive to provide associates in pro bono cases with mentors and supervisors, as appropriate, but we encourage associates to take on as much responsibility in these cases as they feel they can handle."

— *Patton Boggs LLP*

Paul, Hastings, Janofsky & Walker LLP

515 South Flower Street, 25th Floor
Los Angeles, CA 90071-2228
Phone: (213) 683-6000
www.paulhastings.com

LOCATIONS

Atlanta, GA
Los Angeles, CA
New York, NY
Orange County, CA
San Diego, CA
San Francisco, CA
Stamford, CT
Washington, DC
Beijing
Hong Kong
London
Shanghai
Tokyo

MAJOR DEPARTMENTS & PRACTICES

Corporate
Employment
Litigation
Real Estate
Tax

THE STATS

No. of attorneys worldwide: 860 +
No. of offices worldwide: 13
Firm Chair: Seth M. Zachary
Managing Partner: Greg M. Nitzkowski

EMPLOYMENT CONTACT

Ms. Michele Ward
Managing Coordinator of Attorney Recruiting
Phone: (213) 683-5672
E-mail: micheleward@paulhastings.com

WHO'S WHO

Principal pro bono contact(s) at your firm:

Nancy Iredale, Partner
Phone: (213) 683-7232
E-mail: nancyiredale@paulhastings.com

Does the firm have a pro bono coordinator? Yes. Paul Hastings has pro bono coordinators in each of our offices:

Atlanta
Robert Newcomer, Esq.
Joseph Sharp, Esq.

Washington, D.C.
Kirby Behre, Esq.
Judith George, Esq.

San Diego
Tracey DeLange, Esq.

Orange County
John Della Grotta, Esq.
Matthew Lapple, Esq.

Los Angeles
Dennis Ellis, Esq.
Jeffrey Varga, Esq.

Stamford
Charles Lee, Esq.

San Francisco
Peter Meier, Esq.
Emily Kennedy, Esq.

New York
Joshua Sternoff, Esq.
Jonathan Tyras, Esq.

If yes, what percentage of his or her time is spent on pro bono work? It varies.

Does the firm have a pro bono committee? Yes

If yes, how often does the committee meet? Two to three times per year.

Describe the composition of the committee: The committee is comprised of partners, of counsel and associates representing all offices and all legal departments and practice groups.

THE SCOOP

Does your firm have a written pro bono policy? Yes

Has the firm signed on to the Law Firm Pro Bono Challenge? No

What are some of the areas of law in which your firm has performed pro bono legal work in the last two years? Paul Hastings provides pro bono legal services across legal disciplines in which we practice including corporate, employment, real estate, litigation, and tax. In our fiscal year 2003 (February 1, 2002-January 31, 2003) more than 200 pro bono matters were initiated. In this fiscal year 2004 (February 1, 2003 to present) more than 250 matters have already been initiated to date.

What are some of the areas of law in which your firm does not perform pro bono work? We typically do not provide pro bono legal services in areas where we do not currently practice, such as divorce law.

Organizations for which your firm has performed pro bono legal services in the last two years: Intrepid Sea Air Space Museum, Alvin Ailey Dance Foundation, Zoo Atlanta, Korean American Federation of Los Angeles, Superior Court Mental Health Project, The Carriage House/Gates, Public Law Center, Goodwill Industries, Children's Law Center, Inner City Law Center, Meridian International Center, Neighbors of Fire Safety.

List up to three pro bono matters that are representative of the pro bono work your firm participates in.

- Paul Hastings represents adoptive parents in child adoption cases for the Children's Law Center. In addition, our pro bono services have expanded to include the representation of foster parent interests in family court proceedings involving the children in their care, and representation in proceedings seeking special education services for their foster children under the Individuals with Disabilities Education Act (IDEA).

- Paul Hastings has provided pro bono legal representation to the Intrepid Sea Air Space Museum including matters related to corporate, real estate, employment and litigation. Last year, Paul Hastings provided counseling on the acquisition of the U.S.S. Intrepid from the United States Navy and guidance on the day-to-day operation of the museum.

- Paul Hastings has represented Goodwill Industries of Western Connecticut in entering into an asset purchase and license agreement with Goodwill Industries of the Springfield/Hartford area. The partnership agreement enables Goodwill Industries of Western Connecticut, which has stores and employment training programs throughout Fairfield and Litchfield counties, to develop and operate Goodwill Retail Stores and Donation centers in an area covering 38 towns in the greater Hartford area. The firm has been recognized by Goodwill Industries for our pro bono legal efforts and the generosity of the firm in furthering Goodwill's service mission.

BY THE NUMBERS

What is the total number of hours that lawyers in U.S. offices at your firm spent performing pro bono legal services in 2000, 2001 and 2002?

Total number of hours in 2000: 14,786 hours
Total number of hours in 2001: 13,878 hours
Total number of hours in 2002: 17,666 hours

Average number of pro bono hours per attorney in U.S. offices per year (including associates, partners, counsels, but not summer associates):

    Average number of hours per attorney in 2000: 23.5 hours
    Average number of hours per attorney in 2001: 20.0 hours
    Average number of hours per attorney in 2002: 27.4 hours

What percentage of attorneys in this firm's U.S. offices did pro bono work in 2002? 63 percent

What percentage of attorneys in this firm's U.S. offices did at least 20 hours of pro bono work in 2002? 26 percent

Does the firm encourage its lawyers to perform a minimum number of pro bono hours? No

SUPERVISION AND EVALUATIONS

Is there partner supervision on each pro bono matter? Yes

Do partner supervisors or, if applicable, senior associates provide written evaluations of associates' work on pro bono matters? No

If so, are those evaluations taken into account in determining salary, bonuses or advancement in the firm? N/A

If not, does the firm consider pro bono work generally in associate evaluations? Yes

HOURS

Does the firm give billable hour credit for pro bono work? Yes

Does the firm have a maximum number of pro bono hours that can be applied toward the billable hour target? No

If so, what is the maximum? N/A

If your firm uses hours to determine bonuses, does it consider pro bono hours when determining bonuses? Yes

PRO BONO POINTS

What training opportunities are open to associates working on pro bono matters? All training opportunities are open to associates. Associates are also encouraged to attend training offered by pro bono organizations.

Can associates bring matters of interest to the firm? Yes

Does the firm offer the use of support staff in carrying out pro bono matters? Yes

What pro bono opportunities are available for summer associates? All pro bono matters are open to participation by summer associates.

Does the firm have established programs, such as externships, that enable its associates to work in a public interest setting? Yes

If so, where and for up to how long? Settings and length vary depending on the needs of the firm and the interests of the associates.

Has your firm won any special recognition or awards in the last two years for its pro bono work? Yes

If so, please list. The firm has been recognized by Goodwill Industries of Western Connecticut for our pro bono legal efforts and the generosity of the firm in furthering Goodwill's service mission.

THE FIRM SAYS

Since its founding, Paul Hastings has been committed both to the community and to pro bono service. As the firm has grown, so has its commitment. In support of the firm's strong commitment to pro bono, the pro bono budget was significantly increased in 2002 and doubled for 2003. All attorneys are encouraged to participate in pro bono work and every approved pro bono matter is given full "billable" hours credit for all attorneys and paralegals. Pro bono hours also count as billable hours when determining associate bonuses. Our commitment to pro bono extends to clients that can include individuals, groups or classes of individuals, government agencies, tax-exempt organizations, and interest groups regarding matters related to (1) an important social or legal issue; (2) an injustice; or (3) advice or representation about legal options, duties or rights for those who may not be able to afford our legal services. An associate in each office serves as the pro bono coordinator for that office. Each local office coordinator promotes pro bono, publicizes pro bono opportunities and reviews and approves all pro bono matters for the office. Three times a year, the firm publishes a pro bono newsletter highlighting pro bono work and accomplishments for all offices. In addition to highlighting pro bono work, the newsletter also includes volunteer and community activities in which Paul Hastings attorneys and staff have participated (e.g., Habitat for Humanity, AIDS Walk LA, Heart Walk, Dress for Success Clothing Donation Program). Many Paul Hastings attorneys also serve on the boards of nonprofit organizations and volunteer extensively in their communities.

OUR SURVEY SAYS

"The firm is committed to permitting opportunities, but fortunately does not require attorneys to render pro bono service."

"There is a program established in the firm for pro bono; it is just a matter of taking advantage of it."

"While the firm proclaims to have a strong commitment to pro bono activities, when it gets down to actually working on them, there are limited resources available and they really only support small pro bono matters – nothing that would involve too much time."

"The firm provides regular opportunities to get involved in pro bono work and has granted 1:1 billable hour reimbursement regardless of whether it was a firm-sponsored opportunity or an opportunity that I brought to the firm. The only real limitation is your own commitment to get out there and do it."

"Associates get credit for approved pro bono work towards billable hour requirements."

"There is a budget for pro bono work and a supportive committee."

"The pro bono budget is there, but is skimpy. It is virtually impossible to work on a large pro bono case – most tend to be small fries (adoption, unlawful detainers)."

"You get hour for hour credit. The pro bono committee is very interested in opportunities. You are able to bring in stuff. It's really a great program."

"Pro bono is tolerated, but definitely not encouraged."

"I have been working with the same pro bono client since I arrived and have never had trouble getting pro bono allocations each year. Pro bono work counts as billable time."

[The firm reports that several of the above comments may have preceded the expansion of the firm's pro bono program.]

Paul, Weiss, Rifkind, Wharton & Garrison LLP

1285 Avenue of the Americas
New York, NY 10019
Phone: (212) 373-3000
www.paulweiss.com

LOCATIONS

New York, NY (HQ)
Washington, DC
Beijing
Hong Kong
London
Paris
Tokyo

MAJOR DEPARTMENTS & PRACTICES

Antitrust
Bankruptcy & Corporate Reorganization
Communications & Technology
Employee Benefits & Executive Compensation
Entertainment
Environmental
Financing
Insurance
Intellectual Property
Internet, Media & Technology
Investment Funds
Litigation
Mergers & Acquisitions
Personal Representation
Private Equity
Pro Bono & Public Matters
Project Finance
Real Estate
Securities & Capital Markets Practice
Structured Finance & Securitization
Tax

THE STATS

No. of attorneys worldwide: 500
No. of offices worldwide: 7
Chairman: Alfred D. Youngwood

EMPLOYMENT CONTACTS

Ms. Patricia J. Morrissy
Legal Recruitment Director
Phone: (212) 373-2548
Fax: (212) 373-2205
E-mail: pmorrissy@paulweiss.com

Ms. Joanne Ollman
Legal Personnel Director
Phone: (212) 373-2480
Fax: (212) 373-2515
E-mail: jollman@paulweiss.com

WHO'S WHO

Principal pro bono contact(s) at your firm:

Maria T. Vullo, Esq.
Partner
Phone: (212) 373-3346
E-mail: mvullo@paulweiss.com

Does the firm have a pro bono coordinator? Yes. The firm has a committee with the chairperson serving as coordinator along with administrative assistance. Associates also coordinate particular pro bono projects throughout the firm.

Does the firm have a pro bono committee? Yes

If yes, how often does the committee meet? Approximately three times a year.

Describe the composition of the committee: Partners, counsel and associates.

THE SCOOP

Does your firm have a written pro bono policy? Yes

Has the firm signed on to the Law Firm Pro Bono Challenge? Yes

What are some of the areas of law in which your firm has performed pro bono legal work in the last two years? Civil rights, reproductive rights, minority small businesses, death penalty, 9/11 cases, family matters, housing projects, not-for-profit organizations, discrimination cases, criminal appeals, asylum and immigration matters.

What are some of the areas of law in which your firm does not perform pro bono work? Paul Weiss has an open policy about pro bono work.

Organizations for which your firm has performed pro bono legal services in the last two years: Lawyers Committee for Human Rights, Urban Justice Center, Volunteer Lawyers for the Arts, Asian American Legal Defense and Education Fund, New York Lawyers for the Public Interest (NYLPI), Sanctuary for Families, Planned Parenthood Federation, Volunteers of Legal Services (VOLS), Business Resource and Investment Service Center (BRISC), Community Law Offices – Legal Aid Society, Lawyers Committee for Civil Rights under Law.

List up to three pro bono matters that are representative of the pro bono work your firm participates in. Our pro bono practice is so varied and extensive that providing only three representative examples does not accurately represent our pro bono work.

BY THE NUMBERS

What is the total number of hours that lawyers in U.S. offices at your firm spent performing pro bono legal services in 2000, 2001 and 2002?

    Total number of hours in 2000: 34,070 hours
    Total number of hours in 2001: 30,974 hours
    Total number of hours in 2002: 40,824 hours

Average number of pro bono hours per attorney in U.S. offices per year (including associates, partners, counsels, but not summer associates):

    Average number of hours per attorney in 2000: 84.4 hours
    Average number of hours per attorney in 2001: 71.9 hours
    Average number of hours per attorney in 2002: 93.1 hours

What percentage of attorneys in this firm's U.S. offices did pro bono work in 2002? 79 percent

What percentage of attorneys in this firm's U.S. offices did at least 20 hours of pro bono work in 2002? 59 percent

Does the firm encourage its lawyers to perform a minimum number of pro bono hours? The firm has no hourly minimums or maximums. The firm strongly encourages lawyers to get involved in pro bono projects and has neither minimum nor maximum hour standards.

If so, how many hours per year or what percentage of lawyers' billable hours? N/A

SUPERVISION AND EVALUATIONS

Is there partner supervision on each pro bono matter? Yes

Do partner supervisors or, if applicable, senior associates provide written evaluations of associates' work on pro bono matters? Yes

If so, are those evaluations taken into account in determining salary, bonuses or advancement in the firm? Yes

If not, does the firm consider pro bono work generally in associate evaluations? N/A

HOURS

Does the firm give billable hour credit for pro bono work? Yes

Does the firm have a maximum number of pro bono hours that can be applied toward the billable hour target? No

If so, what is the maximum? N/A

If your firm uses hours to determine bonuses, does it consider pro bono hours when determining bonuses? Not applicable

PRO BONO POINTS

What training opportunities are open to associates working on pro bono matters? The firm has an open policy about associates attending training programs for pro bono work. In addition, the firm trains associates in pro bono work as part of associate orientation programs; there are regular luncheons and meetings to discuss pro bono matters; there is partner supervision on individual cases and availability of case-specific training through organizations that invite our associates to their training programs.

Can associates bring matters of interest to the firm? Yes

Does the firm offer the use of support staff in carrying out pro bono matters? Yes

What pro bono opportunities are available for summer associates? Summer associates may work on any pro bono matters as with any assignments during the summer.

Does the firm have established programs, such as externships, that enable its associates to work in a public interest setting? No

Has your firm won any special recognition or awards in the last two years for its pro bono work? Yes

If so, please list. The firm has received numerous awards for its pro bono commitment, including:

- In November 2003, The Legal Aid Society presented several partners and associates of Paul Weiss with the Training and Education Award at the Society's annual awards reception, in recognition of the exceptional training that they have provided to The Legal Aid Society over the years.

- In 2002 and 2003, the firm was recognized for exceeding the Volunteers of Legal Service Pro Bono Pledge.

- In 2003, Paul Weiss was selected as the recipient of the U.S. Small Business Administration's "Minority Small Business Advocate of the Year" Award for its significant contributions on behalf of the minority small business community.

- Paul Weiss was also honored in 2003 at the 21st Birthday Celebration of the Association of Community Organizations for Reform Now ("ACORN"). The firm was presented with a "Community Champion" award for its pro bono achievements.

- In 2003 Paul Weiss ranked 8th in the nation in The American Lawyer "Pro Bono Honor Roll."

- In 2002, Paul Weiss was recognized for its "Assistance to Victims of the WTC Tragedy" at The Legal Aid Society's "2002 Pro Bono Awards Ceremony."

- The Sanctuary for Families Center for Battered Women Legal Services (Associates Committee) presented Paul, Weiss associates Irit Tau and Carmen Cheung with an award for excellence in pro bono advocacy on behalf of battered women and children.

- *The American Lawyer* ranked Paul, Weiss third in the 2003 "A List" of U.S. law firms, where one of the principal criteria employed was the firm's pro bono performance.

- The Lawyers Committee for Human Rights awarded partner Sidney Rosdeitcher one of the first annual Marvin E. Frankel Pro Bono Awards for his extraordinary work in representing refugee asylum-seeking clients.

- The Legal Aid Society awarded partners Edwin Maynard and Marco Masotti and associates Binyomin Kaplan, Matias Milet and Edward Nelson with one of The Legal Aid Society's 2003 Pro Bono Awards at their annual Pro Bono Awards and Law Firm Recognition Ceremony.

- Meredith Kane was honored for her "outstanding commitment and pro bono contributions" to The Legal Aid Society, for her representation of The Legal Aid Society in lease negotiations to relocate its headquarters away from 90 Church Street following the World Trade Center disaster.

THE FIRM SAYS

Paul Weiss continues to rank among the top firms in New York City and the nation in pro bono hours, and has been noted consistently for its pro bono work. From helping Thurgood Marshall prepare and argue Brown v. Board of Education in the 1950s, winning landmark victories in civil rights and death row cases in the 1970s and 1980s, to, more recently, the successful representation of reproductive healthcare workers, victims of human rights abuses in Bosnia, Herzegovina, and the preparation of an amicus brief supporting the University of Michigan Law School's affirmative action program, the firm's pro bono work has contributed to significant progress and changes in the law. We also provide pro bono legal services to nonprofit organizations and minority business owners on a regular basis. In addition to significant high-profile cases with broad impact, Paul Weiss has been steadfast in its commitment to represent hundreds of individual clients with matters of pressing importance. Our associates have a wide-range of opportunities to provide pro bono legal services, and we encourage our lawyers to make pro bono work part of their every day caseload.

OUR SURVEY SAYS

"The firm has a very strong commitment to pro bono. It was also one of the first firms to introduce a pro bono program for corporate lawyers."

"We could always do more pro bono work, but Paul Weiss' reputation for pro bono work is definitely well deserved. My supervising partner, although very busy, spends a lot of time reviewing my work and always gives me meaningful, substantive feedback."

"I have billed tons of pro bono and no one seems to mind."

"The firm is definitely committed to pro bono work – but with the enormous amount of work from fee-paying clients, it is hard to find the time to do pro bono work."

"I have been encouraged to work on pro bono matters since arriving at the firm. I feel that I am able to take time to work on these matters and that they are valued by those more senior to me."

"Everyone who wants to does pro bono work, and most people want to. We represent several death row inmates and numerous asylum seekers, among others."

"Pro bono hours are billable and encouraged. I am hard-pressed to think of an associate who does not do pro bono work."

"I believe that the firm is genuinely enthusiastic about its pro bono commitments, that most lawyers here either do substantial pro bono work or try to, and I don't believe that any firm this size could do better in providing valuable pro bono experience to its associates and services to a vast array of recipients."

"In addition to the highly acclaimed litigation work, Paul Weiss is also actively involved in transactional pro bono. We have worked on small businesses affected by 9/11 and we receive new small business pro bono clients monthly from BRISC, a division of the Upper Manhattan Empowerment Zone, in Harlem."

"In addition to significant high-profile cases with broad impact, Paul Weiss has been steadfast in its commitment to represent hundreds of individual clients with matters of pressing importance."

— *Paul, Weiss, Rifkind, Wharton & Garrison LLP*

Perkins Coie LLP

1201 Third Avenue, 48th Floor
Seattle, WA 98101-3099
Phone: (206) 359-8000
www.perkinscoie.com

LOCATIONS

Seattle, WA (HQ)
Anchorage, AK
Bellevue, WA
Boise, ID
Chicago, IL
Denver, CO
Los Angeles, CA
Menlo Park, CA
Olympia, WA
Portland, OR
San Francisco, CA
Washington, DC
Beijing
Hong Kong

MAJOR DEPARTMENTS & PRACTICES

Business Law
Corporate Finance
Environment & Natural Resources
Estate Planning & Trust Services
Intellectual Property
Labor & Employment
Litigation
Product Liability
Real Estate & Land Use
Regulatory & Government Affairs
Tax
Trademark & Copyright

THE STATS

No. of attorneys worldwide: 575
No. of offices worldwide: 14
Managing Partner: Robert E. Giles

EMPLOYMENT CONTACT

Ms. Laura MacDougall Kader
Lawyer Personnel Recruiter for Law Student Hiring
Phone: (206) 583-8888
Fax: (206) 583-8500
E-mail: lkader@perkinscoie.com

WHO'S WHO

Does the firm have a pro bono coordinator? Yes

Julia Parsons Clarke, Esq.
Partner and Pro Bono Coordinator
Phone: (206) 359-3171
E-mail: jpclarke@perkinscoie.com

If yes, what percentage of his or her time is spent on pro bono work? 100 percent

Does the firm have a pro bono committee? Yes

If yes, how often does the committee meet? Approximately six times a year as a firm-wide committee. We also have a number of subcommittees that meet periodically.

Describe the composition of the committee: The committee has partner, associate and of counsel representatives from throughout the firm.

THE SCOOP

Does your firm have a written pro bono policy? Yes

Has the firm signed on to the Law Firm Pro Bono Challenge? Yes

What are some of the areas of law in which your firm has performed pro bono legal work in the last two years? We are involved in a broad range of pro bono work including direct representation of low-income clients in a variety of litigation matters, representation of low-income clients in immigration matters, work with seniors and low-income clients on estate planning matters, impact litigation to protect constitutional and public rights (and/or the rights of low-income persons), provision of advice to clients in neighborhood legal clinics, and we are engaged in community development by providing advice and representation to nonprofit clients a variety of non-litigation matters.

What are some of the areas of law in which your firm does not perform pro bono work? N/A

Organizations for which your firm has performed pro bono legal services in the last two years: A few of the organizations we have worked with in the last year include: Alaska Legal Services, the ACLU, the Chicago Legal Clinic, King County CASA, KCBA Community Legal Services Program, Idaho Volunteer Lawyers Program, Legal Foundation of Washington, Northwest Immigrants Rights Project, Oregon Law Center and San Francisco Volunteer Legal Services Program.

List up to three pro bono matters that are representative of the pro bono work your firm participates in.

- Over the last five years, a team of Perkins Coie lawyers has represented the Legal Foundation of Washington in Brown v. Legal Foundation of Washington, a federal court case in which the plaintiffs challenged the constitutionality of the Washington Interest in Lawyer Trust Account (IOLTA) program as it applies to limited practice officers in the State of Washington. In 2003, the Supreme Court ruled in this case that the IOLTA program, which provides hundreds of millions of dollars to legal services programs in the United States each year, does not violate the Fifth Amendment's Just Compensation Clause.

- We provide direct legal services to low-income clients in a variety of matters. For example, lawyers in a number of our offices work with low-income victims of domestic violence, assisting them in obtaining restraining orders to protect their safety and assisting them with immigration filings under the Violence Against Women Act.

- A number of our lawyers provide legal advice in non-litigation matters to support community development. In one recent matter, one of our corporate lawyers represented a group of low-income public housing tenants in a transaction that transferred ownership of their housing to a trust controlled by the tenants and resulted in a guarantee that the housing would be available to low-income tenants for perpetuity.

BY THE NUMBERS

What is the total number of hours that lawyers in U.S. offices at your firm spent performing pro bono legal services in 2000, 2001 and 2002?

Total number of hours in 2000: 13,899 hours
Total number of hours in 2001: 15,040 hours
Total number of hours in 2002: 24,694 hours

Average number of pro bono hours per attorney in U.S. offices per year (including associates, partners, counsels, but not summer associates):

Average number of hours per attorney in 2000: 33 hours
Average number of hours per attorney in 2001: 28.2 hours
Average number of hours per attorney in 2002: 45.6 hours

What percentage of attorneys in this firm's U.S. offices did pro bono work in 2002? 72 percent

What percentage of attorneys in this firm's U.S. offices did at least 20 hours of pro bono work in 2002? 62 percent

Does the firm encourage its lawyers to perform a minimum number of pro bono hours? Yes

If so, how many hours per year or what percentage of lawyers' billable hours? The firm's pro bono committee recognizes lawyers who provide 50 or more hours of pro bono services to our clients per year.

SUPERVISION AND EVALUATIONS

Is there partner supervision on each pro bono matter? No

Do partner supervisors or, if applicable, senior associates provide written evaluations of associates' work on pro bono matters? Yes

If so, are those evaluations taken into account in determining salary, bonuses or advancement in the firm? Yes

If not, does the firm consider pro bono work generally in associate evaluations? Yes

HOURS

Does the firm give billable hour credit for pro bono work? Yes

Does the firm have a maximum number of pro bono hours that can be applied toward the billable hour target? No

If so, what is the maximum? N/A

If your firm uses hours to determine bonuses, does it consider pro bono hours when determining bonuses? Yes

PRO BONO POINTS

What training opportunities are open to associates working on pro bono matters? Our pro bono program provides excellent training opportunities for our lawyers in all facets of their practice development. We encourage associates to use pro bono strategically to develop their skills. For litigators, there are many opportunities to work on matters which will involve trial advocacy. Pro bono can also provide non-litigators with great training in client counseling and other skills. The firm also hosts a number of formal training programs in-house in relation to pro bono projects.

Can associates bring matters of interest to the firm? Yes

Does the firm offer the use of support staff in carrying out pro bono matters? Yes

What pro bono opportunities are available for summer associates? We encourage summer associates to become engaged in pro bono projects while at the firm. To facilitate this, we contact summer associates prior to their arrival regarding their interest in pro bono and try to match with them matters they are interested in during the time at the firm. We schedule a number of pro bono training sessions in the summer for summer associates to attend and also provide them with presentations regarding our pro bono program. In the last few years, summer associates have been actively involved in working with us on a number of matters including impact litigation (such as the IOLTA case) and have provided direct service to our low-income clients in immigration matters and litigation matters. A number of our summer associates have also represented guardians ad litem in trials involving allegations of child abuse and neglect.

Does the firm have established programs, such as externships, that enable its associates to work in a public interest setting? Yes

If so, where and for up to how long? The firm established the Perkins Coie Community Service Fellowship Program in 1987 as part of the firm's celebration of its 75th anniversary. The program allows associates to spend up to six months working full-time on a pro bono project for a community organization of their choice. In the last year, we have had associates do fellowships with the King County Prosecutors Office trying felony drug cases, the Northwest Women's Law Center working on reproductive rights issues, and Washington Attorneys Assisting Community Organizations working on the launch of a project in Washington that assists community-based nonprofits find pro bono attorneys.

Has your firm won any special recognition or awards in the last two years for its pro bono work? Yes

If so, please list. The team of lawyers working on the IOLTA case have been honored with the following awards: 2002 King County Bar Foundation Champions of Justice Award, 2003 King County Bar Association ("KCBA") President's Award, 2003 Washington State Bar Association Award of Merit and 2003 American Bar Association IOLTA Litigation Team Award. The firm has been honored with the following awards in last two years: 2002 David W. Soukup Award for Outstanding Legal Advocacy from the CASA program, 2002 KCBA Pro Bono Law Firm of the Year, 2002 Community

Impact Award from the Chief Seattle Council of the Boy Scouts, 2003 Certificate of Achievement from the Washington Council on Economic Education. In addition, the Somali grocer case team was recognized as Volunteers of the Month in October 2002 by the KCBA and Karol Brown was given the 2003 Litigation Award by the Washington Chapter of American Immigration Lawyers.

THE FIRM SAYS

At Perkins Coie, we encourage and strongly support pro bono work. This commitment to pro bono is an outgrowth of Perkins Coie's long tradition of public service. We believe in sharing our expertise and resources to improve communities where our firm has offices. Lawyers and staff are encouraged to engage in community service through nonprofit board membership, participating in firm-sponsored volunteer projects, participating in volunteer projects on an individual basis, charitable giving and providing pro bono legal services to those in need who would not otherwise have access to the legal system. To emphasize the importance of pro bono at our firm, we have a partner in charge of the pro bono program. This partner works full time overseeing the program and supporting attorneys in their pro bono efforts. A major theme of our program is independence. Attorneys are urged to choose and develop projects that match their beliefs and philosophies. The result is a diverse range of work. Partner supervision is available for associates in all pro bono cases but is not typically required unless an associate is in his or her first three years of practice. Pro bono hours are considered positively in evaluating the progress of attorneys at the firm. The pro bono committee continues to explore ways to make it easier and more rewarding for Perkins Coie attorneys to engage in pro bono work.

In 2002, pro bono legal work undertaken by lawyers at Perkins Coie ranged from impact cases involving constitutional issues and protection of public rights, to representation of low-income political refugees seeking asylum, participation in legal clinics through local bar associations and homeless shelters, representation of low-income clients in a variety of litigation matters, and general corporate, intellectual property and employment law counseling for social services organizations, arts organizations and other nonprofit organizations. A unique feature of our pro bono program is the opportunity for associates to apply for Perkins Coie community service fellowships. Recipient of fellowships spend up to six months working for a community organization on a significant public service project. While doing this, the associate is freed from all other work responsibilities. Fellowships enable associates to make a significant contribution to organizations and causes they care deeply about. In addition, the fellowships expand associate legal horizons, by enabling associates to develop legal and other skills they otherwise would not have acquired in day-to-day practice.

For more information about pro bono at Perkins Coie, go to the firm's web site at perkinscoie.com or contact the firm's pro bono coordinator at jpclarke@perkinscoie.com.

OUR SURVEY SAYS

"This is what drew me to the firm initially. We have a partner who devotes all her time to coordinating pro bono work within the firm. We do an amazing array of work, from nationwide impact litigation to appellate work to local legal aid work. The firm views our pro bono work as an integral part of our culture, and it is definitely supported institutionally. That being said, when the salary hikes took effect, the number of pro bono hours which can count toward your billable hours decreased (basically, only 50 hours count toward your billable target, and the rest are considered 'legal time,' which is part of the calculus for merit-based bonuses and salary increases but doesn't count toward your billable goal)."

"The firm's application of pro bono hours to [the] billable requirement is probably too low, discouraging associates from working over 100 hours per year on pro bono cases."

"There is good morale and community support for pro bono if you don't mind taking the hourly hit. The addition of a pro bono coordinator has made a huge difference, but commitment to pro bono remains largely practice group-specific, with little support in the business groups."

"The firm is supportive of pro bono work and there is a great deal of excellent work being done in our Seattle office. Unfortunately, however, there is less encouragement for pro bono work in my local office."

"The firm is pretty well committed to pro bono, but does not give an hour-for-hour credit on pro bono work. You can get up to a 50-hour credit automatically, but you have to go through a cumbersome process to get more. The pro bono matters the firm handles tilt heavily toward liberal causes; very rarely will be firm allow the handling of a conservative cause."

"[The firm] makes an effort, but it doesn't strike me as a huge priority."

"Pro bono hours do not count unless you have reached 1,800 billable hours and even then, you only receive 50 percent credit for every hour spent."

"Part of our billable hours can go to pro bono, a huge incentive, and with a full-time lawyer doing nothing but creating pro bono work for the firm, it is a great place to work if you are interested in giving back to the community."

"The only thing missing is full credit for pro bono. Other than that, the commitment is incredible, and there is tremendous support for a wide range of pro bono work."

Pillsbury Winthrop LLP

1540 Broadway
New York, NY 10036
Phone: (212) 858-1000

50 Fremont Street
San Francisco, CA 94105
Phone: (415) 983-1000
www.pillsburywinthrop.com

LOCATIONS

Century City, CA • Costa Mesa, CA • Houston, TX • Los Angeles, CA • New York, NY • Palo Alto, CA • Sacramento, CA • San Diego, CA • San Francisco, CA • Stamford, CT • McLean, VA • Washington, DC • London • Sydney • Tokyo

MAJOR DEPARTMENTS & PRACTICES

Industry Areas:

Aviation & Aerospace • Global Energy • Health Care • Hotels & Tourism • Insurance & Re-insurance • Life Sciences • Media & Entertainment • Nanotechnology • Restaurant, Food & Beverage • Telecommunications • Affordable Housing • Antitrust & Competition Counseling & Litigation • Appellate Practice • Arbitration & Mediation • Asset Securitization • Aviation & Aerospace Law • Bank Finance • Business Restructure & Reorganization • Commerce & Technology • Construction Law • Copyrights • Corporate & Securities • Corproate Investigations & White Collar Defense • Derivatives • Emerging Companies • Employment & Labor • Environment, Land Use & Natural Resources • Equipment Finance & Leasing • ERISA Litigation • Executive Compensation & Employee Benefits • Finance • Financial Services • Franchising & Distribution • Government Disputes/Government Contracts • Insolvency & Creditors' Rights • Intellectual Property Litigation & Counseling • International Trade • Iraq Reconstruction • Land Use • Licensing Litigation • Marketing, Advertising & Promotions • Mergers & Acquisitions • Outsourcing • Patents • Political Law • Privacy & Data Protection • Private Equity Funds • Product Liability • Project Finance • Public Finance • Real Estate, Project Development & Construction • Securities • Securities Litigation • Tax • Trade Secrets • Trademark • Wealth Management & Individual Client Services • Wine, Beer & Spirits Law

THE STATS

No. of attorneys worldwide: 749
No. of offices worldwide: 16
Firm Chair: Mary B. Cranston
Managing Partner: Marina Park
Executive Vice Chair: David R. Snyde

EMPLOYMENT CONTACTS

Los Angeles & Century City
Ms. Mary Ellen Hatch
E-mail: mhatch@pillsburywinthrop.com

New York
Ms. Dorrie Ciavatta
E-mail: dciavatta@pillsburywinthrop.com

San Francisco
Ms. Sela Seleska
E-mail: sseleska@pillsburywinthrop.com

See firm web site for employment contacts at other offices.

WHO'S WHO

Principal pro bono contact(s) at your firm:

Max Friedman, Esq.
Partner & Co-Chair, Pro Bono Committee
Phone: (212) 858-1555
E-mail: mfriedman@pillsburywinthrop.com

Thomas V. Loran III, Esq.
Partner & Co-Chair, Pro Bono Committee
Phone: (415) 983-1865
E-mail: tloran@pillsburywinthrop.com

Does the firm have a pro bono coordinator? Yes. Each of 13 U.S. offices has at least one pro bono coordinator:

Houston – David R. Tippetts, Esq.
Los Angeles & Century City – Kent B. Goss, Rebecca N. Kaufman and Seth D. Levy, Esqs.
New York – Andrew Behrman, Karen B. Dine and Susan J. Kohlmann, Esqs.
Northern Virginia – Susan T. Brown, Esq.
Orange County – Christine Scheuneman, Esq.
Sacramento – Warren Binford and John S. Poulos, Esqs.
San Francisco – Joan S. Burns, Kevin Fong, Henry S. Noyes and Linda C. Williams, Esqs.
Silicon Valley – William F. Abrams and Nicole M. Townsend, Esqs.
San Diego, Carmel Valley – Eric A. Kremer and Jan H. Webster, Esqs.
Stamford – Kent S. Nevins, Esq.
Washington, DC – Aileen Meyer, Esq.

If yes, what percentage of his or her time is spent on pro bono work? It varies.

Does the firm have a pro bono committee? Yes

If yes, how often does the committee meet? Committees meet on a periodic basis; frequency varies from office to office.

Describe the composition of the committee: Partners and associates from each of the firm's U.S. offices.

THE SCOOP

Does your firm have a written pro bono policy? Yes

Has the firm signed on to the Law Firm Pro Bono Challenge? Yes

What are some of the areas of law in which your firm has performed pro bono legal work in the last two years? Representation of death row inmates in ABA death penalty appeals; civil rights class actions on behalf of prisoners; civil rights class actions on behalf of indigent individuals; representation of indigent clients seeking asylum and resisting deportation under U.S. immigration laws; attorneys throughout the firm are involved in the ABA Young Lawyers Division's Tolerance Through Education Program, which is directed to preventing hate crimes and school violence; provision of general legal advice on housing, benefits and employment matters to indigent individuals; representation of organizations that are devoted to the advancement of women's rights, including Casa Cornelia, which represents indigent and immigrant women in immigration and political asylum cases, and San Francisco Women Against Rape.

Organizations for which your firm has performed pro bono legal services in the last two years: Housing Works and the HIV Law Project, Lawyers Committee for Civil Rights of the San Francisco Bay Area, Horizon Student Enrichment Program, Pro Bono Institute at Georgetown University Law Center, ABA Death Penalty Representation Project, ABA Young Lawyers Division's Tolerance Through Education Program, Equal Justice Works, Volunteers of Legal Service Children's Project.

List up to three pro bono matters that are representative of the pro bono work your firm participates in.

- Henrietta D. v. Guiliani. Represented 25,000 New Yorkers against the city's Division of AIDS Services and Income Support for failing to provide critical benefits and services. Plaintiffs won in landmark decision.

- Lawyers Committee for Civil Rights of the San Francisco Bay Area. For the past 30 years, provided civil legal services to low-income clients by hosting bimonthly clinics in the areas of eviction defense, uninsured motorists claims, school expulsion, tort defense, collections and public benefits, as well as providing translation services.

- ABA Death Penalty Representation Project. In Alabama, offered support of the ABA's general moratorium on execution cases involving mentally retarded people and juveniles and provided defense for death-row inmates denied their fundamental constitutional rights.

BY THE NUMBERS

What is the total number of hours that lawyers in U.S. offices at your firm spent performing pro bono legal services in 2000, 2001 and 2002?

    Total number of hours in 2000: 22,125 hours
    Total number of hours in 2001: 23,977 hours
    Total number of hours in 2002: 23,385 hours

Average number of pro bono hours per attorney in U.S. offices per year (including associates, partners, counsels, but not summer associates):

    Average number of hours per attorney in 2000: 30 hours
    Average number of hours per attorney in 2001: 33 hours
    Average number of hours per attorney in 2002: 36 hours

What percentage of attorneys in this firm's U.S. offices did pro bono work in 2002? 60.9 percent

What percentage of attorneys in this firm's U.S. offices did at least 20 hours of pro bono work in 2002? 33.4 percent

Does the firm encourage its lawyers to perform a minimum number of pro bono hours? Yes

If so, how many hours per year or what percentage of lawyers' billable hours? The firm encourages lawyers to perform a minimum number of pro bono hours by providing billable hours credits for all pro bono hours billed in excess of 20 hours. The firm encourages all of its lawyers to meet the Pro Bono Challenge of 3-to-5 percent of billable hours.

SUPERVISION AND EVALUATIONS

Is there partner supervision on each pro bono matter? Yes

Do partner supervisors or, if applicable, senior associates provide written evaluations of associates' work on pro bono matters? Yes

If so, are those evaluations taken into account in determining salary, bonuses or advancement in the firm? Yes

If not, does the firm consider pro bono work generally in associate evaluations? N/A

HOURS

Does the firm give billable hour credit for pro bono work? Yes

Does the firm have a maximum number of pro bono hours that can be applied toward the billable hour target? No

If so, what is the maximum? N/A

If your firm uses hours to determine bonuses, does it consider pro bono hours when determining bonuses? Yes

PRO BONO POINTS

What training opportunities are open to associates working on pro bono matters? In addition to the partner supervision given to pro bono matters, there are training programs conducted from time to time in each of the firm's offices. The firm also encourages attorneys to participate in training programs sponsored by pro bono organizations.

Can associates bring matters of interest to the firm? Yes

Does the firm offer the use of support staff in carrying out pro bono matters? Yes

What pro bono opportunities are available for summer associates? Summer associates are encouraged to work on active pro bono matters. In addition, certain offices of the firm have sponsored arrangements through which summer associates are given the opportunity to work at legal service and pro bono organizations for several weeks during the summer.

Does the firm have established programs, such as externships, that enable its associates to work in a public interest setting? Yes

If so, where and for up to how long? Established over 10 years ago, Pillsbury Winthrop's Sutro and Stimson Fellowships provide an annual stipend to their recipients, allowing them to conduct pro bono projects. The Sutro Fellowship is coordinated by the firm through Equal Justice Works. The 2003 Sutro Fellowship recipient was Abby McClelland, working at Neighborhood Legal Services of Los Angeles County. During 2003, the firm supported five Stimson Fellows in a variety of legal service and charitable organizations, including the Legal Aid Society, the New York Civil Liberties Union and the Financial Services Corporation. In addition, the firm loans litigation associates to local public defender offices.

Has your firm won any special recognition or awards in the last two years for its pro bono work? Yes

If so, please list. 2003 Fair Housing Leadership Award from Fair Housing of Marin; NAACP Legal Defense and Educational Fund's Pro Bono Legal Services Award; Pro Bono Legal Services Award from the Prison Law Office;

Distinguished Legal Services Award of the American Jewish Congress. Andrew Smith, an associate in the New York office, received the Legal Aid Society 2003 Pro Bono Award for his work in representing homeless individuals. In 2002, Los Angeles associate Seth Levy received the ABA Young Lawyers Division "Star of the Year" award for his work on the Division's Tolerance Through Education Program.

THE FIRM SAYS

Lawyers at all Pillsbury Winthrop offices participate in a wide range of professional, community, civic and pro bono activities, and all attorneys are strongly encouraged to participate in pro bono representation. Pillsbury Winthrop strongly encourages its attorneys to provide legal services for disadvantaged members of our communities. Some of these activities arise from our long-standing support for not-for-profit legal service providers, while others are chosen by individual attorneys with the firm's approval and support. All pro bono clients become clients of the firm, and the firm's considerable resources are available as needed to support each matter. Such work has traditionally provided valuable experience and personal satisfaction to those who have undertaken it and has been a positive factor in evaluating an attorney's development. Pillsbury Winthrop also encourages its lawyers to serve the legal profession. Many of our lawyers publish papers and books and lecture on a variety of legal topics. Others teach at law schools or participate as judges in law school moot court programs. Still others act as judges in small claims courts or as arbitrators in federal court, or participate on panels to resolve attorney fee disputes or to decide attorney disciplinary proceedings.

The core of our pro bono work is the provision of basic legal services to the poor. We also handle pro bono litigation involving important public policy issues. For example, since the 1980s firm attorneys have spent hundreds of pro bono hours on behalf of indigent clients seeking asylum and resisting deportation under U.S. immigration laws. We also advise nonprofit organizations on a variety of legal matters, including incorporation, tax-exempt status, employee matters, leases and contracts. Many of our lawyers serve on the boards of hospitals, educational institutions and charitable organizations.

Some additional examples of our pro bono work include the following:

- In 1993, the firm established the John A. Sutro, Sr. Public Service Fellowship. Recipients have worked on projects to overcome "not-in-my-backyard" (NIMBY) opposition to affordable housing, to develop a nonprofit organization to advocate on behalf of the developmentally disabled, to provide information on workplace rights to immigrant workers and to develop a youth employment law project.

- Share Our Strength (SOS) is a national hunger relief organization that provides grants to over 800 organizations through its leadership forums and nationwide direct service initiative. Since SOS was founded in 1984, Pillsbury Winthrop has assisted in its day-to-day corporate legal matters and has done all of the trademark registration and licensing work associated with its national campaigns such as the Charge Against Hunger, Taste of the Nation and Dine Across America.

OUR SURVEY SAYS

"Associates are encouraged to devote time to pro bono. The firm does not merely pay lip service to this important endeavor. Time spent beyond the first 20 hours on pro bono is counted toward the billable hour requirement. I have personally participated in pro bono representation and seen a good number of my colleagues doing the same."

"The firm as a whole is committed to pro bono work. Pro bono hours count as billable hours, but our bonus policy was recently changed to eliminate pro bono hours from counting towards the first hours-bonus level."

"The commitment to pro bono isn't as strong as in the Winthrop days — and bureaucratic hurdles make doing pro bono work more complicated than in the past — but for associates who want to do pro bono work the firm is still quite supportive."

"They have a long and proud history of doing pro bono but they do not tend to meet their goals and sometimes send mixed messages about how pro bono hours count in your yearly assessment."

"The firm has been emphasizing profitability over the past several years to increase our rank. As a result, associates in busy groups are encouraged only to do pro bono above and beyond meeting their billable hours."

"Pro bono hours count towards hours bonuses! I had over 300 hours my first year. Also, each associate is directed to take a turn at the bimonthly in-house clinic, where indigent clients are retained."

"The policy is good: after the first 20 hours, all pro bono time is fully creditable toward 1,950 hours requirement. However, in practice, there is strong pressure not to rely on pro bono in order to 'make' one's hours. For 2002, I utilized about 40 pro bono hours in order to hit a total of 1,970 hours and was told by a very senior partner, 'Nice try ... you almost made your hours last year!'"

"Pro bono is permitted to the extent that it does not interfere with billable work."

"Our firm has a generous pro bono policy (hours are credited as billable after the first 20 in a calendar year), but that is certainly balanced against the need to represent paying clients."

"The firm has worked hard to improve its pro bono commitment and has been successful in increasing its commitment to pro bono."

Piper Rudnick LLP

1200 Nineteenth Street, NW
Washington, DC 20036-2412
Phone: (202) 861-3900
www.piperrudnick.com

LOCATIONS

Washington, DC (HQ)
Baltimore, MD
Boston, MA
Chicago, IL
Dallas, TX
Easton, MD
Edison, NJ
Las Vegas, NV
Los Angeles, CA
Miami, FL
New York, NY
Philadelphia, PA
Reston, VA
San Francisco, CA
Tampa, FL

MAJOR DEPARTMENTS & PRACTICES

Corporate & Securities
ERISA, Employee Benefits & Executive Compensation
Finance
Franchise & Distribution
Government Affairs
Intellectual Property
International Commerce & Litigation
Labor
Litigation
Private Client Services
Real Estate
Tax

THE STATS

No. of attorneys worldwide: 950 +
No. of offices worldwide: 14
Chairmen: Francis B. Burch Jr. and Lee I. Miller

EMPLOYMENT CONTACTS

Ms. Marguerite Strubing
Legal Recruiting Manager
Phone: (312) 368-8928
E-mail: marguerite.strubing@piperrudnick.com

Ms. Lindy Hilliard
Legal Recruiting Manager
Phone: (410) 580-4664
E-mail: lindy.hilliard@piperrudnick.com

WHO'S WHO

Does the firm have a pro bono coordinator? Yes. The firm has a pro bono counsel and pro bono manager who work together to administer the firm's pro bono program, office pro bono coordinators who act as point persons on local projects and, in some of the larger offices, pro bono partners who spend up to one-third of their time on pro bono projects.

Lisa Dewey, Pro Bono Counsel/Partner
E-mail: elizabeth.dewey@piperrudnick.com

Ms. Leah Medway, Pro Bono Manager
E-mail: leah.medway@piperrudnick.com

Office Pro Bono Coordinators:
Kathleen Ellis and Gina Zawitoski (Baltimore)
Lisa Goodheart (Boston)
Richard Klawiter (Chicago)
Laurie Carroll (Dallas)
Neil David Walters (Edison)
Fred Heather (Los Angeles)
Edward Maluf (New York)
Dan Ansa (Philadelphia)
Mike Bedke (Tampa)
David Bamberger (Washington)
Robert Fries (San Francisco)
Frank Connolly and Stu Mendelsohn (Reston)

Office Pro Bono Partners:
Sheldon Krantz, Esq. (Washington)
Stan Adelman, Esq. (Chicago)

If yes, what percentage of his or her time is spent on pro bono work? 100 percent for pro bono counsel and pro bono manager.

Does the firm have a pro bono committee? Yes

If yes, how often does the committee meet? Approximately once per quarter.

Describe the composition of the committee: The committee consists of the pro bono counsel, pro bono manager, pro bono partners and office pro bono coordinators.

THE SCOOP

Does your firm have a written pro bono policy? Yes

Has the firm signed on to the Law Firm Pro Bono Challenge? Yes

What are some of the areas of law in which your firm has performed pro bono legal work in the last two years? We perform pro bono work in virtually every legal area such as civil rights and public rights, community economic development, poverty law, family law, international and human rights, immigration, real estate, intellectual property, legislative assistance and lobbying, and nonprofit governance.

What are some of the areas of law in which your firm does not perform pro bono work? While we have no set policy against taking certain types of matters, the firm is generally unable to take employment or medical malpractice pro bono cases due to conflicts.

Organizations for which your firm has performed pro bono legal services in the last two years: Asian American Legal Services Clinic, Bay Area Legal Services, The Children's Law Center, Community Economic Development Law Project, Dallas Volunteer Attorney Program, D.C. Bar Pro Bono Clinic, Lawyers Committee for Human Rights, Legal Counsel for the Elderly, Maryland Disability Law Center and Maryland Volunteer Lawyers Service.

List up to three pro bono matters that are representative of the pro bono work your firm participates in.

- Special Education Project with D.C. Appleseed Center. Approximately 30 lawyers, staff and family members of partners analyzed the D.C. public school system due process hearing procedures used to determine special education needs and assignments, and prepared a major report with important findings and recommendations. The team is now working to help implement its recommendations.

- Signature Project with The Children's Law Center. In 2001, the D.C. office of the firm committed to provide up to 5,000 hours in legal services to address significant problems confronting the city (including adoption project, corporate counsel representation and more).

- Chicago Lawyers Committee for Civil Rights HUD matter. The firm worked with the Chicago Lawyers Committee for Civil Rights Under Law in representation of a class of plaintiffs who had purchased homes through an entity that intentionally defrauded HUD, lenders and low-income homebuyers, resulting in a settlement of over $1 million.

BY THE NUMBERS

What is the total number of hours that lawyers in U.S. offices at your firm spent performing pro bono legal services in 2000, 2001 and 2002?

> **Total number of hours in 2000:** 30,105 hours*
> **Total number of hours in 2001:** 31,781 hours*
> **Total number of hours in 2002:** 39,790 hours*

Average number of pro bono hours per attorney in U.S. offices per year (including associates, partners, counsels, but not summer associates):

> **Average number of hours per attorney in 2000:** 28.84 hours*
> **Average number of hours per attorney in 2001:** 36.31 hours*
> **Average number of hours per attorney in 2002:** 29.03 hours*

What percentage of attorneys in this firm's U.S. offices did pro bono work in 2002? 62.5 percent*

What percentage of attorneys in this firm's U.S. offices did at least 20 hours of pro bono work in 2002? 30.45 percent*

Does the firm encourage its lawyers to perform a minimum number of pro bono hours? Yes

If so, how many hours per year or what percentage of lawyers' billable hours? The firm encourages its lawyers each to contribute at least 50 hours of pro bono work each year. Associates receive credit for up to 100 hours of pro bono work and for all pro bono hours once 2,000 billable hours have been reached.

SUPERVISION AND EVALUATIONS

Is there partner supervision on each pro bono matter? Yes

Do partner supervisors or, if applicable, senior associates provide written evaluations of associates' work on pro bono matters? Yes

If so, are those evaluations taken into account in determining salary, bonuses or advancement in the firm? Yes

If not, does the firm consider pro bono work generally in associate evaluations? N/A

HOURS

Does the firm give billable hour credit for pro bono work? Yes

Does the firm have a maximum number of pro bono hours that can be applied toward the billable hour target? Yes

If so, what is the maximum? 100 hours*

If your firm uses hours to determine bonuses, does it consider pro bono hours when determining bonuses? Yes

PRO BONO POINTS

What training opportunities are open to associates working on pro bono matters? The firm offers a wide range of training opportunities including seminars, training lunches, partner supervision and training by members of legal service providers with whom we are working.

Can associates bring matters of interest to the firm? Yes

Does the firm offer the use of support staff in carrying out pro bono matters? Yes

What pro bono opportunities are available for summer associates? For the most part, all pro bono opportunities are available for summer associates and the firm encourages their involvement.

Does the firm have established programs, such as externships, that enable its associates to work in a public interest setting? Yes

If so, where and for up to how long? We participate in the Public Interest Law Initiative (PILI) which provides fellowships for law students and new graduates who want to work at public interest law agencies in Chicago. Incoming associates can spend time prior to joining the firm at one of 44 PILI-affiliated agencies. We also participate in the D.C. Bar Pro Bono Program's Graduate Student Fellowship Program in which incoming associates can spend time prior to joining the firm at one of 10 different public interest agencies.

Has your firm won any special recognition or awards in the last two years for its pro bono work? Yes

If so, please list. D.C. Bar Pro Bono Law Firm of the Year Award (2002) and Pro Bono Lawyer of the Year Award (to Sheldon Krantz) (2003); Pro Bono Resource Center of Maryland's Pro Bono Law Firm of the Year Award (2002) and Pro Bono Service Award (to Kathleen Ellis) (2003); Leadership Washington Community Partnership Award (2003); Federal Judiciary Honor by D.C. Circuit Judicial Conference Standing Committee on Pro Bono Legal Services (2003); WORCforce Partner Appreciation Award (2002 and 2003); Yonkers Martin Luther King Commission Acknowledgement (2003); Dallas Volunteer Attorney Program Special Recognition (2003); American Jewish Committee's Judge Learned Hand Award (to Jeffrey Liss) (2003); Anti-Defamation League's Distinguished Community Service Award (to Jan Anne Dubin in 2003); Chicago Bar Association Alliance for Women's Alta May Hulett Award (to Kathleen Nooney) (2003); National Network to End Domestic Violence Partners for Peaceful Homes Advocacy Award (2003); Anti-Defamation League's Civil Rights Award (to Stephen Landsman) (2002); New Jersey State Historical Trust Award (2002); Washington Lawyers Committee for Civil Rights and Urban Affairs Outstanding Achievement Award in Public Education (2002); Community Service Award from Staten Island Children's Museum (2002); Mercedes Mentor Award for Outstanding Community Service (to Janice Duban) (2002); Equal Justice Council of the Legal Aid Bureau of Maryland's Young Lawyer's Division Leadership Award (2002); Coordinated Advice and Referral Program for Legal Services (CARPLS) Golden Gavel Award (2002).

THE FIRM SAYS

Piper Rudnick has ranked in the top third of the 100 largest law firms by the AmLaw 100 Survey in 2001 and 2002. Pro bono service is ingrained in our culture. In 1969, one of our predecessors, Piper & Marbury, established a storefront office in East Baltimore to offer legal services to low-income people. Our other predecessor, Rudnick & Wolfe, served as general counsel to Bethel New Life, Inc., a national nonprofit housing and community institution, for 20 years. Since then, we've been involved in pro bono projects for hundreds of charities including food banks, women's shelters, immigration help centers and emergency assistance organizations. The firm supports this commitment by: (1) Recognizing up to 100 hours of associate pro bono time as equivalent to billable hours for all purposes (and in some cases more than 100 hours); (2) Awarding bonuses each year to associates in recognition of outstanding pro bono contributions; (3) Providing a full-service pro bono program, which includes, but is not limited to: (a) a full-time pro bono counsel and manager, as well as local pro bono partners with dedicated time given to the program; (b) an attorney who acts as the pro bono coordinator in each of the firm's major offices; and (c) a firm-wide pro bono committee and pro bono committees in certain of the firm's offices. Together, these dedicated individuals manage firm-wide efforts, act as liaisons with nonprofit organizations and ensure that the necessary mentoring, training and lawyer and staff resources are in place for the firm's pro bono clients to receive the same high quality of legal services as clients of the firm's other practice areas do.

In the fall of 2002, Piper Rudnick joined together with Verner Liipfert, a law firm that distinguished itself with a deep commitment to public service. This merger has added an important new dimension to our pro bono program — a legislative/lobbying component. Piper Rudnick's federal affairs practice has been engaged in a variety of pro bono projects. For example, the firm represents the transitional government of Afghanistan before the U.S. Congress and executive branch, working with the embassy and President Karzai's administration. Former Senator George Mitchell of the firm served, pro bono, as the Independent Overseer of the American Red Cross Liberty Disaster Relief Fund for victims of the 9/11 attacks, and the federal affairs group represents the New York Police Department before Congress with respect to homeland security efforts.

The legal service organizations with whom we work provide the skills and resources to strengthen our communities. Some projects and organizations we are involved with include: working with food banks and food rescue organizations across the nation to fight hunger; participating in local legal service provider clinics serving indigent clients and taking on pro bono cases through a variety of other organizations; conducting major special education policy initiative in conjunction with the Appleseed Foundation's D.C. office; in times of serious crisis, helping the victims of the September 11 disaster; providing legislative assistance and lobbying before Congress on behalf of various clients; representing international clients, as well as persons seeking political asylum and protection in the U.S. based on human rights abuses; representing various classes of people who have experienced racial discrimination and sexual harassment; helping small community groups with corporate structure and tax issues, as well as developing projects focused on the most economically vulnerable in our society; and working with The Children's Law Center to provide legal services to reduce a sizable backlog in adoption cases in D.C. Superior Court.

Note that responses to these questions include approximations and some include a minimal amount of pro bono work not strictly within the ABA definition, but for which our firm gives pro bono credit.

OUR SURVEY SAYS

"The commitment is real, encouraged and a factor in partner and associate compensation."

"The application of up to 100 pro bono hours towards bonuses provides a great amount of encouragement for associates to take on pro bono work."

"The firm gives billable hour credit for pro bono work and has strongly encouraged associate participation. The Baltimore and D.C. offices were both given awards as the pro bono offices of the year by the Maryland and D.C. bar associations, respectively."

"I have been heavily involved in pro bono work with the firm's blessing. I have seen others doing a lot of pro bono work as well."

"The firm is very supportive of pro bono activity and provides unlimited financial support for any kind of pro bono work you want to do. Recently, the firm began giving up to 100 hours billable credit for pro bono work, another indication of their support."

"So far, I've been allowed and even asked to do a fair amount of pro bono, so it appears to me the commitment's pretty high."

"Firm management wants the firm to participate in as much pro bono work as possible — all lawyers can count up to 100 hours of pro bono time toward bonus eligibility."

"The firm is very committed to pro bono. If a particular practice or partner is not as committed, it can be difficult for associates who otherwise would like to be more involved."

"The firm's pro bono commitment is great. It has committed to removing the backlog of adoption cases in Washington, D.C., and all first-years take a case. The firm has an amazing pro bono coordinator."

"The firm is fine with pro bono, as long as you reach the minimum billable hour requirement. The analysis of an associate begins with the billable hour requirement."

Preston Gates & Ellis LLP

925 Fourth Avenue, Suite 2900
Seattle, WA 98104-1158
Phone: (206) 623-7580
www.prestongates.com

LOCATIONS

Seattle, WA (HQ)
Anchorage, AK • Coeur d'Alene, ID • Irvine, CA • Portland, OR • San Francisco, CA • Spokane, WA • Washington, DC* • Hong Kong

*As Preston Gates Ellis & Rouvelas Meeds LLP

MAJOR DEPARTMENTS & PRACTICES

Antitrust & Trade Regulation
Appellate Practice
Bankruptcy, Insolvency & Reorganization
Business
Construction, Design & Public Contracting
E-Commerce
Emerging Business
Employee Benefits, Employment & Labor
Energy & Utilities
Environmental Law
Family Law
Government Contracts, Policy & Ethics
Health Care
Homeland Security
Immigration
Intellectual Property & Technology
Life Sciences
Litigation
Maritime
Mergers & Acquisitions
Private Equity
Public Finance
Real Estate & Finance
Securities
Tax
Telecommunications
Transportation
Trusts & Estates

THE STATS

No. of attorneys worldwide: 424
No. of offices worldwide: 9
Chairman: William H. Neukom
Managing Partner: B. Gerald Johnson

EMPLOYMENT CONTACT

Ms. Kristine Immordino
Director, Legal Recruiting
Phone: (206) 623-7580
Fax: (206) 623-7022
E-mail: krisi@prestongates.com

WHO'S WHO

Principal pro bono contact(s) at your firm:

Susan Delanty Jones, Esq.
Pro Bono Partner
Phone: (206) 623-7580
E-mail: susanj@prestongates.com

Does the firm have a pro bono coordinator? Yes
Susan Delanty Jones

If yes, what percentage of his or her time is spent on pro bono work? Half time

Does the firm have a pro bono committee? Yes

If yes, how often does the committee meet? Monthly

Describe the composition of the committee: Partners and associates from all U.S.-based offices of the firm, together with one staff person from the marketing department.

THE SCOOP

Does your firm have a pro bono policy? Yes

Has the firm signed on to the Law Firm Pro Bono Challenge? Yes

What are some of the areas of law in which your firm has performed pro bono legal work in the last two years? Homelessness, immigration, affirmative action, debtor/creditor, nonprofits, family law (domestic violence and termination of parental rights), criminal appeals, class action appeals.

What are some of the areas of law in which your firm does not perform pro bono work? Criminal trial work.

Organizations for which your firm has performed pro bono legal services in the last two years: Northwest Immigration Rights Project, Court-appointed Special Advocate Project, King County Bar Association Legal Clinics, Kidney Cancer Association, Outside-In (drop-in legal clinic for homeless youth).

List up to three pro bono matters that are representative of the pro bono work your firm participates in.

- University of Michigan Affirmative Action case. We filed an amicus brief on behalf of members of Congress in United States Supreme Court.

- Grand Aerie v. Fraternal Order of Eagles. We filed a successful opposition to a petition for certiorari in the United States Supreme Court in this gender discrimination case.

- Homeless Clinics. With the King County Bar Association we established and staff a monthly legal clinic for residents of a transitional housing facility.

BY THE NUMBERS

What is the total number of hours that lawyers in U.S. offices at your firm spent performing pro bono legal services in 2000, 2001 and 2002?

    Total number of hours in 2000: N/A
    Total number of hours in 2001: N/A
    Total number of hours in 2002: N/A

Average number of pro bono hours per attorney in U.S. offices per year (including associates, partners, counsels, but not summer associates):

    Average number of hours per attorney in 2000: 22 hours
    Average number of hours per attorney in 2001: 27 hours
    Average number of hours per attorney in 2002: 31 hours

What percentage of attorneys in this firm's U.S. offices did pro bono work in 2002? 76 percent

What percentage of attorneys in this firm's U.S. offices did at least 20 hours of pro bono work in 2002? 37 percent

Does the firm encourage its lawyers to perform a minimum number of pro bono hours? Yes

If so, how many hours per year or what percentage of lawyers' billable hours? 50 hours per year.

SUPERVISION AND EVALUATIONS

Is there partner supervision on each pro bono matter? Yes

Do partner supervisors or, if applicable, senior associates provide written evaluations of associates' work on pro bono matters? Yes

If so, are those evaluations taken into account in determining salary, bonuses or advancement in the firm? Yes

If not, does the firm consider pro bono work generally in associate evaluations? Yes

HOURS

Does the firm give billable hour credit for pro bono work? Yes

Does the firm have a maximum number of pro bono hours that can be applied toward the billable hour target? Yes

If so, what is the maximum? 50 hours

If your firm uses hours to determine bonuses, does it consider pro bono hours when determining bonuses? Yes

PRO BONO POINTS

What training opportunities are open to associates working on pro bono matters? Many organizations sponsor training in specific legal areas and the firm encourages and supports attendance. The firm also recently sponsored an in-house training on ethics and pro bono.

Can associates bring matters of interest to the firm? Yes

Does the firm offer the use of support staff in carrying out pro bono matters? Yes

What pro bono opportunities are available for summer associates? Summer associates are encouraged to, and do, take pro bono cases (with supervision).

Does the firm have established programs, such as externships, that enable its associates to work in a public interest setting? Yes

If so, where and for up to how long? Columbia Legal Services (Seattle): one year; ACLU (Chicago): one year.

Has your firm won any special recognition or awards in the last two years for its pro bono work? Yes

If so, please list. 1. Seattle Urban League: 2003 Annual "Spirit" Award for successful pro bono litigation on behalf of the League in connection with the establishment of an African-American museum and cultural center. 2. Young Lawyers' Division of Washington State Bar Association: 2003 Outstanding Young Lawyer of the Year to Anthony Miles for his pro bono services to those in need, including his amicus brief to the United States Supreme Court in the University of Michigan affirmative action case.

THE FIRM SAYS

Preston Gates & Ellis LLP believes that providing pro bono service is a vital element of every attorney's professional responsibility. Such service provides an invaluable contribution to the community and particularly to those who otherwise cannot afford such services. Thus, the firm's policy is to strongly encourage its attorneys and staff to undertake pro bono and community service in areas of their choice and interest. The firm encourages each lawyer to perform at least 60 hours per year of pro bono work and other community service, with 50 hours of pro bono representation of clients. The firm has a Pro Bono and Public Service Committee with representation from all of its U.S. offices and a pro bono partner who spends half her time on pro bono cases and administration of the pro bono program. There is a written pro bono policy with detailed procedures for undertaking pro bono assignments and ongoing efforts to match up pro bono cases with the individual interests expressed by the lawyers. Associates may earn up to 50 billable hours for pro bono work, and extraordinary efforts in pro bono matters are seriously considered in the annual discretionary bonuses for both associates and partners.

OUR SURVEY SAYS

"The firm strongly encourages pro bono. I wish that the billable hours credit for pro bono were more than 50 hours, however."

"Fifty hours is all that's officially credited to billable work, but I sense that a substantial project would be well received."

"An attorney can credit 50 hours of pro bono time to the billable hour requirement, and we have a full-time pro bono litigator."

"I was told at my review that the firm encourages us to work at least 50 hours each year on pro bono matters."

"There's a lot of lip service to pro bono, but the firm only counts 50 hours towards billable hours requirements, which is a huge disincentive to take on a big case (or, in my case, a career-limiting move when you do take on a big case and spend 200+ hours on it)."

"The firm definitely talks it up, and 50 hours a year of pro bono counts to the billable hour requirement."

"The firm encourages each lawyer to perform at least 60 hours per year of pro bono work and other community service, with 50 hours of pro bono representation of clients."

— *Preston Gates & Ellis LLP*

Proskauer Rose LLP

1585 Broadway
New York, NY 10036-8299
Phone: (212) 969-3000
www.proskauer.com

LOCATIONS

New York, NY (HQ)
Boca Raton, FL
Los Angeles, CA
Newark, NJ
Washington, DC
Paris

MAJOR DEPARTMENTS & PRACTICES

Antitrust
Banking & Financial Services
Bankruptcy & Reorganization
Corporate & Securities
Criminal Defense & Corporate Investigations
Employee Benefits & ERISA
Entertainment, Sports & Media
Estates, Wills, Trusts & Probate
Health Care
Immigration
Intellectual Property
International Arbitration
Labor & Employment
Litigation
Nonprofit/Exempt Organizations
Personal Planning
Private Equity Funds
Real Estate, Environmental & Zoning
Taxation

THE STATS

No. of attorneys worldwide: 590
No. of offices worldwide: 6
Chairman: Alan S. Jaffe

EMPLOYMENT CONTACT

Ms. Diane M. Kolnik
Manager of Legal Recruiting
Phone: (212) 969-5060
E-mail: dkolnik@proskauer.com

WHO'S WHO

Principal pro bono contact(s) at your firm:

John W. Ritchie, Esq.
Senior Counsel
Phone: (212) 969-3530
E-mail: jritchie@proskauer.com

Does the firm have a pro bono coordinator? No

Does the firm have a pro bono committee? Yes

If yes, how often does the committee meet? As needed.

Describe the composition of the committee: Two partners, one senior counsel, one associate and the director of associate affairs.

THE SCOOP

Does your firm have a written pro bono policy? Yes

Has the firm signed on to the Law Firm Pro Bono Challenge? Yes

What are some of the areas of law in which your firm has performed pro bono legal work in the last two years? Family court matters for victims of domestic abuse, Social Security appeals for low income claimants, housing discrimination, wills for HIV-AIDS sufferers, assistance to victims of the World Trade Center disaster, ongoing post-conviction work for death row inmate. The firm is participating in two new pro bono projects devoted to facilitating adoption of foster children in New York.

What are some of the areas of law in which your firm does not perform pro bono work? Plaintiffs' employment discrimination, actions against the City of New York.

Organizations for which your firm has performed pro bono legal services in the last two years: Legal Aid Society, Volunteer Lawyers for the Arts, Sanctuary for Families, Lawyers Alliance of New York, Gay Men's Health Crisis, New York Lawyers for the Public Interest, American Civil Liberties Union, Now Legal Defense and Education Fund, Office of the Corporation Counsel of the City of New York

List up to three pro bono matters that are representative of the pro bono work your firm participates in.

- Since June 2000, Proskauer has devoted hundreds of hours of pro bono attorney time to representation of the plaintiffs in a housing discrimination class action, King, et al. v. City of Blakely Housing Authority, et al., pending in the U.S. District Court for the Middle District of Georgia. With the Lawyers' Committee for Civil Rights Under Law and local counsel in Georgia, Proskauer is counsel for four individual plaintiffs, three of whom are also class representatives, and the Concerned Citizens Committee of Blakely & Early County, Georgia, in prosecuting claims for declaratory and injunctive relief and incidental damages on behalf of each of the plaintiffs and a class of past, present and future African-American tenants and applicants for public housing operated by the defendant Blakely Housing Authority. After extensive discovery, in September 2003, the court certified a plaintiff class. The parties are now engaged in post-discovery motion practice.

- The firm's current work with Sanctuary for Families includes an associate's representation of a battered woman who was brought to this country by her husband, who repeatedly raped and beat her, even while she was pregnant, until he eventually divorced her and threw her out of her home. He also gave her HIV. The matter at present involves opposition to the former husband's request for unsupervised child visitation rights on the grounds, among others, of his continued harassment and menacing of the woman, in violation of her Family Court Order of Protection.

- Another associate, working with the Legal Aid Society, is currently representing an autistic girl in foster care, responsible for ensuring that the girl receives all the educational services to which she is entitled under the Individuals with Disabilities Act. Other associates have recently filed Violence Against Women Act self-petitions and successfully represented indigent persons at Social Security disability benefits hearings.

BY THE NUMBERS

What is the total number of hours that lawyers in U.S. offices at your firm spent performing pro bono legal services in 2000, 2001 and 2002?

Total number of hours in 2000: 15,420 hours
Total number of hours in 2001: 18,161 hours
Total number of hours in 2002: 21,030 hours

Average number of pro bono hours per attorney in U.S. offices per year (including associates, partners, counsels, but not summer associates):

Average number of hours per attorney in 2000: 31 hours
Average number of hours per attorney in 2001: 35 hours
Average number of hours per attorney in 2002: 40 hours

What percentage of attorneys in this firm's U.S. offices did pro bono work in 2002? 65 percent

What percentage of attorneys in this firm's U.S. offices did at least 20 hours of pro bono work in 2002? N/A

SUPERVISION AND EVALUATIONS

Is there partner supervision on each pro bono matter? There is senior lawyer supervision of all matters.

Do partner supervisors or, if applicable, senior associates provide written evaluations of associates' work on pro bono matters? Yes

If so, are those evaluations taken into account in determining salary, bonuses or advancement in the firm? Yes

If not, does the firm consider pro bono work generally in associate evaluations? N/A

HOURS

Does the firm give billable hour credit for pro bono work? Yes

Does the firm have a maximum number of pro bono hours that can be applied toward the billable hour target? No

If so, what is the maximum? N/A

If your firm uses hours to determine bonuses, does it consider pro bono hours when determining bonuses? Yes

PRO BONO POINTS

What training opportunities are open to associates working on pro bono matters? The firm invites various pro bono clearinghouse organizations to conduct training in the firm's offices. In addition, associates may use a training allowance to register for pro bono training programs for which there is a registration fee.

Can associates bring matters of interest to the firm? Yes

Does the firm offer the use of support staff in carrying out pro bono matters? Yes

What pro bono opportunities are available for summer associates? Proskauer is an active participant in the Courtroom Advocates Project ("CAP") in which summer associates are trained to assist victims of domestic violence in obtaining orders of protection against their abusers in family court. The firm has also offered pro bono externship opportunities from time to time.

Does the firm have established programs, such as externships, that enable its associates to work in a public interest setting? No

If so, where and for up to how long? N/A

Has your firm won any special recognition or awards in the last two years for its pro bono work? Yes

If so, please list. Proskauer's pro bono assistance to struggling artists and arts organizations was recognized by Volunteer Lawyers for the Arts, which awarded the firm the 2001 Outstanding Pro Bono Service Award. In 2002, the firm received a pro bono award from the Legal Aid Society in connection with its work helping victims of the World Trade Center tragedy. In addition, in 2003, individual attorneys were honored for pro bono contrigutions to The Legal Aid Society, Sanctuary for Families, and Lawyers Alliance for New York.

THE FIRM SAYS

Proskauer has a long-standing and strong commitment to pro bono activities, with a major emphasis on providing legal services to the poor. That commitment is manifested both in the structure of the firm's procedures for handling pro bono matters and in the scope and diversity of its pro bono docket. The firm's pro bono program in New York is coordinated by three senior lawyers. They communicate pro bono opportunities to attorneys, coordinate the staffing of each project and, along with other senior attorneys in the firm, supervise the matters. Additionally, subject to conflict procedures and firm policies, individual attorneys also have the discretion to engage in pro bono activities of their own choice. Our offices outside New York have similar procedures. The firm maintains ongoing referral relationships with many organizations, including the Legal Aid Society, Sanctuary for Families, Volunteer Lawyers for the Arts, Lawyers Alliance for New York, the Gay Men's Health Crisis, Volunteers of Legal Services, New York Lawyers for the Public Interest and the pro se clerk's office of the U.S. District Court for the Southern District of New York.

In order to introduce new lawyers to the personal and professional satisfaction of handling pro bono work, each first-year associate is assigned his or her own pro bono matter from one of the above organizations. The assignment is given out at the conclusion of the Proskauer Institute, the firm's week-long intensive introductory training program for new associates. Our hope is that introducing associates to pro bono work early in their careers will help instill in them a long-term commitment to including pro bono work as part of their professional lives. The firm treats hours recorded to pro bono matters as client hours as if they were billable, and does not impose a fixed limit on the number of hours that may be so treated. Our pro bono docket includes large matters as well as small, individual clients as well as not-for-profit organizations, litigated matters as well as transactional. We offer personal planning assistance to persons in need of wills, labor and tax advice to community groups, immigration as well as political asylum representation. Our recent docket includes assistance to individuals and small businesses affected by the World Trade Center disaster, representation of a prisoner on Florida's death row and representation of a class of current and former African-American tenants of a federally-funded housing authority in rural Georgia alleging federal claims of overt housing discrimination and retaliation.

Proskauer has recently committed to two new pro bono initiatives in New York City dedicated to improving the availability of legal services for the adoption of children now in foster care and helping to expedite the adoption process. Participation in these initiatives – involving The Legal Aid Society and MFY Legal Services – was available only to a limited number of New York law firms. The projects have the potential of facilitating the adoptions of thousands of children who are now in foster care. Proskauer is proud to be among the firms chosen to participate in these projects.

OUR SURVEY SAYS

"Although I was working on several projects, all of the partners and more senior associates made sure that I had time to do my pro bono work and that I had help if I had questions."

"The firm regularly publicizes pro bono opportunities, counts work on them as billable and enabled me to bring in my own pro bono client."

"They let you count up to 150 hours towards billable requirements, but they aren't always happy about it."*

"While e-mails are often sent around, pro bono work is always put off since there are always so many urgent assignments in litigation."

"It's great that we can count 150 hours of pro bono as billables per year, but it would be even better if they would just allow all pro bono hours to count (obviously there would need to be some limits)."*

"The firm is committed to pro bono work in its larger offices, but that commitment is not as strong in the smaller offices."

"They give you pro bono hours but it always comes second to billable work."

"The mandatory pro bono program for first-years is great; the firm always sends out e-mails asking for people to respond to pro bono opportunities."

"We're doing well here — all first-years get their own pro bono case the day they walk in to their office and get to run with it. The firm has been very supportive of the long hours I've logged on a pair of pro bono criminal appeals."

"Partners regularly encourage associates to take on pro bono work. However, more of them could lead by example."

* The firm points out that its policy has changed since these comments were made, and there is now no fixed limit on the pro bono hours that may be counted as billable hours.

"In order to introduce new lawyers to the personal and professional satisfaction of handling pro bono work, each first-year associate is assigned his or her own pro bono matter."

— *Proskauer Rose LLP*

Ropes & Gray LLP

One International Place
Boston, MA 02110-2624
Phone: (617) 951-7000
www.ropesgray.com

LOCATIONS

Boston, MA (HQ)
New York, NY
Providence, RI*
San Francisco, CA
Washington, DC
London*

Conference centers

MAJOR DEPARTMENTS & PRACTICES

Antitrust
Bankruptcy & Creditors' Rights
Corporate
Government Relations & Regulatory
Intellectual Property
International
Labor & Employment
Litigation
Private Client Group
Tax & Benefits

THE STATS

No. of attorneys worldwide: 580 +
No. of offices worldwide: 4
Chairman and Managing Partner: Douglass N. Ellis Jr.

EMPLOYMENT CONTACT

Mr. Thomas A. Grewe
Director of Legal Recruiting
Phone: (617) 951-7239
Long Distance: (800) 951-4888, ext. 7239
Fax: (617) 951-7050
E-mail: hiringprogram@ropesgray.com

WHO'S WHO

Principal pro bono contact(s) at your firm:

Ana M. Francisco, Esq.
Chair, Pro Bono Committee
Phone: (617) 951-7541
E-mail: afrancisco@ropesgray.com

Does the firm have a pro bono coordinator? No

If yes, what percentage of his or her time is spent on pro bono work? N/A

Does the firm have a pro bono committee? Yes.

If yes, how often does the committee meet? The committee meets as needed.

Describe the composition of the committee: Our pro bono committee comprises partners from our Boston, Washington, New York and San Francisco offices. In all, there are 10 members on the committee.

THE SCOOP

Does your firm have a written pro bono policy? Yes

Has the firm signed on to the Law Firm Pro Bono Challenge? No

What are some of the areas of law in which your firm has performed pro bono legal work in the last two years? We have performed pro bono legal work in a wide variety of areas. In the litigation area, we have represented indigent individuals seeking asylum in the United States, we have worked on two Alabama death penalty appeals, we have done civil rights cases (recently especially in the area of gay rights) and we have represented indigent clients in a variety of forums, including through referral programs administered by local homeless shelters. In the non-litigation area, we provide advice to a number of not-for-profit organizations. Most recently our focus has been on general representation and advice, real estate acquisition and zoning matters, and incorporating and obtaining tax-exempt status for not-for-profit organizations.

What are some of the areas of law in which your firm does not perform pro bono work? We have no hard and fast rule excluding any category of pro bono work.

Organizations for which your firm has performed pro bono legal services in the last two years: The Political Asylum/Immigration Representation Project ("PAIR"), The Volunteer Lawyers Project of the Boston Bar Association, Artists for Humanity, Physicians for Human Rights, The Lawyers Committee for Civil Rights Under the Law, GLAD, Massachusetts Legal Clinic for the Homeless, District of Columbia Public Library Foundation, Massachusetts Appleseed Center for Law and Justice, Conservation Law Foundation of N.E., Inc., Chelsea Neighborhood Housing Services.

List up to three pro bono matters that are representative of the pro bono work your firm participates in.

- For the last several years, the firm has made a significant commitment to representing asylum seekers through the PAIR program. We have represented dozens of individuals, many of whom have been granted asylum.

- Ropes & Gray has acted as counsel to Artists for Humanity, an entrepreneurial after school visual arts program for teenagers in the Boston public school system. Most recently the firm has represented Artists for Humanity in the acquisition, zoning and development of a new state of the art facility providing studio, gallery and performance space.

- Over the last few years the firm has also provided pro bono legal services to GLAD (Gay & Lesbian Advocates & Defenders) and other advocacy groups in support of equal rights for gays and lesbians. Most recently, attorneys at Ropes & Gray filed an amicus curiae brief in the Massachusetts Supreme Judicial Court ("SJC") presenting constitutional and international law arguments in favor of equal marriage rights for gays and lesbians. The brief was filed on behalf of a number of, inter alia, international and domestic gay rights groups (including, for example, the Coalition Gaie et Lesbienne du Quebec and the Japan Association for the Lesbian and Gay Movement). The SJC decided the appeal in which the amicus brief was filed, Goodridge, et al. v. Department of Public Health, on November 18, 2003; the SJC's decision that any ban on gay marriage is unconstitutional under the Massachusetts constitution is the first ruling of its kind in the country.

BY THE NUMBERS

What is the total number of hours that lawyers in U.S. offices at your firm spent performing pro bono legal services in 2000, 2001 and 2002?

>**Total number of hours in 2000:** 8,900 hours
>**Total number of hours in 2001:** 12,050 hours
>**Total number of hours in 2002:** 12,800 hours

Average number of pro bono hours per attorney in U.S. offices per year (including associates, partners, counsels, but not summer associates):

>**Average number of hours per attorney in 2000:** N/A *See note below
>**Average number of hours per attorney in 2001:** N/A
>**Average number of hours per attorney in 2002:** N/A

*Note: These numbers are not available and cannot accurately be derived from the hours totals because the number of lawyers at Ropes & Gray has changed over the relevant period of time because of expansions in our practice in certain areas.

What percentage of attorneys in this firm's U.S. offices did pro bono work in 2002? N/A **See note below

**Note: Again, this number is not available and would not be meaningful at this point because of the expansions in our practice referenced above. Every attorney is encouraged to participate in pro bono work to the extent that he or she wishes and is able to do so.

What percentage of attorneys in this firm's U.S. offices did at least 20 hours of pro bono work in 2002? N/A

Does the firm encourage its lawyers to perform a minimum number of pro bono hours? No

If so, how many hours per year or what percentage of lawyers' billable hours? Not applicable

SUPERVISION AND EVALUATIONS

Is there partner supervision on each pro bono matter? Yes

1) Every pro bono matter has a partner assigned to it. The actual amount of supervision varies, however, depending on the nature of the matter and the experience and level of skill of the associates involved.

Do partner supervisors or, if applicable, senior associates provide written evaluations of associates' work on pro bono matters? Yes

2) Where appropriate, such evaluations are given as part of our normal associate review process, in which we review all of an associates work during the relevant marking period, both his or her pro bono and non-pro bono work.

If so, are those evaluations taken into account in determining salary, bonuses or advancement in the firm? Yes

3) The evaluations are considered equally with the evaluations of the associate's other work.

If not, does the firm consider pro bono work generally in associate evaluations? N/A

HOURS

Does the firm give billable hour credit for pro bono work? Yes

Does the firm have a maximum number of pro bono hours that can be applied toward the billable hour target? No

If so, what is the maximum? Not applicable

If your firm uses hours to determine bonuses, does it consider pro bono hours when determining bonuses? Not applicable

PRO BONO POINTS

What training opportunities are open to associates working on pro bono matters? Where are pro bono opportunities come from a sponsoring organization, such as PAIIR, that organization will provide training session and all lawyers participating in the PAIR Project are encouraged to attend the training session.

Can associates bring matters of interest to the firm? Yes

Does the firm offer the use of support staff in carrying out pro bono matters? Yes

What pro bono opportunities are available for summer associates? There are no pro bono programs aimed specifically at summer associates. Of course, they are encouraged to participate in our normal pro bono work and many do.

Does the firm have established programs, such as externships, that enable its associates to work in a public interest setting? Yes

If so, where and for up to how long? Each year, the firm sends two litigation associates to work for six months as an assistant district attorney in Middlesex County.

Has your firm won any special recognition or awards in the last two years for its pro bono work? Yes

If so, please list. Over the last several years we have consistently won awards from the PAIR project for our pro bono representation of indigent clients seeking asylum in this country.

THE FIRM SAYS

All lawyers are encouraged to participate in pro bono work to the extent that they desire and are able to. Pro bono clients are treated like any other client of the firm, including in terms of level of legal services provided and for purposes of associate reviews and compensation. As with all matters, department head approval is required for any new pro bono matter. A member of the pro bono committee also must approve the matter, and partner supervision is required for each pro bono matter. There are no hard and fast rules respecting what kinds of matters the firm will take on a pro bono basis. Generally, accepted representations involve either legal work for individuals or organizations with very limited resources who could not otherwise afford the firm's services, or the advancement of legal principles important to society.

OUR SURVEY SAYS

"I do a number of pro bono projects, and I have received great input, support and encouragement in these endeavors."

"The firm is making an effort, including the recent founding of two pro bono awards to be given to associates pursuing pro bono efforts."

"There is no pressure to participate and absolutely no backlash for doing so. The firm participates in many pro bono organizations and is very good about disseminating pro bono opportunities. We are then responsible for electing to participate. There is also a process for bringing pro bono work into the firm outside of the established channels. I personally participate in multiple pro bono projects and spend a considerable amount of time on pro bono activities."

"It is made available, but I never have any time to do it."

"The firm is extremely committed to pro bono work initiatives and encourages lawyers to get involved to the extent that this does not interfere with their primary commitment to billable hours."

"Associates are encouraged to do pro bono work and are given credit for it in the review process. The firm recently instituted an annual awards dinner for lawyers participating in pro bono work."

"I've been able to do as many hours of pro bono work as I wanted."

"The firm supports pro bono efforts with all of its capabilities (treated as a client matter just like other client matters), though initiating these matters is entirely within the individual conscience of each lawyer."

"With renewed emphasis on billables, the firm's pro bono commitment has suffered a great deal."

"I am stunned at how much time I've been able to spend doing pro bono work."

"Ropes & Gray has acted as counsel to Artists for Humanity, an entrepreneurial after school visual arts program for teenagers in the Boston public school system."

— *Ropes & Gray LLP*

Schulte Roth & Zabel LLP

919 Third Avenue
New York, NY 10022
Phone: (212) 756-2000
www.srz.com

LOCATIONS
New York, NY (HQ)
London

MAJOR DEPARTMENTS & PRACTICES
Business Reorganization
Corporate
Employment & Employee Benefits
Environmental
Individual Client Services
Intellectual Property
Litigation
Real Estate
Tax

THE STATS
No. of attorneys worldwide: 305
No. of offices worldwide: 2
Executive Committee: Martin Perschetz, Paul Roth, Alan Waldenberg, Paul Weber and Marc Weingarten

EMPLOYMENT CONTACT
Ms. Lisa Drew
Director of Recruiting
Phone: (212) 756-2000
Fax: (212) 593-5955
E-mail: lisa.drew@srz.com

WHO'S WHO

Principal pro bono contact(s) at your firm:

Brooks R. Burdette, Esq.
Partner and Chair of Pro Bono Committee
Phone: (212) 756-2272
E-mail: brooks.burdette@srz.com

Susan R. Galligan, Esq.
Special Counsel and Director of Professional Development
Phone: (212) 756-2218
E-mail: susan.galligan@srz.com

Does the firm have a pro bono coordinator? Yes. The director of professional development, assisted by the legal personnel coordinator, act as pro bono coordinators.

If yes, what percentage of his or her time is spent on pro bono work? 20 to 30 percent.

Does the firm have a pro bono committee? Yes

If yes, how often does the committee meet? Quarterly; communicates more frequently by e-mail.

Describe the composition of the committee: The committee consists of one partner and one associate from each of the firm's practice groups, the director of professional development and the legal personnel coordinator.

THE SCOOP

What are some of the areas of law in which your firm has performed pro bono legal work in the last two years? Asylum and human rights; education; environmental; prisoner's rights; litigation; family law; corporate; real estate; not-for-profit incorporation; elder law and estate planning.

What are some of the areas of law in which your firm does not perform pro bono work? Immigration.

Organizations for which your firm has performed pro bono legal services in the last two years: New York Legal Assistance Group, Volunteer Lawyers for the Arts, Lawyers Committee for Human Rights, Legal Services for the Elderly, New York Lawyers for the Public Interest, Natural Resource Defense Council, Human Rights Watch, Asian American Legal Defense and Education Fund, inMotion and Neighborhood Housing Service.

List up to three pro bono matters that are representative of the pro bono work your firm participates in.

- SRZ secured an important decision on behalf of our client, the National Resource Defense Council, when a federal judge in Los Angeles ruled that the National Environmental Policy Act applies to oceans beyond the territorial borders of the United States. The court's ruling, which resolved an unsettled area of law, denied the U.S. Navy's request to continue its naval sonar testing program.

- SRZ was co-counsel to a plaintiff class of thousands of abused and neglected New York City children in which plaintiffs alleged that systematic deficiencies in the child welfare system violated federal and state law and resulted in serious harm to children.

- We served as pro bono counsel, along with another law firm, assisting the plaintiffs' attorneys in Hamilton v. Accu-tek, a landmark case involving gun manufacturers' liability for negligent distribution of firearms.

BY THE NUMBERS

What is the total number of hours that lawyers in U.S. offices at your firm spent performing pro bono legal services in 2000, 2001 and 2002?

      Total number of hours in 2000: 10,500 hours
      Total number of hours in 2001: 12,778 hours
      Total number of hours in 2002: 10,127 hours

Average number of pro bono hours per attorney in U.S. offices per year (including associates, partners, counsels, but not summer associates):

      Average number of hours per attorney in 2000: 52 hours
      Average number of hours per attorney in 2001: 44 hours
      Average number of hours per attorney in 2002: 34 hours

What percentage of attorneys in this firm's U.S. offices did pro bono work in 2002? 39 percent

What percentage of attorneys in this firm's U.S. offices did at least 20 hours of pro bono work in 2002? 10.5 percent

Does the firm encourage its lawyers to perform a minimum number of pro bono hours? No

If so, how many hours per year or what percentage of lawyers' billable hours? N/A

SUPERVISION AND EVALUATIONS

Is there partner supervision on each pro bono matter? Yes

Do partner supervisors or, if applicable, senior associates provide written evaluations of associates' work on pro bono matters? Yes

If so, are those evaluations taken into account in determining salary, bonuses or advancement in the firm? Yes

If not, does the firm consider pro bono work generally in associate evaluations? N/A

HOURS

Does the firm give billable hour credit for pro bono work? Yes

Does the firm have a maximum number of pro bono hours that can be applied toward the billable hour target? No

If so, what is the maximum? N/A

If your firm uses hours to determine bonuses, does it consider pro bono hours when determining bonuses? Yes

PRO BONO POINTS

What training opportunities are open to associates working on pro bono matters? Associates are encouraged to attend CLE sessions on subjects relating to their pro bono assignments. In addition, associates working on pro bono matters often have significant responsibility for managing the case, client interaction and the opportunity to take depositions and appear in court.

Can associates bring matters of interest to the firm? Yes

Does the firm offer the use of support staff in carrying out pro bono matters? Yes

What pro bono opportunities are available for summer associates? Our summer program includes a mandatory pro bono week, during which each summer associate actually works at the office of a public interest organization. Each summer associate is matched with an organization according to his or her interests and is expected to work full time on projects assigned by the organization. In addition to their pro bono internships, summer associates often assist attorneys at the firm on pro bono matters. We also sponsor two 1-L summer associate fellowships in conjunction with New York Lawyers for the Public Interest.

Does the firm have established programs, such as externships, that enable its associates to work in a public interest setting? No

Has your firm won any special recognition or awards in the last two years for its pro bono work? Yes

If so, please list. Two of our attorneys in the employment and employee benefits department were honored by Neighborhood Housing Services of New York City. Mark Brossman received the 2003 Lawyers Alliance Cornerstone Award for pro bono excellence, and William Zabel received the 2003 Human Rights Award from Lawyers Committee for Human Rights.

THE FIRM SAYS

At Schulte Roth & Zabel LLP, our partners, associates and summer associates are committed to sharing their knowledge and time with organizations that represent the elderly, the indigent and the disenfranchised.

We are a signatory firm to the Volunteers of Legal Service pro bono commitment, and we are proud to have been the first firm in New York to include a pro bono week in our summer program.

Attorneys at the firm handle a variety of pro bono matters in conjunction with numerous public interest organizations and every effort is made to match associates with projects in areas that interest them. Every case is supervised by a partner and all firm resources are available to attorneys working on pro bono matters. Our attorneys have assumed leadership roles in legal aid organizations and have received awards for their pro bono service. In recent years we have sponsored a number of Equal Justice Works Fellowships. These fellowships provide the funding to enable recent law school graduates to work in the public interest for two years on a project of his or her own creation. The supported projects not only provide services to needy individuals but also educate and empower larger numbers of people.

Schulte Roth & Zabel also supports various public service initiatives. Our partners and attorneys are involved with the Legal Outreach program which consists of a one-week paid internship during the summer for eight students who attend various high schools in Manhattan and Brooklyn. Throughout the school year our associates participate in a mentoring

program for high school students and act as coaches for students from Louis D. Brandeis High School in the moot court competition which is held in the fall and a mock trial competition in the spring.

We encourage each of our associates to perform pro bono service and count all pro bono time towards an attorney's yearly target hours. All time spent by SRZ attorneys on pro bono cases is treated by the firm in the same way as billable client work.

OUR SURVEY SAYS

"[The commitment] varies among departments. Whereas the downturn in the economy may have encouraged pro bono at other firms, we're very busy with billable work — so we haven't been able to take advantage of this as much."

"One unique quality of SRZ is that pro bono time counts toward your billables for the year. I think that's a pretty clear commitment. At the same time, they aren't going to throw good money after bad on cases that have little or no merit."

"It is provided but not pushed for corporate associates."

"The firm is very committed to pro bono. Any work done for a pro bono client counts toward target annual hours. The firm is constantly invited to various charitable events and celebrations and extends this invitation to all attorneys in the firm."

"The firm is very committed; I personally help coach a high school mock trial team."

"We get full billable credit for pro bono work, but at the same time there is little respect for commitments to your pro bono cases when a partner wants you to work on something billable."

"No real effort — all window dressing."

"All pro bono hours count towards target hours."

"Many pro bono opportunities are available to associates, some of which are fully entrusted to the associates."

"Pro bono is available if you seek it."

Schulte Roth & Zabel LLP

"We are proud to have been the first firm in New York to include a pro bono week in our summer program."

— *Schulte Roth & Zabel LLP*

Shaw Pittman LLP

2300 N Street, NW
Washington, DC 20037
Phone: (202) 663-8000
www.shawpittman.com

LOCATIONS

Washington, DC (HQ)
Los Angeles, CA
McLean, VA
New York, NY
London

MAJOR DEPARTMENTS & PRACTICES

Business & Finance
Disputes
Government Regulation
Technology

THE STATS

No. of attorneys worldwide: 370
No. of offices worldwide: 5
Managing Partner: Stephen B. Huttler

EMPLOYMENT CONTACT

Ms. Kathleen A. Kelly
Chief Recruiting Officer & Director of Professional Programs
Phone: (202) 663-8394
Fax: (202) 663-8007
E-mail: kathy.kelly@shawpittman.com

WHO'S WHO

Principal pro bono contact(s) at your firm:

Deborah Baum, Esq.
Chair, Pro Bono Committee and Programs
Phone: (202) 663-8772
E-mail: deborah.baum@shawpittman.com

Ms. Elizabeth Kersey
Manager of Pro Bono Programs
Phone: (202) 663-9412
E-mail: elizabeth.kersey@shawpittman.com

Does the firm have a pro bono coordinator? Yes
Elizabeth Kersey

If yes, what percentage of his or her time is spent on pro bono work? 30 percent

Does the firm have a pro bono committee? Yes

If yes, how often does the committee meet? Shaw Pittman's pro bono committee has regular frequent meetings to discuss both the program in general as well as the status of projects we have undertaken.

Describe the composition of the committee: Shaw Pittman's pro bono committee is comprised of the chair of pro bono programs, manager of pro bono programs, the chair of legal recruiting, the coordinator of community relations and an extensive cross-section of lawyers who are interested in pro bono work.

THE SCOOP

Does your firm have a written pro bono policy? Yes

Has the firm signed on to the Law Firm Pro Bono Challenge? Yes

What are some of the areas of law in which your firm has performed pro bono legal work in the last two years? Shaw Pittman's pro bono program is anchored in the firm's work with community legal services providers. The institutional focus has enabled us to form important and long-lasting relationships with providers serving the poor and needy. Among the areas of law we have performed pro bono legal work on in the last two years are death penalty cases, equal employment opportunity, public accommodations, fair housing, disability rights, public benefits, domestic violence and veterans affairs. Our lawyers have also spearheaded the September 11th Pro Bono Legal Relief Project, which provides a wide range of legal services to the victims and surviving family members of anyone injured or killed in the September 11th attacks on the Pentagon.

Organizations for which your firm has performed pro bono legal services in the last two years: The Legal Aid Society of the District of Columbia, Washington Lawyers' Committee for Civil Rights and Urban Affairs, Zacchaeus Free Clinic, Bread for the City, Whitman Walker Clinic, D.C. Coalition Against Domestic Violence, Gay and Lesbian Immigration Task Force, Washington Area Lawyers for the Arts, D.C. Central Kitchen.

List up to three pro bono matters that are representative of the pro bono work your firm participates in.

- The Legal Aid Society of the District of Columbia. Shaw Pittman supports the Legal Aid Society of D.C. by providing attorneys who assist the organization in serving the poorest residents of Washington, D.C., in the areas of family law (including custody, visitation, child support and domestic violence issues), landlord-tenant (including defending against evictions), public benefits (Medicaid, General Assistance for Children, TANF, food stamps and POWER) and special education cases. Additionally, one of our partners serves as the secretary to the board of trustees and member of the executive committee while another serves as a board member on the president's council for the organization. We also provide pro bono legal assistance to the organization itself in the areas of employment and real estate and are in the process of creating a program whereby our lawyers staff the intake at Legal Aid one day per week.

- Washington Lawyers' Committee for Civil Rights and Urban Affairs. Shaw Pittman has been heavily involved in several landmark cases involving violations of civil rights in public accommodation cases including McKnight v. Circuit City Stores, Inc., a case tried in federal district court in Richmond where the firm represented African-American employees claiming discrimination based on race. We have also worked with the Washington Lawyers' Committee in matters involving public accommodations against Footlocker and Sharper Image stores where the firm represented African-American customers and successfully changed both stores' policies and obtained substantial payments to the plaintiffs. One of our partners is the co-chair of the board of trustees and another partner serves on the board.

- September 11th Pro Bono Legal Relief Project. Shaw Pittman attorneys spearheaded the establishment of the September 11th Pro Bono Legal Relief Project which provides, free of charge, legal services to the victims and family survivors of anyone injured or killed in the September 11th attack on the Pentagon. We developed the program material, recruited lawyers from other law firms, established a wide-range of referral networks and have assisted with over 140 cases covering a variety of issues, including wills, trusts and estates, child custody and guardianship, and insurance coverage and claim issues.

BY THE NUMBERS

What is the total number of hours that lawyers in U.S. offices at your firm spent performing pro bono legal services in 2000, 2001 and 2002?

Total number of hours in 2000: 11,859 hours
Total number of hours in 2001: 21,430 hours
Total number of hours in 2002: 13,222 hours

Average number of pro bono hours per attorney in U.S. offices per year (including associates, partners, counsels, but not summer associates):

Average number of hours per attorney in 2000: 32.95 hours
Average number of hours per attorney in 2001: 54.1 hours
Average number of hours per attorney in 2002: 34.7 hours

What percentage of attorneys in this firm's U.S. offices did pro bono work in 2002? 49.2 percent

What percentage of attorneys in this firm's U.S. offices did at least 20 hours of pro bono work in 2002? 29.9 percent

Does the firm encourage its lawyers to perform a minimum number of pro bono hours? Yes

If so, how many hours per year or what percentage of lawyers' billable hours? A minimum of 25 hours.

SUPERVISION AND EVALUATIONS

Is there partner supervision on each pro bono matter? Yes

Do partner supervisors or, if applicable, senior associates provide written evaluations of associates' work on pro bono matters? Yes

If so, are those evaluations taken into account in determining salary, bonuses or advancement in the firm? Yes

If not, does the firm consider pro bono work generally in associate evaluations? N/A

HOURS

Does the firm give billable hour credit for pro bono work? Yes

Does the firm have a maximum number of pro bono hours that can be applied toward the billable hour target? No

If so, what is the maximum? N/A

If your firm uses hours to determine bonuses, does it consider pro bono hours when determining bonuses? Yes

PRO BONO POINTS

What training opportunities are open to associates working on pro bono matters? Training at Shaw Pittman is a constant, organic process. We offer formal training programs, both firm-wide and within discrete areas of pro bono opportunities. We also offer daily opportunities to learn in one-on-one interactions with more senior lawyers. Programs on pro bono are presented by outside experts and sometimes by the firm's experienced practitioners. Associates are encouraged to supplement these in-firm training opportunities with outside seminars, particularly those sponsored by pro bono organizations such as Lawyers for Children America and WEAVE.

Can associates bring matters of interest to the firm? Yes

Does the firm offer the use of support staff in carrying out pro bono matters? Yes

What pro bono opportunities are available for summer associates? Shaw Pittman's Summer Program is designed to let each of our summer associates get a serious introduction to the practice of law and to begin to develop into a first-rate lawyer. We have a variety of programs and procedures designed to achieve these objectives and actively encourage participation in our pro bono programs. We offer training designed especially for summer associates and offer opportunities that permit them to select assignments that are of the greatest interest to them. We also allow summer associates to split their summer between Shaw Pittman and a public interest organization.

Does the firm have established programs, such as externships, that enable its associates to work in a public interest setting? Yes

If so, where and for up to how long? Shaw Pittman's pro bono program is anchored in the firm's work with community legal services providers. The institutional focus of the pro bono program has enabled Shaw Pittman to form important and long-lasting relationships with providers serving the poor and needy. Shaw Pittman has participated in a rotation program with the Legal Aid Society, assigning an associate to work full-time for six months on-site at Legal Aid. Shaw Pittman lawyers staff a walk-in advice and referral clinic at Zacchaeus Free Clinic and volunteer monthly at the Whitman Walker Clinic.

Has your firm won any special recognition or awards in the last two years for its pro bono work? Yes

If so, please list. Shaw Pittman's recent awards include the LAMP Distinguished Service Award from the American Bar Association for the September 11th Pro Bono Legal Relief Project. The project was also awarded the District of Columbia Bar's Best Bar Project Award for 2002 and was honored with a 2002 Pro Bono Award from The National Law Journal. In years past, we have been honored with other awards including being voted Pro Bono Firm of the year by the D.C. Bar, Legal Services Award from Washington Area Lawyers for the Arts, Servant of Justice Award from the Legal Aid Society and Outstanding Achievement from the Washington Lawyers' Committee for Civil Rights for our "unflagging commitment to see justice prevail" in the case of Lowery v. Circuit City Stores, Inc., which involved claims of African-American Circuit City employees who alleged a pattern and practice of racial discrimination at the company.

THE FIRM SAYS

Shaw Pittman encourages everyone at the firm to become active in the life of the community, through pro bono legal projects and other public service activities. As a signatory to the American Bar Association's Law Firm Pro Bono Challenge, Shaw Pittman has committed to provide pro bono legal services to those who are in need and otherwise unable to afford legal services. The firm's pro bono legal work is diverse and expansive; our lawyers represent organizations serving the community and the needy, engage in important national-impact litigation and partner with local legal services providers to represent individuals who otherwise would not have access to the justice system. In addition to providing legal services, our lawyers and staff organize activities at the firm to benefit local community groups and needy individuals and families, raise money to benefit worthwhile national causes and participate in grassroots work projects in our poorest communities, which efforts are in addition to our traditional "pro bono hours" reflected. We are proud of our firm management support of our pro bono program, best demonstrated by our continuing willingness to pay associates for their pro bono work as though it were billable. Shaw Pittman "puts its money where its mouth is."

OUR SURVEY SAYS

"Attorneys receive hour-for-hour credit for all pro bono work. It counts just as billable hours in meeting yearly hour requirements and in calculating bonuses."

"Pro bono is treated as billable, and [there are] lots of opportunities for pro bono work."

"There is no pro bono work in the Northern Virginia office at all."

"Pro bono hours count as billable hours, but you may not have the time to do pro bono work and manage your caseload."

"Full credit toward our yearly requirement for all pro bono hours worked."

"Many pro bono opportunities are available."

"The firm counts pro bono toward billable hours, but discourages too much pro bono."

"Our lawyers represent organizations serving the community and the needy, engage in important national-impact litigation and partner with local legal services providers to represent individuals who otherwise would not have access to the justice system."

— *Shaw Pittman LLP*

Shearman & Sterling LLP

599 Lexington Avenue
New York, NY 10022
Phone: (212) 848-4000
www.shearman.com

LOCATIONS

New York, NY (HQ)
Menlo Park, CA
San Francisco, CA
Washington, DC
Abu Dhabi
Beijing
Brussels
Dusseldorf
Frankfurt
Hong Kong
London
Mannheim
Munich
Paris
Rome
São Paulo
Singapore
Tokyo
Toronto

MAJOR DEPARTMENTS & PRACTICES

Antitrust
Asset Management
Bank Finance
Bankruptcy & Reorganization
Capital Markets
Executive Compensation & Employee Benefits
Litigation
Mergers & Acquisitions
Private Clients
Project Development & Finance
Property
Securitization & Derivatives
Tax

THE STATS

No. of attorneys worldwide: 1,000 +
No. of offices worldwide: 19
Senior Partner: David W. Heleniak

EMPLOYMENT CONTACT

Ms. Suzanne Ryan
Manager, Professional Recruiting
Phone: (212) 848-4592
Fax: (212) 848-7179
E-mail: sryan@shearman.com

WHO'S WHO

Does the firm have a pro bono coordinator? Yes

Saralyn M. Cohen, Esq.
Pro Bono Attorney
Phone: (212) 848-8772
E-mail: scohen@shearman.com

If yes, what percentage of his or her time is spent on pro bono work? 100 percent

Does the firm have a pro bono committee? Yes

If yes, how often does the committee meet? The Pro Bono Attorney communicates with the other members of the committee daily.

Describe the composition of the committee: Partners J. J. Stevenson III and Henry Weisburg, and Saralyn M. Cohen, Pro Bono Attorney.

THE SCOOP

Does your firm have a written pro bono policy? Yes

Has the firm signed on to the Law Firm Pro Bono Challenge? Yes

What are some of the areas of law in which your firm has performed pro bono legal work in the last two years? September 11 disaster relief, international, arts, immigration, micro-credit, criminal law, family law, civil rights, education, community development, nonprofit law, death penalty.

What are some of the areas of law in which your firm does not perform pro bono work? Shearman & Sterling LLP considers all pro bono matters which are of interest to its legal staff.

Organizations for which your firm has performed pro bono legal services in the last two years: Legal staff at Shearman & Sterling LLP's U.S. offices represent over 60 nonprofit organizations. Shearman & Sterling has taken numerous pro bono matters from the following legal service providers and clearinghouses: inMotion, Lawyers for Children, Lawyers Committee for Civil Rights Under Law, Lawyers Committee for Human Rights, The Legal Aid Society, New York Lawyers for the Public Interest, The Robin Hood Foundation, Sanctuary for Families, Volunteer Lawyers for the Arts, Volunteers of Legal Service.

List up to three pro bono matters that are representative of the pro bono work your firm participates in.

- More than 200 members of our legal staff provided pro bono assistance to the victims of September 11, including representing more than 20 families before the Federal Victim Compensation Fund. In addition, our property group assisted residential and commercial tenants who were unable to return to their homes or offices, and the private clients group assisted with trust and estates matters. The legal staff also provided assistance to four FDNY firehouses that lost members on September 11.

- Each year Shearman & Sterling LLP legal teams represent approximately 20 political asylum applicants fleeing persecution in their countries. Additionally, attorneys from the firm represent numerous immigrant victims of physical

and mental abuse in battered spouse waivers and Violence Against Women Act petitions. Attorneys also assisted those subjected to the Department of Justice's Special Registration program.

- Shearman & Sterling LLP provides post-conviction representation to four inmates on death row: two clients in Florida, one in Alabama and one in Ohio.

BY THE NUMBERS

What is the total number of hours that lawyers in U.S. offices at your firm spent performing pro bono legal services in 2000, 2001 and 2002?

>Total number of hours in 2000: 25,257 hours*
>Total number of hours in 2001: 25,137 hours**
>Total number of hours in 2002: 19,993 hours***

* The firm's legal staff worldwide contributed an additional 9,000 hours of pro bono work that doesn't qualify under this survey's definition
** The firm's legal staff worldwide contributed an additional 13,000 hours of pro bono work that doesn't qualify under this survey's definition
*** The firm's legal staff worldwide contributed an additional 11,000 hours of pro bono work that doesn't qualify under this survey's definition

Average number of pro bono hours per attorney in U.S. offices per year (including associates, partners, counsels, but not summer associates):

>Average number of hours per attorney in 2000: 47.5 hours
>Average number of hours per attorney in 2001: 37.2 hours
>Average number of hours per attorney in 2002: 32.3 hours

What percentage of attorneys in this firm's U.S. offices did pro bono work in 2002? 52 percent

What percentage of attorneys in this firm's U.S. offices did at least 20 hours of pro bono work in 2002? 27 percent

Does the firm encourage its lawyers to perform a minimum number of pro bono hours? Yes

If so, how many hours per year or what percentage of lawyers' billable hours? 25

SUPERVISION AND EVALUATIONS

Is there partner supervision on each pro bono matter? Yes

Do partner supervisors or, if applicable, senior associates provide written evaluations of associates' work on pro bono matters? Yes

If so, are those evaluations taken into account in determining salary, bonuses or advancement in the firm? Yes

If not, does the firm consider pro bono work generally in associate evaluations? N/A

HOURS

Does the firm give billable hour credit for pro bono work? No

Does the firm have a maximum number of pro bono hours that can be applied toward the billable hour target? No

If so, what is the maximum? N/A

If your firm uses hours to determine bonuses, does it consider pro bono hours when determining bonuses? Not applicable

PRO BONO POINTS

What training opportunities are open to associates working on pro bono matters? Numerous training sessions are hosted at the offices of the firm. Examples of sessions hosted on site in 2003 are sessions on nonprofit corporate governance, Violence Against Women Act, political asylum and uncontested divorces. Additionally, monthly listings of available pro bono training sessions in the New York, Washington, D.C., and Bay Area are circulated by e-mail from Probono.net.

Can associates bring matters of interest to the firm? Yes

Does the firm offer the use of support staff in carrying out pro bono matters? Yes

What pro bono opportunities are available for summer associates? Summer associates are strongly encouraged to take on a pro bono matter. More than 68 percent of the 2003 summer class did pro bono work during their summer. Summers contributed 1,700 hours on death penalty cases, did research for the International Criminal Tribunal for Rwanda, represented battered women in uncontested divorces, drafted employee manuals for nonprofits, assisted victims of September 11 and appeared before immigration judges on political asylum cases. These hours are not included in firm totals above due to the definition itself.

Does the firm have established programs, such as externships, that enable its associates to work in a public interest setting? Yes

If so, where and for up to how long? Shearman & Sterling LLP sends one attorney each month to the International Criminal Tribunal for Rwanda in Arusha, Tanzania, to assist the Office of the Prosecution. Additionally, one of the options available in the firm's external development program is a one-month off-site pro bono project of one's choosing.

Has your firm won any special recognition or awards in the last two years for its pro bono work? Yes

If so, please list.

- **2003:** Sanctuary for Families pro bono award to two associates for their work representing a battered woman in a gender asylum case. 2003 Legal Aid Society — Pro Bono Coordinator of the Year. 2002 inMotion Commitment to Justice Award — Law Firm of the Year.

- **2002:** Legal Aid Society — Outstanding Pro Bono Assistance to the Victims of the WTC Tragedy. 2001 inMotion — Pro Bono Coordinator of the Year.

- **2001:** Washington D.C. Lawyers for Children America — Lawyer of the Year.

THE FIRM SAYS

Legal staff from all offices worldwide are encouraged to take on pro bono matters. Each year the firm's legal staff worldwide contribute thousands of additional hours of pro bono work that do not qualify under this survey's definition, including hours of legal assistants (over 5,000 in 2002) and lawyers in offices outside of the United States. Lawyers in the London, Paris, Frankfurt, Singapore, Hong Kong and Tokyo offices have volunteered their time on pro bono matters, such as assistance to FINCA, a micro-credit organization that operates in over 15 countries. Attorneys in the Asia offices provided assistance in the wake of the Bali bombing tragedy and assisted small business enterprise in Tibet. Attorneys from offices around the world did research for the International Criminal Tribunal for Rwanda. Pro bono work was done for local non-governmental organizations in the localities where Shearman & Sterling LLP has its offices — arts organizations in France and Germany, schools in Rome and Paris. Staff in the London office and in New York worked with primary and secondary school students. Volunteers from the firm's London office raised funds for, and aided in completing a renovation project at a local school. Legal staff in New York worked with high school students at the International High School in Queens and their families. Immigration law clinics were held with nonprofit legal services providers. S&S employees spoke to the students at the school about career opportunities and worked with them on their English. The New York office also hosted 15 high school students for one week of activities during the summer, exposing the students to the law. Activities included a mock trial in the United States District Court before a federal court judge, a trip to meet the legal team at Viacom and small group sessions with partners, associates and legal assistants.

OUR SURVEY SAYS

"We have a dedicated pro bono coordinator (in both senses) and pro bono opportunities are regularly offered and zealously supported."

"As a general matter the firm is strongly committed and involved in a wide variety of projects. The pro bono attorney, Saralyn Cohen, is a truly an incredible woman and works on a number of the projects herself and with a core group of associates and partners. It is unfortunate that at the departmental level there is not the same amount of support. It is often difficult to pursue the pro bono opportunities available because of the lack of support within the department."

"Pro bono work is certainly available for those who want it."

"The firm has an attorney who exclusively coordinates pro bono activities for Shearman attorneys. There are literally hundreds of opportunities to become involved in pro bono activities, and the partners appear generally to be supportive of pro bono endeavors."

"Pro bono hours do not count as 'billable hours,' but the firm does not base bonuses or other things on billable hours. S&S has a vigorous pro bono attorney's office that connects our attorneys with very good pro bono opportunities. Partners actively encourage pro bono and appear to really mean it."

"The firm has a very active pro bono coordinator and plenty of attorneys who are enthusiastic about doing pro bono."

"[The firm is] very committed, but only to the type of projects that pass the New York liberal acceptability filter. Don't go asking, for example, to be allowed to do pro bono for the National Rifle Association, or even something as soft as the rights of divorced fathers, because it won't happen."

"Shearman's pro bono work is, as far as I can tell, without equal. From hands-on litigation work and in-court representation to drafting constitutions and monitoring elections to advising international criminal tribunals, the firm offers and supports it all."

"The firm in general is great in terms of pro bono, although in practice it depends upon the head of each department. My department is not particularly interested in pro bono work."

"I know of partners who have sometimes placed pro bono work over regular billable work."

Simpson Thacher & Bartlett LLP

425 Lexington Avenue
New York, NY 10017-3954
Phone: (212) 455-2000
www.SimpsonThacher.com

LOCATIONS

New York, NY (HQ)
Los Angeles, CA
Palo Alto, CA
Hong Kong
London
Tokyo

MAJOR DEPARTMENTS & PRACTICES

Bankruptcy
Corporate (M&A, Private Equity, Securities, Banking & Project Finance)
Executive Compensation & Benefits
Exempt Organizations
Intellectual Property
Litigation
Personal Planning
Real Estate
Tax

THE STATS

No. of attorneys worldwide: 681
No. of offices worldwide: 6
Chairman: Richard I. Beattie

EMPLOYMENT CONTACT

Ms. Dee Pifer
Director of Legal Employment
Phone: (212) 455-2687
Fax: (212) 455-2502
E-mail: dpifer@stblaw.com

WHO'S WHO

Does the firm have a pro bono coordinator? Yes.

Victoria B. Bjorklund, Partner
Phone: (212) 455-2875
E-mail: vbjorklund@stblaw.com

William T. Russell Jr., Partner
Phone: (212) 455-3979
E-mail: wrussell@stblaw.com

If yes, what percentage of his or her time is spent on pro bono work? It varies.

Does the firm have a pro bono committee? Yes

If yes, how often does the committee meet? Every two months in person, but daily by e-mail to discuss and approve pro bono project proposals.

Describe the composition of the committee: The committee includes eight partners of varying seniority from a variety of practice groups.

THE SCOOP

Does your firm have a written pro bono policy? Yes

What are some of the areas of law in which your firm has performed pro bono legal work in the last two years? We have performed pro bono work in a variety of areas including, but not limited to, education finance reform; not-for-profit incorporation and tax exemption; landlord/tenant disputes; child custody, divorce and order of protection proceedings in family court; political asylum proceedings; discrimination law; environmental law; and criminal appeals, including capital defense work.

What are some of the areas of law in which your firm does not perform pro bono work? We do not, as a policy, limit ourselves to any particular areas of the law.

Organizations for which your firm has performed pro bono legal services in the last two years: The Campaign for Fiscal Equity, The Lawyers Alliance for New York, Doctors Without Borders, The Natural Resources Defense Council, InMotion, The Robin Hood Foundation, New York Lawyers for the Public Interest, Volunteer Lawyers for the Arts, The Lawyers Committee for Human Rights, The Legal Aid Society.

List up to three pro bono matters that are representative of the pro bono work your firm participates in.

- The firm has represented the Campaign for Fiscal Equity since 1995 in its successful constitutional challenge to the system by which the State of New York allocates funds for public education. The firm, which has devoted more than $14 million in time and disbursements to this matter, recently obtained a ruling from the New York State Court of Appeals affirming the successful result obtained from the trial judge after a seven month bench trial.

- We successfully represented professional golfer Casey Martin before the United States Supreme Court in a matter regarding the application of the Americans with Disabilities Act to the PGA Tour. The Supreme Court upheld Mr. Martin's right to use a golf cart in tournaments.

- The firm did the legal work to create, and continues to advise, The Robin Hood Relief Fund, which has expended over $50 million in 9/11 relief funds targeted to the poorer survivors of the attack.

BY THE NUMBERS

What is the total number of hours that lawyers in U.S. offices at your firm spent performing pro bono legal services in 2000, 2001 and 2002?

Total number of hours in 2000: 33,454 hours
Total number of hours in 2001: 26,348 hours
Total number of hours in 2002: 38,069 hours

Average number of pro bono hours per attorney in U.S. offices per year (including associates, partners, counsels, but not summer associates):

Average number of hours per attorney in 2000: 56.32 hours
Average number of hours per attorney in 2001: 40.22 hours
Average number of hours per attorney in 2002: 55.58 hours

What percentage of attorneys in this firm's U.S. offices did pro bono work in 2002? 63 percent

What percentage of attorneys in this firm's U.S. offices did at least 20 hours of pro bono work in 2002? 57 percent

Does the firm encourage its lawyers to perform a minimum number of pro bono hours? We strongly encourage all lawyers to get involved in pro bono work but do not set maximum or minimum levels of commitment.

If so, how many hours per year or what percentage of lawyers' billable hours? N/A

SUPERVISION AND EVALUATIONS

Is there partner supervision on each pro bono matter? Yes

Do partner supervisors or, if applicable, senior associates provide written evaluations of associates' work on pro bono matters? Yes

If so, are those evaluations taken into account in determining salary, bonuses or advancement in the firm? Yes

If not, does the firm consider pro bono work generally in associate evaluations? N/A

HOURS

Does the firm give billable hour credit for pro bono work? Yes

Does the firm have a maximum number of pro bono hours that can be applied toward the billable hour target? No

If so, what is the maximum? N/A

If your firm uses hours to determine bonuses, does it consider pro bono hours when determining bonuses? Not applicable

PRO BONO POINTS

What training opportunities are open to associates working on pro bono matters? The training opportunities generally available to Simpson Thacher lawyers are, in many instances, as applicable to pro bono work as they are to billable work. In addition, the firm offers training that is specifically designed for various areas of pro bono practice. For example, every year lawyers from Legal Services for New York City — Manhattan come to the firm to provide a half-day training session on representing tenants in eviction proceedings, and the firm's exempt organizations group provides training on forming and qualifying charitable organizations.

Can associates bring matters of interest to the firm? Yes

Does the firm offer the use of support staff in carrying out pro bono matters? Yes

What pro bono opportunities are available for summer associates? The same opportunities available to our full-time associates are also available to our summer associates, but since most summer associates are here for such a limited time period they often work on existing pro bono matters with our full-time lawyers. In addition, many of our summer associates work under the supervision of more experienced lawyers on uncontested divorce proceedings referred by InMotion, most of which can be concluded during the summer.

Does the firm have established programs, such as externships, that enable its associates to work in a public interest setting? No

If so, where and for up to how long? We do not currently have any externships or other similar programs. We do, however, provide a wide range of opportunities for associates to work with public interest groups as part of their every day practice.

Has your firm won any special recognition or awards in the last two years for its pro bono work? Yes

If so, please list. The firm has been recognized with awards in the past two years by, among others: The Legal Aid Society, Legal Services for New York City — Manhattan, The 2002 MFY Legal Services Scales of Justice Award, 2002 New York State Bar Association's President's Pro Bono Service Law Firm Award, 2002 Lawyers Alliance for New York Cornerstone Award, The National Law Journal Pro Bono Award, Herbert A. Birch Services 2002 Voice of Hope Award, New York Society for Ethical Culture 2002 Distinguished Community Service Award.

In addition, each year many individual Simpson Thacher lawyers and practice groups are recognized by a variety of organizations for the pro bono work that they have performed including: Victoria Bjorklund received in 2003 both the Commissioner's Award from the Commissioner of Internal Revenue and the Tax Exempt/Government Entities Division Commissioner's Award in connection with her work relating to the 9/11 tragedy; William Russell received the 2002 Legal Aid Society Outstanding Pro Bono Leadership Award; and the firm's exempt organizations group was honored in September 2002 for its 9/11-related work at an event hosted by the Nonprofit Coordinating Committee of New York and The Lawyers Alliance for New York.

THE FIRM SAYS

Our commitment to community service is deep and abiding. In recent years, Simpson Thacher partners, associates and summer associates have devoted more than 35,000 hours annually to pro bono projects, and our efforts have been recognized with awards from such distinguished organizations as InMotion, the United Federation of Teachers, The Legal Aid Society, the New York State Bar Association, Volunteer Lawyers for the Arts, the Puerto Rico Legal Defense Fund and the Lawyers Alliance First Cornerstone Award for Public Service. The firm's commitment to pro bono activities and community service is further illustrated by its sponsorship of fellows at the NOW Legal Defense and Education Fund and MFY Legal Services, Inc. Commitment to public service and pro bono legal work is a defining characteristic of Simpson Thacher & Bartlett LLP. Lawyers in the firm at every level make significant contributions to legal service programs, government and not-for-profit groups throughout the year. We approach our pro bono projects with the same commitment to excellence as we do all our work and credit our lawyers' contributions on these matters equally with other engagements.

We have long-standing relationships with a number of organizations for whom we regularly do pro bono work, including The Legal Aid Society, Bronx and Queens Legal Services, the Lawyers' Committee for Human Rights, the Office of the Appellate Defender, the Natural Resources Defense Council, New Visions for Public Schools, Volunteer Lawyers for the Arts, Doctors Without Borders (Nobel Peace Prize Laureate), The Robin Hood Foundation and the Dance Theatre of Harlem. We have handled matters as diverse as assisting a Nicaraguan Indian tribe negotiating timber contracts and representing prison inmates challenging death sentences in Missouri and Florida. Beyond our high-profile projects and work for major community service organizations, many of our pro bono efforts are on behalf of indigent individuals, assisting them in obtaining the basic necessities of life, including housing, public benefits and freedom from abusive spouses. Pro bono projects are regularly handled directly by associates, and summer associates have played significant roles in many of our most important efforts.

Simpson Thacher & Bartlett LLP attorneys have worked on an extraordinary range of pro bono matters, including:

- providing counsel to numerous individuals and a host of nonprofit organizations in connection with the September 11 terrorist attack;

- representing battered women in seeking orders of protection, in obtaining child support payments and in divorce proceedings;

- representing low-income tenants in housing court to preclude evictions and to obtain basic building services such as heat and hot water;

- providing corporate and tax counsel to a wide range of nonprofit organizations, including organizations devoted to reform of New York City's schools, providing health care to impoverished areas and improving legal services for the poor;

- representing victims of political oppression abroad in seeking political asylum;

- representing criminal defendants in appeals of criminal convictions;

- providing corporate counsel to community development organizations undertaking the economic revitalization of some of New York City's poorest neighborhoods;

- representing plaintiffs in environmental actions seeking to protect endangered species and to protect the nation's wilderness areas;

- serving in leadership positions in numerous community service organizations and committees;

- representing the victims of discrimination and prejudice in numerous forums throughout the country.

The firm's pro bono committee ensures that all our lawyers are kept apprised of the many opportunities for pro bono work, offers support and guidance, and solicits proposals for new pro bono projects.

OUR SURVEY SAYS

"I doubt there is a firm anywhere in the U.S. that can honestly say it is more strongly committed to pro bono work. Everyone handles pro bono matters — and some of them are huge like the New York City schools case. It is expected and the firm seems to consider pro bono activity a big positive rather than to penalize lawyers who devote much of their time to pro bono."

"Pro bono cases are given the same resources, commitment and importance as any other case."

"Pro bono is important to the firm and it is counted as billable time for associates, so nobody worries that their time spent on pro bono matters doesn't count. I have spent about 100 hours on pro bono each year (and I'm a corporate person)."

"You can take on as much or as little as you want. As a corporate associate, I am handling my own litigation pro bono matter, and I have both associates and partners in the litigation department helping me out."

"One of the reason why I came to Simpson was because I heard that this firm strongly encourages pro bono work, and since I've been here, I have been extremely impressed. It has lived up to its reputation. Everyone who wishes that they just had more time should make time, because I get e-mails about great pro bono work at least three times a week."

"There are numerous pro bono activities and, with the general economic slowdown, more associates have the opportunity to undertake them."

"They seem supportive if people choose to do it; however, it is hard to manage with your regular work."

"The firm has a very active pro bono practice. Partners as well as associates are encouraged to do pro bono work. The firm as an institution devotes significant resources to pro bono matters. We represent many charities and other not-for-profit companies on a pro bono basis."

"I have freely worked on numerous matters and I have never been asked to push a pro bono case aside for a paying client. The firm expects the same top-quality work product for pro bono cases and makes all of its resources available. Many associates have a true public interest spirit. [This is] a source of pride for me and many at the firm."

"Pro bono is strongly encouraged. Since corporate associates are slow in their other work, partners almost expect that they will take on pro bono projects with their down time. Partners are often deeply involved in pro bono cases as well. All pro bono time is billable and is treated no differently from paying clients."

"They're almost fanatical with their support for pro bono — it is really true. They want you to do it."

Skadden, Arps, Slate, Meagher & Flom LLP and Affiliates

Four Times Square
New York, NY 10036-6522
Phone: (212) 735-3000
www.skadden.com

LOCATIONS

New York, NY (HQ)
Boston, MA
Chicago, IL
Houston, TX
Los Angeles, CA
Newark, NJ
Palo Alto, CA
San Francisco, CA
Washington, DC
Wilmington, DE
Beijing
Brussels
Frankfurt
Hong Kong
London
Moscow
Paris
Singapore
Sydney
Tokyo
Toronto
Vienna

MAJOR DEPARTMENTS & PRACTICES

Antitrust/Sports Law
Banking & Finance
Corporate Restructuring
E-Commerce
Intellectual Property & Technology
Investment Management
Litigation
M&A
Mass Torts
Real Estate
Tax, Trusts & Estates
White Collar Criminal Litigation

THE STATS

No. of attorneys worldwide: 1,750
No. of offices worldwide: 22
Executive Partner: Robert C. Sheehan

EMPLOYMENT CONTACT

Ms. Carol Sprague
Director of Legal Hiring
Phone: (212) 735-3815
Fax: (212) 777-3815
E-mail: csprague@skadden.com

WHO'S WHO

Does the firm have a pro bono coordinator? Yes

Ronald J. Tabak, Esq.
Special Counsel
Phone: (212) 735-2226
E-mail: rtabak@skadden.com

There are also coordinators in particular offices.

If yes, what percentage of his or her time is spent on pro bono work? 100 percent

Does the firm have a pro bono committee? Yes

If yes, how often does the committee meet? The firm-wide committee meets infrequently, because the pro bono coordinator usually secures needed guidance from the firm's managing partner or the chair of the pro bono committee.

Describe the composition of the committee: Partners from various offices.

THE SCOOP

Does your firm have a written pro bono policy? Yes

Has the firm signed on to the Law Firm Pro Bono Challenge? Yes

What are some of the areas of law in which your firm has performed pro bono legal work in the last two years? Contract, merger, organizational and intellectual property work for nonprofits; representing political asylum applicants; representing indigent death row inmates; will, tax and senior citizen clinics; adoptions; representing battered women in Violence Against Women Act, order of protection and divorce matters; copyright applications for artists; disability and housing termination hearings.

What are some of the areas of law in which your firm does not perform pro bono work? None, as a category. Conflicts of interest, by party or issue, are determined on a matter-by-matter basis.

Organizations for which your firm has performed pro bono legal services in the last two years: Bet Tzedek, Lawyers' Alliance for New York, Lawyers' Committee for Civil Rights Under Law, Lawyers' Committee for Human Rights, Legal Aid Society, inMotion, New York Legal Assistance Group, New York Lawyers for the Public Interest, Public Counsel, Volunteer Lawyers for the Arts, NAACP Legal Defense & Educational Fund, Inc.

List up to three pro bono matters that are representative of the pro bono work your firm participates in.

- Attorneys are representing plaintiffs in a class action under Title II of the Americans With Disabilities Act and Section 504 of the Rehabilitation Act, alleging that a school district's facilities are plagued by a host of structural barriers that deny persons with disabilities access to the district's programs, services and activities.

- An attorney represented five Vietnamese electronics assembly workers who had wage and hour claims. The attorney settled the matter, as a result of which the claimants received $42,000.

- Attorneys defended Big Brothers Big Sisters of Greater Los Angeles in a case in which it was sued for breach of contract by someone who had bid unsuccessfully at its charity auction. The Superior Court judge held that plaintiff's claim was barred by the statute of frauds, and dismissed the claim without leave to amend.

- In addition, there are numerous non-litigation matters.

BY THE NUMBERS

What is the total number of hours that lawyers in U.S. offices at your firm spent performing pro bono legal services in 2000, 2001 and 2002?

>   **Total number of hours in 2000:** 56,232 hours
>   **Total number of hours in 2001:** 71,827 hours
>   **Total number of hours in 2002:** 92,450 hours

Average number of pro bono hours per attorney in U.S. offices per year (including associates, partners, counsels, but not summer associates):

>   **Average number of hours per attorney in 2000:** 44 hours
>   **Average number of hours per attorney in 2001:** 51 hours
>   **Average number of hours per attorney in 2002:** 63 hours

What percentage of attorneys in this firm's U.S. offices did pro bono work in 2002? 49 percent

What percentage of attorneys in this firm's U.S. offices did at least 20 hours of pro bono work in 2002? 32 percent

Does the firm encourage its lawyers to perform a minimum number of pro bono hours? No. All attorneys are encouraged to do pro bono work, but not a minimum number or percentage.

If so, how many hours per year or what percentage of lawyers' billable hours? N/A

SUPERVISION AND EVALUATIONS

Is there partner supervision on each pro bono matter? No

Do partner supervisors or, if applicable, senior associates provide written evaluations of associates' work on pro bono matters? Yes

If so, are those evaluations taken into account in determining salary, bonuses or advancement in the firm? Yes

If not, does the firm consider pro bono work generally in associate evaluations? N/A

HOURS

Does the firm give billable hour credit for pro bono work? Yes

Does the firm have a maximum number of pro bono hours that can be applied toward the billable hour target? No

If so, what is the maximum? N/A

If your firm uses hours to determine bonuses, does it consider pro bono hours when determining bonuses? Yes

PRO BONO POINTS

What training opportunities are open to associates working on pro bono matters? There are numerous training programs held about pro bono. Many of the trainings are also videotaped. There is also mentoring from most of the source organizations, and often from other lawyers at the firm. The firm's intranet includes training manuals and other training materials.

Can associates bring matters of interest to the firm? Yes

Does the firm offer the use of support staff in carrying out pro bono matters? Yes

What pro bono opportunities are available for summer associates? Handling administrative hearings; preparing political asylum applications; preparing Violence Against Women Act self-petitions; preparing applications for nonprofit incorporations and tax-exemption; preparing papers for uncontested divorces; and assisting attorneys on pre-existing pro bono matters.

Note: The data and percentages in response to earlier questions would be substantially higher were summer associate time included.

Does the firm have established programs, such as externships, that enable its associates to work in a public interest setting? Yes

If so, where and for up to how long? Four-month externship at New York's Legal Aid Society. Four-month externship at Lawyers' Alliance for New York. Six-month externship at Washington's Legal Aid Society.

Has your firm won any special recognition or awards in the last two years for its pro bono work? Yes

If so, please list. Outstanding Law Firm of the Year awards from Public Counsel, Volunteer Lawyers for the Arts and New York Legal Assistance Group. Bet Tzedek. Legal Services' Volunteer Law Firm of the Year Cornerstone Award, given to only one firm, by Lawyers' Alliance for New York.

THE FIRM SAYS

The firm's philosophy is to make it as easy as possible for its attorneys, summer associates and legal assistants to undertake pro bono matters of interest to them effectively. Toward this end, we survey people regarding their areas of interest and try to find matters fitting those interests; we send frequent announcements of available pro bono matters and pro bono trainings; and we encourage people to handle pro bono matters that they locate themselves. In addition, we provide training materials and ensure that there is mentoring on pro bono matters, because we recognize that the single greatest disincentive to doing pro bono work is the belief that one lacks substantive knowledge regarding unfamiliar areas of law. We regularly check with those working on each pro bono matter to make sure that if any problems arise, we can deal with them, such as by finding additional staff or asking the source group to ask the client to be more responsive.

Due to our usually not using the firm name on pro bono matters (although the pro bono work "counts" and is evaluated, and our malpractice coverage covers it), we permit attorneys to handle controversial matters. Our relationships with present and former Skadden Fellows provide our attorneys with interesting pro bono opportunities and able mentors. We make great efforts to evaluate the quality of pro bono work and to give constructive criticism, particularly since pro bono is often the arena in which our lawyers handle particular types of matters for the first time.

The firm's overall pro bono coordinator has to approve each pro bono matter's intake in any of our domestic or international offices. Using a computerized tracking system for pro bono matters, the firm's overall pro bono coordinator and the coordinators in each office can advise attorneys about others at the firm who have handled similar matters. Lawyers who have completed our externships are valuable sources of insight and mentoring with regard to various kinds of pro bono work. The firm's overall pro bono coordinator has regular conference calls with those responsible for coordinating pro bono work in the firm's various offices. To the extent that time devoted to legal work is considered in determining salaries and bonuses, those who make such decisions are given only the combined billable plus pro bono total of hours for each attorney — not separate breakdowns. Finally, we stress and re-stress the fact that pro bono is not only litigation and is not only for litigators. We make extraordinary efforts to find matters that non-litigators will find interesting and that they can handle effectively.

OUR SURVEY SAYS

"I've always got at least one pro bono matter going."

"Our pro bono coordinator sends e-mails at least once a day with pro bono opportunities for attorneys. Most people I know participate to some degree. The firm also holds an annual reception honoring those attorneys who have worked more than a certain number of hours on pro bono assignments."

"The firm's pro bono commitment is real and you frankly generally need to justify why you are not doing pro bono, as opposed to the opposite."

"The firm is committed. Individual departments, however, vary significantly, and in some there simply is no time for associates to participate in pro bono activities, because the demand for their time to do department work is already excessive."

"The firm is very proud of its pro bono efforts and is very supportive of pro bono work, but you are expected to put billable work first."

"The office makes it very easy to take such projects and publicly rewards those who participate. This year a donation was made to the charity of choice for individuals who billed a certain number of pro bono hours. On the other hand, if you don't want to participate you are not looked down upon either. The only difficulty is balancing billing work with pro bono — i.e., finding the time."

"Our pro bono practice has grown to one of the best in town. We've received numerous awards from local public interest organizations. In fact, over the last 12 months a number of our associates have completed just over 100 non-contested adoptions in connection with Public Counsel's Adoption Project."

"Pro bono hours are treated the same as hours billed to any client, and there is a huge range of pro bono opportunities, which are really encouraged. Everything from bar association involvement to death penalty cases to Supreme Court amicus briefs, political involvement, asylum cases — you name it, if you are interested in it and they don't have it yet, they will find what you want for you. A full-time pro bono administrator, an associate who works on pro bono half-time and a firm-wide pro bono coordinator in New York, as well as a partner in the Chicago office, all ensure that opportunities are widely publicized and encouraged. The managing partner personally gave an address at a firm-wide lunch on pro bono, and they had a fair where nonprofits came and had tables about their pro bono opportunities."

"Skadden is great about pro bono. Not only are all hours billed to pro bono work considered billables (and therefore count toward your bonus), but Skadden also participates in a number of externships whereby Skadden lends a few associates every year to places like Legal Aid and Lawyers Alliance for New York. Those externs work full-time at such places for at least four months (while continuing to make their full Skadden salary), gaining a lot of pro bono experience which they can use to help people when they come back to the firm."

"The work is billable and better be high quality. The variety of possible assignments means that there is something for everyone to get into and get behind."

Sonnenschein Nath & Rosenthal LLP

8000 Sears Tower
Chicago, IL 60606
Phone: (312) 876-8000
www.sonnenschein.com

LOCATIONS

Chicago, IL (HQ)
Kansas City, MO
Los Angeles, CA
New York, NY
San Francisco, CA
Short Hills, NJ
St. Louis, MO
Washington, DC
West Palm Beach, FL

MAJOR DEPARTMENTS & PRACTICES

Antitrust, Franchising & Distribution
Bankruptcy & Restructuring
Corporate & Securities
E-Business
Employee Benefits & Executive Compensation
Energy
Environmental
Food & Drug Law
Government Contracts
Health Care
Import-Export Trade
Information Security & Anti-Privacy
Insolvency, Bankruptcy & Reorganization
Insurance
Intellectual Property & Technology
International
Labor & Employment
Life Sciences
Litigation & Business Regulation
Privacy & Security
Public Finance & Government Law
Public Law & Policy Strategies
Real Estate
Taxation
Telecommunications
Trusts & Estates

THE STATS

No. of attorneys worldwide: 650
No. of offices worldwide: 9
Chairman: Duane C. Quaini

EMPLOYMENT CONTACT

Chicago
Ms. Barbara Petri
Recruitment Coordinator
Phone: (312) 876-8000
Fax: (312) 876-7934
E-mail: bpetri@sonnenschein.com

* *See firm web site for employment contacts in other cities.*

WHO'S WHO

Does the firm have a pro bono coordinator? Yes

Terrance A. Norton, Esq.
Partner
Phone: (312) 876-7939
E-mail: tnorton@sonnenschein.com

If yes, what percentage of his or her time is spent on pro bono work? 100 percent

Does the firm have a pro bono committee? Yes

If yes, how often does the committee meet? Monthly

Describe the composition of the committee: The committee is made up of partners from each of the firm's offices (12 members in total), and it is chaired by the former firm-wide managing partner.

THE SCOOP

Does your firm have a written pro bono policy? Yes

Has the firm signed on to the Law Firm Pro Bono Challenge? Yes

What are some of the areas of law in which your firm has performed pro bono legal work in the last two years? Corporate, real estate, litigation, intellectual property, asylum cases; civil rights cases; criminal appeals; representation of homeless persons; guardianship cases; and housing cases.

What are some of the areas of law in which your firm does not perform pro bono work? None

Organizations for which your firm has performed pro bono legal services in the last two years: The Latino Institute, Lawyers for the Creative Arts, Lawyers Alliance of New York, Community Economic Development Law Project, Chicago Coalition for the Homeless, Public Counsel, National Poverty Law Center, National Immigration Law Center, Chicago Coalition for the Homeless.

List up to three pro bono matters that are representative of the pro bono work your firm participates in. We have represented several children who had been excluded from public school entrance because of their status as homeless persons. We have also represented numerous not-for-profit entities which sought to obtain tax exempt status or needed other legal assistance.

BY THE NUMBERS

What is the total number of hours that lawyers in U.S. offices at your firm spent performing pro bono legal services in 2000, 2001 and 2002?

    Total number of hours in 2000: 14,204 hours
    Total number of hours in 2001: 10,688 hours
    Total number of hours in 2002: 12,201 hours

Average number of pro bono hours per attorney in U.S. offices per year (including associates, partners, counsels, but not summer associates):

    Average number of hours per attorney in 2000: 31.85 hours
    Average number of hours per attorney in 2001: 22.45 hours
    Average number of hours per attorney in 2002: 21.69 hours

What percentage of attorneys in this firm's U.S. offices did pro bono work in 2002? 48.9 percent

What percentage of attorneys in this firm's U.S. offices did at least 20 hours of pro bono work in 2002? 18.14 percent

Does the firm encourage its lawyers to perform a minimum number of pro bono hours? Yes

If so, how many hours per year or what percentage of lawyers' billable hours? 100 hours

SUPERVISION AND EVALUATIONS

Is there partner supervision on each pro bono matter? Yes

Do partner supervisors or, if applicable, senior associates provide written evaluations of associates' work on pro bono matters? Yes

If so, are those evaluations taken into account in determining salary, bonuses or advancement in the firm? Yes

If not, does the firm consider pro bono work generally in associate evaluations? N/A

HOURS

Does the firm give billable hour credit for pro bono work? Yes

Does the firm have a maximum number of pro bono hours that can be applied toward the billable hour target? Yes

If so, what is the maximum? 100 hours

If your firm uses hours to determine bonuses, does it consider pro bono hours when determining bonuses? N/A

PRO BONO POINTS

What training opportunities are open to associates working on pro bono matters? The firm sends interested attorneys to training sessions provided by organizations located in the cities where the firm has offices. For example, the firm has sent attorneys to the Lawyers Committee for Better Housing, where the attorneys were trained in handling cases in eviction court.

Can associates bring matters of interest to the firm? Yes

Does the firm offer the use of support staff in carrying out pro bono matters? Yes

What pro bono opportunities are available for summer associates? Same availability as other groups.

Does the firm have established programs, such as externships, that enable its associates to work in a public interest setting? Yes

If so, where and for up to how long? In Chicago, the firm sends recent law school grads to work at any one of a number of public interest law firms during the summer before they formally begin work at the firm. The firm has a similar arrangement in Kansas City, whereby new hires work for the public aid organization. The firm also has a program by which associates can apply to work at a local public defender's office for several months.

THE FIRM SAYS

Our firm has recently considered and promulgated new guidelines for pro bono work. These new guidelines state strongly the value which Sonnenschein places on pro bono efforts. They stress that pro bono work is "strongly encouraged." The position of pro bono partner was created and Terry Norton, an experienced public interest lawyer, was hired to direct the firm's pro bono efforts on a national basis. The pro bono partner periodically circulates notices of opportunities for pro bono work and also welcomes opportunities of which the firms lawyers make him aware. In addition, the firm arranges for presentations by officers from public interest law firms, in order to familiarize firm lawyers with the kinds of pro bono work that is available. Each pro bono matter is staffed with a supervising partner and is considered, along with other firm work, in yearly evaluations. The firm is in the process of expanding the amount of pro bono work done and also expanding the breadth of such work. Partners, as well as associates, are expected to take our pro bono obligation seriously and support is provided for that purpose.

OUR SURVEY SAYS

"The firm has always been committed to its pro bono work. Recently, the firm has been making greater efforts to encourage its more junior associates to get involved in pro bono assignments."

"The firm allows it, but only if it is above and beyond [the] normal billable requirement."

"The firm recently has made a much greater effort to encourage associates to undertake pro bono activities and has apparently been quite successful in getting interested associates involved, from individual local matters to high-profile national and international cases (including landmine survivors). Prior to the 2003 commitment, associates wishing to do pro bono work had to find the work themselves, usually through local bar association sections, because the firm made no effort to find and staff pro bono matters."

"Pro bono opportunities run the gamut from traditional litigation to drafting documents or negotiating deals for struggling artists. All pro bono assignments are open to all lawyers. Also, lawyers are openly and enthusiastically encouraged to step outside the lines of their normal practice group(s) to have fun and learn something new."

"The contribution and commitment is demonstrable at every level. Partners are as actively encouraged to participate in pro bono assignments as associates are."

"The Kansas City office has a long-standing commitment to Legal Aid, with our office's founding partner serving as chairman of the organization's fundraising committee, and opportunities like this encourage associates to develop a strong interest in pro bono service."

"Though the firm now actively encourages and compensates pro bono work with billable hours credit, associates like myself generally feel that a leopard doesn't change its spots overnight, and traditional commercial litigation types do not understand pro bono work that is not likely to lead to client development.... These impressions have led me to assume that I will need to bill the same number of billable hours as always, and to disregard the pro bono work as 'real time' even though the firm awards billable credit for pro bono hours, because the firm still tallies pro bono hours separately from billable hours and I suspect these billable hours mean more to partners than billable hours credit for non-paying work."

"That pro bono work is good for the individual and the firm habitually is repeated to all lawyers. There is zero pressure to contribute but every incentive and encouragement to do so."

Sonnenschein Nath & Rosenthal LLP

"Partners, as well as associates, are expected to take our pro bono obligation seriously and support is provided for that purpose."

— *Sonnenschein Nath & Rosenthal LLP*

Steptoe & Johnson LLP

1330 Connecticut Avenue, NW
Washington, DC 20036-1795
Phone: (202) 429-3000
www.steptoe.com

LOCATIONS

Washington, DC (HQ)
Los Angeles, CA
Phoenix, AZ
Brussels
London

MAJOR DEPARTMENTS & PRACTICES

Business Solutions
Energy, Environment & Natural Resources
International Trade & Investment
Litigation
Technology, Internet & Media

THE STATS

No. of attorneys worldwide: 350 +
No. of offices worldwide: 5
Chairman: J.A. (Lon) Bouknight Jr.

EMPLOYMENT CONTACT

Ms. Rosemary Kelly Morgan
Director of Attorney Services & Recruiting
Phone: (202) 429-8036
E-mail: legal_recruiting@steptoe.com

WHO'S WHO

Does the firm have a pro bono coordinator? Yes

Barbara Kagan, Esq.
Public Service Counsel
Phone: (202) 429-6258
E-mail: bkagan@steptoe.com

If yes, what percentage of his or her time is spent on pro bono work? 100 percent

Does the firm have a pro bono committee? Yes

If yes, how often does the committee meet? Periodically

Describe the composition of the committee: The committee is comprised of partners and associates plus the Public Service Counsel.

THE SCOOP

Does your firm have a written pro bono policy? Yes

Has the firm signed on to the Law Firm Pro Bono Challenge? Yes

What are some of the areas of law in which your firm has performed pro bono legal work in the last two years? Discrimination, political asylum/immigration, adoption, custody, guardian ad litem, divorce, child support, landlord/tenant, housing, public benefits, tax, nonprofit corporate work, HIV/AIDS, veterans appeals, education, human rights, criminal, arts, Hatch Act, children's issues, prisoners' rights, employment, environmental/conservation, attorneys fees, consumer, medical issues, animal rights, and estates.

What are some of the areas of law in which your firm does not perform pro bono work? no areas completely "off limits."

Organizations for which your firm has performed pro bono legal services in the last two years: American Bar Association; American Indian Foundation; American Civil Liberties Union; Animal Legal Defense Fund; Archdiocesan Legal Network; Boys and Girls Club; California Lawyers for the Arts; Capital Area Immigrants' Rights Coalition; Central American Refugee Center; District of Columbia Children's Law Center; Phoenix, Arizona Children's Law Center; Phoenix, Arizona Community Legal Services; Washington, DC Region Community Tax Aid; District of Columbia Council for Court Excellence; District of Columbia Prisoners' Legal Services Project; District of Columbia Appleseed; District of Columbia Bar; District of Columbia Employment Justice Center; Federalist Society; Florence, Arizona Immigration and Refugee Rights Project; Phoenix, Arizona Homeless Legal Assistance Project; Virginia Innocence Project; Human Rights First (formerly Lawyers' Committee for Human Rights); Lawyers for Children America; Legal Aid Society of the District of Columbia; District of Columbia Legal Counsel for the Elderly; Phoenix, Arizona Modest Means Project; National Parks Foundation; National Peace Corps Association; National Trust for Historic Preservation; Nature Conservancy; Los Angeles Public Counsel Law Center; District of Columbia Public Defender Service; Save the Children Federation; Veterans' Consortium Pro Bono Project; Phoenix, Arizona Volunteer Lawyers Program; Washington, DC Legal Clinic for the Homeless; Washington Lawyers' Committee for Civil Rights and Urban Affairs; Washington, District of Columbia Whitman Walker HIV/AIDS Clinic.

List up to three pro bono matters that are representative of the pro bono work your firm participates in.

- Steptoe & Johnson LLP represents a number of clients in discrimination matters, including for example, an African-American electric utility lineman in a racial discrimination and harassment action. Our client was subjected to years of horrific treatment, including persistent taunting, racial epithets and a mock lynching.

- The firm also represents numerous refugees from many different countries around the world, including for example, a Tibetan Buddhist nun who walked across the Himalayas to escape from China so she could practice her religion. These refugees are seeking political asylum in the United States because of religious, ethnic, racial, or political persecution in their country of origin.

- Another major area of our pro bono work involves family law issues, including child custody, guardian ad litem appointments and, in particular, adoption cases. The adoption work involves representing foster parents in proceedings to terminate the rights of biological parents who have abused and/or neglected their children, moving forward with the adoption, and ensuring that the adoptive parents receive financial subsidies that might be necessary to ensure the child is able to access any needed special services.

Does the firm encourage its lawyers to perform a minimum number of pro bono hours? Yes

If so, how many hours per year or what percentage of lawyers' billable hours? Attorneys are encouraged to take on at least one pro bono representation each year, and a minimum of 100 pro bono hours are credited toward their billable hours target.

SUPERVISION AND EVALUATIONS

Is there partner supervision on each pro bono matter? Yes

Do partner supervisors or, if applicable, senior associates provide written evaluations of associates' work on pro bono matters? Yes

If so, are those evaluations taken into account in determining salary, bonuses or advancement in the firm? Yes

If not, does the firm consider pro bono work generally in associate evaluations? Yes

HOURS

Does the firm give billable hour credit for pro bono work? Yes

Does the firm have a maximum number of pro bono hours that can be applied toward the billable hour target? No

If so, what is the maximum? Discretionary over 100 hours.

If your firm uses hours to determine bonuses, does it consider pro bono hours when determining bonuses? Yes

PRO BONO POINTS

What training opportunities are open to associates working on pro bono matters? There are numerous training sessions throughout each year offered by a variety of legal service providers that attorneys are encouraged to attend, as well as a number of in-house professional development programs.

Can associates bring matters of interest to the firm? Yes, and are encouraged to do so.

Does the firm offer the use of support staff in carrying out pro bono matters? Yes, attorneys representing clients in pro bono matters utilize the same resources they would in any other case.

What pro bono opportunities are available for summer associates? There are many pro bono matters available for summer associates to work on, and most of our summer associates take advantage of this opportunity, including accompanying attorneys to client meetings and court appearances. The firm also has a program through which it funds summer associates to spend up to three weeks working at a public service organization.

Does the firm have established programs, such as externships, that enable its associates to work in a public interest setting? Yes

If so, where and for up to how long? Steptoe has a rotation program through which the firm continuously staffs a full-time attorney position at The Legal Aid Society of the District of Columbia, with associates serving a six-month term. These attorneys carry a full Legal Aid case load (and have no responsibilities for firm matters), handling family law, landlord/tenant, and public benefits cases.

Has your firm won any special recognition or awards in the last two years for its pro bono work? Yes

If so, please list. The firm has been recognized for its work in the areas of public education, political asylum, disability rights and family law.

THE FIRM SAYS

Steptoe & Johnson has a long and rich tradition of public service. Our pro bono program is broad-based and directed both at serving individuals in need and assisting public service organizations. The firm was one of the very first in the country to have its pro bono program directed by an attorney on a full-time basis. Our public service counsel works with the firm's attorneys — associates and partners alike — to find pro bono opportunities that match their interests. Matters are referred to the firm by dozens of different public service organizations, and attorneys are also encouraged to bring pro bono matters to the firm.

Pro bono work is performed in all of Steptoe's offices, which are located in the District of Columbia (the firm's main office), Phoenix, Los Angeles and London. The firm's pro bono cases are treated like any other representation undertaken by the firm, and are allocated whatever time and resources necessary. All pro bono matters are supervised by a partner, and every attorney is encouraged to take on at least one pro bono representation a year. Associates receive a minimum of 100 hours of credit toward their billable target for time spent on pro bono work. In addition to the pro bono work performed at the firm, Steptoe has a loaned associate program through which the firm staffs a full-time attorney position at the Legal Aid Society of the District of Columbia, with each associate serving a six-month term. We also offer summer associates the opportunity to spend a portion of their summer working for a public interest organization in addition to working on pro bono matters during their time at the firm.

Steptoe is a charter signatory to the Law Firm Pro Bono Challenge, and has been recognized by numerous public interest organizations for our pro bono efforts. In addition to our legal public service work, Steptoe has a partnership program with a local public elementary school. Attorneys and staff tutor young students on a regular basis throughout the school year, participate in school activities and collect toys, books and supplies for the benefit of the school's needy families.

OUR SURVEY SAYS

"Of the 1,950 base billable hours, 100 of those can be pro bono. That's a big incentive. There is a full-time lawyer who coordinates pro bono and there is no end to opportunities."

"The firm commitment is strong but seems to have waned a bit with the increase in salaries and billable hours requirements."

"Our commitment to pro bono, especially work by individual associates on individual projects, has really suffered since the salary structure was altered in 2000. Although we can count 100 pro bono hours toward our billable budget, this creates a disincentive for individual associates to attempt much beyond an occasional clinic. I get the sense that working on a complex pro bono matter that might go to trial is discouraged unless the effort s spearheaded by an influential partner."

"I have already been placed in charge of a pro bono client and my hours count toward my billable requirements."

"The firm permits associates to credit up to 100 hours of pro bono work toward their billable goal of 1,950 hours. However, an associate's other non-billable work, such as writing articles and speeches for partners, also comes out of this 100 hours, so pro bono credit can be curtailed by this consideration. I worked on a rewarding pro bono case last year that the firm made a significant commitment to."

"Good commitment to pro bono work in headquarters office."

"They encourage pro bono, but on your own time; if pro bono interferes with your billables, [there's] less encouragement or downright rudeness."

"Pro bono hours receive credit toward bonuses, up to a certain amount. Two associates per year receive a Steptoe salary to work at Legal Aid for six months."

"Some associates do fellowships with Legal Aid on the firm's dollar. We have a full-time coordinator who oversees the firm's pro bono efforts. I am currently working on a major civil rights case."

"In addition to the pro bono work performed at the firm, Steptoe has a loaned associate program through which the firm staffs a full-time attorney position at the Legal Aid Society of the District of Columbia, with each associate serving a six-month term."

— *Steptoe & Johnson LLP*

Stroock & Stroock & Lavan

180 Maiden Lane
New York, NY 10038-4982
Phone: (212) 806-5400
www.stroock.com

LOCATIONS
New York, NY (HQ)
Los Angeles, CA
Miami, FL

MAJOR DEPARTMENTS & PRACTICES
Commodities & Derivatives
Employment Law
Energy & Project Finance
Entertainment
Financial Restructuring
Financial Services Litigation
Insurance
Intellectual Property
Investment Management
Litigation
Mergers, Acquisitions & Joint Ventures
Personal Client Services
Real Estate
Securities
Structured Finance
Tax
Technology & Emerging Companies

THE STATS
No. of attorneys worldwide: 362
No. of offices worldwide: 3
Managing Partners: Stuart H. Coleman, Thomas E. Heftler

EMPLOYMENT CONTACT
Ms. Bernadette Miles
Director of Legal Personnel & Recruiting
Phone: (212) 806-6640
Fax: (212) 806-6006
E-mail: bmiles@stroock.com

WHO'S WHO

Principal pro bono contact(s) at your firm:

Kevin J. Curnin, Esq.
Special Counsel and Attorney Director, The Public Service Project

Does the firm have a pro bono coordinator? Yes

If yes, what percentage of his or her time is spent on pro bono work? Almost 100 percent

Does the firm have a pro bono committee? Yes

If yes, how often does the committee meet? Biannually on a formal basis; more frequently on an informal basis.

Describe the composition of the committee: The Pro Bono committee consists of four partners, one managing attorney and the attorney director.

THE SCOOP

Does your firm have a written pro bono policy? No

Has the firm signed on to the Law Firm Pro Bono Challenge? No

What are some of the areas of law in which your firm has performed pro bono legal work in the last two years? 9/11 efforts, including Small Business Initiative, Adopt-a-Firehouse Program and the Small Business Court Assistance Project; plus traditional and emerging pro bono areas including asylum cases, community economic development, criminal appeals, disability rights and children's advocacy, and legal issues around domestic violence.

What are some of the areas of law in which your firm does not perform pro bono work? There are no areas in which we do not, a priori, perform pro bono work.

Organizations for which your firm has performed pro bono legal services in the last two years: Association of the Bar of the City of New York, inMotion, Lawyers Alliance for New York, NAACP-LDF, New York Lawyers for the Public Interest, Pratt Area Community Council, Sanctuary for Families, Legal Information for Families Today, The Legal Aid Society, Volunteer Lawyers for the Arts, Volunteer of Legal Services, Lawyers Committee for Human Rights, Kings County District Attorney's Office.

List up to three pro bono matters that are representative of the pro bono work your firm participates in.

- Mount Hope Housing Company (MHHC). A team of Stroock attorneys is providing comprehensive legal assistance for the development of the Mount Hope Community Center. MHHC has rehabilitated over 1,200 units of affordable housing and has provided assistance to first time homebuyers. In addition, MHHC operates a thrift shop, health clinic and an array of job readiness, job training and social programs. MHHC is developing a community center that will be a 70,500 square foot facility serving the children of the Bronx. It will include a gymnasium, auditorium space for the general public, office space for other nonprofits and outdoor space for safe play.

- Paynter Amicus Brief. Stroock represented the NAACP Legal Defense and Educational Fund, Inc. and the New York Civil Liberties Union in this appeal. The basis of the appeal was that all students in the Rochester City School District are not receiving the constitutionally mandated sound basic education to which they are entitled, under the Education

Article of the New York State Constitution as a result of the poverty-concentration and racial isolation of students in the district.

- Pratt Area Community Council (PACC). Stroock lawyers provide business counsel (corporate, IP, tax, insolvency, real estate) to PACC micro-entrepeneurs in Brooklyn (Bed-Stuy, Clinton Hill, Fort Greene) as well as counsel and legal support to PACC itself. To make this work more efficient, Stroock has created corporate and real estate "PACC Teams" to handle intake and run new matters — these teams have also created educational materials, form libraries, FAQs and other resources for PACC's internal use and counseling. In addition, Stroock lawyers have presented seminars to local businesspeople on a variety of legal topics.

BY THE NUMBERS

What is the total number of hours that lawyers in U.S. offices at your firm spent performing pro bono legal services in 2000, 2001 and 2002?

Total number of hours in 2000: 11,480 hours
Total number of hours in 2001: 15,720 hours
Total number of hours in 2002: 18,278 hours

Average number of pro bono hours per attorney in U.S. offices per year (including associates, partners, counsels, but not summer associates):

Average number of hours per attorney in 2000: 39.6 hours
Average number of hours per attorney in 2001: 52.6 hours
Average number of hours per attorney in 2002: 57.7 hours

What percentage of attorneys in this firm's U.S. offices did pro bono work in 2002? 204 attorneys (60 percent)

What percentage of attorneys in this firm's U.S. offices did at least 20 hours of pro bono work in 2002? 35 percent

Does the firm encourage its lawyers to perform a minimum number of pro bono hours? No. Stroock actively encourages participation, without assigning a minimum number of hours.

If so, how many hours per year or what percentage of lawyers' billable hours? N/A

SUPERVISION AND EVALUATIONS

Is there partner supervision on each pro bono matter? Yes

Do partner supervisors or, if applicable, senior associates provide written evaluations of associates' work on pro bono matters? Yes, as appropriate

If so, are those evaluations taken into account in determining salary, bonuses or advancement in the firm? Yes

If not, does the firm consider pro bono work generally in associate evaluations? Yes

HOURS

Does the firm give billable hour credit for pro bono work? Yes

Does the firm have a maximum number of pro bono hours that can be applied toward the billable hour target? No

If so, what is the maximum? N/A

If your firm uses hours to determine bonuses, does it consider pro bono hours when determining bonuses? Yes

PRO BONO POINTS

What training opportunities are open to associates working on pro bono matters? Training opportunities, by design, span a broad range that closely approximates and anticipates our associates' experiences working on billable matters: from briefing, oral argument and trial work to structuring and running various transactions, and including working closely with the client, strategizing and overall case/transaction management.

Can associates bring matters of interest to the firm? Yes

Does the firm offer the use of support staff in carrying out pro bono matters? Yes

What pro bono opportunities are available for summer associates? Examples from summer 2003 include: domestic violence/uncontested divorce proceedings, children's Social Security disability hearings and appeals, disability rights advocacy for New York City schoolchildren (special education hearings), summer law intern mentoring (with nonprofit partner Legal Outreach).

Does the firm have established programs, such as externships, that enable its associates to work in a public interest setting? No

Has your firm won any special recognition or awards in the last two years for its pro bono work? Yes

If so, please list.

- **2003:** New York State Bar Association's President's Pro Bono Service Award (Large Firm); New York AIDS Coalition's Vanguard Award; Legal Information for Families Today's Pro Bono Award.

- **2002:** inMotion Deborah E. Smith Award; The Legal Aid Society's Award for Assistance to Victims of the WTC Tragedy; The Legal Aid Society's Community Revitalization Awards (3 categories); The Legal Aid Society's Pro Bono Service Award; Lawyers' Alliance Cornerstone Award; New York State Bar Association's President's Pro Bono Service Award (Individual); Fordham Law School's Louis J. Lefkowitz Public Service Award.

THE FIRM SAYS

The Public Service Project (PSP) is the cornerstone of Stroock's longtime commitment to serving the public interest. Created in March 2001 after decades of firm service to pro bono matters, organizations and advocacy, the Public Service Project provides legal assistance to underserved communities and individuals. Stroock attorneys engage a full range of matters, including asylum cases, criminal appeals, disability rights, education law, mother and child advocacy, and community economic development.

Our innovative approach builds our pro bono practice in much the same way we build our commercial practice areas. The Public Service Project has identified certain areas of concentration, such as children, education and impoverished communities, while still handling a broad array of matters. A principal goal of the PSP is to involve more non-litigators (both associates and partners) in pro bono matters. Transactional opportunities frequently pair pro bono clients and teams of attorneys with a range of experience in tax, financial restructuring, intellectual property, employment and general corporate law.

The Project is directed by Kevin J. Curnin, a special counsel at Stroock. Rather than act as a coordinator only for the distribution of pro bono work, the attorney director is devoted full-time to managing the Project, actively supervising ongoing matters and handling a personal caseload of pro bono work. Since its founding, the Public Service Project has been repeatedly recognized and awarded as an innovative, citywide leader in pro bono services.

OUR SURVEY SAYS

"Excellent pro bono program! The opportunities are endless, and the firm is very supportive."

"They want you to do it, but it's hard to get the time."

"The pro bono coordinator, Kevin Curnin, has been lauded across the city for all that he has done in bringing Stroock's Public Service Project to the forefront of pro bono big law practices."

"The firm permits associates to count pro bono towards their billable hours. As a practical matter, however, as at many large firms, associates have to do pro bono on their own time. The firm does not significantly reduce other work to accommodate a pro bono matter."

"I bill over 300 hours per year to pro bono work. This firm is very committed to pro bono — it has a full-time attorney that directs the pro bono program and develops a supportive relationship with any attorneys who want to work on pro bono."

"The firm is ALL about pro bono — practically everyone does it over the course of a year and between 50 and 100 hours are encouraged."

"Our full-time pro bono attorney makes sure the firm is very active in pro bono work, and pro bono work counts toward associates' billable hours, which further encourages people to take pro bono assignments."

"Instead of worrying about how a partner will react if you take on a pro bono matter, this firm actually makes you feel embarrassed if you don't, but that's a good thing."

"Associates are permitted to work on just about any pro bono project they like."

"Our firm makes a huge pro bono investment. Finding pro bono work to do is very easy and always encouraged and the hours count toward your billable total."

"Stroock attorneys engage a full range of matters, including asylum cases, criminal appeals, disability rights, education law, mother and child advocacy, and community economic development."

— *Stroock & Stroock & Lavan*

Sullivan & Cromwell LLP

125 Broad Street
New York, NY 10004-2498
Phone: (212) 558-4000
www.sullcrom.com

LOCATIONS

New York, NY (HQ)
Los Angeles, CA
Palo Alto, CA
Washington, DC
Beijing
Frankfurt
Hong Kong
London
Melbourne
Paris
Sydney
Tokyo

MAJOR DEPARTMENTS & PRACTICES

Commercial Real Estate
Corporate & Financial
E-Business & Technology
Estates & Personal
Executive Compensation
Financial Institutions
Litigation
Mergers & Acquisitions
Project Finance
Tax

THE STATS

No. of attorneys worldwide: 717
No. of offices worldwide: 12
Chairman: H. Rodgin Cohen

EMPLOYMENT CONTACT

Ms. Nicole Adams
Manager of Legal Recruiting
Phone: (212) 558-3518
Fax: (212) 558-3588
E-mail: adamsn@sullcrom.com

WHO'S WHO

Principal pro bono contact(s) at your firm:

Stuart Meiklejohn, Esq.
Pro Bono Committee Chair

Does the firm have a pro bono coordinator? Yes.

Ms. Karen Biehl
Legal Assistant Pro Bono Coordinator

If yes, what percentage of his or her time is spent on pro bono work? 50 percent

Does the firm have a pro bono committee? Yes

If yes, how often does the committee meet? As needed.

Describe the composition of the committee: Three litigation partners and two corporate partners.

THE SCOOP

Does your firm have a written pro bono policy? Yes

Has the firm signed on to the Law Firm Pro Bono Challenge? Yes

What are some of the areas of law in which your firm has performed pro bono legal work in the last two years? Assistance to not-for-profit corporations, artists and arts groups; representation of victims of domestic violence; asylum applications; death penalty cases; prisoners' rights matters; criminal matters; civil rights issues; legal assistance to AIDS patients.

What are some of the areas of law in which your firm does not perform pro bono work? N/A

Organizations for which your firm has performed pro bono legal services in the last two years: Lawyers Alliance of New York, Lawyers Committee for Human Rights, The Legal Aid Society, inMotion, Inc., Sanctuary for Families, Volunteer Lawyers for the Arts, Volunteers of Legal Service, New York Lawyers for the Public Interest, The American Civil Liberties Union, Lawyers Committee for Civil Rights Under Law.

List up to three pro bono matters that are representative of the pro bono work your firm participates in.

- As co-counsel to the ACLU Reproductive Freedom Project, challenging Florida's "Scarlett Letter Law," which requires a mother to make public her sexual history if she seeks to place her child for adoption but does not know the identity or whereabouts of the father

- Providing varied legal services to survivors of the World Trade Center attack (with specific emphasis on the needs of non-U.S. nationals) and to owners of small businesses that were destroyed in the attack

- Representing capital and other indigent defendants in various stages of their criminal or post-conviction proceedings, including capital defendants in Oklahoma, Alabama, Georgia and North Carolina

BY THE NUMBERS

What is the total number of hours that lawyers in U.S. offices at your firm spent performing pro bono legal services in 2000, 2001 and 2002?

>Total number of hours in 2000: 28,961 hours
>Total number of hours in 2001: 47,201 hours
>Total number of hours in 2002: 55,089 hours

Average number of pro bono hours per attorney in U.S. offices per year (including associates, partners, counsels, but not summer associates):

>Average number of hours per attorney in 2000: 52 hours
>Average number of hours per attorney in 2001: 72 hours
>Average number of hours per attorney in 2002: 80 hours

What percentage of attorneys in this firm's U.S. offices did pro bono work in 2002? 66.5 percent

What percentage of attorneys in this firm's U.S. offices did at least 20 hours of pro bono work in 2002? 45.5 percent

Does the firm encourage its lawyers to perform a minimum number of pro bono hours? N/A

If so, how many hours per year or what percentage of lawyers' billable hours? N/A

SUPERVISION AND EVALUATIONS

Is there partner supervision on each pro bono matter? Yes. At least one partner is available to answer questions and discuss issues that arise in all pro bono matters. Some matters are also formally supervised by partners.

Do partner supervisors or, if applicable, senior associates provide written evaluations of associates' work on pro bono matters? Yes

If so, are those evaluations taken into account in determining salary, bonuses or advancement in the firm? Yes

If not, does the firm consider pro bono work generally in associate evaluations? N/A

HOURS

Does the firm give billable hour credit for pro bono work? Yes

Does the firm have a maximum number of pro bono hours that can be applied toward the billable hour target? No

If so, what is the maximum? N/A

If your firm uses hours to determine bonuses, does it consider pro bono hours when determining bonuses? N/A

PRO BONO POINTS

What training opportunities are open to associates working on pro bono matters? Training opportunities referred to us by the monthly NYC Pro Bono & Legal Service Training Calendar (a joint project of The Legal Aid Society, the Legal Support Unit of Legal Services for New York City, Probono.net and Volunteers of Legal Service) in addition to opportunities sent to us by other pro bono referral organizations.

Can associates bring matters of interest to the firm? Yes

Does the firm offer the use of support staff in carrying out pro bono matters? Yes

What pro bono opportunities are available for summer associates? The Courtroom Advocates Project (helping victims of domestic violence file petitions for protective orders); inMotion Summer Associate Program (representation of victims of domestic violence with uncontested divorces and custody proceedings); City Bar Refugee Assistance Project; Lawyers Committee for Human Rights Summer Associate Program; and research projects regarding death penalty, civil rights and other legal issues. Summer associates are also encouraged to work on all pro bono matters at the firm that are in need of assistance.

Does the firm have established programs, such as externships, that enable its associates to work in a public interest setting? No

If so, where and for up to how long? N/A

Has your firm won any special recognition or awards in the last two years for its pro bono work? Yes

If so, please list. In August 2002, the Administrative Office of the U.S. Courts recognized the firm's work on behalf of a capital defendant as among the most significant habeas corpus cases of the year. In May of 2001, Sullivan & Cromwell received a Cornerstone Award from Lawyers Alliance for New York for research and technical work on behalf of the Community Development and Nonprofit Law Library on the probono.net web site and for longstanding support of Lawyers Alliance projects.

THE FIRM SAYS

Sullivan & Cromwell actively encourages its lawyers to participate in pro bono and other public service activities, and makes the firm's facilities and personnel fully available to assist in these efforts. In recognition of the varying interests of individual lawyers, the firm recognizes as "public service" work participation in such diverse activities as pro bono litigation and legal advice, civil rights programs, bar association and related professional work, and other governmental, legal, educational, charitable, cultural and religious endeavors.

While public service is encouraged, the firm also believes that each lawyer must individually decide the nature and extent of his or her participation in such activities. An individual lawyer's decision as to participation or non-participation in public service activities will not affect that lawyer's standing or progress in the firm. A lawyer undertaking a pro bono or other public service matter is expected to devote sufficient time and effort to conform to the high professional standards to which the firm adheres on all client representations, and work on public service matters is taken into account in evaluating a lawyer's overall professional performance and potential. The firm does not impose any limitations on the amount or percentage of time a lawyer may devote to pro bono or other public service activities, but rather leaves that question to the good judgment of the individual lawyer. Lawyers at the firm engaged in public service activities have made varying time commitments to such activities, ranging from a relatively small percentage of the individual's professional workload to a leave of absence to devote full time to such an activity.

As a general rule, the firm does not seek an award of attorney's fees in public service matters and discourages its lawyers from doing so in such matters undertaken by them individually. An exception to this rule may be considered on a case-by-case basis, on the recommendation of the lawyer involved, where substantial time and effort have been devoted or other considerations indicate that such an application is appropriate. Where a fee is received, the balance of the fee, after deducting the firm's disbursements, will be donated to a suitable law-related charitable organization.

A Sullivan & Cromwell partner is the coordinator of public service activities. A committee, consisting of this individual and four other partners, exercises general supervision over such activities. In addition, the firm has designated a senior day-to-day coordinator of pro bono activities. The coordinators seek out challenging and rewarding public service opportunities and periodically circulate that information to those who have expressed interest in learning of such opportunities. Individual lawyers at the firm are encouraged to (and do) bring public service opportunities to the attention of the coordinators. Individual lawyers are also encouraged to advise the coordinators of their particular interests in public service opportunities so that those with common interests can jointly respond to outside requests for assistance.

In 2003, Sullivan & Cromwell engaged in extensive pro bono activities, with continued growth in the number and kinds of pro bono projects, in the involvement of legal and support staff, in the resources dedicated to such projects and — most importantly — in the number of needy persons, groups and interests that benefited by the high quality legal representation provided by our lawyers and paraprofessionals. This growth in pro bono activities may be attributed to the success of the firm's established pro bono policy, which is designed to encourage and support varied forms of pro bono work, to the firm's commitment to certain innovative pro bono projects, and to the significant efforts of the many individuals at the firm who avail themselves of the opportunity to do this important work.

OUR SURVEY SAYS

"I've taken three trips to Oklahoma working on a death penalty case. When the firm takes on a pro bono matter, its full resources are used."

"I regularly do pro bono work. There has never been a problem with being able to meet the obligations of my pro bono work. Firm resources are always available."

"My first 300+ month was mostly pro bono."

"The New York office seems very committed. It is practically affirmatively discouraged in Los Angeles."

"Pro bono is strongly encouraged and pro bono matters are given equal attention to paying clients. I've billed over 100 hours so far this year and it has earned me accolades within the firm."

"The firm is actually quite devoted to pro bono work, but quietly. They will commit a great deal of firm resources to pro bono matters, especially things like death penalty cases. But the pressure to work on client work isn't relieved by doing pro bono — the firm will support you, but you have to be willing to give up a lot of personal time if you work on pro bono matters."

"Pro bono is, and should be, a big deal at the firm. I have been very impressed with the opportunities to do pro bono, and firm management puts their money where their mouths are — pro bono is taken very seriously."

"The firm as a whole is very committed to pro bono, although it is hard to find time for it when hours are very long."

"S&C is unbelievably committed to pro bono work. I have had wonderful pro bono experiences and have been able to argue in court. It's usually given the same respect as client work. The firm strongly encourages everyone to take on some pro bono activity."

"They will spend large amounts of money on pro bono cases if you just ask for it."

Swidler Berlin Shereff Friedman, LLP

3000 K Street, NW, Suite 300
Washington, DC 20007-5118
Phone: (202) 424-7500

The Chrysler Building
405 Lexington Avenue
New York, NY 10174
Phone: (212) 973-0111
www.swidlaw.com

LOCATIONS

Washington, DC (HQ)
New York, NY

MAJOR DEPARTMENTS & PRACTICES

Antitrust & Trade Regulation
Bankruptcy & Creditors' Rights
Corporate
Energy
Environmental
Government Affairs
Insurance Coverage
Intellectual Property
Investment Management & Private Investment Funds
Litigation
Real Estate & Structured Finance
Tax/ERISA
Telecommunications

THE STATS

No. of attorneys worldwide: 273
No. of offices worldwide: 2
Managing Partner: Barry B. Direnfeld

EMPLOYMENT CONTACTS

Washington, DC
Ms. Kai Wilson
Recruiting Coordinator
Phone: (202) 424-7658
Fax: (202) 424-7664
E-mail: kewilson@swidlaw.com

New York
Ms. Judith Abraham
Recruiting Manager
Phone: (212) 891-9325
Fax: (212) 891-9598
E-mail: jmabraham@swidlaw.com

WHO'S WHO

Does the firm have a pro bono coordinator? Yes

David Lubitz, Esq.
Pro Bono Counsel
Phone: (202) 424-7716
E-mail: dmlubitz@swidlaw.com

If yes, what percentage of his or her time is spent on pro bono work? 100 percent

Does the firm have a pro bono committee? Yes

If yes, how often does the committee meet? Often, on an as-needed basis.

Describe the composition of the committee: The committee consists of the pro bono counsel and the partner in charge of the pro bono program.

THE SCOOP

Does your firm have a written pro bono policy? Yes

Has the firm signed on to the Law Firm Pro Bono Challenge? Yes

What are some of the areas of law in which your firm has performed pro bono legal work in the last two years? Civil rights, civil liberties, death penalty, disability rights, immigration, intellectual property, nonprofit and tax exemption, telecommunications, veterans benefits.

List up to three pro bono matters that are representative of the pro bono work your firm participates in.

- Representation of immigrants before the Department of Homeland Security, Immigration Courts, Board of Immigration Appeal and United States courts.
- Representation of churches, temples and other faith-based entities in various matters.
- Representation of individuals and entities in civil rights and civil liberties matters.

Does the firm encourage its lawyers to perform a minimum number of pro bono hours? Yes

If so, how many hours per year or what percentage of lawyers' billable hours? The firm encourages lawyers to meet bar and law firm pro bono project recommendations.

SUPERVISION AND EVALUATIONS

Is there partner supervision on each pro bono matter? Yes

Do partner supervisors or, if applicable, senior associates provide written evaluations of associates' work on pro bono matters? Yes

If so, are those evaluations taken into account in determining salary, bonuses or advancement in the firm? Yes

If not, does the firm consider pro bono work generally in associate evaluations? N/A

HOURS

Does the firm give billable hour credit for pro bono work? Yes

Does the firm have a maximum number of pro bono hours that can be applied toward the billable hour target? Yes

If so, what is the maximum? 100 hours (more credit may be obtained by approval)

If your firm uses hours to determine bonuses, does it consider pro bono hours when determining bonuses? N/A

PRO BONO POINTS

What training opportunities are open to associates working on pro bono matters? Attorneys are encouraged to attend bar and legal services provider sponsored trainings when taking on a pro bono matter. On occasion, the firm sponsors in-house pro bono trainings.

Can associates bring matters of interest to the firm? Yes

Does the firm offer the use of support staff in carrying out pro bono matters? Yes

What pro bono opportunities are available for summer associates? Summer associates are encouraged to work with attorneys on existing pro bono matters. In addition, each summer the pro bono counsel endeavors to find matters suitable for completion by summer associates during the time that they are at the firm.

Does the firm have established programs, such as externships, that enable its associates to work in a public interest setting? No

Has your firm won any special recognition or awards in the last two years for its pro bono work? Yes

If so, please list. The Judge David L. Bazelon Center for Mental Health Law and Washington Lawyers Committee for Civil Rights Under Law have recognized the firm for its disability and immigration work.

THE FIRM SAYS

In keeping with the firm's commitments to ensure access to justice and contribute to the communities in which it operates, attorneys are encouraged to do pro bono work. A full-time pro bono counsel is available to help with all aspects of performing pro bono work: finding a pro bono client or matter that is of interest to an attorney; obtaining the necessary approvals and performing necessary administrative tasks to enable the attorney to represent the pro bono client; and accessing appropriate resources to competently represent the pro bono client. The firm also sponsors a number of community service projects, such as tutoring elementary school students, providing food and clothing to homeless persons and toys for needy children during the holiday season, as well as a public interest fellowship program, whereby up to four summer associates, two each from the D.C. and New York offices, are permitted to spend half their summer at a public interest organization of their choice, at full summer associate salary.

OUR SURVEY SAYS

"We have a great pro bono director, and many opportunities are presented."

"The firm has a pro bono coordinator and allows each associate to include 100 hours of pro bono work towards an associate's annual billable requirements."

"The firm could do a lot better in supporting the pro bono coordinator, who is a great guy and attorney. The problem is that too many partners don't care about pro bono work and don't encourage you at all to do it."

"One hundred hours of pro bono work counts towards your billable and the firm really does seem to care about being involved in the community."

"We get about five e-mails a week listing various pro bono projects to work on. We get billable credit (for bonus purposes) for up to 100 hours of pro bono work."

"Swidler has a full-time pro bono coordinator, and he does a great job of working with the D.C. Bar pro bono committee and pulling in a lot of quality work."

"Most associates in the litigation group do pro bono work regularly. [There is] wide flexibility in type of work, depending on one's interest."

"The firm is ambivalent here. We have a full-time pro bono coordinator, and he's very active in soliciting attorneys for projects and drumming up cases in areas of interest. But compensation is still tied to billables, which puts a damper on associate participation."

"I have had a number of pro bono proposals approved with more encouragement than difficulty. Certain pro bono promoters here bring many opportunities for work on pro bono projects to the attention of associates."

"Swidler has a pro bono counsel who is incredibly helpful and approachable and whose sole job is to provide pro bono opportunities for the attorneys."

Thelen Reid & Priest LLP

875 Third Avenue
New York, NY 10022-6225
Phone: (212) 603-2000
www.thelenreid.com

LOCATIONS

New York, NY (HQ)
Los Angeles, CA
Morristown, NJ
San Francisco, CA
San Jose, CA
Washington, DC

MAJOR DEPARTMENTS & PRACTICES

Commercial Litigation
Construction
Corporate
Corporate Governance
Employee Benefits & ERISA
Energy, Utility & Infrastructure
Entertainment & Media
Government Affairs
Homeland Security
Hospitality Industry Services
Insurance
Intellectual Property & Trade Regulation
International
Labor & Employment
Project Development & Finance
Real Estate
Tax

THE STATS

No. of attorneys worldwide: 400+
No. of offices worldwide: 6
Chairman: Thomas J. Igoe Jr.

EMPLOYMENT CONTACTS

New York & New Jersey
Ms. Diane Amato
Attorney Recruiting Manager
Phone: (212) 603-8996
E-mail: attorneysny@thelenreid.com

See firm web site for employment contacts in other cities.

THE SCOOP

Thelen Reid & Priest is currently in the process of restructuring its pro bono program. Details about the program will be included in the next edition of the *Vault Guide to Law Firm Pro Bono Programs.*

In the meantime, for information about the firm's pro bono work and community service, please visit the careers section of the firm's web site.

Torys LLP

237 Park Avenue
New York, NY 10017-3142
Phone: (212) 880-6000

Suite 3000
Box 270, TD Centre
79 Wellington Street W.
Toronto, Ontario
M5K 1N2 Canada
Phone: (416) 865-7500
www.torys.com

LOCATIONS

New York, NY
Toronto

MAJOR DEPARTMENTS & PRACTICES

Administrative & Regulatory • Antitrust & Competition • Arbitration • Class Actions • Communications • Constitutional • Construction • Corporate/Commercial • Criminal • Employment & Compensation • Energy & Power • Environmental, Health & Safety • Financial Institutions • Government Relations • Health Care • Insolvency & Restructuring • Institutional Lending • Intellectual Property • Investment Funds & Management
Life Sciences • Litigation & Dispute Resolution • Mergers & Acquisitions • Pension & Benefits • Privacy • Private Client, Tax & Estate Planning • Privatization • Products Liability • Professional Negligence & Discipline • Project Finance • Public-Private Partnerships • Real Estate • Secured Transactions • Securitization • Sports & Entertainment • Tax • Technology • Trade • Trusts & Estates

THE STATS

No. of attorneys worldwide: 300
No. of offices worldwide: 2
Managing Partner, New York: Charles E. Dorkey III
Managing Partner, Toronto: Les Viner

EMPLOYMENT CONTACT

New York
Ms. Marie McHale (for litigation and summer associate positions)
Phone: (212) 880-6289
E-mail: mmchale@torys.com

Ms. Angela DeCato (for all other attorney positions)
Phone: (212) 880-6084
E-mail: adecato@torys.com

Toronto
Ms. Sarah MacKenzie
Phone: (416) 865-7504
E-mail: smackenzie@torys.com.

WHO'S WHO

Does the firm have a pro bono coordinator? No. We do not have a full time pro bono coordinator. Partners on the pro bono committee coordinate pro bono matters within the firm.

Jeffrey Gracer, Esq.
Partner
Phone: (212) 880-6262
E-mail: jgracer@torys.com

David Wawro, Esq.
Partner
Phone:: (212) 880.6288
E-mail: dwawro@torys.com

If yes, what percentage of his or her time is spent on pro bono work? Approximately 5 percent

Does the firm have a pro bono committee? Yes

If yes, how often does the committee meet? Twice a year and as needed.

Describe the composition of the committee: Two partners and two associates.

THE SCOOP

Does your firm have a written pro bono policy? Yes

Has the firm signed on to the Law Firm Pro Bono Challenge? No

What are some of the areas of law in which your firm has performed pro bono legal work in the last two years? Political asylum cases (referred by the Lawyers Committee for Human Rights); disability rights (referred by New York Lawyers for the Public Interest); 9/11 victims (referred by the Association of the Bar of the City of New York); arts organizations (referred by Volunteer Lawyers for the Arts).

What are some of the areas of law in which your firm does not perform pro bono work? We do not have any categorical exclusions.

Organizations for which your firm has performed pro bono legal services in the last two years: Lawyers Committee for Human Rights, New York Lawyers for the Public Interest, Volunteer Lawyers for the Arts, 9/11 Program, Association of the Bar of the City of New York, Children's Advocacy Center of Manhattan, Participant Inc. (performance art space and gallery) For South Asian Arts, Catholic Big Sisters, Youth Education Through Sports, National Stroke Association.

List up to three pro bono matters that are representative of the pro bono work your firm participates in. One of our associates secured political asylum for a democracy advocate from Sierra Leone who was arrested, tortured and threatened with death after he spoke out against military rule. We then helped reunify our client with his wife and young child. A partner and associate successfully defended a nonprofit school in a AAA arbitration arising from environmental conditions in a construction project. An associate helped a mentally disabled adult obtain the return of funds that were improperly taken from him by persons entrusted with his care.

BY THE NUMBERS

What is the total number of hours that lawyers in U.S. offices at your firm spent performing pro bono legal services in 2000, 2001 and 2002?

    Total number of hours in 2000: Data not available
    Total number of hours in 2001: 1,048.7 hours
    Total number of hours in 2002: 1,383.7 hours

Average number of pro bono hours per attorney in U.S. offices per year (including associates, partners, counsels, but not summer associates):

    Average number of hours per attorney in 2000: Data not available
    Average number of hours per attorney in 2001: 19.8 hours
    Average number of hours per attorney in 2002: 22.7 hours

What percentage of attorneys in this firm's U.S. offices did pro bono work in 2002? 43 percent

What percentage of attorneys in this firm's U.S. offices did at least 20 hours of pro bono work in 2002? 15 percent

Does the firm encourage its lawyers to perform a minimum number of pro bono hours? No. The firm's goal is to annually contribute an amount equal to 3 percent of U.S. billable hours. We are actively encouraging participation in pro bono matters at a level that will reach that goal.

If so, how many hours per year or what percentage of lawyers' billable hours? N/A

SUPERVISION AND EVALUATIONS

Is there partner supervision on each pro bono matter? Yes

Do partner supervisors or, if applicable, senior associates provide written evaluations of associates' work on pro bono matters? Yes

If so, are those evaluations taken into account in determining salary, bonuses or advancement in the firm? Yes

If not, does the firm consider pro bono work generally in associate evaluations? N/A

HOURS

Does the firm give billable hour credit for pro bono work? Yes

Does the firm have a maximum number of pro bono hours that can be applied toward the billable hour target? No

If so, what is the maximum? N/A

If your firm uses hours to determine bonuses, does it consider pro bono hours when determining bonuses? Yes

PRO BONO POINTS

What training opportunities are open to associates working on pro bono matters? Training is often offered by provider organizations. Training is also provided by the firm as part of the matter's supervision.

Can associates bring matters of interest to the firm? Yes

Does the firm offer the use of support staff in carrying out pro bono matters? Yes

What pro bono opportunities are available for summer associates? Summer associates are encouraged to participate in ongoing pro bono matters and routinely do so. The firm also offers summer associates the opportunity to spend half of their summer at a public interest organization with their salary paid by the firm.

Does the firm have established programs, such as externships, that enable its associates to work in a public interest setting? Yes

If so, where and for up to how long? The firm offers split summers at public interest organizations for summer associates.

Has your firm won any special recognition or awards in the last two years for its pro bono work? Yes

If so, please list. Torys attorneys who have spent 100 hours or more hours on pro bono matters have been recognized by the Association of the Bar of the City of New York. In addition, one of our partners has been actively involved in efforts by the Vance Center for International Justice at the Association of the Bar of the City of New York to promote pro bono work by law firms in Latin America.

THE FIRM SAYS

Torys believes involvement in pro bono activities is an important professional obligation. We encourage our lawyers to be active in pro bono matters and have adopted a written pro bono policy. In addition to litigation opportunities, we seek out pro bono matters for our corporate lawyers involving tax, technology, intellectual property, financing and other issues. Our pro bono policy is implemented by a pro bono committee consisting of two partners and two associates. The committee is responsible for fostering relationships with public interest and community organizations, promoting pro bono work within the firm, screening and approving pro bono matters, assisting with the supervision and staffing of pro bono matters, and preparing reports on the firm's pro bono activities. The pro bono committee works with provider organizations to identify pro bono opportunities, and circulates notices of available pro bono matters to all attorneys on a regular basis. We also encourage attorneys to develop their own pro bono opportunities.

Pro bono matters are opened and handled just as they are for any client. All matters are supervised by a partner. Pro bono matters are included in the evaluation process. Pro bono hours are credited as billable hours for evaluation, compensation and bonuses. One of our partners is involved in efforts to promote pro bono work by law firms in Latin America. He has participated in delegations to Argentina and Chile and will participate in an upcoming delegation to Brazil. These efforts are being carried forward by the Association of the Bar of the City of New York, through the Vance Center for International Justice. In addition to our pro bono legal activity, Torys' partners serve on the boards of several public entities and nonprofit organizations dedicated to promoting the public good. Our managing partner is chair of the Hudson River Park and also serves on the board of the New York Historical Society, the New York Parks and Conservancy Association, and several other civic and charitable organizations. Other Torys partners serve on the boards of the Citizen's Union, the National Stroke Association, New York Lawyers for the Public Interest, Children's Rights, Inc., MFY Legal Services, Inc., Legal Services of New York City, Pecadillo Theater Company, and Orpheus Performing Arts and Conference Center, Inc.

OUR SURVEY SAYS

"The firm has a strong commitment to pro bono work at all levels and there is a genuine interest among both associates and partners."

"A majority of associates have worked on pro bono matters in the firm. Pro bono work is encouraged and many people take it on especially if they have down time. At least one of the associates has devoted most of her hours to pro bono work and this is well respected."

"Associates have tremendous latitude in which type of case they take on. We receive weekly e-mails containing different pro bono opportunities that the pro bono coordinator forwards from the New York Lawyers for the Public Interest and the Lawyer's Committee for Human Rights. Most of the cases the firm takes on are of the small-scale type, helping individuals without financial means, and small non-profit organizations."

"I have been very satisfied with my [pro bono] experiences. I have been able to develop a case from the start, work independently, yet have partner support when needed. I have gained valuable hands-on experience very early on. I took on these cases on my own volition with the approval of the pro bono committee."

"The pro bono cases I have worked on were treated as if billable. I had all the firm's resources available to me when I needed them. Asylum cases, particularly detained cases, can take a considerable amount of time, but I never felt any pressure not to work more than a certain number of hours. My colleagues were very supportive."

"All the firm resources are available for pro bono matters. The hours associates spend are counted as billable."

"Pro bono matters are considered very important: an integral part of associate development and a valuable service."

"In addition to litigation opportunities, we seek out pro bono matters for our corporate lawyers involving tax, technology, intellectual property, financing and other issues."

— *Torys LLP*

Vinson & Elkins L.L.P.

2300 First City Tower
1001 Fannin
Houston, TX 77002-6760
Phone: (713) 758-2222
www.velaw.com

LOCATIONS

Houston, TX (HQ)
Austin, TX
Dallas, TX
New York, NY
Washington, DC
Beijing
Dubai
London
Moscow
Singapore

MAJOR DEPARTMENTS & PRACTICES

Administrative/Texas Regulatory Law
Alternative Dispute Resolution & Arbitration
Appellate
Biotechnology
Class Actions
Corporate Governance & Compliance
Employee Benefits & Executive Compensation
Employment Litigation & Labor
Energy
Environmental Law
Financial Institutions
Government
Health Industry
Insolvency & Reorganization
Insurance
Intellectual Property/Technical Litigation
International
Litigation
Products Liability
Project Finance & Development
Public Policy
Real Estate
Securities Litigation
Tax
Telecommunications
White Collar Criminal Defense

THE STATS

No. of attorneys worldwide: 800 +
No. of offices worldwide: 10
Managing Partner: Joseph C. Dilg

EMPLOYMENT CONTACT

Ms. Patty H. Calabrese
Director of Attorney Employment
Phone: (713) 758-4544
Fax: (713) 615-5245
E-mail: pcalabrese@velaw.com

WHO'S WHO

Principal pro bono contact(s) at your firm:

William E. Lawler, Esq.
Chairman of Pro Bono Committee
Phone: (202) 639-6676
E-mail: wlawler@velaw.com

Does the firm have a pro bono coordinator? No. V&E does not have an individual pro bono coordinator, but coordination of work and policy issues is handled through the pro bono committee.

Does the firm have a pro bono committee? Yes

If yes, how often does the committee meet? The full committee meets at least once a quarter. Individual office committees and other sub-committees meet as needed.

Describe the composition of the committee: V&E's firm-wide pro bono committee is made up of 27 attorneys representing all the firm's domestic offices, as well as one representative from the international offices. The associates that serve on the pro bono committee make up the pro bono advisory committee which has certain separate responsibilities in regard to identifying and screening new legal services providers and other pro bono initiatives. The pro bono committee has 13 partners and 14 associates.

THE SCOOP

Does your firm have a written pro bono policy? Yes

Has the firm signed on to the Law Firm Pro Bono Challenge? Yes

What are some of the areas of law in which your firm has performed pro bono legal work in the last two years? Vinson & Elkins lawyers have undertaken pro bono representation in a variety of civil, criminal and transactional matters, including civil rights and federal habeas corpus, consumer protection, corporate law and contracts, immigration and political asylum, indigent criminal defense, intellectual property, international human rights, labor and employment, landlord-tenant, low-income housing, real estate and tax-exempt organizations.

What are some of the areas of law in which your firm does not perform pro bono work? Vinson & Elkins does not have categorical prohibitions on its lawyers undertaking pro bono work in any particular areas of law. To the extent an area of law is not within the expertise of members of our firm, Vinson & Elkins lawyers typically consult with a referring pro bono clearinghouse organization that has expertise in the applicable area of law.

Organizations for which your firm has performed pro bono legal services in the last two years: Vinson & Elkins lawyers have provided pro bono legal services for a variety of individuals and organizations including: Austin Volunteer Legal Services Program, Dallas Volunteer Attorney Program, Houston Volunteer Lawyers' Program, Human Rights Initiative, International Human Rights Law Group, Lawyers Alliance for New York, National Center for Missing and Exploited Children, Texas Community Building with Attorney Resources (or Texas C-BAR), Volunteer Legal Services of Central Texas and Washington D.C.'s Operation Crackdown Program.

List up to three pro bono matters that are representative of the pro bono work your firm participates in. Vinson & Elkins lawyers have undertaken a variety of civil, criminal and transactional pro bono matters for both individuals and organizations. A few representative matters include:

- In 2002 and 2003, a team of lawyers in several domestic offices of Vinson & Elkins successfully used the Hague Convention on the Civil Aspects of International Child Abduction to reunite mothers in Canada and Mexico with their minor children who were unlawfully abducted by their fathers and held in the United States.

- Beginning in the Spring of 2002, several lawyers in Vinson & Elkins' Austin office took on the representation of an inmate in a federal court proceeding for a writ of habeas corpus based, in part, on the ineffective assistance received by the inmate from his trial counsel. Based on evidence presented by the Vinson & Elkins team at an evidentiary hearing, the magistrate judge recommended that the petition be granted.

- During 2002 and 2003, lawyers in several domestic and international offices of Vinson & Elkins worked on a variety of international human rights and constitutional research projects and analyses with respect to the countries of Afghanistan, Nicaragua and Somalia.

BY THE NUMBERS

What is the total number of hours that lawyers in U.S. offices at your firm spent performing pro bono legal services in 2000, 2001 and 2002?

> **Total number of hours in 2000:** 33,116 hours
> **Total number of hours in 2001:** 37,252 hours
> **Total number of hours in 2002:** 34,750 hours

Average number of pro bono hours per attorney in U.S. offices per year (including associates, partners, counsels, but not summer associates):

> **Average number of hours per attorney in 2000:** 50.1 hours
> **Average number of hours per attorney in 2001:** 50.3 hours
> **Average number of hours per attorney in 2002:** 42.8 hours

What percentage of attorneys in this firm's U.S. offices did pro bono work in 2002? 68 percent

What percentage of attorneys in this firm's U.S. offices did at least 20 hours of pro bono work in 2002? 40 percent

Does the firm encourage its lawyers to perform a minimum number of pro bono hours? The firm, as a matter of policy and practice, encourages all of its attorneys to make pro bono work a significant part of their professional activity. The firm subscribes to the American Bar Association of Code of Responsibility for principles regarding pro bono work and also subscribes to the pro bono policies of the various state bars to which its lawyers belong. The firm has not established a minimum hour target.

If so, how many hours per year or what percentage of lawyers' billable hours? N/A

SUPERVISION AND EVALUATIONS

Is there partner supervision on each pro bono matter? Yes

Do partner supervisors or, if applicable, senior associates provide written evaluations of associates' work on pro bono matters? Pro bono cases are handled like any other client matter. As such, work that associates do on these matters is included in their evaluations.

If so, are those evaluations taken into account in determining salary, bonuses or advancement in the firm? Yes

If not, does the firm consider pro bono work generally in associate evaluations? N/A

HOURS

Does the firm give billable hour credit for pro bono work? Yes

Does the firm have a maximum number of pro bono hours that can be applied toward the billable hour target? No

If so, what is the maximum? N/A

If your firm uses hours to determine bonuses, does it consider pro bono hours when determining bonuses? Not applicable

PRO BONO POINTS

What training opportunities are open to associates working on pro bono matters? Pro bono matters are treated by the firm exactly the same as any other client matter, and associates working on these matters have available to them a full range of training opportunities. V&E has a very significant in-house professional education department, and pro bono matters are a regular part of the curriculum of V&E's in-house training. New associates receive information and training about the firm's pro bono program shortly after their arrival at the firm. For particular substantive areas of pro bono work, such as political asylum and child custody cases, specialized training is available either through in-house training or through training provided by legal services providers with whom V&E works.

The goal of V&E's pro bono training is to ensure that every attorney doing pro bono work has the resources and background necessary to fully represent our pro bono clients.

Can associates bring matters of interest to the firm? Yes

Does the firm offer the use of support staff in carrying out pro bono matters? Yes

What pro bono opportunities are available for summer associates? Summer associates receive information about the pro bono program and are encouraged to participate in pro bono work during the time that they are at the firm.

Does the firm have established programs, such as externships, that enable its associates to work in a public interest setting? Yes

If so, where and for up to how long? The firm has a program whereby associates can spend up to six months working in the Dallas district attorney's office. The program began in 1999.

Has your firm won any special recognition or awards in the last two years for its pro bono work? Yes

If so, please list. Over the years, V&E and its attorneys have received many awards for pro bono work. Within the last two years, some of the most significant awards are:

- The 2003 Mexican American Legal Defense and Education Fund's Legal Service Award for exemplary work to advance the civil rights of Latinos and improving the legal standing of the Latino community.

- 2003 Award of Merit for the National Center for missing and exploited children for pro bono work in child recovery actions.

- 2003 Pro Bono Gold Service award from the Dallas Volunteer Attorney Program for extraordinary service.

- The 2001 State Bar of Texas W. Frank Newton Award given for outstanding contributions in provision of or access to legal services to the poor.

- The 2001 Community Builder Award for the state-wide Texas C-BAR recognizing V&E for its role in launching C-BAR and providing pro bono services to community-based nonprofit groups.

- During 2001-2003, many individual attorneys were recognized for pro bono work by groups including the State Bar of Texas, the District of Columbia Bar, the local bars of Austin, Dallas, Houston, New York, and Washington, D.C., the American Bar Association, the Texas Appleseed Foundation, the Human Rights Initiative, the Houston Grand Opera and the Council for Court Excellence.

THE FIRM SAYS

Since its inception, V&E has been committed to providing superior legal services to our community and to those who otherwise could not afford legal counsel. The pro bono program at V&E involves lawyers at the pinnacle of the profession, lawyers only months out of law school and everyone in between. Whether a partner is arguing an appeal before the U.S. Court of Appeals for the Fifth Circuit or a first-year associate is on the telephone advocating for a community besieged by drugs, pro bono at V&E is a firm-wide endeavor that utilizes the talent available at every level.

V&E does not merely boast that it is a firm committed to pro bono service. We back up our words by crediting all pro bono hours, on all firm-wide reports, as billable time that has been reported, billed and collected at standard hourly rates. Pro bono work and community involvement are among the factors considered in evaluation and compensation decisions.

Since our founding in 1917, V&E has participated in cases that have affected our society. The cases described below are certainly noteworthy, but it is impossible to give a fair picture of the quantity and quality of V&E's pro bono work over the years.

In 1938, firm founder William Vinson joined a team of lawyers that represented Edgar Smith, an African-American before the U.S. Supreme Court. Mr. Smith had been indicted by an all-white grand jury and convicted by an all-white jury for raping a white woman. The court eventually overturned the conviction, agreeing that grand juries, like juries, were required to "be a body truly representative of the community."

In 1963, V&E represented Rice University in a challenge to the amendment of the university charter to allow African-Americans to attend the school. The charter was successfully amended to allow non-white students to attend Rice University.

In 1994, Harry Reasoner led a team of V&E lawyers that represented the University of Texas School of Law in a challenge to its affirmative action program in Hopwood v. Texas. In Hopwood, four white applicants sued the law school. V&E

defended the University of Texas through two trials and two appeals to the U.S. Court of Appeals for the Fifth Circuit. V&E also worked with the Texas attorney general to prepare a second petition for certiorari, which was filed in the U.S. Supreme Court.

V&E is dedicated to encouraging all of its lawyers to actively participate in pro bono work specifically and community service generally. Every lawyer receives a copy of the firm's pro bono manual when starting work at the firm. This manual is also available on the firm's intranet site. Bill Lawler, the firm's pro bono partner gives every newly-hired lawyer a presentation on the importance of pro bono work, V&E's commitment to it and how to get involved. A similar presentation is made to each summer associate class, so that they are exposed to the V&E pro bono tradition whether or not they eventually join the firm.

V&E is consistently ranked the number one law firm in Texas in The American Lawyer AmLaw 100 ranking of large law firms' pro bono performance. While we are proud of what we have accomplished, V&E is committed to increasing the number of hours our attorneys spend on pro bono work.

The real strength of our program is its growth and change in response to the interests of attorneys and the needs of our communities. In the last several years, for example, we have had tremendous growth in our international pro bono work, such as political asylum cases, international civil rights and constitutional law surveys, and child recovery cases under the Hague Convention. This work has come about largely through the initiative of associates in our international offices who want to work in these areas.

V&E presents only one annual firm-wide award. The Outstanding Pro Bono Lawyer Award is presented each year at V&E's annual firm-wide all attorney meeting. The fact that this is V&E's only firm-wide award demonstrates our high regard for pro bono work.

OUR SURVEY SAYS

"Wonderful support. One hundred percent of all pro bono time is treated as billable. The firm actively supports and promote pro bono activities. Success stories are shared internally firm-wide on a regular basis. The firm presents awards for pro bono work every year."

"The firm has a great pro bono policy."

"The firm is strongly committed, gives full billable credit for pro bono work and encourages associates to take pro bono projects."

"The firm provides true credit for pro bono hours worked, with no minimum billable that one must hit before pro bono hours are treated as billables for record keeping (not that it matters much since billables seem so unimportant). The firm also seems very willing to reimburse necessary expenses to guarantee that pro bono clients are given the same level of representation as paying clients."

"All pro bono hours are reported as billed and collected time, period. The commitment to pro bono work is incredibly strong."

"V&E consistently leads the bar in pro bono commitments. The firm solicits pro bono opportunities from agencies and courts. The firm clearly believes that pro bono is not only the right thing to do, but a necessary component of associate development."

Vinson & Elkins L.L.P.

"I chose to come to V&E because of its attitude towards pro bono — that is, counting pro bono hours as regular billable hours. I have found that partners and associates have been extremely encouraging of pro bono work. I recently won an important asylum case and received upwards of 30 e-mails from people congratulating me. They were genuinely delighted for me (and the client), and I was mightily impressed."

"The hours we bill working on pro bono projects are treated the same as the hours we bill for billable clients. The firm doesn't distinguish between the two in calculating our annual hours."

"The fact that pro bono hours count to billables is just one way that the firm shows its view on the importance of pro bono work. There are more than enough ways to get involved in pro bono work."

"Full billable credit for pro bono hours; very supportive atmosphere, although it is sometimes hard to find the time given other demands."

Vinson & Elkins L.L.P.

"Whether a partner is arguing an appeal before the U.S. Court of Appeals for the Fifth Circuit or a first-year associate is on the telephone advocating for a community besieged by drugs, pro bono at V&E is a firm-wide endeavor that utilizes the talent available at every level."

— *Vinson & Elkins L.L.P.*

Wachtell, Lipton, Rosen & Katz

51 West 52nd Street
New York, NY 10019-6188
Phone: (212) 403-1000
www.wlrk.com

LOCATIONS
New York, NY

MAJOR DEPARTMENTS & PRACTICES
Antitrust
Corporate
Creditors' Rights
Executive Compensation & Benefits
Litigation
Real Estate
Tax

THE STATS
No. of attorneys worldwide: 193
No. of offices worldwide: 1
Chairman: Daniel A. Neff

EMPLOYMENT CONTACT
Ms. Elizabeth F. Breslow
Director of Recruiting & Legal Personnel
Phone: (212) 403-1334
Fax: (212) 403-2334
E-mail: recruiting@wlrk.com

WHO'S WHO

Principal pro bono contact(s) at your firm:

Marc Wolinsky, Esq.
Partner
Phone: (212) 403-1000

SUPERVISION AND EVALUATIONS

Is there partner supervision on each pro bono matter? Yes

Do partner supervisors or, if applicable, senior associates provide written evaluations of associates' work on pro bono matters?

If so, are those evaluations taken into account in determining salary, bonuses or advancement in the firm?

If not, does the firm consider pro bono work generally in associate evaluations? Yes

PRO BONO POINTS

What training opportunities are open to associates working on pro bono matters? The organizations we work with have training programs that our associates participate in.

Can associates bring matters of interest to the firm? Yes

Does the firm offer the use of support staff in carrying out pro bono matters? Yes

What pro bono opportunities are available for summer associates? AHC NY (ACORN Housing Corp.) Housing Court Program and Project on the Homeless and all firm pro bono matters.

Does the firm have established programs, such as externships, that enable its associates to work in a public interest setting? No

Has your firm won any special recognition or awards in the last two years for its pro bono work? No

THE FIRM SAYS

We are committed to supporting attorneys who undertake pro bono projects. Pro bono clients are clients of the firm, and no distinction is made between hours spent on pro bono or other client matters. As part of our pro bono practice, in the last year, our attorneys have argued criminal appeals on behalf of indigent defendants in New York state court; represented a Russian immigrant barber who was fired for wearing a yarmulke on the job; drafted an amicus brief to the New York State Appellate Division in an important school funding case; advised a community-based organization that provides social services in underprivileged areas in South Africa; represented a New York artist in protecting her First Amendment rights; assisted in the representation of an Arizona woman sentenced to capital punishment; provided legal counsel to public AM and FM radio stations in New York City, the National Lawyers' Committee for Civil Rights Under Law, Queens College; and provided tax and corporate advice to a number of small museums and research centers.

In addition, we have participated in a program with the Office of Corporation Counsel of the City of New York whereby we "loaned" one of our litigation associates to the New York City Law Department to assist that department's torts division in its trial work. We are also proud of the considerable contributions the firm has made to the legal profession and the positive impact we have had on our community both through financial support and through leadership of numerous philanthropic and public policy causes. In addition, the firm's partners, counsel and associates have taught courses at Harvard, New York University and the University of Pennsylvania in fields such as constitutional law, ethics, advanced criminal procedure and corporations.

OUR SURVEY SAYS

"Much of our pro bono comes in the form of giving money."

"The firm is encouraging about taking on pro bono matters but the time commitment involved on top of regular work makes it tough for associates to sign on."

"I've had a few very interesting pro bono matters. The partners and associates take them very seriously. They often consume as much time as matters for paying clients."

"No one is going to deter your from doing pro bono, but no one is pushing it either — and that's the way it should be."

"Pro bono is certainly permitted and opportunities provided, but nobody has ever actually encouraged me to do any."

"The firm supports those who want to do pro bono work, but you need to seek it out. Bar association work is treated similarly."

"The firm contributes a great deal of money to charitable causes, but few attorneys are able to devote their time to pro bono."

"Although associates are not always actively encouraged to take on pro bono work, those who do have all of the resources of the office at their disposal."

"It's impossible to make time to do pro bono."

"There are many opportunities available, and summer associates and pre-bars get to do quite a bit. I also think that some partners make this a priority as well. Regular associates do not often have time and, while they would like to do pro bono work, feel that they are unable to make that sort of commitment because of the volume of their other matters."

"Pro bono clients are clients of the firm, and no distinction is made between hours spent on pro bono or other client matters."

— *Wachtell, Lipton, Rosen & Katz*

Weil, Gotshal & Manges LLP

767 Fifth Avenue
New York, NY 10153
Phone: (212) 310-8000
www.weil.com

LOCATIONS

New York, NY (HQ)
Austin, TX
Boston, MA
Dallas, TX
Houston, TX
Miami, FL
Silicon Valley, CA
Washington, DC
Brussels
Budapest
Frankfurt
London
Munich
Paris
Prague
Singapore
Warsaw

MAJOR DEPARTMENTS & PRACTICES

Weil Gotshal is organized into six departments:

Corporate • Litigation • Regulatory • Restructuring/Distress • Management/Insolvency • Tax and Trust & Estates

*There are more than 20 practice areas within these departments, namely, antitrust/competition, appellate, banking & finance, bankruptcy litigation, capital markets, complex commercial litigation, consumer financial services, corporate governance, crisis management, employment, environmental, global dispute resolution, government/regulatory, intellectual property/media, mergers & acquisitions, patent, private equity, product liability/mass tort, propertytransactions and finance, securities litigation, and structured finance/derivatives.

THE STATS

No. of attorneys worldwide: 1,150
No. of offices worldwide: 17
Executive Partner and Chairman: Stephen J. Dannhauser

EMPLOYMENT CONTACT

Ms. Nancy Fishkin
Legal Recruiting Coordinator
Fax: (212) 735-4502
E-mail: nancy.fishkin@weil.com

WHO'S WHO

Principal pro bono contact(s) at your firm:

Steven Alan Reiss, Esq.
Chair, Pro Bono Committee

Harris J. Yale, Esq.
Pro Bono Counsel

Ms. Barbara Nichols
Pro Bono Coordinator

Does the firm have a pro bono coordinator? Yes
Barbara Nichols

If yes, what percentage of his or her time is spent on pro bono work? Full-time position.

Does the firm have a pro bono committee? Yes

If yes, how often does the committee meet? Every six weeks.

Describe the composition of the committee: Partners, counsel and associates from each department and office of the firm.

THE SCOOP

Does your firm have a written pro bono policy? Yes

Has the firm signed on to the Law Firm Pro Bono Challenge? Yes

What are some of the areas of law in which your firm has performed pro bono legal work in the last two years? Corporate, litigation, tax and real estate matters; constitutional rights; children/families/elder representation; criminal appeals; discrimination matters; death penalty cases; economic community development projects; educational matters; housing/homeless rights; intellectual property issues; nonprofit general counsel representation; political asylum cases; representation of low-income artists.

What are some of the areas of law in which your firm does not perform pro bono work? Occasionally, there are areas in which a pro bono matter presents a conflict issue and therefore the firm cannot take on that matter.

Organizations for which your firm has performed pro bono legal services in the last two years: Lawyers Alliance for New York, New York Lawyers for the Public Interest, Legal Services for New York City, Legal Aid Society, Association of the Bar of the City of New York, Lawyers Committee for Human Rights, Lawyers Committee for Civil Rights Under Law, New York Legal Assistance Group, Volunteers of Legal Service, Volunteer Lawyers for the Arts.

List up to three pro bono matters that are representative of the pro bono work your firm participates in.

- Weil Gotshal attorneys have provided significant corporate, tax, real estate and intellectual property legal services to The Microenterprise Project which works with economic community development corporations that assist existing and start-up businesses in Harlem and North Brooklyn, particularly those that are minority and women owned. We also act as volunteer general counsel to numerous nonprofit organizations that deliver crucial social services to disadvantaged communities.

- Several of our offices have worked together on litigation cases regarding racial discrimination. Our attorneys successfully litigated to compel a school district in Pennsylvania to comply with a federal court order to equalize educational opportunities for minority students. Also, working alongside the NAACP, our attorneys have successfully litigated cases which involved the improper convictions of African Americans in Tulia, Texas, on false drug charges.

- The firm's commitment to educational efforts has led to its representation of the New York Performance Standards Consortium in its efforts to overturn a decision by the Commissioner of Education to force consortium schools to abandon their highly successful curriculum in favor of a state-mandated, standardized form of assessment (the "Regents" exams). Also, Weil Gotshal attorneys handle a significant number of children's cases which deal with the rights and educational needs of New York City students with learning disabilities and, on Long Island, provides legal services to a Hispanic economic development group which provides educational programs, vocational training, and youth and tutorial services.

BY THE NUMBERS

What is the total number of hours that lawyers in U.S. offices at your firm spent performing pro bono legal services in 2000, 2001 and 2002?

      Total number of hours in 2000: 18,500 hours
      Total number of hours in 2001: 25,000 hours
      Total number of hours in 2002: 28,000 hours

Average number of pro bono hours per attorney in U.S. offices per year (including associates, partners, counsels, but not summer associates):

      Average number of hours per attorney in 2000: 30 hours
      Average number of hours per attorney in 2001: 36 hours
      Average number of hours per attorney in 2002: 37 hours

What percentage of attorneys in this firm's U.S. offices did pro bono work in 2002? 53 percent

What percentage of attorneys in this firm's U.S. offices did at least 20 hours of pro bono work in 2002? 26 percent

Does the firm encourage its lawyers to perform a minimum number of pro bono hours? Yes

If so, how many hours per year or what percentage of lawyers' billable hours? 50 hours

SUPERVISION AND EVALUATIONS

Is there partner supervision on each pro bono matter? Yes

Do partner supervisors or, if applicable, senior associates provide written evaluations of associates' work on pro bono matters? Yes

If so, are those evaluations taken into account in determining salary, bonuses or advancement in the firm? Yes

If not, does the firm consider pro bono work generally in associate evaluations? N/A

HOURS

Does the firm give billable hour credit for pro bono work? Yes

Does the firm have a maximum number of pro bono hours that can be applied toward the billable hour target? No

If your firm uses hours to determine bonuses, does it consider pro bono hours when determining bonuses? Yes

PRO BONO POINTS

What training opportunities are open to associates working on pro bono matters? There are mandatory training programs for all junior associates. In addition, attorneys are encouraged to participate in all pro bono training matters available to them in-house — i.e., not-for-profit incorporations and tax exemption filings, guardianship workshop and political asylum trainings. Also, attorneys can participate in any one of the training programs offered by the following organizations: Practicing Law Institute, Volunteers of Legal Service, Volunteer Appellate Defender Program, Lawyers Committee for Human Rights, Legal Aid Society, New Associate Pro Bono Day at the Association of the Bar of the City of New York, Lawyers Alliance for New York, New York Lawyers for the Public Interest, New York Legal Assistance Group, and any of the trainings offered in the cities where our offices are located.

Can associates bring matters of interest to the firm? Yes

Does the firm offer the use of support staff in carrying out pro bono matters? Yes

What pro bono opportunities are available for summer associates? Summer associates are invited to participate in a two-week extern program at the offices of leading public services providers, such as Lawyers Alliance for New York, New York Lawyers for the Public Interest, Legal Aid Society, Harlem Legal Services and Legal Services for New York City. Also, summer associates work on a number of pro bono matters when rotating through the firm's departments.

Does the firm have established programs, such as externships, that enable its associates to work in a public interest setting? Yes

If so, where and for up to how long? Lawyers Alliance for New York – four-month full-time rotations; Legal Services for New York City – four-month full-time rotations; New York City Law Department – four-month full-time rotations; New York Legal Assistance Group — one full semester part-time for third-year law students.

Has your firm won any special recognition or awards in the last two years for its pro bono work? Yes

If so, please list. Lawyers' Committee for Civil Rights Under Law — Robert F. Mullen Pro Bono Award. Federal Bar Council Award for Partner's work as Chair of Public Service Committee for the past three years which included the establishment of a significant number of new programs. New York State Bar Association President's Pro Bono Service Award for Large Law Firms. Legal Aid Society Annual Law Firm Recognition Award. Volunteer Lawyers for the Arts — Attorney Volunteer Service Award.

THE FIRM SAYS

Weil, Gotshal & Manges LLP is committed to the principle that pro bono service is part of a lawyer's professional responsibility, and the firm believes that pro bono work can be an enriching personal and professional experience.

It is the firm's goal that each lawyer, partners and associates alike, contribute a minimum of 50 hours of pro bono work each year, a majority of which should be on work that assists people of limited means. Pro bono hours are to be handled with the same level of professional responsibility and resources that the firm gives to its regular clients, and the annual attorney evaluation process includes each lawyer's performance in satisfying the firm's pro bono goals.

In deciding which matters to accept on a pro bono basis, the firm considers all proposed matters, regardless of size or manner of referral. Moreover, absent a conflict situation, the firm encourages its attorneys to pursue their individual pro bono interests. In addition, the firm believes that, because of its size and resources, it should undertake some substantial matters that may have significant impact on the community.

In recognition of the growing need for free legal services to the members of the community, the pro bono work handled by Weil Gotshal includes both litigation and transactional projects. The firm represents individuals seeking political asylum, indigent criminal defendants on appeals matters, constitutional rights issues, death penalty cases, homeless rights initiatives, children's disability rights issues, struggling artists in need of a variety of legal services and the elderly in planning their estates. Weil Gotshal attorneys also work with a wide variety of clients advising on matters ranging from economic community development projects, contract and lease negotiations, mergers of nonprofit and financial reorganizations, incorporation and tax exemption filings for not-for-profit organizations, and act as volunteer general counsel to numerous nonprofit organizations that deliver crucial social services to low-income and disadvantaged neighborhoods.

In addition to the extraordinary amount of work taken on by Weil Gotshal attorneys to assist the families affected by the September 11th tragedy, the firm was appointed pro bono counsel to the Board of Lower Manhattan Development Corporation, a joint state/city corporation responsible for overseeing the revitalization and rebuilding of lower Manhattan. Attorneys from all departments spend a significant amount of hours working on this important project.

Finally, the firm-wide structure of the pro bono committee allows all of our offices to make an effort to take on pro bono matters together, utilizing all the resources of the firm. Our European offices have been increasing their pro bono efforts and recently our London office has worked extensively on projects with both Oxfam and Crisis.

We welcome the opportunity to speak with law students about any aspect of our pro bono program as we are proud to continue our long-standing obligation to ensure that the legal system is accessible and fair to all clients.

OUR SURVEY SAYS

"The firm overall is very committed to pro bono work but it is rarely discussed, if ever, at a department level (nor would it be feasible given workloads)."

"The opportunities are there to be as involved as one wants to be. No one can complain that this firm does not do its part in support of pro bono causes."

"We do it, but it's expressly less important than paying clients. My impression, rightly or wrongly, is that this is an issue of paying especially close attention to work for clients whose satisfaction will translate directly into more paying work, rather than a specific devaluing of our pro bono clients."

"We get weekly updates on available pro bono projects, as well as notices of particularly urgent or significant matters. The firm encourages associates to take on pro bono work and recognizes that it's real work."

"The firm is very committed to pro bono. The firm has an attorney who is of counsel to the firm who oversees the pro bono programs. Monthly, the firm circulates a list of pro bono case offerings. The firm also offers pro bono externships."

"If you can swing the workload, it's readily available."

"Don't be fooled by the averages: the pro bono professionals put in most of those hours and the rest of us are told that it wouldn't fit into our schedules."

"Pro bono opportunities are often provided, but it takes a good deal of individual initiative to get involved in pro bono work."

"From its massive-scale assistance efforts related to post-9/11 issues, to the small, individual pro bono matters, Weil Gotshal leads other law firms in its dedication to and promotion of pro bono work."

"I know several associates that have participated in three-month pro bono rotations outside the office. Moreover, there are a tremendous number of pro bono cases, deals and other opportunities for which associates get full billable credit."

"Overall the firm is extremely committed to pro bono work and is involved in numerous pro bono projects. It is up to the associates to seek these opportunities out. I have billed between 100 and 200 hours to pro bono per year and the firm has been very supportive of my pro bono work."

White & Case LLP

1155 Avenue of the Americas
New York, NY 10036-2787
Phone: (212) 819-8200
www.whitecase.com

LOCATIONS

New York, NY (HQ)
Los Angeles, CA
Miami, FL
Palo Alto, CA
San Francisco, CA
Washington, DC
+31 other offices worldwide

MAJOR DEPARTMENTS & PRACTICES

Antitrust
Banking
Corporate
Employee Benefits & Executive Compensation
Environmental
Financial Restructuring & Insolvency
Insurance
Intellectual Property
International
Labor & Employment
Legislative/Law Reform
Litigation
Mergers & Acquisitions
Private Clients
Project & Infrastructure Finance
Public Finance
Real Estate
Securities
Tax
Telecommunications

THE STATS

No. of attorneys worldwide: 1,736
No. of offices worldwide: 37
Managing Partner: Duane D. Wall

EMPLOYMENT CONTACT

Office of Attorney Recruiting & Employment
Phone: (212) 819-8200
Fax: (212) 354-8113
E-mail: recruit@whitecase.com

WHO'S WHO

Principal pro bono contact(s) at your firm:

James Stillwaggon, Esq.
Pro Bono Committee Chair
Phone: (212) 819-8854
E-mail: jstillwaggon@whitecase.com

Mr. Byrne Harrison
Pro Bono Coordinator, New York
Phone: (212) 819-8787
E-mail: bharrison@whitecase.com

Ms. Felicity Kirk
Pro Bono Director, London
Phone: 44 (20) 7397-3818
E-mail: fkirk@whitecase.com

Does the firm have a pro bono coordinator? Yes
Byrne Harrison, Pro Bono Coordinator
Felicity Kirk, Pro Bono Director

If yes, what percentage of his or her time is spent on pro bono work? 100 percent

Does the firm have a pro bono committee? Yes

If yes, how often does the committee meet? Virtual meetings (e-mail and conference calls) approximately twice a month. Regular meetings approximately six times per year.

Describe the composition of the committee: The committee includes partners and associates from various departments in New York, Washington, D.C., Los Angeles, Mexico City and Miami. It also includes the New York pro bono coordinator and managing clerk and the London director of pro bono.

THE SCOOP

Does your firm have a written pro bono policy? Yes

Has the firm signed on to the Law Firm Pro Bono Challenge? Yes

What are some of the areas of law in which your firm has performed pro bono legal work in the last two years? Children's rights, asylum, community development, micro-entrepreneurial assistance, trust and estates, domestic violence, divorce, not-for-profit incorporation, impact litigation.

Organizations for which your firm has performed pro bono legal services in the last two years: Inner City Law Center, Legal Aid Society, Lawyers Alliance for New York, inMotion, Lawyers Committee for Human Rights, Lawyers' Committee for Civil Rights Under Law, Volunteer Lawyers for the Arts, Volunteers of Legal Service, Women's World Banking, Doctors Without Borders.

List up to three pro bono matters that are representative of the pro bono work your firm participates in.

- Assisting a husband and wife in opening a fast food franchise in an economic empowerment zone in the South Bronx. This included setting up a limited liability company, negotiating a lease and reviewing loan documentation. The franchise has been operating successfully for over a year.

- Serving as co-counsel in a class action lawsuit against New Jersey's Division of Youth and Family Services on behalf of children in New Jersey foster care. The settlement agreement in the case provided for immediate funding to hire workers, obtain facilities and equipment for DYFS, as well as for recruitment of foster parents. It also provides for an immediate review of licensing standards, hiring processes and safety assessments of children in foster care.

- Successfully defending an indigent client in a custody battle with her ex-husband, who was attempting to sever all ties between the child and his mother.

BY THE NUMBERS

What is the total number of hours that lawyers in U.S. offices at your firm spent performing pro bono legal services in 2000, 2001 and 2002?

Total number of hours in 2000: 32,699 hours
Total number of hours in 2001: 33,286 hours
Total number of hours in 2002: 29,937 hours

Average number of pro bono hours per attorney in U.S. offices per year (including associates, partners, counsels, but not summer associates):

Average number of hours per attorney in 2000: 50 hours
Average number of hours per attorney in 2001: 49 hours
Average number of hours per attorney in 2002: 42 hours

What percentage of attorneys in this firm's U.S. offices did pro bono work in 2002? 55 percent

What percentage of attorneys in this firm's U.S. offices did at least 20 hours of pro bono work in 2002? 33 percent

Does the firm encourage its lawyers to perform a minimum number of pro bono hours? No

SUPERVISION AND EVALUATIONS

Is there partner supervision on each pro bono matter? Yes

Do partner supervisors or, if applicable, senior associates provide written evaluations of associates' work on pro bono matters? Yes

If so, are those evaluations taken into account in determining salary, bonuses or advancement in the firm? Yes

If not, does the firm consider pro bono work generally in associate evaluations? N/A

HOURS

Does the firm give billable hour credit for pro bono work? Yes

Does the firm have a maximum number of pro bono hours that can be applied toward the billable hour target? No

If so, what is the maximum? N/A

If your firm uses hours to determine bonuses, does it consider pro bono hours when determining bonuses? Yes

PRO BONO POINTS

What training opportunities are open to associates working on pro bono matters? Training is available through most of the legal service providers from which we accept cases. This can be either in the form of CLE classes or comprehensive training materials. White & Case also has an in-house mentoring program.

Can associates bring matters of interest to the firm? Yes

Does the firm offer the use of support staff in carrying out pro bono matters? Yes

What pro bono opportunities are available for summer associates? All summer associates are encouraged to participate in ongoing pro bono matters based on their interests. In addition, the New York office participates in two domestic violence projects that are specifically for summer associates.

Does the firm have established programs, such as externships, that enable its associates to work in a public interest setting? Yes

If so, where and for up to how long? White & Case has an externship program with inMotion, a New York City-based nonprofit organization that provides free legal services to low-income, under-served or abused women. Each extern serves for a three-month rotation.

Has your firm won any special recognition or awards in the last two years for its pro bono work? Yes

If so, please list. New York State Bar Association President's Pro Bono Service Special Recognition Award (2001); Lawyers Alliance for New York Cornerstone Award (2001); Holborn Law Society and the City of London Law Society's Wig & Pen Prize awarded to London associate Lucy McCullagh for her work on behalf of Medecins Sans Frontieres (2001); The Lawyer magazine names Lucy McCullagh one of the top three "Assistant Solicitors of the Year" for her outstanding pro bono work (2001); Queens Legal Services Corporation Community Service Recognition Award (2001); Legal Aid Society recognized JoAnn DiSanti, managing clerk, for her work in the Early Intervention Project (2001); InMotion's Commitment to Justice Award (2001); Lawyers Alliance for New York Cornerstone Award given to associate Mario Fulgieri for his work related to the World Trade Center attacks (2002); InMotion Commitment to Justice Award for outstanding Pro Bono Coordinator given to Byrne Harrison (2002); Volunteer Lawyers for the Arts Pro Bono Service Award for work done on behalf of low-income artists (2002); Tiffany Fox II Homeowners' Association recognized firm for obtaining a $1.2 million settlement for claims of faulty construction (2002); Legal Aid Society's Pro Bono Publico Award given to partner Jeffrey Temple for assistance in the aftermath of the World Trade Center attack (2002); Orphans International honors associate Una Cho for pro bono work (2002); White & Case recognized for World Trade Center-related pro bono assistance given to New York City Fire Department Engine 16, Ladder 7 (2002); Orphans International presents Certificate of Appreciation to White & Case for work done on their behalf (2003); Legal Aid Society's Pro Bono Publico

Award given to partner Jeffrey Temple and associate Harsha Barot (2003); Mexico City partner Alexis E. Rovzar named chairman of the board of governors of the Center on Philanthropy at Indiana University in Indianapolis (2003).

THE FIRM SAYS

Throughout our firm's history, White & Case lawyers have committed themselves to pro bono work as a way to improve society and deepen their experience. From the firm's standpoint, time devoted to pro bono matters is equivalent in importance to time spent on matters involving our other practice areas. Each year, our legal professionals worldwide dedicate more than 40,000 hours to pro bono service, and we continually renew that tradition through interesting initiatives. For example, in 2000, we started an "externship" program that lets lawyers spend up to several months working for public-service legal services organizations. In 2001, we became the first U.S. law firm in London to create the full-time position of director of pro bono. In 2002, White & Case elevated the position of chairman of the pro bono committee to a full-time role and named a senior lawyer, widely recognized for his contributions to pro bono law, to the position. White & Case also includes and encourages our summer associates and legal assistants to participate in the firm's pro bono projects.

In recent years, our lawyers have devoted a significant amount of time to pro bono work in the U.S. alone. We are very proud that the firm's Los Angeles, Miami, New York and Washington, D.C., offices have been recognized and won awards for their pro bono contributions. Additionally, in 2003, the executive partner of our Mexico City office was named chairman of the board of governors of the Center on Philanthropy at Indiana University — one of the premier institutions in the United States for the study of philanthropic and nonprofit activities as well as for the training of professionals in the sector. In our pro bono work we help protect children from harm, work with political refugees to gain asylum, provide the destitute with access to their rightful benefits and seek respite from capital penalties for death-row inmates. Some recent non-litigation matters have included working on behalf of international human rights organizations, providing a legal clinic for the families of pediatric AIDS patients, serving as a member of the Legal Advisory Group for NYC2012, advising entrepreneurs on start-up financing and alternative business structures and representing not-for-profit community groups.

At White & Case our partners believe doing pro bono work is a great way to accelerate a young lawyer's training and development and to give lawyers at every level opportunities to contribute. Our partners encourage, recognize and mentor associates who embrace our long-standing and genuine commitment to pro bono. The firm includes the pro bono program as part of our new associate orientation. We have also taken on pro bono matters associates have brought with them from law school. We work with a number of legal services organizations that refer matters to us and from which we seek out matters. Lists are also regularly circulated so lawyers are aware of needs, and we encourage our lawyers to contact our full-time pro bono coordinators to share their pro bono interests. The truest measure of the impact of our pro bono efforts is the gratitude of the people and institutions we help and the rich experience we gain as individuals and as a firm.

OUR SURVEY SAYS

"The firm puts its money where its mouth is by counting pro bono hours as billable hours, by sponsoring externships, by holding an annual pro bono awards dinner and in countless other ways. The firm is, and has been since I started here, passionate about its pro bono commitment."

"The firm is strongly committed to pro bono, but it is unclear whether or not pro bono hours officially count towards billables in a tight job market."

"Pro bono, in the corporate department, means 'on your own time.'"

"Pro bono is highly encouraged, if not for the good of the world, then definitely because of the experience that associates can gain early on."

"Seems like the seventh practice group at W&C — has been an active area of late with the slow economy."

"The firm is constantly giving its associates opportunities to do pro bono work and in very diverse areas."

"[I] recently concluded a long-term pro bono project and received absolutely no help at all from senior associates or 'pro bono' partners."

"The firm often promotes pro bono opportunities and there appears to be no 'cap' on credit for pro bono hours."

"I think the firm is committed to pro bono work but with the crazy hours in litigation it makes it challenging for the litigators to do much pro bono work."

"There seem to be some mixed messages on how much pro bono actually counts towards billable hours."

Williams & Connolly LLP

725 Twelfth Street, NW
Washington, DC 20005
Phone: (202) 434-5000
www.wc.com

LOCATION

Washington, DC

MAJOR DEPARTMENTS & PRACTICES

Litigation
Corporate, Tax & Sports

THE STATS

No. of attorneys worldwide: 212
No. of offices worldwide: 1
Management: By Committee

EMPLOYMENT CONTACT

Ms. Donna M. Downing
Hiring Recruiting Manager
Phone: (212) 434-5605
E-mail: ddowning@wc.com

WHO'S WHO

Principal pro bono contact(s) at your firm:

Robin Jacobsohn, Esq.
Co-Chair, Pro Bono Committee
Phone: (202) 434-5000
E-mail: rjacobsohn@wc.com

Does the firm have a pro bono coordinator? No

Does the firm have a pro bono committee? Yes

If yes, how often does the committee meet? As needed.

Describe the composition of the committee: Three partners and one associate.

THE SCOOP

Does your firm have a written pro bono policy? Yes

Has the firm signed on to the Law Firm Pro Bono Challenge? No

What are some of the areas of law in which your firm has performed pro bono legal work in the last two years? Criminal defense, death penalty, political asylum, protection of endangered species, civil rights, advice to nonprofit organizations.

What are some of the areas of law in which your firm does not perform pro bono work? Domestic relations.

Organizations for which your firm has performed pro bono legal services in the last two years: Montgomery County Public Defenders' Office, Washington Lawyers' Committee for Civil Rights & Urban Affairs, ABA Death Penalty Representation Project, Center for Biological Diversity.

List up to three pro bono matters that are representative of the pro bono work your firm participates in.

- Criminal cases obtained through the firm's partnership with the Public Defenders Office in Montgomery County, Maryland. This partnership, characterized by the Public Defenders Office as an "amazing success," has encompassed a wide range of criminal matters, most involving felonies and other serious offenses.

- Post-conviction representation of a mentally retarded man who has been sentenced to death in Louisiana. The case may be one of the first to test implementation of the Supreme Court's opinion last year curtailing execution of mentally retarded individuals.

- Successful representation, in an evidentiary hearing before the Immigration Court, of an Egyptian family seeking asylum in the U.S. in order to protect women in the family from the threat of female genital mutilation.

BY THE NUMBERS

What is the total number of hours that lawyers in U.S. offices at your firm spent performing pro bono legal services in 2000, 2001 and 2002?

The firm does not disclose information about hours, whether pro bono or otherwise.

    Total number of hours in 2000: See above
    Total number of hours in 2001: See above
    Total number of hours in 2002: See above

Average number of pro bono hours per attorney in U.S. offices per year (including associates, partners, counsels, but not summer associates):

    Average number of hours per attorney in 2000: See above
    Average number of hours per attorney in 2001: See above
    Average number of hours per attorney in 2002: See above

What percentage of attorneys in this firm's U.S. offices did pro bono work in 2002? See above

What percentage of attorneys in this firm's U.S. offices did at least 20 hours of pro bono work in 2002? See above

Does the firm encourage its lawyers to perform a minimum number of pro bono hours? The firm encourages pro bono and volunteer work but does not set minimums or maximums; time spent is left to the discretion of individual attorneys.

If so, how many hours per year or what percentage of lawyers' billable hours? See above

SUPERVISION AND EVALUATIONS

Is there partner supervision on each pro bono matter? Yes

Do partner supervisors or, if applicable, senior associates provide written evaluations of associates' work on pro bono matters? No

If so, are those evaluations taken into account in determining salary, bonuses or advancement in the firm? N/A

If not, does the firm consider pro bono work generally in associate evaluations? Yes, the work is evaluated in the same manner as all other work.

HOURS

Does the firm give billable hour credit for pro bono work? Yes

Does the firm have a maximum number of pro bono hours that can be applied toward the billable hour target? N/A

If so, what is the maximum? No maximum/no target

If your firm uses hours to determine bonuses, does it consider pro bono hours when determining bonuses? Not applicable

PRO BONO POINTS

What training opportunities are open to associates working on pro bono matters? Special training is offered in some substantive areas (e.g., criminal cases in Montgomery County program; asylum cases), plus supervision by a partner for all pro bono matters.

Can associates bring matters of interest to the firm? Yes

Does the firm offer the use of support staff in carrying out pro bono matters? Yes

What pro bono opportunities are available for summer associates? Summer associates are welcomed and encouraged to participate in pro bono matters, suitable to their skills and abilities, that are available during their time at the firm.

Does the firm have established programs, such as externships, that enable its associates to work in a public interest setting? No

Has your firm won any special recognition or awards in the last two years for its pro bono work? Yes

If so, please list. Recognition by ABA Death Penalty Representation Project as the 100th pro bono law firm enlisted to assist with its cases; recognition by the D.C. Bar Foundation for firm's contribution to special fundraising drive.

THE FIRM SAYS

The law firm encourages its attorneys to undertake pro bono matters that serve the public interest, that are matched to the talents of our attorneys, and that provide good experiences for our young lawyers.

Pro bono work at the firm covers a broad array of criminal and civil issues, and over the years has ranged from death penalty and race discrimination cases, to representation of media and mental health organizations, and preparation of amicus briefs on constitutional issues.

Pro bono representation must be approved by the firm's Pro Bono Committee. Once approved, it is treated as a professional commitment of equal importance to paying work (including dedication of firm resources, treatment as billable time, partner supervision, and so on.).

Some examples of current/recent pro bono cases:

- Criminal cases, most involving felonies and other serious offenses, obtained through the firm's partnership with the Public Defenders' Office in Montgomery County, Maryland. Over 40 W&C lawyers, the majority of whom are associates, have participated in this program to date. The Public Defenders' Office has called the partnership an "amazing success."

- Post-conviction representation of a mentally retarded man who has been sentenced to death in Louisiana. The case, brought to us by the ABA Death Penalty Representation Project, may be one of the first to test implementation of the Supreme Court's opinion last year curtailing execution of mentally retarded individuals.

- Successful representation, in an evidentiary hearing before the Immigration Court, of an Egyptian family seeking asylum in the United States based on the fear that women in the family will face female genital mutilation if forced to return to Egypt.

- Representation, in Grutter v. Bollinger, of a group of law school deans in an amicus brief, in the Sixth Circuit and in the U.S. Supreme Court, in support of the admission program utilized by the University of Michigan Law School. The Supreme Court recently rendered its decision in that case, upholding the constitutionality of the law school's admission program.

- Challenges, under the Endangered Species Act, seeking protection of the Puerto Rican guajon and Atlantic white marlin.

- Representation of the Association of Defense Counsel for the International Criminal Tribunal for Former Yugoslavia (ADC-ICTY), the official bar of defense lawyers practicing before the ICTY, in connection with efforts by the Treasury Department and its Office of Foreign Assets Control (OFAC) to regulate American attorneys practicing before the ICTY.

In addition to the pro bono cases undertaken by the firm, Williams & Connolly LLP attorneys are involved in a wide variety of charitable and community service activities. The firm contributes financially to a large number of charitable endeavors and recently received special recognition for its $25,000 contribution to the D.C. Bar Foundation, which provides grants to 25 legal services providers in the District of Columbia.

Both lawyers and staff have been actively involved in the D.C. public schools. The firm was selected by the Washington Lawyers' Committee for Civil Rights & Urban Affairs to be a recipient of the Committee's 1999 Outstanding Achievement Award, in recognition of the firm's commitment and success in building a pro bono partnership with Dunbar Senior High School. In recent years, attorneys and staff have also volunteered their time at Thurgood Marshall Academy, a law-oriented public charter high school — mentoring students, organizing fundraising activities and serving on the school's governing body.

Williams & Connolly LLP attorneys and staff serve their communities outside the firm as well — volunteering, leading and giving their financial support to a wide range of charities, religious organizations and schools in their communities.

OUR SURVEY SAYS

"We have an informal pro bono program, but the firm has taken more steps to establish it more visibly and to ensure that we are active in the community."

"I think the firm will allow you to do as much pro bono as you want, as long as you finish up your other work, too."

"It's not formally encouraged, but such formality is against the firm's culture. Lawyers who want to do pro bono work can easily do so and it's billable."

"The firm has a neutral attitude toward pro bono — the firm won't dissuade you from doing it or won't persuade you either. If you want to, you have to take the initiative and go for it. I have heard the firm is attempting to make more of a coordinated effort in this area but don't know much about it."

"[We have a] partnership with the Montgomery County public defender's office."

"It's up to the attorney, and that's how it should be."

* The firm asserts that this quote is inaccurate, noting that many attorneys have handled pro bono cases, including cases that individual attorneys identified and received firm approval to undertake.

"Pro bono work at the firm covers a broad array of criminal and civil issues, and over the years has ranged from death penalty and race discrimination cases, to representation of media and mental health organizations, and preparation of amicus briefs on constitutional issues."

— *Williams & Connolly LLP*

Willkie Farr & Gallagher LLP

787 Seventh Avenue
New York, NY 10019-6099
Phone: (212) 728-8000
www.willkie.com

LOCATIONS

New York, NY (HQ)
Washington, DC
Brussels
Frankfurt
London
Milan
Paris
Rome

MAJOR DEPARTMENTS & PRACTICES

Business Reorganization & Restructuring
Corporate & Financial Services
Environmental
Executive Compensation & Employee Benefits
Government Relations
Intellectual Property
International Trade
Litigation
Pro Bono
Real Estate
Tax
Telecommunications
Trusts & Estates

THE STATS

No. of attorneys worldwide: 530
No. of offices worldwide: 8
Chairman: Jack H. Nusbaum

EMPLOYMENT CONTACT

Ms. Jeanine Salvatore
Director of Legal Personnel and Recruiting
Phone: (212) 728-8460
Fax: (212) 728-8111
E-mail: jsalvatore@willkie.com

WHO'S WHO

Does the firm have a pro bono coordinator? Yes

Martin Klotz, Esq.
Phone: (212) 728-8688
E-mail: mklotz@willkie.com

Does the firm have a pro bono committee? Yes

If yes, how often does the committee meet? As needed.

Describe the composition of the committee: Eight partners, four associates.

THE SCOOP

Does your firm have a written pro bono policy? No

Has the firm signed on to the Law Firm Pro Bono Challenge? Yes

What are some of the areas of law in which your firm has performed pro bono legal work in the last two years? World Trade Center victims: compensation claims, estate administration and related matters; womens' rights, including divorce, custody, support and protection matters; criminal defense (pre-trial, trial and appeal), including cases for indigent defendants assigned through the Criminal Justice Act; housing; youth mentoring; artists' rights.

Organizations for which your firm has performed pro bono legal services in the last two years: MFY Legal Services, inMotion (f/k/a Network for Women's Services), Habitat for Humanity, Legal Aid Society, Criminal Justice Act Panel (SDNY), Volunteer Lawyers for the Arts, Women In Need, Constitutional Education Foundation, Puerto Rican Legal Defense and Education Fund.

List up to three pro bono matters that are representative of the pro bono work your firm participates in.

- In United States v. Padilla, our partner, a former U.S. attorney, filed an amicus brief in the Second Circuit on behalf of the Association of the Bar of the City of New York in support of the rights of a detainee charged with terrorist-related crimes to complete access to counsel.

- In Ryan v. Miller, we obtained the release on a petition for habeas corpus (denied by the district court, but granted in a reversal by the Court of Appeals for the Second Circuit) of a convicted murderer on the ground that the admission at trial of testimony alluding to a co-defendant's confession implicating him violated his rights under the Confrontation Clause.

- In United States v. Vitabile, et al., we were appointed to represent an alleged captain of an organized crime family in a multi-defendant RICO case. We obtained the dismissal of two homicide counts of the indictment on statute of limitations grounds not previously considered in the district and represented the client in a six-week jury trial earlier this year.

BY THE NUMBERS

What is the total number of hours that lawyers in U.S. offices at your firm spent performing pro bono legal services in 2000, 2001 and 2002?

    Total number of hours in 2000: 10,200 hours
    Total number of hours in 2001: 9,700 hours
    Total number of hours in 2002: 11,500 hours

    (All numbers are New York office only.)

Average number of pro bono hours per attorney in U.S. offices per year (including associates, partners, counsels, but not summer associates):

    Average number of hours per attorney in 2000: 31 hours
    Average number of hours per attorney in 2001: 30 hours
    Average number of hours per attorney in 2002: 33 hours

    (All numbers are New York office only.)

What percentage of attorneys in this firm's U.S. offices did pro bono work in 2002? Not available

What percentage of attorneys in this firm's U.S. offices did at least 20 hours of pro bono work in 2002? Not available

Does the firm encourage its lawyers to perform a minimum number of pro bono hours? No, but the firm encourages associates to take on pro bono matters and solicits volunteers for pro bono matters on a regular basis.

If so, how many hours per year or what percentage of lawyers' billable hours? N/A

SUPERVISION AND EVALUATIONS

Is there partner supervision on each pro bono matter? Yes

Do partner supervisors or, if applicable, senior associates provide written evaluations of associates' work on pro bono matters? Yes, on major matters.

If so, are those evaluations taken into account in determining salary, bonuses or advancement in the firm? Yes

If not, does the firm consider pro bono work generally in associate evaluations? N/A

HOURS

Does the firm give billable hour credit for pro bono work? Yes

Does the firm have a maximum number of pro bono hours that can be applied toward the billable hour target? Willkie has no billable hours target. Once accepted by the firm, pro bono matters are treated in all respects the same as all other matters.

If so, what is the maximum? N/A

If your firm uses hours to determine bonuses, does it consider pro bono hours when determining bonuses? Not applicable

PRO BONO POINTS

What training opportunities are open to associates working on pro bono matters? Training sessions are provided by several major pro bono partner organizations, and Willkie hosts a number of these sessions both for Willkie associates and for associates of other firms. Individual pro bono assignments provide the same training by partners and senior associates as billable matters.

Can associates bring matters of interest to the firm? Yes

Does the firm offer the use of support staff in carrying out pro bono matters? Yes

What pro bono opportunities are available for summer associates? Summer associates are assigned to current pro bono matters in the same way and to the same degree as to non-pro bono matters. In addition, we offer approximately 12 one-week internships at one of three or four pro bono organizations.

Does the firm have established programs, such as externships, that enable its associates to work in a public interest setting? Yes

If so, where and for up to how long? For approximately ten years we have had an externship at MFY Legal Services. The flexible externship, typically lasting about four months and typically given to a third- or fourth-year associate, allows the associate to work full time at MFY in a program relating primarily to housing rights while remaining a Willkie associate for purposes of salary, benefits and seniority. Each departing extern is replaced by an incoming Willkie extern. Historically, the externship has been filled about equally by litigation associates and non-litigation associates.

Has your firm won any special recognition or awards in the last two years for its pro bono work? Yes

If so, please list. In the past two years, Willkie or Willkie associates have been awarded the Legal Aid Society's Pro Bono Award, inMotions's Commitment to Justice Award and MFY Legal Services' Scales of Justice Award.

THE FIRM SAYS

Willkie Farr & Gallagher LLP strongly encourages attorneys, both individually and collectively, to devote a significant portion of their professional time to legal matters of public interest, especially on behalf of individuals and organizations who otherwise would have limited access to legal services. The firm supports this commitment as a firm, through the individual activities of attorneys in leadership positions and through policies and procedures intended to foster a commitment to pro bono work.

As a firm, Willkie has long-term partnerships with established pro bono organizations such as the Legal Aid Society and inMotion, an organization devoted to the legal rights of indigent women. These partnerships allow Willkie attorneys to volunteer legal services on a recurring basis in areas with which the firm has an established familiarity. Willkie also serves as counsel to a number of pro bono organizations, including Women In Need and City Harvest. Finally, Willkie has maintained an externship at MFY Legal Services for more than 10 years through which, on a revolving basis, Willkie maintains a full-time attorney permanently on assignment at MFY. This highly popular externship is one of the oldest and most successful of its kind among large New York firms.

Numerous individual Willkie attorneys have commitments of long standing to specific organizations or causes, including Habitat for Humanity, the Puerto Rican Legal Defense and Education Fund, Lincoln Center, the Criminal Justice Act Panel, the United Nations Food and Agriculture Organization and many others. These commitments involve significant contributions of time and other resources to pro bono matters and create models for all attorneys for making pro bono activity an integral part of one's professional life.

To encourage pro bono work and to help ensure that all attorneys are free to pursue their individual pro bono interests, Willkie treats pro bono matters as equivalent in all respects to fee-paying matters, including full billable hours credit for pro bono matters, no cap on time devoted to pro bono matters and the commitment of the same level of support services and disbursements to pro bono matters as to fee-paying matters. All Willkie attorneys, including new associates, are encouraged to introduce their own pro bono matters which, if accepted, are supported fully by the firm.

OUR SURVEY SAYS

"We have taken on a tremendous amount of 9/11 cases and both partners and associates alike have been giving of themselves to help victims of the tragedy."

"Pro bono counts as billable hours and is treated as important as work for paying clients."

"One month I worked almost solely on pro bono work and nobody said a word about it."

"Generally, I don't think Willkie strongly encourages pro bono, but they support any associate who seeks it out. Pro bono hours are counted like any others. Also, Willkie has at least one (if not two) relationship where it sends an associate to a legal aid association for a period of months. There is a rotating position at MFY, so there is always a Willkie associate working there."

"Willkie is very committed to pro bono and has won many awards for its involvement. Associates are encouraged to do pro bono and the work counts as full billable hours."

"There are tons of pro bono opportunities and such work is not looked down upon."

"Opportunities are out there but it falls on the shoulders of the associate to initiate the process."

"All pro bono counts as billable hours and the firm will commit as much money and time to pro bono as to any paying client."

"This needs work. The partner who's the head of the pro bono committee simply forwards e-mails from nonprofit organizations with pro bono opportunities. If you have a pro bono case you want to work on, the firm will gladly let you do it, but there is no affirmative push to work on pro bono matters and I never hear partners discuss pro bono matters that they're working on."

"They don't discourage attorneys from doing too much pro bono work as long as they're getting other stuff done."

Willkie Farr & Gallagher LLP

"As a firm, Willkie has long-term partnerships with established pro bono organizations such as the Legal Aid Society and inMotion, an organization devoted to the legal rights of indigent women."

— *Willkie Farr & Gallagher LLP*

Wilmer Cutler Pickering LLP

2445 M Street, NW
Washington, DC 20037-1420
Phone: (202) 663-6000
www.wilmer.com

LOCATIONS

Washington, DC (HQ)
Baltimore, MD
New York, NY
McLean, VA
Berlin
Brussels
London

MAJOR DEPARTMENTS & PRACTICES

Antitrust & Competition
Bankruptcy & Workout
Communications & Electronic Commerce
Corporate
Financial Institutions
International Aviation, Defense & Aerospace
Litigation
Securities
Tax
Trade

THE STATS

No. of attorneys worldwide: 580
No. of offices worldwide: 7
Chairman: William J. Perlstein

EMPLOYMENT CONTACT

Washington, Baltimore and Northern Virginia
Ms. Mary W. Kiley
Manager of Lawyer Recruitment
Fax: (202) 247-3377
E-mail: JoinWCPLawyers@wilmer.com

New York
Ms. Marian Freed
Office Administrator
Fax: (212) 230-8888
E-mail: Marian.Freed@wilmer.com

WHO'S WHO

Principal pro bono contact(s) at your firm:

A. Stephen Hut Jr., Esq.
Partner
Phone: (202) 663-6235
E-mail: stephen.hut@wilmer.com

Christopher J. Herrling, Esq.
Pro Bono Counsel
Phone: (202) 663-6780
E-mail: christopher.herrling@wilmer.com

Does the firm have a pro bono coordinator? Yes
Christopher J. Herrling

If yes, what percentage of his or her time is spent on pro bono work? 100 percent

Does the firm have a pro bono committee? Yes

If yes, how often does the committee meet? Meetings of the pro bono committee are scheduled monthly.

Describe the composition of the committee: The committee is chaired by a partner in the firm's litigation group. Membership includes the firm's pro bono counsel and associate representation.

THE SCOOP

Does your firm have a written pro bono policy? Yes

Has the firm signed on to the Law Firm Pro Bono Challenge? Yes

What are some of the areas of law in which your firm has performed pro bono legal work in the last two years? Capital cases, campaign finance reform, victims' rights, First Amendment issues, civil rights, environmental law, international human rights, charter schools and voucher programs, asylum, community economic development, and representation of individual clients of limited financial means.

What are some of the areas of law in which your firm does not perform pro bono work? There are no areas in which we categorically refuse pro bono work.

Organizations for which your firm has performed pro bono legal services in the last two years: International Human Rights Law Group, Lawyers Committee for Civil Rights Under Law, National Parks and Conservation Association, The Center for Individual Rights, Migrant Farmworker Justice Project, National Organization for Women, Center for Community Interest, American Civil Liberties Union, Urban Public Libraries Coalition, Iranian-American Bar Association.

List up to three pro bono matters that are representative of the pro bono work your firm participates in.

- We represented Senators McCain and Feingold and other members of the U.S. Congress who are intervenors in McConnell v. Federal Election Commission defending the Bipartisan Campaign Reform Act. The firm was counsel before the three-judge special panel and again before the Supreme Court.

- Along with the NAACP Legal Defense Fund and co-counsel, we achieved justice for 38 residents of Tulia, Texas, who were arrested and convicted of alleged drug charges and sentenced to as much as 90 years in prison based solely on the uncorroborated testimony of one undercover agent. After a dramatic, week-long habeas hearing that discredited the agent as a racist and a perjurer, the legal team persuaded the state to join in a request to overturn all of the convictions. On June 16, 2003, at a nationally televised hearing, all those imprisoned were released on bail and, on August 22, 2003, the governor of Texas granted full pardons to virtually all of the defendants.

- We represented migrant farmworkers before the U.S. Court of Appeals for the Eleventh Circuit in a Fair Labor Standards Act ("FLSA") minimum wage case. The issue in the case, which was one of first impression, was whether the FLSA permits an employer to require employees to bear the costs of the employer's recruitment program (in this case, visa fees, immigration fees and travel costs), when those costs, if the workers were required to bear them, would have the effect of reducing the employees' wages below the statutory minimum. The Eleventh Circuit held (Arriaga v. Florida Pacific Farms, LLC) that the defendant agribusinesses were required by the FLSA to reimburse the costs at issue because the costs were incurred primarily for the benefit of the employer.

BY THE NUMBERS

What is the total number of hours that lawyers in U.S. offices at your firm spent performing pro bono legal services in 2000, 2001 and 2002?

Total number of hours in 2001: 37,323 hours
Total number of hours in 2002: 53,440 hours
Total number of hours in 2003: 51,807 hours

Average number of pro bono hours per attorney in U.S. offices per year (including associates, partners, counsels, but not summer associates):

Average number of hours per attorney in 2001: 95.3 hours
Average number of hours per attorney in 2002: 126.7 hours
Average number of hours per attorney in 2003: 99.8 hours

What percentage of attorneys in this firm's U.S. offices did pro bono work in 2003? 72 percent

What percentage of attorneys in this firm's U.S. offices did at least 20 hours of pro bono work in 2003? 52 percent

Does the firm encourage its lawyers to perform a minimum number of pro bono hours? Yes

If so, how many hours per year or what percentage of lawyers' billable hours? Attorneys are encouraged to fulfill their ethical obligations regarding the provision of pro bono legal services.

SUPERVISION AND EVALUATIONS

Is there partner supervision on each pro bono matter? Yes

Do partner supervisors or, if applicable, senior associates provide written evaluations of associates' work on pro bono matters? Yes

If so, are those evaluations taken into account in determining salary, bonuses or advancement in the firm? Yes

If not, does the firm consider pro bono work generally in associate evaluations? N/A

HOURS

Does the firm give billable hour credit for pro bono work? Yes

Does the firm have a maximum number of pro bono hours that can be applied toward the billable hour target? See firm narrative below.

If so, what is the maximum? See firm narrative below.

If your firm uses hours to determine bonuses, does it consider pro bono hours when determining bonuses? Yes

PRO BONO POINTS

What training opportunities are open to associates working on pro bono matters? Available training includes in-house formal programs, hands-on supervisory training and training offered by the local bar and organizations with whom we partner on pro bono matters.

Can associates bring matters of interest to the firm? Yes

Does the firm offer the use of support staff in carrying out pro bono matters? Yes

What pro bono opportunities are available for summer associates? Pro bono opportunities are made available to summer associates in the same manner that they are made available to full-time associates, and those opportunities are plentiful.

Does the firm have established programs, such as externships, that enable its associates to work in a public interest setting? No

Has your firm won any special recognition or awards in the last two years for its pro bono work? Yes

If so, please list. Wilmer Cutler Pickering LLP received the D.C. Bar's 2003 Law Firm Pro Bono Award and The National Law Journal's 2002 Pro Bono Award. Associate Christopher Meade received the "President's Pro bono Service Award" from the New York State Bar Association on May 1, 2003.

THE FIRM SAYS

Commitment to pro bono work and public service has been an integral part of the firm's culture from its founding. While all lawyers are encouraged to undertake pro bono matters, participation is strictly voluntary. Pro bono assignments are generated by attorney interest, requests from legal service organizations and court appointments. All matters are cleared through the same process that applies to billable matters. Pro bono matters are staffed and supported in the same manner in which billable matters are handled. While every pro bono matter has a responsible partner assigned, it is often the case that another lawyer on the team will take the lead on maintaining the client relationship, making strategic decisions and relating to opposing counsel.

The firm is very supportive of general volunteer work by our lawyers, but we strictly adhere to the definition of "pro bono" as crafted by the Law Firm Pro Bono Challenge. In general, and somewhat oversimplifying the process, after billing 1,850 hours associates can receive full credit toward the next bonus level and very generous credit, and often full credit, toward further bonus levels. In addition, when an associate takes on a pro bono matter of such a size that he or she could not reasonably be expected to bill 1,850 hours, that requirement is waived. U.S. lawyer time is reported for purposes of fulfilling our commitment under the Challenge (i.e. that our pro bono hours will be an equivalent of 5 percent of our billable time).

We actively encourage and support pro bono work by lawyers in our European offices. There are several pro bono matters in which our legal team is comprised of lawyers from both our U.S. and European offices.

OUR SURVEY SAYS

"The number of pro bono opportunities is overwhelming. The work is treated almost as billable work, both in terms of allowing associates the time and resources they need to complete pro bono projects and in terms of counting pro bono hours toward the hours-based bonuses."

"Wilmer remains strongly committed to pro bono work, though associates tend not to take on quite as much pro bono work now that the firm has implemented an hours-based bonus. But to the firm's credit, pro bono hours are counted toward the second-tier bonus and, in exceptional cases, toward the first-tier bonus also."

"Pro bono is a big part of the firm's training."

"The firm spends a huge amount of its resources on pro bono and is very committed to promoting good causes. Among many other issues, this year the firm is doing many pro bono Supreme Court representations, including representing University of Michigan in defending its affirmative action program and defending the constitutionality of the McCain-Feingold case. Associates who worked hard on these and other pro bono cases last year received large performance bonuses even though they often had very few 'billable' hours."

"High-profile pro bono is treated differently from run-of-the-mill help for the under-represented."

"On the one hand, pro bono work is touted as a great way to get hands-on experience at the district and appellate level (and several associates in the New York office have recently had appellate arguments in pro bono cases). One partner is particularly dedicated to helping associates with pro bono briefs. On the other hand, several associates were reprimanded for doing too much pro bono work last year. Granted, these associates had worked several hundred pro bono hours — but many other associates do no pro bono at all, and so when amortized [it] is not that much time. I think the firm in general is moving toward becoming more bottom-line-oriented, and that dedication to pro bono has begun to suffer as a result."*

"I am amazed at the support for pro bono projects that there is at this firm and have not seen any backlash for people who are strongly committed to pro bono work."

"The firm is very committed to pro bono and puts its money where its mouth is by allowing associates to count 150 hours pro bono towards the 2,000 hour requirement (at 2,000 [hours] associates receive a bonus)."

"The firm's outstanding commitment to pro bono is one of the reasons I came here. The bonus structure is such that almost everyone here does pro bono work. The pro bono matters vary, so there is something for all interests. We have a full-time pro bono partner who gets us great work and is very accessible and helpful."

* The firm reports, "We ask associates to reduce their pro bono time only in the are instances where an associate accumulates pro bono matters in a way that has consistently resulted in high pro bono and low billable hours. But we take great pride in associates who have, in some instances, billed hundreds of hours to a pro bono matter for two or more years."

Wilson Sonsini Goodrich & Rosati

650 Page Mill Road
Palo Alto, CA 94304-1050
Phone: (650) 493-9300
www.wsgr.com

LOCATIONS

Palo Alto, CA (HQ)
Austin, TX
Seattle, WA
New York, NY
Reston, VA
Salt Lake City, UT
San Francisco, CA

MAJOR DEPARTMENTS & PRACTICES

Antitrust & Trade Regulation
Corporate Finance
Corporate Law & Governance
Employee Benefits/Compensation
Employment Law
Fund Services
Intellectual Property
Life Sciences
Litigation
Mergers & Acquisitions
Real Estate/Environmental
Tax
Venture Capital
Wealth Management

THE STATS

No. of attorneys worldwide: 600
No. of offices worldwide: 7
Chairman and CEO: Larry W. Sonsini

EMPLOYMENT CONTACT

Attorney Recruiting Department
Phone: (650) 493-9300
Fax: (650) 493-6811
E-mail: attorneyrecruiting@wsgr.com

WHO'S WHO

Does the firm have a pro bono coordinator? Yes

Mark Parnes, Esq.
Assistant General Counsel
Phone: (650) 493-9300
E-mail: mparnes@wsgr.com

Ms. Candida Malferrari
Pro Bono Coordinator
Phone: (650) 493-9300
E-mail: cmalferrari@wsgr.com

If yes, what percentage of his or her time is spent on pro bono work? Mark Parnes: 40 percent; Candida Malferrari: 25 percent.

Does the firm have a pro bono committee? Yes

If yes, how often does the committee meet? Monthly

Describe the composition of the committee: Five partners, five associates, two paralegals, one of counsel.

THE SCOOP

Does your firm have a written pro bono policy? Yes

Has the firm signed on to the Law Firm Pro Bono Challenge? Yes

What are some of the areas of law in which your firm has performed pro bono legal work in the last two years? General corporate, employee benefits & compensation, employment & labor law, litigation, real estate/environmental, technology transactions, trademark, trusts & estates.

What are some of the areas of law in which your firm does not perform pro bono work? Criminal, family (with the exception of guardianship).

Organizations for which your firm has performed pro bono legal services in the last two years: Disabilities Rights Education and Defence Fund (DREDF), AIDS Legal Referral Panel, Lawyer's Committee for Civil Rights Asylum Program, Bar Association of San Francisco, Center for Justice & Accountability, National Center for Youth Law.

List up to three pro bono matters that are representative of the pro bono work your firm participates in.

- **Emma C. v. Eastin.** A recent important victory for children with disabilities by negotiating a new consent decree with Ravenswood School District, with greater protections for the plaintiff class, including greater visibility into the operations of the school district, and clear procedures for identifying problems and righting them.

- **Zita Cabello Barrueto v. Armando Fernadez Larios.** Recent victory for the surviving family members of Winston Cabello, killed by Pinochet regime death squad known as the "Caravan of Death." A federal jury found in favor of our clients on all claims.

- **Peninsula Open Space Trust** – a variety of corporate matters.

BY THE NUMBERS

What is the total number of hours that lawyers in U.S. offices at your firm spent performing pro bono legal services in 2000, 2001 and 2002?

>Total number of hours in 2000: 14,388
>Total number of hours in 2001: 14,526
>Total number of hours in 2002: 24,614

Average number of pro bono hours per attorney in U.S. offices per year (including associates, partners, counsels, but not summer associates):

>Average number of hours per attorney in 2000: 17.9
>Average number of hours per attorney in 2001: 20.5
>Average number of hours per attorney in 2002: 36.7

What percentage of attorneys in this firm's U.S. offices did pro bono work in 2002? N/A

What percentage of attorneys in this firm's U.S. offices did at least 20 hours of pro bono work in 2002? 26.1

Does the firm encourage its lawyers to perform a minimum number of pro bono hours? Yes

If so, how many hours per year or what percentage of lawyers' billable hours? 50 hours

SUPERVISION AND EVALUATIONS

Is there partner supervision on each pro bono matter? Yes

Do partner supervisors or, if applicable, senior associates provide written evaluations of associates' work on pro bono matters? Yes

If so, are those evaluations taken into account in determining salary, bonuses or advancement in the firm? Yes

If not, does the firm consider pro bono work generally in associate evaluations? N/A

HOURS

Does the firm give billable hour credit for pro bono work? Yes

Does the firm have a maximum number of pro bono hours that can be applied toward the billable hour target? No

If so, what is the maximum? N/A

If your firm uses hours to determine bonuses, does it consider pro bono hours when determining bonuses? Yes

PRO BONO POINTS

What training opportunities are open to associates working on pro bono matters? Periodic training on particular legal matters – i.e., guardianship, asylum, estate planning and nonprofit incorporation.

Can associates bring matters of interest to the firm? Yes

Does the firm offer the use of support staff in carrying out pro bono matters? Yes

What pro bono opportunities are available for summer associates? They are given the opportunity to work with the attorneys, who assign the summer associates their projects.

Does the firm have established programs, such as externships, that enable its associates to work in a public interest setting? No

Has your firm won any special recognition or awards in the last two years for its pro bono work? Yes

If so, please list:

- Disabilities Rights Education and Defence Fund (DREDF) Award in May 2002 for advancing disability rights.
- Ronald McDonald House "Ronnie Award" for exceptional commitment to the House and its community.
- Lawyers Committee for Civil Rights Asylum Program Award in January 2004.

THE FIRM SAYS

Recognizing the growing severity of the unmet needs of the poor and disadvantaged in the community we serve, Wilson Sonsini Goodrich & Rosati believes that pro bono activities should be primarily focused on providing access to the justice system for persons otherwise unable to afford it. We also believe that providing pro bono legal services is an important part of our professional responsibility. Consequently, the firm encourages and recognizes the work performed on such activities. Individuals who undertake pro bono work not only receive the opportunity to expand their knowledge of the law and to enhance their work experience, but oftentimes such work fosters great personal satisfaction. Wilson Sonsini Goodrich & Rosati encourages each individual to set aside time each year to devote to pro bono work, recognizing that the actual number of hours devoted to pro bono work will depend on the particular matter(s) undertaken. We suggest a guideline of 50 hours a year. The maximum amount of time an individual may devote to pro bono matters has not been predetermined. Wilson Sonsini Goodrich & Rosati recognizes that each individual has particular interests and will choose to devote his/her time differently. Participation in the firm's pro bono program is voluntary; it is also strongly encouraged. Opportunities exist with numerous nonprofit organizations who are our clients: San Francisco Museum of Modern Art, Project Read, Civic Ventures, Aspire Public Schools, Schools Online, Earthjustice, The Natural Step, Lenders for Community Development, Plugged In, Austin Music Foundation, Washington Toxics Coalition, Until There's A Cure Foundation, The Imagine Bus Project, Global Peace Congress, Decision Education Foundation, Celiac Sprue Research Foundation and the Dalai Lama Foundation.

OUR SURVEY SAYS

"They're very supportive with any project I've ever wanted to work on."

"Pro bono hours count like any other billable hours. People are free to pursue their causes."

"All time billed to pro bono counts as billable hours at the firm for purposes of billing targets, quarterly bonuses and year-end bonuses."

"I know that pro bono is a strong firm value and has been since our firm was founded. It is just difficult for associates to commit to non-billable work right now, when we need to be readily available for any billable work that may come in."

"Certain individuals are quite visible in this area, but client work (billable work) is definitely emphasized. Again, typical of a large firm."

"Overall, the firm is committed; however, there are some partners that have been vocal about their opposition to associates working on pro bono matters."

"There are many opportunities to work in pro bono but the encouragement to do that comes from the pro bono contacts, and not the partners I actually work for."

"The firm has a special pro bono committee with a target of 3 percent of billable hours for pro bono work. One hundred percent of pro bono hours count towards an associate's billable hours. For associates who want to take advantage of the opportunities, they are encouraged for the most part."

"The commitment level has skyrocketed with the increase in idle associates. Not sure whether the levels could be sustained if we became busy again."

"As long as nothing interferes with your billables, the firm couldn't care less what you do."

"Individuals who undertake pro bono work not only receive the opportunity to expand their knowledge of the law and to enhance their work experience, but oftentimes such work fosters great personal satisfaction."

— *Wilson Sonsini Goodrich & Rosati*

Winston & Strawn LLP

35 West Wacker Drive
Chicago, IL 60601-9703
Phone: (312) 558-5600
www.winston.com

LOCATIONS

Chicago, IL (HQ)
Los Angeles, CA
New York, NY
San Francisco, CA
Washington, DC
Geneva
London
Paris

MAJOR DEPARTMENTS & PRACTICES

Corporate & Financial
Employee Benefits & Executive Compensation
Energy
Environmental
Government Relations & Regulatory Affairs
Health Care
Intellectual Property
International
Labor & Employment Relations
Litigation
Maritime & Admiralty
Real Estate
Tax
Trusts & Estates

THE STATS

No. of attorneys worldwide: 900
No. of offices worldwide: 8
Chairman: Gov. James R. Thompson
Managing Partner: James M. Neis

EMPLOYMENT CONTACT

Ms. Deborah S. Cusumano
Legal Recruitment Manager
Phone: (312) 558-6151
Fax: (312) 558-5700
E-mail: dcusumano@winston.com

WHO'S WHO

Does the firm have a pro bono coordinator? Yes

Greg McConnell, Esq.
Director of Public Interest Law
Phone: (312) 558-8068
E-mail: gmcconnell@winston.com

If yes, what percentage of his or her time is spent on pro bono work? The director spends 100 percent of his time on pro bono work — approximately 80 percent managing and administering the firm's pro bono activities, and 20 percent working on or supervising active pro bono client matters.

Does the firm have a pro bono committee? Yes

If yes, how often does the committee meet? Approximately once a quarter.

Describe the composition of the committee: The firm's pro bono committee is comprised of 22 attorneys, including a partner and associate from each office. The chair of the committee is a member of the firm's executive committee.

THE SCOOP

Does your firm have a written pro bono policy? Yes

Has the firm signed on to the Law Firm Pro Bono Challenge? Yes

What are some of the areas of law in which your firm has performed pro bono legal work in the last two years? Winston & Strawn is providing pro bono legal work in many areas, including but not limited to: domestic relations, real estate and housing, consumer advocacy, asylum, employment law, criminal trial, criminal appeals, First Amendment, tax, prisoner rights, death penalty and post-conviction matters, special education and corporate.

What are some of the areas of law in which your firm does not perform pro bono work? Winston & Strawn does not categorically exclude any practice area from its pro bono work. The firm gives closer scrutiny to plaintiff's employment and consumer bankruptcy matters where actual and business conflicts regularly develop.

Organizations for which your firm has performed pro bono legal services in the last two years: Winston & Strawn has performed pro bono work for over 100 pro bono organizations in the last two years, including but not limited to the D.C. Bar Pro Bono Program, Archdiocesan Legal Network, Legal Aid Society of New York, Lawyers Alliance of New York, Chicago Volunteer Legal Services Foundation, Midwest Immigrants Human Rights Center, Public Counsel (LA), and the Bar Association of San Francisco.

List up to three pro bono matters that are representative of the pro bono work your firm participates in.

- Winston & Strawn recently secured political asylum for a citizen of Guinea in a removal proceeding before an immigration judge.

- Over 20 Winston & Strawn lawyers have accepted assignments as a guardian ad litem representing the interests of children involved in custody disputes.

- Winston & Strawn represents a charter school, providing services for the acquisition of property, securing tax exempt status, developing appropriate employment policies and confirming appropriate corporate status and registration.

BY THE NUMBERS

What is the total number of hours that lawyers in U.S. offices at your firm spent performing pro bono legal services in 2000, 2001 and 2002?

>Total number of hours in 2000: 24,480 hours
>Total number of hours in 2001: 21,217 hours
>Total number of hours in 2002: 26,983 hours

Average number of pro bono hours per attorney in U.S. offices per year (including associates, partners, counsels, but not summer associates):

>Average number of hours per attorney in 2000: 33.8 hours
>Average number of hours per attorney in 2001: 28.4 hours
>Average number of hours per attorney in 2002: 36.1 hours

What percentage of attorneys in this firm's U.S. offices did pro bono work in 2002? 56 percent

What percentage of attorneys in this firm's U.S. offices did at least 20 hours of pro bono work in 2002? 34 percent

Does the firm encourage its lawyers to perform a minimum number of pro bono hours? Yes

If so, how many hours per year or what percentage of lawyers' billable hours? In 2003, in connection with the celebration of the firm's 150th anniversary, the firm developed an individual pledge that requested all lawyers to perform a minimum of 35 hours pro bono work. The pledge has become an annual institutional goal.

SUPERVISION AND EVALUATIONS

Is there partner supervision on each pro bono matter? Yes

Do partner supervisors or, if applicable, senior associates provide written evaluations of associates' work on pro bono matters? Yes

If so, are those evaluations taken into account in determining salary, bonuses or advancement in the firm? Yes

If not, does the firm consider pro bono work generally in associate evaluations? Yes

HOURS

Does the firm give billable hour credit for pro bono work? Yes

Does the firm have a maximum number of pro bono hours that can be applied toward the billable hour target? Yes

If so, what is the maximum? The firm will credit up to 35 hours toward billable hour goals. All pro bono hours are credited to bonus goals.

If your firm uses hours to determine bonuses, does it consider pro bono hours when determining bonuses? Yes

PRO BONO POINTS

What training opportunities are open to associates working on pro bono matters? In addition to the extensive practice-related training offered associates, associates also receive training opportunities relating to specific pro bono practice areas and skills. Most of these pro bono trainings are developed in conjunction with local pro bono agencies. Many of these training events are sponsored by the firm and conducted in our offices. Associates are also encouraged to attend other training events that may be conducted off-site.

Can associates bring matters of interest to the firm? Yes

Does the firm offer the use of support staff in carrying out pro bono matters? Yes

What pro bono opportunities are available for summer associates? Winston & Strawn has developed specific pro bono programming for summer associates that allows them to work with local agencies and meet with clients on an individual basis. This programming varies from office to office, depending on the work of the local agencies. For example, New York associates participate in a domestic violence advocacy project. Chicago associates provide intake and assistance to low-income persons seeking custody over children through the Cook County pro se desk. Los Angeles associates assist homeless persons receive benefits and housing. In addition, summer associates are regularly asked to participate on existing teams of attorneys staffing pro bono cases.

Does the firm have established programs, such as externships, that enable its associates to work in a public interest setting? No

Has your firm won any special recognition or awards in the last two years for its pro bono work? Yes

If so, please list.

- 2003 — Partner Kimball Anderson receives the American Bar Association Pro Bono Publico Award.
- 2003 — Partners Kimball Anderson, David Doyle and David Koropp receive the Excellence in Pro Bono Service Award from the Northern District of Illinois in conjunction with the Federal Bar Association.
- 2003 — Partner Pat Doyle received the Distinguised Service Award from Chicago Volunteer Legal Services.
- 2003 — Partner Susan Longstreet received the Commercial Real Estate Women (REW) Public Service Award.
- 2003 — Chairman James R. Thompson received the Distinguished Service Award from the Metropolitan Family Services Legal Aid Bureau.
- 2002 — Partner Anna Masters receives the Volunteer Attorney of the Year from the Western Law Center for Disability Rights.
- 2002 — Associates Stephen Moncarz Schmidt, Patricia Gopaul, Andrea Moore and Jonathon Levine receive Cornerstone Award from the Lawyers Alliance for New York.
- 2002 — Paralegal Ken Berry receives Most Valuable Paralegal from the Center for Disability and Elder Law.
- 2001 — Winston & Strawn receives the Golden Gavel Award from Coordinated Advice and Referral Program for Legal Services (CARPLS).
- 2001 — Winston & Strawn receives Outstanding Achievement Award from Chicago Legal Clinic.

THE FIRM SAYS

Winston & Strawn strongly supports and encourages pro bono work by all of its lawyers, regardless of their practice area or experience. The firm believes it is the responsibility of lawyers to use their skills and talents on behalf of the many persons and organizations that are unable to afford legal counsel. The firm also recognizes that pro bono work provides lawyers at all stages of their careers the opportunity for personal and professional development that makes them better lawyers and better citizens of the communities where they live and practice. Acknowledging that lawyers face tremendous time demands, Winston & Strawn has taken steps to make sure that lawyers can quickly and easily find a wide variety of matters that appeal to their own personal interests and are compatible with their work schedules.

OUR SURVEY SAYS

"For its 150th anniversary, the firm has asked every attorney (partners included) to pledge 35 hours of pro bono work this year."

"The majority of the pro bono effort comes from the associate ranks in our office; however, the partners recognize and praise our efforts."

"The firm highly encourages pro bono participation and makes getting referrals quite easy. Individual department heads (whose bottom lines are affected by non-billable hours, like pro bono) could be more on board with the program."

"Most attorneys have committed to perform at least 35 pro bono hours this year. We have a full-time attorney who serves as our pro bono director."

"Winston's commitment to pro bono is a big reason for my loyalty to the firm. In a very competitive market, Winston continues to support pro bono work. Not only that, they reward it — in the form of recognition assemblies, pro bono reporters and including such work in your bonus."

"The firm makes an effort to undertake a wide array of pro bono work in all practice areas. If pro bono hours counted toward minimum billable hours, the package would be complete."*

"Winston is very devoted to pro bono work. Our full-time coordinator makes sure that there is a variety of interesting and challenging pro bono assignments."

"Once you reach the client billable hours requirement of 1,950, hours above that count on an hour-for-hour basis toward your bonus."*

"While no one is pressured to do pro bono work, most attorneys take advantage of the pro bono opportunities available."

"We don't get any billable hour credit for pro bono work, although we are otherwise encouraged to do it."*

* The firm notes that it has changed its policy to provide credit to billable goals in addition to bonus goals as the policy previously provided.

"Acknowledging that lawyers face tremendous time demands, Winston & Strawn has taken steps to make sure that lawyers can quickly and easily find a wide variety of matters that appeal to their own personal interests and are compatible with their work schedules."

— *Winston & Strawn LLP*

Use the most **targeted** job search tools for lawyers on the Internet.

Vault's Law Job Board and VaultMatch™ Resume Database

■ **Law Job Board**

The most comprehensive and convenient job board for legal professionals. Target your search by practice area, function, and experience level, and find the job openings that you want. No surfing required.

■ **VaultMatch™ Resume Database**

Vault takes match-making to the next level: post your resume and customize your search by practice area, trial experience, level and more. We'll match job listings with your interests and criteria and e-mail them directly to your in-box.

> the most trusted name in career information™

Find out more at
www.law.vault.com

[they told him it was a "lifestyle" firm]

Vault Law Channel >
- Law Firm Profiles
- Message Boards
- Law Member Network
- Law Job Board
- Law Resume Database

VAULT
> the most trusted name in career information™

Visit www.vault.com
AOL Keyword: Vault.com

Wondering what it's like to work at a specific employer?

Read what EMPLOYEES have to say about:

- Workplace culture
- Compensation
- Hours
- Diversity
- Hiring process

Read employer surveys on THOUSANDS of top employers.

> the most trusted name in career information™

Go to www.vault.com

VAULT LAW CAREER LIBRARY

You are reading just one title from Vault's Law Career Library - the complete resource for legal careers. To see a full list of legal career titles, go to law.vault.com.

"With reviews and profiles of firms that one associate calls 'spot on,' [Vault's] guide has become a key reference for those who want to know what it takes to get hired by a law firm and what to expect once they get there."
– *New York Law Journal*

"To get the unvarnished scoop, check out Vault."
– *SmartMoney magazine*

the most trusted name in career information™

"Vault is indispensable for locating insider information."
- *Metropolitan Corporate Counsel*